Digital Entrepreneurship and Co-Creating Value Through Digital Encounters

Farag Edghiem
Manchester Metropolitan University, UK

Mohammed Ali
University of Salford, UK

Robert Wood
University of Manchester, UK

A volume in the Advances in Logistics, Operations, and Management Science (ALOMS) Book Series

IGI Global
PUBLISHER of TIMELY KNOWLEDGE

Published in the United States of America by
IGI Global
Business Science Reference (an imprint of IGI Global)
701 E. Chocolate Avenue
Hershey PA, USA 17033
Tel: 717-533-8845
Fax: 717-533-8661
E-mail: cust@igi-global.com
Web site: http://www.igi-global.com

Library of Congress Cataloging-in-Publication Data

Names: Edghiem, Farag, 1974- editor. | Ali, Mohammed Banu, 1983- editor. | Wood, James Robert, 1949- editor.
Title: Digital entrepreneurship and co-creating value through digital encounters / edited by Farag Edghiem, Mohammed Banu Ali and James Robert Wood.
Description: Hershey, PA : Business Science Reference, [2023] | Includes bibliographical references and index. | Summary: "Digital Entrepreneurship and Co-Creating Value Through Digital Encounters contributes to the services' digital transformation and digital entrepreneurship domain by uncovering contemporary innovations used in the modern service industry. It supports modern applications of industry 4.0, digital transformation, and entrepreneurship to facilitate value co-creation for contemporary businesses. Covering topics such as big data management, industrial relations, and tourist destination selection, this premier reference source is an ideal resource for entrepreneurs, business owners and managers, government officials, policy makers, students and educators of higher education, librarians, researchers, and academicians"-- Provided by publisher.
Identifiers: LCCN 2023000653 (print) | LCCN 2023000654 (ebook) | ISBN 9781668474167 (hardcover) | ISBN 9781668474174 (paperback) | ISBN 9781668474181 (ebook)
Subjects: LCSH: Service industries--Technological innovations. | Industrial management--Technological innovations. | Tourism--Management. | Big data. | Value added.
Classification: LCC HD9980.5 .D5164 2023 (print) | LCC HD9980.5 (ebook) | DDC 338/.064--dc23/eng/20230105
LC record available at https://lccn.loc.gov/2023000653
LC ebook record available at https://lccn.loc.gov/2023000654

This book is published in the IGI Global book series Advances in Logistics, Operations, and Management Science (ALOMS) (ISSN: 2327-350X; eISSN: 2327-3518)

British Cataloguing in Publication Data
A Cataloguing in Publication record for this book is available from the British Library.

Advances in Logistics, Operations, and Management Science (ALOMS) Book Series

John Wang
Montclair State University, USA

ISSN:2327-350X
EISSN:2327-3518

Mission

Operations research and management science continue to influence business processes, administration, and management information systems, particularly in covering the application methods for decision-making processes. New case studies and applications on management science, operations management, social sciences, and other behavioral sciences have been incorporated into business and organizations real-world objectives.

The **Advances in Logistics, Operations, and Management Science** (ALOMS) Book Series provides a collection of reference publications on the current trends, applications, theories, and practices in the management science field. Providing relevant and current research, this series and its individual publications would be useful for academics, researchers, scholars, and practitioners interested in improving decision making models and business functions.

Coverage

- Information Management
- Risk Management
- Marketing engineering
- Networks
- Finance
- Production Management
- Political Science
- Operations Management
- Services management
- Decision analysis and decision support

The Advances in Logistics, Operations, and Management Science (ALOMS) Book Series (ISSN 2327-350X) is published by IGI Global, 701 E. Chocolate Avenue, Hershey, PA 17033-1240, USA, www.igi-global.com. This series is composed of titles available for purchase individually; each title is edited to be contextually exclusive from any other title within the series. For pricing and ordering information please visit http://www.igi-global.com/book-series/advances-logistics-operations-management-science/37170. Postmaster: Send all address changes to above address.

Titles in this Series

For a list of additional titles in this series, please visit: www.igi-global.com/book-series

Entrepreneurship Ecosystems and Their Opportunities and Challenges
Mohammed El Amine Abdelli (University of Brest, France) Shajara Ul-Durar (University for Creative Arts, UK) and Hala Wasef Hattab (British University in Egypt, Egypt)
Business Science Reference • © 2023 • 300pp • H/C (ISBN: 9781668471401) • US $250.00

Change Management During Unprecedented Times
Kyla Latrice Tennin (College of Doctoral Studies, University of Phoenix, USA & Forbes School of Business, USA & World Business Angels Investment Forum (WBAF)-G20, USA & Lady Mirage Global, Inc., USA)
Business Science Reference • © 2023 • 413pp • H/C (ISBN: 9781668475096) • US $250.00

Multidisciplinary Approaches to Organizational Governance During Health Crises
Carla Sofia Vicente Negrão (CeBER, University of Coimbra, Portugal) Isabel Guerreiro Pimentel Maia (University of Coimbra, Portugal) and João António Furtado Brito (University of Cape Verde, Cape Verde)
Business Science Reference • © 2023 • 300pp • H/C (ISBN: 9781799892137) • US $250.00

Considerations and Characteristics of the Millennial Leader in Today's Global Society
Tymon M. Graham (TMGraham Consulting, LLC, USA)
Business Science Reference • © 2023 • 300pp • H/C (ISBN: 9781668447116) • US $240.00

Handbook of Research on Blockchain Technology and the Digitalization of the Supply Chain
Tharwa Najar (Gafsa University, Tunisia) Yousra Najar (Manar University, Tunisia) and Adel Aloui (EM Normandie Business School, France)
Business Science Reference • © 2023 • 520pp • H/C (ISBN: 9781668474556) • US $295.00

Perspectives on Women in Management and the Global Labor Market
Elisabete S. Vieira (GOVCOPP, University of Aveiro, Portugal) Mara Madaleno (GOVCOPP, University of Aveiro, Portugal) and João Teodósio (Polytechnic Institute of Santarém, Portugal)
Business Science Reference • © 2023 • 382pp • H/C (ISBN: 9781668459812) • US $240.00

Perspectives and Strategies of Family Business Resiliency in Unprecedented Times
Hotniar Siringoringo (Gunadarma University, Indonesia) and Ravindra Hewa Kuruppuge (University of Peradeniya, Sri Lanka)
Business Science Reference • © 2023 • 322pp • H/C (ISBN: 9781668473948) • US $240.00

IGI Global
PUBLISHER of TIMELY KNOWLEDGE

701 East Chocolate Avenue, Hershey, PA 17033, USA
Tel: 717-533-8845 x100 • Fax: 717-533-8661
E-Mail: cust@igi-global.com • www.igi-global.com

Table of Contents

Detailed Table of Contents

Entrepreneurship has a long history. The terms entrepreneurship and entrepreneurs are defined in various ways. Entrepreneurs are considered individuals who lead innovation, show outstanding initiative, coordinate social and economic structures, convert resources and circumstances into feasible assets, and embrace risks associated with such ventures, as well as a concept in which entrepreneurs are primarily focused on the notion of profitability and opportunity identification. This chapter delves into the realm of digital entrepreneurship in the context of the UK and German online business communities.

Within the past decade there has been a paradigm shift in complex innovation in organisations through the adoption of contemporary technologies, which has brought us into the age of digital transformation (DT). The authors adopt a conceptual approach to analysing complex innovation models based on bibliographic analysis and integrate existing concepts and theories related to complex innovation in the DT context. The main innovation models (e.g., 4Ps and open/closed) are analysed through the lens of DT and multiple perspective theory. The outcome of this chapter is the categorization of modern innovation models in DT from multiple perspectives (technical, organisational, and personal), which has revealed that DT is the foundation of the modern innovation ecosystem. The chapter's uniqueness is its conceptual nature, which does not rely on empirical data collection but instead integrates pre-existing concepts and theories such as DT, complex innovation, and multiple perspective theory.

Although digital entrepreneurship (DE) emerged in the early 1990s because of digital technologies and entrepreneurship, current researchers consider it a recent phenomenon. This chapter proposes to extend the concept of DE to include the concept of dimensions of DE. Using literature in the areas of digital knowledge base and ICT market, digital business environment, digital skills and e-leadership, corporate culture, and access to finance, the chapter proposes a conceptual model for digital entrepreneurship, identifying the components of such a model as well as specific indications of size overlaps in different domains. This model implies that digital transformation in SMEs is intertwined with other activities and entrepreneurial behaviours in small firms, and it argues that understanding digital transformation or the adoption of digital technologies in SMEs requires an understanding of its context, particularly in relation to diffusion innovation theory, innovation system theory, and entrepreneurial approaches to the digital transformation towards digital corporate success.

This chapter explores the current challenges and transitional needs required to regulate digital entrepreneurship within the illicit economy by examining digital entrepreneurship relating to commercial sex and trafficking in human beings for the purpose of sexual exploitation. As such, new innovative digital technologies are transforming serious and organised crime operations and, thus, need to also change the way the law, enforcement, and the wider criminal justice system combat crime. The chapter seeks to expose contemporary practises of digitally-facilitated commercial sex and trafficking in human beings for the purpose of sexual exploitation, recent developments in law and policy in the area, emerging investigative and prosecution practises within digital online environments, as well as necessary future changes to the law and enforcement.

Despite growing scholarly interest in the impact of the digital economy on economic recovery in the midst of the current global crisis and regional development situations, research on the effects of the global crisis on developing digital economies in the Gulf Cooperation Council Region (GCC) and the resulting future uncertainty is limited. Thus, this chapter examines the developing GCC countries' digital infrastructure, openness, innovation environment, competitiveness, and digital divide to determine how the digital economy affects economic growth during a global crisis. This chapter demonstrates how the GCC economies are still developing and attempting to diversify away from oil, with the digital economy serving as a major driving force in achieving the region's goals. Furthermore, while the recent pandemic has harmed GCC digital industries, it has also increased demand, creating an excellent opportunity to develop the region's digital infrastructure to compete with developed digital economies. Policy implications have been proposed as a potential impact mechanism.

Business and IT alignment has been a critical issue for researchers, consultants, and practitioners seeking to improve demand and delivery management by executing business requirements in real-life systems that benefit end-users. Companies using IT to enable their business must improve their business and information technology alignment (BITA) by implementing best practices and frameworks. This study focuses on one area of improvement in the BITA model, which is project software delivery using Agile as a project management methodology. Agile methodology allows for collaboration and dynamic requirements, which benefits aligning businesspeople with IT delivery within the software development lifecycle (SDLC) framework.

In view of the fierce competition and rapidly changing business environment in the banking and finance industries, many banks have been progressively shifting their retail banking services online. With the aim of streamlining operations and improving customer service, the burgeoning use of artificial intelligence (AI) in the banking industry accelerates the adoption of various AI-based technologies. This chapter conducted a case study on Fubon Bank, researching the adoption of chatbots in the Hong Kong banking industry. A chatbot development framework for e-banking is being developed. Lastly, a comparison of chatbot services among three local banks in Hong Kong is provided.

Foreword

Digital entrepreneurship has transformed the business landscape, as the emergence of digital technologies has opened up new opportunities for entrepreneurs to create innovative products and services that cater to the needs and expectations of customers. With the rise of digital platforms and tools, entrepreneurs can now connect with customers, suppliers, and other stakeholders in real-time, enabling them to co-create value through digital encounters. The concept of co-creation has become increasingly important in the digital entrepreneurship ecosystem, as it enables entrepreneurs to leverage the collective intelligence of their customers and other stakeholders to create value.

Co-creation involves a collaborative process where entrepreneurs work together with their customers and other stakeholders to design, develop, and deliver products and services that meet their needs and expectations. Co-creation has many benefits for entrepreneurs. By involving customers and other stakeholders in the product development process, entrepreneurs can gain valuable insights into their needs and preferences. This can help them create products and services that are better aligned with the needs and expectations of their target market, leading to increased customer satisfaction and loyalty. Furthermore, co-creation can help entrepreneurs create a sense of community and loyalty among their customers and other stakeholders. By involving them in the product development process, entrepreneurs can build a sense of ownership and engagement among their customers, leading to increased brand loyalty and advocacy. Co-creation has become an essential component of digital entrepreneurship. By leveraging the power of digital technologies to connect with customers and other stakeholders, entrepreneurs can co-create value and drive innovation in their respective industries.

This book *Digital Entrepreneurship and Co-Creating Value Through Digital Encounters* by Dr. Farag Edgheim, Dr. Mohammed Ali, and Prof. Bob Wood is a comprehensive guide to digital entrepreneurship that emphasises the importance of co-creation. The book covers a range of topics, from business innovation management to industry 4.0. The authors take a holistic approach to the subject, considering the challenges and opportunities that entrepreneurs face as they navigate the digital landscape. The book is divided into 12 chapters, each of which focuses on a different aspect of digital entrepreneurship.

Some of the major themes include the history, evolution, and current state of digital entrepreneurship. The book also covers key drivers of digital entrepreneurship, such as technological innovation, globalisation, and changing consumer behaviour. Other chapters delve into the key skills and competencies required for success in digital entrepreneurship, as well as the importance of creativity, innovation, and agility, and the need for digital literacy and business acumen. Co-creation is another central theme of the book, in which its importance in digital entrepreneurship is stressed. The book also provides useful and practical examples on how entrepreneurs engage with their customers and other stakeholders to co-create value, leading to increased customer loyalty, engagement, and profitability. The challenges and opportunities that entrepreneurs face as they navigate the digital landscape, in addition to the impact of emerging technologies, such as artificial intelligence and blockchain, on digital entrepreneurship and the ethical and social implications of digital entrepreneurship are also discussed in the book.

One of the key strengths of this book is its emphasis on practical insights and real-world examples. The authors draw on the latest research and practical experience of digital entrepreneurs to provide a comprehensive guide to this exciting field. The book is written in a clear and accessible style, making it suitable for a wide range of readers, from aspiring entrepreneurs and academics to established business owners looking to expand into the digital realm. The authors' expertise and insights are invaluable, and the book is sure to become a go-to resource for anyone interested in digital entrepreneurship and co-creating value through digital encounters.

Marie Griffiths
Salford Business School, University of Salford, UK

Preface

OVERVIEW

In the 21st century, digital technology has dramatically transformed the business landscape, creating new opportunities and challenges for entrepreneurs. In this book, *Digital Entrepreneurship and Co-Creating Value Through Digital Encounters*, we explore how digital technology can be harnessed to co-create value with customers and other stakeholders. As digital technologies continue to evolve at a breakneck pace, the ability to adapt and innovate has become increasingly critical for businesses. In this context, entrepreneurship has emerged as a key driver of growth and change, with digital entrepreneurs leading the way in creating new businesses and disrupting established industries. However, digital entrepreneurship is not just about starting a new venture or using digital tools to sell products and services. It is also about creating value in new ways, through collaboration and co-creation with customers and other stakeholders. In this book, we explore how digital entrepreneurs are leveraging the power of digital technology to co-create value with customers, build strong communities, and drive innovation. Drawing on cutting-edge research and real-world case studies, this book provides a comprehensive overview of the theory and practice of digital entrepreneurship. We explore the key concepts and frameworks that underpin successful digital entrepreneurship, including design thinking, lean startups, and agile development. We also examine the strategies and tactics that digital entrepreneurs can use to engage with customers and co-create value, from social media marketing to crowdsourcing and open innovation. Ultimately, this book is about how digital entrepreneurship can be a force for positive change, both for businesses and for society as a whole. By embracing the opportunities and challenges of the digital age, entrepreneurs can create new value for customers and other stakeholders and drive innovation that transforms the way we live and work.

CONTEXTUAL FIT

The rise of digital technology has fundamentally transformed the business landscape, creating new opportunities and challenges for entrepreneurs. In this context, entrepreneurship has emerged as a key driver of growth and innovation, with digital entrepreneurs leading the way in creating new businesses and disrupting established industries. However, digital entrepreneurship is not just about using technology to sell products and services. It is also about creating value in new ways, through collaboration and co-creation with customers and other stakeholders. This requires a deep understanding of the evolving digital landscape, as well as the ability to adapt and innovate in response to changing customer needs and market conditions. The book *Digital Entrepreneurship and Co-Creating Value Through Digital Encounters* is designed to provide entrepreneurs with the tools and insights they need to thrive in this rapidly changing environment. Drawing on cutting-edge research and real-world case studies, the book explores the theory and practice of digital entrepreneurship, with a particular focus on the strategies and tactics that entrepreneurs can use to co-create value with customers and other stakeholders. At its core, this book is about how digital entrepreneurs can leverage the power of digital technology to create new value for their customers and drive innovation that transforms the way we live and work. By embracing the opportunities and challenges of the digital age, entrepreneurs can unlock new sources of growth and value and help shape a more prosperous and sustainable future for all.

TARGET AUDIENCE

The book *Digital Entrepreneurship and Co-Creating Value Through Digital Encounters* is intended for a wide range of readers who are interested in exploring the opportunities and challenges of entrepreneurship in the digital age. The book is particularly relevant for entrepreneurs and aspiring entrepreneurs who are looking to start and grow digital businesses, as well as for established businesses that are seeking to innovate and adapt to the rapidly changing digital landscape. The book will also be of interest to academics and researchers who are studying entrepreneurship and innovation, as well as to policymakers who are seeking to foster an environment of innovation and entrepreneurship in their communities. In addition, the book will be useful for anyone who is interested in understanding the impact of digital technology on business and society and how entrepreneurs can leverage these changes to create value and drive positive change. The book is written in a clear and accessible style, with a focus on practical insights and real-world examples. Whether you are an entrepreneur, a researcher, or simply a curious reader, this book will provide you with valuable insights into the theory and practice of digital entrepreneurship and the ways in which entrepreneurs can use digital technology to co-create value with their customers and other stakeholders.

ORGANISATION OF THE BOOK

The book is organised into 12 chapters, with a summary of each as follows:

Chapter 1: Digital Entrepreneurship Behaviour: How Patterns Shape Co-Creation

The entrepreneurship literature has recognised the impact of entrepreneurial behaviour and the contribution towards co-creating value by entrepreneurs within business communities. As such, entrepreneurs' behaviour within an online business community platform has been centre to recent academic debate marking contemporary digital transformation in multiple business sectors. A wide spectrum of entrepreneurship behaviour patterns may be unravelled to leverage value for business and to be influenced by dynamic determinants of online business communities. Given the paucity of research on this topic, this chapter intends to shed light on the behaviour patterns of digital entrepreneurs and the potential to co-create value within online business communities.

Chapter 2: Taxonomy of Industry 4.0 Technologies in Digital Entrepreneurship and Co-Creating Value

The chapter proposes a taxonomy of Industry 4.0 (I4.0) technologies that are key enabling technologies (KETs) of I4.0. These technologies range from cyber-physical systems and the Internet of Things (IoT) to big data and cloud computing, among others. The chapter explores how these technologies can be used in digital entrepreneurship and co-creating value, and how they can be integrated to create innovative business models and enhance business operations. The taxonomy provides a comprehensive framework for understanding the different Industry 4.0 technologies and their applications in the constantly evolving landscape of digital entrepreneurship and co-creating value.

Chapter 3: Digital Entrepreneurship: Insights from Online Business Communities

Entrepreneurship and entrepreneurs may be conceptualised in various ways. By bare definition, entrepreneurs could be conceived as individuals who lead innovation, develop outstanding initiatives, coordinate social and economic structures, convert resources and circumstances into feasible assets, and embrace risks associated with such ventures and primarily focused on generating profitability. The impact of entrepreneurship and entrepreneurs transformed, in line with advancements in digital business networks, to a wider realm to include cross-sector collaboration and easier access to business resources. In essence, this chapter delves into the scope of digital entrepreneurship and the implications for digital entrepreneurs in online business communities.

Chapter 4: Multi-Perspectives of Contemporary Digital Transformation Models of Complex Innovation Management

Over the past ten years, there has been a significant shift in the way organisations approach complex innovation as they have begun to adopt modern technologies and move into the era of digital transformation. To examine complex innovation models in the context of digital transformation, we take a conceptual approach that involves analysing existing concepts and theories related to complex innovation. Specifically, we examine how well-known innovation models, like the 4Ps and open/closed models, fit within the framework of digital transformation and multiple perspective theory. Our analysis leads us to categorise modern innovation models in the context of digital transformation from various perspectives, including technical, organisational, and personal. Ultimately, our chapter concludes that digital transformation is the cornerstone of modern innovation, and our unique approach to examining this subject integrates existing concepts and theories without relying on empirical data collection.

Chapter 5: Developing an Innovation-Based Framework of Digital Entrepreneurship Strategy for Small and Medium-Sized Enterprises – An Innovation-Based Framework of Digital Entrepreneurship Strategy for SMEs

The emergence of digital entrepreneurship (DE) in the early 1990s, driven by digital technologies and entrepreneurship, is now considered a recent phenomenon by current researchers. This chapter proposes expanding the concept of DE by introducing dimensions of DE. By drawing on literature from the digital knowledge base, the ICT market, the digital business environment, digital skills and e-leadership, corporate culture, and access to finance, the chapter proposes a conceptual model for digital entrepreneurship. This model identifies the components of DE and highlights specific overlaps in different domains. The chapter argues that digital transformation in SMEs is interconnected with other entrepreneurial activities in small firms. To understand digital transformation and the adoption of digital technologies in SMEs, it is essential to consider their context, especially in relation to diffusion innovation theory, innovation system theory, and entrepreneurial approaches to digital transformation for corporate success.

Chapter 6: Tackling Digital Entrepreneurship Within the Illicit Economy – The Evolving Fight Against Serious and Organized Crime Within a Digitally Facilitated Sex Industry

This chapter delves into the challenges and changes required to regulate digital entrepreneurship in the illegal economy by examining digital entrepreneurship in commercial sex and human trafficking for sexual exploitation. As new innovative digital technologies transform organised crime operations, there is a need to change the approach of law enforcement and the criminal justice system to combating crime. The chapter aims to shed light on current practises of digitally facilitated commercial sex and human trafficking for sexual exploitation, recent legal and policy developments in this area, emerging investigative and prosecution practises in digital online environments, and the necessary changes to law enforcement and policy in the future.

Chapter 7: Shifting Paradigms in the Rapidly Developing Global Digital Ecosystem – A GCC Perspective

Although there is increasing scholarly interest in the impact of the digital economy on economic recovery during the current global crisis and regional development situations, limited research has been conducted on the effects of the crisis on developing digital economics in the Gulf Cooperation Council (GCC) region and the resulting future uncertainty. This chapter addresses this gap by examining the digital infrastructure, openness, innovation environment, competitiveness, and digital divide in the developing GCC countries to determine how the digital economy impacts economic growth during a global crisis. The chapter highlights that the GCC economies are still developing and attempting to diversify away from oil, with the digital economy playing a significant role in achieving these goals. Despite the recent pandemic's negative impact on GCC digital industries, it has also increased demand, providing an excellent opportunity to develop the region's digital infrastructure and compete with developed digital economies. The chapter proposes policy implications as a potential impact mechanism.

Chapter 8: Improving the Business and IT Alignment Through Software Delivery Methodology

Meeting the expectations of business owners in delivering their requirements has always been a difficult task, irrespective of the technology employed and resources allocated. To ensure that the outcomes of delivery meet business expectations, it is imperative to improve delivery methodologies. In this regard, the agile methodology has emerged as a preferred approach in recent times, as it helps overcome the challenges and limitations of the traditional waterfall methodology in terms of aligning business and technical delivery through scope management and collaboration. These two factors are practical advantages of the agile methodology, as they facilitate better alignment between business and IT. This chapter proposes how business and its alignment through agile methodology can be enhanced.

Chapter 9: Strategic Outlook for Big Data Management

Over the past two decades, big data has gained prominence across various sectors, including politics and business. It is considered a valuable resource for improving business operations and increasing employee efficiency by simplifying the process of collecting and distributing information using IT. As a result, there is a growing trend where everyone from major web companies to traditional entrepreneurs to physical and social scientists is either already experiencing or expecting a significant increase in available data, along with new opportunities and untapped value. Despite the extensive research and discussion surrounding the role of big data in our interconnected world, our understanding of its potential is still in its early stages. There is significant untapped potential for big data from an organisational perspective. Therefore, the main objective of this chapter is to use a systematic literature review with content analysis to discuss the strategic outlook for managing big data.

Chapter 10: The Role of Social Manufacturing for Entrepreneurship in the Industry 4.0 Transformation

Social manufacturing is an online platform that utilises social networks, enabling manufacturers with similar capabilities to collaborate and form communities. These communities can be either horizontal, where manufacturers with similar resources and capabilities are grouped together, or vertical, where manufacturers with different capabilities work together to produce a product from start to finish. By creating these communities, social manufacturing reduces the bargaining power of the main producer. This platform serves as a virtual showcase for small-scale entrepreneurs to showcase their skills and talents, an effective cost management tool for customers, and a collaborative and sharing tool that enhances production efficiency for countries. Therefore, this chapter explores the role of social manufacturing for entrepreneurship in the Industry 4.0 transformation.

Chapter 11: How Do Various Social Media Platforms Influence Chinese Tourists' Destination Selection? From Information Searching and Sharing Perspectives

This chapter explores the impact of social media on tourists' destination selection in China, with a focus on the different types of tourism information available on various Chinese social media platforms. The study analyses the application and influence of these platforms on destination selection across three stages of travel. The chapter highlights that tourists require different types of tourism information from individual tourists, destination marketing organisations, and tourism businesses to make informed destination choices. Chinese social media platforms have been designed with different functions to cater to tourists' destination choices across these three stages of travel. However, the characteristics of information on these platforms, such as positive and negative comments, information variation, richness, and credibility, generate both positive and negative influences on tourists' destination selection. Based on these findings, a social media framework for destination selection is proposed, which has several theoretical and managerial implications.

Chapter 12: An Analysis on the Adoption of Chatbots in the Banking Sector of Hong Kong – A Contemporary System for Improving Customer Experiences in E-Banking

Given the intense competition and swiftly evolving business landscape in the banking and finance sectors, several banks have gradually transitioned their retail banking services to online platforms. To streamline their operations and enhance customer services, many banks are increasingly utilising artificial intelligence (AI) technologies, which are being adopted at a rapid pace. This chapter presents a case study on the implementation of chatbots in the Hong Kong banking industry, focusing on Fubon Bank. The study proposes a framework for developing chatbots for e-banking services and concludes with a comparison of chatbot services among three local banks in Hong Kong.

CONCLUSION

The book *Digital Entrepreneurship and Co-Creating Value Through Digital Encounters* offers a comprehensive and practical guide to entrepreneurship in the digital age. By exploring the theory and practice of digital entrepreneurship and the ways in which entrepreneurs can co-create value with their customers and other stakeholders, this book provides valuable insights into the opportunities and challenges of entrepreneurship in the digital age. Through a combination of cutting-edge research and real-world case studies, this book demonstrates how digital entrepreneurs can use digital technology to create new value for their customers, build strong communities, and drive innovation that transforms the way we live and work. It highlights the importance of adaptability and innovation in the face of rapid technological change and provides entrepreneurs with the tools and insights they need to succeed in this dynamic and rapidly evolving landscape. Ultimately, this book is a call to action for entrepreneurs to embrace the opportunities and challenges of the digital age and to use their skills and creativity to create a more prosperous and sustainable future for all. By working together to co-create value with their customers and other stakeholders, entrepreneurs can help drive positive change and create a better world for generations to come.

Farag Edghiem
Manchester Metropolitan University, UK

Mohammed Ali
University of Salford, UK

Robert Wood
University of Manchester, UK

Chapter 1
Digital Entrepreneurship Behaviour:
How Patterns Shape Co-Creation

Farag Edghiem
Manchester Metropolitan University, UK

Nicholas George
Manchester Metropolitan University, UK

ABSTRACT

The entrepreneurship literature has recognised the impact of entrepreneurial behaviour and the contribution towards co-creating value by entrepreneurs within business communities. As such, entrepreneurs' behaviour within an online business community platform has been centre to recent academic debate marking contemporary digital transformation in multiple business sectors. A wide spectrum of entrepreneurship behaviour patterns may be unravelled to leverage value for business and to be influenced by dynamic determinants of online business communities. Given the paucity of research on this topic, this chapter intends to shed light on the behaviour patterns of digital entrepreneurs and the potential to co-create value within online business communities.

INTRODUCTION

Entrepreneurship has been widely acknowledged as the most pertinent way to contend with major social, technological, environmental, and economic challenges (Akpan and Ibidunni, 2021). Whilst entrepreneurship refers to the recognition, assessment, and exploitation of novel ideas and opportunities (Ajdari et al., 2016), the transition towards encouraging entrepreneurship has impacted industry policies leading to promoting new business ventures and innovation within existing ones. Aided by an enhanced entrepreneurial culture (Baranauskas and Raišienė, 2022), it also became a determinant of improved economic indicators, employment opportunities and encouraging the participation of individuals in the entrepreneurial conduct (Zaheer et al., 2019; Steininger et al., 2022). Being entrepreneurial may not be

DOI: 10.4018/978-1-6684-7416-7.ch001

necessarily related to new start-ups; instead, it has become a critical aspect of existing businesses as to leverage growth, competitive advantage, and sustainability (Manea et al., 2021; Kollmann et al., 2022).

The literature on entrepreneurship has identified multiple aspects of entrepreneurial behaviour such as risk-taking, innovativeness, and pro-activeness (Fernandes et al., 2022; Laitsou et al., 2020). The nature of these behaviour patterns, however, varies among individuals depending on their entrepreneurial intentions and available opportunities (Herman, 2022). We opt to in this chapter to focus on the aspect of digital entrepreneurs' behaviour by discussing models of behaviour and the prospect of knowledge sharing within digital entrepreneurship networks. In this vein, the emergence of the digital business environment facilitates new collaborative opportunities and challenges for entrepreneurs (Gavrila & Ancillo, 2022). From one perspective, it allows collaboration to enable the acquisition of a wide range of resources; while from another, it requires the adoption of a digital strategy and a mindset change in traditional business by promoting digital entrepreneurship (Jha et al., 2022).

Digital technologies instigated a transition in the existing patterns of doing business and ultimately resulted in improved products, higher revenues, market diversification, and improved product/service delivery (Manjon, 2022). Therefore, these changes have transformed traditional business practices towards an enhanced model of digital entrepreneurship (Nambisan et al., 2019). Digital business platforms and communities provide unconventional opportunities for collaborative knowledge sharing and idea generation and as a means of co-creating value (Fernandes et al., 2022). Moreover, it has also developed forward the type of skills and capabilities required for being a successful entrepreneur (Lin and Maruping, 2022).

Digital entrepreneurship is mainly built on the evolution of the digital ecosystem and offers numerous benefits, including user participation, reduced cost, higher accessibility and connectivity and sustainable growth and development (Gregori and Holzmann, 2020; Lichtenthaler, 2021; Zhai et al., 2022). The critical success factors of entrepreneurship are dependent on the aspect of networking through online platforms and exploitation of relevant digital technologies (i.e. cloud computing, social media, the Internet of things, big data, etc.) (Ali, 2019, 2020; M. Ali, 2019a, 2019b, 2021; Ali, 2022; Ali & Abdel-Haq, 2021; Ali & Edghiem, 2021; Ali et al., 2022; M. B. Ali, 2021; Ali et al., 2020a, 2020b; Kraus et al., 2019). The current literature on digital entrepreneurship has stressed the importance of this phenomenon (Awawdeh et al., 2022; Baran et al., 2021; Bican et al., 2020; Fernandes et al., 2022; Jha et al., 2022; Zhai et al., 2022). However, we contemplate the concept of digital entrepreneurship to be evolving and requires further empirical investigation in various directions. In essence, the research discussing the key factors of entrepreneurs' behaviour patterns and intentions of setting up a business and networking through online platforms is lacking. Thus, this chapter aims to draw the attention of researchers to digital entrepreneurial behaviour from varied perspectives. Specifically, the entrepreneurial motivations and intentions to take part in online business communities and the behaviour patterns of digital entrepreneurs.

BEHAVIOURIST PERSPECTIVE OF ENTREPRENEURSHIP

Entrepreneurs' behaviour on an online community platform might be influenced by unconscious and unintended factors; however, more emphasis is placed on the intentional act of establishing a business and how this decision is made (Bird, 1988; Krueger et al., 2000). Intentions are recognised as the best determinant of behaviour in the pre-decision stage of becoming an entrepreneur (Fishbein and Ajzen, 1975). The probability of behaviour is directly affected by the ratio of the entrepreneurship intention (Ajzen, 1991). Several elements, such as needs, values, wants, habits, and beliefs, can influence the intention to engage in entrepreneurial behaviour (Bird, 1988; Lee and Wong, 2004). Entrepreneurship has also been considered a major element in alleviating poverty, addressing unemployment issues, leading to innovations, and improving the economic indicators of a community (Nakara et al., 2020; Si et al., 2020). These factors can be considered as the entrepreneurs' intentions of setting up a business and networking through online platforms; hence, these factors can be used to identify the purpose of entrepreneurs when joining online community platforms. It is governed by several models that have been categorised as cultural, economic, psychological, and sociological theories (Mwange, 2018). Here is a set of entrepreneur theories and models to generate an understanding of the entrepreneurial behavioural aspect and the factors that either influence or shape the entrepreneur's journey on an online community platform.

Ajzen's Theory of Planned Behaviour

The entrepreneurial intention has seen multiple theories and models (Krueger and Carsrud, 1993). The theory of planned behaviour model, depicted in Figure 1, has been the most utilised theory within entrepreneurial research due to its capacity for projecting entrepreneurial intention (Ajzen, 1991) and has been frequently cited for projections of social behaviour of human beings (Ajzen, 2011). It has extended the previous Theory of Reasoned Action and focuses more on the prediction of behaviours (Fishbein and Ajzen, 1977). The planned behaviour theory elaborates the prediction mechanisms of behaviours based on three parameters, including those of a) favourable or unfavourable attitude towards the behaviour, b) perceived behavioural control, dependent on the individual's ability as well as the challenges faced by them, and c) the norms of the subject as a result of social pressure. These components regulate the tendency of an individual in adopting a particular behaviour.

Figure 1. Theory of planned behaviour
Source: Ajzen (2011)

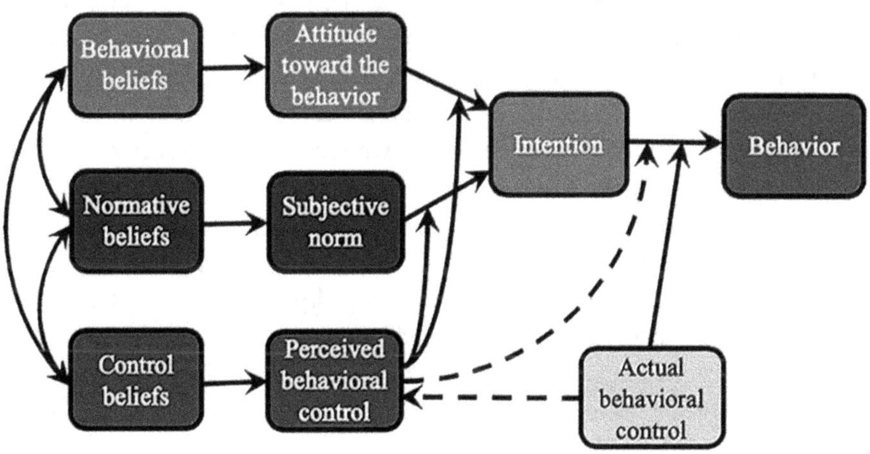

Although the theory of planned behaviour has been extensively used, it may contain random measurement errors (Ajzen, 2011). Among other criticisms, the irrational approach of not considering cognitive and affective processes and abandoning the effect and emotions has been put forward (Zhang et al., 2020). Manstead and Parker (1995) have also indicated two issues, namely a) the use of direct against belief-based assessments of Theory of Planned Behaviour components, and b) measuring perceived control. Similarly, even though the theory of planned behaviour has been employed in the realm of entrepreneurship (Tornikoski and Maalaoui, 2019; Pejic Bach et al., 2018; Wang et al., 2021), yet small and medium enterprises have seen less of it (Southey, 2011).

Van Gelderen et al. (2008) further describe entrepreneurial intentions through two crucial factors: entrepreneurial vigilance and financial security concerns. The entrepreneurs who set up multiple ventures once established can be described as serial entrepreneurs (Van Gelderen et al., 2008). Therefore, gaps remain in the implementation of this theory in the domain of serial entrepreneurship, where entrepreneurs perceive setting up exciting new ventures regularly as career progression, and also research the quality and quantity of the ventures (Van Gelderen et al., 2008). This study can provide effective perceptions and create a better understanding of entrepreneurs' behaviour and intentions. The theory of planned behaviour can also help the researcher in generating questionnaires and setting semi-structured interview questions, as it helps to measure the intentions and behaviour of digital entrepreneurs in the setting of online communities.

Bourdieu's Theory of Practice: Habitus

Pierre Bourdieu investigated different sociological phenomena through the creation of thinking tools and formulated interrelated concepts in understanding and dissecting prevalent inequalities in society (Bourdieu, 1977). One of Bourdieu's major thinking tools and factors of this theory, habitus, has risen in prominence in recent years (Lyke, 2017; Huang, 2019; Shimoni, 2017; Bourdieu, 2018). Bourdieu's attempt to reconcile the contradiction between construction and activity while recognising the exterior and historical forces that compel, restrict, and drive variation is reflected in the concept of habitus (Öztürk, 2011). The habitus particularly enables academics and researchers to better understand in what way and where for societal mediators to conceptualise and renovate the social environment in which they find themselves (Rehbein, 2017). It also investigates internalised behaviours, perceptions, and beliefs which are transcribed in the personality of individuals (Stahl and McDonald, 2021). In conclusion, habitus is a combination of experiences that illustrate people's viewpoints, principles, activities, and societal situations (Costa and Murphy, 2015) (see Figure 2).

The Bourdieusian framework's failure to foresee change is perhaps its most serious flaw (Yang, 2014). Bourdieu's attempts to defy determinist critique, such as the imitation approach, reflexiveness, and hysteresis effect, are also points of concern. The incongruity between some domains and habits that can stimulate conscious experience can be investigated systematically, and explicit pedagogy, which is a method of habit formation that has been neglected but is incredibly important, can be fully appreciated and tacitly acknowledged as being important (Clarkin-Phillips, 2018; Nobbs, 2017). Kozinets and Gambetti (2020) have further elaborated and connected the theory to the axiological research perspective with netnography analysis.

Figure 2. Bourdieu's theory of practice
Source: Harker (1990, p. 101)

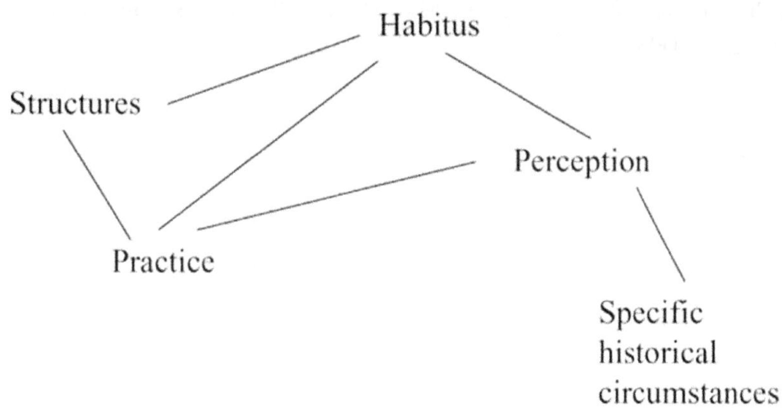

Communities of Practice (COP) Theory

Recently, online start-up communities have emerged as a significant way of obtaining, distributing, and sharing information; facilitating knowledge exchange and problem-solving, widely recognised as 'Communities of Practice' (Wenger et al., 2002). The members of the community are actively seeking knowledge and sharing knowledge about their common interests or providing solutions to challenges, thus learning, and continually developing as a community over time. Communities of Practice (COP) theory (see Figure 3), which Lave and Wenger first proposed in 1991, is a social learning theory that emphasises how social networks and interpersonal interactions shape knowledge, behaviour, and attitudes. It is frequently employed to research organisational change, knowledge management, and learning (Wenger and Snyder, 2000). Individuals can improve their self-efficacy, a crucial factor in determining entrepreneurial behaviour and intentions, by participating in shared activities and working for shared objectives (Bandura, 1977). Also, digital entrepreneurs can find assistance in online groups, where they can overcome obstacles and take part in activities that boost their self-efficacy (Gist and Mitchell, 1992).

KNOWLEDGE GENERATION AND SHARING ENDEAVOURS

There are codified and tacit dimensions to knowledge, but contemporary research tends to focus on one or the other; however, Polanyi (1983) has explicitly stated that knowledge has both codified and non-codified dimensions (Empson, 2001; Hardy and Palmer, 2000; Hazlett et al., 2005). In other words, knowledge can either be viewed as an object entity that can be codified and transferred or as having a high level of tacit elements which can be difficult to capture and transfer (Davenport and Prusak, 1998). Knowledge can also be viewed as unique, personal, socially created, situated, and rooted in practice (Sole and Edmondson, 2002; Orlikowski, 2002; Tsoukas, 2005). Due to the knowledge-making process, it can be difficult to classify knowledge as either "codified" or "tacit" as it is multidimensional and can have elements of both codified and tacit knowledge at the same time (Guzman and Trivelato, 2008). However, the transfer of codified knowledge requires a distinct set of techniques than the transfer of tacit knowledge, thus, there are different theories that can shed more light on the processes involved (Guzman and Trivelato, 2008).

Figure 3. Communities of practice theory
Source: Wenger et al. (2002)

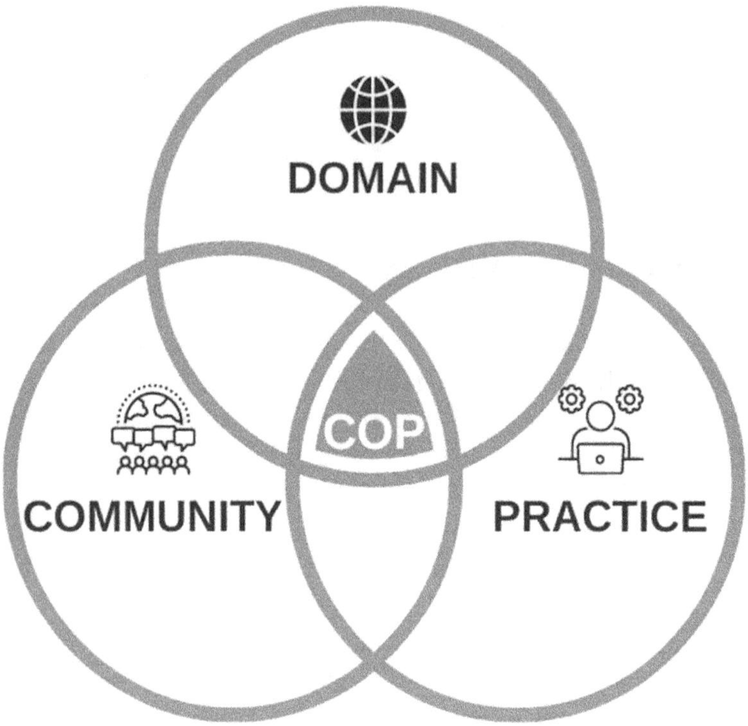

Theories of knowledge sharing have progressed from an emphasis on domains (Senge, 1993), key processes (Leonard, 1995), and structure (Dougherty, 1999) to a changing focus on institutional cognitive procedures (Walsh and Ungson, 1991). Individuals, resources, and activities can all be seen as part of the "reservoirs" of knowledge theory, along with processors of knowledge generating and transferring knowledge (Argote and Ingram, 2000; Zack, 1999a). Figure 4 below illustrates the framework of knowledge creation processes. Using this concept, the process of knowledge formation can be represented as a series of transitions between two categories of knowledge: explicit and tacit. Thus, the knowledge generation process is characterised in literature as a series of continuous and dynamic exchanges between tacit and explicit categories of information, rather than as a single event (Sharma and Goswami, 2009).

Knowledge is transmitted across the entirety of the start-up community platform via a knowledge-sharing process, integrating both people and technology in knowledge production, transfer, and accumulation (Oyemomi et al., 2019). Entrepreneurs share both codified and tacit knowledge and other resources mutually, generating new patterns of merged knowledge collectively (Van Den Hooff and De Ridder,

2004). Ardichvili et al. (2003) have named the knowledge subjects within the communities as suppliers and demanders, while Van Den Hooff and De Ridder (2004) attribute them as knowledge contributors and collectors. The knowledge sharing intention, behaviour, and motivation have been described as a voluntary act in earlier studies (Gagné, 2009). Successful online communities have amassed an extensive and rich knowledge library, an engaged user base, and a vibrant community over time (Ardichvili et al., 2006). Figure 5 represents the knowledge-sharing processes within an online community where user interactions are the key to building effective knowledge-sharing systems, identifying patterns (Ardichvili et al., 2006).

Figure 4. Framework of knowledge creation processes
Source: Wan et al. (2011, p. 336)

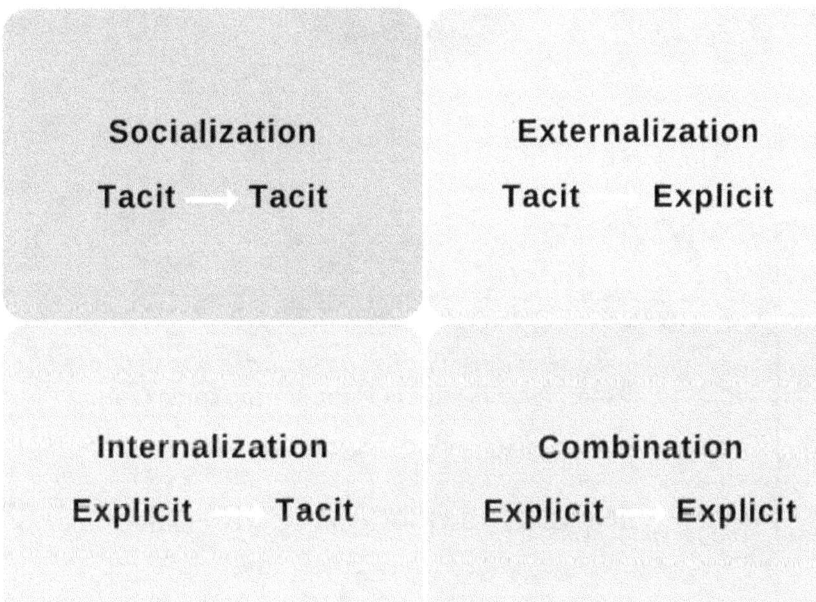

ENTREPRENEURS AS ROLE MODELS

Considering the theoretical and functional significance of the topic of the study, the creation and growth of entrepreneurial networks have drawn limited interest from researchers so far (Batjargal, 2006). However, the present research has highlighted that the entrepreneurial network complexities can depend on the industry sector, market lifecycle, and resource availability (Batjargal, 2006). The Boulder Thesis illustrated in Figure 6 comprises four principal concepts and is a prominent yet powerful model for start-up communities where entrepreneurs can be the leaders (Feld, 2020). It can help keep the momentum going when entrepreneurs are classified as leaders, but other members of the community may feel inferior (Feld, 2020). However, both the entrepreneur and participants are indispensable parts of the development of the start-up communities (Feld, 2020).

Figure 5. Online communities knowledge-sharing processes
Source: Adapted from Ardichvili et al. (2006)

Figure 6. The boulder thesis
Source: Adapted from Feld (2020, p. 7)

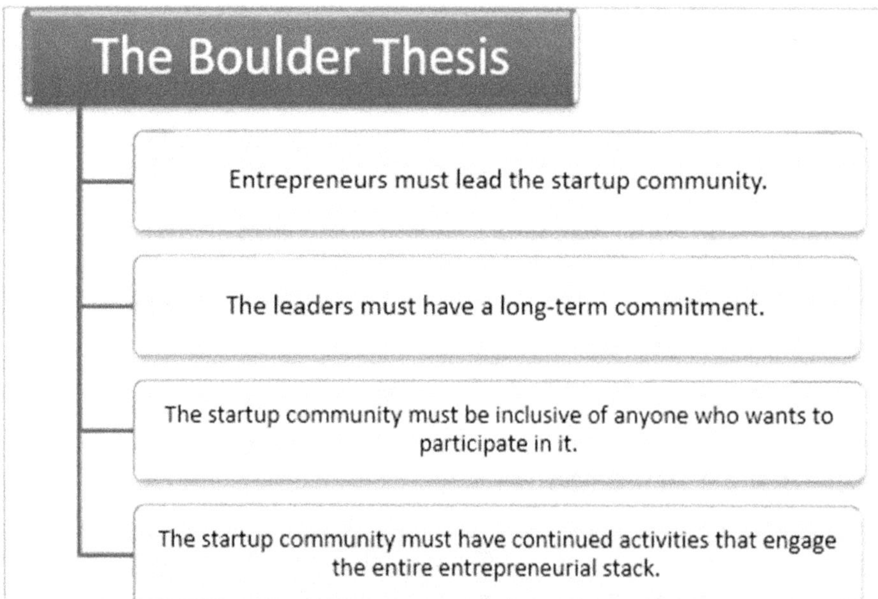

Researchers found that the presence of role models influenced the decision to start a business or to become an entrepreneur (Bosma et al., 2012). Role models can encourage entrepreneurialism or the desire to develop as an entrepreneur among young people on online start-up community platforms (Van Auken et al., 2006). This can help young entrepreneurs seek guidance, resource knowledge to fund their ventures. As well, they may serve as a source of anthropological and social capital or as a source of knowledge that helps to minimise the uncertainty surrounding the start-up process. Nevertheless, the connection between student entrepreneurship intention and entrepreneurial role models remains unexplored. According to research, role models may be better understood by using philosophies of (role) identification and social learning (Gibson, 2004). There are four interconnected tasks that entrepreneurs may do in theory: inspiration and motivation, self-efficacy improvement and learning by example, and helping others in their entrepreneurial endeavours, respectively. To properly understand entrepreneurship intention, it is helpful to understand the first two functions, which are connected to role identification theory. Business role models can provide information and expertise or practical assistance (Granovetter, 1973). Comparative studies in the entrepreneurial literature are an emerging area (Moore, 2004). The current literature has identified that there are four main factors for entrepreneurs' motivation; independence (Alstete, 2003; Cassar, 2007; Wilson et al., 2004), financial gains (Alstete, 2003), self-employment (Clain, 2000), and time flexibility (Georgellis and Wall, 2005). Other researchers have suggested that motivation factors can vary and depend on the entrepreneurship process (Shane et al., 2003). Consequently, as the motivational factors are diverse, there are key literature disparities to identify these influences using an interpretive approach (Kirkwood, 2009). This study can help fill the gaps and help understand the motivational aspects from a different perspective. This research is set out to explore the entrepreneurial intentions to engage in online communities, their motivations, and how the online platforms can aid the entrepreneurs on their entrepreneurial journey.

Exploration of Opportunities

When businesses decide to explore new technology opportunities, it is based on the idea that both internal and external variables have a direct influence on innovation and entrepreneurial behaviour. Resources and capabilities have been studied in the past as they relate to the creation and performance of technologies and inventions (Beckman et al., 2012; Katila and Shane, 2005). In the organisational context, for example, consideration is given to the impression of novel strategies on technological advances and innovation methods in different nations (Zhou et al., 2005). Many authors have called for greater research on types of innovations and different strategic orientations (Spyropoulou et al., 2018). It is similar to how entrepreneurial literature tends to explain the creation of new technology opportunities and how they are converted to business ventures (Guerrero and Urbano, 2017). This is where the importance of entrepreneurial orientation comes in (Wang et al., 2017). Researchers found that it was necessary to better understand how new or established companies explore or exploit technology potential (Busenitz et al., 2014). The environment plays a role in the creation of new technologies and provides an important framework (Spyropoulou et al., 2018), and entrepreneurship (Autio et al., 2014). Due to serious resource constraints and uncertain market conditions, environmental factors have posed major obstacles to companies' growth-through-innovation business strategies (Kuratko et al., 2015). Autio et al. (2014) point out that it is difficult to determine if environmental conditions foster entrepreneurship and innovation or whether economic cycles influence the elements that affect technical entrepreneurship (Fernández-Olmos and Ramírez-Alesón, 2017).

The origin of potential entrepreneurs, and their relationship to entrepreneurial behaviour in conditions of adversity, is a hot topic of discussion (Shepherd and Williams, 2020; Ajiwibawani and Subroto, 2017). Whether or not markets are in equilibrium, entrepreneurship has traditionally been seen to be about discovering and utilising profit opportunities that exist outside of individuals (Thompson and Byrne, 2020), although others argue that entrepreneurial activities may also generate such flaws. Most academics agree on the general description of opportunities as profitable business defects, whether they be prior causes or final results of entrepreneurial effort (Rapp and Olbrich, 2020; Ramoglou, 2021). Researchers are having a hard time conceptualising opportunities in ways that may be utilised to drive empirical research and entrepreneurial activity (Berglund et al., 2020), despite the rising consensus. This problem arises because opportunities like these can only be discovered after entrepreneurs have succeeded, and they are so abstractly conceptualised that "it will always be possible after an opportunity is formed to describe the actions of a particular entrepreneur in both 'discovery' and 'creation terms,' which have no empirical content in and of themselves" (Alvarez and Barney, 2007). Fundamentally, digital entrepreneurship has changed how venture opportunities can be discovered, transformed, and exploited, as well as the definition and modes of entrepreneurship throughout the world (Giones and Brem, 2017). The previous research has also focused on digital technology entrepreneurship in the field of innovation by Giones and Brem (2017). The article covers the entrepreneurship theme profoundly and stipulates further research to highlight how community dynamics can influence the activity of entrepreneurs in an emergent and developing ecosystem. Beliaeva et al. (2019) suggest that future researchers can apply a comparative country context to determine the country-level factors that shape and promote innovation ecosystems in the context of digital entrepreneurship.

Learning Opportunities and Possibilities

Entrepreneurs with a higher education level are seen as more essential in rising regional economies than those with a lower education level (Boldureanu et al., 2020). It also shows that entrepreneurs with a better academic upbringing are more likely to be inventive, adopt current business methods, and build their enterprises around new technologies (Baumol et al., 2009). It is vital to remark here that although education has impacted the entrepreneurship sphere, and many of the start-up owners have good education backgrounds, yet many innovators without formal schooling have also led to successful businesses (Douglass, 1976). Education, however, provides them with a better idea of how to incorporate them into a business in the future as they gain experience in their respective fields. As a result, academic entrepreneurs are not required to have any prior commercial experience. Utilising and developing high-level personnel while starting a new firm is crucial to its success (Minniti and Lévesque, 2008). Many people with a college education want to pursue an entrepreneurial career for economic reasons. Entrepreneurship in higher education suffers from several weaknesses, as observed in the European Union where around 24 percent of students at the university level have access to entrepreneurial courses. A student's entrepreneurial talents are less likely to develop the more specialised their subject of study is. Entrepreneurship education has limited time and knowledge from academic staff. Taking meaningful efforts to boost the number of entrepreneurs with a college education is essential (European Survey of Higher Education Institutions, 2008).

Neither inductive nor deductive, abduction is a way of gathering knowledge in real-life situations (Thagard and Croft, 2012). Abduction becomes a knowledge-creating process because it requires the acquirer to create innovative principles or depictions of connotations based on the acquired and integrated bits of evidence (Kakas and Riguzzi, 1997). Student entrepreneurs learn and grow as a consequence of their real-life experiences by coming up with inventive solutions to new issues. For similar reasons (Römer-Paakkanen and Pekkala, 2008), students are highly motivated to complete their projects as well. Abductive thinking is circular in nature and creates new knowledge continuously because learning should be internalised, the entrepreneurial learning cycle is characterised by a lack of externally driven learning. Sincere interest and encouragement from the student's environment will result in great internal drive in the entrepreneurial domain. The established entrepreneurs can also provide intellectual capital and learning opportunities for other entrepreneurs on the online start-up platforms, where intellectual capital can be viewed as an intermediary between the entrepreneurial learning and activities that promote knowledge-seeking (Scarmozzino et al., 2017).

The prospective entrepreneurial opportunities can be described in two distinct interpretations: discovery and creation theories (Alvarez and Barney, 2007), where discovery theory conveys that the presence of opportunities is regardless of entrepreneurs, and creation theory contends that opportunities arise through the actions of entrepreneurs. Both theories imply that opportunities arise when there are competitive flaws in a market or sector and the aim of entrepreneurs is to create, exploit, and capitalise on these opportunities (Shane and Venkataraman, 2000; Shane, 2003). Effective entrepreneurs understand market dynamics (Eckhardt et al., 2018), possess a very open attitude and an entrepreneurial inclination that allows them to recognise and grab opportunities (Yun et al., 2018). Eftekhari and Bogers (2015) suggest that it requires an entrepreneurial mentality for open innovation to discover and exploit possibilities, as well as build and design business models based on information gathered from external sources. The entrepreneurial mindset is motivated through educational abilities that result in maintaining innovative entrepreneurial aptitudes (Bissola et al., 2017). However, in order to establish sustainable and open innovation opportunities, technological strategy and entrepreneurial talents are required to engage collectively (Clausen and Rasmussen, 2011). Flamini et al. (2021) have indicated that open innovation literature requires further research to determine the affiliation between entrepreneurs and an organisational entity, where the entrepreneur transforms information into knowledge, manages various information and knowledge flows, and influences the innovation course through his or her capabilities (Au et al., 2013; Hsieh and Wu, 2019). Therefore, this research can fill the gap in the literature by determining the key factors associated with online start-up communities, entrepreneur's behaviour, and opportunity identification.

Innovative Tendencies Among Entrepreneurs

Intentionality is a mental state in which one focuses one's attention (and hence one's experience and behaviour) on a specified object (goal) or techniques for accomplishing it (Bird, 1988). According to numerous empirical studies, the strongest predictor of entrepreneurship is someone's future aim to convert oneself into an entrepreneur (Krueger Jr et al., 2000). Entrepreneurial ambitions, according to general ideas, are influenced by an individual's attitude toward entrepreneurship, cultural norms connected with entrepreneurship, and self-efficacy, among other things. There were no creative concepts included in intention-based models before; however, a long-standing association between entrepreneurship and inventiveness has existed (Braunerhjelm, 2010). Few studies have been conducted on the specific components of these programmes that are most effective in fostering entrepreneurial desires since (Braunerhjelm, 2010; Souitaris et al., 2007). Entrepreneurial education programmes place an emphasis on creative problem-solving and fresh idea generation activities. It has been said for a very long time that entrepreneurialism and innovative commercial activity are acts of creativity. Innovation and originality are key components of entrepreneurial activity (Davidsson, 2002). These characteristics can significantly influence the market process; what you want to sell, and how to market it.

Entrepreneurs must consider themselves as explorers, unlike traditional businessmen who usually rely on set principles and rarely explore further opportunities (Brenkert, 2009). Similarly, entrepreneurs have always been leaving their comfort zones, therefore, this is another way of enhancing creativity among entrepreneurs (Baucus and Human, 1995). Risk-taking is another approach that forms the foundation of entrepreneurship (Vereshchagina and Hopenhayn, 2009). This trait, however, must be an essential fragment of the commercial prototype rather than just being the motivation in the start and should keep on contributing to the execution and success of the start-up. Similarly, immediate response to social needs would also improve creativity among entrepreneurs (Muñoz et al., 2020). In conclusion, entrepreneurship business models depend on creativity and must keep on following the same principles.

Schumpeter (1934) presented the idea of creative destruction that further developed occupying niches concept (Wiklund, 1998), exploiting commercial opportunities (Zott et al., 2011), being radical (Lassen et al., 2006), innovative (Gartner, 1990), and risk-taking (Palich and Bagby, 1995). Entrepreneurs are pushed beyond their capabilities to distinguish themselves by being more visible and solution-oriented when resources are scarce (McDougall and Oviatt, 2000). Richter et al. (2017) have offered insights into digital entrepreneurship in the aspects of creativity and innovation with a qualitative research approach where 14 companies from 3 different countries were studied. The research was aimed at exploring the sharing economy phenomenon and presented findings that it has been affected by a number of factors such as economy, social orientation, digitalised environment, new urban solutions, new mindsets, various working conditions, and the driver of the sharing economy. Richter et al. (2017) mentioned further research to explore the sharing economy approach while incorporating cultural variables present in different countries.

CONCLUSION

This chapter ultimately aimed to explore and synthesise the perspective of digital entrepreneurship behaviour linked with online start-up communities, opportunity recognition and entrepreneurial intentions. We encourage further identification and integration of digital entrepreneurship central themes to provide a comprehensive understanding of the behavioural aspect of entrepreneurs, including their perceptions, intentions and motivation. Although the boundaries of digital technologies are still undefined, the dissemination of digitalisation has resulted in a new horizon of digital entrepreneurship by reshaping the traditional practices and procedures of seeking novel entrepreneurial opportunities. The emergence of digitalisation in entrepreneurship has also affected the criteria of competitive advantage and sustainability for national as well as global competition.

The theoretical underpinning implicated in this chapter may prove to be valuable for both academic researchers and management practitioners; this chapter contributes to the extant literature on digital entrepreneurship by highlighting the behaviour aspect involved in digital entrepreneurship and how the collaboration to co-create value may be conducted within digital online business communities. We hope, by doing this, to inspire further research on digital entrepreneurship and relevant behaviour patterns leading to collaborative co-creation of value. For management practitioners, the main concern would be to realise business competitive advantages through nurturing collaborative digital entrepreneurial behaviour.

We also encourage a thorough investigation of the determining factors of digital entrepreneurial behaviour and provide various solutions for utilising digital technologies for creating online communities through the development of digital ecosystems and innovative business models, which optimally maximise the individual, organisational as well as societal outcomes of digital entrepreneurship. Additionally, the drivers behind the development of an effective ecosystem reside in various elements, i.e. deep-rooted entrepreneurial culture, openness to innovation, highly motivated and skilful human capital, informative systems, uninterrupted communication, and cooperative managerial philosophy. Hence, this chapter sets a stage for future investigations to take the lead and further explore the dynamics and potential benefits of digital entrepreneurship while networking within online business platforms.

REFERENCES

Ajdari, P., Soltanifar, E., & Ansari, M. (2016). International opportunity recognition among Iranian practitioners: Analysis and practical application. *Journal for International Business and Entrepreneurship Development*, *9*(4), 379–397. doi:10.1504/JIBED.2016.080017

Ajiwibawani, M. P., & Subroto, W. T. (2017). The effect of achievement motivation, adversity quotient, and entrepreneurship experience on students entrepreneurship attitude. *International Journal of Academic Research in Business & Social Sciences*, *7*(9), 441–450. doi:10.6007/IJARBSS/v7-i9/3339

Ajzen, I. (1991). The theory of planned behavior. *Organizational Behavior and Human Decision Processes*, *50*(2), 179–211. doi:10.1016/0749-5978(91)90020-T

Ajzen, I. (2011). The theory of planned behaviour: Reactions and reflections. *Psychology & Health*, *26*(9), 1113–1127. doi:10.1080/08870446.2011.613995 PMID:21929476

Akpan, I. J., & Ibidunni, A. S. (2021). Digitization and technological transformation of small business for sustainable development in the less developed and emerging economies: A research note and call for papers. *Journal of Small Business and Entrepreneurship*, 1–7. doi:10.1080/08276331.2021.1924505

Ali, M. (2019a). The Barriers and Enablers of the Educational Cloud: A Doctoral Student Perspective. *Open Journal of Business and Management*, *7*(1).

Ali, M. (2019b). Cloud Computing at a Cross Road: Quality and Risks in Higher Education. *Advances in Internet of Things*, *9*(3), 33–49. doi:10.4236/ait.2019.93003

Ali, M. (Ed.). (2021). *Remote Work and Sustainable Changes for the Future of Global Business*. IGI Global. doi:10.4018/978-1-7998-7513-0

Ali, M. (2022). *Future Role of Sustainable Innovative Technologies in Crisis Management*. IGI Global. doi:10.4018/978-1-7998-9815-3

Ali, M., & Abdel-Haq, M. K. (2021). Bibliographical Analysis of Artificial Intelligence Learning in Higher Education: Is the Role of the Human Educator a Thing of the Past? In *Fostering Communication and Learning With Underutilized Technologies in Higher Education* (pp. 36–52). IGI Global. doi:10.4018/978-1-7998-4846-2.ch003

Ali, M., & Edghiem, F. (2021). Sustainable Business and Collaboration Driven by Big Data Analytics Amidst the Emergence of the Remote Work Culture. In *Remote Work and Sustainable Changes for the Future of Global Business* (pp. 15–32). IGI Global. doi:10.4018/978-1-7998-7513-0.ch002

Ali, M., Edghiem, F., & Alkhalifah, E. S. (2022). Cultural Challenges of ERP Implementation in Middle-Eastern Oil & Gas Sector: An Action Research Approach. *Systemic Practice and Action Research*. PMID:35668863

Ali, M. B. (2021). Internet of Things (IoT) to Foster Communication and Information Sharing: A Case of UK Higher Education. *Fostering Communication & Learning With Underutilized Technologies in Higher Education*, 1-20.

Ali, M. B., Wood-Harper, T., & Ramlogan, R. (2020a). A Framework Strategy to Overcome Trust Issues on Cloud Computing Adoption in Higher Education. In Modern Principles, Practices, and Algorithms for Cloud Security (pp. 162-183). IGI Global. doi:10.4018/978-1-7998-1082-7.ch008

Ali, M. B., Wood-Harper, T., & Ramlogan, R. (2020b). *The Role of SaaS Applications in Business IT Alignment: A Closer Look at Value Creation in Service Industry*. UKAIS.

Ali. (2019). Multiple Perspective of Cloud Computing Adoption Determinants in Higher Education a Systematic Review. *International Journal of Cloud Applications and Computing, 9*(3), 89-109.

Ali. (2020). Multi-Perspectives of Cloud Computing Service Adoption Quality and Risks in Higher Education. In D. B. A. Mehdi Khosrow-Pour (Ed.), *Handbook of Research on Modern Educational Technologies, Applications, and Management* (2nd ed.). IGI Global.

Alstete, J. (2003). Trends in corporate knowledge asset protection. *Journal of Knowledge Management Practice*, *4*(1).

Alvarez, S. A., & Barney, J. B. (2007). Discovery and creation: Alternative theories of entrepreneurial action. *Strategic Entrepreneurship Journal*, *1*(1-2), 11–26. doi:10.1002ej.4

Ardichvili, A., Cardozo, R., & Ray, S. (2003). A theory of entrepreneurial opportunity identification and development. *Journal of Business Venturing*, *18*(1), 105–123. doi:10.1016/S0883-9026(01)00068-4

Ardichvili, A., Maurer, M., Li, W., Wentling, T., & Stuedemann, R. (2006). Cultural influences on knowledge sharing through online communities of practice. *Journal of Knowledge Management*, *10*(1), 94–107. doi:10.1108/13673270610650139

Argote, L., & Ingram, P. (2000). Knowledge transfer: A basis for competitive advantage in firms. *Organizational Behavior and Human Decision Processes*, *82*(1), 150–169. doi:10.1006/obhd.2000.2893

Au, K., Chiang, F. F., Birtch, T. A., & Ding, Z. (2013). Incubating the next generation to venture: The case of a family business in Hong Kong. *Asia Pacific Journal of Management*, *30*(3), 749–767. doi:10.100710490-012-9331-7

Autio, E., Kenney, M., Mustar, P., Siegel, D., & Wright, M. (2014). Entrepreneurial innovation: The importance of context. *Research Policy*, *43*(7), 1097–1108. doi:10.1016/j.respol.2014.01.015

Awawdeh, H., Abulaila, H., Alshanty, A., & Alzoubi, A. (2022). Digital entrepreneurship and its impact on digital supply chains: The mediating role of business intelligence applications. *International Journal of Data and Network Science*, *6*(1), 233–242. doi:10.5267/j.ijdns.2021.9.005

Bandura, A. (1977). Self-efficacy: Toward a unifying theory of behavioral change. *Psychological Review*, *84*(2), 191–215. doi:10.1037/0033-295X.84.2.191 PMID:847061

Baran, G., & Berkowicz, A. (2021). Digital platform ecosystems as living labs for sustainable entrepreneurship and innovation: A conceptual model proposal. *Sustainability (Basel), 13*(11), 6494. doi:10.3390u13116494

Baranauskas, G., & Raišienė, A. G. (2022). Transition to digital entrepreneurship with a quest of sustainability: Development of a new conceptual framework. *Sustainability (Basel), 14*(3), 1104. doi:10.3390u14031104

Batjargal, B. (2006). The dynamics of entrepreneurs' networks in a transitioning economy: The case of Russia. *Entrepreneurship and Regional Development, 18*(4), 305–320. doi:10.1080/08985620600717448

Baucus, D. A., & Human, S. E. (1995). Second-career entrepreneurs: A multiple case study analysis of entrepreneurial processes and antecedent variables. *Entrepreneurship Theory and Practice, 19*(2), 41–71. doi:10.1177/104225879501900204

Baumol, W. J., Schilling, M. A., & Wolff, E. N. (2009). The superstar inventors and entrepreneurs: How were they educated? *Journal of Economics & Management Strategy, 18*(3), 711–728. doi:10.1111/j.1530-9134.2009.00227.x

Beckman, C., Eisenhardt, K., Kotha, S., Meyer, A., & Rajagopalan, N. (2012). Technology entrepreneurship. *Strategic Entrepreneurship Journal, 6*(2), 89–93. doi:10.1002ej.1134

Beckman, G. D., & Essig, L. (2012). Arts entrepreneurship: A conversation. *Artivate, 1*(1), 1–8. doi:10.1353/artv.2012.0000

Beliaeva, T., Ferasso, M., Kraus, S., & Damke, E. J. (2019). Dynamics of digital entrepreneurship and the innovation ecosystem: A multilevel perspective. *International Journal of Entrepreneurial Behaviour & Research, 26*(2), 266–284. doi:10.1108/IJEBR-06-2019-0397

Berglund, H., Bousfiha, M., & Mansoori, Y. (2020). Opportunities as artifacts and entrepreneurship as design. *Academy of Management Review, 45*(4), 825–846. doi:10.5465/amr.2018.0285

Bican, P. M., & Brem, A. (2020). Digital business model, digital transformation, digital entrepreneurship: Is there a sustainable "digital"? *Sustainability (Basel), 12*(13), 5239. doi:10.3390u12135239

Bird, B. (1988). Implementing entrepreneurial ideas: The case for intention. *Academy of Management Review, 13*(3), 442–453. doi:10.2307/258091

Bissola, R., Imperatori, B., & Biffi, A. (2017). A rhizomatic learning process to create collective knowledge in entrepreneurship education: Open innovation and collaboration beyond boundaries. *Management Learning, 48*(2), 206–226. doi:10.1177/1350507616672735

Boldureanu, G., Ionescu, A. M., Bercu, A. M., Bedrule-Grigoruță, M. V., & Boldureanu, D. (2020). Entrepreneurship education through successful entrepreneurial models in higher education institutions. *Sustainability (Basel), 12*(3), 1267. doi:10.3390u12031267

Bosma, N., Hessels, J., Schutjens, V., Van Praag, M., & Verheul, I. (2012). Entrepreneurship and role models. *Journal of Economic Psychology, 33*(2), 410–424. doi:10.1016/j.joep.2011.03.004

Bourdieu, P. (1977). *Outline of a theory of practice; translated by Richard Nice*. Cambridge University Press. doi:10.1017/CBO9780511812507

Bourdieu, P. (2018). Structures, habitus, practices. In *Rethinking the Subject* (pp. 31–45). Routledge. doi:10.4324/9780429497643-2

Braunerhjelm, P. (2010). *Entrepreneurship, Innovation and Economic Growth-past experience, current knowledge and policy implications*. Academic Press.

Brenkert, G. G. (2009). Innovation, rule breaking and the ethics of entrepreneurship. *Journal of Business Venturing*, *24*(5), 448–464. doi:10.1016/j.jbusvent.2008.04.004

Busenitz, L. W., Plummer, L. A., Klotz, A. C., Shahzad, A., & Rhoads, K. (2014). Entrepreneurship research (1985–2009) and the emergence of opportunities. *Entrepreneurship Theory and Practice*, *38*(5), 1–20. doi:10.1111/etap.12120

Cassar, G. (2007). Money, money, money? A longitudinal investigation of entrepreneur career reasons, growth preferences and achieved growth. *Entrepreneurship and Regional Development*, *19*(1), 89–107. doi:10.1080/08985620601002246

Clain, S. H. (2000). Gender differences in full-time self-employment. *Journal of Economics and Business*, *52*(6), 499–513. doi:10.1016/S0148-6195(00)00032-1

Clarkin-Phillips, J. (2018). Explicit pedagogy for transforming habitus: Early childhood teachers as mediators of affordances for parents. *New Zealand Journal of Educational Studies*, *53*(1), 83–99. doi:10.100740841-018-0104-9

Clausen, T., & Rasmussen, E. (2011). Open innovation policy through intermediaries: The industry incubator programme in Norway. *Technology Analysis and Strategic Management*, *23*(1), 75–85. doi:10.1080/09537325.2011.537109

Costa, C., & Murphy, M. (Eds.). (2015). *Bourdieu, habitus and social research: The art of application*. Springer. doi:10.1057/9781137496928

Davenport, T. H., & Prusak, L. (1998). *Working knowledge: How organizations manage what they know*. Harvard Business Press.

Davidsson, P., & Henrekson, M. (2002). Determinants of the prevalance of start-ups and high-growth firms. *Small Business Economics*, *19*(2), 81–104. doi:10.1023/A:1016264116508

Dougherty, D. (1999). Organizing for innovation. Managing organizations: Current issues, 174-189.

Douglas, J. D. (1976). Investigative social research: Individual and team field research. *Sage (Atlanta, Ga.)*.

Douglass, M. E. (1976, August). Entrepreneurial Education Level Related to Business Performance. In Academy of Management Proceedings (Vol. 1976, No. 1, pp. 461-464). Academy of Management. doi:10.5465/ambpp.1976.4975936

Eckhardt, J. T., Ciuchta, M. P., & Carpenter, M. (2018). Open innovation, information, and entrepreneurship within platform ecosystems. *Strategic Entrepreneurship Journal*, *12*(3), 369–391. doi:10.1002ej.1298

Eftekhari, N., & Bogers, M. (2015). Open for entrepreneurship: How open innovation can foster new venture creation. *Creativity and Innovation Management*, *24*(4), 574–584. doi:10.1111/caim.12136

Empson, L. (2001). Introduction: Knowledge management in professional service firms. *Human Relations*, *54*(7), 811–817. doi:10.1177/0018726701547001

European Survey of Higher Education Institutions. (2008). *Entrepreneurship in higher education, especially within non-business studies.* Final Report for the European Commission DG Education and Culture.

Feld, B. (2020). *Startup communities: Building an entrepreneurial ecosystem in your city*. John Wiley & Sons.

Fernandes, C., Pires, R., & Gaspar Alves, M. C. (2022). Digital Entrepreneurship and Sustainability: The State of the Art and Research Agenda. *Economies*, *11*(1), 3. doi:10.3390/economies11010003

Fernández-Olmos, M., & Ramírez-Alesón, M. (2017). How internal and external factors influence the dynamics of SME technology collaboration networks over time. *Technovation*, *64*, 16–27. doi:10.1016/j.technovation.2017.06.002

Fishbein, M., & Ajzen, I. (1977). *Belief, attitude, intention, and behavior: An introduction to theory and research.* Addison-Wesley.

Flamini, G., Pellegrini, M. M., Fakhar Manesh, M., & Caputo, A. (2022). Entrepreneurial approach for open innovation: Opening new opportunities, mapping knowledge and highlighting gaps. *International Journal of Entrepreneurial Behaviour & Research*, *28*(5), 1347–1368. doi:10.1108/IJEBR-01-2021-0079

Gagné, M. (2009). A model of knowledge-sharing motivation. *Human Resource Management, 48*(4), pp.571-589.

Gartner, W. B. (1990). What are we talking about when we talk about entrepreneurship? *Journal of Business Venturing*, *5*(1), 15–28. doi:10.1016/0883-9026(90)90023-M

Gavrila Gavrila, S., & De Lucas Ancillo, A. (2022). Entrepreneurship, innovation, digitization and digital transformation toward a sustainable growth within the pandemic environment. *International Journal of Entrepreneurial Behaviour & Research*, *28*(1), 45–66. doi:10.1108/IJEBR-05-2021-0395

Georgellis, Y., & Wall, H. J. (2005). Gender differences in self-employment. *International Review of Applied Economics*, *19*(3), 321–342. doi:10.1080/02692170500119854

Gibson, D. E. (2004). Role models in career development: New directions for theory and research. *Journal of Vocational Behavior*, *65*(1), 134–156. doi:10.1016/S0001-8791(03)00051-4

Giones, F., & Brem, A. (2017). Digital technology entrepreneurship: A definition and research agenda. *Technology Innovation Management Review*, *7*(5), 44–51. doi:10.22215/timreview/1076

Gist, M. E., & Mitchell, T. R. (1992). Self-efficacy: A theoretical analysis of its determinants and malleability. *Academy of Management Review*, *17*(2), 183–211. doi:10.2307/258770

Granovetter, M. S. (1973). The strength of weak ties. *American Journal of Sociology*, *78*(6), 1360–1380. doi:10.1086/225469

Gregori, P., & Holzmann, P. (2020). Digital sustainable entrepreneurship: A business model perspective on embedding digital technologies for social and environmental value creation. *Journal of Cleaner Production*, *272*, 122817. doi:10.1016/j.jclepro.2020.122817

Guerrero, M., & Urbano, D. (2017). The impact of Triple Helix agents on entrepreneurial innovations' performance: An inside look at enterprises located in an emerging economy. *Technological Forecasting and Social Change*, *119*, 294–309. doi:10.1016/j.techfore.2016.06.015

Guzman, G., & Trivelato, L. F. (2008). Transferring codified knowledge: Socio-technical versus top-down approaches. *The Learning Organization*, *15*(3), 251–276. doi:10.1108/09696470810868873

Hardy, C., Palmer, I., & Phillips, N. (2000). Discourse as a strategic resource. *Human Relations*, *53*(9), 1227–1248. doi:10.1177/0018726700539006

Harker, R. (1990). Bourdieu-education and reproduction. An introduction to the work of Pierre Bourdieu: The practice of theory, 86-108.

Hazlett, S. A., Mcadam, R., & Gallagher, S. (2005). Theory building in knowledge management: In search of paradigms. *Journal of Management Inquiry*, *14*(1), 31–42. doi:10.1177/1056492604273730

Herman, E. (2022). The interplay between digital entrepreneurship and sustainable development in the context of the EU digital economy: A multivariate analysis. *Mathematics*, *10*(10), 1682. doi:10.3390/math10101682

Hsieh, Y. J., & Wu, Y. J. (2019). Entrepreneurship through the platform strategy in the digital era: Insights and research opportunities. *Computers in Human Behavior*, *95*, 315–323. doi:10.1016/j.chb.2018.03.033

Huang, X. (2019). Understanding Bourdieu-cultural capital and habitus. *Review of European Studies*, *11*(3), 45. doi:10.5539/res.v11n3p45

Jha, A., Sindhwani, R., Dwivedi, A., & Saddikuti, V. (2022). Sustainable recovery for digital entrepreneurs with shared resources: Enablers, challenges and solutions. *Journal of Asia Business Studies*, *16*(3), 515–537. doi:10.1108/JABS-05-2021-0214

Kakas, A. C., & Riguzzi, F. (1997, September). Learning with abduction. In ILP (pp. 181-188). doi:10.1007/3540635149_47

Katila, R., & Shane, S. (2005). When are new firms more innovative than established firms? *Academy of Management Journal*, *48*(5), 814–829. doi:10.5465/amj.2005.18803924

Katila, R., & Shane, S. (2005). When does lack of resources make new firms innovative? *Academy of Management Journal*, *48*(5), 814–829. doi:10.5465/amj.2005.18803924

Kirkwood, J. (2009). Motivational factors in a push-pull theory of entrepreneurship. *Gender in Management*, *24*(5), 346–364. doi:10.1108/17542410910968805

Kollmann, T., Kleine-Stegemann, L., de Cruppe, K., & Strauss, C. (2022). Eras of digital entrepreneurship: connecting the past, present, and future. In *Handbook of Digital Entrepreneurship* (pp. 49–73). Edward Elgar Publishing. doi:10.1007/978-3-658-37260-6

Kozinets, R. V., & Gambetti, R. (Eds.). (2020). *Netnography unlimited: Understanding technoculture using qualitative social media research.* Routledge. doi:10.4324/9781003001430

Kraus, S., Palmer, C., Kailer, N., Kallinger, F. L., & Spitzer, J. (2019). Digital entrepreneurship: A research agenda on new business models for the twenty-first century. *International Journal of Entrepreneurial Behaviour & Research*, *25*(2), 353–375.

Krueger, N. F., & Carsrud, A. L. (1993). Entrepreneurial intentions: Applying the theory of planned behaviour. *Entrepreneurship and Regional Development*, *5*(4), 315–330. doi:10.1080/08985629300000020

Krueger, N. F. Jr, Reilly, M. D., & Carsrud, A. L. (2000). Competing models of entrepreneurial intentions. *Journal of Business Venturing*, *15*(5-6), 411–432. doi:10.1016/S0883-9026(98)00033-0

Kuratko, D. F., Morris, M. H., & Schindehutte, M. (2015). Understanding the dynamics of entrepreneurship through framework approaches. *Small Business Economics*, *45*(1), 1–13. doi:10.100711187-015-9627-3

Laitsou, E., Kargas, A., & Varoutas, D. (2020). Digital competitiveness in the European Union era: The Greek case. *Economies*, *8*(4), 85. doi:10.3390/economies8040085

Lassen, A. H., Gertsen, F., & Riis, J. O. (2006). The nexus of corporate entrepreneurship and radical innovation. *Creativity and Innovation Management*, *15*(4), 359–372. doi:10.1111/j.1467-8691.2006.00406.x

Lee, S. H., & Wong, P. K. (2004). An exploratory study of technopreneurial intentions: A career anchor perspective. *Journal of Business Venturing*, *19*(1), 7–28. doi:10.1016/S0883-9026(02)00112-X

Leonard, D. (1995). *Wellsprings of knowledge* (Vol. 16). Harvard Business School Press.

Lichtenthaler, U. (2021). Digitainability: The combined effects of the megatrends digitalization and sustainability. *Journal of Innovation Management*, *9*(2), 64–80. doi:10.24840/2183-0606_009.002_0006

Lin, Y. K., & Maruping, L. M. (2022). Open source collaboration in digital entrepreneurship. *Organization Science*, *33*(1), 212–230. doi:10.1287/orsc.2021.1538

Lyke, A. (2017). Habitus, doxa, and saga: Applications of Bourdieu's theory of practice to organizational history. *Management & Organizational History*, *12*(2), 163–173. doi:10.1080/17449359.2017.1329091

Manea, D. I., Istudor, N., Dinu, V., & Paraschiv, D. M. (2021). Circular economy and innovative entrepreneurship, prerequisites for social progress. *Journal of Business Economics and Management*, *22*(5), 1342–1359. doi:10.3846/jbem.2021.15547

Manjon, M., Aouni, Z., & Crutzen, N. (2022). Green and digital entrepreneurship in smart cities. *The Annals of Regional Science*, *68*(2), 1–34. doi:10.100700168-021-01080-z

Manstead, A. S., & Parker, D. (1995). Evaluating and extending the theory of planned behaviour. *European Review of Social Psychology*, *6*(1), 69–95. doi:10.1080/14792779443000012

McDougall, P. P., & Oviatt, B. M. (2000). International entrepreneurship: The intersection of two research paths. *Academy of Management Journal*, *43*(5), 902–906. doi:10.2307/1556418

Minniti, M., & Lévesque, M. (2008). Recent developments in the economics of entrepreneurship. *Journal of Business Venturing*, *23*(6), 603–612. doi:10.1016/j.jbusvent.2008.01.001

Muñoz, P., Kibler, E., Mandakovic, V., & Amorós, J. E. (2022). Local entrepreneurial ecosystems as configural narratives: A new way of seeing and evaluating antecedents and outcomes. *Research Policy, 51*(9), 104065. doi:10.1016/j.respol.2020.104065

Mwange, A. (2018). An evaluation of entrepreneurship intention theories. *Journal of Social Science and Humanities Research, 3*(9), 127–160.

Nakara, W. A., Laouiti, R., Chavez, R., & Gharbi, S. (2020). An economic view of entrepreneurial intention. *International Journal of Entrepreneurial Behaviour & Research, 26*(8), 1807–1826. doi:10.1108/IJEBR-12-2019-0693

Nambisan, S., Wright, M., & Feldman, M. (2019). The digital transformation of innovation and entrepreneurship: Progress, challenges and key themes. *Research Policy, 48*(8), 103773. doi:10.1016/j.respol.2019.03.018

Nobbs, A. (2017). *Habitus, ontology and misrecognition: Addressing the issue of structural injustice within the university context* [Doctoral dissertation]. Auckland University of Technology.

Orlikowski, W. J. (2002). Knowing in practice: Enacting a collective capability in distributed organizing. *Organization Science, 13*(3), 249–273. doi:10.1287/orsc.13.3.249.2776

Oyemomi, O., Liu, S., Neaga, I., Chen, H., & Nakpodia, F. (2019). How cultural impact on knowledge sharing contributes to organizational performance: Using the fsQCA approach. *Journal of Business Research, 94*, 313–319. doi:10.1016/j.jbusres.2018.02.027

Öztürk, Ş. (2011). Pierre Bourdieu's theory of social action. *Habitus Toplumbilim Dergisi*, (1), 63–77.

Palich, L. E., & Bagby, D. R. (1995). Using cognitive theory to explain entrepreneurial risk-taking: Challenging conventional wisdom. *Journal of Business Venturing, 10*(6), 425–438. doi:10.1016/0883-9026(95)00082-J

Pejic Bach, M., Aleksic, A., & Merkac-Skok, M. (2018). Examining determinants of entrepreneurial intentions in Slovenia: Applying the theory of planned behaviour and an innovative cognitive style. *Economic research-. Ekonomska Istrazivanja, 31*(1), 1453–1471. doi:10.1080/1331677X.2018.1478321

Perrin Moore, D. (2004). The entrepreneurial woman's career model: Current research and a typologicalframework. *Equal Opportunities International, 23*(7/8), 78–98. doi:10.1108/02610150410787864

Polanyi, M. (1983). *The tacit dimension.* Peter Smith.

Ramoglou, S. (2021). Knowable opportunities in an unknowable future? On the epistemological paradoxes of entrepreneurship theory. *Journal of Business Venturing, 36*(2), 106090. doi:10.1016/j.jbusvent.2020.106090

Rapp, D. J., & Olbrich, M. (2020). On entrepreneurial decision logics under conditions of uncertainty: An attempt to advance the current debate. *Journal of Innovation and Entrepreneurship, 9*(1), 21. doi:10.118613731-020-00131-7

Rehbein, B. (2017). *Society in Contemporary Laos: Capitalism, Habitus and Belief* (Vol. 88). Taylor & Francis. doi:10.4324/9781315229539

Richter, C., Kraus, S., Brem, A., Durst, S., & Giselbrecht, C. (2017). Digital entrepreneurship: Innovative business models for the sharing economy. *Creativity and Innovation Management, 26*(3), 300–310. doi:10.1111/caim.12227

Römer-Paakkanen, T., & Pekkala, A. (2008). Generating entrepreneurship from students' hobbies. In *Promoting Entrepreneurship by Universities, The Proceedings of the 2nd International FINPIN 2008 Conference, Hämeenlinna, Finland, April* (Vol. 20, No. 22, p. 340). Academic Press.

Scarmozzino, E., Corvello, V., & Grimaldi, M. (2017). Entrepreneurial learning through online social networking in high-tech startups. *International Journal of Entrepreneurial Behaviour & Research, 23*(3), 406–425. doi:10.1108/IJEBR-12-2015-0302

Schumpeter, J. A. (1934). *The Theory of Economic Development: An Inquiry into Profits, Capital, Credit, Interest, and the Business Cycle*. Harvard University Press.

Schumpeter, J. A., & Nichol, A. J. (1934). Robinson's economics of imperfect competition. *Journal of Political Economy, 42*(2), 249–259. doi:10.1086/254595

Senge, P. M. (1993). Transforming the practice of management. *Human Resource Development Quarterly, 4*(1), 5–32. doi:10.1002/hrdq.3920040103

Shane, S., Locke, E. A., & Collins, C. J. (2003). Entrepreneurial motivation. *Human Resource Management Review, 13*(2), 257–279. doi:10.1016/S1053-4822(03)00017-2

Shane, S., & Venkataraman, S. (2000). The promise of entrepreneurship as a field of research. *Academy of Management Review, 25*(1), 217–226. doi:10.5465/amr.2000.2791611

Shane, S. A. (2003). *A general theory of entrepreneurship: The individual-opportunity nexus*. Edward Elgar Publishing. doi:10.4337/9781781007990

Sharma, N. L., & Goswami, S. (2009). The nuances of knowledge creation and development in Indian pharmaceutical industry. *Journal of Knowledge Management, 13*(5), 319–330. doi:10.1108/13673270910988132

Shepherd, D. A., & Williams, T. (2020). Entrepreneurship responding to adversity: Equilibrating adverse events and disequilibrating persistent adversity. *Organization Theory, 1*(4). doi:10.1177/2631787720967678

Shimoni, B. (2017). What is resistance to change? A habitus-oriented approach. *The Academy of Management Perspectives, 31*(4), 257–270. doi:10.5465/amp.2016.0073

Si, S., Zahra, S. A., Wu, X., & Jeng, D. J. F. (2020). Disruptive innovation and entrepreneurship in emerging economics. *Journal of Engineering and Technology Management, 58*, 101601. doi:10.1016/j.jengtecman.2020.101601

Sole, D., & Edmondson, A. (2002). Situated knowledge and learning in dispersed teams. *British Journal of Management, 13*(S2), S17–S34. doi:10.1111/1467-8551.13.s2.3

Souitaris, V., Zerbinati, S., & Al-Laham, A. (2007). Do entrepreneurship programmes raise entrepreneurial intention of science and engineering students? The effect of learning, inspiration and resources. *Journal of Business Venturing, 22*(4), 566–591. doi:10.1016/j.jbusvent.2006.05.002

Southey, G. (2011). The Theories of Reasoned Action and Planned Behaviour Applied to Business Decisions: A Selective Annotated Bibliography. *Journal of New Business Ideas and Trends*, *9*(1).

Spyropoulou, S., Katsikeas, C. S., Skarmeas, D., & Morgan, N. A. (2018). Strategic goal accomplishment in export ventures: The role of capabilities, knowledge, and environment. *Journal of the Academy of Marketing Science*, *46*(1), 109–129. doi:10.100711747-017-0519-8

Stahl, G., & McDonald, S. (2021). Thinking with habitus in the study of learner identities. In *The Handbook of Critical Theoretical Research Methods in Education* (pp. 199–211). Routledge. doi:10.4324/9780429056963-13

Steininger, D. M., Kathryn Brohman, M., & Block, J. H. (2022). Digital entrepreneurship: What is new if anything? *Business & Information Systems Engineering*, *64*(1), 1–14. doi:10.100712599-021-00741-9

Thagard, P., & Croft, D. (2012). *Scientific Discovery and Technological Innovation: Ulcers, Dinosaur Extinction, and the Programming*. Model-Based Reasoning in Scientific Discovery.

Thompson, N. A., & Byrne, O. (2020). Advancing entrepreneurship as practice: Previous developments and future possibilities. In *Research handbook on entrepreneurial behavior, practice and process* (pp. 30–55). Edward Elgar Publishing.

Tornikoski, E., & Maalaoui, A. (2019). Critical reflections–The Theory of Planned Behaviour: An interview with Icek Ajzen with implications for entrepreneurship research. *International Small Business Journal*, *37*(5), 536–550. doi:10.1177/0266242619829681

Tsoukas, H., 2005. Do we really understand tacit knowledge. *Managing knowledge: An essential reader*, *107*, 1-18.

Van Auken, H., Fry, F. L., & Stephens, P. (2006). The influence of role models on entrepreneurial intentions. *Journal of Developmental Entrepreneurship*, *11*(02), 157–167. doi:10.1142/S1084946706000349

Van Den Hooff, B., & De Ridder, J. A. (2004). Knowledge sharing in context: The influence of organizational commitment, communication climate and CMC use on knowledge sharing. *Journal of Knowledge Management*, *8*(6), 117–130. doi:10.1108/13673270410567675

Van Gelderen, M., Brand, M., Van Praag, M., Bodewes, W., Poutsma, E., & Van Gils, A. (2008). Explaining entrepreneurial intentions by means of the theory of planned behaviour. *Career Development International*, *13*(6), 538–559. doi:10.1108/13620430810901688

Vereshchagina, G., & Hopenhayn, H. A. (2009). Risk taking by entrepreneurs. *The American Economic Review*, *99*(5), 1808–1830. doi:10.1257/aer.99.5.1808

Walsh, J. P., & Ungson, G. R. (1991). Organizational memory. *Academy of Management Review*, *16*(1), 57–91. doi:10.2307/258607

Wan, J., Wan, D., Luo, W., & Wan, X. (2011). Research on explicit and tacit knowledge interaction in software process improvement project. *Journal of Software Engineering and Applications*, *4*(06), 335–344. doi:10.4236/jsea.2011.46038

Wang, M., Jin, Z., Fan, S., Ju, X., & Xiao, X. (2021). Chinese residents' preferences and consuming intentions for hotels after COVID-19 pandemic: A theory of planned behaviour approach. *Anatolia, 32*(1), 132–135. doi:10.1080/13032917.2020.1795894

Wang, T., Thornhill, S., & De Castro, J. O. (2017). Entrepreneurial orientation, legitimation, and new venture performance. *Strategic Entrepreneurship Journal, 11*(4), 373–392. doi:10.1002ej.1246

Wenger, E., McDermott, R., & Snyder, W. (2002). Cultivating communities of practice: a guide to managing knowledge. Harvard Business School.

Wiklund, J. (1998). *Small firm growth and performance: Entrepreneurship and beyond* [Doctoral dissertation]. Internationella Handelshögskolan.

Wilson, F., Marlino, D., & Kickul, J. (2004). Our entrepreneurial future: Examining the diverse attitudes and motivations of teens across gender and ethnic identity. *Journal of Developmental Entrepreneurship, 9*(3), 177.

Yang, Y. (2014). Bourdieu, practice and change: Beyond the criticism of determinism. *Educational Philosophy and Theory, 46*(14), 1522–1540. doi:10.1080/00131857.2013.839375

Yun, J. J., Won, D., & Park, K. (2018). Entrepreneurial cyclical dynamics of open innovation. *Journal of Evolutionary Economics, 28*(5), 1151–1174. doi:10.100700191-018-0596-y

Zack, M. H. (1999). Developing a knowledge strategy. *California Management Review, 41*(3), 125–145. doi:10.2307/41166000

Zaheer, H., Breyer, Y., & Dumay, J. (2019). Digital entrepreneurship: An interdisciplinary structured literature review and research agenda. *Technological Forecasting and Social Change, 148*, 119735. doi:10.1016/j.techfore.2019.119735

Zhai, Y., Yang, K., Chen, L., Lin, H., Yu, M., & Jin, R. (2023). Digital entrepreneurship: Global maps and trends of research. *Journal of Business and Industrial Marketing, 38*(3), 637–655. doi:10.1108/JBIM-05-2021-0244

Zhang, X., Liu, S., Wang, L., Zhang, Y., & Wang, J. (2020). Mobile health service adoption in China: Integration of theory of planned behavior, protection motivation theory and personal health differences. *Online Information Review, 44*(1), 1–23. doi:10.1108/OIR-11-2016-0339

Zhou, K. Z., Yim, C. K., & Tse, D. K. (2005). The effects of strategic orientations on technology-and market-based breakthrough innovations. *Journal of Marketing, 69*(2), 42–60. doi:10.1509/jmkg.69.2.42.60756

Zott, C., Amit, R., & Massa, L. (2011). The business model: Recent developments and future research. *Journal of Management, 37*(4), 1019–1042. doi:10.1177/0149206311406265

Chapter 2
Taxonomy of Industry 4.0 Technologies in Digital Entrepreneurship and Co-Creating Value

Mohammed Ali
University of Salford, UK

ABSTRACT

This chapter proposes a taxonomy of Industry 4.0 (I4.0) technologies in the context of digital entrepreneurship and co-creating value. The I4.0 taxonomy ranges from cyber-physical systems and the internet of things (IoT) to big data and cloud computing, among others, which are key enabling technologies (KETs) of I4.0. The chapter examines how these technologies are utilised in digital entrepreneurship and co-creating value, and how they can be integrated to create innovative business models and enhance business operations. The taxonomy offers a comprehensive framework for understanding the different Industry 4.0 technologies and their applications in the rapidly evolving landscape of digital entrepreneurship and co-creating value.

INTRODUCTION

Businesses today face a growing need to adapt to changing market demands and remain competitive. Thanks to advancements in technology, companies can improve their productivity and efficiency through digital transformation. The availability of smart sensors, computing power, robotics, and ICT has enabled the rise of Industry 4.0, or the fourth industrial revolution (I4.0). I.40 is the fourth model of digital transformation (Marcon et al., 2022). The first model focused on automating individual tasks and processes, while the second model focused on connecting these tasks and processes through the use of enterprise resource planning (ERP) systems. The third model focused on leveraging digital technologies to create new business models and revenue streams. I.40 builds on these previous models by

DOI: 10.4018/978-1-6684-7416-7.ch002

integrating advanced technologies such as the Internet of Things (IoT), artificial intelligence (AI), and big data analytics to create smart, interconnected, and autonomous systems. This enables manufacturers to optimize their production processes, increase efficiency, and reduce costs by leveraging real-time data and insights. The shift towards intelligent manufacturing relies on the integration of digitalization into the industrial sector through the use of IoT. The success of I.40 depends on the implementation of key enabling technologies, as shown in Figure 1 (Ryalat et al., 2023; Singh et al., 2023).

Figure 1. Pillars of I.40

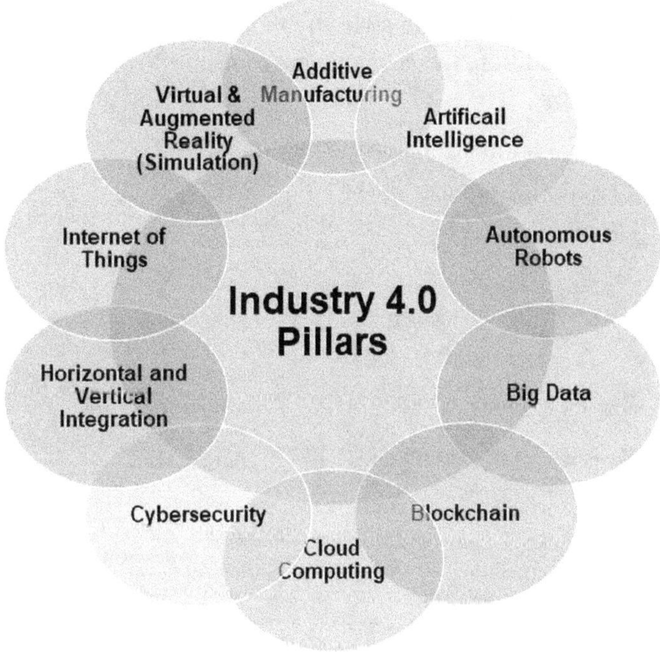

I.40 has significant implications for digital entrepreneurship and business by opening new doors for innovation and operational excellence. By utilising digital technologies, entrepreneurs can create products and services that are tailored to their customers, cost-effective, and environmentally sustainable. They can also optimise their processes to minimise waste, enhance quality, and increase efficiency. Innovation is a key driver of I4.0 in digital entrepreneurship and business, enabling entrepreneurs to invent new business models and solutions that leverage emerging technologies. By fostering a culture of innovation, entrepreneurs can maintain a competitive edge and deliver value to their customers. Operations management is equally vital to I4.0 in digital entrepreneurship and business, helping entrepreneurs optimise their processes and streamline their operational efficiency. By leveraging data analytics, entrepreneurs can gain insights into their operations and make informed decisions that propel their businesses forward (Duggal et al., 2022; Matt et al., 2020; Ng, 2021; Singh et al., 2023).

I4.0 is a transformative force in digital entrepreneurship and business, offering unprecedented opportunities for innovation and operational excellence. Through the integration of cyber-physical systems, the Internet of Things (IoT), Big Data, cloud computing, artificial intelligence (AI), robotics, and smart factories, entrepreneurs can co-create value and build sustainable and profitable businesses that are responsive to the needs of their customers and competitive on a global scale (M. Ali, 2019, 2021; Ali & Abdel-Haq, 2021; Ali & Edghiem, 2021; M. B. Ali, 2021; Ali et al., 2020a, 2020b). Therefore, this chapter delves into the main building blocks and facilitators of I.40 in the context of digital entrepreneurship and co-creating value.

Evolution and Development of I4.0

The first industrial revolution began around 1760 and was one of four major revolutions in human history, each bringing its own advancements and improvements. During this period, the discovery of steam engines greatly enhanced human lifestyles by reducing the need for manual labour and increasing workflow efficiency. In addition, the development of steamships allowed for faster travel over long distances (Singh et al., 2023).

Figure 2. Evolution and development of I.40
Source: InfoSys (2023)

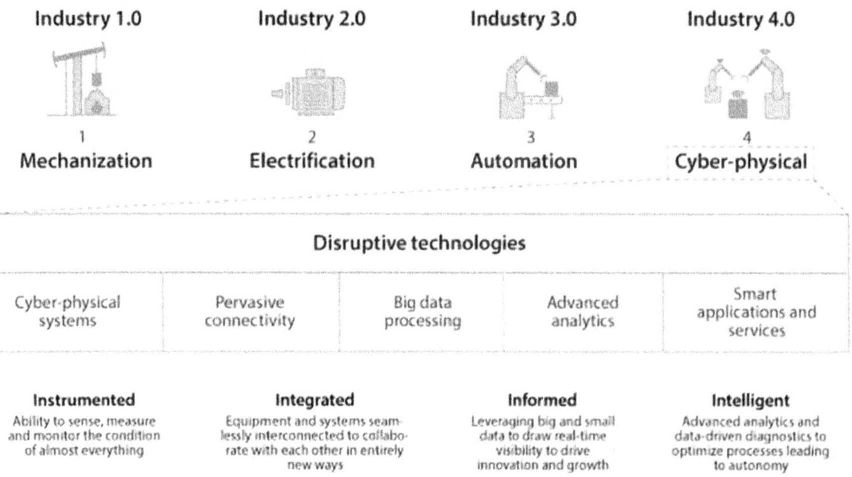

The second industrial revolution, which occurred in the 19th century, introduced electric power and mass production assembly, revolutionising the production of cars. The third industrial revolution, in the 1970s, utilised electronic, IT, and computer automation to automate production processes. The fourth industrial revolution, I.40, is marked by smart industrialisation, where digital computers and sensing devices strengthen production processes. The integration of cyber-physical production systems with industry leads to more reliable and smart manufacturing units where the interaction between processes, components, and people is almost independent. In I.40, self-repair processes, self-organised logistics, and automatic defect reduction are accomplished without human intervention (Grabowska et al., 2022; Singh et al., 2023; Tortorella et al., 2020; Xu et al., 2021). Figure 2 provides a summary of the four industrial revolutions.

I4.0 Pillars

I.40 integrates digital technologies like IoT, AI, machine learning, big data, and cloud computing with traditional industrial processes to create a more efficient and connected system of production, distribution, and consumption. Smart machines, systems, and processes optimise performance, reduce waste, and improve quality by communicating with each other and with humans in real-time. The core technologies of I.40 are IoT, big data, AI, and cloud computing. These enable real-time communication and collaboration between machines, systems, and people, optimising production and improving product quality. The goal is a fully automated and self-optimising production system. Modern hardware infrastructure, wireless devices, and smart mobile technologies have transformed connectivity and enabled cost-effective services (Ryalat et al., 2023; Singh et al., 2023). Key components of I.40 include IoT, big data, cloud computing, AI, ML, smart sensing, 3D printing, mobile technology, and blockchain. These components are essential for growth and efficiency in industrial manufacturing. The I4.0 pillars are summarised below:

Additive Manufacturing

Additive manufacturing is a method of building objects by joining materials together in layers using a 3D computer model as a guide. It is different from traditional manufacturing methods, which often involve cutting or subtracting materials from a larger piece (Godec et al., 2022). Additive manufacturing, or 3D printing, is also an innovative technology that has the potential to revolutionise the manufacturing industry. It enables the production of complex and customised products while reducing costs and waste. In the automotive and aerospace industries, 3D printing can reduce the weight of parts and increase fuel efficiency. However, the high initial investment, limited material options, and quality control issues can be challenges.

Table 1. Benefits and challenges of additive manufacturing

Benefits	Challenges
Increased Design Flexibility: Additive manufacturing allows for the creation of highly complex geometries and custom designs that may not be possible with traditional manufacturing methods.	Limited Material Selection: Although the range of materials available for additive manufacturing has grown significantly in recent years, there are still limitations in terms of the types of materials that can be used.
Faster Time to Market: With additive manufacturing, products can be designed and produced more quickly than with traditional manufacturing methods, allowing businesses to get products to market faster.	High Initial Investment: The cost of acquiring and maintaining additive manufacturing equipment can be high, which can be a barrier for some businesses.
Reduced Waste: Additive manufacturing creates less waste than traditional manufacturing methods, as only the necessary amount of material is used to produce a given product.	Limited Production Volume: Additive manufacturing may not be suitable for producing high volumes of products, as the process can be slower than traditional manufacturing methods.
Personalisation and Customisation: Additive manufacturing allows for the creation of highly personalised and customised products, which can be a competitive advantage for businesses.	Quality Control Challenges: Quality control can be more difficult with additive manufacturing, as the process can be more variable than traditional manufacturing methods.
Distributed Manufacturing: Additive manufacturing can be done anywhere with the appropriate equipment, allowing for decentralised production, and reducing the need for transportation and logistics.	Intellectual Property Concerns: The ease of reproducing digital designs with additive manufacturing raises concerns about intellectual property protection and counterfeiting.

Figure 3. Model of additive manufacturing
Source: Tashi et al. (2018)

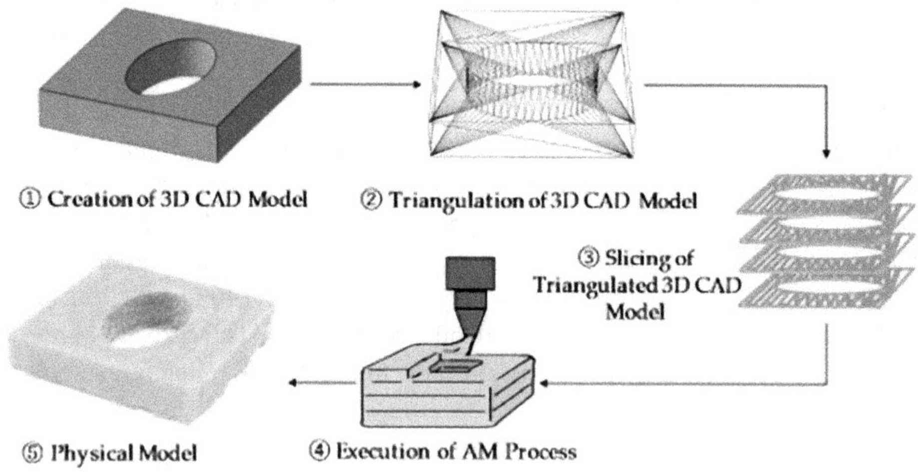

Digital business plays a crucial role in additive manufacturing by providing digital design and file sharing, streamlining the ordering and delivery processes, and offering real-time visibility into the manufacturing process. Furthermore, digital technologies such as artificial intelligence and machine learning can optimise the design and production processes for additive manufacturing, leading to more efficient supply chain management and quality control. It is important for businesses to invest in the necessary infrastructure and personnel to effectively leverage additive manufacturing in I.40. This technology has the potential to disrupt traditional manufacturing processes and create new business models, making it an essential part of the digital transformation journey (Davila Delgado et al., 2019; Godec et al., 2022; Ngo et al., 2018; Oettmeier & Hofmann, 2017; Tashi et al., 2018). See Table 1 for a summary of the benefits and challenges of additive manufacturing.

Artificial Intelligence

AI refers to systems programmed to think and act like humans to solve problems and learn. It is used in various sectors like banking, finance, health, and communication to make informed decisions and reduce errors (see Figure 4). The integration of AI in devices allows them to operate automatically 24/7 (Ryalat et al., 2023; Singh et al., 2023). Machines have the ability to perform tasks that typically require human intelligence, such as decision-making, speech recognition, and visual perception. There are two types of AI: narrow or weak AI, which is designed to perform a specific task, and general or strong AI, which has the ability to perform any intellectual task that a human can. The benefits of AI in digital business include increased efficiency and productivity, cost savings, improved decision-making, personalised customer experiences, and the ability to process vast amounts of data quickly and accurately.

However, challenges associated with AI include potential bias in decision-making, job displacement, data privacy concerns, and the need for significant investments in infrastructure and talent. The implications of AI for digital business are significant, as AI can enable the automation of various business processes, the creation of new products and services, and valuable insights into customer behaviour and preferences. However, responsible implementation is necessary to ensure ethical use and fair distribution of benefits across society (Ali & Abdel-Haq, 2021; Han et al., 2023; Li et al., 2022; Manickam, 2020; Ryalat et al., 2023; Singh et al., 2023). See Table 2 for a summary of the benefits and challenges of artificial intelligence.

Table 2. Benefits and challenges of artificial intelligence

Benefits	Challenges
Improved Efficiency: AI can automate routine tasks, such as data entry and analysis, freeing up employees to focus on higher-level tasks.	Data Privacy and Security: The use of AI involves collecting and analysing vast amounts of data, which raises concerns about data privacy and security.
Enhanced Customer Experience: AI-powered chatbots and virtual assistants can provide 24/7 support, personalised recommendations, and more, leading to an improved customer experience.	Bias and Fairness: AI algorithms can be biased, perpetuating unfairness and discrimination, and there is a need to ensure that AI is used ethically and fairly.
Predictive Analytics: AI can analyse data and make predictions, allowing businesses to make informed decisions and optimise operations.	Integration with Existing Systems: Integrating AI with existing business systems can be challenging, requiring specialised expertise and resources.
Competitive Advantage: AI can provide a competitive advantage, allowing businesses to stay ahead of the competition and respond quickly to changing market conditions.	Lack of Transparency: AI algorithms can be complex and difficult to understand, making it challenging to explain their decisions and actions.
Innovation and Creativity: AI can support innovation and creativity, allowing businesses to explore new ideas and solutions.	Talent Shortage: There is a shortage of skilled professionals with expertise in AI, making it challenging for businesses to find and retain talent.

Figure 4. Classifications of AI
Source: Manickam (2020)

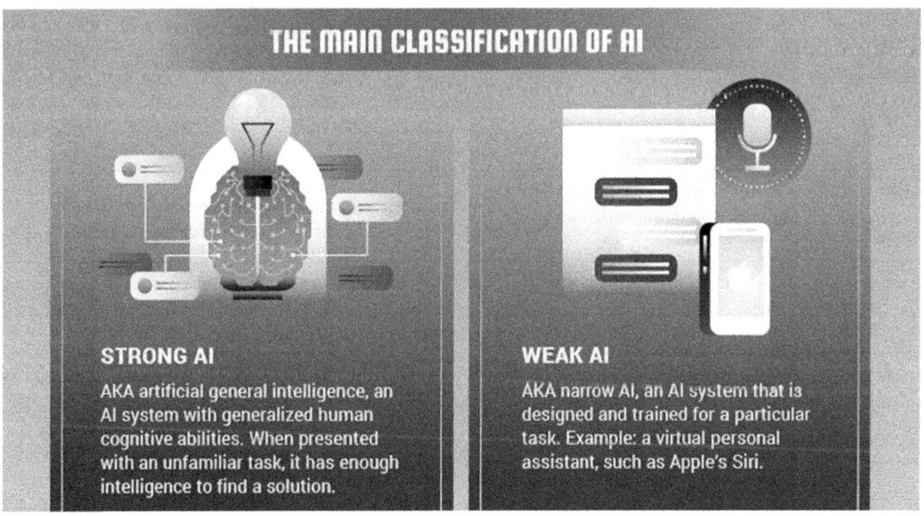

Autonomous Robots

Autonomous robots are self-operating machines that use artificial intelligence and sensors to perform tasks without human intervention. For an autonomous robot to be a human's life partner, it should be able to communicate its actions and goals in a way that humans can easily understand (see Figure 5). To achieve this, the robot should be able to assess the human's internal state and adjust its behaviour, actions, and way of presenting information accordingly (Sakai & Nagai, 2022). By developing such mechanisms, robots can earn the trust of humans as they become more considerate of human needs. They offer several benefits to digital businesses, including increased efficiency, reduced labour costs, and improved safety. They can perform repetitive, dangerous, or unpleasant tasks and operate in hazardous environments or emergency scenarios. For example, in the manufacturing industry, robots can perform assembly and packaging tasks, while in the healthcare industry, they can aid in surgery and medication management. However, the use of autonomous robots also presents ethical and social implications. The displacement of human workers can lead to job loss and reduced job security.

Additionally, safety and reliability must be carefully considered, as any malfunction or error could result in injury or damage to property. Companies must also consider potential legal liability in the event of an accident involving an autonomous robot. Despite these challenges, the use of autonomous robots can enable companies to automate operations and increase productivity. Investment in development and deployment is required, but the potential benefits can be significant, particularly in industries where efficiency and safety are critical factors. Digital businesses that adopt autonomous robots may also gain a competitive advantage, as they can reduce costs and improve customer experiences (Rahal et al., 2023; Sakai & Nagai, 2022). See Table 3 for a summary of the benefits and challenges of automated robots.

Table 3. Benefits and challenges of automated robots

Benefits	Challenges
Increased Efficiency: Autonomous robots can work 24/7 without breaks, leading to increased efficiency and productivity.	High Initial Investment: The cost of acquiring and maintaining autonomous robots can be high, which can be a barrier for some businesses.
Improved Quality: Autonomous robots can perform tasks with a high level of accuracy and consistency, improving the quality of products and services.	Safety Concerns: Autonomous robots can pose safety risks to employees and customers if not properly designed and tested.
Cost Savings: Autonomous robots can reduce labour costs and improve operational efficiency, leading to cost savings for businesses.	Technical Limitations: Autonomous robots may not be suitable for all tasks, and there may be technical limitations that prevent them from performing certain functions.
Scalability: Autonomous robots can be easily scaled up or down as needed, allowing businesses to adapt to changing demand.	Legal and Regulatory Issues: The use of autonomous robots raises legal and regulatory issues, such as liability and insurance concerns.
Flexibility: Autonomous robots can be programmed to perform a wide range of tasks, making them highly flexible and adaptable.	Public Perception: The use of autonomous robots can raise concerns among the public, such as job displacement and ethical concerns.

Figure 5. Autonomous robot example
Source: Rahal et al. (2023)

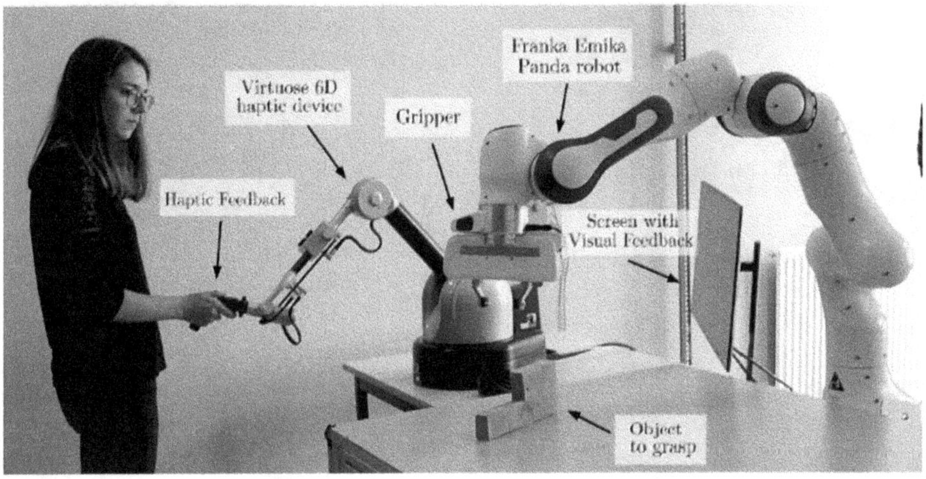

Big Data

Big data refers to large sets of data, often with high volume, speed, and diversity, that need a flexible and efficient system for storage, processing, and examination (Grady et al., 2014). These are large and complex data sets that traditional processing methods are unable to efficiently handle. They can come from various sources and be analysed to identify patterns, trends, and insights that can inform decision-making and improve business outcomes. Big data can be best represented through the 9 vs (see Figure 6). The increasing use of digital technologies generates a large volume of data that can provide a competitive advantage for digital businesses. However, businesses must consider challenges such as data privacy and security, as well as the need for skilled personnel to analyse and interpret data. To effectively leverage big data analytics, organisations must invest in the necessary infrastructure and personnel.

Table 4. Benefits and challenges of big data

Benefits	Challenges
Improved Decision Making: Big data can provide insights into customer behavior, market trends, and other factors that can inform business decisions.	Data Quality and Consistency: Big data is only valuable if it is accurate, consistent, and relevant. Poor data quality can lead to incorrect insights and decisions.
Enhanced Customer Experience: Big data can be used to personalise marketing, improve customer service, and provide a better overall customer experience.	Privacy and Security Concerns. The collection and use of big data can raise concerns about privacy and security, especially in light of recent data breaches and scandals.
Increased Efficiency and Productivity: Big data can automate routine tasks and optimise operations, leading to increased efficiency and productivity.	Skills and Expertise Shortage: Big data requires specialised skills and expertise, and there is a shortage of professionals with these skills.
Competitive Advantage: Big data can provide a competitive advantage by identifying new opportunities, predicting market trends, and optimising pricing strategies.	Technical Infrastructure and Integration: The processing and analysis of big data requires significant technical infrastructure and integration with existing systems, which can be challenging.
Innovation and Creativity: Big data can support innovation and creativity by providing new insights and opportunities.	Ethical Concerns: The use of big data can raise ethical concerns, such as the potential for discrimination and bias in decision-making.

Figure 6. 9vs of big data
Source: Federico (2018)

Big data analytics is crucial for achieving high production efficiency in I.40 and can help create intelligent analysis models and algorithms for smart manufacturing. The value of big data in a data-driven world is significant and is gaining traction in digital business. With proper implementation and management, big data can provide valuable insights and inform strategic business decisions. The potential benefits of big data include increased efficiency, improved customer experiences, and optimised operations, leading to a competitive advantage in the marketplace (Ali & Edghiem, 2021; Davenport et al., 2012; Federico, 2018; Grady et al., 2014; Marr, 2016, 2017, 2020). See Table 4 for a summary of the benefits and challenges of big data.

Blockchain

Simply put, blockchain is a type of technology that uses a decentralised shared ledger to store data in a specific order that cannot be changed or faked due to cryptographic measures (Sharmeela et al., 2023) (see the example in Figure 7). It is a distributed ledger technology that has the potential to disrupt traditional business models by offering a decentralised and secure alternative to traditional intermediaries such as banks and financial institutions. This technology allows for faster and more efficient transactions, reducing the need for manual intervention and increasing overall productivity. The transparency and accountability of blockchain can help build trust among customers and partners, leading to increased adoption and usage of blockchain-based solutions.

However, the scalability of blockchain remains a challenge as the computational requirements for verifying transactions increase with network size. Regulatory and legal issues also need to be addressed as the technology evolves, with many countries still unsure about how to regulate blockchain-based solutions. Additionally, the lack of interoperability among different blockchain platforms can limit their usefulness. In digital business, blockchain can enable new business models that eliminate intermediaries and reduce costs, leading to increased competition and innovation. Decentralised autonomous organisations, governed by smart contracts, can be created on the blockchain, potentially disrupting traditional corporate governance structures. The creation of new markets and asset classes, such as cryptocurrencies and digital assets, can also be facilitated by blockchain. Overall, the adoption and implementation of blockchain-based solutions in digital business will require careful consideration of these benefits and challenges (Li et al., 2022; Raj, 2023; Sharmeela et al., 2023; Statista, 2022; Yazdinejad et al., 2023). See Table 5 for a summary of the benefits and challenges of blockchain.

Figure 7. Example model of blockchain
Source: Raj (2023)

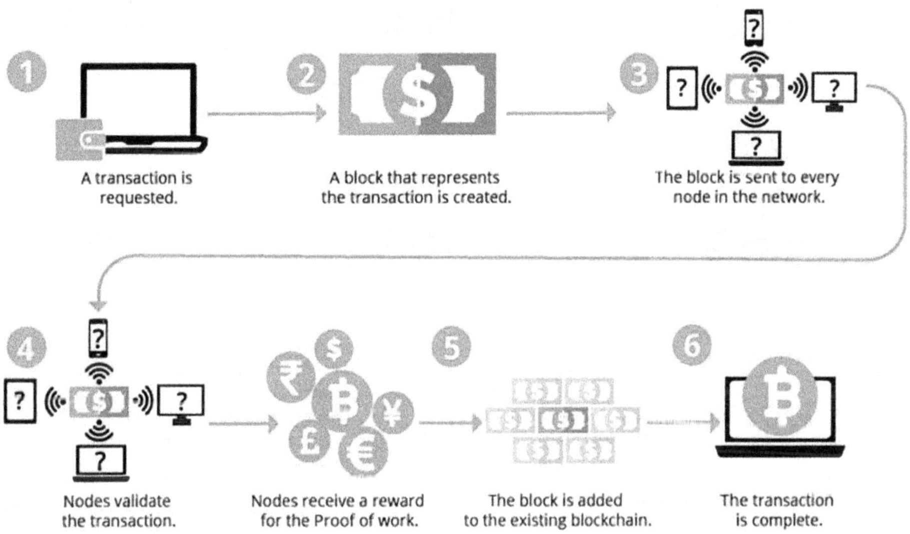

Table 5. Benefits and challenges of blockchain

Benefits	Challenges
Increased Transparency: Blockchain provides a transparent and tamper-proof ledger of transactions, improving transparency and accountability in business operations.	Technical Complexity: Blockchain is a complex technology that requires specialised expertise and technical infrastructure.
Enhanced Security: Blockchain uses cryptography and decentralised storage to ensure the security and integrity of transactions, reducing the risk of fraud and cyber-attacks.	Scalability: Blockchain currently has limited scalability, which can be a barrier to adoption in high-volume transaction environments.
Reduced Costs: Blockchain can reduce transaction costs by eliminating intermediaries and streamlining processes, resulting in cost savings for businesses.	Regulatory and Legal Uncertainty: The regulatory and legal landscape surrounding blockchain is still uncertain, which can create challenges for businesses.
Improved Efficiency: Blockchain can automate processes and reduce manual intervention, leading to improved efficiency and productivity.	Energy Consumption: The energy consumption required for blockchain transactions is currently high, which can raise environmental concerns.
Increased Trust: Blockchain enables trust between parties by providing a transparent and immutable record of transactions, reducing the need for trust-based relationships.	Lack of Standardisation: There is currently a lack of standardisation in the blockchain industry, which can make interoperability and integration difficult.

Cloud Computing

Cloud computing refers to a system that provides access to a shared and easily configurable set of computing resources such as servers, networks, storage, applications, and services. This access can be quickly granted or revoked with minimal management involvement or interaction with the service provider (Mell & Grance, 2009; Willcocks et al., 2014) (see Figure 8). Cloud computing is also a model where users can access and store data and applications over the internet rather than on their local hardware. This model allows for benefits such as cost savings, scalability, and access to the latest technology. As well as the five key characteristics (see Figure 9), there are three primary service models in cloud computing: infrastructure as a service (IaaS), platform as a service (PaaS), and software as a service (SaaS) (see Figure 10), and four deployment models: public, private, hybrid, and multi-cloud (see Figure 11).

Table 6. Benefits and challenges of cloud computing

Benefits	Challenges
Scalability and Flexibility: Cloud computing allows businesses to scale up or down their computing resources as needed, providing flexibility and cost savings.	Security and Privacy Concerns: Cloud computing raises concerns about data security and privacy, especially in public cloud environments.
Cost Savings: Cloud computing eliminates the need for businesses to invest in expensive hardware and software infrastructure, reducing costs and increasing efficiency.	Downtime and Outages: Cloud computing is vulnerable to downtime and outages, which can disrupt business operations and impact productivity.
Increased Collaboration: Cloud computing enables real-time collaboration and data sharing across geographically dispersed teams, improving productivity and innovation.	Vendor Lock-in: Cloud computing can create vendor lock-in, where businesses are dependent on a single provider and unable to easily switch to another provider.
Improved Disaster Recovery: Cloud computing provides businesses with automatic backup and recovery options, improving disaster recovery and business continuity.	Data Access and Control: Cloud computing raises concerns about data ownership, control, and access, especially in public cloud environments.
Access to Advanced Technologies: Cloud computing provides businesses with access to advanced technologies and capabilities, such as artificial intelligence and machine learning.	Compliance and Regulation: Cloud computing raises compliance and regulatory concerns, especially in industries with strict data protection requirements.

Figure 8. Typology of cloud computing ecosystem
Source: Willcocks et al. (2014)

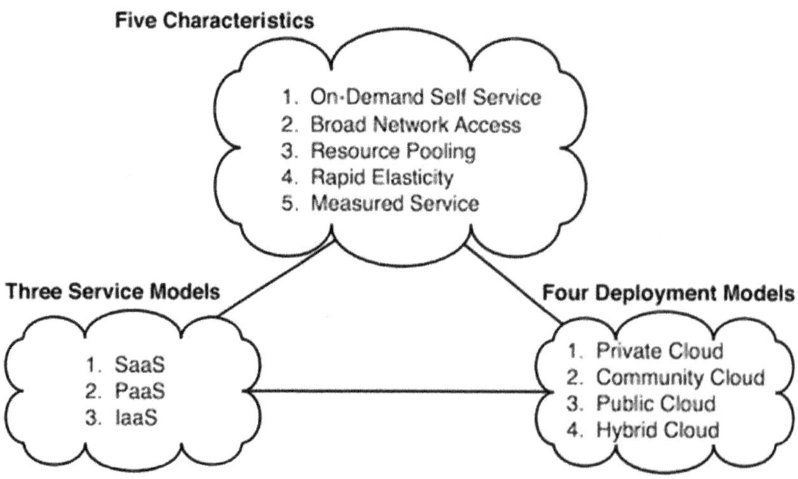

Figure 9. Cloud computing characteristics
Source: Willcocks et al. (2014)

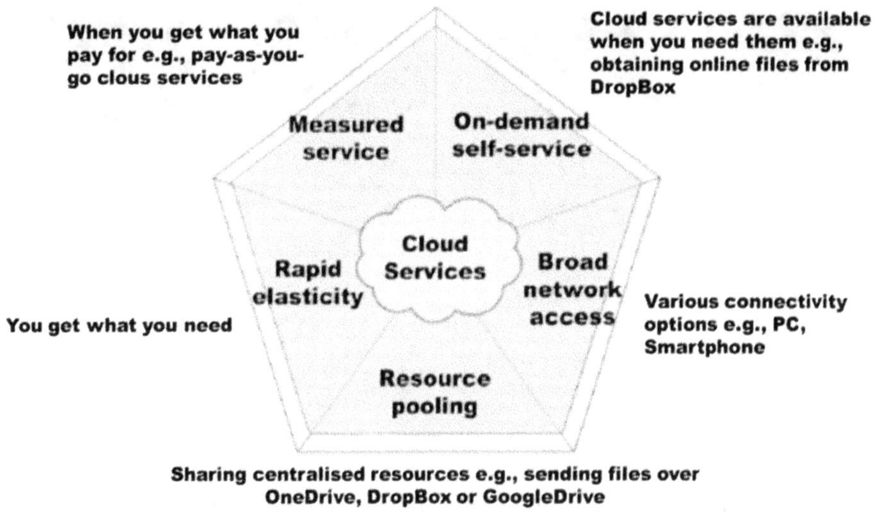

One significant benefit of cloud computing is the ability for remote work and collaboration, allowing employees to access work-related files and applications from anywhere with an internet connection. Additionally, cloud computing offers disaster recovery and easy data backup and recovery, reducing the risk of data loss in the event of hardware failure or other disasters. However, businesses must also consider potential risks when using cloud computing, such as data security and privacy concerns.

Figure 10. Cloud computing service models

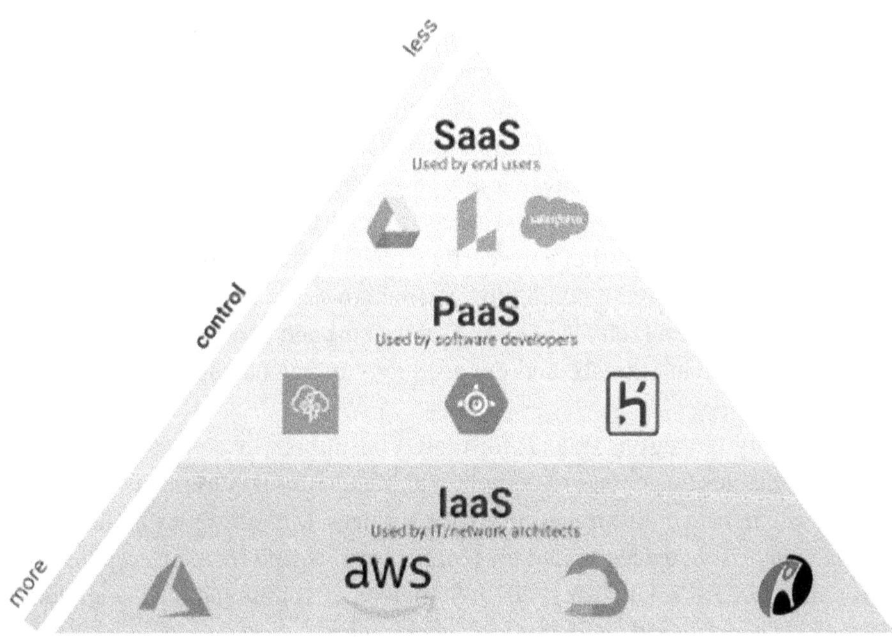

Figure 11. Cloud computing deployment models

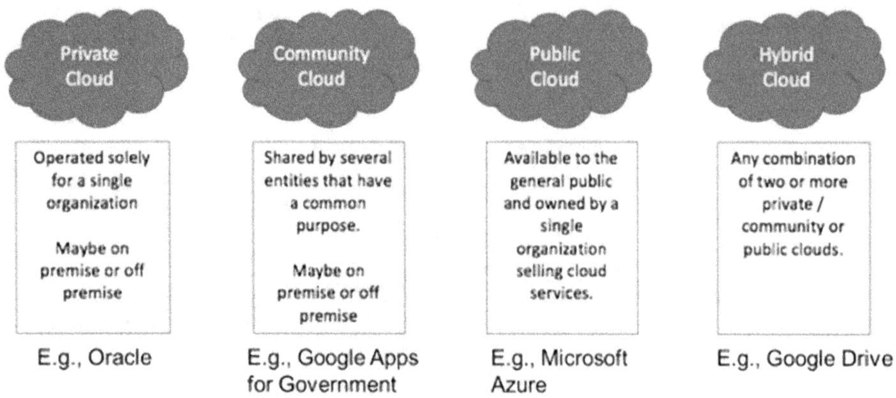

As data is stored on third-party servers, businesses must ensure that their data is protected from unauthorised access or data breaches. Vendor lock-in is another potential risk where businesses may become reliant on a particular cloud provider and have difficulty switching to a different provider. Additionally, businesses may have limited control over their data as it is stored on third-party servers, and potential downtime or service disruptions can occur, leading to lost productivity and revenue. Overall, cloud computing has significant implications for digital business, including increased efficiency, agility, and innovation, but businesses must also consider the potential risks and challenges associated with using it (Ali, 2019, 2020; Ali, 2018; M. Ali, 2019; Ali et al., 2017; Ali et al., 2020a; Willcocks et al., 2014; Willcocks et al., 2016). See Table 6 for a summary of the benefits and challenges of cloud computing.

Cybersecurity

To safeguard systems and information from harm, unauthorised usage, modifications, or exploitation is known as a process or activity of cybersecurity (Shoemaker et al., 2023) (see Figure 12). Cybersecurity is a vital practise that protects computer systems and sensitive information from cyber threats, such as hacking, malware, and phishing attacks. It involves various technologies, processes, and procedures to ensure the confidentiality, integrity, and availability of digital assets. Cyber-physical systems (CPSs) integrate computation, networking, and physical assets to create a communicative interface between the digital and physical worlds. Benefits of cybersecurity include protecting digital assets, ensuring confidentiality and privacy, complying with regulations, maintaining customer trust, and avoiding financial and reputational damage. However, challenges such as the cost and complexity of implementation and maintenance, constantly evolving threats, and the need for continuous education and training must be considered.

A robust cybersecurity strategy is crucial for digital businesses to protect their data and systems from cyber threats. It enables businesses to comply with regulatory requirements and ensures the trust and confidence of customers in online transactions and services. Measures may include access controls, encryption, firewalls, intrusion detection and prevention systems, and incident response plans (Furfaro et al., 2018; Okereafor, 2021; Paul & Wang, 2019; Schreider, 2020; Siregar & Chang, 2022). See Table 7 for a summary of the benefits and challenges of cybersecurity.

Table 7. Benefits and challenges of cybersecurity

Benefits	Challenges
Protection Against Cyber Attacks: Cybersecurity measures protect digital businesses against cyber-attacks, such as malware, phishing, and ransomware.	Complexity: Cybersecurity is complex and requires specialised expertise, making it challenging for businesses to implement and maintain effective cybersecurity measures.
Compliance with Regulations: Cybersecurity measures help businesses comply with data protection and privacy regulations, such as GDPR and CCPA.	Constantly Evolving Threats: Cyber threats are constantly evolving, making it difficult for businesses to keep up with the latest threats and vulnerabilities.
Maintaining Business Reputation: Effective cybersecurity measures can help maintain a business's reputation by protecting against data breaches and cyber-attacks.	Cost: Implementing and maintaining effective cybersecurity measures can be expensive, especially for small and medium-sized businesses.
Protection of Sensitive Information: Cybersecurity measures protect sensitive business and customer information, such as financial data and personal information.	Human Error: Human error, such as weak passwords and phishing scams, can undermine cybersecurity measures and make businesses vulnerable to cyber-attacks.
Competitive Advantage: Strong cybersecurity measures can provide a competitive advantage for businesses, as customers are more likely to trust businesses with their sensitive information.	Lack of Awareness: Lack of awareness and education about cybersecurity among employees can make businesses vulnerable to cyber-attacks.

Figure 12. Types of cybersecurity
Source: Mathrick (2023)

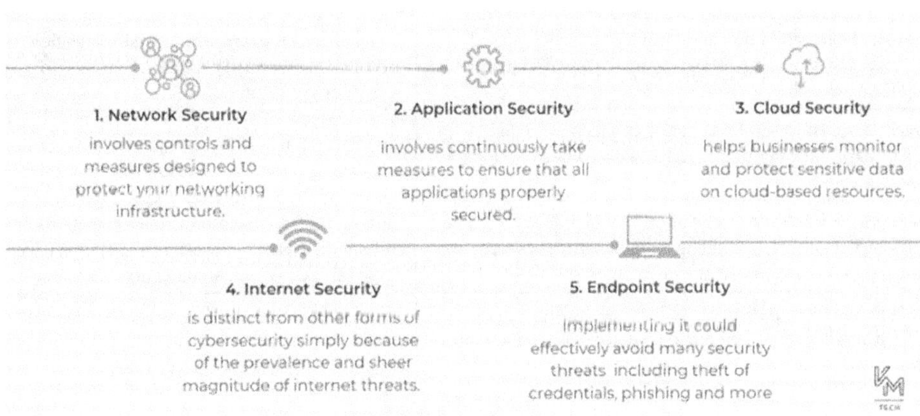

Horizontal and Vertical Integration

Horizontal integration is a strategy that involves merging or acquiring similar businesses to expand market share and gain economies of scale. This can result in increased profitability and reduced competition. On the other hand, vertical integration is the combination of companies at different stages of the same production process, which can lead to improved efficiency, greater control over the supply chain, and reduced transaction costs (Pérez-Lara et al., 2020) (see Figure 13). However, both forms of integration present challenges. Horizontal integration can lead to cultural clashes and increased complexity, and vertical integration can lead to reduced flexibility and increased dependence on suppliers. Digital technologies can facilitate integration, but they also bring cybersecurity risks and data privacy concerns that must be managed.

In the context of digital business, horizontal integration can lead to increased market power and profitability, while vertical integration can reduce transaction costs and improve product quality. However, integration can also present challenges such as cultural clashes and data privacy concerns that must be managed to ensure long-term success. Digital businesses must carefully consider the benefits and risks of integration and develop strategies to manage these challenges effectively (Dalenogare et al., 2018; Grossmann et al., 2013; Pérez-Lara et al., 2020). See Table 8 for a summary of the benefits and challenges of horizontal and vertical integration.

Table 8. Benefits and challenges of horizontal and vertical integration

Benefits	Challenges
Horizontal Integration	
Diversification of Products and Services: Horizontal integration allows digital businesses to diversify their products and services by acquiring or merging with other companies in the same industry.	Integration Challenges: Horizontal integration can be challenging to implement and integrate different systems, processes, and cultures of merged companies.
Economies of Scale: Horizontal integration can lead to economies of scale, reducing costs and increasing efficiency by sharing resources and eliminating duplicate processes.	Competitive Pressures: Horizontal integration can lead to increased competitive pressures, as it may trigger similar actions by competitors.
Increased Market Share: Horizontal integration can increase a digital business's market share, allowing it to capture a larger share of the market and generate more revenue.	Regulatory Barriers: Horizontal integration can face regulatory barriers, such as antitrust laws and regulations.
Access to New Markets: Horizontal integration can provide access to new markets and customer segments, expanding a digital business's reach and revenue streams.	Cultural Differences: Horizontal integration can lead to cultural differences between merged companies, affecting employee morale and productivity.
Reduced Risk: Horizontal integration can reduce risk by diversifying a digital business's revenue streams and reducing dependence on a single product or service.	Brand Dilution: Horizontal integration can lead to brand dilution, as merged companies may have different brand identities and customer perceptions.
Vertical Integration	
Control Over Supply Chain: Vertical integration allows digital businesses to have more control over their supply chain, from sourcing raw materials to distributing finished products.	Higher Costs: Vertical integration can be expensive to implement, as it requires investments in infrastructure and resources.
Improved Efficiency: Vertical integration can lead to improved efficiency, as digital businesses can optimise their operations and eliminate inefficiencies.	Risks of Overinvestment: Vertical integration can lead to overinvestment in areas where businesses lack expertise or market knowledge.
Competitive Advantage: Vertical integration can provide a competitive advantage by improving product quality and reducing costs.	Reduced Flexibility: Vertical integration can reduce a digital business's flexibility and responsiveness to changes in the market.
Innovation: Vertical integration can foster innovation by allowing digital businesses to control the entire product development and distribution process.	Potential for Conflict: Vertical integration can lead to conflicts between different parts of the supply chain, such as between manufacturers and distributors.
Difficulties in Managing: Vertical integration can be challenging to manage, especially if digital businesses lack experience in managing multiple aspects of the supply chain.	Supply Chain Disruptions: Vertical integration can lead to supply chain disruptions if one part of the supply chain experiences operational issues.

Figure 13. Example model of horizontal/vertical integration
Source: Grossmann et al. (2013)

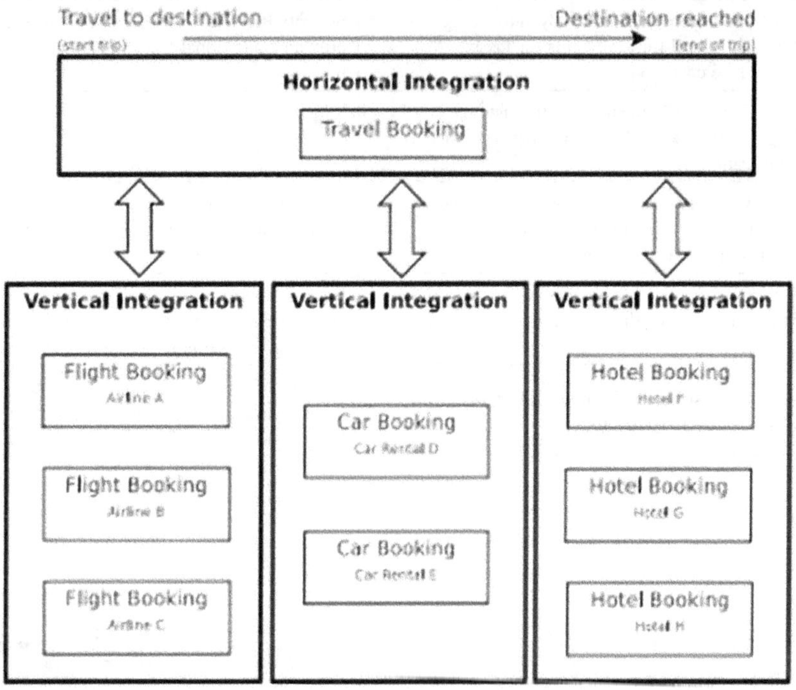

Internet of Things

The Internet of Things (IoT) is a network of physical devices, appliances, and other objects that are embedded with sensors, software, and connectivity, enabling them to communicate with each other and with people (M. B. Ali, 2021; Singh et al., 2023; Syed et al., 2021). It has wide-ranging applications across various industries, offering opportunities for increased efficiency, automation, and new services (see Figure 14).

The IoT enables the monitoring of real-time data, the prediction of low-cost maintenance, and the creation of additional value through data-driven methods. IoT offers customised services using big data and is advantageous for energy efficiency, predictive maintenance, quality, and personalisation in digital transformation. In I.40, IoT devices can communicate with other objects to make informed decisions, optimising operations, reducing costs, and improving the customer experience. IoT also creates new revenue streams and provides valuable insights for data-driven decision-making. However, the adoption of IoT also raises concerns around data privacy, security, and ethical considerations, which must be addressed. Organisations need to invest in the necessary infrastructure and security measures to effectively leverage the potential of IoT in digital businesses (Agrawal, 2017; M. B. Ali, 2021; Singh et al., 2023; Syed et al., 2021). See Table 9 for a summary of the benefits and challenges of the Internet of Things.

Table 9. Benefits and challenges of the internet of things

Benefits	Challenges
Improved Efficiency: IoT can improve efficiency by automating processes and collecting data in real-time, allowing businesses to optimise operations and reduce costs.	Security Risks: IoT devices can create security risks by providing additional entry points for cyber-attacks and data breaches.
Enhanced Customer Experience: IoT can enhance the customer experience by providing personalised and proactive services, such as automatic alerts and notifications.	Complexity: IoT can be complex and difficult to manage, especially if businesses use multiple devices and platforms.
New Revenue Streams: IoT can create new revenue streams by enabling businesses to offer value-added services and solutions, such as predictive maintenance and remote monitoring.	Interoperability Issues: IoT devices may have interoperability issues, which can make it difficult to integrate with existing systems and platforms.
Real-Time Data Analytics: IoT can provide businesses with real-time data analytics, allowing them to make informed decisions and improve business processes.	Privacy Concerns: IoT devices may collect personal data, raising privacy concerns and requiring businesses to comply with data protection regulations.
Cost Savings: IoT can lead to cost savings by reducing energy consumption and optimising resource utilisation.	Implementation Costs: IoT implementation can be costly, requiring businesses to invest in infrastructure, software, and training.

Figure 14. The internet of things value chain
Source: Agrawal (2017)

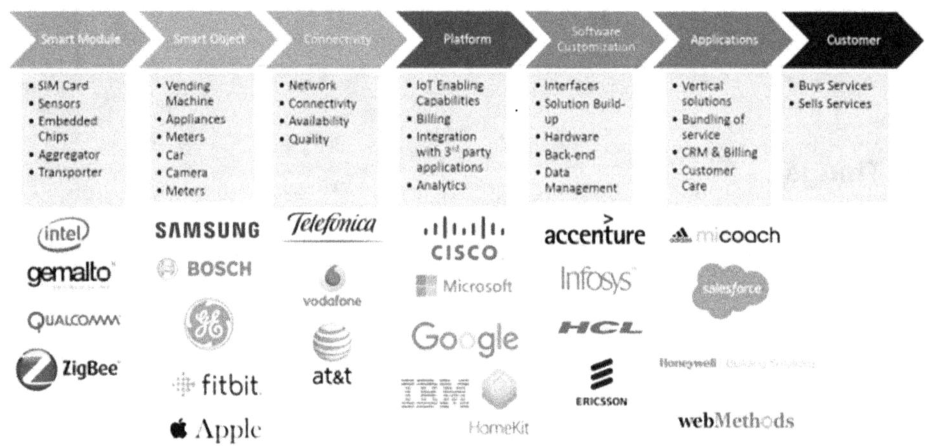

Virtual and Augmented Reality (Mixed Reality/Simulation)

Virtual reality (VR) and augmented reality (AR) are two immersive technologies that are increasingly used in digital business. VR creates a fully simulated environment that allows users to experience a world that doesn't exist, while AR overlays digital information onto the real world (Ryalat et al., 2023; Singh et al., 2023) (see Figure 15). Both technologies have benefits such as enhancing customer experiences, improving training and education, and creating new revenue streams. However, they also face challenges such as high costs, limited accessibility, and privacy concerns. VR and AR are widely used in industries such as gaming, entertainment, and education, but they also have applications in healthcare, real estate, and manufacturing.

Table 10. Benefits and challenges of mixed realities

Benefits	Challenges
Enhanced Customer Experience: VR/AR can enhance the customer experience by providing immersive and interactive experiences, such as virtual try-ons and product demonstrations.	Technical Limitations: VR/AR technology is still evolving, and businesses may face technical limitations, such as hardware requirements and compatibility issues.
Improved Training: VR/AR can improve employee training by providing realistic simulations and hands-on experience, reducing the risk of accidents and errors.	Costly Development: Developing VR/AR applications can be costly, requiring specialised skills and equipment.
Increased Engagement: VR/AR can increase engagement by providing interactive and entertaining content, improving brand awareness and customer loyalty.	Limited Adoption: VR/AR technology is still relatively new, and there may be limited adoption by customers and employees.
Personalisation: VR/AR can provide personalised experiences based on customer preferences and behaviours, improving customer satisfaction and retention.	Health Concerns: VR/AR can cause health concerns, such as motion sickness and eye strain, requiring businesses to ensure user safety.
New Revenue Streams: VR/AR can create new revenue streams by enabling businesses to offer premium content and services, such as virtual events and tours.	Ethical Issues: VR/AR can raise ethical concerns, such as privacy violations and digital addiction, requiring businesses to consider the ethical implications of their use.

Figure 15. Mixed reality continuum
Source: Brassea (2021)

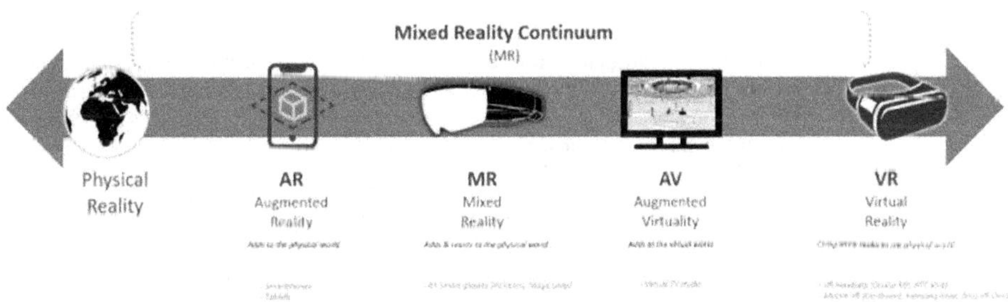

In healthcare, for example, VR and AR can be used to simulate medical procedures and train healthcare professionals. In real estate, they can be used to give virtual tours of properties to potential buyers. In manufacturing, they can be used to simulate product designs and identify potential issues before production. Digital businesses that invest in VR and AR can gain a competitive advantage by providing immersive and engaging experiences to customers. However, implementing these technologies can be expensive and require specialised skills. Additionally, businesses must consider privacy and security concerns, such as data protection and ethical use of technology. Overall, VR and AR have the potential to transform the way businesses operate and interact with customers, but careful planning and execution are essential to their success (Brassea, 2021; Damiani et al., 2018; Jung & Tom Dieck, 2019; Jung et al., 2016; Jung & Tom Dieck, 2017; Ryalat et al., 2023; Singh et al., 2023). See Table 10 for a summary of the benefits and challenges of mixed realities.

Practical Models of I4.0 Innovation for Operations Management

This section presents a series of practical scenarios of I4.0 innovation for operations management through the lens of digital entrepreneurship and co-creating value (see Figure 16). Table 11 provides a summary of the key scenarios covered in this section.

Table 11. Taxonomy of I4.0 real-world scenarios

Model	Scenario
Revolutionising Operations Management with Additive Manufacturing	Adidas has transformed their operations management using 3D printing to produce customised products on-demand and create a co-creation platform called "MakerLab," while overcoming challenges such as specialised skills, quality control, and cost savings
Intelligent Systems Streamlining Operations	AI-powered chatbots in customer service can enhance customer experience, collect data on interactions and preferences, and optimise supply chain management
Transforming Operations with Autonomous Robots	Autonomous robots are transforming Operations Management by automating and optimising tasks, such as manufacturing, inventory management, and order fulfilment, but also present challenges such as the need for specialised skills and quality control.
Transforming Operations Management through Big Data	Big data analytics enables a custom-made athletic shoe company (e.g., Nike) to optimise their supply chain operations, improve production efficiency and quality, and offer personalised products to customers, resulting in increased customer satisfaction and loyalty, and ultimately, greater profitability and success in the digital entrepreneurship landscape
Blockchain Security Opportunities for Operations Management	Blockchain is transforming and securing Operations Management in the supply chain industry by providing transparency and security through an immutable and decentralised ledger that tracks the movement of goods and information, as seen in examples such as Walmart's implementation for food products and the diamond industry's use of blockchain for secure and ethical sourcing
Strategies for Enhanced Operations Management and Efficiency in the Cloud	How cloud computing transforms operations management in startup e-commerce business selling handmade artisanal goods to improve inventory and order management, website hosting, and payment processing, automate processes, optimise inventory levels, reduce stockouts, improve order fulfilment, provide a fast, reliable, and secure shopping experience to its customers, and ultimately, achieve increased sales and growth
Securing Business Operations through Cybersecurity Strategies and Risk Management	Investing in a robust cybersecurity framework is essential for digital startups to protect their platforms and customer data, build trust with customers, differentiate themselves in the market, and create new opportunities for growth and innovation
Strengthening Business Competitiveness and Operations through Horizontal and Vertical Integration	A company's horizontal and vertical integration through acquisition of a microprocessor startup and building its own distribution centers, along with investment in digital technologies such as an ERP system and data analytics tools, leads to improved operational efficiency, cost reduction, and better customer experience
Internet of Things for Operational Excellence	By leveraging IoT technology, a manufacturing company has transformed its operations management by collecting real-time data to optimise production schedules, prevent equipment failures, reduce waste, and offer predictive maintenance services, ultimately co-creating value with its customers by offering customised products tailored to their specific needs
Enhancing Business Operations and the Customer Experience through Mixed Realities	Mixed reality technology in the retail industry allows a clothing retailer to provide a virtual fitting room for customers to try on clothes, expanding the customer base and improving the shopping experience, while also reducing the need for physical inventory and store space, and enabling more personalised production and services.

Note: the above scenarios are just a snapshot of examples to illustrate the context of this chapter. Snapshot examples of cases used in this section can be found in the following sources and bibliography list at the end of the chapter (Adidas, 2021; Ali, 2020; M. Ali, 2019, 2021; Ali, 2022; Ali et al., 2022; Barseghian, 2019; Dutta et al., 2020; Javaid et al., 2021; Malik, 2022).

Revolutionising Operations Management With Additive Manufacturing

The sporting brand Adidas has been using additive manufacturing (AM) or 3D printing to transform their operations management in the context of digital entrepreneurship and co-creating value. They launched the "Futurecraft 4D" shoe in 2018, which was designed using customer feedback and 3D printed using Carbon's Digital Light Synthesis technology.

By using 3D printing, Adidas can produce customised shoes on demand without the need for tooling or moulds. This reduces inventory costs and waste, as they can produce shoes only when they are needed. They also have the ability to quickly iterate on designs based on customer feedback, which leads to faster time-to-market and improved customer satisfaction. Moreover, Adidas has created a co-creation platform called "MakerLab," which allows customers to customise and 3D print their own shoes. This enables customers to create personalised products that meet their specific needs while also providing Adidas with valuable customer data and insights. Adidas has also leveraged 3D printing to create new revenue streams and differentiate itself in the market. They offer 3D printing services to other companies as well as selling 3D printable designs through their online store. However, implementing 3D printing in operations management also presents challenges. One challenge is the need for specialised skills and knowledge to operate and maintain the 3D printing equipment. Adidas had to invest in training their staff to ensure that the equipment was used efficiently and effectively. Another challenge is the need to balance cost savings with quality control. 3D printing can enable businesses to produce products at a lower cost, but the quality of the products may not meet customer expectations. Adidas needs to ensure that the quality of their 3D-printed shoes meets their standards and customer expectations.

Overall, 3D printing has transformed Adidas' operations management by enabling them to produce customised products on demand, facilitating co-creation with customers, and developing new business models. They have overcome challenges such as specialised skills, quality control, and cost savings to fully realise the benefits of additive manufacturing.

Intelligent Systems Streamlining Operations

One real-world scenario of how artificial intelligence (AI) transforms operations management from the perspective of digital entrepreneurship and co-creating value is the use of AI-powered chatbots in customer service.

For example, a clothing retailer can implement an AI-powered chatbot on their website or social media platforms to interact with customers and assist them with their inquiries. The chatbot can answer frequently asked questions, provide product recommendations, and help customers navigate the website. By doing so, the chatbot enhances the customer experience and improves customer satisfaction. Additionally, the chatbot can collect data on customer interactions and preferences, such as the types of questions asked and products searched for. This data can be used to improve the retailer's operations, such as by identifying areas for improvement in customer service or popular products that can be restocked. Moreover, AI can be used to optimise supply chain management by analysing large amounts of data on factors such as demand forecasting, inventory levels, and supplier performance. This can lead to better decision-making, improved efficiency, and cost savings for businesses. However, the implementation of AI in operations management also presents challenges, such as the need for specialised skills to develop and maintain AI systems, the potential for bias in algorithms, and the need to ensure data privacy and security.

Overall, the use of AI has the potential to transform operations management and improve competitiveness for businesses in the context of digital entrepreneurship and co-creating value.

Transforming Operations with Autonomous Robots

Autonomous robots are transforming operations management in the context of digital entrepreneurship and co-creating value. They can automate and optimise a variety of tasks, such as manufacturing, inventory management, and order fulfilment.

A real-world example of this is Amazon's use of autonomous robots in their fulfilment centres. The robots, called "drive units," are designed to carry stacks of inventory shelves to workers, who then pick items for customer orders. This system has significantly increased efficiency and reduced the time it takes to fulfil orders, enabling Amazon to offer same-day or even two-hour delivery in some areas. Autonomous robots can also be used in manufacturing processes to improve efficiency and productivity. For example, car manufacturers are using robots to automate tasks such as welding and painting, resulting in improved quality and reduced costs. Moreover, autonomous robots can facilitate co-creation with customers, as businesses can collaborate with customers to design and produce customised products using robotics technology. This can lead to increased customer satisfaction and loyalty. However, the implementation of autonomous robots in operations management also presents challenges. One challenge is the need for specialised skills and knowledge to operate and maintain the robots. Businesses may need to invest in training or hire specialised staff to ensure that the robots are used efficiently and effectively. Another challenge is the need to balance cost savings with quality control. While autonomous robots can reduce labour costs and improve efficiency, businesses need to ensure that the quality of their products or services meets the required standards and customer expectations.

Overall, autonomous robots have the potential to transform operations management in the context of digital entrepreneurship and co-creating value by automating and optimising tasks, facilitating co-creation with customers, and improving efficiency and productivity. However, businesses need to overcome challenges such as specialised skills and quality control to fully realise the benefits of autonomous robots.

Transforming Operations Management Through Big Data

One real-world scenario of how big data transforms operations management from the perspective of digital entrepreneurship and co-creating value is the use of predictive analytics for supply chain optimisation.

A company that specialises in manufacturing custom-made athletic shoes (e.g., Nike) collects large amounts of data from various sources, such as online customer orders, production processes, inventory, and shipping information. By using big data analytics tools, the company is able to extract insights from this data and use them to optimise its supply chain operations. For example, the company uses predictive analytics to forecast demand for each type of shoe based on past sales data and online trends. This helps them adjust production capacity, inventory levels, and shipping schedules to ensure they have the right number of materials and products at the right time while minimising waste and excess inventory. The company also uses real-time data from sensors on their production equipment to monitor performance and identify potential issues before they cause downtime or quality problems. This enables them to take proactive measures to optimise production efficiency and quality. Furthermore, the company uses data analytics to personalise their product offerings for individual customers. By analysing customer data such as preferences, purchase history, and browsing behaviour, they are able to offer customised shoe designs that meet the unique needs of each customer. This leads to increased customer satisfaction and loyalty, which can result in higher revenue and market share.

In summary, big data analytics enables this company to optimise their supply chain operations, improve production efficiency and quality, and offer personalised products to customers, resulting in increased customer satisfaction and loyalty and, ultimately, greater profitability and success in the digital entrepreneurship landscape.

Blockchain Security Opportunities for Operations Management

One real-world scenario of how blockchain is transforming and securing operations management is in the supply chain industry. Blockchain can provide transparency and security by creating an immutable and decentralised ledger that tracks the movement of goods and information across the supply chain.

For example, Walmart implemented a blockchain-based system to track the origin and journey of food products from farm to store. By scanning a QR code on the product, customers can access information on the product's origin, processing, and shipping, providing transparency and accountability. This system not only enhances the customer experience by providing them with detailed information, but it also ensures food safety and helps prevent fraud and counterfeit products from entering the supply chain. Another example is the diamond industry, where blockchain is being used to create a secure and transparent supply chain. Each diamond is assigned a unique digital identity that is stored on the blockchain, including information on its origin, quality, and journey through the supply chain. This ensures that each diamond is ethically sourced and not a conflict diamond, providing transparency and accountability for customers and industry regulators.

By using blockchain technology, operations management can improve supply chain efficiency, reduce costs, enhance the customer experience, and increase trust and security in the supply chain.

Strategies for Enhanced Operations Management and Efficiency in the Cloud

A startup e-commerce business selling handmade artisanal goods has experienced rapid growth in sales but is struggling to keep up with the increasing demand. They currently manage their inventory and orders through a combination of spreadsheets and manual processes, which are becoming inefficient and error-prone. They also face challenges in managing their website traffic and processing payments securely.

Transformation with Cloud Computing: The business decides to implement cloud computing to transform their operations management and enhance the customer experience. They move their inventory and order management systems to a cloud-based platform, which allows them to automate processes and provides real-time data analytics to optimise inventory levels, reduce stockouts, and improve order fulfilment. This also enables them to scale their operations quickly and cost-effectively to keep up with demand. In addition, they move their website hosting to a cloud-based server, which provides scalability, reliability, and security. They also integrate their payment processing with a cloud-based payment gateway, which ensures secure and fast transactions for their customers. Impact on Customer Experience: With the implementation of cloud computing, businesses are able to provide a better customer experience. The real-time data analytics provided by the cloud-based inventory management system enable them to accurately forecast demand and maintain optimal inventory levels, reducing stockouts and improving order fulfilment times. The website's hosting on a cloud-based server ensures that the website is fast, reliable, and secure, providing a seamless shopping experience for their customers. The integration with a cloud-based payment gateway ensures that payments are processed securely and quickly, improving customer trust and loyalty.

Overall, the implementation of cloud computing transforms the business's operations management and enhances the customer experience, leading to increased sales and growth.

Securing Business Operations through Cybersecurity Strategies and Risk Management

A digital startup has developed a cloud-based platform that allows small and medium-sized businesses to manage their operations and supply chains in a more efficient and streamlined way. The platform integrates with various IoT devices and sensors to collect data on inventory levels, equipment performance, and other key metrics. However, with the increasing reliance on cloud-based technology and IoT devices, the startup faces a significant cybersecurity risk. Any breach in their platform could result in a loss of data, privacy violations, and damage to their reputation.

To mitigate this risk, the startup invests in a robust cybersecurity framework that includes regular vulnerability assessments, firewalls, encryption, and intrusion detection systems. They also train their employees on best practises for data security and implement strict access controls to limit who can access sensitive information. In addition to protecting their own platform, the startup also works with their customers to ensure that their data is secure when using the platform. They provide clear guidelines on data privacy and security and work with their customers to implement best practises for securing their own IoT devices and networks. As a result of their strong cybersecurity measures, the startup is able to build trust with their customers and differentiate itself in the market. They are able to attract more customers who value security and privacy and can charge a premium for their services.

Overall, cybersecurity is essential for digital entrepreneurship and co-creating value, as it enables startups to protect their own platforms and the data of their customers. By investing in cybersecurity, startups can build trust, differentiate themselves in the market, and create new opportunities for growth and innovation.

Strengthening Business Competitiveness and Operations through Horizontal and Vertical Integration

Horizontal and vertical integration can transform operations management and competitiveness from the perspective of digital entrepreneurship and co-creating value by streamlining supply chains, improving operational efficiency, and enabling faster and more accurate decision-making. Here's a real-world scenario:

A company that designs and manufactures electronic devices for consumers wants to streamline its supply chain and improve operational efficiency. The company decides to pursue both horizontal and vertical integration. Horizontal integration: The company acquires a small startup that specialises in designing and manufacturing microprocessors, which are a key component of its electronic devices. This acquisition allows the company to bring the microprocessor design and production in-house, reducing its dependence on external suppliers and streamlining the supply chain. Vertical integration: The company also decides to integrate vertically by building its own distribution centres and logistics network. By bringing logistics in-house, the company can reduce lead times and delivery times, improving the customer experience. The company also invests in digital technologies to support its integration efforts. It implements an enterprise resource planning (ERP) system to better manage inventory, production, and logistics across its supply chain. It also uses data analytics tools to monitor supplier performance and identify areas for improvement. As a result of these integration efforts, the company is able to improve operational efficiency, reduce costs, and improve the customer experience. It is also able to quickly adapt to changes in the market and customer demand by leveraging data analytics and other digital tools.

Overall, horizontal and vertical integration, when combined with digital technologies, can transform operations management and competitiveness by streamlining supply chains, improving operational efficiency, and enabling faster and more accurate decision-making.

Internet of Things for Operational Excellence

The Internet of Things (IoT) is transforming operations management from the perspective of digital entrepreneurship and co-creating value by enabling businesses to collect and analyse real-time data to optimise their operations and co-create value with their customers. For example, smart manufacturing with IoT

A manufacturing company is looking to optimise its operations by leveraging IoT technology. The company has installed sensors on its machines and production lines, allowing it to collect real-time data on machine performance, production speed, and product quality. This data is transmitted to a central platform, where it is analysed using big data analytics tools. The company is now able to use this data to identify and diagnose potential issues with its machines and production lines in real-time, reducing downtime and improving efficiency. It can also optimise production schedules and inventory levels based on real-time demand data, reducing waste and improving customer satisfaction. In addition, the company is exploring new business models enabled by IoT technology. It has started offering predictive maintenance services to its customers, using the data it collects from its machines to proactively identify potential issues and prevent equipment failures. This has enabled the company to create a new revenue stream and differentiate itself in the market. Moreover, the company is co-creating value with its customers by offering customised products that are tailored to their specific needs. By collecting data on customer preferences and usage patterns, the company can design and produce products that are better suited to its customers' needs, improving customer satisfaction and loyalty.

Overall, the company has transformed its operations management by leveraging IoT technology to collect and analyse real-time data, optimise its operations, and co-create value with its customers.

Enhancing Business Operations and the Customer Experience Through Mixed Realities

Mixed reality (MR), which combines virtual and augmented reality, is transforming operations management and the customer experience from the perspective of digital entrepreneurship and co-creating value. One real-world scenario is the use of MR in the retail industry.

A clothing retailer could use MR technology to create a virtual fitting room where customers could try on clothes without physically being in a store. This would allow the retailer to expand its customer base beyond those who are able to visit a physical store and provide a unique customer experience. The MR technology would allow customers to upload a picture of themselves and see how different clothes look on their virtual bodies. The technology could also incorporate data such as the customer's measurements, style preferences, and previous purchases to suggest items that may fit well and complement their existing wardrobe. The use of MR technology in this scenario can also benefit operations management by reducing the need for physical inventory and store space. The retailer could produce items on demand using additive manufacturing, reducing the need for inventory and the cost of storing excess inventory. Additionally, the retailer could use the data collected from the MR technology to better understand customer preferences and adjust production accordingly. This would enable the retailer to optimise its production processes, reduce waste, and provide more personalised products and services to customers.

Overall, the use of MR technology can transform operations management and the customer experience by providing a unique and convenient shopping experience, reducing inventory and production costs, and enabling personalised production and services.

Figure 16. Taxonomy of I4.0 in digital business innovation and operations

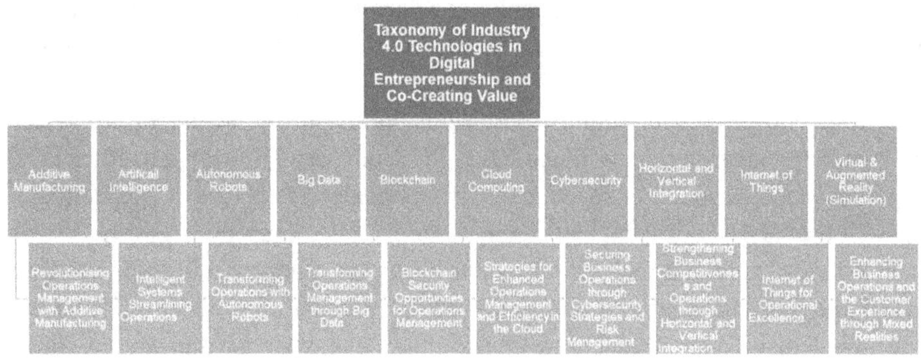

CONCLUSION: THE FUTURE OF I4.0 AND THE I5.0 REVOLUTION

This chapter delved into I.40 in the context of digital entrepreneurship and co-creating value, as well as from the perspective of operations management and innovation (see Figure 16). We have come to know that I.40, also known as the Fourth Industrial Revolution, has transformed digital business and created value by integrating digital technologies like big data analytics, the Internet of Things (IoT), artificial intelligence (AI), and additive manufacturing. However, as the digital landscape evolves, the buzz around Industry 5.0 (I5.0) grows louder. I5.0 focuses on human-machine collaboration, where advanced technologies such as AI, robotics, and automation work alongside human workers to create new value and drive innovation.

From the perspective of operations management and innovation, the I5.0 revolution represents a new wave of technological advancements that will significantly impact how businesses operate and compete in the digital landscape. I5.0 is characterised by the integration of advanced technologies such as AI, augmented reality, and IoT into the manufacturing process, enabling greater automation and customisation. One key benefit of I5.0 is increased efficiency and productivity in manufacturing operations. AI and IoT can optimise production processes and reduce waste, leading to higher throughput and lower costs. The ability to customise products at scale through advanced technologies like augmented reality can help businesses better meet customers' evolving needs, increasing satisfaction and loyalty. Innovation will play a critical role in the I5.0 revolution. As businesses adopt new technologies and processes, they must continuously innovate to stay ahead of the competition. This will require a culture of experimentation and risk-taking, as well as a willingness to invest in new technologies and talent.

From the perspective of digital entrepreneurship and co-creating value, I5.0 presents opportunities and challenges. The integration of advanced technologies with human workers can lead to greater efficiency, productivity, and profitability for businesses. For example, collaborative robots (cobots) can assist workers in physically demanding or repetitive tasks, allowing them to focus on more creative and innovative aspects of their job. The use of AI and machine learning can help businesses gain valuable insights into consumer behaviour and preferences, enabling them to personalise products and services and deliver a more targeted and effective customer experience. However, the integration of advanced technologies with human workers raises concerns around job displacement and the need for new skills and training. As more tasks become automated, there is a risk that some jobs may become redundant, leaving workers without the necessary skills to find new employment. Therefore, businesses and governments must work together to ensure workers are equipped with the skills and training necessary to adapt to the changing digital landscape and thrive in the Industry 5.0 revolution.

Overall, Industry 5.0 represents an exciting new chapter in the evolution of the manufacturing industry. It offers tremendous opportunities for businesses to enhance efficiency, productivity, and profitability while also posing challenges that must be addressed through collaboration and innovation.

REFERENCES

Adidas. (2021). *4DFWD: Data-Driven 3d Printed Performance Technology Designed To Move You Forward*. Retrieved 21st April from https://news.adidas.com/running/4dfwd--data-driven-3d-printed-performance-technology-designed-to-move-you-forward/s/514baddb-1029-4686-abd5-5ee3985a304a#:~:text=adidas%204D%20footwear%20is%20amongst,new%20adidas%204DFWD%20lattice%20midsole

Agrawal, M. (2017). *Internet of Things – Business Models*. Retrieved 19th April from https://www.linkedin.com/pulse/internet-things-business-models-mohit-agrawal

Ali, M. (2018). The Barriers and Enablers of the Educational Cloud: A Doctoral Student Perspective. *Open Journal of Business and Management*, *7*(1), 1–24. doi:10.4236/ojbm.2019.71001

Ali, M. (2019). Cloud Computing at a Cross Road: Quality and Risks in Higher Education. *Advances in Internet of Things*, *9*(3), 33–49. doi:10.4236/ait.2019.93003

Ali, M. (Ed.). (2021). *Remote Work and Sustainable Changes for the Future of Global Business*. IGI Global. doi:10.4018/978-1-7998-7513-0

Ali, M. (2022). *Future Role of Sustainable Innovative Technologies in Crisis Management*. IGI Global. doi:10.4018/978-1-7998-9815-3

Ali, M., & Abdel-Haq, M. K. (2021). Bibliographical Analysis of Artificial Intelligence Learning in Higher Education: Is the Role of the Human Educator and Educated a Thing of the Past? In Fostering Communication and Learning With Underutilized Technologies in Higher Education (pp. 36-52). IGI Global.

Ali, M., & Edghiem, F. (2021). Sustainable Business and Collaboration Driven by Big Data Analytics Amidst the Emergence of the Remote Work Culture. In *Remote Work and Sustainable Changes for the Future of Global Business* (pp. 15–32). IGI Global. doi:10.4018/978-1-7998-7513-0.ch002

Ali, M., Edghiem, F., & Alkhalifah, E. S. (2022). Cultural Challenges of ERP Implementation in Middle-Eastern Oil & Gas Sector: An Action Research Approach. *Systemic Practice and Action Research.* PMID:35668863

Ali, M., Wood-Harper, A., & Ramlogan, R. (2017). Benefits and Challenges of Cloud Computing Adoption in Higher Education: A Systematic Literature Review. *British Academy of Management Conference Proceedings, 14*(4).

Ali, M. B. (2021). Internet of Things (IoT) to Foster Communication and Information Sharing: A Case of UK Higher Education. *Fostering Communication & Learning With Underutilized Technologies in Higher Education*, 1-20.

Ali, M. B., & Wood-Harper, T. (Eds.). (2020). *Fostering communication and learning with underutilized technologies in higher education*. IGI Global.

Ali, M. B., Wood-Harper, T., & Ramlogan, R. (2020a). A Framework Strategy to Overcome Trust Issues on Cloud Computing Adoption in Higher Education. In Modern Principles, Practices, and Algorithms for Cloud Security (pp. 162-183). IGI Global. doi:10.4018/978-1-7998-1082-7.ch008

Ali, M. B., Wood-Harper, T., & Ramlogan, R. (2020b). *The Role of SaaS Applications in Business IT Alignment: A Closer Look at Value Creation in Service Industry*. UKAIS.

Ali. (2019). Multiple Perspective of Cloud Computing Adoption Determinants in Higher Education a Systematic Review. *International Journal of Cloud Applications and Computing, 9*(3), 89-109.

Ali. (2020). Multi-Perspectives of Cloud Computing Service Adoption Quality and Risks in Higher Education. In D. B. A. Mehdi Khosrow-Pour (Ed.), *Handbook of Research on Modern Educational Technologies, Applications, and Management* (2nd ed.). IGI Global.

Barseghian, A. (2019). *How Nike Is Using Analytics To Personalize Their Customer Experience*. Retrieved 21st April from https://www.forbes.com/sites/forbestechcouncil/2019/10/07/how-nike-is-using-analytics-to-personalize-their-customer-experience/?sh=402ac85b1611

Brassea, M. (2021). *Augmented Reality vs Virtual Reality for Manufacturers*. Retrieved 22nd April from https://www.tacton.com/cpq-blog/augmented-reality-vs-virtual-reality/

Dalenogare, L. S., Benitez, G. B., Ayala, N. F., & Frank, A. G. (2018). The expected contribution of Industry 4.0 technologies for industrial performance. *International Journal of Production Economics, 204*, 383–394. doi:10.1016/j.ijpe.2018.08.019

Damiani, L., Demartini, M., Guizzi, G., Revetria, R., & Tonelli, F. (2018). Augmented and virtual reality applications in industrial systems: A qualitative review towards the industry 4.0 era. *IFAC-PapersOnLine, 51*(11), 624–630. doi:10.1016/j.ifacol.2018.08.388

Davenport, T. H., Barth, P., & Bean, R. (2012). *How 'big data' is different*. Academic Press.

Davila Delgado, J. M., Oyedele, L., Ajayi, A., Akanbi, L., Akinade, O., Bilal, M., & Owolabi, H. (2019). Robotics and automated systems in construction: Understanding industry-specific challenges for adoption. *Journal of Building Engineering*, *26*, 100868. doi:10.1016/j.jobe.2019.100868

Duggal, A. S., Malik, P. K., Gehlot, A., Singh, R., Gaba, G. S., Masud, M., & Al-Amri, J. F. (2022). A sequential roadmap to Industry 6.0: Exploring future manufacturing trends. *IET Communications, 16*(5), 521-531. doi:10.1049/cmu2.12284

Dutta, P., Choi, T. M., Somani, S., & Butala, R. (2020). Blockchain technology in supply chain operations: Applications, challenges and research opportunities. *Transportation Research Part E, Logistics and Transportation Review*, *142*, 102067. doi:10.1016/j.tre.2020.102067 PMID:33013183

Federico, G. (2018). *The origin of Big Data*. Retrieved 18th April from https://www.federicomassarottomason.com/2018/01/31/big-data/

Furfaro, A., Piccolo, A., Parise, A., Argento, L., & Saccà, D. (2018). A Cloud-based platform for the emulation of complex cybersecurity scenarios. *Future Generation Computer Systems*, *89*, 791–803. doi:10.1016/j.future.2018.07.025

Godec, D., Pilipović, A., Breški, T., Ureña, J., Jordá, O., Martínez, M., Gonzalez-Gutierrez, J., Schuschnigg, S., Blasco, J. R., & Portolés, L. (2022). Introduction to Additive Manufacturing. In D. Godec, J. Gonzalez-Gutierrez, A. Nordin, E. Pei, & J. Ureña Alcázar (Eds.), *A Guide to Additive Manufacturing* (pp. 1–44). Springer International Publishing. doi:10.1007/978-3-031-05863-9_1

Grabowska, S., Saniuk, S., & Gajdzik, B. (2022). Industry 5.0: Improving humanization and sustainability of Industry 4.0. *Scientometrics*, *127*(6), 3117–3144. doi:10.100711192-022-04370-1 PMID:35502439

Grady, N. W., Underwood, M., Roy, A., & Chang, W. L. (2014, October 27-30). Big Data: Challenges, practices and technologies: NIST Big Data Public Working Group workshop at IEEE. *Big Data*.

Grossmann, G., Jordan, A., Muruganandha, R., Selway, M., & Stumptner, M. (2013). *Enabling Information Interoperability through Multi-domain Modeling*. Practice-Driven Research on Enterprise Transformation. doi:10.1007/978-3-642-38774-6_2

Han, H., Shiwakoti, R. K., Jarvis, R., Mordi, C., & Botchie, D. (2023). Accounting and auditing with blockchain technology and artificial Intelligence: A literature review. *International Journal of Accounting Information Systems*, *48*, 100598. doi:10.1016/j.accinf.2022.100598

InfoSys. (2023). *Industry 4.0 as an evolution, not a revolution*. Retrieved 22nd April from https://www.infosys.com/iki/perspectives/industry-4-0-evolution.html

Javaid, M., Haleem, A., Singh, R. P., & Suman, R. (2021). Substantial capabilities of robotics in enhancing industry 4.0 implementation. *Cognitive Robotics*, *1*, 58–75. doi:10.1016/j.cogr.2021.06.001

Jung, T., & tom Dieck, M. C. (2019). *Augmented Reality and Virtual Reality: The Power of AR and VR for Business*. Springer International Publishing.

Jung, T., tom Dieck, M. C., Lee, H., & Chung, N. (2016). Effects of virtual reality and augmented reality on visitor experiences in museum. In *Information and communication technologies in tourism 2016* (pp. 621–635). Springer. doi:10.1007/978-3-319-28231-2_45

Jung, T. H., & tom Dieck, M. C. (2017). Augmented reality, virtual reality and 3D printing for the co-creation of value for the visitor experience at cultural heritage places. *Journal of Place Management and Development.*

Li, J., Herdem, M. S., Nathwani, J., & Wen, J. Z. (2022). Methods and Applications for Artificial Intelligence, Big Data, Internet-of-Things, and Blockchain in Smart Energy Management. *Energy and AI*, 100208.

Malik, P. (2022). *Improve your customer service with AI-powered chatbots*. Retrieved 20th April from https://www.sprinklr.com/blog/customer-service-chatbots/

Manickam, V. (2020). *Weak, Strong AI — Do these Terms Matter?* Retrieved 21st April from https://medium.com/@vjmanickam/weak-strong-ai-do-these-terms-matter-4bb57ce3a61f

Marcon, É., Le Dain, M.-A., & Frank, A. G. (2022) Designing business models for Industry 4.0 technologies provision: Changes in business dimensions through digital transformation. Technological Forecasting and Social Change, 185.

Marr, B. (2016). *Big Data in Practice: How 45 Successful Companies Used Big Data Analytics to Deliver Extraordinary Results*. Wiley. doi:10.1002/9781119278825

Marr, B. (2017). *Data Strategy: How to Profit from a World of Big Data, Analytics and the Internet of Things*. Kogan Page.

Marr, B. (2020). *Tech Trends in Practice: The 25 Technologies that are Driving the 4th Industrial Revolution*. Wiley.

Mathrick, S. (2023). *Understanding The 5 Types Of Cyber Security*. Retrieved 21st April from https://kmtech.com.au/information-centre/understanding-the-5-types-of-cyber-security/

Matt, D. T., Modrák, V., & Zsifkovits, H. (2020). *Industry 4.0 for SMEs: Challenges, Opportunities and Requirements*. Springer International Publishing. doi:10.1007/978-3-030-25425-4

Mell, P., & Grance, T. (2009). The NIST definition of cloud computing. *National Institute of Standards and Technology*, *53*(6), 50.

Ng, H. S. (2021). Opportunities, challenges, and solutions for industry 4.0. In *Research Anthology on Cross-Industry Challenges of Industry 4.0* (pp. 1–20). IGI Global. doi:10.4018/978-1-7998-8548-1.ch001

Ngo, T. D., Kashani, A., Imbalzano, G., Nguyen, K. T. Q., & Hui, D. (2018). Additive manufacturing (3D printing): A review of materials, methods, applications and challenges. *Composites. Part B, Engineering*, *143*, 172–196. doi:10.1016/j.compositesb.2018.02.012

Oettmeier, K., & Hofmann, E. (2017). Additive manufacturing technology adoption: An empirical analysis of general and supply chain-related determinants. *Journal of Business Economics*, *87*(1), 97–124. doi:10.100711573-016-0806-8

Okereafor, K. (2021). *Cybersecurity in the COVID-19 Pandemic*. CRC Press.

Paul, J. A., & Wang, X. (2019). Socially optimal IT investment for cybersecurity. *Decision Support Systems*, *122*, 113069.

Pérez-Lara, M., Saucedo-Martínez, J. A., Marmolejo-Saucedo, J. A., Salais-Fierro, T. E., & Vasant, P. (2020). Vertical and horizontal integration systems in Industry 4.0. *Wireless Networks, 26*(7), 4767–4775. doi:10.100711276-018-1873-2

Rahal, R., Ghalamzan-E, A. M., Abi-Farraj, F., Pacchierotti, C., & Robuffo Giordano, P. (2023). Haptic-guided grasping to minimise torque effort during robotic telemanipulation. *Autonomous Robots*. Advance online publication. doi:10.100710514-023-10096-7

Raj, R. (2023). *How does Blockchain work?* Retrieved 20th April from https://intellipaat.com/blog/tutorial/blockchain-tutorial/how-does-blockchain-work/

Ryalat, M., ElMoaqet, H., & AlFaouri, M. (2023). Design of a Smart Factory Based on Cyber-Physical Systems and Internet of Things towards Industry 4.0. *Applied Sciences (Basel, Switzerland), 13*(4), 2156. doi:10.3390/app13042156

Sakai, T., & Nagai, T. (2022). Explainable autonomous robots: A survey and perspective. *Advanced Robotics, 36*(5-6), 219–238. doi:10.1080/01691864.2022.2029720

Schreider, T. (2020). Cybersecurity Law, Standards and Regulations. Rothstein Publishing.

Sharmeela, C., Sanjeevikumar, P., Joseph, M., & Sivaraman, P. (2023). IoT, Machine Learning and Blockchain Technologies for Renewable Energy and Modern Hybrid Power Systems. River Publishers.

Shoemaker, D., Sigler, K., & Shoemaker, T. (2023). *Teaching Cybersecurity: A Handbook for Teaching the Cybersecurity Body of Knowledge in a Conventional Classroom*. CRC Press.

Singh, M., Goyat, R., & Panwar, R. (2023). Fundamental pillars for industry 4.0 development: implementation framework and challenges in manufacturing environment. *The TQM Journal*.

Siregar, S., & Chang, K. (2022). External Social Capital, Cybersecurity Incident Flexibility, and Cybersecurity Incident Management Effectiveness. *PACIS 2022 Proceedings*.

Statista. (2022). *Size of the blockchain technology market worldwide from 2018 to 2025*. Retrieved 10th June from https://www.statista.com/statistics/647231/worldwide-blockchain-technology-market-size/#:~:text=Blockchain%20technology%20market%20size%20worldwide%20 2018%2D2025&text=Forecasts%20suggest%20that%20global%20blockchain,dollars%20in%20size%20 by%202025

Syed, A. S., Sierra-Sosa, D., Kumar, A., & Elmaghraby, A. (2021). IoT in Smart Cities: A Survey of Technologies, Practices and Challenges. *Smart Cities, 4*(2).

Tashi, U., Ullah, A. M. M., Watanabe, M., & Kubo, A. (2018). Analytical Point-Cloud Based Geometric Modeling for Additive Manufacturing and Its Application to Cultural Heritage Preservation. *Applied Sciences (Basel, Switzerland), 8*(5), 656. doi:10.3390/app8050656

Tortorella, G. L., Cawley Vergara, A. M., Garza-Reyes, J. A., & Sawhney, R. (2020). Organizational learning paths based upon industry 4.0 adoption: An empirical study with Brazilian manufacturers. *International Journal of Production Economics, 219*, 284–294. doi:10.1016/j.ijpe.2019.06.023

Willcocks, L., Venters, W., & Whitley, E. (2014). *Moving to the Cloud Corporation*. Palgrave Macmillan. doi:10.1057/9781137347473

Willcocks, L. P., Sauer, C., & Lacity, M. C. (2016). *Enacting Research Methods in Information Systems* (Vol. 1). Palgrave Macmillan.

Xu, X., Lu, Y., Vogel-Heuser, B., & Wang, L. (2021). Industry 4.0 and Industry 5.0—Inception, conception and perception. *Journal of Manufacturing Systems*, *61*, 530–535. doi:10.1016/j.jmsy.2021.10.006

Yazdinejad, A., Dehghantanha, A., Parizi, R. M., Srivastava, G., & Karimipour, H. (2023). Secure intelligent fuzzy blockchain framework: Effective threat detection in iot networks. *Computers in Industry*, *144*, 103801. doi:10.1016/j.compind.2022.103801

ADDITIONAL READING

Ali, M. (2018). The Barriers and Enablers of the Educational Cloud: A Doctoral Student Perspective. *Open Journal of Business and Management*, *7*(1), 1–24. doi:10.4236/ojbm.2019.71001

Ali, M. (2019). Cloud Computing at a Cross Road: Quality and Risks in Higher Education. *Advances in Internet of Things*, *9*(3), 33–49. doi:10.4236/ait.2019.93003

Ali, M. (Ed.). (2021). *Remote Work and Sustainable Changes for the Future of Global Business*. IGI Global. doi:10.4018/978-1-7998-7513-0

Ali, M. (2022). *Future Role of Sustainable Innovative Technologies in Crisis Management*. IGI Global. doi:10.4018/978-1-7998-9815-3

Ali, M., & Abdel-Haq, M. K. (2021). Bibliographical Analysis of Artificial Intelligence Learning in Higher Education: Is the Role of the Human Educator and Educated a Thing of the Past? In Fostering Communication and Learning With Underutilized Technologies in Higher Education (pp. 36-52). IGI Global.

Ali, M., & Edghiem, F. (2021). Sustainable Business and Collaboration Driven by Big Data Analytics Amidst the Emergence of the Remote Work Culture. In *Remote Work and Sustainable Changes for the Future of Global Business* (pp. 15–32). IGI Global. doi:10.4018/978-1-7998-7513-0.ch002

Ali, M., Edghiem, F., & Alkhalifah, E. S. (2022). Cultural Challenges of ERP Implementation in Middle-Eastern Oil & Gas Sector: An Action Research Approach. *Systemic Practice and Action Research*. PMID:35668863

Ali, M., Wood-Harper, A., & Ramlogan, R. (2017). Benefits and Challenges of Cloud Computing Adoption in Higher Education: A Systematic Literature Review. *British Academy of Management Conference Proceedings, 14*(4).

Ali, M. B. (2021). Internet of Things (IoT) to Foster Communication and Information Sharing: A Case of UK Higher Education. *Fostering Communication & Learning With Underutilized Technologies in Higher Education*, 1-20.

Ali, M. B., & Wood-Harper, T. (Eds.). (2020). *Fostering communication and learning with underutilized technologies in higher education*. IGI Global.

Ali, M. B., Wood-Harper, T., & Ramlogan, R. (2020a). A Framework Strategy to Overcome Trust Issues on Cloud Computing Adoption in Higher Education. In Modern Principles, Practices, and Algorithms for Cloud Security (pp. 162-183). IGI Global. doi:10.4018/978-1-7998-1082-7.ch008

Ali, M. B., Wood-Harper, T., & Ramlogan, R. (2020b). *The Role of SaaS Applications in Business IT Alignment: A Closer Look at Value Creation in Service Industry*. UKAIS.

Ali. (2019). Multiple Perspective of Cloud Computing Adoption Determinants in Higher Education a Systematic Review. *International Journal of Cloud Applications and Computing, 9*(3), 89-109.

Ali. (2020). Multi-Perspectives of Cloud Computing Service Adoption Quality and Risks in Higher Education. In *Handbook of Research on Modern Educational Technologies, Applications, and Management* (2nd ed.). IGI Global.

Chapter 3
Digital Entrepreneurship: Insights From Online Business Communities

Nicholas George
Manchester Metropolitan University, UK

Farag Edghiem
Manchester Metropolitan University, UK

ABSTRACT

Entrepreneurship has a long history. The terms entrepreneurship and entrepreneurs are defined in various ways. Entrepreneurs are considered individuals who lead innovation, show outstanding initiative, coordinate social and economic structures, convert resources and circumstances into feasible assets, and embrace risks associated with such ventures, as well as a concept in which entrepreneurs are primarily focused on the notion of profitability and opportunity identification. This chapter delves into the realm of digital entrepreneurship in the context of the UK and German online business communities.

INTRODUCTION

Entrepreneurship evolved throughout a rich heritage and has become centre to modern economic development (Hisrich, 1990; Shane & Venkataraman, 2000). One perspective characterises entrepreneurs as individuals who lead innovation, exhibit exceptional initiative, coordinate social and economic structures, convert resources and circumstances into viable assets, and assume the risks associated with such ventures (Hisrich, 1990). Another distinctive characteristic of entrepreneurship is primarily centred around the ideas of profitability and opportunity identification, where entrepreneurs recognise opportunities, establish new ventures, or redevelop existing businesses and lead to initiating and managing innovation across various sectors (Shane & Venkataraman, 2000). Similarly, digital entrepreneurship involves designing, launching, or running a business on digital systems to sell digital products and services across

DOI: 10.4018/978-1-6684-7416-7.ch003

electronic networks. Technological advancements, networks, and easily accessible internet connections have leveraged entrepreneurship to an unprecedented level, merging conventional entrepreneurship with digital technology (Onuoha, 2007; Drucker, 2014).

As technology advances, further research is needed to uncover factors that nurture digital entrepreneurship and identify potential constraints and risk-mitigation opportunities (Mitchelmore & Rowley, 2010). In view of this, entrepreneurship is widely perceived to lead to open innovation, help economies overcome challenges and shape online communities (Kuratko, 2005; Lackéus, 2015). Digital entrepreneurial online communities consist of networks and actors collaborating to support innovative entrepreneurship, leading to significant economic development (Stam & Spigel, 2016). This incorporation of digital technologies has fostered innovation and the growth of digital start-ups, transforming industries and business models (Omorede, 2014). Omorede (2014) further proposed that entrepreneurship is not only based on economic benefits, but social entrepreneurship is driven by the motivation of social benefit, focusing extensively on societal contributions and developments rather than profits and growth.

The rapid growth of online start-up communities and digital ecosystems contributed to open innovation and promoted the development of digital skills among entrepreneurs (Kuratko, 2005; Lackéus, 2015). Social digital entrepreneurship, a subset of digital entrepreneurship is accordingly based on creating a positive social impact using digital technology in its business model (Omorede, 2014). While some views emphasise the economic aspects of entrepreneurship, diverse views perceive that social entrepreneurship is driven by the motivation for social benefit, focusing specifically on societal contributions and developments rather than profits and growth (Harding et al., 2002).

It is essential to consider that entrepreneurship and entrepreneurial activities are significantly influenced by an entrepreneur's individual intentions, motivations, aspirations, and goal-oriented behaviour. Consequently, entrepreneurs have been classified into two categories: necessity-based and opportunity-based, which helps identify their reasons for embarking on an entrepreneurial conduct (Harding et al., 2002). The extant literature on entrepreneurship has primarily focused on the processes of identifying, evaluating, and exploiting opportunities to develop future goods and services (Shane & Venkataraman, 2000). Therefore, more emphasis should be placed on exploring digital entrepreneurship and entrepreneurial ecosystems (Stam & Spigel, 2016). In this chapter, we aim to highlight the concept of digital entrepreneurship and the implications associated with this evolving phenomenon, that changed the ways businesses operate and opened up opportunities for growth and innovation (Drucker, 2014), hoping to pave the way for further investigation of these implications.

DIGITAL ENTREPRENEURSHIP

Entrepreneurship studies are divided and diversified, and this has been extended to the research of digital entrepreneurship (Karlsson et al., 2021). Digital entrepreneurship is an entity of the conventional entrepreneurship in which one or all segments have been digitised with the help of technologies (Hull et al., 2007). Elia et al. (2020) cited that the diffusion of digital technologies assists in creating new contexts where entrepreneurship and digital technology are giving rise to a new breed of entrepreneurs that facilitate to use of digital technology to create new ventures. Fernandes et al. (2022) cited that digital entrepreneurship creates new enterprises and digitalises existing business processes. Trongtorsak et al. (2021) outline digital entrepreneurship as a subcategory of entrepreneurship where part or all of the traditional physical business venture has been digitalised. In this, traditional entrepreneurs should try transforming their traditional businesses, products and services into digital models. In support, Zaheer et al. (2019) define digital entrepreneurship as creating a digital start-up as a new business venture or within an established venture. Moreover, in this paper, "digital entrepreneurship" is understood as designing, launching or running a business on digital systems where it sells digital products and services across electronic networks. Moreover, digital entrepreneurship can be seen as a new way of creating and doing business in the digital era (Kraus et al., 2019).

Le Dinh et al. (2018) claim that technological advancements, networks, and easily accessible internet connections have contributed to the phenomenon of digital entrepreneurship, thus synthesising new innovative methods of creating endeavours with a fusion of conventional entrepreneurship in the digital era. In the early stages of venture creation, it's difficult to conceptualise it (Sopjani, 2019), whilst it is unclear what level of desire is required to qualify as an entrepreneurial firm rather than a small business (Mason and Brown, 2014). The success of a recently launched enterprise can rely heavily on the support available on a digital platform (Srinivasan and Venkatraman, 2018). Zaheer et al. (2019) clarify that the 'entrepreneurial ecosystems' are unique in digital entrepreneurship. Elia et al. (2020) emphasised that the digital entrepreneurial ecosystem, which associated with four dimensions; digital actors (who), digital activities (what), digital motivations (why) and digital organisation (how).

Entrepreneurs may not follow any established principles or norms, instead, the unique experiences shape the entrepreneurial process as they embark on their entrepreneurial journey (Morris and Schindehutte, 2012). For this reason, Ghezzi and Cavallo (2020) argue that digital start-ups should continuously undergo innovation to their business model as digital entrepreneurs need to tackle internal resources to the external conditions. The findings of Ghezzi and Cavallo (2020) further confirm that the learn start-up approaches can adopt an agile method where it allows business model innovation in digital entrepreneurship. Kraus et al. (2019) state that the digital business model works differently than the traditional business models. Hence, digital entrepreneurs should be aware of the opportunities, differences and threats to mitigate the risk of failure and succeed in the digital era.

Morris and Schindehutte (2012) have explored entrepreneur's experiences based on Affective Events Theory (AET) through a unique perspective, where entrepreneur's pre-venture experience, important events, experiential processing, knowledge, affective results, and decision making have been concluded as all linked in this paradigm and collection of concepts. Not all entrepreneurs pursue the high growth or profit model when starting a business, for some, it is basically a survival tactic or additional income source (Morris and Schindehutte, 2012). The literature findings of Zaheer et al. (2019) suggest that digital entrepreneurship needs more in-depth studies of start-ups across countries, industries, and regions. The research study of Bican and Brem (2020) reveals that digital entrepreneurship plays a leading role in achieving the sustainability goals of the United Nations Sustainable Development Goals, where it contributes to solving economic and environmental issues in future. Digital business models minimise resource utilisations towards a circular economy. Soluk et al. (2021) emphasise entrepreneurship as a support factor towards solving ongoing challenges of poverty among the rural populations in developing countries. The research findings of Soluk disclose that digital technologies positively affect entrepreneurship, where digital infrastructure is strengthened to create new ventures.

SOCIAL DIGITAL ENTREPRENEURSHIP

Recently, social entrepreneurship has attracted the attention of academics, policymakers, and entrepreneurs. An emphasis on money generation, as well as a focus on social innovation and the management of social organisations, ensures the sustainability of such initiatives (Ghatak et al., 2020; Ratten, 2018). Skivko (2021) reveals that social entrepreneurship can solve social and environmental problems by creating sustainable business solutions. Sustainable business goals are difficult to achieve without digital technologies. As Kraus et al. (2019) discussed, digital technologies create more opportunities for entrepreneurs; mobile devices, social platforms, web and e-commerce are drivers for digital social entrepreneurship. These digital platforms encourage individuals to start ventures that satisfy social needs and create sustainable innovations. These business models use digital technologies to create social values and execute social missions (Skivko, 2021).

These characteristics can help the entrepreneurs and online start-up communities in supporting each other. A mix of market and non-market activities are defined as socially beneficial entrepreneurship (Haugh, 2005). It is an excellent career choice because of its relevance in the social welfare sector. Digital technology has become more widely available and more affordable, which has benefitted social entrepreneurship. Digital social entrepreneurship is the future of social enterprise (Dacin et al., 2011). It has been increasingly common to develop corporate strategies that significantly rely on digital technology in the last decade (Mubarak and Petraite, 2020; Bharadwaj et al., 2013; Kiron et al., 2016).

There is a vast amount of literature claiming that the digital environment aids entrepreneurship, and reduces barriers, however, social inequalities and hierarchies do impose further obstacles for entrepreneurs at the early stages (Dy et al,. 2017). Therefore, these barriers exist whether the entrepreneurs are offline, or online as social structures remain the same. The research gap for social digital entrepreneurs and digital entrepreneurship is expanding frequently as technological innovations are advancing on a fast pace, therefore, Kraus et al. (2019) suggests that further research can be conducted to uncover other variables that boost digital entrepreneurship in the context of identifying potential constraints, risk-mitigation opportunities, and positive facilitators.

Social, digital entrepreneurship uses digital technology in its business model to make a positive social impact (Ghataka et al., 2020). Martin and Osberg (2007) have described social entrepreneurs as individuals working to improve the lives of marginalised groups and society as a whole by bringing positive change to the institutions in which they operate. The interaction between entrepreneurial activity and social structure within online communities generates networked resources recognised as social capital (Lin, 2002). Social capital in the context of online communities can be described as a sort of goodwill that is developed through the network of community interactions (Adler and Kwon, 2002). Economic sociology has consistently established that social capital within online communities can be managed and generated by knowledgeable individuals i.e., entrepreneurs, and this is consistent with conventional social capital literature (Bourdieu, 1986; Bourdieu 2011; Lin, 2002; Burt, 2000; Wellman and Wortley, 1990). A new age of social and entrepreneurial connections is emerging in online communities, in which many entrepreneurs can share resources and operate under new provisions and methods, however, the communities can lack imperial objective or aptitude (Lin, 1999). According to Wellman et al. (2003), there is minimal social management in online communities since entrepreneurs may easily quit communities with restrictive limitations or lack of resources.

Entrepreneurship and Open Innovation

Entrepreneurship has led to open innovation and assisted disintegrating economies overcome challenges; however, the growth of the entrepreneur innovation can be limited by lack of core knowledge and external sources (Eisenhardt and Schoonhoven, 1996; Presutti et al, 2011). Open innovation helps influence and shape online communities through recognition of opportunities and technology (Chesbrough and Bogers, 2014; West and Bogers, 2014). Open innovation facilitates access to new knowledge through networking, providing development of new strategies on online community platforms that can be suitable for acting in response to volatile conditions that present in global marketplaces (Chesbrough, 2007). To generate innovation, the online community platforms rely heavily on entrepreneurial user ecosystem, hence, the platform success is dependent on user innovation and networking (Gawer and Cusumano, 2002; Eisenmann et al., 2009; Kenney and Pon, 2011). By regulating the flows of innovation-related knowledge and technology beyond organisational boundaries, open innovation entails harnessing external knowledge and commercial and economic prospects (Chesbrough and Bogers, 2014; West and Bogers, 2014). The online platforms that embrace open innovation ecosystems can also enhance their platform value through technology dynamics and resource availability (Gawer and Cusumano, 2014). Abbate et al. (2019) suggests that further research can highlight how platform users (i.e., entrepreneurs) are connected to the platform (e.g., online start-up community) to analyse the activities, resources, technology, and services to strategize using open innovation approach.

Digital Entrepreneurial Ecosystems

The digitalisation of almost every industry has led to remarkable growth in software-driven digital start-ups and supporting communities. This can create significant economic development; however, the software-propelled digital trade can also diminish the traditional high street organisations (Schroeder, 2013). The digital entrepreneurs and the online start-ups operate in the entrepreneurial ecosystem/system or the entrepreneurship's regional system. Within the entrepreneurial ecosystem, the actors' networks can function under the institutional infrastructure. The regulations can support the online start-ups by offering financial incentives and tax benefits or the low number of rules that the online start-ups should comply with (Nordina et al., 2019). The supportive culture improves the rewards for the online start-ups to take the risk that thinks creatively and the behaviour opportunities. The online start-ups conform to norms, and the values presented in institutional infrastructure gain legitimacy.

As depicted in Figure 1, the topic can be explored further by combing the two crucial factors: digital and entrepreneurial ecosystems; and how the collaboration of institutions and agents helps to create a perspective on consumer and social behaviours (Sussan and Acs, 2017). As shown in Figure 1, there are four components of the digital entrepreneurial ecosystem that can be used as a theoretical framework to grasp the understanding of the topic and explore the propositions at hand (Sussan and Acs, 2017). In determining the benefits of the online start-up communities, it is crucial to understand that one should fulfil the online start-ups for success. Some of those criteria have been related to the individual entrepreneur using the literature on entrepreneurship as described.

Figure 1. Digital entrepreneurial ecosystem
Source: Sussan and Acs (2017, pp. 55-73)

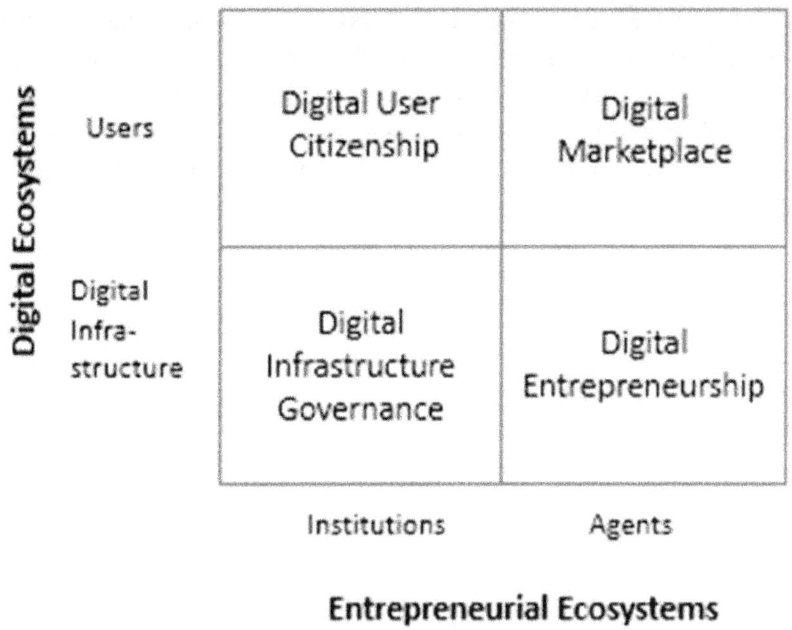

Entrepreneurial ecosystem is defined by Prahalad (2005) as a structure that encourages entrepreneurs, businesses, and communities to work together to create economic progress and success. Entrepreneurship can be an efficient way of introducing diverse and sustainable growth on online community platforms through its ecosystem, interactions, and social capital resources (Youssef et al., 2018). A sustainable entrepreneurial ecosystem requires several crucial elements to thrive and expand such as formal networks, informal networks, specialist support services, universities, government, investment services, and talent pool (Cohen, 2005). According to Tiba et al. (2020), start ups perform exceptionally well in areas that have a high concentration of entrepreneurial activity, also recognised as entrepreneurial ecosystems. Although 'Silicon Valley' has always been viewed as the greatest global entrepreneurial ecosystem, however European entrepreneurial ecosystems, especially in Berlin (Germany), London (UK) and Tallinn (Estonia) have outgrown Silicon Valley with a higher number of start-ups (Tiba et al., 2020).

The Isenberg entrepreneurial ecosystem can be described with 6 factors that can interact with other various components and create a complex strategy for analysis. The correlated factors can be explained well through the illustration above (see Figure 2). The quality of the new venture can be directly affected by the availability of funds as shown in Figure 2. The government and its policies intend to offer equal opportunities and funds to all new ventures, however, not all projects can utilise the resources (Isenberg., 2011). The resources may also feel wasted on some projects where novice entrepreneurs can be on a test and trial approach and taking unnecessary risks. To equalise the resources the policymakers can be encouraged to identify the worthy and non-worthy enterprises, rather than providing a blanket of safety with favourable regulations. If a worthy enterprise can meet the necessary requirements, it can create a support system to self-fund future ventures (Isenberg, 2011). The circumstances and influencing factors can be hard to identify, however, under the right conditions, the online start-up communities can provide many benefits to the entrepreneurial ecosystem, the individual digital entrepreneurs, and the start-ups (see Figure 3). Therefore, if these requirements cannot be balanced, start-up communities can lead to the malfunctioning of online communities and may create risks (Ngoasong, 2018). The main benefit of entrepreneurship can be that the successful entrepreneurs can reinvest their finances, capabilities, knowledge, and time in to support new ventures; thus, increasing the prospects of more successful enterprises (Mason and Brown, 2014). Successful entrepreneurs can engage in more projects and even make them venture junkies, where they can start treating entrepreneurship as a hobby, thus the experience creates a sustainable ecosystem that can maximise capital gains and reduce risks related to the early stages of new ventures (Isenberg, 2011).

Figure 2. The Isenberg entrepreneurial ecosystem
Source: Isenberg (2011, p. 7)

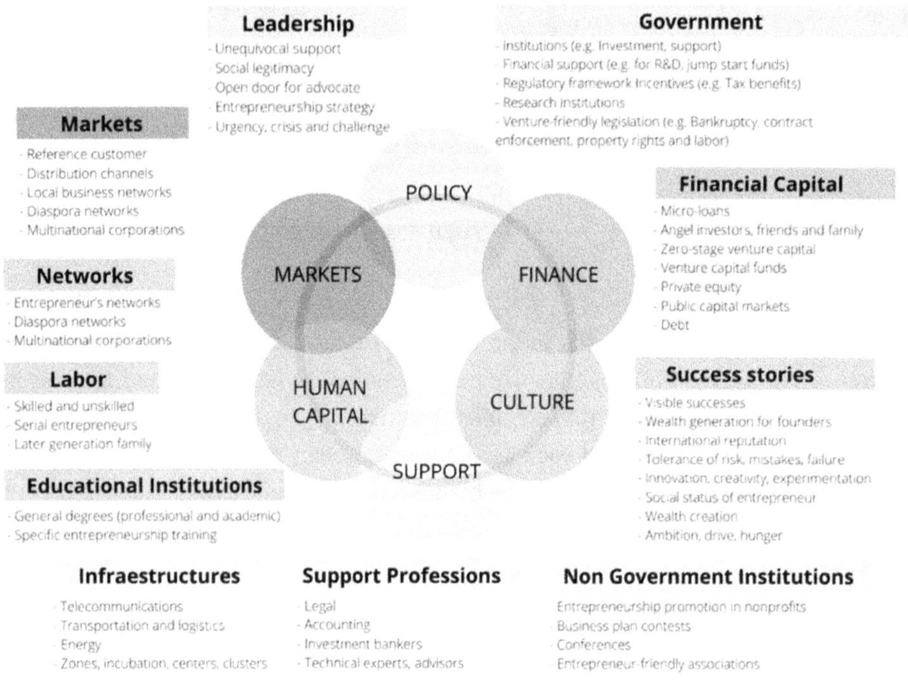

Entrepreneurship ecosystem can be described as is a collection of mutually reliant actors and factors that work together to support innovative entrepreneurship (Stam, 2015). The actors can be defined as advisors, entrepreneurs, workers and mentors and factors can be identified as networks, research and development systems, policies, strategies, and cultural viewpoints (Acs et al., 2014; Autio and Levie, 2017; Stam, 2015). Mason and Brown (2014) and OECD (2010) emphasise that researchers have widely concentrated on high-growth entrepreneurship models and networks as it provides economic growth, job opportunities, drives employment throughout developing and established economies. Therefore, a literature gap can be identified in start-up or emerging entrepreneurship models and networking platforms to address open innovation. The shifts of innovation and economic benefits attract policymakers to entrepreneurial ecosystems (Mason and Brown, 2014; Spigel, 2017). The entrepreneurial ecosystems do not necessitate investments for physical infrastructure; however, they intend to establish an active community of entrepreneurial actors who can assist creative new businesses start and expand by co-creating the support they need (Feld, 2012). Entrepreneurial ecosystems' composition and continuing relationships among the components that make them up are not static, rather they develop as biological ecosystems do (Autio et al., 2014; Hayter et al., 2018), It has been suggested, further research is required to apply a dynamic approach to understand the evolving factors that influence the entrepreneurs and online start-up communities.

Figure 3. Sustainable entrepreneurial ecosystem
Source: Isenberg (2011, p. 4)

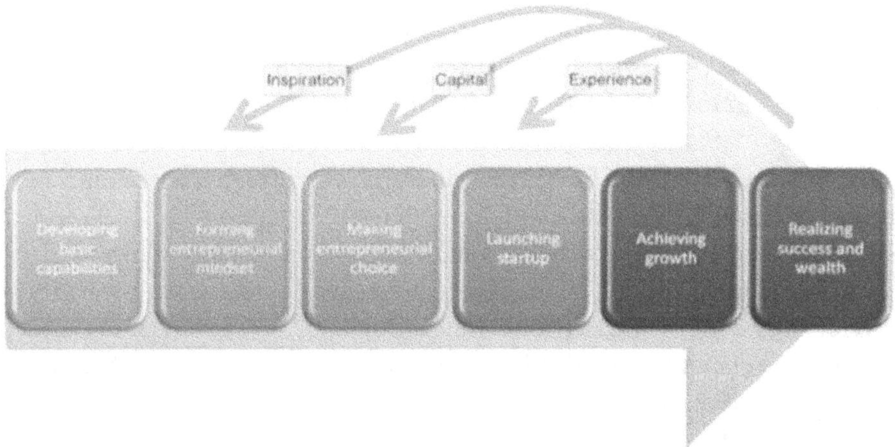

ROLE OF TECHNOLOGY IN DIGITAL ENTREPRENEURSHIP

A plethora of research has been second steered to investigate and find the options to address the issues of entrepreneur uncertainty. Flexible boundaries, as well as the outcomes, are two imperative considerations, where arrival of technology has helped entrepreneurship in addressing the uncertainties, improving the processes, and enhancing the results (Muñoz and Kibler, 2016, Tomy and Pardede, 2018). Digitisation has opened new horizons in entrepreneurship in a more than ever connected world (Hisrich and Soltanifar, 2021), led to an enhanced exchange of knowledge as well as introducing new methods of business procedures and development. Novelty in the utilisation of resources (Marchant et al., 2008), collaborations, production, and financial dealings are an advantage of technology in entrepreneurship (Tony, 2012).

Integration of digital technologies-led digital entrepreneurship has been a source of innovation as well as many diverse startups (Szalavetz, 2020; Gregori and Holzmann, 2020; Sussan and Acs, 2017). Digital start-ups have seen a rise recently due to the COVID-19 circumstances and enhanced accessibility of the technology. Entrepreneurs see this opportunity of using digital technologies based on the prospects as mentioned in the social cognitive theory (Oppong et al., 2020). Opportunities in the digital world are quick to appear as well as disappear and there is a lot of competition due to the time factor (Rathee and Rajain, 2017). The novelty of every business model is at stake until pursued and testing and validation becomes an imperative aspect of digital startups (Vang et al., 2021).

Multiple strategies, for example, lean startup approaches and lean startups have been used to validate the business models. The validation strategies usually rely on the principles of breaking out of the structures, minimum viable product, verified learning, quick iteration, and pivot if required (Ries, 2011). The incorporation of digital technologies has not only led to the start of digital startups, but also digital transformation is on its way in recent times (Hilbert, 2022). New business models, innovative solutions, and unprecedented involvement of the customers have seen the rise (Spremic, 2017). The digital transformation era has also brought forward the need of equipping the existing initiatives to come up with digital transformations through which they will be able to survive in emerging landscapes (Berger et al. 2021; Kraus et al., 2019). Digital revolution has been found to depend on digital organizational setup, digital institutional organizations, and digital established structure (Hinings et al., 2018). Digitization has also enhanced the opportunities for entrepreneurs (Samara and Terzian, 2021), providing the startups with a variety of business models, new products and increased their preferences for collaborators, outlets and theoretical frameworks (Ali, 2019, 2020; M. Ali, 2019a, 2019b, 2021; Ali, 2022; Ali & Abdel-Haq, 2021; Ali & Edghiem, 2021; Ali et al., 2022; M. B. Ali, 2021; Ali et al., 2020a, 2020b; Recker and Von Briel, 2019).

The technology, however, has also brought up some problems in entrepreneurship for example many of the startups, as well as business models, no longer fall under the domains of local regulations so there has been an institutional conflict with many new initiatives (Chambers and Munemo, 2019). Similarly, accountability in an online sphere or with the novel entrepreneurs' projects has been a very difficult job alongside a lack of monitoring of the cash flows (Hanna, 2018). Likewise, the new instances of the shared economy as well as the platform revolution have led to unparalleled scalability (Acquier et al., 2019).

Among other issues at the intersection of technology and entrepreneurship is the limited availability of diverse information technology skills; which have seen an increase due to the extensive integration of technology in entrepreneurship (Amjad et al., 2020). Similarly, rising matters of cybersecurity, data analytics, and dynamic business models are among the issues that need to be resolved (Bianchini and Michalkova, 2019; Plachkinova and Pittz, 2021). The effectiveness of digital transformation might also be obstructed by outdated organizational structures, inefficient procedures, and restrictive leadership styles (Cinnioğlu, 2020) and this has been more evident since the pandemic started (Feghali et al., 2022). COVID-19 has also directed to people relying extensively on their laptops and smartphones, and as a result, clients are pickier and demanding than they have ever been (Thukral and Ratten, 2021). Another issue that occurs when an entrepreneurial venture doesn't have a defined approach to create or keep a budget, and as a response to modification requests and changing client demands, a scope deviation can be projected (Qermane and Mancha, 2021). Similarly, one of the cornerstones of digital transformation is handling customer data, and in recent times, it might be tough to process the data with outdated systems (Denoo and Yli-Renko, 2019). The technology helps create a digital competitive online environment for budding entrepreneurs and expand into international ventures (Rathee and Rajain, 2017). This can also provide a wide range of resources, knowledge, opportunities, and ease of digital funding to entrepreneurs of all ages on an online start-up community platform (Rathee and Rajain, 2017).

Traditionally, the technology entrepreneurs faced a crucial decision dilemma on whether to licence their technology to avoid copyrights, or to fully develop the technology to capture the commercial product value (Gans and Stern, 2003). However, the modern digital technology entrepreneurs engage themselves in an interlinked platform systems and network to take advantage of commercialising their solutions to aid other products (Srinivasan et al., 2004; Kyprianou, 2016), emphasising that platforms and networks are correlatedly linked. Giones and Brem (2017) indicate that further research can highlight how platform dynamics can influence the entrepreneurs' activity in an evolving and developing ecosystem, also indicating how the user activity on a platform can help generate new open innovation. The research can help expand on the growth patterns studied by Hesse and Sternberg (2017) on the topic of technology entrepreneurship. The authors indicate that future analysis should focus on how the user activity on a community can help generate new open innovation, and exploration of growth patterns on the domain of technology entrepreneurship (Hesse and Sternberg, 2017).

Digital Innovation and Entrepreneurship

A relevant theoretical framework for discussing the nature of digital entrepreneurship is provided by the rising debate on digital innovation and digital artefacts. Previously non-digital artefacts in an industrial environment have been heavily documented in several studies on the digital invention (Yoo et al., 2010). Whereas digital innovation and digital entrepreneurship have certain similarities with Shumpeter (1942) and Schumpeter (2017)'s four additional categories of innovations-new manufacturing methods, innovative foundations of source, manipulation of fresh markets, and a new way of managing business-they are also distinct from one another. Digital innovation is characterised by re-programmability, consistency of data, and self-referentiality (Yoo et al., 2010; Kallinikos et al., 2013). The convergence and generativity of these features have opened up previously unimaginable prospects for inventors and businesses. As a result of convergence, formerly distinct infrastructures, services, and appliances may now be combined (Tilson et al., 2010a).

Due to being purposefully unfinished and hence flexible, digital technology is characterised by its ability to stimulate future inventions and may be combined in many different ways (Fenwick and Edwards, 2016). However, digital artefacts are challenging to regulate because of their dynamic nature. According to the study, while being objects, they lack the wholeness and solidity of traditional products and gadgets (Kallinikos et al., 2013). The idea of a generative matrix is born out of this understanding of digitalization as a continual evolution of technology (Kallinikos, 2012). A substantial reallocation of resources as well as a reorganisation of routines, market connections, and patterns of goods and services flow emerged as a result of this opportunity (Bughin and Van Zeebrocck, 2017). Businesses are reorganising their strategy to take advantage of market possibilities because of the rising digitization; as growing digitization changes the value of knowledge assets, which in turn decreases the value of some legal protections and raises the value of new techniques for deploying information in creative ways (Atanasova, 2019). It is necessary to modify the incentives for innovation and creativity (Peukert, 2019; Atanasova, 2019).

Also, digital infrastructure has an auto-emergent, recursive nature, and different components of the system contribute to its continued growth (Henfridsson and Bygstad, 2013). Because the system may be reconfigured very quickly, this indicates the flexibility of digital infrastructure (Tilson et al., 2010b). However, because digital infrastructures are self-emerging, the system is subject to drifting. During the growth of infrastructure, there are often unintended side effects, unintentional consequences, and unanticipated uses (Ciborra et al., 2000). Digital innovation and technology have supported entrepreneurs and online start-up communities in identifying challenges and converting them to opportunities during unprecedented times of the covid-19 pandemic (Chen and Roldan, 2021). As demonstrated in Figure 4, there are several popular services and applications that have been introduced to the digital market as a result of the no-code and low-code innovation within the digital entrepreneurship (Luo et al., 2021).

Figure 4. No-code and low-code services and applications
Source: Adapted from Luo et al. (2021, p. 5)

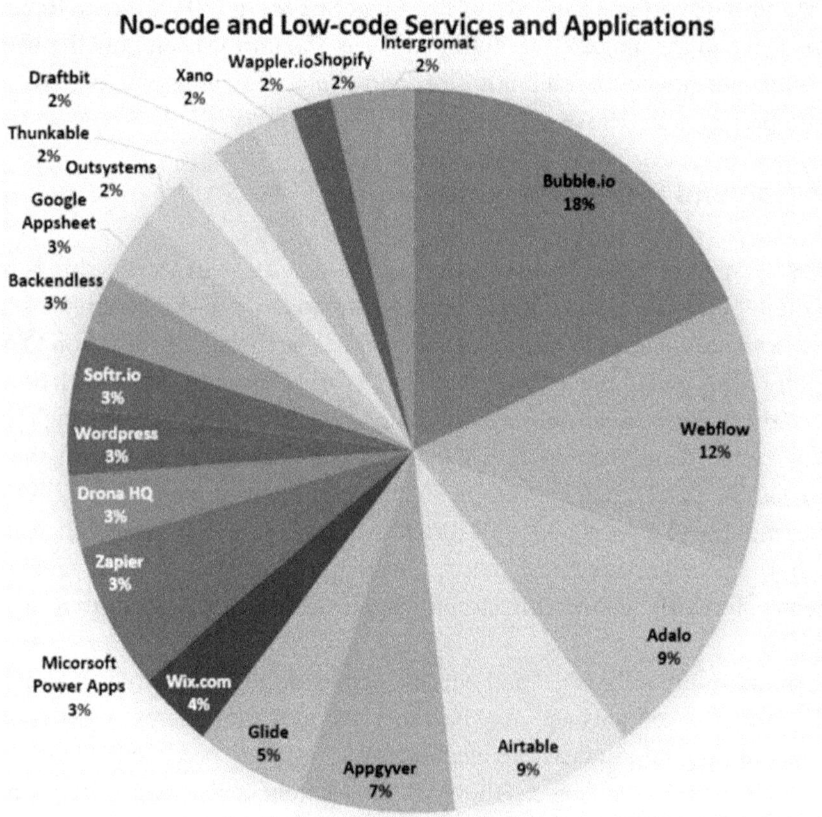

Digital Start-Ups (DSS)

Entrepreneurs create entrepreneurial ecosystems that are specifically focused on digital start-ups that use digital technology to create innovative business models. These digital start-ups are quite diverse in their nature. Small and medium-sized enterprises (SMEs) with low-to-medium tech manufacturing and so-called high-tech new enterprises that specialise in translating scientific breakthroughs into marketable products and services make up this technology-intensive sector. Digitization-based start-ups, as a category of new enterprises, are not tied to any one industry or technology. The innovative business models they conjure can target clients in nearly any sector (Basu and Fernald, 2007). Digitization has made it possible to integrate any corporate resource with a digital interface since digital technologies and infrastructures are flexible and adaptable. Service and business model innovations are more important to digital start-ups than technology, product, or innovation strategy as the primary source of chances for start-up and scale-up. Entrepreneurship refers to the design and development of innovative organisational architectures that coordinate and utilise demarcation interactions for value co-creation. It is defined as "the execution of non-trivial modifications to at least two business model elements resulting in a new business strategy design for the organization's industry and market" (Bock and George, 2017).

As a foundation of competitive benefit, digital start-ups look to ecosystem architecture for support (Rosenstand, 2021). The success of these start-ups is highly dependent on cheap costs or distinctiveness, or both, according to Porter's value chain and strategy for competitive advantage (Porter, 1980). As a competitive environment, their strategies presume a modular vertical value chain structure, in which they attempt to position themselves relative to complementary assets (Teece, 1986). The digital start-ups, on the other hand, work in an architecture of layers and modules in which digitalization takes a horizontalizing impression on the organisation of value-generating activities. Start-ups that are digitally enabled are important vehicles for converting digital technologies into economic and societal advantages (Faludi, 2020). These enterprises are also more likely to expand up and become high-growth businesses. Start-ups are important drivers of an economy's innovation process and can provide ideas for existing businesses (Steiber and Alänge, 2020). Steiber and Alänge (2020) also indicate that innovative goods and fresh ideas are not just popular among start-ups, but also provide a vital impetus for older firms' digitisation efforts. Digital start-ups can also directly assist established businesses with their innovation and commercial operations. Interactions between existing firms and digital start-ups can have consequences in the development of novel business models in established industries, or start-up business models might function as digitalisation drivers (Margiono, 2020; Steiber and Alänge, 2020). Creative solutions and technology supplied by start-ups can help established firms become more competitive. Start-ups that employ big data and smart data solutions may assist established firms in making better use of their current data and reducing the increasing complexity of a linked and digitised environment. By providing innovative consumer interfaces, start-ups may dramatically improve customer interactions and communication for established businesses (Oppong-Tawiah and Bassellier, 2017; Danarahmanto et al., 2020). By collaborating with established businesses, start-ups can benefit from increased sales and corporate growth. For example, a start-up can benefit from improved reputation, higher awareness, and improved business image, as well as extended sales techniques and a larger target audience (Beisheim and Langner, 2021). As digital start-ups may take use of digital affordances, they are unique from traditional new enterprises. A digital firm follows a certain operational logic to develop its business model, which is based on a variety of management guidelines. They require different structural components, resource dynamics, and management techniques in order to create and utilise a common information and resource base at the landscape scale to serve this aim (Bashir et al., 2016). The digital start-ups can also have an advantage due to their vast resource dynamic, support available through the online start-up community, strong personalities, and information base (Autio and Cao, 2019)

CONCLUSION

Digital entrepreneurship has been a prominent phenomenon due to its enormous benefits not only for entrepreneurs and organisations, in the form of higher profits and improved product and services, but also for the society as a whole by ensuring the attainment of sustainable growth and development goals. This chapter intended to draw readers' attention to this distinctive construct and highlight the current paucity in the literature to provide better understanding of the key co-dependent actors and factors that have influence on digital entrepreneurship, online platforms, and entrepreneurial ecosystems by synthesising the literature on digital entrepreneurship and then bringing together key relevant themes as explained in the extant literature.

The diffusion of digital technologies brings in new entrepreneurial phase which has evidently preceded and altered the traditional ways of searching for entrepreneurial opportunities. This digital transformation resulted in initiating different institutional provisions, setting off unique structures, practices, and values, challenging existing logics and influenced the standards of conventional business.

Consequently, entrepreneurs have to incorporate new proficiencies of digital nature including both hard and soft skills, which make them able to retain, undertake, lead, and develop digital technologies and their innate knowledge for online networking, problem solving, and a positive socio-economic impact. For this purpose, the establishment of digital ecosystems may facilitate the successful development and growth of digital startups, as ecosystem links the entrepreneurs to a network of highly capable and specialized actors having diverse knowledge, skills and abilities, and in this way digital ecosystems ultimately foster open innovations. The focal point of an ecosystem is not a particular venture or individual, instead it focus on the development and opportunities for the entire region and community, thus it is connected to whole external environment with a view to construct a bridge among various actors by establishing firm and effective connections among them in order to institute entrepreneurial networks and best practices communities.

Moreover, the development of a thriving ecosystem is determined by industry conditions and innovations diffusion (i.e. more disruptive technological discontinuities often result in prime opportunities). Therefore, it has become obligatory for enablers of entrepreneurship to connect the entrepreneurial ecosystem to the innovation dynamics and digital technological transformations. To reap the maximum benefits of digital entrepreneurship through the adoption of online platforms and the development of prospering ecosystems, the entrepreneurs and organizations have to build high levels of intellectual (i.e. organizational, relational, and human components) as well as social capital. To sum up, the ways how the businesses are conducted by the entrepreneurs today have been shifted drastically due to digitalization and online networking platforms, and resulted in remarkable growth in software-driven digital start-ups and supporting communities in almost every industry. Through online communities, entrepreneurs can share resources and operate under new provisions and procedures, however, the communities can lack imperial objective or aptitude. Thus, this chapter has highlighted the underlying themes, changes, and challenges to unveil the importance of digital entrepreneurship as an emerging line of extreme significance and also provide directions to facilitate more research in the field of digital entrepreneurship.

REFERENCES

Abbate, T., Codini, A. P., & Aquilani, B. (2019). Knowledge co-creation in open innovation digital platforms: Processes, tools and services. *Journal of Business and Industrial Marketing*, *34*(7), 1434–1447. doi:10.1108/JBIM-09-2018-0276

Acquier, A., Carbone, V., & Massé, D. (2019). How to create value (s) in the sharing economy: Business models, scalability, and sustainability. *Technology Innovation Management Review*, *9*(2), 5–24. doi:10.22215/timreview/1215

Acs, Z. J., Autio, E., & Szerb, L. (2014). National systems of entrepreneurship: Measurement issues and policy implications. *Research Policy*, *43*(3), 476–494. doi:10.1016/j.respol.2013.08.016

Adler, P. S., & Kwon, S. W. (2002). Social capital: Prospects for a new concept. *Academy of Management Review, 27*(1), 17–40. doi:10.2307/4134367

Amjad, T., Rani, S. H. B. A., & Sa'atar, S. B. (2020). Entrepreneurship development and pedagogical gaps in entrepreneurial marketing education. *International Journal of Management Education, 18*(2), 100379. doi:10.1016/j.ijme.2020.100379

Atanasova, I. (2019). Copyright infringement in digital environment. *Economics & Law, 1*(1), 13–22.

Autio, E., & Cao, Z. (2019). *Fostering digital start-ups: Structural model of entrepreneurial ecosystems.* Academic Press.

Autio, E., Kenney, M., Mustar, P., Siegel, D., & Wright, M. (2014). Entrepreneurial innovation: The importance of context. *Research Policy, 43*(7), 1097–1108. doi:10.1016/j.respol.2014.01.015

Autio, E., & Levie, J. (2017). Management of entrepreneurial ecosystems. The Wiley handbook of entrepreneurship, 423-449. doi:10.1002/9781118970812.ch19

Bashir, T., Usman, I., & ur Rehman, J. (2016). Secure digital watermarking using optimized improved spread spectrum and BCH coding for DIBR 3D-TV system. *Multimedia Tools and Applications, 75*(13), 7697–7713. doi:10.100711042-015-2689-z

Basu, S., & Fernald, J. (2007). Information and communications technology as a general-purpose technology: Evidence from US industry data. *German Economic Review, 8*(2), 146–173. doi:10.1111/j.1468-0475.2007.00402.x

Beisheim, M., & Langner, C. (2021). *Lean Startup as a Tool for Digital Business Model Innovation: Enablers and Barriers for Established Companies.* Academic Press.

Berger, E. S., Von Briel, F., Davidsson, P., & Kuckertz, A. (2021). Digital or not–The future of entrepreneurship and innovation: Introduction to the special issue. *Journal of Business Research, 125*, 436–442. doi:10.1016/j.jbusres.2019.12.020

Bharadwaj, A., El Sawy, O. A., Pavlou, P. A., & Venkatraman, N. V. (2013). Digital business strategy: Toward a next generation of insights. *Management Information Systems Quarterly, 37*(2), 471–482. doi:10.25300/MISQ/2013/37:2.3

Bianchini, M., & Michalkova, V. (2019). *Data analytics in SMEs: Trends and policies.* Academic Press.

Bican, P. M., & Brem, A. (2020). Digital Business Model, Digital Transformation, Digital Entrepreneurship: Is There A Sustainable "Digital"? *Sustainability (Basel), 12*(13), 1–15. doi:10.3390u12135239

Bock, A. J., & George, G. (2017). The Business Model Book: Design, build and adapt business ideas that drive business growth. Pearson UK.

Bourdieu, P. (2011). The forms of capital. *Cultural theory: An anthology, 1*, 81-93.

Bughin, J., & Van Zeebroeck, N. (2017). The best response to digital disruption. *MIT Sloan Management Review.*

Burt, R. S. (2000). The network structure of social capital. *Research in Organizational Behavior, 22*, 345–423. doi:10.1016/S0191-3085(00)22009-1

Chambers, D., & Munemo, J. (2019). Natural resource dependency and entrepreneurship: Are nations with high resource rents cursed? *Journal of International Development, 31*(2), 137–164. doi:10.1002/jid.3397

Chen, Y., & Roldan, M. (2021). Digital innovation during COVID-19: Transforming challenges to opportunities. *Communications of the Association for Information Systems, 48*(1), 3. doi:10.17705/1CAIS.04803

Chesbrough, H. (2007). Business model innovation: It's not just about technology anymore. *Strategy and Leadership, 35*(6), 12–17. doi:10.1108/10878570710833714

Chesbrough, H., & Bogers, M. (2014). *Explicating open innovation: Clarifying an emerging paradigm for understanding innovation. New Frontiers in Open Innovation*. Oxford University Press. doi:10.1093/acprof:oso/9780199682461.003.0001

Ciborra, C., & Hanseth, O. (2000). Towards a contingency view of infrastructure and knowledge: an exploratory study. Business Information Technology Management Alternative and Adaptive Futures, 178-194.

Cinnioğlu, H. (2020). A Review of Modern Leadership Styles in Perspective of Industry 4.01. *Agile Business Leadership Methods for Industry, 4*(0), 1–23. doi:10.1108/978-1-80043-380-920201002

Cohen, J. (2006). Social, emotional, ethical, and academic education: Creating a climate for learning, participation in democracy, and well-being. *Harvard Educational Review, 76*(2), 201–237. doi:10.17763/haer.76.2.j44854x1524644vn

Dacin, M. T., Dacin, P. A., & Tracey, P. (2011). Social entrepreneurship: A critique and future directions. *Organization Science, 22*(5), 1203–1213. doi:10.1287/orsc.1100.0620

Danarahmanto, P. A., Primiana, I., Azis, Y., & Kaltum, U. (2020). The sustainable performance of the digital start-up company based on customer participation, innovation, and business model. *Business: Theory and Practice, 21*(1), 115–124. doi:10.3846/btp.2020.11053

Denoo, L., & Yli-Renko, H. (2019). Entrepreneurship in a new digital industry: The emergence and growth of mobile health. Digital Entrepreneurship: Interfaces Between Digital Technologies and Entrepreneurship, 79-98.

Drucker, P. (2014). *Innovation and entrepreneurship*. Routledge. doi:10.4324/9781315747453

Dy, A. M., Marlow, S., & Martin, L. (2017). A Web of opportunity or the same old story? Women digital entrepreneurs and intersectionality theory. *Human Relations, 70*(3), 286–311. doi:10.1177/0018726716650730

Eisenhardt, K. M., & Schoonhoven, C. B. (1996). Resource-based view of strategic alliance formation: Strategic and social effects in entrepreneurial firms. organization. *Science, 7*(2), 136–150.

Eisenmann, T.R., Parker, G., & Van Alstyne, M. (2009). Opening platforms: How, when and why. *Platforms, Markets and Innovation, 6*, 131-162.

Elia, G., Margherita, A., & Passiante, G. (2020). Digital entrepreneurship ecosystem: How digital technologies and collective intelligence are reshaping the entrepreneurial process. *Technological Forecasting and Social Change, 150*, 119791. doi:10.1016/j.techfore.2019.119791

Faludi, J., Hoffenson, S., Kwok, S. Y., Saidani, M., Hallstedt, S. I., Telenko, C., & Martinez, V. (2020). A research roadmap for sustainable design methods and tools. *Sustainability (Basel), 12*(19), 8174. doi:10.3390u12198174

Feghali, K., Matta, J., & Moussa, S. (2022). Digital transformation of accounting practices and behavior during COVID-19: MENA evidence. *Accounting and Management Information Systems, 21*(2), 236–269. doi:10.24818/jamis.2022.02005

Feld, B. (2020). *Startup communities: Building an entrepreneurial ecosystem in your city*. John Wiley & Sons.

Fenwick, T., & Edwards, R. (2016). Exploring the impact of digital technologies on professional responsibilities and education. *European Educational Research Journal, 15*(1), 117–131. doi:10.1177/1474904115608387

Fernandes, C., Ferreira, J., Veiga, P., Kraus, S., & Dabić, M. (2022). Digital entrepreneurship platforms: Mapping the field and looking towards a holistic approach. *Technology in Society, 70*, 101979. doi:10.1016/j.techsoc.2022.101979

Gans, J. S., & Stern, S. (2003). The product market and the market for "ideas": Commercialization strategies for technology entrepreneurs. *Research Policy, 32*(2), 333–350. doi:10.1016/S0048-7333(02)00103-8

Gartner, W. B. (1988). "Who is an entrepreneur?" is the wrong question. *American Journal of Small Business, 12*(4), 11–32. doi:10.1177/104225878801200401

Gawer, A., & Cusumano, M. A. (2002). *Platform leadership: How Intel, Microsoft, and Cisco drive industry innovation* (Vol. 5). Harvard Business School Press.

Ghataka, A., Chatterjee, S., & Bhowmick, B. (2020). Intention Towards Digital Social Entrepreneurship: An Integrated Model. *Journal of Social Entrepreneurship*, 1–22. doi:10.1080/19420676.2020.1826563

Ghezzi, A., & Cavallo, A. (2020). Agile Business Model Innovation in Digital Entrepreneurship: Lean Startup Approaches. *Journal of Business Research, 110*, 519–537. doi:10.1016/j.jbusres.2018.06.013

Giones, F., & Brem, A. (2017). Digital Technology Entrepreneurship: A Definition and Research Agenda. *Technology Innovation Management Review, 7*(5), 44–51. doi:10.22215/timreview/1076

Gregori, P., & Holzmann, P. (2020). Digital sustainable entrepreneurship: A business model perspective on embedding digital technologies for social and environmental value creation. *Journal of Cleaner Production, 272*, 122817. doi:10.1016/j.jclepro.2020.122817

Hanna, N. (2018). A role for the state in the digital age. *Journal of Innovation and Entrepreneurship, 7*(1), 5. doi:10.118613731-018-0086-3

Harding, R., Hart, M., Jones-Evans, D., & Levie, J. (2002). *Global entrepreneurship monitor*. London Business School.

Haugh, H. (2005). A research agenda for social entrepreneurship. *Social Enterprise Journal, 1*(1), 1–12. doi:10.1108/17508610580000703

Hayter, C. S., & Link, A. N. (2018). Why do knowledge-intensive entrepreneurial firms publish their innovative ideas? *The Academy of Management Perspectives, 32*(1), 141–155. doi:10.5465/amp.2016.0128

Henfridsson, O., & Bygstad, B. (2013). The generative mechanisms of digital infrastructure evolution. *Management Information Systems Quarterly, 37*(3), 907–931. doi:10.25300/MISQ/2013/37.3.11

Hesse, N., & Sternberg, R. (2017). Alternative growth patterns of university spin-offs: Why so many remain small? *The International Entrepreneurship and Management Journal, 13*(3), 953–984. doi:10.100711365-016-0431-6

Hilbert, M. (2022). Digital technology and social change: The digital transformation of society from a historical perspective. *Dialogues in Clinical Neuroscience.* PMID:32699519

Hinings, B., Gegenhuber, T., & Greenwood, R. (2018). Digital innovation and transformation: An institutional perspective. *Information and Organization, 28*(1), 52–61. doi:10.1016/j.infoandorg.2018.02.004

Hisrich, R. D. (1990). Entrepreneurship/intrapreneurship. *The American Psychologist, 45*(2), 209–222. doi:10.1037/0003-066X.45.2.209

Hisrich, R. D., & Soltanifar, M. (2021). Unleashing the creativity of entrepreneurs with digital technologies. Digital Entrepreneurship: Impact on Business and Society, 23-49. doi:10.1007/978-3-030-53914-6_2

Hull, C. E. K., Hung, Y. T. C., Hair, N., Perotti, V., & DeMartino, R. (2007). Taking advantage of digital opportunities: A typology of digital entrepreneurship. *International Journal of Networking and Virtual Organisations, 4*(3), 290–303. doi:10.1504/IJNVO.2007.015166

Isenberg, D. (2011). Introducing the entrepreneurship ecosystem: Four defining characteristics. *Forbes, 14*, 1–8.

Kallinikos, J., Hasselbladh, H., & Marton, A. (2013). Governing social practice: Technology and institutional change. *Theory and Society, 42*(4), 395–421. doi:10.100711186-013-9195-y

Karlsson, C., Rickardsson, J., & Wincent, J. (2021). Diversity, innovation and entrepreneurship: Where are we and where should we go in future studies? *Small Business Economics, 56*(2), 759–772. doi:10.100711187-019-00267-1

Kenney, M., & Pon, B. (2011). Structuring the smartphone industry: Is the mobile internet OS platform the key? *Journal of Industry, Competition and Trade, 11*(3), 239–261. doi:10.100710842-011-0105-6

Kiron, D., Kane, G. C., Palmer, D., Phillips, A. N., & Buckley, N. (2016). Aligning the organization for its digital future. *MIT Sloan Management Review, 58*(1).

Kraus, S., Palmer, C., Kailer, N., Kallinger, F. L., & Spitzer, J. (2019). Digital entrepreneurship: A research agenda on new business models for the twenty-first century. *International Journal of Entrepreneurial Behaviour & Research, 25*(2), 353–375.

Kuratko, D. F. (2005). The emergence of entrepreneurship education: Development, trends, and challenges. *Entrepreneurship Theory and Practice, 29*(5), 577–597. doi:10.1111/j.1540-6520.2005.00099.x

Kyprianou, C. (2016). Getting to network effects: Social club and open door strategies in two-sided marketplaces. In Academy of management proceedings (Vol. 2016, No. 1, p. 17343). Academy of Management.

Lackéus, M., & Williams Middleton, K. (2015). Venture creation programs: Bridging entrepreneurship education and technology transfer. *Education + Training*, *57*(1), 48–73. doi:10.1108/ET-02-2013-0013

Le Dinh, T., Vu, M. C., & Ayayi, A. (2018). Towards a living lab for promoting the digital entrepreneurship process. *International Journal of Entrepreneurship*, *22*(1), 1–17.

Lima, E., Lopes, R. M., Nassif, V., & Silva, D. (2015). Opportunities to Improve Entrepreneurship Education:Contributions Considering Brazilian Challenges. *Journal of Small Business Management*, *53*(4), 1033–1051. doi:10.1111/jsbm.12110

Lin, N. (1999). Social networks and status attainment. *Annual Review of Sociology*, *25*(1), 467–487. doi:10.1146/annurev.soc.25.1.467

Lin, N. (2002). *Social capital: A theory of social structure and action* (Vol. 19). Cambridge university press.

Luo, Y., Liang, P., Wang, C., Shahin, M., & Zhan, J. (2021, October). Characteristics and challenges of low-code development: the practitioners' perspective. In *Proceedings of the 15th ACM/IEEE international symposium on empirical software engineering and measurement (ESEM)* (pp. 1-11). Academic Press.

Marchant, C. A., Briggs, K. A., & Long, A. (2008). In silico tools for sharing data and knowledge on toxicity and metabolism: Derek for windows, meteor, and vitic. *Toxicology Mechanisms and Methods*, *18*(2-3), 177–187. doi:10.1080/15376510701857320 PMID:20020913

Margiono, A. (2021). Digital transformation: Setting the pace. *The Journal of Business Strategy*, *42*(5), 315–322. doi:10.1108/JBS-11-2019-0215

Martin, R.L., & Osberg, S. (2007). *Social entrepreneurship: The case for definition*. Academic Press.

Mason, C., & Brown, R. (2014). Entrepreneurial ecosystems and growth oriented entrepreneurship. *Final report to OECD, 30*(1), 77-102.

Mitchelmore, S., & Rowley, J. (2010). Entrepreneurial competencies: A literature review and development agenda. *International Journal of Entrepreneurial Behaviour & Research*, *16*(2), 92–111. doi:10.1108/13552551011026995

Morris, M. H., Pryor, C. G., & Schindehutte, M. (2012). *Entrepreneurship as experience: How events create ventures and ventures create entrepreneurs*. Edward Elgar Publishing. doi:10.4337/9781781005187

Mubarak, M. F., & Petraite, M. (2020). Industry 4.0 technologies, digital trust and technological orientation: What matters in open innovation? *Technological Forecasting and Social Change*, *161*, 120332. doi:10.1016/j.techfore.2020.120332

Muñoz, P., & Kibler, E. (2016). Institutional complexity and social entrepreneurship: A fuzzy-set approach. *Journal of Business Research*, *69*(4), 1314–1318. doi:10.1016/j.jbusres.2015.10.098

Ngoasong, M. Z. (2018). Digital entrepreneurship in a resource-scarce context: A focus on entrepreneurial digital competencies. *Journal of Small Business and Enterprise Development, 25*(3), 483–500. doi:10.1108/JSBED-01-2017-0014

Nordina, N., Normanb, H., Zainic, H., Hamdand, F., Md, M., & Yunuse, N.H.A. (n.d.). *Online Innovation of Business Start-up Training for Marginalised Communities via MOOCS*. Academic Press.

Omorede, A. (2014). Exploration of motivational drivers towards social entrepreneurship. *Social Enterprise Journal, 10*(3), 239–267. doi:10.1108/SEJ-03-2013-0014

Onuoha, G. (2007). Entrepreneurship. *AIST International Journal, 10*, 20-32.

Oppong, G. Y. S., Singh, S., & Kujur, F. (2020). Potential of digital technologies in academic entrepreneurship–a study. *International Journal of Entrepreneurial Behaviour & Research, 26*(7), 1449–1476. doi:10.1108/IJEBR-06-2019-0401

Oppong-Tawiah, D., & Bassellier, G. (2017). *Digital innovation, platform orientation and the performance of IT startups*. Academic Press.

Peukert, C. (2019). The next wave of digital technological change and the cultural industries. *Journal of Cultural Economics, 43*(2), 189–210. doi:10.100710824-018-9336-2

Plachkinova, M., & Pittz, T. (2021). Assessing the Awareness of Cybersecurity Within Entrepreneurship Students: The Cyberpreneurship Project. *Entrepreneurship Education and Pedagogy, 4*(3), 564–582. doi:10.1177/2515127420913056

Porter, M. E. (1980). Industry structure and competitive strategy: Keys to profitability. *Financial Analysts Journal, 36*(4), 30–41. doi:10.2469/faj.v36.n4.30

Prahalad, C. K., Prahalad, C. K., Fruehauf, H. C., & Prahalad, K. (2005). *The Fortune at the Bottom of the Pyramid*. Wharton School Pub.

Presutti, M., Boari, C., & Majocchi, A. (2011). The importance of proximity for the start-ups' knowledge acquisition and exploitation. *Journal of Small Business Management, 49*(3), 361–389. doi:10.1111/j.1540-627X.2011.00331.x

Qermane, K., & Mancha, R. (2021). WHOOP, Inc.: Digital entrepreneurship during the Covid-19 pandemic. *Entrepreneurship Education and Pedagogy, 4*(3), 500–514. doi:10.1177/2515127420975181

Rathee, R., & Rajain, P. (2017). Entrepreneurship in the digital era. *Asia Pacific Journal of Research in Business Management, 8*(6), 52–63.

Ratten, V. (2018). *Sport entrepreneurship: Developing and sustaining an entrepreneurial sports culture*. Springer. doi:10.1007/978-3-319-73010-3

Rauch, A., & Hulsink, W. (2015). Putting Entrepreneurship Education Where the Intention to Act Lies: An Investigation Into the Impact of Entrepreneurship Education on Entrepreneurial Behavior. *Academy of Management Learning & Education, 14*(2), 187–204. doi:10.5465/amle.2012.0293

Recker, J., & Von Briel, F. (2019, November). *The Future of Digital Entrepreneurship Research*. Existing and Emerging Opportunities. In ICIS.

Ries, E. (2011). *The lean startup: How today's entrepreneurs use continuous innovation to create radically successful businesses*. Currency.

Rosenstand, C. A. F. (2021, June). Governance framework for performance measurement of a regional digital ecosphere. In *Event Proceedings: ISPIM Innovation Conference–Innovating Our Common Future*. LUT Scientific and Expertise Publications.

Samara, G., & Terzian, J. (2021). Challenges and opportunities for digital entrepreneurship in developing countries. *Digital Entrepreneurship, 283*.

Schroeder, H., Burch, S., & Rayner, S. (2013). Novel multisector networks and entrepreneurship in urban climate governance. *Environment and Planning. C, Government & Policy, 31*(5), 761–768. doi:10.1068/c3105ed

Schumpeter, J. A. (2017). *Essays: On entrepreneurs, innovations, business cycles and the evolution of capitalism*. Routledge. doi:10.4324/9781351311489

Shane, S., & Venkataraman, S. (2000). The promise of entrepreneurship as a field of research. *Academy of Management Review, 25*(1), 217–226. doi:10.5465/amr.2000.2791611

Shumpeter, J. A. (1942). *Capitalism. Socialism and Democracy*. Harper and Row.

Skivko, M. (2021). Digital Technologies, Social entrepreneurship and Governance for Sustanable Development. *Research in Social Change, 13*(1), 165–173. doi:10.2478/rsc-2021-0016

Soluk, J., Kammerlander, N., & Darwin, S. (2021). Digital entrepreneurship in developing countries: The role of institutional voids. *Technological Forecasting and Social Change, 170*, 1–13. doi:10.1016/j.techfore.2021.120876

Sopjani, X. (2019). *Challenges and opportunities for startup innovation and entrepreneurship as tools towards a knowledge-based economy: The case of Kosovo*. Academic Press.

Spigel, B. (2017). The relational organization of entrepreneurial ecosystems. *Entrepreneurship Theory and Practice, 41*(1), 49–72. doi:10.1111/etap.12167

Spremic, M. (2017). Governing digital technology–how mature IT governance can help in digital transformation? *International Journal of Economics and Management Systems, 2*.

Srinivasan, A., & Venkatraman, N. (2018). Entrepreneurship in digital platforms: A network-centric view. *Strategic Entrepreneurship Journal, 12*(1), 54–71. doi:10.1002ej.1272

Stam, E. (2015). Entrepreneurial ecosystems and regional policy: A sympathetic critique. *European Planning Studies, 23*(9), 1759–1769. doi:10.1080/09654313.2015.1061484

Stam, F. C., & Spigel, B. (2016). *Entrepreneurial ecosystems*. Utrecht School of Economics Working Papers, (16-13).

Steiber, A., & Alänge, S. (2020). Corporate-startup co-creation for increased innovation and societal change. *Triple Helix (Heidelberg), 7*(2-3), 227–249. doi:10.1163/21971927-bja10004

Sussan, F., & Acs, Z. J. (2017). The digital entrepreneurial ecosystem. *Small Business Economics, 49*(1), 55–73. doi:10.100711187-017-9867-5

Szalavetz, A. (2020). Digital transformation–enabling factory economy actors' entrepreneurial integration in global value chains? *Post-Communist Economies, 32*(6), 771–792. doi:10.1080/14631377.2020.1722588

Teece, D. J. (1986). Profiting from technological innovation: Implications for integration, collaboration, licensing and public policy. *Research Policy, 15*(6), 285–305. doi:10.1016/0048-7333(86)90027-2

Thukral, E., & Ratten, V. (2021). COVID-19: Entrepreneurial ecosystem approach to bounce back: Implications for the sport industry. In Innovation and entrepreneurship in sport management (pp. 148-158). Edward Elgar Publishing.

Tiba, S., van Rijnsoever, F. J., & Hekkert, M. P. (2020). The lighthouse effect: How successful entrepreneurs influence the sustainability-orientation of entrepreneurial ecosystems. *Journal of Cleaner Production, 264*, 121616. doi:10.1016/j.jclepro.2020.121616

Tilson, D., Lyytinen, K., & Sørensen, C. (2010). Research commentary—Digital infrastructures: The missing IS research agenda. *Information Systems Research, 21*(4), 748–759. doi:10.1287/isre.1100.0318

Tomy, S., & Pardede, E. (2018). From uncertainties to successful start ups: A data analytic approach to predict success in technological entrepreneurship. *Sustainability (Basel), 10*(3), 602. doi:10.3390u10030602

Tony Yu, F. L. (2012). Turning trash papers into gold: Entrepreneurship and international coordination of China's paper queen, Zhang Yin. *Journal of Chinese Entrepreneurship, 4*(1), 88–96. doi:10.1108/17561391211200957

Trongtorsak, S., Saraubon, K., & Nilsook, P. (2021). Collaborative Experiential Learning Process for Enhancing Digital Entrepreneurship. *Higher Education Studies, 11*(1), 137. doi:10.5539/hes.v11n1p137

Walter, S. G., & Block, J. H. (2016). Outcomes of entrepreneurship education: An institutional perspective. *Journal of Business Venturing, 31*(2), 216–233. doi:10.1016/j.jbusvent.2015.10.003

Wellman, B., Quan-Haase, A., Boase, J., Chen, W., Hampton, K., Díaz, I., & Miyata, K. (2003). The social affordances of the Internet for networked individualism. *Journal of Computer-Mediated Communication, 8*(3), JCMC834. doi:10.1111/j.1083-6101.2003.tb00216.x

Wellman, B., & Wortley, S. (1990). Different strokes from different folks: Community ties and social support. *American Journal of Sociology, 96*(3), 558–588. doi:10.1086/229572

West, J., & Bogers, M. (2014). Leveraging external sources of innovation: A review of research on open innovation. *Journal of Product Innovation Management, 31*(4), 814–831. doi:10.1111/jpim.12125

Yoo, Y., Henfridsson, O., & Lyytinen, K. (2010). Research commentary—the new organizing logic of digital innovation: An agenda for information systems research. *Information Systems Research, 21*(4), 724–735. doi:10.1287/isre.1100.0322

Youssef, A. B., Boubaker, S., & Omri, A. (2018). Entrepreneurship and sustainability: The need for innovative and institutional solutions. *Technological Forecasting and Social Change, 129*, 232–241. doi:10.1016/j.techfore.2017.11.003

Zaheer, H., Breyer, Y., & Dumay, J. (2019). Digital entrepreneurship: An interdisciplinary structured literature review and research agenda. *Technological Forecasting and Social Change, 148*, 119735. doi:10.1016/j.techfore.2019.119735

ADDITIONAL READING

Ali, M. (2019a). The Barriers and Enablers of the Educational Cloud: A Doctoral Student Perspective. *Open Journal of Business and Management, 7*(1).

Ali, M. (2019b). Cloud Computing at a Cross Road: Quality and Risks in Higher Education. *Advances in Internet of Things, 9*(3), 33–49. doi:10.4236/ait.2019.93003

Ali, M. (Ed.). (2021). *Remote Work and Sustainable Changes for the Future of Global Business*. IGI Global. doi:10.4018/978-1-7998-7513-0

Ali, M. (2022). *Future Role of Sustainable Innovative Technologies in Crisis Management*. IGI Global. doi:10.4018/978-1-7998-9815-3

Ali, M., & Abdel-Haq, M. K. (2021). Bibliographical Analysis of Artificial Intelligence Learning in Higher Education: Is the Role of the Human Educator a Thing of the Past? In *Fostering Communication and Learning With Underutilized Technologies in Higher Education* (pp. 36–52). IGI Global. doi:10.4018/978-1-7998-4846-2.ch003

Ali, M., & Edghiem, F. (2021). Sustainable Business and Collaboration Driven by Big Data Analytics Amidst the Emergence of the Remote Work Culture. In *Remote Work and Sustainable Changes for the Future of Global Business* (pp. 15–32). IGI Global. doi:10.4018/978-1-7998-7513-0.ch002

Ali, M., Edghiem, F., & Alkhalifah, E. S. (2022). Cultural Challenges of ERP Implementation in Middle-Eastern Oil & Gas Sector: An Action Research Approach. *Systemic Practice and Action Research*. PMID:35668863

Ali, M. B. (2021). Internet of Things (IoT) to Foster Communication and Information Sharing: A Case of UK Higher Education. *Fostering Communication & Learning With Underutilized Technologies in Higher Education*, 1-20.

Ali, M. B., Wood-Harper, T., & Ramlogan, R. (2020a). A Framework Strategy to Overcome Trust Issues on Cloud Computing Adoption in Higher Education. In Modern Principles, Practices, and Algorithms for Cloud Security (pp. 162-183). IGI Global. doi:10.4018/978-1-7998-1082-7.ch008

Ali, M. B., Wood-Harper, T., & Ramlogan, R. (2020b). *The Role of SaaS Applications in Business IT Alignment: A Closer Look at Value Creation in Service Industry*. UKAIS.

Ali. (2019). Multiple Perspective of Cloud Computing Adoption Determinants in Higher Education a Systematic Review. *International Journal of Cloud Applications and Computing, 9*(3), 89-109.

Ali. (2020). Multi-Perspectives of Cloud Computing Service Adoption Quality and Risks in Higher Education. In *Handbook of Research on Modern Educational Technologies, Applications, and Management* (2nd ed.). IGI Global.

Chapter 4
Multi-Perspectives of Contemporary Digital Transformation Models of Complex Innovation Management

Mohammed Ali
University of Salford, UK

Trevor Wood-Harper
Alliance Manchester Business School, UK

Maria Kutar
University of Salford, UK

ABSTRACT

Within the past decade there has been a paradigm shift in complex innovation in organisations through the adoption of contemporary technologies, which has brought us into the age of digital transformation (DT). The authors adopt a conceptual approach to analysing complex innovation models based on bibliographic analysis and integrate existing concepts and theories related to complex innovation in the DT context. The main innovation models (e.g., 4Ps and open/closed) are analysed through the lens of DT and multiple perspective theory. The outcome of this chapter is the categorization of modern innovation models in DT from multiple perspectives (technical, organisational, and personal), which has revealed that DT is the foundation of the modern innovation ecosystem. The chapter's uniqueness is its conceptual nature, which does not rely on empirical data collection but instead integrates pre-existing concepts and theories such as DT, complex innovation, and multiple perspective theory.

DOI: 10.4018/978-1-6684-7416-7.ch004

INTRODUCTION

In the late 20th century, digital technologies began to significantly infiltrate all aspects of society (Ali, 2019, 2020; M. Ali, 2019a, 2019b, 2021; Ali, 2022; Ali & Abdel-Haq, 2021; Ali & Edghiem, 2021; Ali et al., 2022; M. B. Ali, 2021; Ali et al., 2020a, 2020b). Experts and scholars began discussing the shift towards a new system of operation founded on digital technologies, referred to as "society 5.0 and "industry 4.0 (Bordeleau et al., 2020; De Felice et al., 2021; Ramírez-Montoya et al., 2022). Meanwhile, the effects of digital transformation (DT) are being felt by numerous nations, along with all economic sectors, industries, and types of organisations. The introduction of digital technologies has had a significant impact on the innovation process, a crucial aspect of technological organisation development (Ludbrook et al., 2019). The utilisation of advanced supercomputers, virtual reality (VR) technologies, and robotic systems in research, science, and production has resulted in significant modifications in the way innovation activities are organised. Digital technologies have hastened the dissemination of information, decreased the expenses associated with acquiring and exchanging information, and created the foundation for innovation models. In turn, innovations have also influenced the digital economy (Teece, 2018).

"Innovation" is a popular term used in many industries, particularly due to DT and disruption. It involves a creative process that introduces a new solution to the world and enhances entrepreneurship. Innovation is often associated with entrepreneurship and is the catalyst for creating world-changing solutions to problems. To ensure the long-term integration of innovations and their effective involvement in global transformation processes, it is important to consider the impact of major trends in the economy and society. This includes the widespread adoption of the idea of sustainable development. Contemporary scientific literature has begun to explore the links between Industry 4.0, Society 5.0, and the Sustainable Development Goals (SDGs) (Beltrami et al., 2021; Ejsmont et al., 2020; Piccarozzi et al., 2022). This represents the first effort to examine how these concepts are interrelated. The swift advancement of digital technologies is at odds with the existing models and techniques of innovation management. Furthermore, some countries and regions are already experiencing a discrepancy between the level of development of their digital infrastructure and the efficacy of their innovation management methods. This necessitates a re-evaluation of several conceptual approaches.

The purpose of this chapter is to explore complex innovation models in the context of DT for innovation management. By complex, we refer to innovation as a complex or multifaceted process (Zukin, 2020) that considers the wider technical, organisational, and personal perspectives. Hence, the aim is to identify contemporary concepts that influence innovation activity, pinpoint promising domains and types of innovation, and evaluate the multifaceted role of innovation from multiple perspectives (technical, organisational, and personal). The chapter first introduces the concept of DT, then moves to complex innovation models, then the taxonomy of innovation models in the DT context, and finally the future DT challenges facing innovation models.

Digital Transformation

Digital transformation (DT) refers to the integration of digital technologies into all areas of an organisation, fundamentally changing how organisations operate and deliver value to customers. While DT can lead to significant benefits such as increased efficiency, improved customer experience, and enhanced innovation, it also poses challenges that organisations must address (Ahn & Chen, 2022; Nadkarni & Prügl, 2021; Oztemel & Gursev, 2020; Ulas, 2019; Verhoef et al., 2021).

One of the key debates in DT is whether technology should be viewed as an enabler or a driver of change (Tsiavos & Kitsios, 2022). While some argue that DT is primarily driven by technological advancements, others argue that it is driven by the need to solve organisational problems and improve the customer experience. Technology is only one of the four key drivers of DT, with the other three being customer behaviour, regulatory requirements, and competition. Therefore, organisations should focus on addressing organisational problems and delivering value to customers rather than just implementing the latest technologies. DT requires significant changes in organisational culture and leadership, as it involves adopting new ways of working and embracing a culture of innovation. The most successful DTs are those that have a strong leadership vision, a culture of innovation, and an agile and collaborative approach to decision-making. Therefore, organisations should invest in developing a culture of innovation and empowering employees to drive DT.

DT also poses significant risks related to cybersecurity, data privacy, and regulatory compliance (Ahmad & Gupta, 2021). Organisations must ensure that they have robust risk management processes and cybersecurity measures in place to protect their assets and data. Organisations that prioritise cybersecurity during their DT are more likely to achieve positive outcomes and avoid costly breaches. DT can also have a significant impact on the workforce, as it may require new skills and ways of working. Organisations must invest in upskilling and reskilling their employees to ensure that they have the necessary skills to adapt to new technologies and work processes. Organisations that invest in upskilling their workforce are more likely to succeed in their DT efforts.

In conclusion, DT is a complex and multifaceted process that requires organisations to address various challenges related to technology, culture, leadership, risk management, and workforce skills. Organisations that prioritise delivering value to customers, developing a culture of innovation, and investing in risk management and workforce skills are more likely to succeed in their DT efforts.

Complex Innovation Management Models

Schumpeter and Backhaus (2003) are widely regarded as the pioneers of innovation theory. The mechanisms of creating novel knowledge and innovations have always exerted a significant impact on human life, especially during critical periods of economic development (Fagerberg et al., 2012; Mingaleva et al., 2020; Mingaleva et al., 2019). This section discusses the complex models of innovation, such as the 4Ps model (product, process, position, and paradigm), introduced by Joe Tidd and John R. Bessant, that can help organise and focus innovation efforts (Tidd & Bessant, 2014). Open and closed innovation are other models of innovation discussed in this section.

4Ps Innovation Model

Tidd and Bessant (2014) developed the 4Ps model as a typology to guide organisations in managing complex innovation in the areas of product, process, position, and paradigm. These areas of complex innovation were also considered from a radical and incremental perspective, with radical being the development of completely new and disruptive products, services, or processes that fundamentally change the way things are done, and incremental being the amendments to existing products, services, or processes to enhance their performance or functionality.

Figure 1. 4Ps innovation model
Source: Tidd and Bassant (2014)

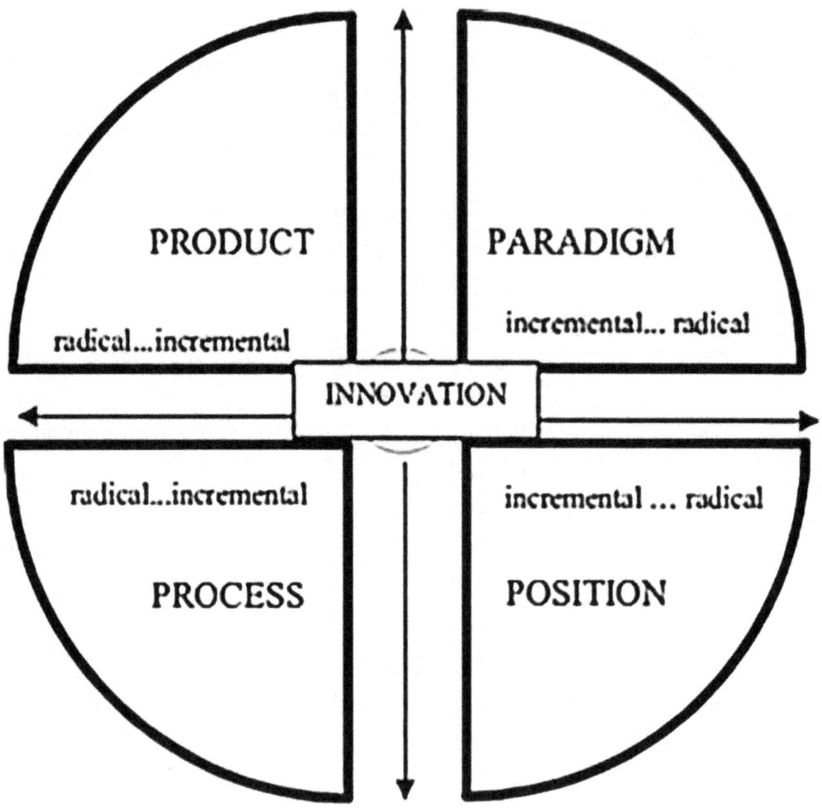

The most straightforward of the 4Ps is product innovation, which involves creating new products (radical innovation) or making changes to existing ones (incremental innovation) offered by an organisation. Product innovation is typically what people think of when they talk about innovation, and it can involve changes to the design or the entire product or service. However, it does not always require creating a completely new product to solve a new problem. For example, the first computer was created for a non-existent market, but subsequent generations have been improvements on the original design. Innovation can occur by adding new features to existing products or making improvements to them. Innovation isn't limited to products but can also include services, processes, or organisational models. Recent examples of product innovation in the context of DT include streaming platforms like Amazon Prime, Netflix, and Hotstar, while Airbnb, Uber, and Ola are also examples of this type of innovation.

Tidd and Bessant (2014) define process innovation as a change in the way a product or service is created or delivered. This can involve introducing greater automation in the manufacturing process, rethinking best practises in process management, or changing how improvements are measured. Process innovation is mainly focused on optimisation and can be achieved through continuous improvement over time rather than through occasional radical changes. It is primarily an internal process that can greatly affect an organisation's efficiency and profitability. There are several tools and frameworks available to stimulate process innovation, such as the Flow Process Chart (see Figure 2).

Figure 2. Process innovation model
Source: Preez et al. (2009)

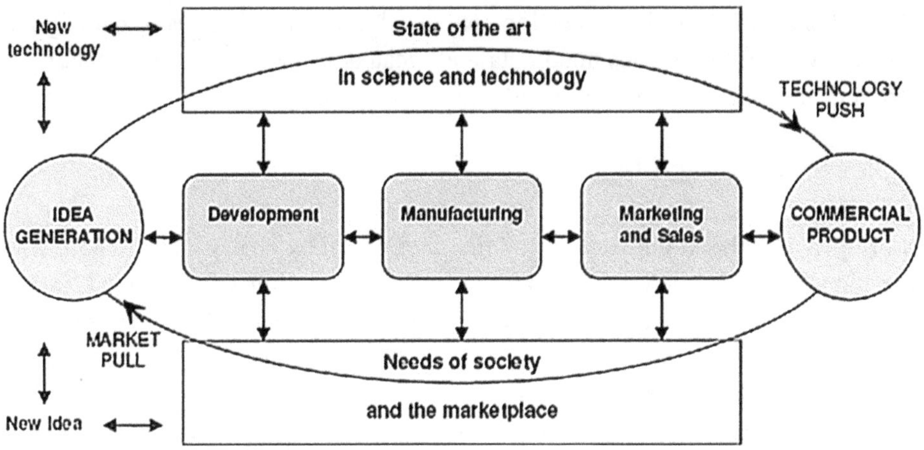

The innovation environment has shifted due to factors like liberalisation, deregulation, globalisation, increasing customer demand, and technological advancements, leading to changes in manufacturing processes within organisations. Process innovation is crucial for organisations to align their processes in a customer-oriented manner, ensuring long-term success. Processes contain four elements: process deliverables, process flow, process management, and technologies. By reforming the production process based on market and technology-related changes, firms can adapt more quickly to changes in the organisational environment. Although the process of change may be challenging, it can result in high earnings. Examples of process innovation in the context of DT include AliExpress, which applied a disruptive innovation to the process of online selling through dropshipping. This involves the manufacturer sending the product directly to the purchaser. Spotify and other music-streaming services and Ford Motors' belt systems are also examples of process innovations.

From an organisation's point of view, position refers to the placement of a product or service in the market. Position innovation involves changing the context in which the product or service is introduced, thereby altering consumers' perceptions of it, according to Tidd and Bessant. Positioning innovation involves repositioning a product or service in a new market or from a new angle. This innovation creates space for other types of innovation to take place. For instance, Airbnb was initially positioned around conferences before moving into the general holiday and travel industry. Position innovation can also involve changing how a specific product or process is perceived or used, leading to new market opportunities. Examples of positioning innovations in the context of DT include the online home rental marketplace Airbnb, low-cost Tata Nano cars, and the rise of low-cost airlines.

Thomas Kuhn coined the term "paradigm shift" to describe a significant change in the core concepts, values, and practises of a scientific community or discipline. Paradigm innovation, which is informed by such a shift, involves fundamentally changing a conceptual model through a common example such as Henry Ford and the motorcar. The common misconception about innovation is that it is similar to invention, but it is actually about improving current products or services. Paradigm innovation is the most significant method of innovation, as it drives all major economic development. For instance, in the context of DT, electric cars are paradigmatic innovations as they change what is possible within the innovation space. Paradigm innovation not only allows for economic growth but also creates new wealth. Organisations constantly shift paradigms, especially when they find more profitable subdivisions. Paradigm innovation reflects a shift in the vital theoretical model through a change in the organisation's status quo. The iPhone and smartphone development are significant examples of paradigm innovation, as they changed how consumers consumed data and created a new market. Smartphone growth and Google advertising are some examples of paradigmatic innovation.

Open and Closed Innovation Model

The concept of open and closed innovation was first introduced by Henry Chesbrough, who proposed the idea of open innovation as a new paradigm for managing innovation. Chesbrough (2003) argued that traditional closed innovation models, which rely on internal research and development, were becoming less effective in a world of increasing technological complexity and interconnectedness. Instead, he suggested that organisations should embrace open innovation by leveraging external sources of knowledge and expertise, such as universities, customers, and suppliers, to accelerate innovation and create more value. Since then, the concept of open innovation has gained widespread attention and has become a key framework for innovation management in many organisations (see Figure 3).

Figure 3. Open and closed innovation model
Source: Chesbrough (2003)

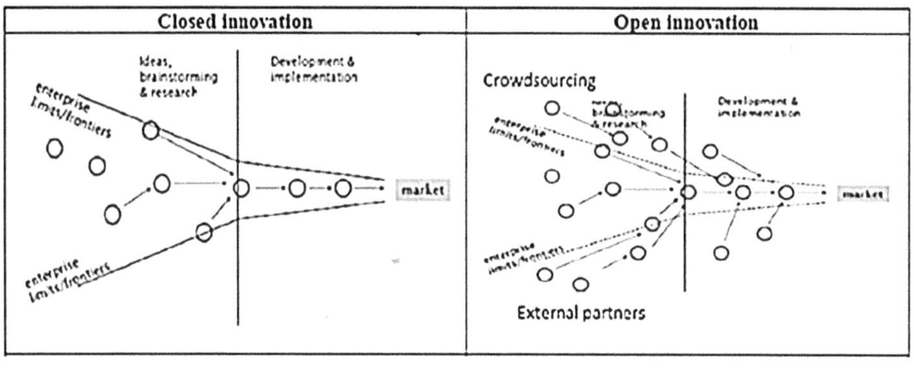

Open and closed innovation models can both be applied in the context of DT. In a closed innovation model, an organisation relies on its internal resources to develop new products or services. The focus is on developing and protecting intellectual property, and ideas and information are kept confidential within the organisation. This approach may be suitable for some DT initiatives that involve improving existing products or services, such as enhancing internal processes or upgrading software systems. However, closed innovation can limit an organisation's access to external expertise, knowledge, and technologies that may be critical for more disruptive DTs. The closed innovation model was successful due to the use of computers and information technology. However, the increasing use of information and communication technologies has led to a shift towards the open innovation model, facilitated by the DT (Bardhan et al., 2013; Cainelli et al., 2020; Choi, 2019; Li et al., 2019).

On the other hand, open innovation involves collaborating with external partners, such as startups, academic institutions, or other organisations, to share ideas, knowledge, and resources. This approach allows an organisation to leverage external expertise and resources to develop new products or services. Open innovation is well-suited for DT initiatives that involve more radical changes, such as developing entirely new digital products or services. For example, an organisation may partner with a startup to develop a new app or use open-source software to build a new platform.

The adoption of information and computer technologies led to a shift from the closed innovation model to the open innovation model, enabling communication and product promotion in markets. While some legal protection of innovation rights remained, the open innovation model brought significant changes to the innovation transfer system (Kesidou et al., 2022). The open innovation model also considers factors such as network interaction between organisations and the local community, environmental norms and standards, and social responsibility. Access to external knowledge has become more important, and interaction with other organisations has also increased (Boh et al., 2020; Saebi & Foss, 2015).

Taxonomy of the Innovation Ecosystem in Digital Transformation

The choice between complex innovation models in the context of DT depends on the nature of the transformation. Organisations need to weigh the benefits of leveraging external expertise and resources against the potential risks of intellectual property leakage and loss of control over the innovation process. The current models of innovation in the context of DT recognise innovation based on different information and communication principles. These models are the closed innovation model (CIM), the open innovation model (OIM), and the 4Ps. In the last twenty years, digitalization and the expansion of sustainable development goals have impacted these models. These global trends have shaped the peculiarities of innovation activity at the present stage of development through various factors that influence innovation management and the applied model of innovation activity in the context of DT. For that reason, this section delves into the taxonomy or categorisation of innovation models in DT from multiple perspectives.

The application of innovation models with complementary theories such as multi-perspective theory can provide a more holistic and detailed lens of how different models of innovation impact innovation activity in the context of DT. Harold Linstone (1989) introduced the theory in the 1980s, which takes on a Kantian perspective that requires us to differentiate between our point of view and the object of our observation. In other words, it emphasises the importance of considering different perspectives when analysing a situation or problem; these perspectives are technical, organisational, and personal. The theory was later adapted by scholars such as David Avison and Trevor Wood-Harper in their Multiview model (Avison et al., 1998; Avison & Wood-Harper, 1990; Wood-Harper & Avison, 1992). The above scholars agree that the technical perspective looks at the tools, methods, and processes needed to complete a task; the organisational perspective examines how work is structured and the roles of individuals in an organisation; and the personal perspective focuses on individual values, motivation, and attitude towards their work. Each perspective highlights different aspects of completing tasks, including efficiency, collaboration, alignment with organisational goals, individual growth and development, work-life balance, and finding meaning in work.

Table 1 presents a taxonomy of innovation models (OIM, CIM, and 4Ps) from multiple perspectives, and thus the corresponding TOP perspective(s) are identified and categorised (see Table 1 and Figure 1). Table 1 corresponds to the link between the innovation models and TOP perspectives:

Table 1. Taxonomy of innovation models from multiple perspectives

Technical (T)	Organisational (O)	Personal (P)
	4Ps	
• Leveraging new technologies or data to create more personalised or efficient products (product) • Leveraging data analytics or automation technologies to streamline workflows and reduce costs (process) • Leveraging new technologies or data to create new market opportunities (position) • Leveraging new technologies or data to create entirely new products or services (paradigm)	• Collaboration between different departments or external partners to bring a new digital products or technologies to market (product) • Changes to organisational structures or workflows and may also require training or upskilling employees (process) • Require a significant shift in organisational culture or structure and may require collaboration with external partners (position) • Require a fundamental shift in the organisation's mission or values and may require collaboration with external partners (paradigm)	• Innovation may require individuals with specialised technical skills, such as software development or data analysis (product) • Require individuals who are comfortable with change and able to learn new technologies or workflows quickly (process) • Require individuals with an entrepreneurial mindset and a willingness to take risks (position) • Require individuals who are comfortable with ambiguity and able to challenge the status quo (paradigm)
	Open/Closed Innovation	
• Provide access to a broader range of knowledge and expertise than closed innovation • By collaborating with external partners, organisations can access cutting-edge research, technology, and expertise • Can accelerate innovation and provide a competitive advantage • Presents challenges related to intellectual property, confidentiality, and control over the innovation process	• Requires a culture of collaboration and willingness to work with external partners by building trust with them and being transparent about goals and expectations. • Organisations must also be willing to share the risks and benefits of innovation with external partners, which can be challenging in some cases. • Closed innovation allows organisations to maintain control over the innovation process and protect intellectual property • Lack of creativity and innovation, as ideas may become stagnant or not fully developed	• Requires individuals who are comfortable collaborating with external partners and working in teams • Willingness to share knowledge and expertise and to learn from external partners. • Closed innovation may appeal to individuals who prefer to work independently or who value control over the innovation process

4Ps of Innovation and Digital Transformation

Innovation plays a critical role in DT, and it can be viewed from different perspectives, including product, process, position, and paradigm innovation. Each perspective presents unique challenges and opportunities that must be carefully evaluated to achieve success in the digital age. Organisations must be agile, adaptable, and willing to invest in research and development, disrupt existing organisational models, and carefully evaluate potential risks and benefits to thrive in the digital age. Ethical and responsible use of new technologies is also crucial for long-term success.

Product

Product innovation refers to the creation and development of new products, as well as improvements to existing ones, to meet the needs and wants of customers in a given market. In DT, product innovation has become even more critical as technology continues to advance and customers' expectations shift towards more digitally enhanced products. One of the benefits of DT is that it allows for faster and more efficient product innovation processes. With the use of digital tools such as computer-aided design (CAD) and simulation software, organisations can rapidly prototype and test new products. Digital platforms and tools also enable collaboration between different teams, including research and development, marketing, and production, leading to more innovative products. Another advantage of product innovation in DT is the ability to leverage data analytics to gain insights into customer behaviour and preferences. Through the use of data collected from customer interactions with digital products, organisations can identify patterns, trends, and opportunities for improvement, leading to more customer-centric product design and development. However, there are also challenges associated with product innovation in the context of DT. One of the most significant challenges is keeping up with the rapid pace of technological change. As new technologies emerge, organisations must be agile and adaptable to incorporate them into their products to stay competitive. This requires significant investment in research and development and a willingness to experiment and take risks. Another challenge is the potential for disruption of existing organisational models. DT has enabled the creation of entirely new markets and the disruption of traditional ones. Organisations must be willing to disrupt their existing organisational models to take advantage of these new opportunities.

From a technical perspective, product innovation often involves leveraging new technologies or data to create more personalised or efficient products. From an organisational perspective, product innovation may require collaboration between different departments or external partners to bring new digital products or technologies to market. From a personal perspective, product innovation may require individuals with specialised technical skills, such as software development or data analysis.

Process

Process innovation involves improving the efficiency and effectiveness of organisational processes. In the context of DT, process innovation can be seen as the adoption and integration of digital technologies to streamline organisational operations and improve productivity. One of the primary benefits of process innovation in DT is the ability to automate routine tasks, reducing the workload on employees and freeing up time for more creative and strategic work. This can lead to significant cost savings and improved efficiency. For example, organisations can use artificial intelligence and machine learning algorithms to automate customer service, reducing the need for human intervention and allowing for faster response times. However, there are also potential drawbacks to process innovation in DT. One concern is the potential for job displacement as routine tasks are automated. This can lead to job losses and a skills gap, as employees may not have the necessary skills to adapt to the new digital environment. It is important for organisations to invest in training and reskilling programs to help employees adapt to the changing technological landscape. Another concern is the potential for increased cyber threats as organisations rely more heavily on digital technologies. Process innovation can increase the risk of cyberattacks, and organisations must invest in robust cybersecurity measures to protect their operations and sensitive data. Finally, process innovation in DT requires careful planning and implementation. It is important for organisations to assess their current processes and identify areas that could benefit from digital integration. It is also crucial to ensure that digital technologies are integrated seamlessly into existing processes to avoid disruption and ensure a smooth transition.

From a technical perspective, process innovation often involves leveraging data analytics or automation technologies to streamline workflows and reduce costs. From an organisational perspective, process innovation may require changes to organisational structures or workflows and may also require training or upskilling employees. From a personal perspective, process innovation may require individuals who are comfortable with change and are able to learn new technologies or workflows quickly.

Position

Position innovation, also known as organisation model innovation, is a critical aspect of DT. It involves creating new organisational models that change the way organisations interact with customers, suppliers, and partners. Position innovation can be seen in the emergence of new digital platforms that allow organisations to deliver products and services in new ways or in the adoption of new revenue models such as subscription-based pricing. One of the key drivers of position innovation in the context of DT is the increasing availability of data. Digital technologies generate a vast amount of data that can be used to gain insights into customer behaviour, market trends, and competitive pressures. Organisations that are able to harness this data and use it to develop new organisational models are more likely to succeed in the digital age. Another important aspect of position innovation is the ability to collaborate with external partners. DT has made it easier for organisations to connect with partners across the globe and to tap into new sources of expertise and innovation. This has led to the emergence of new ecosystems of partners that work together to create value for customers. However, there are also challenges associated with position innovation in the context of DT. One of the biggest challenges is balancing the desire for innovation with the need for stability and continuity. Organisations that are too focused on innovation may lose sight of their core competencies and end up diluting their brand or confusing their customers. Another challenge is the need to manage risk in the face of rapid change. DT is a disruptive force that can fundamentally change the competitive landscape of an industry. Organisations that fail to adapt to these changes risk becoming irrelevant or being left behind by more agile competitors.

From a technical perspective, positioning innovation often involves leveraging new technologies or data to create new market opportunities. From an organisational perspective, position innovation may require a significant shift in organisational culture or structure and may require collaboration with external partners. From a personal perspective, position innovation may require individuals with an entrepreneurial mindset and a willingness to take risks.

Paradigm

Paradigm innovation is a fundamental shift in the way things are done, leading to the creation of new products, services, or processes that change the industry landscape. In the context of DT, paradigm innovation has become increasingly important as technological advancements have revolutionised the way organisations operate and interact with customers. One example of paradigm innovation in DT is the shift from physical to virtual organisation operations. With the rise of e-commerce, many organisations have transformed their entire organisational models to focus on online sales and services. This shift has led to the creation of entirely new industries, such as online marketplaces and subscription-based services. Another example of paradigmatic innovation in DT is the development of artificial intelligence and machine learning technologies. These technologies have revolutionised many industries, including finance, healthcare, and transportation. For example, in finance, AI and machine learning are being used to improve fraud detection and risk management, while in healthcare, these technologies are being used to develop new treatments and diagnostic tools. However, paradigm innovation in DT also presents significant challenges. For example, new technologies may disrupt traditional organisational models and threaten the livelihoods of workers in certain industries. Additionally, there may be ethical and privacy concerns associated with the use of certain technologies, such as facial recognition or predictive analytics.

From a technical perspective, paradigm innovation often involves leveraging new technologies or data to create entirely new products or services. From an organisational perspective, paradigm innovation may require a fundamental shift in the organisation's mission or values and may require collaboration with external partners. From a personal perspective, paradigm innovation may require individuals who are comfortable with ambiguity and able to challenge the status quo.

Open/Closed Innovation and Digital Transformation

Open innovation in the context of DT refers to the process of involving external partners in the innovation process of an organisation. This approach allows organisations to access a wider range of expertise, knowledge, and resources than they would have by relying solely on internal research and development. Open innovation can lead to faster and more efficient innovation as well as more successful market outcomes. However, open innovation also comes with some challenges. One of the biggest challenges is the risk of intellectual property theft. When an organisation shares its ideas and innovations with external partners, there is always a risk that those partners will steal the organisation's intellectual property and use it for their own benefit. This risk can be mitigated by using legal agreements and contracts, but it still remains a potential issue. Another challenge of open innovation in the context of DT is the need for effective collaboration and communication between all parties involved. Organisations must be able to work closely with their external partners to ensure that the innovation process runs smoothly and that everyone is on the same page. This can be difficult when working with partners from different locations, cultures, and backgrounds. Finally, open innovation in the context of DT requires organisations to be open to new ideas and approaches. This means that organisations must be willing to embrace new technologies, processes, and organisational models. Organisations that are resistant to change may struggle to adapt to open innovation and may miss out on the potential benefits it can offer.

Closed innovation is an innovation model that emphasises internal research and development and relies on the firm's internal resources to develop new products or services. It is also characterised by stringent legal regulations governing the monopoly rights to innovation, which may include patents, copyrights, and trade secrets. In the context of DT, closed innovation has some limitations. One of the main limitations is that it restricts a firm's access to external knowledge and expertise. In today's fast-changing digital environment, where technology is evolving rapidly, firms must be agile and flexible enough to adapt to changes quickly. Closed innovation may inhibit a firm's ability to acquire new knowledge and keep up with the latest trends in technology. Another limitation of closed innovation is that it can be expensive to develop and maintain the necessary infrastructure and resources. In the digital age, firms need to invest heavily in digital technologies and infrastructure to remain competitive. Closed innovation can be costly because it requires significant investment in research and development, capital expenditures, and technical regulations. Furthermore, closed innovation can create a culture of silos within a firm where different departments work independently of each other. This siloed culture can impede collaboration and inhibit knowledge sharing, which is crucial for innovation. In contrast, open innovation, which emphasises collaboration and knowledge sharing, can foster a culture of innovation within a firm.

From a technical perspective, open innovation can provide access to a broader range of knowledge and expertise than closed innovation. By collaborating with external partners, organisations can access cutting-edge research, technology, and expertise that they may not have in-house. This can accelerate innovation and provide a competitive advantage. However, open innovation also presents challenges related to intellectual property, confidentiality, and control over the innovation process. From an organisational perspective, open innovation requires a culture of collaboration and a willingness to work with external partners. This involves building trust with partners and being transparent about goals and expectations. Organisations must also be willing to share the risks and benefits of innovation with external partners, which can be challenging in some cases. Closed innovation, on the other hand, allows organisations to maintain control over the innovation process and protect intellectual property. However, it can also lead to a lack of creativity and innovation, as ideas may become stagnant or not fully developed. From a personal perspective, open innovation requires individuals who are comfortable collaborating with external partners and working in teams. This requires a willingness to share knowledge and expertise, as well as a willingness to learn from external partners. Closed innovation may appeal to individuals who prefer to work independently or who value control over the innovation process.

Overall, open innovation in the context of DT can be a valuable tool for organisations looking to stay competitive and innovative in today's fast-paced organisational environment. However, it requires careful consideration of potential risks and challenges, as well as a willingness to adapt to new approaches and ways of working. In conclusion, while closed innovation may have been successful in the past, it is not the most effective innovation model in the context of DT. DT requires firms to be agile, flexible, and adaptive, and closed innovation can be limiting in these regards. Open innovation, on the other hand, provides firms with access to a wider range of knowledge and expertise, fosters collaboration and knowledge-sharing, and enables firms to adapt to changes quickly, making it a more suitable innovation model in the digital age (see Figure 4) (Cenamor & Frishammar, 2021; Colombo et al., 2021; Osorno & Medrano, 2020).

Figure 4. Multiple perspectives innovation in innovation model factors

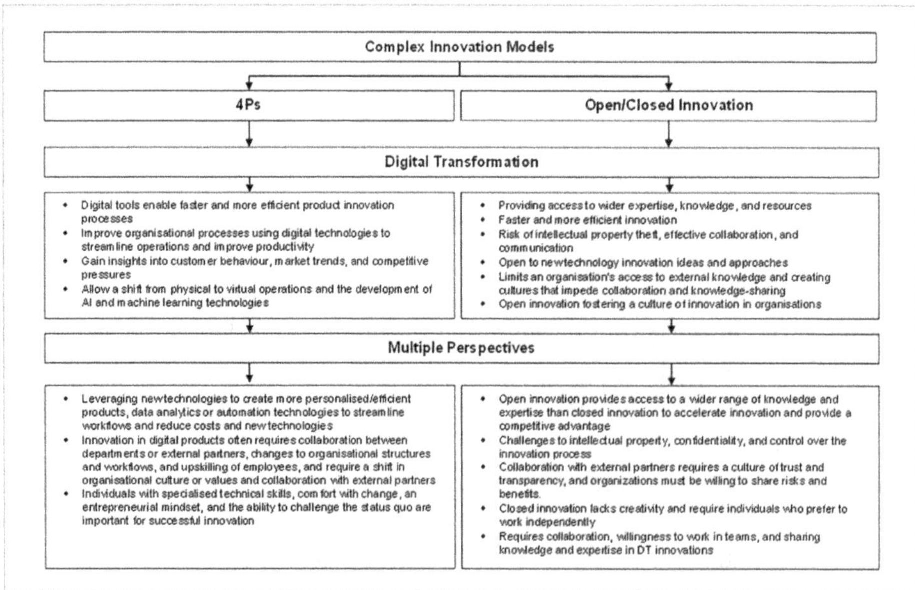

Future of Complex Innovation Management in DT

Indeed, the emergence of innovation ecosystems has brought about a new set of challenges for organisations. One of the key challenges is the issue of intellectual property rights and ownership in a collaborative environment. With the participation of multiple parties in the creation of an innovation, it becomes difficult to determine the individual copyright holder and protect property rights. This is further complicated by the use of emerging technologies such as artificial intelligence, where the question of who owns the copyright becomes even more complex. Addressing these challenges requires a coordinated effort between stakeholders, including governments, industry, and academia, to develop new legal frameworks and mechanisms for protecting intellectual property rights in collaborative innovation ecosystems. At the same time, it is important to address the ethical issues surrounding intellectual property protection, such as ensuring that the benefits of innovation are shared equitably among all parties involved. By doing so, organisations can leverage the full potential of innovation ecosystems to drive growth and competitiveness while ensuring that the rights of all stakeholders are protected (Mingaleva & Mirskikh, 2015; Wang, 2021).

Figure 5. Stages of future innovation in DT

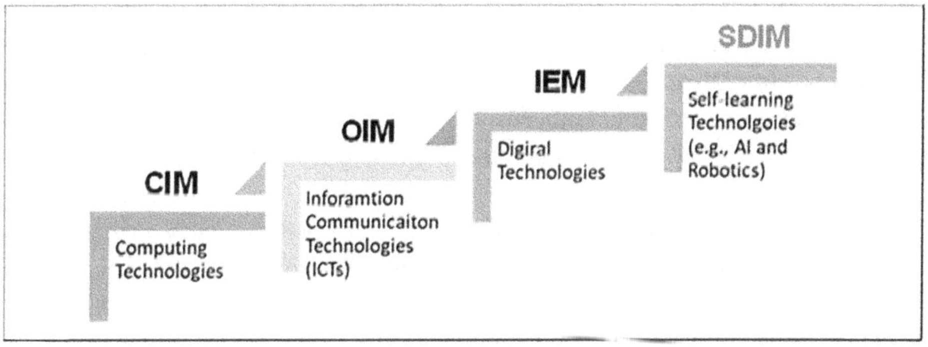

Indeed, the emergence of artificial intelligence raises complex ethical and legal issues, including those related to intellectual property rights (Atabekov & Yastrebov, 2018; Stahl, 2021). As AI systems become increasingly sophisticated and capable of creating original works, there is a growing debate about who should be considered the rightful owner of the resulting intellectual property. Some argue that the creators of the AI systems should be granted ownership of any intellectual property generated by those systems, while others suggest that such works should be considered a product of collaboration between humans and machines and be jointly owned. This issue is particularly relevant in the fields of art, music, and literature, where AI-generated works have already been created and are being sold for significant sums of money. As AI technology continues to advance, it is likely that these debates will intensify and lead to significant changes in the legal and ethical frameworks governing intellectual property rights.

According to various research conducted in the area of predicting the future of information and digital technologies, it is possible to speculate that a novel innovation model will emerge in the future (Ahn & Chen, 2022; Keating et al., 2017; Yang et al., 2018). This model will be founded on robots, artificial intelligence, and computer systems that can develop on their own. This new innovation model can be referred to as the "self-developing" innovation model (SDIM). Figure 4 illustrates the different stages of the transformation of innovation models, which include the emergence of this new model, its features, and how it is connected to the digital and information foundations of its existence.

Overall, the future of complex innovation management in digital transformation will involve a greater emphasis on open innovation and collaboration. Collaboration with external partners, such as universities and startups, will be crucial to accessing cutting-edge research, technology, and expertise. However, this also presents challenges related to intellectual property, confidentiality, and control over the innovation process. To manage innovation effectively in DT, organisations will need to foster a culture of innovation, develop agile structures and workflows, balance short-term and long-term goals, and use emerging technologies such as AI and IoT. Individuals must possess specialised technical skills, an entrepreneurial mindset, and be comfortable with ambiguity and change (see Figure 5).

CONCLUSION

The purpose of this chapter was to explore complex innovation models in the context of DT for innovation management from a wider technical, organisational, and personal perspective. Digital transformation (DT) is a complex process that requires organisations to address challenges related to technology, culture, leadership, risk management, and workforce skills. Prioritising customer value, innovation culture, risk management, and workforce development can lead to success in DT for product, process, position, and paradigm innovation. Similarly, open innovation can provide access to a broader range of knowledge and expertise than closed innovation but presents challenges related to intellectual property, confidentiality, and control over the innovation process. Open innovation requires a culture of collaboration and the willingness to work with external partners. Closed innovation can limit innovation and creativity. Open innovation is more suitable for DT because it enables firms to adapt to changes quickly. As for the future of innovation management in DT, it will involve a greater emphasis on open innovation and collaboration, fostering a culture of innovation, developing agile structures and workflows, balancing short-term and long-term goals, and using emerging technologies such as AI and IoT. Individuals must possess specialised technical skills, an entrepreneurial mindset, and be comfortable with ambiguity and change. Future research could take this chapter to the next level by conducting an empirical study on the multiple perspectives of complex innovation models applied in real-world organisational settings, which could provide some valuable contributions to knowledge and practise in the innovation domain.

REFERENCES

Ahmad, I., & Gupta, S. (2021). *Digital transformation: Key technology, cybersecurity and privacy risks*. Retrieved 13th March from https://www.nortonrosefulbright.com/en/knowledge/publications/4318add0/digital-transformation-key-technology-cybersecurity-and-privacy-risks

Ahn, M. J., & Chen, Y.-C. (2022). Digital transformation toward AI-augmented public administration: The perception of government employees and the willingness to use AI in government. *Government Information Quarterly*, *39*(2), 101664. doi:10.1016/j.giq.2021.101664

Atabekov, A., & Yastrebov, O. (2018). Legal Status of Artificial Intelligence Across Countries: Legislation on the Move. *European Research Studies, 21*(4), 773–782. doi:10.35808/ersj/1245

Avison, D. E., Wood-Harper, A., Vidgen, R. T., & Wood, J. (1998). A further exploration into information systems development: The evolution of Multiview2. *Information Technology & People, 11*(2), 124–139. doi:10.1108/09593849810218319

Avison, D. E., & Wood-Harper, A. T. (1990). *Multiview: An Exploration in Information Systems Development.* Blackwell Scientific Publications.

Bardhan, I., Krishnan, V., & Lin, S. (2013). Research note—Business value of information technology: testing the interaction effect of IT and R&D on Tobin's Q. *Information Systems Research, 24*(4), 1147–1161.

Beltrami, M., Orzes, G., Sarkis, J., & Sartor, M. (2021). Industry 4.0 and sustainability: Towards conceptualization and theory. *Journal of Cleaner Production, 312*, 127733. doi:10.1016/j.jclepro.2021.127733

Boh, W. F., Huang, C. J., & Wu, A. (2020). Investor experience and innovation performance: The mediating role of external cooperation. *Strategic Management Journal, 41*(1), 124–151. doi:10.1002mj.3089

Bordeleau, F.-E., Mosconi, E., & de Santa-Eulalia, L. A. (2020). Business intelligence and analytics value creation in Industry 4.0: A multiple case study in manufacturing medium enterprises. *Production Planning and Control, 31*(2-3), 173–185. doi:10.1080/09537287.2019.1631458

Cainelli, G., De Marchi, V., & Grandinetti, R. (2020). Do knowledge-intensive business services innovate differently? *Economics of Innovation and New Technology, 29*(1), 48–65. doi:10.1080/10438599.2019.1585639

Cenamor, J., & Frishammar, J. (2021). Openness in platform ecosystems: Innovation strategies for complementary products. *Research Policy, 50*(1), 104148. doi:10.1016/j.respol.2020.104148

Chesbrough, H. W. (2003). *Open Innovation: The New Imperative for Creating and Profiting from Technology.* Harvard Business School Press.

Choi, B. (2019). The role of firm size and IT capabilities in open and closed innovation. *Asia Pacific Journal of Information Systems, 29*(4), 690–716.

Colombo, M. G., Foss, N. J., Lyngsie, J., & Lamastra, C. R. (2021). What drives the delegation of innovation decisions? The roles of firm innovation strategy and the nature of external knowledge. *Research Policy, 50*(1), 104134. doi:10.1016/j.respol.2020.104134

De Felice, F., Travaglioni, M., & Petrillo, A. (2021). Innovation Trajectories for a Society 5.0. *Data, 6*(11), 115. doi:10.3390/data6110115

Ejsmont, K., Gladysz, B., & Kluczek, A. (2020). Impact of industry 4.0 on sustainability—Bibliometric literature review. *Sustainability (Basel), 12*(14), 5650. doi:10.3390u12145650

Fagerberg, J., Fosaas, M., & Sapprasert, K. (2012). Innovation: Exploring the knowledge base. *Research Policy, 41*(7), 1132–1153. doi:10.1016/j.respol.2012.03.008

Keating, S. J., Leland, J. C., Cai, L., & Oxman, N. (2017). Toward site-specific and self-sufficient robotic fabrication on architectural scales. *Science Robotics*, *2*(5), eaam8986. doi:10.1126cirobotics.aam8986 PMID:33157892

Kesidou, E., Narasimhan, R., Ozusaglam, S., & Wong, C. Y. (2022). Dynamic openness for network-enabled product and process innovation: A panel-data analysis. *International Journal of Operations & Production Management*, *42*(3), 257–279. doi:10.1108/IJOPM-06-2021-0380

Li, C., Jiang, Y., & Fang, P. (2019). Innovation in advanced manufacturing driven by supercomputing. *Procedia CIRP*, *83*, 584–589. doi:10.1016/j.procir.2019.04.092

Linstone, H. A. (1989). Multiple perspectives: Concept, applications, and user guidelines. *Systems Practice*, *2*(3), 307–331. doi:10.1007/BF01059977

Ludbrook, F., Michalikova, K. F., Musova, Z., & Suler, P. (2019). Business models for sustainable innovation in industry 4.0: Smart manufacturing processes, digitalization of production systems, and data-driven decision making. *Journal of Self-Governance and Management Economics*, *7*(3), 21–26.

Mingaleva, Z., Deputatova, L., & Starkov, Y. (2020). *Management of organisational knowledge as a basis for the competitiveness of enterprises in the digital economy*. Academic Press.

Mingaleva, Z., & Mirskikh, I. (2015). Psychological aspects of Intellectual property protection. *Procedia: Social and Behavioral Sciences*, *190*, 220–226. doi:10.1016/j.sbspro.2015.04.938

Mingaleva, Z. A., Deputatova, L. N., Akatov, N. B., Starkov, Y. V., & Mitrofanova, E. (2019). Application of HADI-cycle for providing sustainability of processes of knowledge and innovation. *Entrepreneurship and Sustainability Issues*, *7*(2), 1628–1640. doi:10.9770/jesi.2019.7.2(58)

Nadkarni, S., & Prügl, R. (2021). Digital transformation: A review, synthesis and opportunities for future research. *Management Review Quarterly*, *71*(2), 233–341. doi:10.100711301-020-00185-7

Osorno, R., & Medrano, N. (2020). Open innovation platforms: A conceptual design framework. *IEEE Transactions on Engineering Management*, *69*(2), 438–450. doi:10.1109/TEM.2020.2973227

Oztemel, E., & Gursev, S. (2020). Literature review of Industry 4.0 and related technologies. *Journal of Intelligent Manufacturing*, *31*(1), 127–182. doi:10.100710845-018-1433-8

Piccarozzi, M., Silvestri, C., Aquilani, B., & Silvestri, L. (2022). Is this a new story of the 'Two Giants'? A systematic literature review of the relationship between industry 4.0, sustainability and its pillars. *Technological Forecasting and Social Change*, *177*, 121511. doi:10.1016/j.techfore.2022.121511

Preez, N. d., Louw, L., & Essmann, H. (2009). *An Innovation Process Model for Improving Innovation Capability*. Academic Press.

Ramírez-Montoya, M. S., Castillo-Martínez, I. M., Sanabria-Z, J., & Miranda, J. (2022). Complex Thinking in the Framework of Education 4.0 and Open Innovation—A Systematic Literature Review. *Journal of Open Innovation*, *8*(1), 4. doi:10.3390/joitmc8010004

Saebi, T., & Foss, N. J. (2015). Business models for open innovation: Matching heterogeneous open innovation strategies with business model dimensions. *European Management Journal, 33*(3), 201–213. doi:10.1016/j.emj.2014.11.002

Schumpeter, J., & Backhaus, U. (2003). *The theory of economic development*. Springer.

Stahl, B. C. (2021). *Artificial intelligence for a better future: an ecosystem perspective on the ethics of AI and emerging digital technologies*. Springer Nature.

Teece, D. J. (2018). Profiting from innovation in the digital economy: Enabling technologies, standards, and licensing models in the wireless world. *Research Policy, 47*(8), 1367–1387.

Tidd, J., & Bessant, J. (2014). *Managing Innovation: Integrating Technological, Market and Organisational Change*. Wiley.

Tsiavos, V., & Kitsios, F. (2022). *Technology as Driver, Enabler and Barrier of Digital Transformation: A Review*. Academic Press.

Ulas, D. (2019). Digital Transformation Process and SMEs. *Procedia Computer Science, 158*, 662–671. doi:10.1016/j.procs.2019.09.101

Verhoef, P. C., Broekhuizen, T., Bart, Y., Bhattacharya, A., Qi Dong, J., Fabian, N., & Haenlein, M. (2021). Digital transformation: A multidisciplinary reflection and research agenda. *Journal of Business Research, 122*, 889–901. doi:10.1016/j.jbusres.2019.09.022

Wang, B. (2021). *Artificial intelligence technology simulation university three whole education moral education model research*. Academic Press.

Wood-Harper, A., & Avison, D. (1992). Reflections from the experience of using Multiview: Through the lens of soft systems methodology. *Systemist, 14*(3), 136–145.

Yang, G.-Z., Bellingham, J., Dupont, P. E., Fischer, P., Floridi, L., Full, R., Jacobstein, N., Kumar, V., McNutt, M., Merrifield, R., Nelson, B. J., Scassellati, B., Taddeo, M., Taylor, R., Veloso, M., Wang, Z. L., & Wood, R. (2018). The grand challenges of science robotics. *Science Robotics, 3*(14), eaar7650. doi:10.1126cirobotics.aar7650 PMID:33141701

Zukin, S. (2020). *The Innovation Complex: Cities, Tech, and the New Economy*. Oxford University Press. doi:10.1093/oso/9780190083830.001.0001

ADDITIONAL READING

Ali, M. (2019a). The Barriers and Enablers of the Educational Cloud: A Doctoral Student Perspective. *Open Journal of Business and Management, 7*(1).

Ali, M. (2019b). Cloud Computing at a Cross Road: Quality and Risks in Higher Education. *Advances in Internet of Things, 9*(3), 33–49. doi:10.4236/ait.2019.93003

Ali, M. (Ed.). (2021). *Remote Work and Sustainable Changes for the Future of Global Business.* IGI Global. doi:10.4018/978-1-7998-7513-0

Ali, M. (2022). *Future Role of Sustainable Innovative Technologies in Crisis Management.* IGI Global. doi:10.4018/978-1-7998-9815-3

Ali, M., & Abdel-Haq, M. K. (2021). Bibliographical Analysis of Artificial Intelligence Learning in Higher Education: Is the Role of the Human Educator a Thing of the Past? In *Fostering Communication and Learning With Underutilized Technologies in Higher Education* (pp. 36–52). IGI Global. doi:10.4018/978-1-7998-4846-2.ch003

Ali, M., & Edghiem, F. (2021). Sustainable Business and Collaboration Driven by Big Data Analytics Amidst the Emergence of the Remote Work Culture. In *Remote Work and Sustainable Changes for the Future of Global Business* (pp. 15–32). IGI Global. doi:10.4018/978-1-7998-7513-0.ch002

Ali, M., Edghiem, F., & Alkhalifah, E. S. (2022). Cultural Challenges of ERP Implementation in Middle-Eastern Oil & Gas Sector: An Action Research Approach. *Systemic Practice and Action Research.* PMID:35668863

Ali, M. B. (2021). Internet of Things (IoT) to Foster Communication and Information Sharing: A Case of UK Higher Education. *Fostering Communication & Learning With Underutilized Technologies in Higher Education*, 1-20.

Ali, M. B., Wood-Harper, T., & Ramlogan, R. (2020a). A Framework Strategy to Overcome Trust Issues on Cloud Computing Adoption in Higher Education. In Modern Principles, Practices, and Algorithms for Cloud Security (pp. 162-183). IGI Global. doi:10.4018/978-1-7998-1082-7.ch008

Ali, M. B., Wood-Harper, T., & Ramlogan, R. (2020b). *The Role of SaaS Applications in Business IT Alignment: A Closer Look at Value Creation in Service Industry.* UKAIS.

Ali. (2019). Multiple Perspective of Cloud Computing Adoption Determinants in Higher Education a Systematic Review. *International Journal of Cloud Applications and Computing, 9*(3), 89-109.

Ali. (2020). Multi-Perspectives of Cloud Computing Service Adoption Quality and Risks in Higher Education. In D*Handbook of Research on Modern Educational Technologies, Applications, and Management* (2nd ed.). IGI Global.

Chapter 5
Developing an Innovation-Based Framework of Digital Entrepreneurship Strategy for Small and Medium-Sized Enterprises

Theoneste Manishimwe
American University of Nigeria, Nigeria

Lukman Raimi
Universiti Brunei Darussalam, Brunei

ABSTRACT

Although digital entrepreneurship (DE) emerged in the early 1990s because of digital technologies and entrepreneurship, current researchers consider it a recent phenomenon. This chapter proposes to extend the concept of DE to include the concept of dimensions of DE. Using literature in the areas of digital knowledge base and ICT market, digital business environment, digital skills and e-leadership, corporate culture, and access to finance, the chapter proposes a conceptual model for digital entrepreneurship, identifying the components of such a model as well as specific indications of size overlaps in different domains. This model implies that digital transformation in SMEs is intertwined with other activities and entrepreneurial behaviours in small firms, and it argues that understanding digital transformation or the adoption of digital technologies in SMEs requires an understanding of its context, particularly in relation to diffusion innovation theory, innovation system theory, and entrepreneurial approaches to the digital transformation towards digital corporate success.

DOI: 10.4018/978-1-6684-7416-7.ch005

INTRODUCTION

A subset of entrepreneurship known as "digital entrepreneurship" involves the digitization of any or all components of a traditional firm. It appears likely that digital entrepreneurship will become more prevalent given the rapid development of digital activities across all countries, societies, industries, and organizations, suggesting a need for a greater knowledge of this phenomenon (Nambisan, 2017; Hannibal & Rasmussen, 2014; Matlay & Westhead, 2007). DE is supposed to result from the fusion of the entrepreneurial and digital technology industries. Figures 1 and 2 illustrate it more graphically by emphasizing the digital technology adoption procedures that lead to digital entrepreneurship success in small and medium firms, respectively. In general, research on digital entrepreneurship has involved both the domains of digital technology and entrepreneurship.

The use of digital technologies to increase organizational performance in terms of organization and management, marketing and sales and production, and the same kind of mediating role that entrepreneurial orientation plays in this context. The adoption of digital technologies to build new ventures that are digitized or to transform existing businesses from traditional organizations to improve their organizational performance and create economic and/or social value has attracted some study attention in general. Although both are present in the literature, little is known about the synergetic effects of both strategies and the impact of digital transformation on them, given that SMEs are entrepreneurial by nature.

Given that digital technology (DT) plays a critical role in the design and success of organizational business models, it also allows for the establishment of new ventures and the survival of the entrepreneurial ecosystem. As a result, DT encourages entrepreneurship (Zahra et al., 2023). Business owners and executives have shown a strong interest in managing the innovation of digital goods and services. This is unsurprising given how digital technologies are changing the way businesses produce, market, and distribute goods and services while also boosting the economy and raising people's living standards. As a result, more opportunities for business owners to benefit from digital transformation are becoming available (Scuotto et al., 2021; Loonam et al., 2018). SMEs must not be left behind as digital technology has transformed society and business activities, as this results in changes in entrepreneurship theory, practice, and education. In response to this interest, the authors present a framework for promoting and tracking digital entrepreneurship among SMEs through digital innovation strategy initiatives.

The significance of focusing on SMEs cannot be overstated. Numerous academics and researchers have demonstrated the importance of SMEs in achieving the 2030 Agenda's Sustainable Development Goals. According to the World Bank, small and medium businesses have between 10 and 49 employees and 50 to 249 employees, respectively (Kushnir et al., 2010). However, because they are also classified based on specific revenue and asset turnover thresholds, the local definition of SMEs varies by country. SMEs are critical components of the larger industrial ecosystem. Start-ups and young businesses, typically small or medium-sized businesses, are the primary drivers of net job creation in many countries. They also serve as the foundation for the private sector's innovation and sustainability. In emerging markets, there are approximately 25-30 million formal SMEs, 55-70 million micro-businesses and 285-345 million informal businesses. SMEs account for approximately 90% of all businesses and more than 50% of all jobs worldwide. In emerging economies, formal SMEs can account for up to 40% of GDP. These numbers are significantly higher when informal SMEs are included. According to projections, 600 million new jobs will be needed by 2030 to accommodate the world's expanding workforce, making SME development a top priority for many governments around the world. The majority of formal jobs are created by small and medium-sized businesses (SMEs), which account for seven out of ten jobs in emerging markets (Raniya, 2019).

The contribution of SMEs to the 2030 Sustainable Development Goals (SDGs) is critical in responding to various business goals. With respect to SDG1, "End poverty in all its forms everywhere", Small and medium-sized enterprises (SMEs) are the economic frontier in terms of socioeconomic improvement and poverty alleviation, which is expected to lead to the zero poverty target (Patwary, 2020; Asikhia, 2016); developing more resilient agri-food small and medium-sized business is critical to poverty alleviation (Ali et al., 2022; Mkwambisi et al., 2021; Bishoge & Suntu, 2018); the success of SMEs, as reflected in their shareholders' well-being, contributes significantly to long-term business growth and job creation, which leads to poverty alleviation (Agyei et al., 2019); entrepreneurship in SMEs provides the best opportunity to make a profound and significant positive difference in poverty situations. (Liu, 2022). Various scholars and researchers (e.g. Daz-Bonilla, 2021; Aravindaraj & Rajan, 2022) have also demonstrated the significant contribution of SMEs to other SDGs; SDG 2 End hunger, achieve food security and better nutrition and promote sustainable agriculture. In general, the Sustainable Development Goals (SDGs) emphasize labour-intensive sectors (SDG 8.2), and improve small business access to affordable credit to support decent job creation and entrepreneurship (SDG 8.3 and 9.3) (Brixiov et al., 2020).

Several SDGs, such as SDG 1: "End poverty in all its forms everywhere," have been established. SDGs 8 and 10 rely on entrepreneurial activity to "promote inclusive and sustainable economic growth, employment, and decent work for all" (Bosma et al., 2020). According to the United Nations' SDG 8, businesses should strive for consistent, inclusive, and sustainable economic growth while also ensuring that everyone has access to decent work and living conditions (Lin & Koh, 2019). Small and medium-sized businesses, which are important contributors to the job creation process, provide two-thirds of all formal jobs in developing countries and 80% in low-income countries. Environmental factors such as public services, sound corporate law, and financial access are required for SMEs to succeed in the long run (EDFI, 2016). Furthermore, SMEs collectively contribute significantly to the national economy (White, 2018), accounting for 60% of employment on average and more than 50% of the GDP of most of Africa (Muiruri, 2017). It is the "missing link" in inclusive growth, employing much of the local labour force. It is also essential to any long term growth strategy (ITC, 2018). African SMEs create around 80% of new jobs but are also responsible for many job losses (ILO, 2019a). Due to its micro-business sector, Ethiopia employs the most people from developing countries (IFC, 2013).

Furthermore, 60% of the SDG targets can be met through SME investment, and an additional $1 trillion in SME investment will help developing countries meet the SDGs. Small and medium-sized businesses support 83% of SDG 8's goals to "promote sustained, inclusive, and sustainable economic growth, full and productive employment, and decent work for all," as well as 88% of SDG 9's goals to "build resilient infrastructure, promote inclusive and sustainable industrialization, and foster innovation" (ITC, 2019). As a result, financial stability in Sub-Saharan Africa promotes the growth of the entrepreneurial sector, which improves economic growth and accelerates the achievement of the SDGs (Babajide et al., 2020).

One of the current major issues confronting all businesses, particularly SMEs, is the need to go digital in order to overcome their limitations without falling behind their competitors due to a lack of technological advancement and limited resources in comparison to established businesses. The current digital transformation has brought about opportunities such as digital presence, adaptive customer engagement, competitive advantage, innovation, and effective resource management. Therefore, this chapter responds to calls for further development and exploration of the concept of digital entrepreneurship toward new ventures, as well as the fact that digital entrepreneurship is under-researched (Nobanee & Dilshad, 2020;

Morabito, 2021; Kraus et al., 2018; Zaheer et al., 2019). The article proposes that the DE paradigm be expanded to include an approach to digital transformation that is grounded in the knowledge bases of not only digital technology adoption, but also entrepreneurship, diffusion innovation theory, and innovation system theory. This philosophical viewpoint is conceptualized through an emphasis on DE dimensions. Thus, the article aims to integrate key aspects of the Digital Knowledge base and ICT market (DK), Digital business environment (DBE), Access to finance (AF), Digital skills and e-leadership (DSE), and Entrepreneurial Culture (EC). This chapter arrived at this conclusion through an extrapolation of the key themes in the DE literature from the SME perspective, as well as a review of the DK, DBE, DSE, AC, and AF pieces of literature. On this foundation, a theoretical framework for digital technology adoption toward digital entrepreneurial success is proposed, as well as a new Digital Entrepreneurship (DE) model.

This chapter first encapsulates DE literature, with an emphasis on its application to digital transformation and innovation in SMEs. The case for including each of the dimension measurement scales from the DK, DBE, DSE, AC, and AF literature is then made. This leads to a proposal for a conceptual model of DE as a foundation for research into DE in SMEs. The article concludes by proposing several areas for future research and development in order to advance the concept of DE.

Digital Entrepreneurship in SMEs

Over the last two decades, SMEs' digital transformation has been actively researched. This research has demonstrated that small firms exhibit different behaviours toward digital technology adoption when compared to well-established firms, and this research has formed the foundation for diffusion innovation theory (DIT) (Rogers, 1995), and the adaptive learning capabilities of these digital technologies, which lead to entrepreneurship as the driver of organizational change (Gunasilan, 2019). This attempt to adapt and apply digital transformation models to SMEs assumes that the fundamental principles of traditional analog operations developed in large businesses are universally applicable and have not proven effective in the digital era. The innovation orientation of SMEs is highly dependent on the small business owner's or entrepreneur's new technical knowledge and learning capabilities, who is solely responsible for providing the organizational learning philosophy, trans-functional beliefs, and strategic direction, which defines organizational technology toward specific innovation-enabling competencies. These innovative small and medium competencies focus on effective resource allocation, optimization of deployed technology, optimization of employee inputs, effective operations, and meeting consumer needs and expectations.

However, there is now recognition that, while the SME's approach to digital transformation may not fit established theories, successful SMEs are able to capitalize on their entrepreneurial behaviours. Nambisan. (2017); Scott. (2021); Kuznetsova et al. (2019) emphasized that the digital transformation of small businesses and new ventures was in fact digital entrepreneurship, a distinct style characterized by a variety of factors such as inherent generativity, affordances, and openness. The concept of digital entrepreneurship is extending to scholarly debates, as reflected in the European Commission's (2005) adopted definition:

Digital entrepreneurship embraces all new ventures and the transformation of existing businesses that drive economic and/or social value by creating and using novel digital technologies. Digital enterprises are characterized by a high intensity of utilization of novel digital technologies (particularly social, big data, mobile and cloud solutions) to improve business operations, invent new business models, sharpen business intelligence, and engage with customers and stakeholders. They create the jobs and growth opportunities of the future. (p. 1)

This approach is the result of a number of factors relating to new ventures, small businesses, or existing non-digitalized organizations, including digital transformation limitations; entrepreneur influence; and a lack of formal organizational technology or formal systems of digital processes, with sometimes no systems at all when it comes to digital transformation. This type of digital transformation is usually responsive to market niches, opportunities, and competition in the direction of value capture and value creation (Chopra, 2020; Proksch et al., 2021). It is also highly dependent on the five diffusion innovation theory attributes of compatibility, observability, trial-ability, relative advantage, and complexity, which are considered by business owners or managers when adopting new technology (Aljarrah et al., 2016; Rogers, 1995; 2005), and organizational learning capabilities to incorporate novel digital technologies as described in the European Commission's DI definition.

Digital Innovation Theories in SMEs

The concept of innovation is linked to the core principles of various theories, including innovation system theory (IST), which describes adaptive learning capabilities (Siyanbola & Olamade, 2012; Egbetokun et al, 2008), and diffusion innovation theory (DIT), which describes a model used in IS research to explain user adoption of new technology, Rogers. (1995, 2005). For many, if not most, organizations, innovation is the central path to long-term value creation. Building an effective funnel for organizational innovation is a common metaphor (Salerno et al., 2015). For successful value creation, organizational management must understand vulnerabilities (opportunities and risks), which lead to the transition within innovation processes. The entrepreneurial mindset necessitates the effective distribution and use of knowledge, which eventually leads to innovation. In Satalkina and Steiner's (2020) systematic review of the role of digital entrepreneurship innovation systems, innovation is defined as a "new combination of factors that determines "creative destruction" and relates to five core spheres, namely products, methods of production, markets, raw material sources, and industry structure. According to the author, the five core spheres lead to the most common three innovation components, which are product innovation, process innovation, market innovation, and innovation system (Kahn 2018). Furthermore, the components of firm innovation are reflected in a definition of innovation as the extent to which a firm can introduce new products and new production processes, modify existing products, and enter new territorial markets and segments within existing markets (Nguyen and Pham, 2009; Bigliardi and Domio, 2009), which is also reflected in Schumpeter's (1934) definition of innovation (Ziemnowicz, 2013).

Entrepreneurial-minded individuals play a critical role in SMEs by bringing innovative ideas and business growth, which leads to economic competitiveness and change. Schumpeter (1934) argued that the search for new opportunities and competitive advantage in business is accompanied by what he called "creative destruction," which distinguishes entrepreneurs based on their economic and technical competencies. Contributions to knowledge formation and dissemination, as well as the perception of opportunities, can be used to assess this. Hansen and Wakonen (1997) identified the entrepreneur's character/skills, organizational strengths, business culture, and business strategy as the primary factors that lead to SMEs' competitive advantage, growth, and change. Whether established businesses or start-ups/SMEs, the current digital era has resulted in technological changes in various organizational functions. They must develop and implement new strategies in order to respond to ongoing change.

The approach of the innovation constituents to understanding digital entrepreneurship is based on the idea that digitalization, with its risks and opportunities, may be considered one of a number of business challenges today, particularly for SMEs. Among these challenges are several significant ones for SMEs: (1) a lack of appropriate IT strategic alignment, (2) a lack of proper management of newly implemented IT, and (3) complexity in the IT ecosystem, which includes the establishment and management of relationships with IT specialists (Pelletier & Cloutier, 2019), apprehension of missing out (social challenge), Go for broke or go home (invest big and be comprehensive), Where do I begin? Who will do digital (in comparison to born-digital organizations that may not need to change entire operations before implementing any digital transformation)? (SMEs attempting to exert control over the process). However, digital transformation provides SMEs with benefits such as access to global markets, reduced manufacturing costs, improved document processing, access to financial and accounting applications, improved internal and external communication, collaboration opportunities among business stakeholders, and digital transformation as a driver of innovation (Rachinger et al., 2019). This is related to the diffusion of innovation theory, which is a model of five attributes used in IS research to explain user adoption of new technology. These attributes are compatibility, observability, trialability, relative advantage, and complexity (Aljarrah et al., 2016; Rogers, 1995; 2005).

Figure 1. Theoretical framework of digital technologies adoption in SMEs towards digital entrepreneurial success

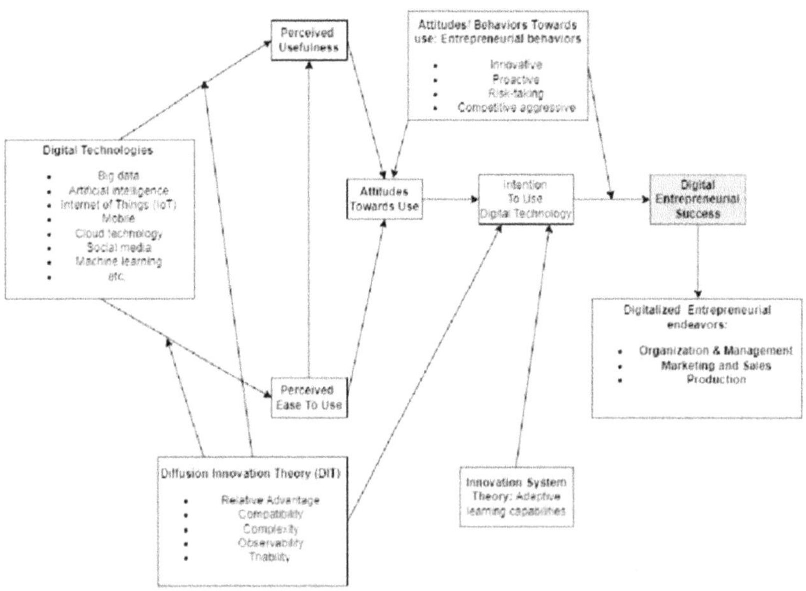

The above theoretical framework explains how the adoption of digital technologies by SMEs leads to digital entrepreneurial success. The framework integrated three popular theories namely: the Technology Acceptance Model, the Diffusion of Innovation Theory and the National Innovation System Theory. The Technology Acceptance Model (TAM) explains the general determinants of technology acceptance in relation to user behaviour in any context. TAM offers a smart approach for technology entrepreneurs or digital entrepreneurship in general. Ultimately, digital business success is achieved by SMEs based on two specific beliefs: Perceived Usefulness (PU) and Perceived Ease to Use (PEU). PU is defined as the potential user's subjective likelihood that the use of a particular technology will improve their action, while PEU denotes the degree to which the potential user expects the target system to be effortless (Ilyas et al., 2023).

Another way in which the introduction of digital technologies by SMEs leads to digital entrepreneurial success is explained by the Diffusion of Innovation Theory (DIT). DIT explains the process by which new technologies or digital innovations are communicated and disseminated to members of a social system for adoption. The DIT explained that innovation and acceptance came after going through five phases identified as understanding, persuading, deciding, implementing and confirming. Ultimately, based on their willingness to accept and adopt new technologies or digital innovations, the SMEs or individuals are classified into five categories within the social system, namely: innovators, early adopters, early majority, late majority and laggards (Dutta & Sarma, 2020; Upadhyay, Upadhyay & Dwivedi, 2022).

The theory of national innovation systems (NIS) is a precursor to the first two theories. Introduced in the 1980s, the term NIS emphasizes the interrelationship between technology and institutional change. NIS theory posits that both innovation and technology development are the result of a complex set of relationships among actors in the system, which include corporations, universities, and government research institutes. The NIS is the network of public and private institutions whose activities and interactions initiate, import, modify, and disseminate new technologies (Freeman, 1995). The NIS is important because it represents all parts and aspects of economic structure and institutional design that affect learning and innovation (Johnson & Lundvall, 2013). Ultimately, in the disruptive digital age, SMEs can achieve effective digital entrepreneurial success if there are enabling national innovation systems.

To achieve digital entrepreneurial success based on the foregoing explanations, SMEs need to acknowledge the existence of digital technologies such as big data, artificial intelligence, internet of things, mobile media, social media, and machine learning as business turning points in the current digital age. According to technology adoption model theory, for an organization like an SME to adopt any of these existing digital technologies, it needs to recognize its usefulness and ease of use (Iyamu, 2021). In terms of its usefulness, an organization should be able to convince itself that using such digital technology would enable it to complete tasks faster, improve company performance, increase productivity, increase employee effectiveness increase and so on before committing to their implementation. They also need to perceive it as an easy-to-use technology in terms of flexibility, agility, etc. Since SMEs have limited resources and risk a new idea, diffusion innovation theory must be used to assess the influence of perception on the intention to use such a technology, considering the relative advantage, compatibility, complexity, observability, and testability of the Explain Technology Digital Technology. So, after accepting our perception of the usefulness of digital technology, they must have or acquire an appropriate attitude towards digital technology. As a result, this attitude towards using digital technologies for SMEs is already embedded in entrepreneurial behaviors such as innovation, proactivity, competitive aggressiveness, and autonomy, which mitigate the impact of the adopted technology on digital entrepreneurial success.

In addition, for an SME to implement an effective digital business venture, it must first ensure that it has or acquires adaptive learning skills as a facilitator. The term digital entrepreneurial success refers to the effective and efficient creation and value creation through the effective implementation of digitized entrepreneurial efforts in the areas of organization and management, marketing and sales, and production.

Reviewing the Pillar Literature

As previously stated, there is growing interest in DE research, and its foundation in both digital technology and entrepreneurship theory and practice is well established. Based on an examination of the DE literature, this section will argue that any discussion of DE must include innovation, customer engagement, and relationships. As a result, previous work on the DK, DB, AF, DSE, and EC scales is summarized and conceptualized in this section with respect to small and medium enterprises. Also identified and discussed are the scales used to inform the components of the proposed DE model.

Digital Knowledge/Skills Base and ICT Market

Digital knowledge-based market (DK) which is used interchangeably with digital literacy, is widely recognized as having a positive effect on the economic development and common wealth creation, and business value (Afele, 2003; Hu et al., 2022; Riera & Iijima, 2018; Son et al., 2022; Morley & Leyton, 2022; Pronina, 2022), on organizational learning (Marchegiani, 2021; Kesti, 2021), on business continuity and efficiency, and on entrepreneurial orientation (Zahra et al., 2023). This has ameliorated the quality, efficiency and power at all levels, organization level, society level and country level, and has become a new driving force to promote the development of common wealth, as digital knowledge has been associated in achieving Sustainable Development Goals (SDGs) (Lee, 2022). European Commission (2013) describes digital knowledge from two lens as digital innovation, commercialization and ICT knowledge for creating new digitalized ventures, fostering the development and digital transformation of existing ones, diffusing digital knowledge to enhance digital innovation, and using ICT as a mechanism for commercialization and diffusion of new business ideas.

Although the literature has provided a variety of definitions of DK most authors emphasized adopting two perspectives such as behavioural and cultural perspectives in term of integrating in organizational culture. For an organization to success in the digital era, they must acquire digital knowledge and develop the culture of using digital technologies in their business operations (Kannisto & Hästbacka, 2022; Maindola & Kumar, 2022). Digital knowledge is described as the know-how of business digital technologies which is having sufficient knowledge in terms of literacy along the ability to use digital technologies in organization and management, marketing and sales, and production strategically and effectively (Vervest & Dunn, 2000; Pan, 2022), noting that SMEs exhibit entrepreneurial-oriented behaviour in their nature (Narver and Slater, 1990; Manishimwe et al., 2022; Raimi & Manishimwe, 2021). This determines their entrepreneurial digital skills which is based on a cultural perspective, identifying three behavioural components: digital competence such as concepts, attitude/behaviour etc.; digital usage (discipline and professional application); and digital transformation (creative/innovative, proactive, risk-taking (Martin, A., & Grudziecki, J., 2006; Phuapan et al., 2015). Different models are rigorously tested, but owing to their robustness, reliability and validity, Martin & Grudziecki DK scale and Phuapan et al., 2015 adapted scale are used in the DK element of the proposed innovation-based DE model. Therefore, the DK dimensions that inform the innovation-based DE model are: entrepreneurial-oriented digital competence, digital usage, and digital transformation (Martin & Grudziecki, J., 2006; Phuapan et al., 2015)

Digital Business Environment

A digital business environment can be described as an internal, virtual location where one or more computer systems are utilized to record or store company data and interactions between people. This is possible through online social networks, also known as digital social environments, which have a single central server that distributes information to all users. According to the European Commission (2013), a digital business environment strengthens the legal system, advances digital infrastructure, and makes doing business easier. The commission placed emphasis on the need for a clear and accommodating regulatory environment in their study. This environment should facilitate market entry, provide active and dynamic demand and supply of digital technologies, and facilitate access to digital markets because of improved ICT infrastructure.

Business environment was defined by Rubin & Dai, (2003) as "a set of external conditions, factors in activities, and features of the environment for each business entity, which directly or indirectly influence the formation of content for a given business entity's activities and its interpersonal relationships with other business entities." This aids in the exploration and comprehension of organizational management in the context of digital business management, which includes dynamical processes in the business environment and allows for the identification of distinctive changes in the theoretical justification of the impact of its state whether internal or external on establishing strategic competitive goals for organization digital entrepreneurial success and on choosing models for their implementation. The difference in how various elements of the business environment affect a company is determined by the economic systems of each nation. Such mechanisms, according to Adam et al. (2019) are a product of economic security and growth, which depend on how well-functioning national entrepreneurial organizations are. The quality of the business environment, in accordance with Caldwell. (1983) is what makes economic processes more efficient, and this, in turn, increases national prosperity and well-being. He continued by saying that it is crucial for every aspect of the business environment to be shared by all countries, companies, organizations, and people.

For businesses to survive and flourish, particularly during periods like the Covid-19 shutdown and beyond, the present tendencies of the pandemic and uncertainty like Covid-19 have sparked what can be regarded as a digital revolution. Every successful business on a worldwide scale has been impacted by this digital shift. Since the present business environment is undergoing rapid change, Mufudza. (2019) acknowledged that there is an intense rivalry. As a result, firms are becoming more dependent on entrepreneurial structures, which strengthens their organizational adaptability. Thus, this is explained using the innovation system theory, particularly in the current digital era where every organization must use the acquired adaptive capabilities to alter and/or accelerate its business strategies, processes, and business model to respond to the disruption of dynamic markets because of disruption by digital technologies and the speed of internet usage. "The future comes faster than management expresses a desire to say goodbye to the present. The capability to adapt is the evolutionary feature of business efficiency, and the ability to adapt quicker than others is a competitive advantage of the future" (Nikolaev, 2018).

Furthermore, according to Drucker (1999), the principles of modern management are applicable to all societal structures and offer sustainable growth under both internal and external conditions of unpredictability in both noncommercial operations and the market environment. As a result, SMEs, have the three main characteristics of uncertainty, variability, and complexity. The diffusion of innovation theory, which distinguished the level at which they affect businesses differently based on compatibility, observability, trial-ability, relative advantage, and complexity that are considered by business owners or managers when adopting new technology (Aljarrah et al., 2016; Rogers, 1995; 2005), and organizational learning capabilities to incorporate novel digital technologies as described by European Commission (2015).

In terms of the digital environment, numerous researchers, including Wiliandri. (2020); Mithas et al. (2013); and Ortiz (2010), described internal and external digital business environmental factors using SLEPT analysis, a similar version of PESTELE, which included social factors like culture, demographics, including gender and age, social lifestyles, domestic structures, affluence or wealth, and religion; legal and ethical factors such as data protection regulation (GDPR), disability and discrimination law, brand and trademark protection, intellectual property rights, contract law, and online advertising law; economic factors such as market condition, inflation rate, interest rates, monetary or fiscal policies, and foreign exchange rate; political factors such as government or leadership, policies, tax laws, and internet governance; and technological factors the availability of technology, and knowledge of the technology. Other internal factors discussed specifically for a digitalized business include organizational, internal IT resources (Nguyen et al., 2013), internal capability compatibility, internal resource compatibility, and business model changes (Tarutė et al. 2018). These factors are in addition to common internal business environmental factors like customers, competitors, suppliers, and intermediaries which directly influence the organization. Therefore, the internal and external aspects highlighted based on the literature comprise the DBE dimensions that inform the innovation-based DE model.

E-Leadership

Lowri Evans, European Commission Director General Internal Market, Industry, Entrepreneurship and SMEs stated that "for Europe to compete, grow and generate jobs, we must ensure that we have the people who can lead the digital innovation and transformation of our industries. New technologies are a key engine for growth fueled by the ideas of highly-skilled professionals and business leaders (e-leaders)." Belitski and Liversage (2019) defined e-leadership as "a social influence process mediated by advanced IT to produce a change in attitudes, feelings, thinking, behavior, and/or performance of individuals, groups, or organizations" (p. 64).

The e-leadership measurement scales and constructs are heavily influenced by e-leadership personality characteristics identified in the body of digital innovation and digital transformation literature. As a result, digital savvy, strategic leadership, and business savvy are frequently incorporated (Hüsing et al., 2013; Belitski & Liversage, 2019; Korte et al., 2015). Investigation of e-leadership in relation to research in SMEs includes (Li et al., 2016) investigation of e-leadership in the digital era through strategic management. Furthermore, Avolio et al. (2014) and Ellermann (2017) stated that alignment thinking is a critical component of effective e-leadership. Gurr. (2004) developed an e-leadership model with sub-constructs, which Avolio re-examined (2014). This scale has since been refined (Liu, 2014; Lead, 2014; Li et al., 2016) and widely cited in the e-leadership literature, with numerous studies praising its reliability and validity. As a result, the discussed e-leadership elements inform the DE model.

Entrepreneurial Culture

EC was defined by the European Commission (2013) as "a pattern of values, assumptions, and practices shared within an organization that is centrally concerned with opportunities, where opportunity is the creation of new value to society in part or in whole," and Danish et al. (2019) defined EC as "the attitude, values, skills, and power of a group or individuals working in an institute or an organization to generate income." Entrepreneurial culture (EC) is also known as entrepreneurial orientation (EO), and the characteristics identified in the body of entrepreneurship literature largely inform the EC measurement scales and constructs. As a result, the dimensions of innovativeness, proactiveness, and risk taking are frequently incorporated (Covin & Slevin, (1991); Khandwalla, (1977); Lumpkin and Dess, (1996); Shane, (2000) investigated market focus, technological posture, and EO in relation to research in SMEs. This scale has been refined over time (Covin and Slevin, 1989;) and is frequently cited in the European Commission literature for its validity and reliability in various studies (Covin and Slevin, 1989; Khandwalla, 1977) developed an EC scale based on previous EC research studies (Morris and Paul, 1987; Miller, 1983; Covin and Slevin, 1989). Among other recent studies, Theoneste et al. (2021) scale 's takes into account propensity to innovate, proactivity, and risk-taking behavior toward opportunities as a measure of entrepreneurial culture.

All researchers' scales reflect the EC literature's consensus view, preferring dimensions' scales known for their reliability and validity, and they have all agreed that creative teams, differentiation, and opportunity identification are essential factors for a vibrant, entrepreneurial culture. They provide the following dimensions to the DE model: innovativeness, proactiveness, risk-taking (Dimitratos et al., 2016), and autonomy (Swierczek, 2003).

Access to Finance

Access to finance has been a critical challenge for both traditional and digitalized SMEs (Wasiuzzaman et al., 2020), and SMEs' lack of access to finance has slowed SMEs' potential and optimization towards poverty alleviation and national development globally, most notably in most Sub-Saharan African countries (Osano, 2015). According to the literature review, dimensions of access to finance for both types of SMEs are collateral (Kaleemullah, 2021; Motta, 2019), condition, capacity (Osano, 2015), capital, and character (Brixiová et al., 2020). Access to finance was defined by the European Commission (2013) as "an act of facilitating access to finance and enhancing digital investments." According to their report, improved access to finance, innovative mechanisms that supplement traditional forms, and fiscal and tax frameworks enable the creation, survival, and growth of digital entrepreneurs, boost digital investments, and enable SMEs to embrace digital technologies. As a result, the DE model is informed by elements of the access to finance dimension such as condition, capacity, collateral, character, capital, innovative mechanisms, enhanced access to finance, and fiscal and tax frameworks.

Towards the DE Model

A number of DK, DBE, DSE, EC, and AF scales were identified in the previous section as being critical to understanding these DE dimensions. The authors propose the DE model in Figure 1 based on these scales and the characteristics of DE identified in the literature. The model depicts five key dimensions, and contends that, any concept of DE that is an accurate reflection of how successful small and medium-sized businesses market must grasp aspects of digital and entrepreneurial behavior that have typically been researched in the digital transformation, digital innovation, and entrepreneurship towards opportunities, and customer engagement. In other words, distinguishing between digital transformation, digital innovation, and entrepreneurship in digitalized small and medium enterprises is both impossible and futile. The overlaps between digital transformation scales in these different fields provide the most compelling evidence for this assertion. Such overlaps have been resolved in Figure 1 as discussed below in order to provide a clear set of dimensions for DE.

Although the DE model is still in its early stages, its model was developed by imploding existing scales to develop a set of dimensions and determining the most important components within each dimension. The authors were guided in this process by the recognition that replication and adaptation of digital technology and entrepreneurship scales is common, and that if done systematically and thoroughly, can provide a useful foundation for future empirical research and the development of new theory (Kraus, 2006). The authors have noticed, in particular, that the removal and realignment of items is adequate where they are conceptually linked.

Figure 2. The SME digital entrepreneurship (DE) conceptualized model

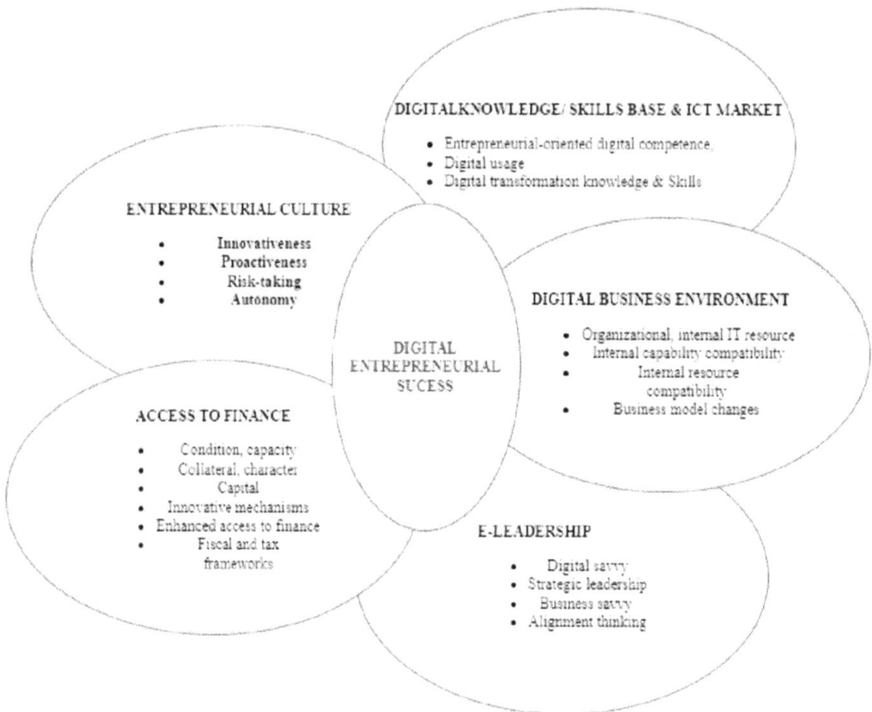

The conceptualized model above simply explains the five success factors and associated sub-factors for digital entrepreneurship. In other words, the success of SME Digital Entrepreneurship (DE) is based on entrepreneurial culture, access to finance, e-leadership, digital business environment and digital knowledge/skills base and ICT market.

The following stages were involved in the model's development:

1. Identifying the key scales for DK, DBE, DSE, EC and AF using relevant literature.

2. Identifying components of each dimension from the items in those scales by deleting and merging components, typically using comparisons between two or more scales from the same panel.
3. A comparison of the dimensions identified in each of the DE dimensions DK, DBE, DSE, EC, and AF to see if any dimensions overlap.
4. A review of the SME and DE literature to identify potential DEs in the formation, survival, growth and development of SMEs.

CONCLUSION

This article attempted to integrate the discussion of DE activities in SMEs into the larger conceptual base and framework of the SME domain by taking a more contextualized view of digital transformation and entrepreneurship, considering the relevant literature from DK, DBE defined, DSE, AF and related literature and theories such as DIT and IST. This model needs to be further tested in a variety of contexts, but it has the potential to influence the development of both practice and theory of digital transformation of SMEs.

Several themes are emerging from the evolving concept of DE, the most important of which is the connection between digital technology and entrepreneurship, as well as how digital entrepreneurs engage in digital transformation. To tie these threads together, this article revisited the discussion of DE, particularly in the context of the SME, as well as the fundamental definitions of DK, DBE, DSE, and AF. This rethinking, in conjunction with evidence of the importance of networks and suggestions for future research, as well as the creation of customer value through digital transformation and digital innovation, suggests that digital technology is a critical dimension of DE. This posture seeks to grasp the intrinsic nature of DE based on what digital entrepreneurs and SMEs do in the digital operations arena. The authors postulate that the elements of DK, DBE, DSE, and AF be adopted and incorporated into the developing DE paradigm while recognizing that these DE dimensions operate perform and interact dynamically depending on the market sector, stage of development, and firm size.

The investigation of the concept of DE has revealed a broad agenda for future research on both DE and related topics:

1. The digital business environment necessitates further investigation, including an examination of the link between the traditional and digital business environments, as well as the extent to which digitalized/traditional businesses are involved in the development and design to respond to market niches, opportunities, and competition for value capture and value creation.
2. Further research within SMEs could be conducted to gain a better understanding of the relationship between digital knowledge and digital skills as they relate to organizational learning capabilities.
3. Further research within SMEs could be conducted to investigate the relationship between e-leadership and international e-leadership and to determine the extent to which the concepts are aligned.
4. Additional research is needed to determine how digital entrepreneurship evolves in SMEs as the business grows, and whether specific digital entrepreneurial competencies are enhanced. And a broad-based DE strategy may not fit all businesses. Therefore, it is necessary to investigate whether different approaches to DE are suitable for various market conditions or sectors.
5. Although the literature suggests that aligning DE activities improves business performance, a more sophisticated understanding of what constitutes digital business performance in SMEs requires

SMART (specific, measurable, achievable, relevant, and time-bound) and conclusive evidence. Female digital transformation literature, for example, is rich with a variety of social factors that influence how digital entrepreneurs plan the development of their company, whereas family-owned or non-entrepreneurial and non-digital-oriented owner-managers may seek to limit firm size to minimize stress risk levels, or due to a lack of know-how while maintaining the advantage of maintaining direct and close digital interaction with customers.

6. Further research is suggested to investigate how larger and more established organizations implement DE by examining existing overlaps of the DK, DBE, DSE, and AF orientation concepts, as well as links between their digital transformation, digital entrepreneurship success, product and service innovation, and customer satisfaction.

REFERENCES

Abbasi, K., Alam, A., Brohi, N. A., Brohi, I. A., & Nasim, S. (2021). P2P lending fintechs and smes' access to finance. *Economics Letters*, *204*, 109890. doi:10.1016/j.econlet.2021.109890

Adam, S., Ramliy, M. K., Thoo, A. C., Mas'od, A., & Muharam, F. M. (2019). Entrepreneurial orientation and organizational performance of e-business in Malaysia: The moderating role of External Environment. *Advanced International Journal of Business, Entrepreneurship and SMEs, 1*(1), 1–17. doi:10.35631/aijbes.11001

Afele, J. S. C. (2003). Digital Bridges and digital opportunities for developing nations. *Digital Bridges*, 85–159. doi:10.4018/978-1-59140-039-4.ch005

Agyei, S. K., Adam, A. M., & Agyemang, O. S. (2019). Financial Literacy, cultural dominance, and financial well-being of SME owners in Ghana. *Poverty & Public Policy*, *11*(3), 222–237. doi:10.1002/pop4.254

Ali, I., Sadiddin, A., & Cattaneo, A. (2022). Risk and resilience in agri-food supply chain smes in the pandemic era: A cross-country study. *International Journal of Logistics Research and Applications*, 1–19. doi:10.1080/13675567.2022.2102159

Aljarrah, E., Elrehail, H., & Aababneh, B. (2016). E-voting in Jordan: Assessing readiness and developing a system. *Computers in Human Behavior*, *63*, 860–867. doi:10.1016/j.chb.2016.05.076

Aravindaraj, K., & Rajan Chinna, P. (2022). A systematic literature review of integration of Industry 4.0 and warehouse management to achieve Sustainable Development Goals (sdgs). *Cleaner Logistics and Supply Chain*, *5*, 100072. doi:10.1016/j.clscn.2022.100072

Asikhia, O. U. (2016). SMEs, wealth creation and poverty alleviation in Nigeria. *Journal of Economics and Behavioral Studies, 8*(4), 17–31. doi:10.22610/jebs.v8i4(J).1360

Avolio, B. J., Sosik, J. J., Kahai, S. S., & Baker, B. (2014). E-leadership: Re-examining transformations in leadership source and transmission. *The Leadership Quarterly*, *25*(1), 105–131. doi:10.1016/j.leaqua.2013.11.003

Babajide, A., Lawal, A., Asaleye, A., Okafor, T., & Osuma, G. (2020). Financial Stability and entrepreneurship development in sub-sahara africa: Implications for sustainable development goals. *Cogent Social Sciences*, *6*(1), 1798330. Advance online publication. doi:10.1080/23311886.2020.1798330

Belitski, M., & Liversage, B. (2019). E-leadership in small and medium-sized enterprises in the developing world. *Technology Innovation Management Review*, *9*(1), 64–74. doi:10.22215/timreview/1212

Bigliardi, B., & Ivo Dormio, A. (2009). An empirical investigation of innovation determinants in Food Machinery Enterprises. *European Journal of Innovation Management*, *12*(2), 223–242. doi:10.1108/14601060910953988

Bishoge, O. K., & Suntu, S. L. (2018). Opportunies of urban horticulture for poverty alleviation in Dar es Salaam City, Tanzania – A case study of Ubungo Municipality. *Journal of Food. Nutrition and Agriculture*, *12–16*, 12–16. Advance online publication. doi:10.21839/jfna.v1i1.123

Bosma, N., Hill, S., Ionescu-Somers, A., Donna Kelley, J. L., & Tarnawa, A. (2020). *Global Entrepreneurship Monitor 2019/2020 global report*. Global Entrepreneurship Research Association.

Brixiová, Z., Kangoye, T., & Yogo, T. U. (2020). Access to finance among small and medium-sized enterprises and job creation in Africa. *Structural Change and Economic Dynamics*, *55*, 177–189. doi:10.1016/j.strueco.2020.08.008

Caldwell, L. K. (1983). The economy and the environment. *Business Horizons*, *26*(6), 2–5. doi:10.1016/0007-6813(83)90038-1

Covin, J. G., & Slevin, D. (1989). Strategic management of small firms in hostile and benign environments. *Strategic Management Journal*, *10*(1), 75–88. doi:10.1002mj.4250100107

Covin, J. G., & Slevin, D. P. (1991). A conceptual model of entrepreneurship as firm behavior. *Entrepreneurship Theory and Practice*, *16*(1), 7–26. doi:10.1177/104225879101600102

Danish, R. Q., Asghar, J., Ahmad, Z., & Ali, H. F. (2019). Factors affecting "Entrepreneurial culture": The mediating role of creativity. *Journal of Innovation and Entrepreneurship*, *8*(1), 14. Advance online publication. doi:10.118613731-019-0108-9

Díaz-Bonilla, E. (2021). *Food Systems Summit Brief prepared by research partners of the Scientific Group for the Food Systems Summit, May 11th, 2021.* https://sc-fss2021.org/wp-content/uploads/2021/06/FSS_Brief_Science_Policy_Interactions.pdf

Dimitratos, P., Johnson, J. E., Plakoyiannaki, E., & Young, S. (2016). SME internationalization: How does the opportunity-based international entrepreneurial culture matter? *International Business Review*, *25*(6), 1211–1222. doi:10.1016/j.ibusrev.2016.03.006

Drucker, P. F. (1999). Peter Drucker on the new business realities. *Antitrust Bulletin*, *44*(4), 795–819. doi:10.1177/0003603X9904400403

Dutta, D., & Sarma, M. K. (2020). Adoption of digital innovation-Formulating adopter categories and levels of adoption in a digital sphere in an emerging economy. *International Journal on Management of Innovation & Technology*, *17*(08), 2050059. https://www.worldscientific.com/doi/epdf/10.1142/S0219877020500595. doi:10.1142/S0219877020500595

EDFI. (2016). *Investing to create jobs, boost growth and fight poverty*. Association of the European Development Finance Institutions.

Egbetokun, A., Siyanbola, W., Olamade, O., Adeniyi, A., & Irefin, I. (2008). Innovation in Nigerian SMEs: types and impact. MPRA Paper 25338, University Library of Munich.

Ellermann, H., Kreutter, P., & Messner, W. (2017). The Palgrave Handbook of Managing Continuous Business Transformation. E-Leadership for SMEs in the Digital Age, 17, 375–416. doi:10.1057/978-1-137-60228-2

European Commission. (2013). *Strategic policy forum for digital entrepreneurship: Fuelling digital entrepreneurship in Europe*. Author.

European Commission. (2015). *European Commission (EC), Digital Transformation of European Industry and Enterprises; A report of the Strategic Policy Forum on Digital Entrepreneurship*. http://ec.europa.eu/DocsRoom/documents/9462/attachments/1/translations/en/renditions/native

Freeman, C. (1995). The 'National System of Innovation' in historical perspective. *Cambridge Journal of Economics*, 5–24. doi:10.1093/oxfordjournals.cje.a035309

Gunasilan, U. (2019). Entrepreneurship as a driver of the digital transformation. *International Review of Management and Marketing*, *9*(5), 23–29. doi:10.32479/irmm.8264

Gurr, D. (2004). ICT, Leadership in Education and E-leadership. *Discourse: Studies in the Cultural Politics of Education, 25*(1), 113–124. . doi:10.1080/0159630042000178518

Hannibal, M., & Rasmussen, E. S. (2014). Digital Entrepreneurship in a traditional production firm. *International Journal of E-Services and Mobile Applications*, *6*(3), 48–66. doi:10.4018/ijesma.2014070104

Hansen, S., & Wakonen, J. (1997). *Innovation, a winning solution?* International Journal of Technology. doi:10.1504/IJTM.1997.001668

Hansen, S. O., & Wakonen, J. (1997). Innovation, a winning solution? *International Journal of Technology Management, 13*(4), 345. doi:10.1504/IJTM.1997.001668

Hu, C., Yan, X., & Zhou, Z. (2022). The Digital Economy, market-based factor allocation and shared prosperity. *Frontiers in Humanities and Social Sciences*, *2*(8), 119–124. doi:10.54691/fhss.v2i8.1667

Hüsing, T., Korte, W. B., Fonstad, N., Lanvin, B., Welsum, D., Cattaneo, G., Kolding, M., & Lifonti, R. (2013). *E-Leadership: E-Skills for Competitiveness and Innovation Vision, Roadmap and Foresight Scenarios*. European Commission.

IFC. (2013). *Assessing private sector contributions to job creation and poverty reduction*. International Finance Corporation.

ILO. (2019a). *Enabling environment for sustainable enterprises in Sierra Leone*. International Labour Organization.

Ilyas, M., ud din, A., Haleem, M., & Ahmad, I. (2023). Digital Entrepreneurial Acceptance: An Examination of technology acceptance model and do-it-yourself behavior. *Journal of Innovation and Entrepreneurship*, *12*(1), 15. Advance online publication. doi:10.118613731-023-00268-1

ITC. (2018). *Promoting SME competitiveness in Africa: Data for de-risking investment.* International Trade Centre.

ITC. (2019). *SME competitiveness outlook 2019: Big money for small business—Financing the sustainable development goals.* International Trade Centre.

Iyamu, T. (2021). Technology acceptance model. *Applying Theories for Information Systems Research*, 143–154. doi:10.4324/9781003184119-9

Johnson, B., & Lundvall, B. Å. (2013). National Innovation Systems (NIS). In E. G. Carayannis (Ed.), *Encyclopedia of Creativity, Invention, Innovation and Entrepreneurship*. Springer. doi:10.1007/978-1-4614-3858-8_458

Kahn, K. B. (2018). Understanding innovation. *Business Horizons*, *61*(3), 453–460. doi:10.1016/j.bushor.2018.01.011

Kannisto, P., & Hästbacka, D. (2022). Digitalized cross-organizational interoperability in industrial business ecosystems: Implications and models for process industry. *Proceedings of the 3rd International Conference on Innovative Intelligent Industrial Production and Logistics*. 10.5220/0011543900003329

Kesti, M. (2021). *The digital twin of an organization by utilizing reinforcing Deep Learning*. Deep Learning Applications. doi:10.5772/intechopen.96168

Khandwalla, P. (1977). *The design of organizations*. Harcourt, Brace.

Korte, W. B., Hüsing, T., & Dashja, E. (Eds.). (2015). *E-Leadership: Digital Skills for SMEs*. European Commission.

Kraus, S., Palmer, C., Kailer, N., Kallinger, F. L., & Spitzer, J. (2018). Digital Entrepreneurship. *International Journal of Entrepreneurial Behavior & Research*. doi:10.1108/IJEBR-06-2018-0425

Kushnir, K., Mirmulstein, M. L., & Ramalho, R. (2010). *Micro, Small, and Medium Enterprises around the World: How Many Are There, and What Affects the Count?* World Bank/IFC.

LEAD (2014). E-*Leadership Skills for Small and Medium Sized Enterprises project.* European Commission, Directorate-General for Enterprise and Industry.

Lee, C. (2022). An analysis of global digital knowledge sharing platforms on National Territorial Policy and its implications. *Journal of the Korean Cadastre Information Association*, *24*(2), 102–127. doi:10.46416/JKCIA.2022.08.24.2.102

Li, W., Liu, K., Belitski, M., Ghobadian, A., & O'Regan, N. (2016). E-Leadership through Strategic Alignment: An Empirical Study of Small- and Medium-sized Enterprises in the Digital Age. *Journal of Information Technology*, *31*(2), 185–206. doi:10.1057/jit.2016.10

Lin, R.-T., & Koh, D. (2019). Small and medium enterprises: Barriers and drivers of managing environmental and occupational health risks. Encyclopedia of environmental health, 682–692. doi:10.1016/B978-0-12-409548-9.11347-8

Liu, K., Belitski, M., & Li, W. (2014). Leading your company to high performance growth. E-Leadership strategies for SMEs driving innovation and competitive edge in digital integration. *The Henley Accelerator High Growth Accelerator, Executive programme*. https://www.henley.ac.uk/executiveeducation/clopenedp/henley-accelerator/high-growth-accelerator/high_growth_accelerator_2013.pdf

Liu, X. (2022). *Targeted poverty alleviation: China's ingenuity to defeat poverty*. Bangladesh Journal of Public Administration. doi:10.1007/978-981-19-4488-8

Loonam, J., Eaves, S., Kumar, V., & Parry, G. (2018). Towards digital transformation: Lessons learned from traditional organizations. *Strategic Change*, *27*(2), 101–109. doi:10.1002/jsc.2185

Lumpkin, G. T., & Dess, G. G. (1996). Clarifying the entrepreneurial orientation construct and linking it to performance. *Academy of Management Review*, *21*(1), 135–172. doi:10.2307/258632

Maindola, S., & Kumar, S. (2022). Employee perception of the effectiveness of digitalized performance management systems. *Disruptive Innovation and Emerging Technologies for Business Excellence in the Service Sector*,186–195. . doi:10.4018/978-1-7998-9194-9.ch009

Manishimwe, T., Raimi, L., & Azubuike, C. J. (2022). Customer-centric influence of entrepreneurial marketing on business performance of hotels in Nigeria during the COVID-19 crisis. *Journal of Revenue and Pricing Management*, *21*(6), 668–683. doi:10.105741272-022-00383-w

Marchegiani, L. (2021). Knowledge and (Digital) learning organizations. *Digital Transformation and Knowledge Management*, 105–148. doi:10.4324/9780367628284-4

Martin, A., & Grudziecki, J. (2006). DigEuLit: Concepts and Tools for Digital LiteracyDevelopment. ITALICS. *Innovations in Teaching & Learning in Information & Computer Sciences*, *5*(4), 246–264.

Matlay, H., & Westhead, P. (2007). Competitive advantage in virtual teams of E-entrepreneurs: Evidence from the European Tourism Industry. *Tourism in the New Europe*, 9–27. doi:10.1016/B978-0-08-044706-3.50005-9

Miller, D. (1983). The Correlates of Entrepreneurship in Three Types of Firms. *Management Science*, *29*(7), 770–791. doi:10.1287/mnsc.29.7.770

Mithas, S., Tafti, A., & Mitchell, W. (2013). How a firm's competitive environment and Digital Strategic Posture Influence Digital Business Strategy. *Management Information Systems Quarterly*, *37*(2), 511–536. doi:10.25300/MISQ/2013/37.2.09

Mkwambisi, D. D., Jew, E. K., & Dougill, A. J. (2021). Farmer Preparedness for Building Resilient Agri-Food Systems: Lessons from the 2015/2016 El Niño drought in Malawi. *Frontiers in Climate*, *2*, 584245. Advance online publication. doi:10.3389/fclim.2020.584245

Morabito, V. (2021). Digital Entrepreneurship and Digital Business. *Digital Entrepreneurship, Management. Systems Practice*, 5–27. doi:10.1017/9781108979917.002

Morley, L., & Leyton, D. (2022). Queering the Digital Knowledge Economy. *Queering Higher Education*, 71–96. doi:10.4324/9781003257431-4

Morris, M., & Paul, G. (1987). The relationship between entrepreneurship and marketing in established Firms. *Journal of Business Venturing*, *2*(3), 247–259. doi:10.1016/0883-9026(87)90012-7

Motta, V., & Sharma, A. (2020). Lending technologies and access to finance for smes in the hospitality industry. *International Journal of Hospitality Management*, *86*, 102371. doi:10.1016/j.ijhm.2019.102371

Mufudza, T. (2019). Dynamic strategy in a turbulent business environment. *Strategic Management - A Dynamic View*. doi:10.5772/intechopen.81250

Muiruri, S. (2017). African small and medium enterprises (SMES) contributions, challenges and solutions. *European Journal of Research and Reflection in Management Sciences*, *5*(1), 36–48.

Nambisan, S. (2017). Digital Entrepreneurship: Toward a digital technology perspective of entrepreneurship. *Entrepreneurship Theory and Practice*, *41*(6), 1029–1055. doi:10.1111/etap.12254

Narver, J., & Slater, S. (1990). The effects of a market orientation on business profitability. *Journal of Marketing*, *5*(4), 20–35. doi:10.1177/002224299005400403

Nguyen, T. U. H., Newby, M., & Macaulay, M. J. (2013). Information technology adoption in small business: Confirmation of a proposed framework. *Journal of Small Business Management*, *53*(1), 207–227. doi:10.1111/jsbm.12058

Nikolaev, M. G. (2018). Strategic company management in the Digital Business Environment. *European Journal of Management Issues*, *26*(3-4), 82–91. doi:10.15421/191809

Nobanee, H., & Dilshad, N. (2020). Digital Entrepreneurship: Concepts, Applications, and future research agenda. *SSRN* Electronic Journal. https://doi.org/ doi:10.1504/IJBG.2010.035479

Ortiz, J. (2010). The global environment through the slept framework. *International Journal of Business and Globalisation*, *5*(4), 475. doi:10.1504/IJBG.2010.035479

Osano & Languitone. (2015). Factors influencing access to finance by SMEs in Mozambique: case of SMEs in Maputo central business district. *Journal of Innovation and Entrepreneurship, 5*(1), 13. . doi:10.1186/s13731-016-0041-0

Pan, L. (2022). Maturity assessment for implementing digital technologies in SMEs. *Proceedings of the International Conference on Big Data Economy and Digital Management*. 10.5220/0011157300003440

Patwary, A. (2020). Private sector SMEs in realizing SDG 1- "no poverty" in the context of Bangladesh. *International Journal of Humanities, Arts, and Social Sciences*, *6*(6), 274–288. doi:10.20469/ijhss.6.20005-6

Phuapan, P., Viriyavejakul, C., & Pimdee, P. (2015). Elements of digital literacy skill: A conceptual analysis. *Asian International Journal of Social Sciences*, *15*(4), 88–99. doi:10.29139/aijss.20150406

Pronina, E. V. (2022). Increasing the level of digital knowledge as the key to the country's energy security. *Uchenyy Sovet*, (9), 557–564. doi:10.33920/nik-02-2209-01

Rachinger, M., Rauter, R., Müller, C., Vorraber, W., & Schirgi, E. (2019). Digitalization and its influence on Business Model Innovation. *Journal of Manufacturing Technology Management*, *30*(8), 1143–1160. doi:10.1108/JMTM-01-2018-0020

Raimi, L., & Manishimwe, T. (2021). *Small Business Survival of Onslaughts of Boko Haram Insurgency, COVID-19 Pandemic, and Economic Crisis in Yola, North-East Nigeria*. Cases on Small Business Economics and Development During Economic Crises. doi:10.4018/978-1-7998-7657-1.ch005

Raniya, S. (2019). *Micro-, Small and Medium-sized Enterprises (MSMEs) and their role in achieving the Sustainable Development Goals.* The United Nations Department of Economic and Social Affairs Division for Sustainable Development Goals.

Riera, C., & Iijima, J. (2018). Does investment in digital technologies yield Digital Business Value? The Digital Investment Paradox and knowledge creation as enabling capability. *Proceedings of the 10th International Joint Conference on Knowledge Discovery, Knowledge Engineering and Knowledge Management*. 10.5220/0006958202080215

Rogers, E. M. (1995). Diffusion of innovations. Academic Press.

Rogers, E. M. (2005). *Diffusion of innovations*. Free Press.

Rubin, S. H., & Dai, W. (2003). An Integrated Knowledge Management Environment: A Study of Counter Terrorism Technologies. *Journal of Information & Knowledge Management*, *02*(03), 203–217. doi:10.1142/S0219649203000401

Salerno, M. S., Gomes, L. A., Silva, D. O., Bagno, R. B., & Freitas, S. L. (2015). Innovation processes: Which process for which project? *Technovation*, *35*, 59–70. doi:10.1016/j.technovation.2014.07.012

Satalkina, L., & Steiner, G. (2020). Digital Entrepreneurship and its role in Innovation Systems: A systematic literature review as a basis for future research avenues for Sustainable Transitions. *Sustainability (Basel)*, *12*(7), 2764. doi:10.3390u12072764

Schumpeter, J. A. (1934). The theory of economic development. Harvard University Press.

Scuotto, V., Nicotra, M., Del Giudice, M., Krueger, N., & Gregori, G. L. (2021). A microfoundational perspective on smes' growth in the Digital Transformation Era. *Journal of Business Research*, *129*, 382–392. doi:10.1016/j.jbusres.2021.01.045

Shane, S. (2000). Prior knowledge and the discovery of entrepreneurial opportunities. *Organization Science*, *11*(4), 448–469. doi:10.1287/orsc.11.4.448.14602

Siyanbola, W., & Olamade, O. (2012). *Innovation Systems and Capabilities in Developing Regions: Concepts, Issues and Cases* (A. Egbetokun, Ed.; 1st ed.). Routledge. doi:10.4324/9781315588674

Son, N. H., Lam, L. B., Van Duong, H., Bac, H. M., Anh, D. D., Thuy, V. T., Quynh, N. T., Tan, N. D., Giang, L. H., Hai, V. S., Van Khanh, T., van Thi Thanh, T., & Lan, N. T. (2022). VNU-LIC Digital Knowledge Center Model: Transforming Big Data Into Knowledge. *From Born-Physical to Born-Virtual: Augmenting Intelligence in Digital Libraries*, 516–522. doi:10.1007/978-3-031-21756-2_44

Swierczek, F. W., & Thai, T. (2003). Motivation, entrepreneurship and the performance of smes in Vietnam. *Journal of Enterprising Culture*, *11*(01), 47–68. doi:10.1142/S0218495803000044

Tarutė, A., Duobienė, J., Klovienė, L., Vitkauskaitė, E., & Varaniūtė, V. (n.d.). *Identifying factors affecting digital transformation of smes*. AIS Electronic Library (AISeL). Retrieved April 4, 2023, from https://aisel.aisnet.org/iceb2018/64

Theoneste, M., & Clinton-Etim, N. (2021). Investigating the level of entrepreneurial orientation and desire for self-employment of students in selected tertiary institutions, north-east nigeria. *The Business and Management Review*, *12*(01). Advance online publication. doi:10.24052/BMR/V12NU01/ART-03

Upadhyay, N., Upadhyay, S., & Dwivedi, Y. K. (2021). Theorizing Artificial Intelligence Acceptance and Digital Entrepreneurship Model. *International Journal of Entrepreneurial Behaviour & Research*, *28*(5), 1138–1166. doi:10.1108/IJEBR-01-2021-0052

Vervest, P., & Dunn, A. (2000). Digital Business Technologies and Total Action. *How to Win Customers in the Digital World*, 21–79. doi:10.1007/978-3-642-57141-1_2

Wasiuzzaman, S., Nurdin, N., Abdullah, A. H., & Vinayan, G. (2020). Creditworthiness and access to finance of smes in Malaysia: Do linkages with large firms matter? *Journal of Small Business and Enterprise Development*, *27*(2), 197–217. doi:10.1108/JSBED-03-2019-0075

White, S. (2018). *Creating better business environments for micro and small enterprises', Technical Report*. Donor Committee for Enterprise Development.

Wiliandri, R. (2020). A conceptual approach to identify factors affecting the digital transformation of micro, small and medium-sized enterprises (msmes) during covid-19 pandemic in Indonesia. *Ekonomi Bisnis*, *25*(2), 66. doi:10.17977/um042v25i2p66-85

Zaheer, H., Breyer, Y., & Dumay, J. (2019). Digital Entrepreneurship: An interdisciplinary structured literature review and research agenda. *Technological Forecasting and Social Change*, *148*, 119735. doi:10.1016/j.techfore.2019.119735

Zahra, S. A., Liu, W., & Si, S. (2023). How Digital Technology promotes entrepreneurship in ecosystems. *Technovation*, *119*, 102457. doi:10.1016/j.technovation.2022.102457

Ziemnowicz, C. (2013). Joseph A. Schumpeter and Innovation. Encyclopedia of Creativity, Invention, Innovation and Entrepreneurship, 1171–1176. doi:10.1007/978-1-4614-3858-8_476

Chapter 6
Tackling Digital Entrepreneurship Within the Illicit Economy:
The Evolving Fight Against Serious and Organized Crime Within a Digitally Facilitated Sex Industry

Alicia Danielsson
Hume Institute for Postgraduate Studies, Switzerland

ABSTRACT

This chapter explores the current challenges and transitional needs required to regulate digital entrepreneurship within the illicit economy by examining digital entrepreneurship relating to commercial sex and trafficking in human beings for the purpose of sexual exploitation. As such, new innovative digital technologies are transforming serious and organised crime operations and, thus, need to also change the way the law, enforcement, and the wider criminal justice system combat crime. The chapter seeks to expose contemporary practises of digitally-facilitated commercial sex and trafficking in human beings for the purpose of sexual exploitation, recent developments in law and policy in the area, emerging investigative and prosecution practises within digital online environments, as well as necessary future changes to the law and enforcement.

INTRODUCTION

Digital technology has had a significant impact on entrepreneurship in recent years, transforming the way that businesses are created, operated, and marketed (Almeida, Santos, & Monteiro, 2020). It has transformed entrepreneurship by increasing accessibility. As such, digital technology has made it easier for anyone to start a business, regardless of their location or resources. With the internet, it is possible

DOI: 10.4018/978-1-6684-7416-7.ch006

to reach a global market and access a wide range of tools and resources (Allen, 2019). Moreover, digital technology has reduced barriers to entry for many businesses, making it easier for new entrepreneurs to enter markets and compete with established players (Lamine et al., 2021; Bradley et al., 2021; Tekic & Koroteev, 2019). Enhanced communication and collaboration have also been an advantage that digital tools have brought to the realm of entrepreneurship, which has made it easier for entrepreneurs to communicate and collaborate with partners, customers, and employees, regardless of their location. It is also often noted that digital technology improves efficiency and productivity, as it helps entrepreneurs streamline their operations and improve their efficiency and productivity (Hisrich & Soltanifar, 2021; Li, 2020). For example, cloud-based tools and automation can help businesses automate routine tasks and reduce the need for manual labor (Tyagi, Fernandez, Mishra, & Kumari, 2021). In addition to these operational benefits, digital technology has also improved access to capital. In this respect, digital platforms have made it easier for entrepreneurs to access capital, including through crowdfunding and peer-to-peer lending (Keyhani et al., 2022; Bollaert et al., 2021). Overall, digital technology has had a transformative impact on entrepreneurship, making it easier for businesses to start, grow, and succeed in the digital age.

However, the opportunities that digital technologies have brought to lawful entrepreneurship have also created opportunities within the illicit economy. As such, digital technology has enabled the creation of online marketplaces that facilitate the buying and selling of illegal goods and services, such as drugs and stolen credit card information. These marketplaces are often hosted on the dark web, which is a part of the internet that is not accessible through standard web browsers and is therefore difficult to monitor and regulate (Liggett et al., 2020; Garcia-Teruel, 2020; Bancroft, 2020). Digital currencies, such as Bitcoin and Ethereum, have been adopted by many people involved in the illicit economy as a means of payment due to their anonymity and the difficulty of tracing transactions (Leuprecht et al., 2022; Kethineni & Cao, 2020). Digital technology has also made it easier for individuals and organizations to engage in cybercrime, such as hacking into systems to steal sensitive information or disrupt services, as well as making it easier for criminals to launder money by transferring funds electronically and obscuring the trail of transactions (Mugarura & Ssali, 2020; Shulzhenko & Romashkin, 2020).

Digital technology has also made it easier for criminal organizations to communicate and coordinate their activities, as well as to hide their tracks. For example, the use of encrypted messaging apps and anonymous web browsing tools can make it more difficult for law enforcement to monitor and intercept the communications of criminal groups (Shekhar & Vincent, 2022; Proulx, 2022).

Overall, the proliferation of digital technology has made it easier for people to engage in illicit activities and has created new challenges for law enforcement agencies around the world.

An area of illicit entrepreneurship that not only harms economies but also involves human rights atrocities and harm and suffering to individuals is the area of trafficking in human beings (Mackay, et al., 2020; Goździak, & Vogel, 2020). Trafficking in human beings (THB), also known as human trafficking, is considered part of the illicit economy because it involves the illegal trade of people for the purpose of exploitation. This can include forced labor, sexual exploitation, and other forms of abuse. Human trafficking is a violation of human rights and is often linked to organized crime. It is illegal in most countries, and international efforts to combat human trafficking have been ongoing for many years.

However, often the divide between the lawful and illicit economies is not as clear, which makes regulating and navigating the cross-sections a difficult task for legislators and law enforcement officials. An example of this can be seen in the sex industry.

The sex industry is a complex and multifaceted sector that encompasses a range of legal, illegal and criminal activities. In many countries, certain aspects of the sex industry, such as the sale of commercial sexual services, are legal, while others, such as pimping and human trafficking, are prohibited under criminal law (Prylinski, 2020; Essien, 2022; Aronowitz & Veldhuizen, 2021).

Prostitution, or the provision of commercial sex services for remuneration, is legal in some countries, but criminal in others. In countries where it is legal, it is regulated by laws that set out the conditions under which it is permitted and the responsibilities of those involved in the industry, such as the requirement to use condoms and to register with the authorities (Danielsson, 2017). In countries where it is criminal, it is often associated with organized crime and operated in the underground economy (Cioboată, 2020; Koufopoulou, 2019).

One of the major ways that digital technology has changed the sex industry is by making it easier for people to find and access sexual services. For example, websites and apps that facilitate the buying and selling of sexual services have made it easier for both clients and providers to connect with one another. This has led to the proliferation of so-called "online red-light districts," where people can easily browse and purchase sexual services from the comfort of their own homes (Strohmayer et al., 2019; Taras, 2001; Grant, 2014).

Digital technology has also changed the way that the sex industry is marketed. Online platforms have made it easier for sex workers to advertise their services, and they have also made it easier for clients to find and compare different providers. In addition, social media and other online platforms have provided sex workers with new ways to build and maintain relationships with their clients, which can be an important source of support and income (Sanders et al., 2016; Campbell et al., 2019).

However, the use of digital technology in the sex industry has also raised a number of concerns, such as the potential for exploitation and abuse, the risk of online predators, and the challenges of regulating and managing online platforms. There are also concerns about the impact of digital technology on the overall safety and well-being of sex workers, as well as on the broader community (Scoular et al., 2019; Yar, 2012).

When it comes to dealing with digital transformations within the sex industry in law and law enforcement, difficulties may arise due to the differing needs of the illicit and lawful sectors of the sex industry. The following chapter seeks to examine some of these challenges from the perspective of the need to tackle digital illicit entrepreneurship within THB for the purpose of sexual exploitation. A combination of doctrinal and sociolegal research methods was used to analyse contemporary regulatory frameworks within the sex industry and state practices seeking to combat technology-facilitated THB for the purpose of sexual exploitation in order to expose contemporary practices of digitally-facilitated commercial sex and THB for the purpose of sexual exploitation, recent developments in law and policy in the area, emerging investigative and prosecution practices within digital online environments, as well as necessary future changes to the law and enforcement.

The Evolution of Digital Entrepreneurship in the Illicit Sex Industry

As has been experienced in most industries over the past decades, technological advancements have had a significant influence on the operations within the sex industry (Strohmayer et al., 2019). Academic studies, as well as research undertaken by NGOs over the past years (see for example, Raets & Janssens, 2021; Thurnhofer, 2022; Carassa, 2022; Atkinson, 2022; International Labour Organization, 2016; Organization for Security and Co-operation in Europe, 2022), demonstrate an increasing transition of commercial sex providers into technology-facilitated, online spheres, whereby commercial sex services are increasingly being offered online. The specific formats vary significantly; however, a widespread component includes most of self-employed commercial sex entrepreneurs offering and promoting their in-person commercial sex services online (Brooks-Gordon & Vickers, 2022; Cubides et al., 2022; Mulvihill, 2022). In addition, the digital era has seen the emergence of a number of new forms of commercial sex services which are provided solely online, such as webcamming (Campbell et al., 2019; Vlase & Preoteasa, 2022).

The Regulatory Framework Pertaining to Online Commercial Sex Entrepreneurship

In terms of the different theoretical regulatory approaches to prostitution and commercial sex entrepreneurship, the legal frameworks used across the world differ significantly between jurisdictions yet can be classified mostly into three leading conceptual models. Prohibitionism, which involves practices which criminalize both the selling and purchase of commercial sex services or the categorical restriction of some behaviors that are intimately associated with selling or buying; Abolitionism, which does not automatically penalize prostitution or closely connected activities, but may only target one side of a relationship in an effort to render the entire interaction obsolete (Danielsson, 2017); and regulationism, which generally involves the adoption of policies which neither criminalize the sale or purchase of commercial sex services nor any other related activities, but rather include the decriminalization and legalization of selling and buying sex itself, yet, with certain embedded legal restrictions that may distinguish prostitution from other commercial activities, such as age restrictions or introducing targeted health regulations (De Marneffe, 2012).

Regardless of the specific approach adopted by a state, it should be noted that any commercial sex services, which fall outside of criminal sanctions could potentially be considered a lawful economic activity. However, as soon as any form of criminal prohibition applies to a situation, these would fall within the illicit economy. A good example from legal practice, which demonstrates the fine line between the two classifications can be found in England and Wales. Here, the provision of commercial sexual services between two consenting adults is not considered criminal within the current legal framework of England and Wales (Sanders et al., 2021). Nevertheless, numerous associated practices, mostly involving a public component, are prohibited under criminal law and involve criminal penalties (Treloar, Cama, Stardust & Kim, 2021; Matolcsi, et al., 2021). The present legal stance within England and Wales still builds heavily upon the discussions and findings of the Wolfenden Committee Report of 1957, which found that "there must remain a domain of private morality and immorality that is, in plain and basic words, not the law's concern" (Wolfenden Committee, 1957, para. 60; Scoular et al., 2019). It was this underpinning view which is still visible in the English and Welsh regulatory approach, which only seeks to intervene in commercial sex when the public may be harmed (Matthews, 1986; Scoular et al., 2019). As also previously highlighted, the consequence has historically been an often-paradoxical scenario in which it is difficult and often impossible for anyone to provide commercial sex securely or without also committing a criminal offence. In particular, the fact that the law merely views commercial sex activities that are offered and undertaken alone, in private settings as permitted has been an often-criticized point. This provision has meant in practice that many commercial sex providers have had to choose between a heightened threat of violence and exploitation due to the increased vulnerability of lone work, on the one hand, or alternatively, increased protection from abuse by joining forces with other commercial sex providers, yet with the increased risk of legal sanctions (Sanders, 2009; Fudge, 2018).

As will be discussed in more detail in the following sections of this chapter, there is a clear divide between the understanding in law and society of vulnerability of commercial sex providers who are viewed as voluntarily providing sex as a service and the vulnerability of people who are identified as victims of modern slavery and sexual exploitation. Although the law relating to sexual exploitation and the prevention thereof has seen a shift towards prioritizing vulnerability (Home Office, 2006; Scoular et al. 2019), contributing factors, such as socio-economic disparities, sex, migration status and law which enhance the vulnerability of commercial sex providers are yet to be effectively considered in government policy (Munro & Scoular, 2012). Yet, the focus on public harm, rather than the security of commercial sex providers makes any effective changes in law and policy in the near future unlikely.

Nevertheless, philosophically, a contradiction emerges here, whereby the safety within commercial sex, which is perceived to be provided voluntarily, is not prioritized in the regulatory efforts to eradicate exploitation, yet commercial sex is, at the same time, viewed as a form of exploitation in and of itself, especially in relation to modern slavery and trafficking for the purpose of sexual exploitation. This philosophical contradiction is not, however, confined to the laws of England and Wales. As such, the contradiction is even found in jurisdictions in which commercial sex is understood to constitute exploitation in itself, such as the neo-abolitionist approaches followed in Sweden and Northern Ireland. According to the neo-abolitionist stance, commercial sex is always a form of sexual exploitation, which is why the purchasing and using of commercial sex services are prohibited under criminal law, whereas the sale and provision are not (Scoular & Carline, 2014; Ellison, 2017). Nevertheless, in Sweden and Northern Ireland, commercial sex which is deemed to have been provided voluntarily, even if the law states that it is impossible to consent, is not considered sufficient exploitation to justify victim status within the laws seeking to tackle THB for the purpose of sexual exploitation (Section 12, Swedish Penal Code; McMenzie, Cook & Laing, 2019; Danielsson, 2021).

As has been the case in many jurisdictions globally, THB for the purpose of sexual exploitation, in contrast to commercial sex, which is deemed to be provided voluntarily, has been prioritized as a serious contemporary issue on both national and international policy agendas, despite the often-inconsistent conflation of commercial sex services and THB (Chuang, 2009).

In relation to digital entrepreneurship within the commercial sex industry, this will be one of the reasons why the sector is rapidly growing outwith national legal regulation. In the UK, a 2016 HASC investigation into commercial sex indicated that indoor and internet-based commercial sex services were bigger industries now than street prostitution (House of Commons Home Affairs Committee, 2016).

In the midst of this rush of efforts to regulate, reduce, and replace markets for sexual labor, internet-based marketplaces seem to have flourished. They are now perhaps the greatest marketplaces, located on a paradoxical axis: extremely visible, but with a mostly concealed community, with no regulation or police information beyond anecdotes (Murphy & Venkatesh, 2006; Jones, 2020).

When examining commercial sex and the regulation thereof through the lens of digital entrepreneurship, the trend of online commercial sex has encouraged academic debate relating to the impact of digital technology on the practices within the sector. As such, a divide in opinions can be found within the available academic literature, whereby it is either predicted that the increase of digital technology will eliminate the necessity for regulation or intensify it. Cunningham and Kendall (2011) or Peppet (2012) argue, for instance, that new technologies could assist in making commercial sex safer. However, others argue that the digital transitions have made the sex industry more volatile to the capitalist market dynamics, whereby neoliberal politics of internet-facilitated commercial sex are often inconsistent and varied (Dean, 2009; Kennedy, 2016).

Experiential Data From the Field: Findings From England and Wales in the Context of Entrepreneurial Practice and the Heightened Threat of Exploitation

A significant academic study into the changing circumstances of the sex industry was carried out by Sanders et al. in 2018, which verified a movement of commercial sex providers into internet-mediated private and public areas and chronicled the influence of technology on both commercial sex providers, as well as those responsible for enforcing regulations. The study included interviews with people engaged in police strategy and operations, managers of commercial sex online platforms, and commercial sex providers in order to examine how policing in the United Kingdom has been attempting to adapt to a rapidly changing market and the effect this has on those who operate in the field (Sanders et al., 2018). A key finding of this study was a heightened susceptibility to exploitative working circumstances and new forms of crime made possible by the Internet. Sanders et al. (2018) examined the ramifications of police methods and ideological discourses and their effect on interactions with commercial sex providers. The results of this study have demonstrated conflicts within the modern regulation of online sex marketplaces, new threats for commercial sex providers, and the ability of the criminal justice system to protect vulnerable individuals.

In particular, what is being found in England and Wales (Sanders et al., 2019), as well as in other jurisdictions (Flowers, 2011; Paché, 2022; Torn and Lister, 2018), is that the transition of commercial sex online and the lack of regulation and enforcement thereof in this area facilitates severely exploitative practices to be carried out unchecked and hidden from view of law and law enforcement. Moreover, as mentioned in the previous section, the transition of commercial sex entrepreneurship practices online has also moved many commercial sex practices outside of criminal prohibition. However, just because something is not prohibited under criminal law, does not mean it is not illegal (Danielsson, 2021). Illegality, when correctly used as a term, refers to something that is outwith legal regulation, which remains the case in online commercial sex activities. Despite not being a crime, commercial sex practices are not considered a form of work within English and Welsh employment law. The consequence of this is that commercial sex providers will not be protected by employment or labor laws either. Thus, commercial sex providers have very few recourses at their disposal for the protection from exploitation and abuse. Law enforcement procedures aimed at trafficking can have a negative impact on all sex workers, including those who are working lawfully. Sex workers, particularly those who are marginalized or who are working in underground or informal settings, may be at greater risk of being targeted by law enforcement or facing discrimination and mistreatment from authorities. This can make it more difficult for them to access resources and support and can also increase the risk of violence and other harm. It is unfortunate, that the international guidance available on tackling THB for the purpose of sexual exploitation does not make much reference to the impact any interference in the sex industry may have on the legitimate sex industry and lawful entrepreneurs in this area. The strong focus on victim identification neglects the threat of commercial sex providers becoming victims of other forms of exploitation during investigations, as well as vulnerability that is not directly related to THB. Due to the clear separation of THB for the purpose of sexual exploitation and the regulation of commercial sex practices in law and law enforcement procedures, there is little guidance on what to do when circumstances overlap. Currently, the only significant acknowledgement of these realities is emerging from practical law enforcement guidelines rather than regulators. An example can be seen in the English National Police Chiefs' Council Guidance on Policing Sex Work and Prostitution (2019). Here it is stated that the "guidance offers practical advice to those dealing with sex-work-related issues. It recognizes the need to address community concerns but also stresses as a priority the duty that police services have to enhance the safety of sex workers and to find practical ways to address crimes against, and exploitation of, those connected to prostitution" (p. 3).

Although outwith the scope of this chapter, it is noted that international and national law will need to address the intersections between illicit and lawful entrepreneurship in the future to ensure that any developments in the legal framework seeking to tackle THB for the purpose of sexual exploitation do not disregard the realities of persons who work within the sex industry lawfully.

A significant conceptual issue that arises now is the distinction between voluntary commercial sex provision and forced prostitution as a component of modern slavery and THB. The contemporary understanding of THB was first defined in international law in 2000. In this sense, according to Annex I and II of Art. 3 of the Protocol to Prevent, Suppress, and Punish Trafficking in Persons, Especially Women and Children, which is attached to the UN Convention Against Transnational Organized Crime (UN General Assembly, 2001), trafficking is defined as "the recruitment, transportation, transfer, harboring, or receipt of persons, by means of threat or use of force or other forms of coercion, of abduction, of fraud, of deception, of the abuse of power or of a position of vulnerability, or of the giving or receiving of payments or benefits to achieve the consent of a person having control over another person, for the purpose of exploitation" (UN General Assembly, 2005). This constitutes a tripartite definition of human trafficking, as it includes three key elements, namely, the action element (the recruitment, transportation, transfer, harboring, or receipt of persons), the means element (by means of threat or use of force or other forms of coercion, of abduction, of fraud, of deception, of the abuse of power or of a position of vulnerability, or of the giving or receiving of payments or benefits to achieve the consent of a person having control over another person), and the purpose (for the purpose of exploitation) element (Bressan, 2012; Gallagher, 2010; National Rapporteur on Trafficking in Human Beings, 2010). Accordingly, contrary to common belief, it is not the trafficking in the sense of the transportation of persons, which is the defining characteristic of THB, but rather the exploitation of someone in a position of vulnerability. This internationally recognized concept of THB was specifically addressed on a regional level within international law in 2005, when the Council of Europe adopted the Convention on Action against Trafficking in Human Beings, which entered into force on 1 February 2008, and has been ratified by almost all European countries. However, if exploitation is the decisive factor in distinguishing between what is considered forced and voluntary prostitution, the new forms of exploitation and abuse experienced by commercial sex providers should, albeit merely hypothetically, blur the lines between legally accepted commercial sex provision and sexual exploitation, THB and modern slavery.

Technology as a Tool for Trafficking: When the Grey Area Darkens

From slavery to sexual exploitation, THB has occurred in some form across the globe throughout recorded history (Lee & Lewis, 2003). It is an inherently difficult activity to assess, not just because of variations in relation to its definition across jurisdictions, but also due to the hidden nature and political sensitivity of the subject matter (de Cock & Woode, 2014).

Investigating and combating THB, especially online THB practices, needs to be undertaken from a global perspective due to the global cross-border nature, not just of THB itself, but also due to the reduced physical borders of the internet itself (O'Neill, 2011; Shelley, 2010), in particular, as the internet removes any barriers for traffickers geographically, as they can run their practices without a core location (McKee, 2010).

Within contemporary society, at least within the Western regions of the world, the internet has become crucial for many people (Marston & van Hoof, 2019; Lai & Widmar, 2021). Nonetheless, during the last two decades, the Internet has spawned new methods of THB and a new mode of operation for traffickers. A research project conducted in eight major cities within the United States of America found that the "widespread availability and rapid expansion of the Internet has redefined the spatial and social limitations of the sex market by introducing new markets of recruitment and advertisement [...]. Offenders report new marketing opportunities for pimps [traffickers] to connect with both recruits and clientele, including online classifieds, social media, and networking websites" (Dank et al., 2014).

Although the internet has the potential to be utilized as a tool to fight THB, a number of aggravating variables continue to make internet-related THB practices a complex issue to address (Schrock, 2022).

As discussed in the first section of this chapter, the increase in usage of digital technologies, such as the Internet, has not only created opportunities for entrepreneurship within the legitimate economic sectors but also for entrepreneurship within the illicit economy. As such, illicit entrepreneurs involved in criminal activities related to THB have also benefited from digital technologies and new ways to bring their products and services to market (Roe-Sepowitz, 2019; Bryant & Landman, 2020), as well as facilitating the recruitment and exploitation of victims, and providing traffickers with new forms of control mechanisms (Council of Europe, 2022). According to the UN Office on Drugs and Crime's Global Report on Trafficking in Persons 2020, the initial stages of digitally facilitated trafficking took place primarily through independent websites which targeted mostly adult victims (UNODC, 2020). However, more recently, the forms of digital technology used to facilitate trafficking have moved towards using social media platforms as the primary tool, including Facebook, WhatsApp, and Xbox Live (UNODC, 2020; see also Hickle, 2017; Schrock, 2022), which are not only used to promote services, but also as a tool for the recruitment of victims, which has also seen a shift from primarily targeting adults towards children becoming a primary focus (UNODC, 2020). In particular in relation to THB for the purpose of sexual exploitation or forced labor, digital technology is used in the recruitment processes through sham job vacancies, which are placed on classified websites (UN Global Initiative to Fight Human Trafficking, 2008; Schrock, 2022). Other forms of illicit online sex services involve live streamed exploitation (UNODC, 2020).

Traffickers operate online both on what is known as the "surface web" and the "dark web." The practices taking place on the surface web include all the commonly accessed websites, including the prominent classifieds webpages, social media platforms, and other social fora (UNODC, 2020). According to the UN Office on Drugs and Crime (2020), no evidence of specific cases of THB on the dark web has been obtained, yet it is presumed that people involved in trafficking offenses utilize this for the purpose of remaining anonymous online when communicating (ICAT, 2019). In addition, in the same way that digital technology has enhanced lawful entrepreneurship, digital technology has also provided several other tools that have enhanced the illicit operations within THB, for instance in relation to the ability to control victims (Gerry, Muraszkiewicz & Vavoula, 2016; Finklea, 2011). As such, technological developments, such as GPS tracking devices or audio and video surveillance are used as monitoring tools, whereas other digital advancements, such as the ease of distribution of digital materials may serve as bases for threats, such as threats to distribute private imagery, for example, which may showcase sexual content involving victims (van Rij & McAlister, 2020; Eaton, 2022; GRETA, 2022). Digital technologies have facilitated the rise and growth of technologically facilitated human trafficking crimes. A particular area within THB that is rapidly growing due to the use of modern technologies is child sexual exploitation. As such, crimes in this area have adapted rapidly to evolving technological advancements, which has seen a stark transition from initial practices involving group file-sharing systems to more contemporary practices such as sextortion, grooming via social media platforms, as well as live streaming facilities to broadcast sex activities within private circles of internet users. In particular, the live broadcasting of streamed content has become a popular format within the illicit online sex industry, as authorities are unable to effectively track it, since there are no records left on devices of the streamed content (Bird et al., 2020).

Within the illicit markets of THB, there is a rising prevalence of digital technology being used for the purpose of exploitation in numerous forms, with numerous implications for business operations, the wider illicit economy, victims, law enforcement, and the wider society. A significant issue is the fact that the anonymity of perpetrators, most notably within their communications with other criminal actors as well as with victims has increased (Vivrette, 2022; Aronowitz & Veldhuizen, 2021).

Encrypted messaging applications, closed chat rooms, as well as other forms of web fora that operate with exclusivity tools, such as invitation-only mechanisms ensure that entrepreneurs operating within the illicit economy, such as THB, as well as any other potential stakeholders may interact anonymously and securely (Europol, 2014). Moreover, as encrypted ICT becomes increasingly accessible, networking structures surrounding THB become less hierarchical, with flatter management structures, as actors within criminal networks are less dependent on highly specialized equipment. This has also meant that crime networks are increasingly becoming less dependent on strictly connected groups, which is resulting in a loosening of personnel structures and group memberships (Meneses Falcón, Urío Rodríguez & Uroz Olivares, 2019; Raets & Janssens, 2019).

This has resulted in a particular transition in entrepreneurship within this illicit economy as well (Europol, 2014). Technological advancements have not only resulted in easier access to specialized technology but have also resulted in decreased risks and administrative expenses, such as those associated with recruiting prospective victims, laundering money, and trading (Europol, 2015). As such, it is becoming increasingly easier to enter the illicit economy in the area of THB, which has resulted in a rise in illicit entrepreneurs in this area.

At the same time, increased access to digital technologies globally has resulted in increased vulnerability of potential victims, who are now easier to approach and recruit, especially for online exploitation. The widespread availability of the internet and a variety of digital technologies on the mass market have rendered victims very susceptible to online trafficking. The plethora of ICT, big data, and the internet of things have opened up new avenues for perpetrators to obtain and collect information, as well as to pinpoint, profile, and recruit a growing amount of targets, especially among vulnerable populations (Bird et al., 2020). The expanded availability of content relating to labor and sexual exploitation on the internet, to both regional and international audiences, has increased market penetration and demand (UNODC, 2015).

Key Challenges in Combatting Technology-Facilitated THB Entrepreneurship in Law and Criminal Justice

The last two decades witnessed a shift in focus in relation to tackling THB for the purpose of sexual exploitation. As such, driven by international law, the approaches have moved away from a border security approach to tackling THB, which focused predominantly on border controls and prosecution mechanisms, towards a human rights approach, which places the key emphasis on victim identification and support (Wieltschnig, Muraszkiewicz & Fenton, 2021; Mancarella, 2021). Yet, detecting and identifying victims of online or internet-facilitated THB remains difficult. A recent report by the Council of Europe's Group of Experts on Action against Trafficking in Human Beings (2022) presents many of the challenges faced by international and national actors and law enforcement agencies, indicating some of the key obstacles faced both nationally and internationally in relation to the growing market for online and digitally facilitated THB. As such, the first obstacle relates to resourcing. Due to the vast prevalence of potential THB related online activity, policing the internet requires significant amounts of resources, financial, technological as well as human resources and expertise. Often, the volume of data, such as internet-based open as well as classified advertisements for sexual as well as non-sexual service provisions, is larger than what is possible to manually search through (GRETA, 2022). The frequent use of anonymization software as well as aliases online further cumber the ability to identify victims or perpetrators. This is further exacerbated by the fact that many conversations between victims and perpetrators take place in closed groups. The time, staffing and specialist know-how, and equipment required to investigate are some of the key resource areas that would require expansion in order to be adequately capable of tackling THB and connected illicit entrepreneurship (GRETA, 2022). However, apart from merely resources, there are other common issues faced by states in combating online or technology-facilitated THB, most notably in the areas of police investigations and prosecution. In the following, each of these three areas will be addressed in turn.

Obstacles Within National Police Investigations of Online THB Cases

According to the accounts of the member states of the Council of Europe, it seems that data encryption is viewed as one of the more prominent issues faced by states seeking to tackle THB, as well as the high quantities of available data (GRETA, 2022). Other challenges include the speed at which digital technology is developing, inadequate technical equipment and insufficient legislative instruments. Moreover, more than 50 percent of the countries in Europe also emphasized a lack of technical understanding amongst the personnel within national law enforcement, and the absence of help from the private sector (GRETA, 2022).

Protocols for data encryption used by popular applications and internet services are frequently regarded as insecure. Additionally, encryption inhibits the ability to monitor conversations. A few nations have hinted at the existence of decryption tools for certain kinds of gadgets. However, this is a dynamic environment that necessitates (considerable) expenditures in training as well as software (Ilbiz & Kaunert, 2021). Among the measures adopted to address this problem is the development of cybercrime units or centers which are entrusted with developing decryption technologies. In addition, there is value in the transnational pooling of resources for the creation of technological tools such as specialized software which can decrypt information as well as so-called web-crawlers, which are internet bots that browse systematically through pages on the World Wide Web for the purpose of data indexing (GRETA, 2022).

As the continuously expanding amount of data from electronic communications or ICT devices place a significant burden on investigators, which, in turn, hinders the capacity of investigators to extract and properly examine any material, which also needs specialized tools and training to effectively review any potential evidence that may be found (GRETA, 2022).

States and investigators across the globe agree that increasing the ability to manage vast volumes of electronic evidence is vital. However, this capability must be continually developed in order to keep up to date with ongoing developments. As such, rapid shifts in behavioral patterns within the use of digital technology place an additional burden on the ability of investigators to sift through the growing volume of data (Casino et al., 2022; Waller et al., 2022; Reedy, 2020). Thus, in order to be able to keep up with the rapid pace of technological progress, specialist hard- and software are essential, yet costly, and police forces struggle to balance the necessary costs without impacting their obligations in other areas, regardless of the economic strength of the state involved (Brown & Marsden, 2013; Schrock, 2022).

However, as indicated previously, human capital is also a vital investment as digital technology, especially as any investigations, even with technology, will require human expertise to run. Moreover, especially in relation to illicit entrepreneurship involving THB for the purpose of sexual exploitation, there is always some form of physical exploitation that needs to be tackled through human intervention. As was discussed in the previous sections, technology-facilitated sexual exploitation mostly uses digital technologies for recruitment purposes as well as to promote physical services online. As such, the abuse itself will still be taking place physically. Investigative technology and expertise are critical for the detection of potential cases of THB for the purpose of sexual exploitation. However, ultimately, the steps taken thereafter will require physical interventions in order to support potential victims. A final, yet noteworthy obstacle to the investigation of illicit digital entrepreneurship can be found in the law itself. As such, the development of laws with the purpose of fostering lawful entrepreneurship and protecting the rights of all netizens may also stifle investigations into illicit online practices. As such, laws seeking to protect people from unnecessary interference into their private lives, such as the provisions contained in the General Data Protection Regulation (GDPR) limit the ability to investigate practices, for instance in relation to accessing private correspondence, data retention requirements, as well as the scope of access to information for web-crawlers (Diamond & Plattner, 2012; Layton & Elaluf-Calderwood, 2019; Deeb-Swihart, Endert & Bruckman, 2022; Gerry, Muraszkiewicz & Vavoula, 2016).

Obstacles for the Ability of Effective Prosecution of Online THB Perpetrators

Generally, the difficulties associated with achieving a prosecution of perpetrators are perceived to be secondary to those associated with investigations. Nevertheless, it is important to note that prosecutions are a vital component within the fight against illicit entrepreneurship. Although there are many underpinning reasons for the need for effective prosecution, some of the most fundamental ones are built on the underpinning concepts on which criminal laws are built in their entirety, which are retribution, incapacitation, deterrence, reparations, and rehabilitation, as well as the philosophical foundations of the rule of law and social contract, which require states to protect the fundamental rights of their subjects, which include the protection of life and liberty (Castiglione et al., 1995; Tamanaha, 2004; Carlsmith, 2001; 2006). As such, effective prosecution and criminal penalties for illicit digital entrepreneurs engaged in THB practices are crucial to deter future market entrants, prevent the already established entrepreneurs from continuing to exploit people, to seek retributive justice and reparations for victims, and to comply with constitutional obligations to protect citizens from harm (Babcock, 2018; Greene, 2003). Yet, similarly to the investigation stage, effective prosecution comes with a number of obstacles for states and law enforcement. One of the first issues to note relates to obtaining evidence. Apart from requirements to have obtained evidence legally, which faces similar challenges as police investigations in relation to GDPR and privacy protection requirements, there is an additional issue when seeking to obtain evidence from other jurisdictions (Farrell et al., 2016; Broad & Muraszkiewicz, 2020; Bowen, 2017). Also, similarly to the issues within the investigation stage, specialized personnel are required, which necessitates continuous training for prosecutors, which remains insufficient. Legislation is also often slow to respond to changing practices, making laws often outdated before they are even enforced (Brunovskis, 2012; GRETA, 2022).

An issue across jurisdictions is a lack of successful prosecutions, as cases need to be particularly strong to succeed over constitutional fair trial safeguards (Hodgson, 2011; Stoykova, 2022). Thus, states highlight the need for effective training for prosecutors to ensure that cases relating to technology-facilitated THB involve correctly obtained electronic evidence, and that the evidence is understood sufficiently to be able to present it to judges and juries convincingly (Didier et al., 2022; Stockhem, 2020; Devasahayam, 2019). In particular, prosecution problems have been reported to arise when handling electronic materials, especially in relation to GDPR responsibilities. As such, not only national legal red tape, but also difficulties relating to foreign data protection rules which may impede the collection, storage, and processing of data gathered via technical investigative methods (such as web crawling, as discussed in the previous section) (GRETA, 2022). These issues may contribute to lengthy processing times for Mutual Legal Assistance (MLA) requests when seeking to prosecute cross-border cases of THB. As explained in earlier sections, technology allows criminal networks to undertake illicit entrepreneurial practices, such as organizing and supervising exploitation operations remotely, such as from another nation, frequently with the knowledge that demands for judicial cooperation would not be met promptly, if at all. Inadequately trained employees to assemble and process requests, as well as the use of obsolete equipment, may further contribute to the difficulty of processing MLAs. In addition, insufficient electronic evidence also does not present enough details to be able to sufficiently determine the jurisdiction in which data is located, which further impacts the ability to complete an MLA request (GRETA, 2022).

Tackling Illicit Digital Entrepreneurs With Their Own Weapons: ICT-Facilitated Investigations Into THB

Some states report a number of techniques to identify online and ICT-facilitated THB incidents (GRETA, 2022). Internet surveillance, including forums and, in certain situations, TOR networks, is also a frequently used tactic (Rawat, 2022; Jardine, 2021). Used in combination with Open-Source Intelligence (OSINT), which is the collection of information from publicly accessible internet sources, such as social media platforms and other websites containing people's online contact networks, living circumstances, as well as financial information (Böhm & Lolagar, 2021). It is also reported that some states have established "cyber-patrols" with personnel specifically trained to conduct online OSINT investigations. Other tools used when permitted under national laws include covert online investigations, also known as cyber-infiltration (GRETA, 2022).

Another tool that can be used involves web-scraping technologies, which have been expressly designed to gather information from websites, notably to assess risk and vulnerability on Adult Services Websites (ASWs) (GRETA, 2022).

Another area in which the tools used by illicit digital entrepreneurs engaged in THB can be used against perpetrators relates to the use of social media platforms. As explained in earlier sections, social media platforms are often used in the recruitment processes within THB, whereby potential victims are approached online via these accounts. During OSINT investigations, social network analysis tools can, thus, be used to gain more information about and piece together both criminal networks as well as victims' networks of relationships and connections between the two as well as, potentially, locations (UNODC, 2020; GRETA, 2022).

Moving reporting mechanisms online for suspected THB-related entrepreneurship is also an increasingly utilised tool. As such, governments across the world are introducing online reporting pages where concerned internet users are able to report any websites containing suspected exploitation. Moreover, many private online platforms, such as social media sites have introduced their own reporting mechanisms for users who come across suspected exploitation (Omand, Bartlett & Miller, 2012; Instagram, 2022; Facebook, 2022). Some jurisdictions, such as France, have embedded this as an obligation for businesses within their national laws (de Streel, 2020; Frosio, 2018).

Law enforcement authorities may at times infiltrate criminal networks via the use of covert procedures and undercover investigations. Internationally, this has been identified as an area in which more covert investigations are necessary, with many states investing increasingly in the training of specialized investigators (Gerry, Muraszkiewicz & Vavoula, 2016).

Another tactic utilized is to tackle illicit entrepreneurship through active counter-campaigning practices. For instance, in destination countries such as the United Kingdom and Belgium, where exploitative service use is more prevalent, alerts on websites which are known to feature advertising for commercial sex services are used, which contain information on the risks associated with encountering THB cases (UNODC, 2020; OSCE, 2021). In countries of origin, in which recruitment stages of THB are more prevalent, such as Poland and Bulgaria, online campaigning is used to educate jobseekers on safe employment alternatives (Volodko, 2020). However, governments are still in the early stages of developing these kinds of "proactive" measures, while the majority of state practices within investigations into technology-facilitated THB remain "reactive" (GRETA, 2022).

International Legal instruments: Opportunities and Challenges

In addition to the general international instruments and initiatives that are aimed at THB, such as the United Nations Protocol to Prevent, Suppress, and Punish Trafficking in Persons, Especially Women and Children, which is a supplement to the United Nations Convention against Transnational Organized Crime, there are also numerous international legal instruments which become relevant when tackling specifically illicit digital entrepreneurship and technology-facilitated THB for the purpose of sexual exploitation. In particular, two international documents are reported to be viewed by states as the most relevant, which include the Convention on Cybercrime and the Mutual Legal Assistance Treaty (GRETA, 2022).

The Convention on Cybercrime

The Convention on Cybercrime, also known as the Budapest Convention, is a legally binding international treaty that aims to combat cybercrimes, including THB. It was adopted by the Council of Europe in 2001 and has been ratified by more than 50 countries.

One of the main strengths of the Convention is that it provides a framework for international cooperation in the investigation and prosecution of cybercrimes, including THB. This is particularly important given the transnational nature of many cybercrimes and the fact that traffickers often use the internet to advertise and facilitate their activities (Clough, 2014; Keyser, 2017; Marion, 2010).

The Convention also requires signatory states to criminalize specific forms of THB, including the use of the internet to facilitate or commit such crimes. This can be an effective way of deterring traffickers from using the internet for their activities (Kunze, 2009; Convention on Cybercrime, 2001; Schrock, 2022).

However, the effectiveness of the Budapest Convention in combating THB depends on a number of factors, including the level of cooperation between countries, the resources and capacity of law enforcement agencies, and the willingness of countries to take action against traffickers. Some countries may have limited resources or may be unwilling to cooperate with other countries in investigations and prosecutions, which can hinder the effectiveness of the Convention (Konrad, 2002; Clough, 2014; Lavorgna, 2015).

Overall, while the Convention on Cybercrime is a useful tool in combating THB, it is not a standalone solution and needs to be supported by other efforts such as robust law enforcement capacity and victim support services.

The Mutual Legal Assistance Treaty

The Mutual Legal Assistance Treaty (MLAT) is a legal agreement between countries that allows for cooperation in the investigation and prosecution of crimes, including THB. It allows for the exchange of evidence and information, as well as the extradition of suspects.

In general, the MLAT is considered an effective tool in tackling THB. It allows for international cooperation and coordination in the investigation and prosecution of traffickers, which can be crucial in cases that involve multiple countries or jurisdictions. It also allows for the sharing of resources and expertise between countries, which can improve the efficiency and effectiveness of investigations and prosecutions (van der Wilt, 2018; Michael & Rose, 2007; Nguyen, 2020; Geldenhuys, 2019).

However, the effectiveness of the MLAT in tackling THB can depend on a number of factors, including the willingness and ability of participating countries to cooperate and share information, as well as the capacity of their law enforcement and judicial systems to effectively investigate and prosecute traffickers. Additionally, the MLAT can be limited by language barriers, cultural differences, and other logistical challenges that can impede cooperation and coordination.

However, the MLAT process can be problematic in combatting THB for several reasons. Firstly, it can be a lengthy process. The MLAT process can be time-consuming, as it involves multiple steps and approvals. This can delay the investigation and prosecution of trafficking cases, which can result in the perpetrators remaining free to continue their illegal activities (Lewis, 2003; Bauer & Erixon, 2020; Quintel & Cole, 2018). Secondly, the ability to use it only has a limited scope. MLATs are limited to requests between two specific countries, which can make it difficult to gather evidence from other countries that may be relevant to a trafficking case. Especially, with digital technology meaning that instances of trafficking can be spread across many different localities, it makes the collection of evidence complex (Hsiao & Weaver-Lee, 2021; Cutler, 1999).

Another issue relates to a lack of consistency. As such, MLATs are not uniform, and the requirements and procedures for obtaining assistance can vary from country to country. This can create confusion and make it difficult to effectively request and receive assistance (Lyman, 2006; Goodman, 2006; Woods, 2016).

As with many other international treaties as well, there is an issue with limited coverage. Not all countries have MLATs with every other country, which can limit the ability to gather evidence from certain countries (Woods, 2015; Cory, Atkinson & Castro, 2019).

Similarly, to the issues mentioned earlier in this chapter in relation to the ability of states to effectively investigate THB offenses, MLATs are impacted by limited resources. In this respect, some countries may have limited resources or expertise to effectively process MLAT requests, which can further delay the investigation and prosecution of THB cases (Kittichaisaree, 2017; Ross, 2018; Selby, 2017).

Other issues involve potential conflicting laws, as different countries may have different laws and definitions of trafficking, which can make it difficult to obtain assistance under the MLAT. This can also make it difficult to prosecute trafficking cases in different countries, as evidence and testimony may not be admissible in one country but may be in another (Nadelmann, 2010; Kranrattanasuit, 2014; Gyandoh, 2001).

The Second Additional Protocol to the Convention on Cybercrime

In light of many of these issues, the Second Additional Protocol to the Convention on Cybercrime, also known as the "Protocol on Matters Specific to Electronic Evidence," was introduced. It is a legal instrument that was adopted by the Council of Europe in 2018 to address the challenges associated with the collection and use of electronic evidence in criminal investigations. The Protocol establishes a legal framework for international cooperation and disclosure of electronic evidence among the Parties to the Convention, with the goal of improving the efficiency and effectiveness of law enforcement in combating cybercrime. This includes issues such as cross-border data access, mutual assistance in investigations, and the extradition of suspects. The Second Additional Protocol aims to provide a more comprehensive and effective approach to combating cybercrime, and to ensure that the Budapest Convention remains relevant and effective in the face of constantly evolving technologies and online threats (Spiezia, 2022; Polyzoidou, 2021; Casino et al., 2022).

Some key changes introduced by the Protocol include the clarification of the legal framework for the collection and disclosure of electronic evidence, an extension of the scope of the Convention to cover new types of electronic evidence, the introduction of new provisions on mutual legal assistance, as well as new provisions on urgent preservation and expedited disclosure of electronic evidence. In particular, the Protocol clarifies the legal framework for the collection and disclosure of electronic evidence, including the types of evidence that may be collected and the processes that must be followed when requesting and disclosing such evidence. Moreover, it extends the scope of the Convention to cover new types of electronic evidence, including evidence stored in the cloud and evidence stored on devices that are not connected to the internet. The Protocol introduces new provisions on mutual legal assistance, which provide for the expeditious exchange of electronic evidence between parties to the Convention and new provisions on the urgent preservation and expedited disclosure of electronic evidence, which allow for the rapid collection and disclosure of electronic evidence in cases where there is a risk that the evidence may be lost or tampered with. Although the protocol has introduced new provisions to accommodate developments in digital technology, many of the issues pertaining to conflicts in law remain untouched. However, it is still to be seen if the amendments to the international legal framework will have the desired impact, and a series of reviews will be necessary in the coming years to closely monitor its impact.

Summary, Recommendations, and Concluding Remarks

Digital technology has had a major impact on the sex industry by making it easier for people to connect with each other and share information and content. With the widespread adoption of the internet, people can now use websites and apps to find and connect with potential partners or clients, as well as share and sell explicit content such as videos and photos. Digital technology has also made it easier for people to purchase and sell sex-related products and services online, which has led to the growth of e-commerce sites and services in this sector. In addition, digital technology has made it possible for people to participate in virtual sex or engage in online sex work, such as through webcamming or other types of online performance.

Digital technology has not only had a significant impact on the lawful parts of the sex industry. Particularly the illicit areas involving THB, have also been transformed by digital technology in several ways. One of the main ways it has changed THB is by making it easier for traffickers to find and recruit victims. For example, traffickers can use social media and online classified ads to lure people, particularly young people, into trafficking situations. They may also use the internet to research potential victims and gather information about them that can be used to manipulate or coerce them.

Digital technology has also made it easier for traffickers to operate and evade detection. They can use encrypted messaging apps and anonymous web browsers to communicate with each other and with their victims, making it more difficult for law enforcement to track their activities. In addition, traffickers can use the internet to buy and sell people and to advertise services such as prostitution, making it easier for them to generate revenue from their criminal activities.

Finally, digital technology has played a role in increasing the demand for trafficking, particularly in the form of sex trafficking. The proliferation of internet pornography and the increased use of social media and other online platforms for buying and selling sex have contributed to the demand for trafficking.

Tackling illicit entrepreneurship in the areas of tackling THB for sexual exploitation online can be a complex and challenging task for law enforcement agencies.

Issues can arise due to difficulties in determining which law enforcement agency has jurisdiction to investigate and prosecute a case involving online trafficking, especially if the activity spans multiple countries. Moreover, it can be challenging to gather sufficient evidence to prosecute traffickers online, as they often use encryption and other methods to conceal their activities. As many traffickers use anonymous online platforms and pseudonyms to hide their identities, it is often difficult to detect them or track them down. The work of enforcement authorities is often further burdened due to limited resources, which means that there may not be enough capacity to investigate and prosecute all cases of online THB. As perpetrators are no longer bound to physical locations close to the exploitative practices, there is a growing dependency on cross-border collaboration. Yet, some countries may not have strong legal frameworks in place to address online trafficking, making it difficult to prosecute cases. Although international law is implementing regulations to close loopholes in this area, there is still too much discretion given to national laws in these areas to accommodate variations in domestic interpretations, definitions, and procedural laws.

Nevertheless, there are also strategies that may be effective in addressing the issues generated by the increase in illicit entrepreneurship within THB for the purpose of sexual exploitation. These strategies include enhanced collaboration, targeting online platforms, enhanced training in digital technologies for law enforcement personnel, and raising public awareness. Law enforcement agencies can work with other organizations, such as non-governmental organizations (NGOs) and international partners, to gather information, share resources, and coordinate efforts to investigate and prosecute traffickers. They can also target online platforms where trafficking is known to occur, such as social media sites, classified ad websites, and message boards. This may involve working with platform providers to identify and remove trafficking-related content, as well as pursuing criminal charges against traffickers who use these platforms. However, any investigation of THB online will require law enforcement agencies to provide training to their personnel to help them recognize and investigate trafficking cases, as well as understand the specific needs of victims. In relation to raising public awareness practices, it is crucial that all internet users are educated on the issue of trafficking, which can help identify potential victims and disrupt the activities of traffickers. Law enforcement agencies can work with the media and other organizations to educate the public about the signs of trafficking and how to report suspected cases. It can also help prevent people from becoming victims, as enhanced knowledge about risks can combat vulnerabilities of exploitation.

REFERENCES

Allen, J. P. (2019). *Digital entrepreneurship*. Routledge. doi:10.4324/9780429506567

Almeida, F., Santos, J. D., & Monteiro, J. A. (2020). The challenges and opportunities in the digitalization of companies in a post-COVID-19 World. *IEEE Engineering Management Review*, *48*(3), 97–103. doi:10.1109/EMR.2020.3013206

Aronowitz, A. A., & Veldhuizen, M. E. (2021). The human trafficking–organized crime nexus. In *The Routledge Handbook of Transnational Organized Crime* (pp. 232–252). Routledge. doi:10.4324/9781003044703-17

Atkinson, T. C. (2022). *Sex-e-Work: An Exploration on the Rise of OnlyFans as a Space for Sexually Explicit Content* [Doctoral dissertation]. Carleton University.

Babcock, H. M. (2018). The Federal Government Has an Implied Moral Constitutional Duty to Protect Individuals from Harm Due to Climate Change: Throwing Spaghetti Against the Wall to See What Sticks. *Ecology Law Quarterly*, *45*, 735.

Bancroft, A. (2020). Crime Is as Smart and as Dumb as the Internet. In *The Darknet and Smarter Crime* (pp. 1–22). Palgrave Macmillan. doi:10.1007/978-3-030-26512-0_1

Bauer, M., & Erixon, F. (2020). *Europe's quest for technology sovereignty: Opportunities and pitfalls* (No. 02/2020). ECIPE Occasional Paper.

Bird, L., Hoang, T., Stanyard, J., Walker, S., & Haysom, S. (2020). *Transformative Technologies*. Academic Press.

Böhm, I., & Lolagar, S. (2021). Open source intelligence. *International Cybersecurity Law Review*, *2*(2), 317–337. doi:10.136543439-021-00042-7

Bollaert, H., Lopez-de-Silanes, F., & Schwienbacher, A. (2021). Fintech and access to finance. *Journal of Corporate Finance*, *68*, 101941. doi:10.1016/j.jcorpfin.2021.101941

Bowen, P. (2017). Prosecution of cases of human trafficking in a common law system. In *Routledge Handbook of Human Trafficking* (pp. 213–223). Routledge. doi:10.4324/9781315709352-17

Bradley, S. W., Kim, P. H., Klein, P. G., McMullen, J. S., & Wennberg, K. (2021). Policy for innovative entrepreneurship: Institutions, interventions, and societal challenges. *Strategic Entrepreneurship Journal*, *15*(2), 167–184. doi:10.1002ej.1395

Bressan, S. (2012). Criminal Law against Human Trafficking withing the EU: A Comparison of an Approximated Legislation. *European Journal of Crime Criminal Law and Criminal Justice*, *20*(2), 137–163. doi:10.1163/092895612X13333546844554

Broad, R., & Muraszkiewicz, J. (2020). The investigation and prosecution of traffickers: Challenges and opportunities. The Palgrave International Handbook of Human Trafficking, 707-723.

Brooks-Gordon, B., & Vickers, E. (2022). Growth and Diversity of the Online Solopreneur and Sexpreneur. *Current Opinion in Psychology*, 101474. PMID:36469962

Brown, I., & Marsden, C. T. (2013). *Regulating code: Good governance and better regulation in the information age*. MIT Press. doi:10.7551/mitpress/8879.001.0001

Brunovskis, A. (2012). *Balancing protection and prosecution in anti-trafficking policies: A comparative analysis of reflection periods and related temporary residence permits for victims of trafficking in the Nordic Countries*. Nordic Council of Ministers. doi:10.6027/TN2012-556

Bryant, K., & Landman, T. (2020). Combatting human trafficking since Palermo: What do we know about what works? *Journal of Human Trafficking*, *6*(2), 119–140. doi:10.1080/23322705.2020.1690097

Campbell, R., Sanders, T., Scoular, J., Pitcher, J., & Cunningham, S. (2019). Risking safety and rights: Online sex work, crimes and 'blended safety repertoires'. *The British Journal of Sociology*, *70*(4), 1539–1560. doi:10.1111/1468-4446.12493 PMID:30318604

Carasa, L. L. (2022). *Enhancing international cooperation to fight gender inequality: A comparative analysis of the effectiveness of internet regulations in tackling online violence against women in the EU and the USA*. Academic Press.

Carlsmith, K. M. (2001). *Why do we punish? Retribution, deterrence, and incapacitation as motives for punishment*. Princeton University.

Carlsmith, K. M. (2006). The roles of retribution and utility in determining punishment. *Journal of Experimental Social Psychology*, *42*(4), 437–451. doi:10.1016/j.jesp.2005.06.007

Casino, F., Pina, C., López-Aguilar, P., Batista, E., Solanas, A., & Patsakis, C. (2022). SoK: Cross-border criminal investigations and digital evidence. *Journal of Cybersecurity*, *8*(1), tyac014. doi:10.1093/cybsec/tyac014

Castiglione, D., Charvet, J., Coole, D., & Forsyth, M. (1995). *The social contract from Hobbes to Rawls*. Routledge.

Chuang, J. A. (2009). Rescuing trafficking from ideological capture: Prostitution reform and anti-trafficking law and policy. *U. Pa. L. Rev.*, *158*, 1655.

Cioboată, M. (2020). The Underground Economy: Determinants and Implications. *Revista tinerilor economişti*, (34), 52-63.

Clough, J. (2014). A world of difference: The Budapest Convention on Cybercrime and the Challenges of Harmonisation. *Monash University Law Review. Monash University. Faculty of Law*, *40*(3), 698–736.

Cory, N., Atkinson, R. D., & Castro, D. (2019). *Principles and Policies for "Data Free Flow With Trust"*. Information Technology and Innovation Foundation.

Council of Europe. (2001, Nov. 23). *Convention on Cybercrime*. Author.

Cubides Kovacsics, M. I., Santos, W., & Siegmann, K. A. (2022). Sex workers' everyday security in the Netherlands and the impact of COVID-19. *Sexuality Research & Social Policy*, 1–15. doi:10.100713178-022-00729-4 PMID:35637773

Cunningham, S., & Kendall, T. D. (2011). Prostitution 2.0: The changing face of sex work. *Journal of Urban Economics*, *69*(3), 273–287. doi:10.1016/j.jue.2010.12.001

Cutler, S. P. (1999). Building International Cases: Tools for Successful Investigations. *FBI L. Enforcement Bull.*, *68*, 1.

Danielsson, A. (2017). Legal philosophical considerations of prostitution: A roadmap to understanding diverse legal approaches to prostitution in Europe. *Strathclyde Law Review*, *3*(1), 24–59.

Danielsson, A. (2017a). Competing Ideas of Regulationism-What Can be Learnt from the German Move to a More Comprehensive Regulation of Prostitution. *International Journal of Advanced Research*, *5*(3), 2149–2166. doi:10.21474/IJAR01/3734

Danielsson, A. (2021). *Economic Activity or Public Order Limitations: The Interplay of the Regulation of Prostitution between National Law, EU Law and Efforts to Combat Human Trafficking* [Thesis].

Dank, M. L., Khan, B., Downey, P. M., Kotonias, C., Mayer, D., Owens, C., ... Yu, L. (2014). *Estimating the size and structure of the underground commercial sex economy in eight major US cities*. Academic Press.

de Cock, M., & Woode, M. (2014). *Profits and Poverty: The Economics of Forced Labour*. Academic Press.

De Marneffe, P. (2012). *Liberalism and prostitution*. OUP USA.

De Streel, A. (2020). *Online Platforms' Moderation of Illegal Content Online*. Policy Department for Economic, Scientific and Quality of Life Policies, European Parliament.

Dean, J. (2009). Democracy and other neoliberal fantasies. In *Democracy and Other Neoliberal Fantasies*. Duke University Press. doi:10.2307/j.ctv11smj29

Deeb-Swihart, J., Endert, A., & Bruckman, A. (2022). Ethical Tensions in Applications of AI for Addressing Human Trafficking: A Human Rights Perspective. *Proceedings of the ACM on Human-Computer Interaction, 6*(2), 1-29. 10.1145/3555186

Devasahayam, T. W. (2019). Sex, Crime and Deceit: Women and Child Trafficking and Sexual Abuse in the Internet Age in Cambodia and Thailand. *Exploring the Nexus Between Technologies and Human Rights*, 1.

Diamond, L., & Plattner, M. F. (Eds.). (2012). *Liberation technology: Social media and the struggle for democracy*. JHU Press. doi:10.1353/book.72079

Didier, E., Hellweger, A., Powell, R. J., & van Kampen, C. (2022). Exploring Legal Accountability of Global Technology and Social Media Companies for the Cyber Exploitation and Online Human Trafficking of Yezidis and Other Minorities By ISIS. *Journal of Human Trafficking, Enslavement, and Conflict-Related Sexual Violence*, *3*(1), 4–44. doi:10.7590/266644722X16563337545111

Eaton, D. (2022). *Human Trafficking: Detection and Transaction Monitoring Techniques* [Doctoral dissertation]. Utica University.

Ellison, G. (2017). Who needs evidence? Radical feminism, the Christian Right and sex work research in Northern Ireland. In *Reflexivity and Criminal Justice* (pp. 289–314). Palgrave Macmillan. doi:10.1057/978-1-137-54642-5_13

Essien, E. D. (Ed.). (2022). *Handbook of Research on Present and Future Paradigms in Human Trafficking*. IGI Global. doi:10.4018/978-1-7998-9282-3

European Police Office. (2015). *Exploring Tomorrow's Organised Crime*. Author.

Europol, I. O. C. T. A. (2014). https:// www.europol.europa.eu/activities-services/main-reports/internet-organised-crime-threat-assessment-iocta-2014

Europol. (2021). *Internet Organised Crime Threat Assessment (IOCTA) 2021*. Publications Office of the European Union.

Facebook. (2022). *Report something: Facebook help centre*. Facebook Help Centre. Retrieved December 9, 2022, from https://en-gb.facebook.com/help/263149623790594

Farrell, A., DeLateur, M. J., Owens, C., & Fahy, S. (2016). The prosecution of state-level human trafficking cases in the United States. *Anti-Trafficking Review*, (6), 48–70. doi:10.14197/atr.20121664

Finklea, K. M. (2011, July). *The interplay of borders, turf, cyberspace, and jurisdiction: Issues confronting US law enforcement*. Congressional Research Service, Library of Congress.

Flowers, R. B. (2011). *Prostitution in the digital age: Selling sex from the suite to the street*. ABC-CLIO.

Frosio, G. F. (2018). Why keep a dog and bark yourself? From intermediary liability to responsibility. *International Journal of Law and Information Technology*, *26*(1), 1–33. doi:10.1093/ijlit/eax021

Fudge, J. (2018). Modern Slavery, Unfree Labour and the Labour Market: The Social Dynamics of Legal Characterization. *Social & Legal Studies, 27*(414).

Gallagher, A. T. (2010). *The international law of human trafficking*. Cambridge University Press. doi:10.1017/CBO97805111761065

Garcia-Teruel, R. M. (2020). Legal challenges and opportunities of blockchain technology in the real estate sector. *Journal of Property, Planning and Environmental Law*.

Geldenhuys, K. (2019). Bilateral tools for fighting transnational organised crime. *Servamus Community-based Safety and Security Magazine*, *112*(8), 32–37.

Gerry, F., Muraszkiewicz, J., & Vavoula, N. (2016). The role of technology in the fight against human trafficking: Reflections on privacy and data protection concerns. *Computer Law & Security Report, 32*(2), 205–217. doi:10.1016/j.clsr.2015.12.015

Goodman, M. (2006). *Mutual Legal Assistance Treaties and Letters Rogatory: A Guide for Judges.* Academic Press.

Goździak, E. M., & Vogel, K. M. (2020). Palermo at 20: A retrospective and prospective. *Journal of Human Trafficking, 6*(2), 109–118. doi:10.1080/23322705.2020.1690117

Grant, M. (2014). *Playing the whore: The work of sex work.* Verso Books.

Greene, A. S. (2013). What is Constitutional Obligation. *BUL Rev., 93*, 1239.

Gyandoh, M. K. (2001). Foreign Evidence Gathering: What obstacles stand in the way of justice. *Temp. Int'l & Comp. LJ, 15*, 81.

Henderson, E. (1995). Of Signifiers and Sodomy: Privacy, public Morality and Sex in the Decriminalisation Debates. *Melb. UL Rev., 20*, 1023.

Hisrich, R. D., & Soltanifar, M. (2021). Unleashing the Creativity of Entrepreneurs with Digital Technologies. In *Digital Entrepreneurship* (pp. 23–49). Springer. doi:10.1007/978-3-030-53914-6_2

Hodgson, J. S. (2011). Safeguarding Suspects' Rights in Europe: A Comparative Perspective. *New Criminal Law Review, 14*(4), 611–665. doi:10.1525/nclr.2011.14.4.611

Home Office (HO). (2006). *A Co-ordinated Prostitution Strategy and a Summary of Responses to `Paying the Price'.* Author.

House of Commons Home Affairs Committee, Third Report, Prostitution, HC (2016±17)

Hsiao, R., & Weaver-Lee, Z. (2021). Mutual Legal Assistance in the Digital Age and Taiwan's New Southbound Policy. *Policy, 21*, 1.

Ilbiz, E., & Kaunert, C. (2021). Europol and cybercrime: Europol's sharing decryption platform. *Journal of Contemporary European Studies*, 1–14.

Instagram. (2022). *Report Violations of our Community Guidelines.* Instagram Help Center. Retrieved December 9, 2022, from https://help.instagram.com/contact/383679321740945

International Labour Organization. (2016). *Occupational Safety and Health Management System: An Applied and Training Guide for Medium and Large Companies.* Available online: https://www.ilo.org/wcmsp5/groups/public/---africa/---ro-abidjan/---sro-cairo/documents/publication/wcms_622420.pdf

Jardine, E. (2021). Policing the cybercrime script of darknet drug markets: Methods of effective law enforcement intervention. *American Journal of Criminal Justice, 46*(6), 980–1005. doi:10.100712103-021-09656-3

Jones, A. (2020). *Camming: Money, power, and pleasure in the sex work industry.* NYU Press. doi:10.18574/nyu/9781479842964.001.0001

Kennedy, E. J. (2016). *Digital desire: Commercial, moral, and political economies of sex work and the internet* [Doctoral dissertation]. University of Kansas.

Kethineni, S., & Cao, Y. (2020). The rise in popularity of cryptocurrency and associated criminal activity. *International Criminal Justice Review, 30*(3), 325–344. doi:10.1177/1057567719827051

Keyhani, M., Robinson, M., Lehar, A., & Ashjari, A. (2022). Digital Entrepreneurship and capital acquisition in the global economy. *Digital Entrepreneurship and the Global Economy*, 91-101.

Keyser, M. (2017). The council of Europe convention on cybercrime. In *Computer Crime* (pp. 131–170). Routledge. doi:10.4324/9781315095493-7

Kittichaisaree, K. (2017). Regulation of Cyberspace and Human Rights. In *Public International Law of Cyberspace* (pp. 45–152). Springer. doi:10.1007/978-3-319-54657-5_3

Konrad, H. (2002). Trafficking in human beings-the ugly face of Europe. *Helsinki Monitor, 13*(3), 260–271. doi:10.1163/157181402401452924

Koufopoulou, P., Williams, C. C., Vozikis, A., & Souliotis, K. (2019). Shadow Economy: Definitions, terms & theoretical considerations. *Advances in Management and Applied Economics, 9*(5), 35–57.

Kranrattanasuit, N. (2014). ASEAN and human trafficking: Case studies of Cambodia, Thailand, and Vietnam. Martinus Nijhoff Publishers. doi:10.1163/9789004265189

Kunze, E. I. (2009). Sex trafficking via the internet: How international agreements address the problem and fail to go far enough. *J. High Tech. L., 10*, 241.

Lai, J., & Widmar, N. O. (2021). Revisiting the digital divide in the COVID-19 era. *Applied Economic Perspectives and Policy, 43*(1), 458–464. doi:10.1002/aepp.13104 PMID:33230409

Lamine, W., Anderson, A., Jack, S. L., & Fayolle, A. (2021). Entrepreneurial space and the freedom for entrepreneurship: Institutional settings, policy, and action in the space industry. *Strategic Entrepreneurship Journal, 15*(2), 309–340. doi:10.1002ej.1392

Lavorgna, A. (2015). Organised crime goes online: realities and challenges. *Journal of Money Laundering Control.*

Layton, R., & Elaluf-Calderwood, S. (2019, November). A social economic analysis of the impact of GDPR on security and privacy practices. In *2019 12th CMI Conference on Cybersecurity and Privacy (CMI)* (pp. 1-6). IEEE. 10.1109/CMI48017.2019.8962288

Lee, I. C., & Lewis, M. (2003). Human trafficking from a legal advocate's perspective: History, legal framework and current anti-trafficking efforts. *UC Davis J. Int'l L. & Pol'y, 10*, 169.

Leuprecht, C., Jenkins, C., & Hamilton, R. (2022). Virtual money laundering: policy implications of the proliferation in the illicit use of cryptocurrency. *Journal of Financial Crime.*

Lewis, J. A. (Ed.). (2003). Cyber security: turning national solutions into international cooperation (No. 25). CSIS.

Li, F. (2020). *Team to market (T2M): Creating high performance teams in the digital age*. Academic Press.

Liggett, R., Lee, J. R., Roddy, A. L., & Wallin, M. A. (2020). The dark web as a platform for crime: An exploration of illicit drug, firearm, CSAM, and cybercrime markets. The Palgrave handbook of international cybercrime and cyberdeviance, 91-116.

Lyman, R. N. (2006). Compulsory process in a globalized era: Defendant access to mutual legal assistance treaties. *Va. J. Int'l L.*, *47*, 261.

Mackay, M., Hardesty, B. D., & Wilcox, C. (2020). The intersection between illegal fishing, crimes at sea, and social well-being. *Frontiers in Marine Science*, *7*, 589000. doi:10.3389/fmars.2020.589000

Mancarella, F. (2021). *Human rights-based approach to sex-trafficking of women and girls: the analysis of prostitution policies in Italy, Sweden, and the Netherlands* [Doctoral dissertation].

Marion, N. E. (2010). The Council of Europe's Cyber Crime Treaty: An exercise in Symbolic Legislation. *International Journal of Cyber Criminology*, 4.

Marston, H. R., & van Hoof, J. (2019). "Who doesn't think about technology when designing urban environments for older people?" A case study approach to a proposed extension of the WHO's age-friendly cities model. *International Journal of Environmental Research and Public Health*, *16*(19), 3525. doi:10.3390/ijerph16193525 PMID:31547204

Matolcsi, A., Mulvihill, N., Lilley-Walker, S. J., Lanau, A., & Hester, M. (2021). The current landscape of prostitution and sex work in England and Wales. *Sexuality & Culture*, *25*(1), 39–57. doi:10.100712119-020-09756-y

Matthews, R. (1986). Beyond Wolfenden? Prostitution, Politics and the Law. In R. Matthews & J. Young (Eds.), Confronting Crime (p. 188). Academic Press.

McKee, K. A. (2010). It's 10: 00 PM Do You Know Where Your Children Are. *Regent UL Rev.*, *23*, 311.

McMenzie, L., Cook, I. R., & Laing, M. (2019). Criminological policy mobilities and sex work: Understanding the movement of the 'Swedish model' to Northern Ireland. *British Journal of Criminology*, *59*(5), 1199–1216. doi:10.1093/bjc/azy058

Meneses Falcón, M. D. C., Urío Rodríguez, S. J., & Uroz Olivares, J. (2019). *Financing of trafficking in human beings in Spain*. Academic Press.

Michael, K., & Rose, G. L. (2007). *Human tracking technology in mutual legal assistance and police inter-state cooperation in international crimes*. Academic Press.

Mugarura, N., & Ssali, E. (2020). Intricacies of anti-money laundering and cyber-crimes regulation in a fluid global system. *Journal of Money Laundering Control*, *24*(1), 10–28. doi:10.1108/JMLC-11-2019-0092

Mulvihill, N. (2022). Female Independent Sex Workers. In *Experiences of the Sex Industry* (pp. 18–42). Bristol University Press. doi:10.2307/j.ctv2sjj08k.6

Munro, V. E., & Scoular, J. (2012). Abusing vulnerability? Contemporary law and policy responses to sex work in the UK. *Feminist Legal Studies*, *20*(3), 189–206. doi:10.100710691-012-9213-x

Murphy, A. K., & Venkatesh, S. A. (2006). Vice careers: The changing contours of sex work in New York City. *Qualitative Sociology*, *29*(2), 129–154. doi:10.100711133-006-9012-2

Nadelmann, E. A. (2010). *Cops across borders: The internationalization of US criminal law enforcement*. Penn State Press.

National Rapporteur on Trafficking in Human Beings. (2010). *Trafficking in Human Beings*. Bureau of the Dutch National Rapporteur.

Nguyen, D. H. (2020). International cooperation and mutual legal assistance in criminal matters in handling with transnational wildlife trafficking crimes in Vietnam. In *E3S Web of Conferences* (Vol. 164, p. 11006). EDP Sciences. doi:10.1051/e3sconf/202016411006

O'Neill, M. C. (2011). The EU legal framework on trafficking in human beings: Where to from here–the UK perspective. *Journal of Contemporary European Research*, *7*(4), 452–467. doi:10.30950/jcer.v7i4.376

Omand, D., Bartlett, J., & Miller, C. (2012). Introducing social media intelligence (SOCMINT). *Intelligence and National Security*, *27*(6), 801–823. doi:10.1080/02684527.2012.716965

Organization for Security and Co-operation in Europe (OSCE), Recommendations on enhancing efforts to identify and mitigate risks of trafficking in human beings online as a result of the humanitarian crisis in Ukraine, Publisher, Organization for Security and Co-operation in Europe, 22 April 2022

OSCE Office of the Special Representative and Co-ordinator for Combating Trafficking in Human Beings. (2021). *Discouraging the demand that fosters trafficking for the purpose of sexual exploitation*. OSCE.

Paché, G. (2022). Prostitution of Underage Girls in France: The Hidden Supply Chain Dimensions. *Journal of Marketing Management*, *10*(1), 1–12.

Peppet, S. R. (2012). Prostitution 3.0. *Iowa Law Review*, *98*, 1989.

Polyzoidou, V. (2021). Combatting the Cybercrime: Thoughts Based on the Second Additional Protocol (Draft) to the Budapest Convention on Cybercrime. In *EU Internet Law in the Digital Single Market* (pp. 355-375). Springer.

Proulx, K. (2022). *Anonymity Online and the Perfect Environment for Cybercrime* [Doctoral dissertation]. Utica University.

Prylinski, K. M. (2020). Tech Trafficking: How the internet has transformed sex trafficking. *J. High Tech. L.*, *20*, 338.

Quintel, T. A., & Cole, M. (2018). Transborder Access to e-Evidence by Law Enforcement Agencies: A first comparative view on the Commission's Proposal for a Regulation on a European Preservation/ Production Order and accompanying Directive. SSRN *Electronic Journal.*

Raets, S., & Janssens, J. (2019). The financial approach to tackling trafficking in human beings. In Financing of organised crime: Human trafficking in focus (pp. 97-108). Center for the Study of Democracy (CSD).

Raets, S., & Janssens, J. (2021). Trafficking and technology: Exploring the role of digital communication technologies in the Belgian human trafficking business. *European Journal on Criminal Policy and Research*, *27*(2), 215–238. doi:10.100710610-019-09429-z

Rawat, R., Garg, B., Mahor, V., Telang, S., Pachlasiya, K., & Chouhan, M. (2022). Organ trafficking on the dark web—the data security and privacy concern in healthcare systems. *Internet of Healthcare Things: Machine Learning for Security and Privacy*, 189-216.

Reedy, P. (2020). Interpol review of digital evidence 2016-2019. *Forensic Science International. Synergy*, *2*, 489–520. doi:10.1016/j.fsisyn.2020.01.015 PMID:33385144

Roe-Sepowitz, D. (2019). A six-year analysis of sex traffickers of minors: Exploring characteristics and sex trafficking patterns. *Journal of Human Behavior in the Social Environment*, *29*(5), 608–629. doi:10.1080/10911359.2019.1575315

Ross, E. (2018). Increasing United States-China cooperation on anti-corruption: Reforming mutual legal assitance. *Geo. Wash. L. Rev.*, *86*, 839.

Sanders, T. (2009). UK sex work policy: eyes wide shut to voluntary and indoor sex work. Regulating Sex for Sale: Prostitution Policy Reform in the UK, 67.

Sanders, T., Connelly, L., & King, L. J. (2016). On our own terms: The working conditions of internet-based sex workers in the UK. *Sociological Research Online*, *21*(4), 133–146. doi:10.5153ro.4152

Schrock, W. (2022). Internet-Era Human Trafficking and the Need for a Better International Legal Instrument. *U. Md. LJ Race, Religion, Race, Gender & Class*, *22*, 120.

Scoular, J., & Carline, A. (2014). A critical account of a 'creeping neo-abolitionism': Regulating prostitution in England and Wales. *Criminology & Criminal Justice*, *14*(5), 608–626. doi:10.1177/1748895814543534

Scoular, J., Pitcher, J., Sanders, T., Campbell, R., & Cunningham, S. (2019). Beyond the gaze and well beyond Wolfenden: The practices and rationalities of regulating and policing sex work in the digital age. *Journal of Law and Society*, *46*(2), 211–239. doi:10.1111/jols.12155

Selby, J. (2017). Data localization laws: Trade barriers or legitimate responses to cybersecurity risks, or both? *International Journal of Law and Information Technology*, *25*(3), 213–232. doi:10.1093/ijlit/eax010

Shekhar, B., & Vincent, V. V. (2022). Technology and human trafficking: Reconstructing the nexus. *Urban Crime. International Journal (Toronto, Ont.)*, *3*(1), 65–101.

Shelley, L. (2010). *Human trafficking: A global perspective*. Cambridge University Press. doi:10.1017/CBO9780511760433

Shulzhenko, N., & Romashkin, S. (2020). Internet fraud and transnational organized crime. *Juridical Tribune*, *10*(1), 162–172.

Spiezia, F. (2022, May). International cooperation and protection of victims in cyberspace: welcoming Protocol II to the Budapest Convention on Cybercrime. In *ERA Forum* (Vol. 23, No. 1, pp. 101-108). Springer Berlin Heidelberg. 10.100712027-022-00707-8

Stockhem, O. (2020). *Improving the international regulation of cybersextrafficking of women and children through the use of data science and artificial intelligence* [Doctoral dissertation].

StoykovaR. (2022). The Right to a Fair Trial as a Conceptual Framework for Digital Evidence Rules in Criminal Investigations. *Available at* SSRN 4232504. doi:10.2139/ssrn.4232504

Strohmayer, A., Clamen, J., & Laing, M. (2019, May). Technologies for social justice: Lessons from sex workers on the front lines. In *Proceedings of the 2019 CHI conference on human factors in computing systems* (pp. 1-14). 10.1145/3290605.3300882

Strohmayer, A., Clamen, J., & Laing, M. (2019, May). Technologies for social justice: Lessons from sex workers on the front lines. In *Proceedings of the 2019 CHI conference on human factors in computing systems* (pp. 1-14). 10.1145/3290605.3300882

Tamanaha, B. Z. (2004). *On the rule of law: History, politics, theory*. Cambridge University Press. doi:10.1017/CBO9780511812378

Taras, D. (2001). *Power and Betrayal in the Canadian Media: Updated Edition*. University of Toronto Press.

Tekic, Z., & Koroteev, D. (2019). From disruptively digital to proudly analog: A holistic typology of digital transformation strategies. *Business Horizons*, *62*(6), 683–693. doi:10.1016/j.bushor.2019.07.002

The Inter-Agency Coordination Group against Trafficking of Persons (ICAT). (2019). *Human Trafficking and Technology: Trends, Challenges and Opportunities*. The Inter-Agency Coordination Group against Trafficking of Persons (ICAT). Retrieved from https://icat.un.org/sites/g/files/tmzbdl461/files/human_trafficking_and_technology_trends_challenges_and_opportunities_web.pdf

Thurnhofer, M. K. (2022). *What we keep in the shadows: Sex work in Germany during the COVID-19 pandemic*. Academic Press.

Torn, A., & Lister, K. (2018, July). Emancipatory sex work research: narratives of a hidden population. *Narrative Matters Annual Conference*.

Treloar, C., Cama, E., Stardust, Z., & Kim, J. (2021). 'I wouldn't call the cops if I was being bashed to death': Sex work, whore stigma and the criminal legal system. *International Journal for Crime. Justice and Social Democracy*, *10*(3), 142–157.

Tyagi, A. K., Fernandez, T. F., Mishra, S., & Kumari, S. (2021). Intelligent automation systems at the core of industry 4.0. In *International conference on intelligent systems design and applications* (pp. 1-18). Springer. 10.1007/978-3-030-71187-0_1

UN Office on Drugs and Crime (UNODC). (2020). *Global Report on Trafficking in Persons*. UNODC.

UNODC. (2015). *Study on the effects of new information technologies on the abuse and exploitation of children*. https://www.unodc.org/documents/ Cybercrime/Study_on_the_Effects.pdf

van der Wilt, H. (2018). Extradition and mutual legal assistance in the draft Convention on Crimes Against Humanity. *Journal of International Criminal Justice*, *16*(4), 795–812. doi:10.1093/jicj/mqy037

van Rij, J., & McAlister, R. (2020). Using Criminal Routines and Techniques to Predict and Prevent the Sexual Exploitation of Eastern-European Women in Western Europe. The Palgrave International Handbook of Human Trafficking, 1689-1708.

Vivrette, A. T. (2022). *Approach to the Global Human Trafficking Crisis: Analyzing Applications of Social Network Analysis* [Doctoral dissertation].

Vlase, I., & Preoteasa, A. M. (2022). Flexi (nse) curity in adult webcamming: Romanian women's experiences selling digital sex services under platform capitalism. *Gender, Place and Culture*, *29*(5), 603–624. doi:10.1080/0966369X.2021.1878114

Volodko, A., Cockbain, E., & Kleinberg, B. (2020). "Spotting the signs" of trafficking recruitment online: Exploring the characteristics of advertisements targeted at migrant job-seekers. *Trends in Organized Crime*, *23*(1), 7–35. doi:10.100712117-019-09376-5

Waller, L., Johnson, S. C., Satchell, N., Gordon, D., Daley, G. L. K., Reid, H., ... Linton, P. (2022). Woe is the dark Web: the main challenges that governments of the Commonwealth Caribbean will face in combating dark Web-facilitated criminal activities. *Transforming Government: People, Process and Policy*.

Wieltschnig, P., Muraszkiewicz, J., & Fenton, T. (2021). Without data we are fighting blind: the need for human security data in defence sector responses to human trafficking. *Journal of Modern Slavery: A Multidisciplinary Exploration of Human Trafficking Solutions, 6*(3).

Wolfenden Committee, Report of the Committee on Homosexual Offences and Prostitution (1957; Cmnd. 247) para. 60.

Woods, A. K. (2015). *Data beyond borders: Mutual legal assistance in the internet era.* Academic Press.

Woods, A. K. (2016). Against data exceptionalism. *Stanford Law Review*, *68*, 729.

Yar, M. (2012). E-Crime 2.0: The criminological landscape of new social media. *Information & Communications Technology Law*, *21*(3), 207–219. doi:10.1080/13600834.2012.744224

KEY TERMS AND DEFINITIONS

Commercial Sex: Activities, such as sexual intercourse, which are sold as services for remuneration.

Commercial Sex Provider: A person who offers and provides commercial sex services.

Illicit Economy: A system of state-prohibited economic activity, such as trafficking in human beings, arms smuggling, money laundering and cybercrime.

Illicit Entrepreneurship: Entrepreneurship that operates within the illicit economy.

Open-Source Intelligence: Open-source intelligence (OSINT) is the collecting and analysis of data from open sources (covert and public sources) to gather actionable intelligence. OSINT is typically utilised within national security and law enforcement, as well as some corporate intelligence operations.

Technology-Facilitated Trafficking: Trafficking practices which are enhanced by the use of digital technology, such as the internet and devices which access the internet.

TOR Network: A network which enables users to access online materials anonymously. It is intended for TCP connections and facilitates the use of anonymous web browsers, IRC, instant messaging, P2P, SSH and email.

Chapter 7
Shifting Paradigms in the Rapidly Developing Global Digital Ecosystem: A GCC Perspective

Mohammed Ali
University of Salford, UK

ABSTRACT

Despite growing scholarly interest in the impact of the digital economy on economic recovery in the midst of the current global crisis and regional development situations, research on the effects of the global crisis on developing digital economies in the Gulf Cooperation Council Region (GCC) and the resulting future uncertainty is limited. Thus, this chapter examines the developing GCC countries' digital infrastructure, openness, innovation environment, competitiveness, and digital divide to determine how the digital economy affects economic growth during a global crisis. This chapter demonstrates how the GCC economies are still developing and attempting to diversify away from oil, with the digital economy serving as a major driving force in achieving the region's goals. Furthermore, while the recent pandemic has harmed GCC digital industries, it has also increased demand, creating an excellent opportunity to develop the region's digital infrastructure to compete with developed digital economies. Policy implications have been proposed as a potential impact mechanism.

INTRODUCTION

The Internet, big data, 5G, and artificial intelligence (AI) are just a few of the digital technologies that are hastening deep integration across industries and ushering in the era of the digital economy (Ali, 2019, 2020; M. Ali, 2019a, 2019b, 2021; Ali, 2022; Ali & Abdel-Haq, 2021; Ali & Edghiem, 2021; Ali et al., 2022; M. B. Ali, 2021; Ali et al., 2020a, 2020b; Afonasova et al., 2019; Williams, 2021). The digital economy has also become a critical area of cooperation for developing countries, particularly those operating in the Gulf Cooperation Council (GCC) countries (Aidrous et al., 2021). The GCC is

DOI: 10.4018/978-1-6684-7416-7.ch007

a regional organisation and political and economic alliance comprised of six member states: Bahrain, Kuwait, Oman, Qatar, Saudi Arabia, and the United Arab Emirates (UAE) (Al-Sayed, 2013). These member countries are developing countries that are currently undergoing socioeconomic, political, and environmental reform in order to compete on the global stage with thriving developed economies.

The digital economy can optimise the industrial structure and increase employment opportunities by leveraging ICT, the Internet, and other forms of smart technology, thereby boosting growth. Although global crisis situations such as the recent COVID-19 pandemic have enabled the digital economy to reduce economic losses and accelerate economic recovery through online entrepreneurship and other digital business opportunities, they have also caused significant disruptions to the global economy due to their effects on production, supply chains, businesses, and financial markets (Gozgor & Lau, 2021; Zhai et al., 2021). The efforts of policymakers to limit social mobility by imposing stringent regulations have the unintended consequence of dampening overall economic activity.

The digital economy, on the other hand, has created a new window of opportunity for the digital transformation of other industries due to its technological advantages and inter-industry integration. In comparison to the traditional economy, the digital sector acts as a vital stabiliser and is thus regarded as a critical response to the crisis and a potential economic growth driver. However, developing countries in the GCC with weaker infrastructures and social development continue to have vastly different levels of digital economic development due to the process of digitalization being often seen simply as the introduction of specific technologies and not as a way of transformation, as well as the process of transformation being hampered by established obsolete technologies and a lack of personnel (Aidrous et al., 2021), resulting in unequal digital development opportunities.

In light of the ongoing trend toward digital transformation amidst global crises (e.g., regional conflicts, pandemics, famine, and crime), it is critical to assess the state of the digital economy in developing countries in the GCC to shed light on the mechanism by which it contributes to economic growth and to define the effects of global crises on digital economy-related sectors. This can serve as a policy reference for bridging the "digital divide" between developing and developed countries and strengthening digital economic cooperation among developing countries amidst global crises.

As new technologies such as big data, the cloud, and the Internet of Things emerge, ICT is increasingly viewed as the "engine" driving economic growth (Appiah-Otoo & Song, 2021), and the digital economy could aid in economic expansion by increasing the productivity of key resources such as capital and labour (Pan et al., 2022). Furthermore, the digital economy represents a paradigm shift in how economic growth is achieved; as a new development model, it will have a positive impact on employment and industrial structure, which will affect economic growth (Pan et al., 2022), yet there is a dearth of knowledge about the mechanism that produces this effect. Although scholarly interest in the impact of the digital economy on economic recovery amidst contemporary global crisis and regional development situations has grown, research on assessing the shifting paradigms in the rapidly developing digital economy, or in this case, the effects of global crisis situations on developing digital economies, is scarce.

Existing literature has revealed a gap pertaining to the impact of the digital economy on economic growth in developing regions of the GCC amidst global crisis situations and regional developments. As a result, the digital economies of these countries face an uncertain future. The contributions to filling the literature gap are twofold:

1. Explore the variations in the digital infrastructure, openness, innovation environment, competitiveness, and digital divide of developing countries in the GCC

2. How these variations can help to uncover the impact mechanism of the digital economy on economic growth during a global crisis.

These contributions can set a good example for how the digital economy can be used to promote high-quality economic growth in developing countries in the GCC. As a result, policymakers will have a better understanding of how to adopt a digital economy mechanism to respond to current global crises and regional development in order to limit future economic damage and accelerate digital industry transformation.

Related Work

Following the agricultural and industrial economies, the digital economy has emerged in recent years as a new economic structure (Pan et al., 2022). Tapscott (2014) proposed the concept of the digital economy, claiming that in the age of networked intelligence, the networking of humans through technology is just as important as the networking of technology. As a result of the integration of digital and network technologies, the digital economy has become more prominent in economic and social activities, giving rise to a richer connotation. The digital economy comprises three components: e-business infrastructure, e-business, and e-commerce. Some academics saw the digital economy as a dynamic rather than a static process (Carlsson, 2004). In recent years, the term "digital economy" has been coined to refer to a segment of the economy that is digitising more broadly than a small portion (Bukht & Heeks, 2017; Williams, 2021). For example, the Organization for Economic Cooperation and Development (OECD) defined "digital economy" as "the digital transformation of economic and social development" and included all traditional industries that were digitising and networking as part of the term (OECD, 2014). Alternatively, the G20 Digital Economy Development and Cooperation Initiative refers to the term "digital economy" as a wide range of economic activities that use digitised knowledge and information as the primary factor of production, modern information networks as a significant area of activity, and effective use of ICT as a key driver of productivity growth and economic structural optimization (G20, 2016). As a result of these ambiguous definitions, the digital economy has no universal definition.

Previous research has shown that both developed and developing countries regard the digital economy as the primary driver of economic growth (Cheng et al., 2021; Pradhan et al., 2019). The digital economy, which is primarily based on ICT, contributes to increased labour and capital productivity as well as lower prices for goods and services (Dahlman et al., 2016). For example, Seo et al. (2009) used a cumulative growth model to examine the positive correlation between ICT investment and economic growth in 29 countries, and they discovered that even countries with low productivity levels could catch up to developed nations by leveraging ICT's knowledge spillover effects. Furthermore, Vu (2011) discovered that ICT can increase output by promoting technological innovation, improving decision-making quality, and lowering production costs. Because of the rapid development of digital technologies such as ICT, more researchers are focusing on the impact of the digital economy on consumer surplus, the e-commerce supply chain, and smart cities (Kitchin, 2015; Liu et al., 2021; Pan et al., 2022). Academics have been studying the impact of the digital economy on economic recovery, particularly since global issues such as the COVID-19 outbreak. The digital economy has had a significant positive impact on economic growth, value-added distribution in global value chains, and pandemic prevention and control (Aidrous et al., 2021; Chauhan et al., 2021; Pan et al., 2022). During the COVID-19 pandemic, a significant portion of the resources reallocated from traditional industries went to digital services, which became a key factor in accelerated growth (Ganichev & Koshovets, 2021). Jiang (2020) also discovered that digital technologies served as the long-term technological foundation for Internet-based business and consumption, enabling short-term pandemic response strategies. Although global crisis situations like COVID-19 served as a catalyst for the adoption of various technologies, the process was contentious, and the outcomes were uncertain. Other scholars, however, have suggested that the digital economy may be harmful to economic growth, particularly in the absence of economic transition (Albiman & Sulong, 2017; Amankwah-Amoah et al., 2021; Nchofoung & Asongu, 2022).

The above literature has revealed some key variations, which are used as the key themes to fulfil the contributions of this chapter (see Table 1).

Table 1. Key variations in the digital economy

Theme	Description
Digital infrastructure	Digital Infrastructure serves as the foundation for the development of places where people want to live, work, and visit.
Openness	Willingness to compete the world stage with digital products and services produced by digital industry
Innovation environment	Extent and capacity of a country to adopt, implement and utilise technologies
Competitiveness	Competing with other digital infrastructures of other countries
Digital divide	Unequal access to digital technologies

In the post-COVID-19 era, the digital economy can both "boost" the local economy and pose a threat to other industries. Based on the body of existing literature, this chapter identifies some research gaps in the current literature. First, there is still disagreement about the definition of the "digital economy." While the current literature focuses on the effects of ICT on economic development in terms of the number of mobile subscribers, fixed broadband Internet users, and Internet users, these indicators do not fully capture the broader implications of the digital economy. The majority of studies on the impact of digitalization on economic development have yielded ambiguous results. Few studies, however, have looked at how the digital economy is influencing the economic development of developing national economies, particularly those that are emerging in the GCC (e.g., Saudi Arabia's 2030 vision aiming to promote economic diversification and less dependence on oil). The GCC member states are gradually making the digital economy a key area of cooperation and analysing how the digital economy has impacted their economic growth can serve as a guide for the economy's recovery and expansion post-COVID-19. More importantly, while some researchers have acknowledged that the epidemic has created new opportunities and challenges for the digital economy, there have been few studies that assess how global crisis situations have affected the digital economies of the GCC through the lens of digital infrastructure, openness, innovation environment, competitiveness, and the digital divide (see Figure 1).

Figure 1. Conceptual model

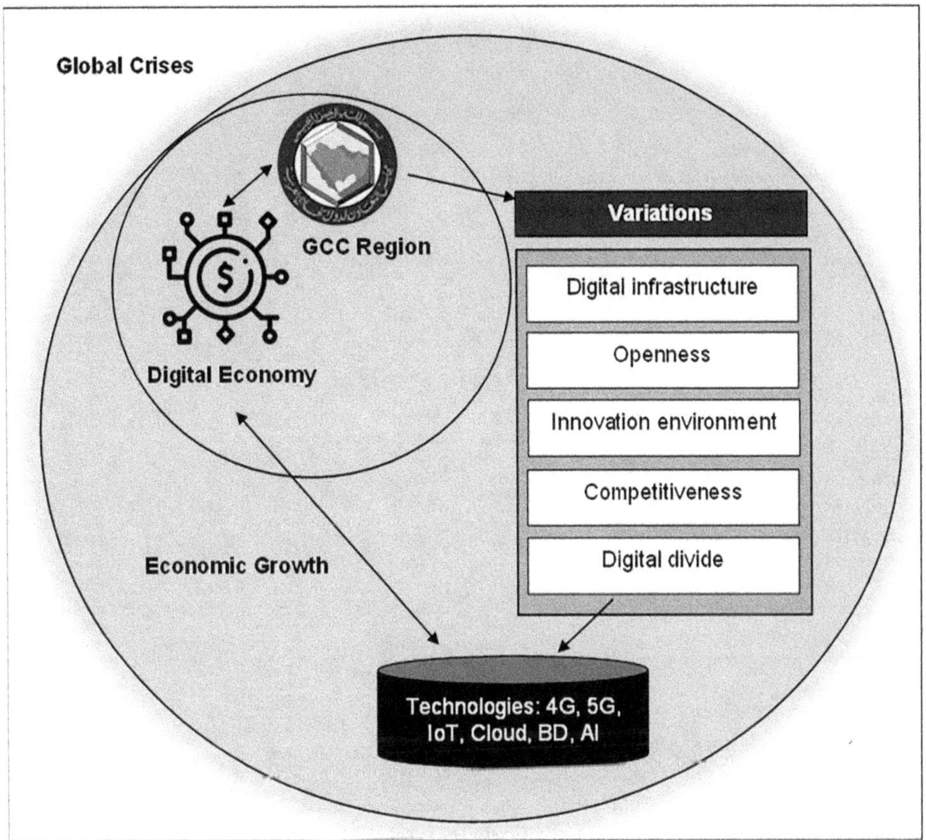

VARIATIONS IN THE DEVELOPING GLOBAL DIGITAL ECONOMY

Digital Infrastructure

The transition to the model of the digital economy is implemented as part of national development strategies in the GCC countries, unlike many developed nations where digitalization issues are reflected in specific government programmes and strategies. The successes of the monarchies in the Gulf have varied. In nations with more developed and diversified economies, digitalization is occurring faster and more actively. Figure 2 shows the penetration of Internet usage among GCC members, showing that the region has come a long way since the 2000s compared to 2022, meaning that their digital infrastructure has shown some positive growth within the past few decades. Saudi Arabia has seen the best growth, with over 35 million people having been exposed to an online presence (Internet World Stats, 2022).

Bahrain has started to actively use the money it has accrued from the sale of oil in recent decades to modernise its economy and enhance social and political life. It caused the economy of Bahrain to be restructured and new technologies to be implemented in order to boost economic growth. Bahrain's government started to alter its approach and adopt a more varied approach. The e-government (eGov) programme is also a part of the Economic Vision 2030 (Aidrous et al., 2021) (see Figure 3).

Figure 2. Digital infrastructure of GCC
Source: Internet World Stats (2022)

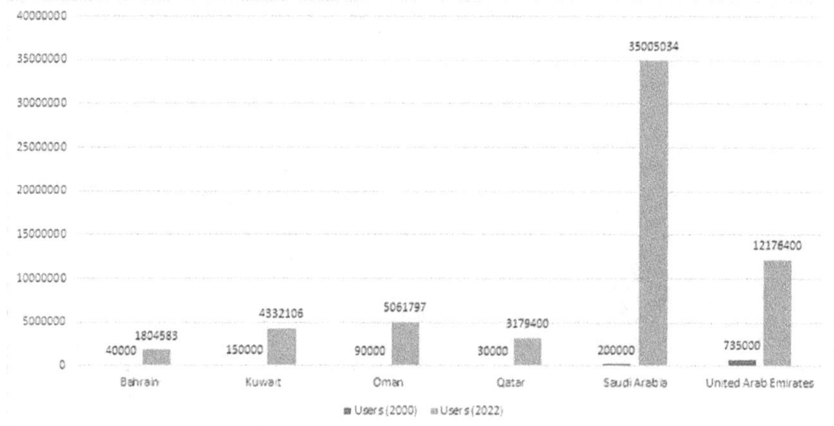

Figure 3. eGov strategy of Bahrain

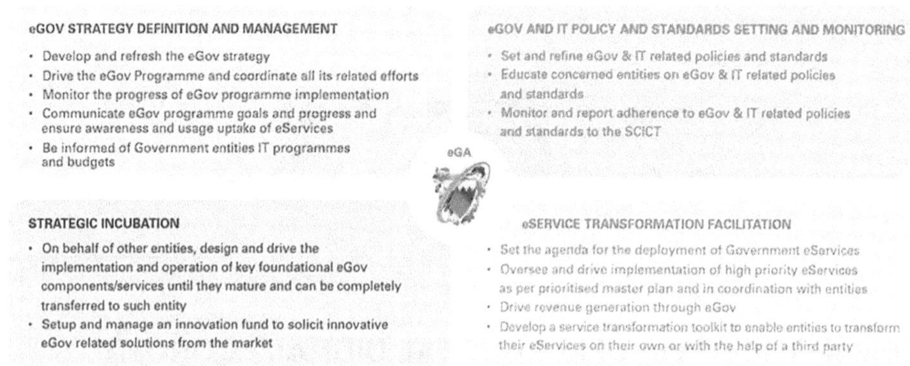

The eGov initiative aims to enhance public Internet services. The plan's level of customer satisfaction must be maintained at 90% or higher. Additionally, it is anticipated that 50% of governmental organisations will communicate with citizens on a weekly basis via social media (Bahrain eGov report, 2016). One of the main objectives of the Bahraini government is to increase the possibility of developing new Internet services and enhancing existing Internet services. Powerful technologies will support the new strategy, assisting in the diversification of the economy. The Kingdom will contribute money to creative projects. The state and private businesses will collaborate to create the eGov projects, which will be overseen by government committees and managed through business IT planning. Online help services are used to manage all electronic services.

Like Bahrain, the government of Qatar made the decision to alter its approach to creating a diversified economy. The gap between the present and the future is being bridged by the Qatar National Program 2030. Qatar keeps making investments in its people so that everyone can take part in the growth of the nation's social, political, and economic life. In order to build a dynamic and diversified economy where the private sector plays a significant role, it is important to create world-class infrastructure (Qatar national vision, 2018). According to the Government of Qatar, the national concept of the state should be based on four pillars: human development, social development, economic development, and environmental development. A safe and stable society, the provision of high-quality services to meet the needs of the population, the preservation of Qatar's heritage and the strengthening of its Arabic and Islamic identity, and the empowerment of women are the key factors. The new Digital Incubation Center was established by the Government of Qatar to aid in the development of new technologies in order to accomplish the aforementioned objectives. The development of technological innovations is the goal of the Digital Incubation Center. In particular, it enables young people to start and grow a tech-related business. The center's goal is to develop technology with the aid of private businesses. The same as in Bahrain, the Qatar e-Government 2020 Strategy was developed. Future residents of Qatar should enjoy better lives thanks to the country's strategy (Aidrous et al., 2021). In general, technology makes life simpler for regular people. Without leaving their homes, citizens will be able to access electronic services via the Internet. This will especially benefit the private sector. The management of an organization's government obligations will be simpler for registered organisations. Time will be saved, which may speed up profit-making and enable them to increase their tax contributions more quickly. Additionally, the bureaucratic time lag should be reduced.

In Kuwait, the country's modernization is primarily focused on creating an environment that supports balanced human development while preserving social values, national identity, and Arab and Islamic cultural values, bolstering the democratic system, adhering to the constitution, and advancing justice (New Kuwait Vision, 2019). While big businesses and government organisations work to boost efficiency and productivity through an expanding number of solutions that streamline processes and enable real-time analysis of consumer behaviour, the state is increasing funding to create an ecosystem that will help to kickstart the development of new technologies. According to the National Development Plan, the government wants to increase investment in their nation to boost competitiveness. Kuwait has started improving its laws, public administration, infrastructure, sustainable habitat, human capital, and position in the world in order to achieve this goal.

In the UAE, it has become one of the GCC's most diverse economies thanks to investments in new technology, particularly smart cities, with goal to build them to improve infrastructure in existing cities (Rajan & Aldhaheri, 2019; Samad & Azar, 2018). UAE is also investing in tourism, as well as desalination plants that have been built for agricultural use, located in arid regions with very little rainfall and no rivers. These plants now generate income from the cultivation of dates, tobacco, melons, and various fruits and vegetables. According to the Vision 2021 programme (UAE Vision, 2010), investing in a child's education is the best way to help a country develop as a whole. The government of the United Arab Emirates is currently at the forefront of digitalization in the Middle East and is comparable to the global digital vanguard in a number of ways (see Figure 3). A productive and competitive economy based on entrepreneurs in a business-friendly environment where the public and private sectors will form useful partnerships is the foundation of the Vision 2021 programme. This programme is based on this ideology. For instance, Dubai Science Park will increase Visions 2021's capabilities. The park is home to 350 national and international companies that work to advance technology in the areas of life sciences, energy, and the environment (Aidrous et al., 2021).

Oil extraction and export have only recently been the sole drivers of the Sultanate of Oman's economy; in 2018, a policy of economic diversification was adopted. Development of the metallurgical sector, tourism, and gas production are among its objectives (Digital Oman Strategy, 2018). In 2008, the Sultan of Oman gave the government instructions to streamline procedures, integrate technology into people's daily lives, and concentrate on providing public services electronically. To support individuals with innovative ideas and small and medium-sized businesses, an incubator was established in Oman. The incubation centre assists businesses in securing their first orders while also offering technical business training for the real world. This will encourage the growth of domestic technologies generally and boost investments from both domestic and foreign businesses.

In Saudi Arabia, a highly developed and sustainable communications infrastructure must be built in order to achieve quick results and changes, inspiring small and medium-sized businesses to launch new ICT goods and services (Vision 2030, 2016; 2020). The direction of the educational system has also changed to emphasise the growth of students' ICT skills. Industry digitalization will ultimately result in higher levels of competition. Since the entire chain, from the moment a product or service is created to the end use of the technology, will be transparent, ICT will aid business processes in generating value more quickly (Al Naimi, 2021).

Figure 4. Pillars and national priorities of the UAE 2021 vision

		PILLARS			
	United in Responsibility	United in Destiny	United in Knowledge	United in Prosperity	
		NATIONAL PRIORITIES			
Cohesive Society & Preserved Identity	Safe Public & Fair Judiciairy	Competitive Knowledge Economy	First-Rate Education System	World-Class Healthcare	Sustainable Environment & Infrastructure

Source: UAE 2021 Vision.

Openness

The GCC member states have recently opened up more about promoting their nations on the global economic stage in an effort to diversify their economies and reduce their reliance on oil. The GCC has not been as competitive on the digital front because of its subpar global economic standing. GCC members like the UAE and Saudi Arabia have impressive technological infrastructures for developing countries, making it an attractive prospect to draw in new revenue sources from Western nations.

To encourage innovation and diversification from oil-based economies, one of the pillars of the national strategies of the majority of GCC countries is building an "Open Data" economy. For instance, big data has gained a lot of attention in the past ten years as many nations seek to gain a competitive edge in this emerging sector. For governments all over the world, this disruptive technology presents a number of opportunities: it can help improve decision-making and service delivery and also support the expansion of a multibillion-dollar industry (Jackson & Dunn-Jensen, 2021; Zhong et al., 2017). Achieving tangible benefits, nations like the UK, the US, and Australia have already demonstrated measurable progress in the implementation of their own Big Data initiatives.

From a regional perspective, the GCC governments have established bold goals for themselves to become leaders in this digital revolution. The majority of GCC nations have acknowledged the significance of this disruptive technology and have developed strategies that look to the future (such as the UAE Smart Data Strategy, Tasmu Qatar, KSA Strategy, and Smart Dubai) to capitalise on the opportunities presented by big data. Some of these nations are still in the planning stage and are putting the finishing touches on practical applications. Gulf nations profit from specific advantages that help them take advantage of big data opportunities. These advantages include having an effective legal framework, committed leadership, and a foundation of cutting-edge infrastructure and technology (Deloitte Report, 2019). As a result, it is crucial for GCC nations to move quickly past the planning stage and begin putting into place the crucial foundations needed to make it possible for Big Data applications to be used at the government level.

Governments in the GCC have acknowledged the potential of big data to spur economic expansion, improve decision-making, and produce competitive advantages in both the public and private sectors. To start their Big Data transformation journeys, they have created elaborate plans. As a result, compared to international standards, GCC countries have progressed through different stages of their roadmap and still have additional milestones to hit. The GCC governments are currently approaching the potential of big data. Significant work has been put into developing comprehensive Big Data strategies and programmes, as well as tactical directions. Each of these nations took a different tack: Examples include the Smart City Strategy for Dubai, the Smart Program for Qatar (TASMU), Bahrain Open Data, and the Open and Big Data Strategies for Saudi Arabia. The GCC nations have prioritised big data on their agendas in anticipation of it becoming a potent tool for realising national visions.

Big Data is being used more effectively by implementing the required technology architecture and analytical capabilities. Few governments, though, have started initiatives to create data registries, standards, and classifications to improve data accessibility and quality. The region's data quality is inconsistent, has scant metadata, and even still exists in non-digital form, making it difficult to draw insightful conclusions.

The GCC governments have recognised the need to develop data specialists' capabilities, train public servants, and update existing educational curricula in order to prepare the current and future generations to handle big data. One of these initiatives in the public sector gave civil servants the tools they needed to use data to deliver higher-quality, more effective services (Deloitte Report, 2019). To promote data science skills in Dubai, enhance community collaboration within the data science community, and identify opportunities to strengthen the data ecosystem, Smart Dubai, for instance, recently partnered with the private sector to build the Data Lab. Government transformation is difficult, though, due to the region's small pool of data science talent.

When using big data to deliver individual services, a delicate balance must be struck between data collection and utilisation, as well as data privacy and security (Tawalbeh & Saldamli, 2019). Given the recent cyberattacks that governments around the world have experienced, cyber security has quickly gained importance for GCC countries. Governments in the GCC are making significant investments to protect national security and inform the general public about the value of cyber security. New laws are being developed by governments throughout the GCC to safeguard not only the interests of individual citizens but also the system's overall security and robustness. The Qatari law N13 of 2016 is an illustration of one of these data protection laws. The law aims to safeguard consumers in an online environment that is becoming more dangerous and to give them confidence in the protection of their personal data. Similar initiatives are also being made in Saudi Arabia and UAE, where new data protection laws are anticipated to be put into effect (Deloitte Report, 2019).

The GCC governments have a crucial understanding before they start their big data journeys: Big Data is a strategic component of the future that goes beyond technology. Before the GCC nations can reap the rewards of big data, five significant obstacles must be overcome:

Figure 5. Big data initiatives in GCC countries

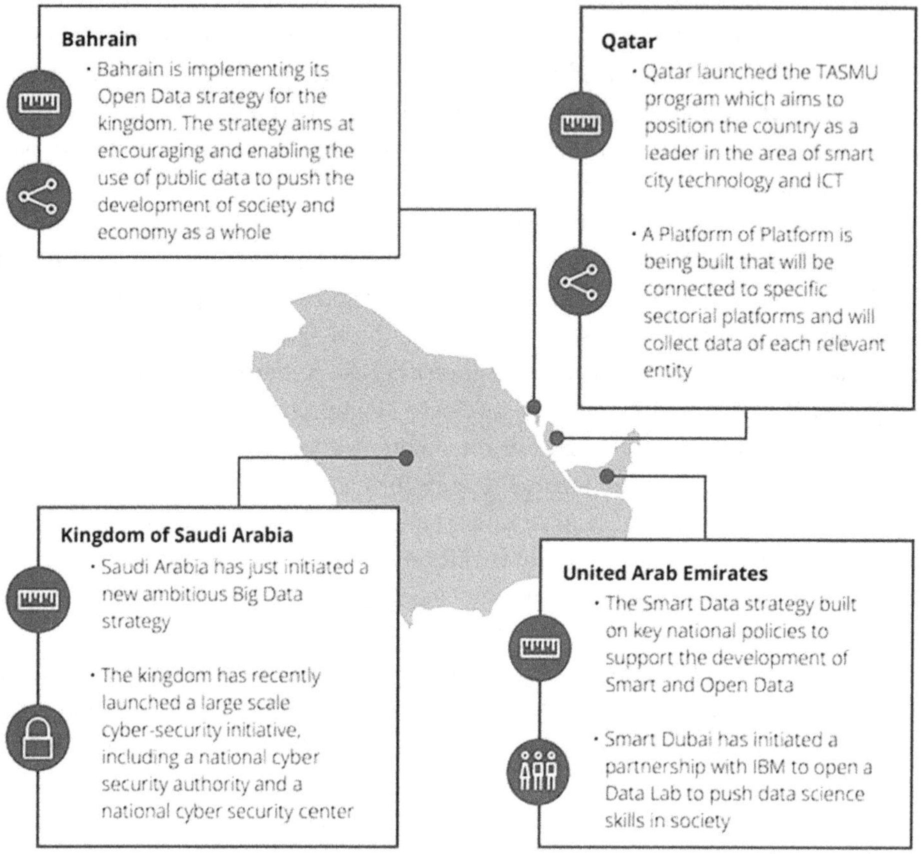

- Limited partnership to profit from data with businesses and entrepreneurs.
- Due to concerns about data residency, the cloud is out of the picture, which drives up the cost of big data.
- Investment still prioritises technology over use cases.
- Expensive human capital because it takes a long time to develop local capabilities and there is a lack of talent locally (and to some extent globally).
- Data usage across the government remains constrained due to fragmentation.

These consequences ultimately prevent stakeholders from realising the full potential of such an investment and, in some cases, discourage others from participating in the project.

Innovation Environment and Competitiveness

The ideas of digital infrastructure and openness have demonstrated the relationship between the innovation environment and member states of the GCC's competitiveness on the global economic stage. A nation's capacity for innovation is crucial for fostering competitiveness and growth in a region like the GCC.

The GCC countries have created national innovation policy programmes because they recognise that merely adopting new technologies is no longer sufficient to sustain high income levels and foster economic growth (Miniaoui & Schiliro, 2016). However, a complex interaction between all innovation actors, policies, and institutions leads to an innovation system approach. This strategy contends that, in addition to encouraging research, the framework conditions for innovation—such as the business environment, access to finance, competition, and trade openness—must be strengthened. Another essential requirement is collaboration, so clusters with the innovation actors involved, public-private partnerships, and collaborative research projects should all be prioritised. Strong human capital and a research base that incorporates knowledge absorption, sophisticated firms and markets, innovation linkages, and research infrastructures are required. A law that promotes future innovation and related markets, as well as the international harmonisation of regulations for new technologies so they can spread more quickly, are additional important factors. As a result, an innovation policy has many facets and encompasses numerous policy areas (such as international trade and education) as well as numerous institutional reforms.

The region can develop advanced digital economies, adding $255 billion to the regional GDP by 2030, with the right policies and by cultivating tech leaders (Harper, 2022). The GCC region's digital economy is growing quickly. However, the region's emphasis is still skewed toward traditional IT, and its tech market is less developed than in other parts of the world. In closing this gap, the emergence of GCC tech champions can be very important. The economies of scale and scope that are required for innovation, talent attraction, job creation, significant investment, and exports are provided by tech champions. The digital economy is expanding six times as quickly as the traditional economy on a global scale. Because of their tech leaders, the superpowers of China and the US currently hold a commanding position within the digital economy. They control 90% of the market capitalization of the top 70 digital businesses worldwide. Even though the GCC's digital economy is expanding quickly, the region will not become globally competitive on its own. The majority of its product development and service delivery is still handled by foreign corporations, and there is still little investment in R&D and start-ups. According to research by Strategy & Middle East, the region's GDP could increase by a cumulative 5% by 2030 with the aid of tech champions, resulting in the creation of about 600,000 technology jobs (Harper, 2022). A large portion of this growth will be driven by digital solutions, including emerging technologies. Developing an anchor portfolio and value propositions, scaling up and expanding geographically, and diversifying and monetizing at scale are the three key stages in the development of a technology champion. To develop a robust digital economy and promote national resilience, Gulf nations must cultivate and support tech leaders. They are primarily buyers and adopters right now, which is an untenable situation. Instead, they should act as tech disruptors by promoting the growth of their own tech leaders, with the assistance of the government.

The GCC nations have not innovated well enough so far. However, in this stage of decline and high volatility in oil prices, the GCC governments are making a great effort to develop and implement national strategies to improve their innovative capacity. Technology, innovation, and high-quality education are major forces in a developed knowledge- and innovation-driven economy, which is the type of economy that GCC countries are attempting to emulate. Therefore, education is crucial for innovation, but it is also a prerequisite for entrepreneurship. The diversification and growth of the GCC countries depend on improving the educational system. In order to foster a favourable environment for innovation, governments in the Gulf region can significantly contribute to the creation of a successful innovation strategy. Furthermore, a nation that seeks to become knowledge-based can greatly benefit from the triple helix approach in terms of generating knowledge and innovation. The GCC countries have a fairly high propensity for entrepreneurship and self-employment, but there are a number of obstacles to starting your own business, the most common of which is a lack of funding. Additionally, GCC nations must support high-tech start-ups as well as SMEs that are open to international markets. UAE is rapidly evolving and diversifying in the right direction. Given the natural differences and varied vocations, all other GCC nations should soon follow.

Digital Divide

As the digital divide grows, developing nations will likely be left behind, which will have a negative effect. Making an effective digital strategy that improves digitization and deepens integration in the digital economy is a challenge that many developing nations, including those in the GCC, must overcome.

Oil and gas production and export revenues have shaped the GCC region's economic development for several decades, with little to no effort being made to diversify output in non-energy sectors (Al-Roubaie, 2021). Rental economies are unsustainable to reduce the risk of global shocks and maintain financial stability, as demonstrated by global crises like the 2020 pandemic. The pandemic's detrimental effects on the regional economies serve as a stark reminder of the region's weak productive capacity and low level of capabilities to reduce the risk of external shocks and maintain growth. To overcome these obstacles and close the digital divide between developed nations with robust digital economies and oil-producing nations, they must develop strategies that allow their economies to take part in the Fourth Industrial Revolution.

A high-tech strategy project for the German government gave rise to Industry 4.0 in 2011 (Grabowska et al., 2022). It developed cyber-physical systems (CPS) into smart factories and cyber-physical production systems (CPPS). Through real-time communication and collaboration between "manufacturing things," CPPS can make intelligent decisions in Industry 4.0, enabling the flexible production of high-quality, customised products at scale. With the adoption of Industry 4.0 by businesses, the Fifth Industrial Revolution (Industry 5.0) began. By respecting the limits of our planet and putting employee well-being first, Industry 5.0 acknowledges the power of the industry to achieve societal goals beyond employment and economic growth and transform into a resilient provider of prosperity. Industry 5.0 is based on the observation that Industry 4.0 prioritises social justice and sustainability over production efficiency and flexibility through the use of digitalization and AI-driven technologies. In order to help the industry serve humanity within the limits of the planet, Industry 5.0 places a strong emphasis on research and innovation (Chauhan et al., 2021; Duggal et al., 2022).

Industry 4.0 transforms human-technology and human-environment interactions, as well as health management, work organisation, lifelong learning, career path models, team structures, and knowledge management, to create new socio-technical infrastructures that can help close the digital divide between countries. However, the increased use of robot-assisted systems and augmented reality (AR) to give workers real-time information to improve decision-making and work procedures reflects the second and third design principles and is expected to change the roles of workers (information transparency and technical assistance).

Industry 4.0, which is driven by technology, and Industry 5.0, which is driven by values, coexist, suggesting that they should be considered together. Given that the term "techno-social system" has been around for a while, it is possible that we are currently experiencing a techno-social revolution (or social-technological revolution), with technology serving as the enabling tools and societal needs serving as the ultimate goal. Many businesses have a journey to complete in the Industry 4.0 era. To emphasise

Industry 5.0 values like sustainability, human-centricity, and resilience, it might need to be modified or repurposed. A company should only make one journey.

Figure 6. Digital divide between developing GCC nations and developed nations
Source: Strategy (2020)

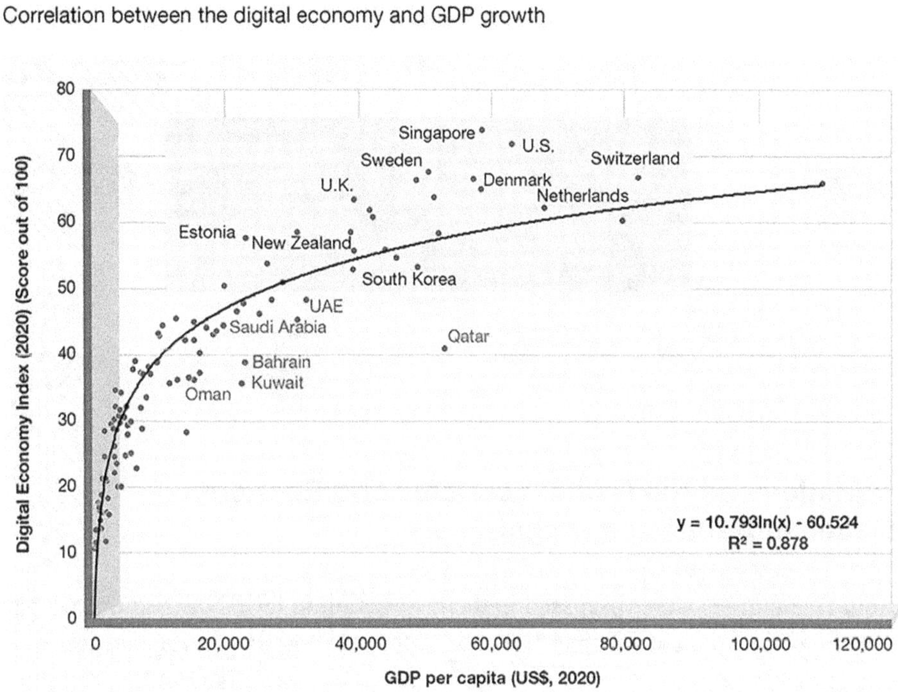

For the GCC, specifically the KSA, UAE, Qatar, Kuwait, Bahrain, and Oman, adoption of Industry 4.0 is still in its early stages due to their economies' ongoing development and the need for economic diversification (Shaiful Fitri Abdul Rahman et al., 2022). This is supported by recent figures shown in Figure 6, which suggest that the GCC is falling behind in the digital economy (Strategy, 2020). Therefore, it is impossible to know with certainty how Industry 4.0 will help close the digital divide. However, recent statistics (see Figure 7) are beginning to show that the digital divide is narrowing in the GCC due to the improved digital transformation efforts in the region with Saudi Arabia (59.26%) and UAE (66.22%) having the greatest growth (Srinivasan, 2022). This growth has been attributed to the roles of science and technology in developing research, development, and innovation (RDI) capacity in order to establish national innovation systems (NIS) for the GCC, which has seen considerable growth.

Global crises, such as the recent COVID-19 pandemic, have hampered and delayed the GCC countries' development in the digital sphere. For that reason, the final section of this chapter discusses how the variations already mentioned can be used to shed light on how the digital economy affects economic growth in times of global crisis, or how can the digital economy be made to grow while the world is in a state of crisis?

Figure 7. Digital transformation performance GCC
Source: Srinivasan (2022)

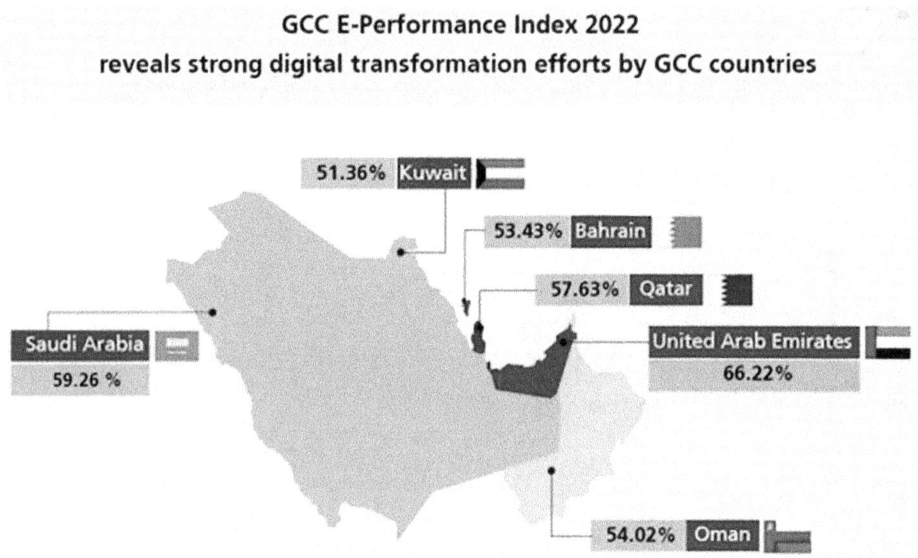

Impact of Variations on the Digital Economy and Economic Growth Relationship During a Global Crisis

The GCC's digital economies were discussed in the last section in terms of their digital infrastructure, openness, innovation environment, competitiveness, and digital divide. In this section, it is discussed how, in times of global crisis, the growth of the digital economy can be strengthened.

The political economy of the Gulf is being disrupted by COVID-19 and historically low oil prices, but the pandemic has shown the region's technological adaptability (Soliman, 2020). The Gulf region has experienced historically high rates of social media and smartphone penetration as well as an upward trend in data outflow since the 2010s. In parallel, governments throughout the GCC, particularly those of the United Arab Emirates (UAE), Bahrain, and Saudi Arabia, have been investing heavily in the digitalization of their infrastructure by setting up the necessary institutions, changing the law, collaborating with "Big Tech," and developing local human capital. The COVID-19 pandemic has undoubtedly been the Gulf's digital infrastructure's toughest test to date, but the region has shown impressive digital resilience (Ben Hassen, 2022).

The pandemic surprised everyone and created major disruptions, particularly as remote work began to take hold. The National Innovation Strategy, the Artificial Intelligence Strategy 2031, and the Blockchain Strategy 2021, among other long-term plans that served as the foundation for the UAE's COVID-19 digital response, all paid off for the country (Soliman, 2020). It is clear that the transition to remote work, study, and business was quick, effective, and resilient. For instance, Dubai's Paperless Strategy gave each of the 300,000 registered users a digital national identity and an account from which they could access 5,000 national public and private services. The openness of the system also made it possible to request and share data digitally with service providers, use digital signatures for documents and transactions, and more.

The health response was more significantly influenced by technology. The TraceCovid app was created by the UAE Department of Health to track down people who had close contact with COVID-19 patients who were later diagnosed (Yasmin et al., 2022). Oyoon, which means "eyes" in Arabic, is a cutting-edge surveillance system used by Dubai police to keep an eye on the emirate's citizens. Oyoon uses a vast network of cameras throughout the city to collect data using facial, voice, and licence plate recognition. The collected data is then fed into a shared government database for cross-referencing. This database and network are being used to impose lockdown regulations in order to combat the pandemic.

The UAE is renowned for its "data sovereignty" doctrine, which was most famously put into practise in 2013 when the government blocked access to VoIP services, including Skype. The country has lifted its ban on VoIP services, as well as that on the well-known video conference apps Teams and Zoom, in an effort to mitigate the economic effects of COVID-19 and assist businesses in making the transition to remote working (Soliman, 2020). However, after the anticipated return to the pre-COVID-19 working environment, there are serious concerns about whether the UAE will continue to permit VoIP services. But there is no doubt that after the crisis, the nation will be more assured in its digital infrastructure and its capacity to withstand a global pandemic.

Bahrain has steadily developed into a technology hub despite its small size and population thanks to institutional investments it has made in legal frameworks and infrastructure for technology. Bahrain competes with other regional tech hubs like the UAE by offering 30–40% lower operating costs as well as a strategic Gulf location and a tech-savvy populace (Soliman, 2020). The regulatory environment in the kingdom, the result of decades of reforms, including the data protection laws, the bankruptcy law, and the acceptance of full foreign ownership in most industries and sectors, is what has helped it become a sought-after hub for global tech giants.

Bahrain is one of the first countries to roll out a nationwide 5G network and a regional leader in digital infrastructure (Bahrain News, 2019). Amazon Web Services opened its first Middle Eastern data centre in Bahrain in 2019 as a direct result of Manama's efforts, expanding the region's enterprise cloud options. Bahrain's digital infrastructure made the transition to remote work, which was necessitated by the COVID-19 pandemic, quick and resilient. The kingdom utilised its digital resources to track down COVID-19 cases. BeAware is a contact-tracing app that Bahrain's eGovernment introduced. It involves infected people wearing GPS-tracked bracelets that alert government monitoring stations to any movement outside of predetermined areas. Self-isolating people may receive random photo requests from the Ministry of Health; they are required to reply with a photo demonstrating that they are wearing the bracelet.

The private sector is actively combating the pandemic's economic effects by making use of Bahrain's robust infrastructure. For instance, to help with the effective distribution of food and medicines in the kingdom and the rest of the GCC market, MVC Global and Cox Logistics will use blockchain and artificial intelligence. The government of Bahrain was able to oversee the shift to remote work thanks to long-term reforms and investments, while the private sector had the opportunity to test and implement its solutions.

In Saudi Arabia, the pandemic-fighting efforts have benefited from the country's technological investments. The kingdom used to lag behind its Gulf counterparts in technological development despite having the largest economy in the Middle East and the largest population on the Arabian Peninsula. Saudi Arabia launched a national transformation strategy with Vision 2030 to transition from an oil-dependent economy to one that is digitally empowered (Al Naimi, 2021; Arab News, 2021; Saudi Vision 2030, 2020; Vision 2030, 2022). It established institutions, enacted laws and frameworks, and built global alliances. With a clear objective of becoming the region's tech leader, the kingdom also concentrated on implementing digital solutions in priority sectors such as justice, health, electricity, culture, and tourism.

Saudi Arabia prioritised digital transformation, which led to the gradual rollout of commercial 5G networks in more than 20 cities in 2019. The rollout of 5G also improved the kingdom's reputation in the tech world among investors eager to make investments in sectors like tech, finance, education, and the public sector that would profit from 5G capabilities (Soliman, 2020). In addition, the government has introduced a variety of clever tools that have been successful in gaining the confidence of the populace. For instance, the Ministry of Education uses the National Education Portal to provide educational resources and digital tools for students at home, while the Ministry of Health updated its app, Mawid, which directs users on self-isolation and hospital visits.

In 2020, the pandemic occurred during Saudi Arabia's G20 forum presidency. By implementing an early lockdown, suspending the hajj and umrah pilgrimages, and using its position as chair to coordinate the international response to COVID-19 on various fronts, especially in the digital sector, Riyadh had the chance to set an example for other countries. A change in Saudi priorities was signalled by the kingdom's support for digital response and recovery as well as its promotion of cooperation with outside agencies and the private sector. The digital infrastructure that increased the kingdom's digital resilience in the face of the pandemic was established by Vision 2030, and as a result of Saudi Arabia's G20 leadership, the country is now establishing itself as a tech leader in the region.

The reforms implemented and institutional investments made throughout the Gulf in the 2010s paved the way for the region's robust digital response to the pandemic and its fallout, even though the GCC states have not yet completely transitioned from oil-powered economies to ones that are fully diversified. For example, the UAE demonstrated that it is a global leader in digital innovation in addition to solidifying its position as a regional tech hub. Despite being the smallest country in the Gulf, Bahrain has developed into one of its most technologically advanced governments thanks to strong support from local and global tech companies. Saudi Arabia, which despite having a sizable economy lag behind its Gulf neighbours in terms of digital development, benefited from Vision 2030 by building a robust digital infrastructure that withstood the crisis. In addition, Riyadh is promoting the use of technology to fight the pandemic as part of the kingdom's G20 presidency.

CONCLUSION

Given that the GCC's economies are still in the early stages of development and are actively working to diversify their revenue sources away from dependence on oil, the discussion of the variations in the digital economy and economic growth reveals: (1) a regional imbalance in the development of the GCC's digital economies. (2) Through its support for the modernization of the industrial structure, the digital economy has the potential to boost the economic growth of GCC member states. (3) COVID-19 has generally increased demand for digital industries in GCC nations, with the demand side of the equation having a much larger impact than the supply side. However, COVID-19 has also had detrimental effects on the digital industries, particularly in the GCC, leading to the following suggested policy implications:

In order to develop effective development strategies and pathways, each GCC nation should assess its strengths and weaknesses based on the digital economy's development scores. In order to help the nations or regions with less advanced digital technologies, it is crucial to reduce and bridge the "digital divide" and improve the network infrastructure. Due to the wide development gaps within regions, the more emerging nations can learn from developing nations like the UK, US, Singapore, and Malaysia and examine the appropriate development models in light of their own status. These nations should prioritise improving specialised talent training, bolstering R&D support for cutting-edge digital technologies like artificial intelligence and 5G, and enhancing the innovation climate for the digital economy.

In the post-COVID-19 era, it is important to focus on how the digital economy is influencing industrial upgrading and employment. To further support the deep integration of the digital economy with conventional primary, secondary, and tertiary industries, economic globalisation and information technology must be combined. The GCC countries must use ICT to improve the digital management and operation of traditional industries, optimise the efficient allocation of industrial resources, boost economic efficiency, and raise the value-added of industries. On the other hand, it is crucial to make good use of the digital economy's significant stabilising effect on the labour market. Demand for digital living, working, and learning will significantly rise in the post-COVID-19 era. This is a unique chance for the growth of the digital economy. Therefore, the GCC nations should promote digital employment through the employment promotion mechanisms of the digital economy, increasing labour productivity and fostering steady economic recovery and growth.

In the era following COVID-19, the GCC nations should promote deep integration between the real economy and the digital economy, industrialization, and information technology in order to enhance digital connectivity, advance information technology, and establish new hubs for collaboration. The COVID-19 pandemic has significantly increased demand for digital life, work, and learning in GCC nations, providing a once-in-a-lifetime opportunity for the growth of the digital economy. As a result, those nations should continue to enhance their digital economy development strategies and optimise and upgrade the development of information infrastructures like artificial intelligence, the internet of things, and the industrial internet. In order to encourage digital firms to invest more in digital technologies, a favourable environment for their growth should also be established.

To create new service trade patterns and boost cooperation in digital trade and e-commerce, the GCC countries must rely on the digital economy. The disruption caused by COVID-19 has forced traditional trade in goods and services to undergo a digital transformation. On the other hand, emerging digital technologies like big data, cloud computing, artificial intelligence, and blockchain will make digital trade the dominant form of international trade. To support the development of a "digital trade community," the GCC countries must enhance their technological innovation capacities and broaden the scope of their service trade cooperation, including cross-border e-commerce, teleconferences and exhibitions, telemedicine, tele-education, and unlimited payment.

Reflecting on the above policy recommendations, other Middle Eastern nations could potentially benefit from studying the Gulf's digital investments in order to develop their own digital economy strategy to promote nationwide growth.

Future Studies

Future research could incorporate a more in-depth empirical examination of the variations discussed in this chapter in relation to the following:

1. Empirical studies can be conducted to validate the conceptual model presented in this chapter (see Figure 1) by using an action-research approach.

2. Conduct individual case studies of each GCC member state in order to deduce the similarities and differences in how the variations impact these member states' digital economies.
3. The above suggested future studies may provide an additional impact mechanism to assist GCC member states in promoting their digital economies on the global stage in order to compete with developing nations' existing digital economies; this will also reinforce the member states' social, economic, and environmental visions, which aim to be more competitive globally in various areas of industry as well as diversify their revenue stream to move away from oil dependence.

REFERENCES

G20. (2016). *G20 digital economy development and cooperation initiative.* G20 Research Group at the University of Toronto.

Afonasova, M. A., Panfilova, E. E., Galichkina, M. A., & Ślusarczyk, B. (2019). Digitalization in economy and innovation: The effect on social and economic processes. *Polish Journal of Management Studies, 19.*

Aidrous, I. A., Asmyatullin, R. R., & Glavina, S. G. (2021). *The Development of the Digital Economy: GCC Countries Experience. Industry Competitiveness: Digitalization*, Management, and Integration.

Al Naimi, S. M. (2021). Economic Diversification Trends in the Gulf: The Case of Saudi Arabia. *Circular Economy and Sustainability*. PMID:34888575

Al-Roubaie, A. (2021). *The Digital Economy: Challenges and Opportunities for Economic Conversion in the Gulf Countries*. Academic Press.

Al-Sayed, K. A. (2013). *GCC and Arab Spring*. The Peninsula Publishing.

Albiman, M. M., & Sulong, Z. (2017). The linear and non-linear impacts of ICT on economic growth, of disaggregate income groups within SSA region. *Telecommunications Policy*, *41*(7-8), 555–572. doi:10.1016/j.telpol.2017.07.007

Amankwah-Amoah, J., Khan, Z., Wood, G., & Knight, G. (2021). COVID-19 and digitalization: The great acceleration. *Journal of Business Research*, *136*, 602–611. doi:10.1016/j.jbusres.2021.08.011 PMID:34538980

Appiah-Otoo, I., & Song, N. (2021). The impact of ICT on economic growth-Comparing rich and poor countries. *Telecommunications Policy*, *45*(2), 102082. doi:10.1016/j.telpol.2020.102082

Arab News. (2021). *Evaluating Saudi Arabia's Vision 2030 at the five-year mark.* Retrieved 25th Nov from https://www.arabnews.com/node/1850041

Bahrain EGov Report. (2016). *E-government of Bahrain: Bahrain national eGovernment strategy*. Retrieved from https://www.bahrain.bh/wps/wcm/connect/fc54be3a-a0d6-43ef-9cbe-7ab640c581d3/New+eGovernment+Strategy+2012-2016.pdf?MOD=AJPERES

Bahrain News. (2019). *Bahrain among the first countries to rollout 5G network, says minister*. Retrieved from https://www.bna.bh/en/Bahrainamongthefirstcountriestorollout5Gnetworksaysminister.aspx?cms=q8FmFJgiscL2fwIzON1%2BDv5AaBoS%2Fg96G32BSZLftMo%3D

Ben Hassen, T. (2022). *A Transformative State in the Wake of COVID-19: What Is Needed to Enable Innovation, Entrepreneurship, and Education in Qatar?* Academic Press.

Bukht, R., & Heeks, R. (2017). *Defining, conceptualising and measuring the digital economy*. Development Informatics working paper.

Carlsson, B. (2004). The Digital Economy: What is new and what is not? *Structural Change and Economic Dynamics, 15*(3), 245–264. doi:10.1016/j.strueco.2004.02.001

Chauhan, C., Singh, A., & Luthra, S. (2021). Barriers to industry 4.0 adoption and its performance implications: An empirical investigation of emerging economy. *Journal of Cleaner Production, 285*, 124809. doi:10.1016/j.jclepro.2020.124809

Cheng, C.-Y., Chien, M.-S., & Lee, C.-C. (2021). ICT diffusion, financial development, and economic growth: An international cross-country analysis. *Economic Modelling, 94*, 662–671. doi:10.1016/j.econmod.2020.02.008

Dahlman, C., Mealy, S., & Wermelinger, M. (2016). *Harnessing the digital economy for developing countries*. Academic Press.

Digital Oman Strategy. (2018). *Ministry of Technology and Communications: Digital Oman strategy 2018*. Retrieved from https://www.ita.gov.om/ITAPortal/eOman/Main_Strategic_Directions.aspx

Duggal, A. S., Malik, P. K., Gehlot, A., Singh, R., Gaba, G. S., Masud, M., & Al-Amri, J. F. (2022). A sequential roadmap to Industry 6.0: Exploring future manufacturing trends. *IET Communications, 16*(5), 521-531. doi:10.1049/cmu2.12284

Ganichev, N. A., & Koshovets, O. B. (2021). Forcing the digital economy: How will the structure of digital markets change as a result of the COVID-19 pandemic. *Studies on Russian Economic Development, 32*(1), 11–22. doi:10.1134/S1075700721010056 PMID:33642845

Gozgor, G., & Lau, C. K. M. (2021). Editorial: Economic Effects of COVID-19 Related Uncertainty Shocks. *Frontiers in Public Health, 9*, 760619. doi:10.3389/fpubh.2021.760619 PMID:34650956

Grabowska, S., Saniuk, S., & Gajdzik, B. (2022). Industry 5.0: Improving humanization and sustainability of Industry 4.0. *Scientometrics, 127*(6), 3117–3144. doi:10.100711192-022-04370-1 PMID:35502439

Harper, J. (2022). *GCC countries must develop 'tech champions' to compete with US and China*. Retrieved from https://www.arabianbusiness.com/industries/technology/gcc-countries-must-develop-tech-champions-to-compete-with-us-and-china

Internet World Stats. (2022). *Internet Usage in the Middle East*. Retrieved from https://www.internetworldstats.com/stats5.htm#me

Jackson, N. C., & Dunn-Jensen, L. M. (2021). Leadership succession planning for today's digital transformation economy: Key factors to build for competency and innovation. *Business Horizons, 64*(2), 273–284. doi:10.1016/j.bushor.2020.11.008

Jiang, X. (2020). Digital economy in the post-pandemic era. *Journal of Chinese Economic and Business Studies, 18*(4), 333–339. doi:10.1080/14765284.2020.1855066

Kitchin, R. (2015). Making sense of smart cities: Addressing present shortcomings. *Cambridge Journal of Regions, Economy and Society, 8*(1), 131–136. doi:10.1093/cjres/rsu027

Liu, Q., Gu, J., Yang, J., Li, Y., Sha, D., Xu, M., Shams, I., Yu, M., & Yang, C. (2021). Cloud, Edge, and Mobile Computing for Smart Cities. In W. Shi, M. F. Goodchild, M. Batty, M.-P. Kwan, & A. Zhang (Eds.), *Urban Informatics* (pp. 757–795). Springer Singapore. doi:10.1007/978-981-15-8983-6_41

Miniaoui, H., & Schilirò, D. (2016). *Innovation and Entrepreneurship for the growth and diversification of the GCC Economies*. Academic Press.

Nchofoung, T. N., & Asongu, S. A. (2022). ICT for sustainable development: Global comparative evidence of globalisation thresholds. *Telecommunications Policy, 46*(5), 102296. doi:10.1016/j.telpol.2021.102296

New Kuwait Vision. (2019). *Government of Kuwait: New Kuwait Vision 2035*. Retrieved from https://www.newkuwait.gov.kw/home.aspx

OECD. (2014). *Measuring the digital economy: A new perspective*. OECD Publishing.

Pan, W., Xie, T., Wang, Z., & Ma, L. (2022). Digital economy: An innovation driver for total factor productivity. *Journal of Business Research, 139*, 303–311.

Pradhan, R. P., Arvin, M. B., Nair, M., Bennett, S. E., & Bahmani, S. (2019). Short-term and long-term dynamics of venture capital and economic growth in a digital economy: A study of European countries. *Technology in Society, 57*, 125–134. doi:10.1016/j.techsoc.2018.11.002

Qatar National Vision. (2018). *Government Communications Office of Qatar: Qatar national vision 2030*. Retrieved from https://www.gco.gov.qa/en/about-qatar/national-vision/

Rajan, R., & Aldhaheri, S. K. (2019). *Digital Nation: How the United Arab Emirates is Building a Future Based on Tech Innovation. Motivate Media Group.*

Report, D. (2019). *Big Data in the GCC: From strategy to global leadership*. Retrieved from https://www2.deloitte.com/ye/en/pages/about-deloitte/articles/revolution/big-data-gcc.html

Samad, W. A., & Azar, E. (2018). Smart Cities in the Gulf: Current State, Opportunities, and Challenges. Springer Singapore.

Saudi Vision 2030. (2020). *Vision 2030*. Retrieved from https://vision2030.gov.sa/en/reports

Seo, H.-J., Lee, Y. S., & Oh, J. H. (2009). Does ICT investment widen the growth gap? *Telecommunications Policy, 33*(8), 422–431. doi:10.1016/j.telpol.2009.04.001

Shaiful Fitri Abdul Rahman, N., Adam Hamid, A., Lirn, T.-C., Al Kalbani, K., & Sahin, B. (2022). The adoption of industry 4.0 practices by the logistics industry: A systematic review of the gulf region. *Cleaner Logistics and Supply Chain*, *5*, 100085. doi:10.1016/j.clscn.2022.100085

Soliman, M. (2020). *COVID-19 and the digital landscape in the Gulf.* Retrieved 27th Dec from https://www.mei.edu/publications/covid-19-and-digital-landscape-gulf

Srinivasan, M. (2022). *GCC E-Performance Index 2022 reveals strong digital transformation efforts by GCC countries*. Retrieved from https://www.sme10x.com/10x-industry/gcc-e-performance-index-2022-reveals-strong-digital-transformation-efforts-by-gcc-countries

Strategy. (2020). *Advancing digital maturity a $100+ billion opportunity for GCC*. Retrieved from https://www.consultancy-me.com/news/4488/advancing-digital-maturity-a-100-billion-opportunity-for-gcc

Tapscott, D. (2014). *The Digital Economy Anniversary Edition: Rethinking Promise and Peril in the Age of Networked Intelligence*. McGraw-Hill Education.

Tawalbeh, L. A. A., & Saldamli, G. (2019). Reconsidering big data security and privacy in cloud and mobile cloud systems. *Journal of King Saud University - Computer and Information Sciences*.

Vision, U. A. E. (2010). *The UAE Government Portal: UAE vision 2021*. Retrieved from https://www.government.ae/en/about-the-uae/strategies-initiatives-and-awards/federal-governments-strategies-and-plans/vision-2021

Vision 2030. (2022). Saudi Vision 2030: Financial Development Programme. *Saudi Arabia, 2022*, 39.

Vu, K. M. (2011). ICT as a source of economic growth in the information age: Empirical evidence from the 1996–2005 period. *Telecommunications Policy*, *35*(4), 357–372. doi:10.1016/j.telpol.2011.02.008

Williams, L. D. (2021). Concepts of Digital Economy and Industry 4.0 in Intelligent and information systems. *International Journal of Intelligent Networks*, *2*, 122–129. doi:10.1016/j.ijin.2021.09.002

Yasmin, T., El Refae, G. A., & Eletter, S. (2022). Digital Healthcare Provision Policies in United Arab Emirates (UAE) Amid COVID-19. In Digital Economy, Business Analytics, and Big Data Analytics Applications (pp. 215-222). Springer.

Zhai, Y., Jiang, D., Gozgor, G., & Cho, E. (2021). The Amplifying Effect of Conflicts on Case Fatality Rate of COVID-19: Evidence From 120 Countries [Brief Research Report]. *Frontiers in Public Health*, *9*, 9. doi:10.3389/fpubh.2021.681604 PMID:34422745

Zhong, R. Y., Xu, X., Klotz, E., & Newman, S. T. (2017). Intelligent Manufacturing in the Context of Industry 4.0: A Review. *Engineering (Beijing)*, *3*(5), 616–630. doi:10.1016/J.ENG.2017.05.015

ADDITIONAL READING

Ali, M. (2019a). The Barriers and Enablers of the Educational Cloud: A Doctoral Student Perspective. *Open Journal of Business and Management*, *7*(1).

Ali, M. (2019b). Cloud Computing at a Cross Road: Quality and Risks in Higher Education. *Advances in Internet of Things*, *9*(3), 33–49. doi:10.4236/ait.2019.93003

Ali, M. (Ed.). (2021). *Remote Work and Sustainable Changes for the Future of Global Business*. IGI Global. doi:10.4018/978-1-7998-7513-0

Ali, M. (2022). *Future Role of Sustainable Innovative Technologies in Crisis Management*. IGI Global. doi:10.4018/978-1-7998-9815-3

Ali, M., & Abdel-Haq, M. K. (2021). Bibliographical Analysis of Artificial Intelligence Learning in Higher Education: Is the Role of the Human Educator a Thing of the Past? In *Fostering Communication and Learning With Underutilized Technologies in Higher Education* (pp. 36–52). IGI Global. doi:10.4018/978-1-7998-4846-2.ch003

Ali, M., & Edghiem, F. (2021). Sustainable Business and Collaboration Driven by Big Data Analytics Amidst the Emergence of the Remote Work Culture. In *Remote Work and Sustainable Changes for the Future of Global Business* (pp. 15–32). IGI Global. doi:10.4018/978-1-7998-7513-0.ch002

Ali, M., Edghiem, F., & Alkhalifah, E. S. (2022). Cultural Challenges of ERP Implementation in Middle-Eastern Oil & Gas Sector: An Action Research Approach. *Systemic Practice and Action Research*. PMID:35668863

Ali, M. B. (2021). Internet of Things (IoT) to Foster Communication and Information Sharing: A Case of UK Higher Education. *Fostering Communication & Learning With Underutilized Technologies in Higher Education*, 1-20.

Ali, M. B., Wood-Harper, T., & Ramlogan, R. (2020a). A Framework Strategy to Overcome Trust Issues on Cloud Computing Adoption in Higher Education. In Modern Principles, Practices, and Algorithms for Cloud Security (pp. 162-183). IGI Global. doi:10.4018/978-1-7998-1082-7.ch008

Ali, M. B., Wood-Harper, T., & Ramlogan, R. (2020b). *The Role of SaaS Applications in Business IT Alignment: A Closer Look at Value Creation in Service Industry*. UKAIS.

Ali. (2019). Multiple Perspective of Cloud Computing Adoption Determinants in Higher Education a Systematic Review. *International Journal of Cloud Applications and Computing, 9*(3), 89-109.

Ali. (2020). Multi-Perspectives of Cloud Computing Service Adoption Quality and Risks in Higher Education. In *Handbook of Research on Modern Educational Technologies, Applications, and Management* (2nd ed.). IGI Global.

Chapter 8
Improving the Business and IT Alignment Through Software Delivery Methodology

SidAli Mohamed Yousfi
Bolton University, UK

Bob Wood
Institute of Management, Bolton, UK

ABSTRACT

Business and IT alignment has been a critical issue for researchers, consultants, and practitioners seeking to improve demand and delivery management by executing business requirements in real-life systems that benefit end-users. Companies using IT to enable their business must improve their business and information technology alignment (BITA) by implementing best practices and frameworks. This study focuses on one area of improvement in the BITA model, which is project software delivery using Agile as a project management methodology. Agile methodology allows for collaboration and dynamic requirements, which benefits aligning businesspeople with IT delivery within the software development lifecycle (SDLC) framework.

INTRODUCTION AND PROBLEM STATEMENT

The digital world brings a variety of products to consumers, and services to facilitate our daily life from many aspects such as telecommunication, e-commerce, digital banking, fintech (finance technology), digital marketing, and many others. Moreover, as authors, consultants, or practitioners got enabled to use our experiences from different business industries and research backgrounds to perform research and write articles, chapters, publications, and books to contribute to this area. Following that, entrepreneurship also shined as one of the trends to encourage business owners to propose ideas to solve an existing problem or discover a future opportunity. Hence, many business owners have the required budget to start their business and transform the idea into action and a product or service. One of the biggest challenges

DOI: 10.4018/978-1-6684-7416-7.ch008

usually faced by the entrepreneurship community is how can they turn and deliver their ideas into a real-life product or service; to do so, the business owner has to be aware of the delivery methodologies to maximize the time to market to start their business and generating an early revenue to operate the business. If not, the business owner has to acquire a consultant to help with that and secure the alignment between the business owners to the final deliverables. The business owners would better have a business and technical understanding to reduce the dependency and act fast to define the business needs. However, is not mandatory to have the functional and technical knowledge to start or manage the business. That is why the market recently mandated a new profession called "Business Analyst" to bridge the gap and secure the alignment between business understanding and the technical mindset.

The Business and Information Technology Alignment topic has been an open subject for authors, consultants, and subject matter experts in the IT area for the last three decades (Henderson and Venkatraman, 1993), it remains elusive (Coltman et al., 2015, Karpovsky and Galliers, 2015, Chan, 2002, Symons, 2005). The BITA subject becomes a concern subject to business leaders due to the negative impact that they are getting as a result of the misalignment between Business and IT as all approaches seem to be time and resources consumed, contrary to what would be desirable nowadays: achieve and maintain BITA quickly, efficiently, and sustainably. The company's leadership is due to the emergence of the need of having effective models, frameworks, and methodologies to improve the alignment. As a result, improve the business and IT alignment regardless of the expected time and the efforts that might be consumed specifically from the leaders who become mature with the value of having a mechanism of practicing the alignment and feel the direct impact of the alignment issues as well on the final outcomes.

This chapter is going to put in place the relationship first between the used methodologies in the project software delivery (in the Software Development Life-Cycle industries as a case study in the Middle East which is the author's area of experience and expertise) which are either waterfall or agile[1] methodologies with the core issue of the business and IT alignment within Telco and Government companies as an example and case study. In order to demonstrate the improvement that happened in the alignment between the business and IT while transforming the delivery framework from the waterfall to agile methodology. The theoretically expected results of this study are that the agile method of software delivery contains an alignment practice as part of its process that gives the advantage to enable the business through IT adequate software delivery method with high efficiency of deliverable's quality and improve the go live. This chapter is constructed to a theoretical comparison between the waterfall and agile methodology, the concept of alignment within a dynamic requirement, and collaboration importance to improve the alignment in the operation model, especially in the agile methodology, and finally a conclusion and recommendation about the effective methods that shall be considered by business leaders to enable their businesses in the software world.

THEORETICAL FRAMEWORK AND METHODOLOGY

Introduction

The context of Project management as a methodology for overseeing every part of a project in the Software Development Lifecycle (SDLC) framework would be introduced as the fundamental of each keyword in this section by giving the definition, objectives, and some use cases from the real world to make it easier for the reader to understand and link the theory with the practical use cases. In another hand, as a starting point to move forward in performing research and practice to both project management methodologies along with the alignment contribution in both methodologies. The alignment factors that shall be measured would be based on the level of collaboration between team members and the coherence between each process step, and scope change during the product life cycle management which is usually called dynamic requirements management.

Project delivery management has been utilized for a thousand years due to the need of organizing and managing humanity's daily life from the generic aspect without considering the project for an organization or enterprise. Project management is a generic term that can be used also in our daily routine tasks to well established and finished our targeted objectives with good quality within a specific time, actions, and amount of money if it is applicable. In addition to that, it has been about mid of last century with the development of the industry and with the discovery and innovation of the tools and techniques in construction for example, and engineering in general, to facilitate the tasks on the human being to achieve enormous outcomes with fewer efforts that enable the humanity to progress in facilitating the life by using such technologies; start applying organized management methods that we called "Project Management" with the definition of each term separately which is as part the Project Management Institute (PMI, PMBOK, v6) "The Project is a temporary endeavour undertaken to create a unique project service or result" tools and techniques to complex initiatives and projects (Carayannis, et al., 2003). Since then, the project management discipline got a massive improvement in those tools and techniques till today.

Initially, the project management used a waterfall methodology which is simply using a sequence of process steps (Shah, et al., 2016) to achieve the delivery of the business objectives from the beginning till the end. However, this methodology got challenged by the practitioners, consultants, and researchers as well as the disputes raised by the end users due to the delay of the value delivery, and unexpected deliverables at the user acceptance stage. That is why the agile methodology had a discussion since around the 70s (Noura et al., 2014) and got introduced formally in 2001 to satisfy the end user and make the project delivery more agile in terms of scope flexibility and introduced many other principles as well. In the next section, the author is going to explain in brief the definition of each method with its objectives.

The research method that has been considered in this study is a comparative research methodology which is based on critical analysis of both software delivery methodologies against the subject research which is improving the alignment in BITA.

Waterfall Methodology

In any industry, the business owner has always business needs that will be expressed either to a problem to be solved regardless of if it is in the existing environment or a problem exists at the end user side or an opportunity to be explored, the results of these would be either a product, service, or results to be delivered and given to the business owner.

Waterfall methodology in project management discipline within the SDLC framework was the main method of this domain as mentioned in the introduction as part of the history, the process simply starts with the initiation, planning, analysis, design, development, and testing (Wantana, et al., 2016) as strictly sequence process steps and cannot be in parallel of any of the phases. From the Figure 1, the process sequence steps are similar to the waterfall effect, which is why it is named as waterfall methodology. This methodology is still being used until today in many industries. The project delivery management methodology is linear with the development process following the specific sequence from start to finish when the final project is delivered, and each phase is a prerequisite for the next phase. Project teams also shall develop, execute and fully complete each process step as described below in the same and exact order (Alexander, et al., 2020).

Figure 1. Waterfall methodology model
Source: Pedersen (2013)

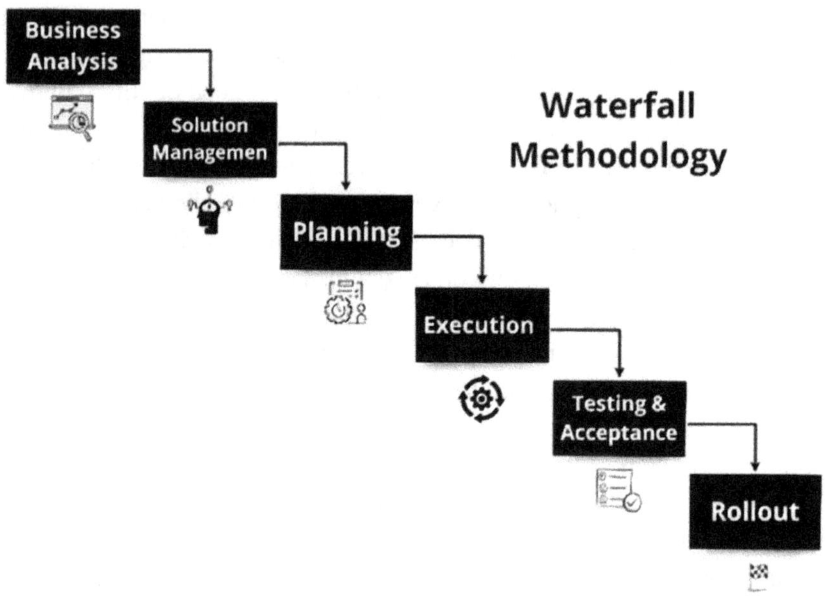

The above method is composed of seven phases linked to each other by processes and sub-processes[2]. Each process step has input(s), output(s), and interrelated activities and actions in between. The inputs are the prerequisites to trigger the functionality of the process, using interrelated activities and actions against the inputs and applying PM tools and techniques which are mixing between the inputs, tools, and techniques in iteration and performing an action to produce the outputs.

Idea Initiation: Process which is the first step that shall be considered to initiate any idea, solving a problem to be solved within the current organization or at the end user level, or exploring an opportunity to be announced to the market in a form of a project, demand, or initiative. (IIBA, CBAP, 2013). The end user might be an internal (Internal cross-section between two divisions such as IT and Business Areas like Marketing or Finance), or an external client.

Requirements Analysis: This process step is to secure that the requirements are effectively captured from clients and other key stakeholders that are divided into functional, non-functional, system requirements, and technical specifications to be considered in the project up-front that the scope shall be signed-off and shall not be changed during the software delivery lifecycle (Ateeq and Shuaib, 2014). There are many tools and techniques stated in the BABOK used in this phase of defining the problem statement, breaking it down into sub-problems, performing a root cause analysis, requirements elicitation and business analysis from stakeholders and securing the alignment, and then performing business, and system impact analysis, and feasibility study from business and technology in order to define a clear scope to be delivered at the end of the project; the final step is to align the business architecture with the agreed business solution.

Solution Design: This process step is the technical design to answer what is the optimum solution that shall fulfill the business requirements that were mentioned in the above step after performing the detailed technical feasibility study and aligning the solution with the information system and technology architecture. If the alignment happens with good quality at this stage, we can say that we succeeded in achieving the BITA in high quality because the solution definition is the primary key stage of business and IT alignment.

Planning: The planning phase where the time, effort estimate, cost, and define the desired accepted quality. In this phase also it is very important to fulfill the business and technical prerequisites and dependencies either as projects (Previous or concurrent projects), or any external factors to produce a project plan for the entire project.

Development: This is the phase in which the execution of the planned activities in the planning phase and based on the requirements specification defined in the requirements analysis step. In the waterfall methodology, another phase would be in parallel which we call it "Monitoring and Controlling" phase (PMBOK). These two phases are in parallel to execute, monitor, and control if the project is going as planned, and manage any changes and scope deviation, creep, or changes.

Testing: Performance, unit, systems, and user acceptance testing is then done to ensure the product meets the identified requirements. If defects or bugs are discovered, then they are addressed before delivery. This phase is crucial to ensure the agreed deliverables with the end user at the beginning are met. Performing this phase in the project delivery method shall pass with many test models, such as unit test, and integration test, before demonstrating the outcomes to the client and regression test before going to production. This is the client and project team alignment stage.

Final Project Delivery: Once the product meets the specifications established at the beginning of the project, the product is delivered to the client. The client would sign off the project in order to release all the project resources and close any procurements, contracts, or agreements that had a relationship with the project charter.

In this method, the alignment between the business and IT team is the ownership of the business analyst or sometimes the project manager who is responsible for the alignment which is happening intermittently during the project life cycle. In another hand, the waterfall methodology lives with a strong documentation and knowledge management process that shall participate in the alignment from the documentation perspective that the agile method does not maintain proper documentation which is described in detail in the next section.

Agile Methodology

Agile terminology is a generic term that is currently being extracted from many methods like Scrum, Kanban, and many others. The definition of agile in the project management domain is delivering requirements iteratively and the value should be incrementally throughout the product life cycle (Muhammad et al., 2014, 64). An important note from the author's opinion is that the agile methodology is still under refinement and improvement and there is not a well-proofed model and has NO generic and unified agreement from the researchers, practitioners, and consultants. However, it is a best practice documented and formulated by some organizations such as Project Management Institute (PMI), PRINCE 2, Scrum Alliance, AgilePM administered by APMG International, and The International Consortium for Agile's (ICAgile). The primary differences between the agile and waterfall methodology are the scope definition and management, and the level of collaboration and alignment between the software delivery team and the client. The purpose of that is instead to discuss the scope at the beginning and freeze the entire scope and leave the client until the final delivery to see the outcomes, agile came to keep the client involved and engaged in the delivery and prioritize the expected deliverables based on the expected values and keep the value incremented till the end (Shahet al., 2016). Agile plays a primary role in delivering the highest value products and features to the end user in the fastest way and an enormous quality of the deliverables. The end-to-end process of the agile methodology in the software delivery field is shown in Figure 2.

Figure 2. Agile (Scrum as a use case) methodology within SDLC

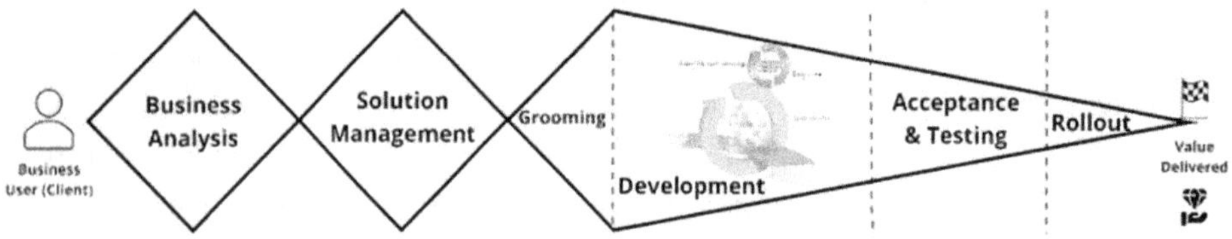

The advantage of the agile methodology is that the stakeholders that are working on either client, product owner[3], scrum master, the development team[4], QC (Quality Control), QA (Quality Assurance), and other cross-function team members, is the agile mindset and level of collaboration that shall be considered. The agile mindset is one of the agile principles, flexible, thinking and adapting fast, and self-motivation. In this case, any member of the team will be self-engaged and seek daily alignment from top to down levels to understand and deliver the daily assigned tasks with the desired quality. The second agile benefit is collaboration, starting from the product backlog where the product owner shall secure the alignment with the client in terms of scope and priority. Once it is done, the product owner prepares the requirements in form of requirements specifications[5] linked to an Epic which is a container of requirements with the same objective, and aligns them with the Scrum Master and technical lead to close the technical alignment and the feasibility study, after that the product owner shall take responsibility to align all the requirements with the stakeholders from the business based on the business impact analysis study and technical perspective based on the system impact analysis. The alignment shall be done with all impacted areas under the governance of the scrum master. Once this phase is done, the capacity planning of the sprint shall be aligned with stakeholders specifically the client to know which features and functionalities shall be delivered at the end of each sprint which usually takes between two to six weeks of development and testing that we call it as "Sprint Planning", once the sprint started, a daily alignment meeting between the product owner who is representing the client (Business Side) in the team and the squad team to discuss what has been done, what shall be done, and finally what are the challenges and blockers, this meeting called "Stand-up meeting" which is very important to align on the day-to-day outcomes and realign with the client's if needed on the requirements changes. Moreover, the accessibility of all team members to the product owner who is representing the client inside the development team is improving the alignment internally on a daily basis to secure value delivery. Once the development is done and certified, the developed features and functionalities by the QC and QA, and the product owner. Hence, the client is ready to test and accept the agreed scope (which is another important level of alignment between stakeholders) which is called "Sprint Review" and so on for each sprint to secure the alignment and value delivery incrementally. The final internal alignment meeting is called "Sprint Retrospective" to evaluate the delivered outcomes and enhance the way of working of the next upcoming sprints. The main role of the product owner in the agile model is the alignment and being a single point of contact between the business which is the client and the technical team which is the squad. With this model, the alignment is improved during the product life cycle within the agile software delivery methodology.

Exploring more on the relationship between alignment and agility, some studies and research have been conducted and the outcome was that agility is the result of alignment (Tallon et al., 2011; Wirat-tanapornkul, 2012). Based on the study held by Chung et al. 2003, among 202 managers, discovered a strong relationship and correlation between IT Agility and IT Business Alignment at the strategic level. This conclusion means that the agility of IT was enough to digest the changes and deliver the quickest applications and new processes that enable the business to move forward and be more agile. As a conclusion of this subject of the linkage between dynamic capabilities, requirements, alignment, and agility; Bigdeli has mentioned that if the enterprise agility has established a proper relationship with the strategic alignment, the results would be an enormous added value to the organization and securing business continuity (Bigdeli et al., 2020).

Conclusion

The alignment in the waterfall methodology is weak due to the low collaboration between each phase as well as the team members during the delivery steps due to the disconnected sequence steps. In another hand, the alignment between the development team and the client is practical not exist during the project delivery. That is why the waterfall methodology got many disputes cases between the development companies and the client in practical life due to low engagement of the client and delayed value delivery. However, the agile method came with a flexible mindset to solve both issues and improve the alignment.

ALIGNMENT FACTORS AND FINDINGS

Introduction

There are many factors that are impacting the BITA within IT companies. The author is concentrating in this chapter to highlight two main factors that are still under study by many consultants and practitioners to demonstrate the positive and negative impacts of considering the dynamic requirements which happen frequently in the projects and the degree of collaboration within the software delivery team.

Dynamic Requirements

Changing the requirements frequently might lead to an alignment issue through the software project delivery processes and requirements quality. The agile methodology practitioners believe that changing the requirements frequently is one of the agile benefits (Novelle, 2016) which is totally wrong. As per the author, agile gives flexibility to the project scope prior to the development execution phase ONLY. After that, for a specific sprint timeframe of the execution, the requirements should be locked to secure the alignment and improve the team focus on the concurrent work that is between their hand to be delivered as per the agreed scope and expected quality.

Requirements changes as a process shall be improved with a dynamic alignment between the end user and the actual delivery team which shall adopt the up-to-date needs with the project analysis, solution definition, and execution phases. Therefore, agile offers this feature which is not existing in the waterfall methodology that believes the scope change is defined up-front (Almazaydehet al., 2022), and as per the author's observation during his work experience going through different companies and business areas, any changes during the signoff of the communicated project plan, it shall be considered as a change request and it shall go through a specific change request process workflow which is usually time-consuming to agree on and if the changes are enormous it might impact the overall project massively and it might hold or cancel the project till the new changes are incorporated to the final plan, circulating, and realigning to the plan again with stakeholders which is a painful and costly process. In another hand, in the agile methodology, there is nothing called scope changes, there is always a principle called "Welcome Changes" or "Welcome Requirements" (Kashumi et al., 2020) by changing the requirements, bringing new business and system capabilities and features, or enhance the existing systems. The dynamic requirement shall NOT be considered within the sprint execution phase as described in the 3.3 section. However, keep generating a new scope and agreeing on the requirements incrementally before each sprint is a huge benefit to all parties to get the expected values at an early stage of each project delivery cycle. In another hand, Laiali has compared six delivery methodologies which are the waterfall, and the other five agile concepts which are Incremental, Iterative, Agile, Spiral, and Scrum. The comparison was driven based on the scope changes and the flexibility of managing the scope (Laiali, 2022). The outcome of this study is that every method has advantages and disadvantages as an overall assessment in this regard. However, from an agility perspective, it was clearly concluded that the waterfall has stable requirements and is unchangeable (Mansoori et al., 2010) that is reduce the level of alignment as stated in the section with very less user involvement, and less collaboration level.

From the above comparison, the conclusion is the waterfall methodology leads to requirements alignment issues between the client and software delivery team due to requirements changes. Alternatively, the agile methods could digest any changes from the client that leads to improving the alignment on the client's expectation, and hence the quality along with the collaboration factor which is described in the below section. In another hand, the waterfall has stability and requirements maintainability much better than agile in terms of documentation (This is another conclusion elicited from Laiali study), traceability, and management in case of no frequent changes in the requirements.

Collaboration

The agile methodology as a practice is improving the alignment between the end user and the software delivery team. However, collaboration between the team members and including the end user and other stakeholders to work proactively to solve the work challenges is extremely needed. Hence, the collaboration shall be planned, managed, and considered as one of the main practice subjects that shall be improved. As Gretchen Anderson, 2019, has mentioned in his book that called "Mastering Collaboration" establishes the right environment and sets a clear direction. The collaboration itself might be failed due to a lack of structure that shall enable the team members to collaborate effectively (as a case study, the telco-companies usually have a very complex structure due to the need for different business segments and technological domains) to manage their time, understand the success factors and how it looks like and set clear expectations.

Enabling the right environments to make a healthy workplace shall be considered based on the following factors *Enlist Everyone* to be part of the decision, dealing with all members with equality, transparency, integrity, and building trust and respect. Setting clear roles and responsibilities and aligning them to the employee's title and job description would improve the process efficiency and reduce role conflict which usually leads to conflict between team members. Hence, this leads to impacting the project and the company directly when the communication got impacted by such role conflict. The same happened to the author in one of his experiences when one of the roles was conflicting with the business analysis role in terms of requirements and client management and engagement which led to a daily conflict and push-back behavior. This matter resulted in the resignation of many business analysts due to the given power to the said role layer. When the company built a healthy workplace that shall give space for any individual to tell his or her opinion without fear, unexpected negative behavior from the management, and complexity, the innovation would be improved automatically as the innovation came from a free and open mind. As stated above the collaboration shall be also managed the same as communication management or stakeholders' management by making a collaboration plan and setting clear guidelines, and objectives that shall be SMART[6] in order to measure success metrics. The key factor in the collaboration is communication which also shall be managed and counting the communication channel among the team members to evaluate the communication complexity and plan for the better. As an example, Figure 3 is a representation of the communication channels for a product owner within the software delivery method:

The formula for calculating the communication channels is demonstrated below as per PMBOK. **N** is the number of stakeholders participating in the project including the project team. Taking Figure 3 as an example and the below formula, the number of communication channels considering the project team as a single point of contact, and the management, is forty-five which is time-consuming to manage, control and secure proper productive communication. However, it can be managed on daily basis within a specific squad team, and probably many squads could be running in parallel which is practically around seven persons. Hence, the communication would be distributed across many squads working on the project at the same time.

Figure 3. Communication channel for the product owner

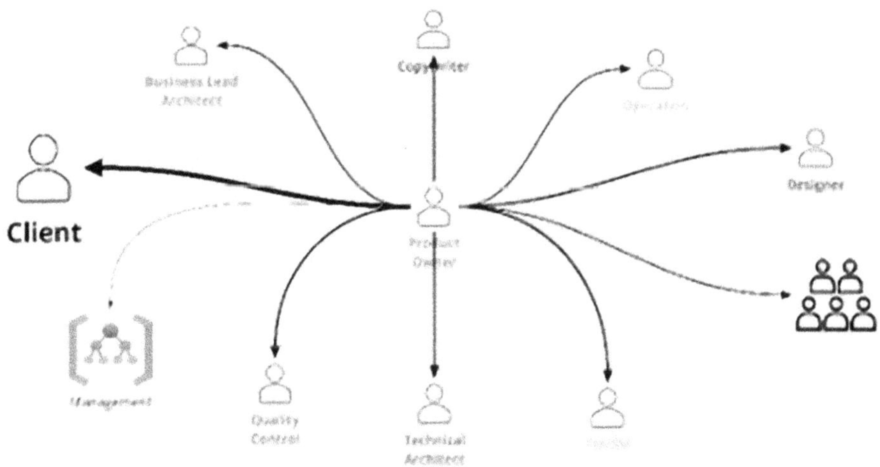

Communication Channels= (N × (N-1)) / 2

The waterfall methodology communication plan is huge as all stakeholders including the project team considered as one project team which makes communication and collaboration extremely difficult to manage when the project is complex in size. However, in the agile method and with the sprint and squad concept from five to seven project team members form a squad team (if we take as an example this squad, the communication channels would equal twenty-one channels considered seven members in the team only) to deliver a very specific feature or functionality. The communication can be calculated easily, and the collaboration would be much easier, and more fruitful with a limited focus group. The remaining project scope can be delivered with other squads and so on. All project teams are working in parallel with better communication and collaboration management tools and techniques.

Conclusion and Findings

One of the concluded benefits of the agile methodology as stated in section 3.3 and based on the proposed software lifecycle below which is describing the level of collaboration between each team member which is also detailed in section 4.3 that the agile proactive mindset that enables everyone in the team including the client to be engaged and work hand-in-hand to deliver the expected value. This attitude came mainly with the agile methodology as one of its principles.

Below is a practice outcome based on the author's experience and based on eights companies that he worked on and the comparison between waterfall and agile methodology within the SDLC framework:

Table 1 demonstrates the Level of Alignment between the Stakeholders for both Methodologies from the Collaboration Impact, and Scope Change Impact perspectives. The adoption of scope changes and level of collaboration is extremely important to improve the business and IT alignment. Going through the idea or prospect problem to be solved by the business owners (sometimes the product manager or marketing) shall start with a Customer Value Proposition (CVP) which is a very high-level idea in order to start communicating it with other stakeholders like product owners, business analysts…etc. and other cross-functions and enablers from IT, and Technology segments. the proposed CVP shall be developed into a detailed proposition that we usually called a business requirement which is the written form of the needs, after the requirements are identified, it shall be analysed and written in a way that the technical person can understand and start executing it after the solution is already defined and aligned between business and IT technical session to accumulate the time, cost, and resources before starting the implementation. Both the waterfall and agile methodologies are considered equal in terms of collaboration at these two stages of the project. From the project kick-off, the client and the business team will be almost disconnected from what is happening on the ground in the waterfall methodology. However, in agile this phase is the golden time to align, accept changes, be flexible…etc. and the collaboration between all stakeholders will be at the highest level even on a daily basis. This is the stage/phase in which this chapter has explained in detail the benefits of the agile methodology to increase the alignment between business and IT from the operation level.

Table 1. Level of alignment between all stakeholders within both methodologies

Collaboration	***Scope Changes** (Dynamic Requriements)*
Agile Alignment Model	
Business to Business Alignment	
Waterfall Alignment Model	
Business to Business Alignment	
Analysis Phase	
Both methods have **strong** collaboration	Scope change is **open** for both methods
Business to IT Alignment (Increment Scope)	
Business to IT Alignment (Entire Scope)	
Design Phase	
Both methods are **strong** but it is very complex in Waterfall	Scope change impact in this stage is **challenged** for both methods
IT to Business Ongoing Alignment (Daily Basis via Standup Meeting)	
No Alignment Except in a Official Change Request	
Development Phase	
Agile is **strong**. The waterfall is **weak** except in the change requests	Agile is **open** (Except within Sprint). Waterfall **does not accept** any scope change.
Business to Business Alignment	
Business to Business Alignment	
Testing, Acceptance, and Rollout Phase	
Agile is **strong**. The waterfall is **challenged** and subjected to client dispute.	Agile is flexible to add the scope changes to the next release. The Waterfall does accept a change request.

GENERAL CONCLUSION AND RECOMMENDATION

The project management methodologies that are used in the world and in the middle east region specifically from different disciplines and industries such as telco-companies, consulting agencies, e-government, and IT companies, in general, have transformed slowly to agile with their different methods like Scrum which is widely used in the region. Some companies still believe that the waterfall methodology is the right framework solution to deliver their business values such as Etisalat in its central IT division (Central IT within Etisalat company which is leading the IT enablement for the entire Etisalat Group Business Strategy and Operation in UAE and other countries such as Mobily-KSA, Etisalat-Egypt, Etisalat-Afghanistan…etc.) due to some factors, the project sizing is medium complexity (As per their internal definition of the complexity) in most of them which delivering in one release is going to be much better to take it in iteration models (Agile). However, the leadership style and cultural limitations of adopting the agile methodology to its business model, and organizational structure complexity led to a failure of adopting the agile methodology. After many years of testing the agile methodology for its business transformation segment and its initiatives, the leadership has seen the quality of delivery versus time was remarkable. Hence, they decided to generalize the agile methodology to all segments along with introducing DevOps[7] to their model to make it fully agile from the initiatives to the operation. Pierre, 2021 discussed the obstacles to using agility in some cases in Middle Eastern companies that are starting from being agile from the leader to developing the leadership skills to be agile. After analysing, assessing, and performing a vertical and horizontal diagnostic phase of the collected data, the findings are practically four main factors that are blocking the agility to be in practice to such organizations which are centralized organization structure that has the benefits of swift decision making. However, it is extremely difficult to transform into agile as restructuring such type of organization with a very high dynamic demand management, can be challenged which is the same case for Etisalat having a central IT that serves the entire company as well as its subsidiaries in the other nineteen countries worldwide (more than a thousand demand in the yearly average). The second finding is related to roles and responsibilities assigned to section heads and leads that are not aligned and part of the decision-making to participate in such transformation as well as they are not empowered enough by the leaders to implement the decision. The author has practiced the same situation in Etisalat as an example. Because it is a weak organization matrix that leads to weak ownership which is landing also to a weak power to enforce the correct practice of the agile framework. Some other reasons such as misalignment between the job description, task assignment and allocation, and work procedures. Finally, the misalignment also between employee performance evaluation and incentives seems random and not defined correctly. Regarding the two last points, Riaz, and Linda have mentioned the same arguments which are related to the compensation alignment with the employee's scorecard in their practical book chapter thirteen "Aligning Compensation" of the "Total Alignment" book, because these factors shall participate and impact the employee's engagement and the culture massively (Riaz, et al., 2017, p. 165).

The alignment issue is a serious subject in most industries that they are using IT as an enabler to their business. In this chapter, the author has taken two parameters to measure the level of alignment based on which are the proactivity of the stakeholders and team members that shall land to the level of collaboration during the product lifecycle, and the requirements changes during the project and product life cycle. The author has projected these two parameters to both products/project delivery methodologies to measure the alignment based on the author's observations and expertise in many companies such as telecommunication, fintech, e-government, and broadcasters within the MENA region (Middle East and North Africa). The waterfall methodology as described in section 3.1, is based on a sequence process that shall be followed and cannot be bypassed which resulted in a limitation of collaboration between team members and stakeholders as well as the mindset being pre-active. The business owner is being disconnected on the delivery after signing the contract and business requirements documents and waiting for the entire scope delivery which most of the time will not be satisfied due to many reasons such as poor requirements gathering and maintaining that results in dissatisfaction of the project deliverables, adding some new ideas during the project execution, and changing the scope that shall result in a long process of a change request. In another hand, the agile methodology has many principles, one of them being to be proactive and collaborative as it is a default mindset in an agile environment (Lynda et al., 2022). Starting from the idea or problem that shall be solved, the business owner would be aligned and the results come incrementally at the end of each iteration (Sprint); the client will start benefiting from the proposed features and functionalities very early so that the alignment on the expectation is becoming more valuable and real as well as solving also the issue of a static scope to become dynamic and the client would be able to change the requirements during the project if any idea or mind changes of any feature or functionality which increase the flexibility and give more relaxation to the client that the engagement and alignment are increased per each progress. The scope freeze at the beginning of the project is the waterfall style. However, some of the agile practitioners are operating in different methods like Scrum, Kanban…etc. believe that the "*Welcome Changes/Requirements*" (Kashumi et al., 2020, 37), which is one of the agile principles is applicable in the entire lifecycle which is NOT correct. The author does not strongly recommend changing the scope within the sprint itself. This means any changes that first shall be analysed, defined as the optimum solution, estimated, and added to the backlog, and then prioritize to be part of the next sprint to avoid disturbing the team and increase the focus that leads to deliverables quality is high.

REFERENCES

Abbas, Gravell, & Wills. (2014). Historical Roots of Agile Methods: Where did "Agile Thinking" Come from? School of Electronics and Computer Science, University of Southampton.

Alexander, M. (2020). *Agile vs. waterfall: Project methodologies compared.* CIO.

Almazaydeh. (2022). Formalization of the prediction and ranking of software development life cycle models. *International Journal of Electrical and Computer Engineering.*

Anderson, G. (2019). Mastering Collaboration. O'Reilly Media, Inc.

Ateeq. (2014). Comparison of various SDLC models. *Global Journal of Multidisciplinary Studies, 3*(11), 176-181.

Babar, M. A., Brown, A. W., & Mistrik, I. (2014). *Agile Software Architecture Aligning Agile Processes and Software Architectures.* Elsevier.

Bigdeli, E., Motadel, M., Eshlaghy, A. T., & Radfar, R. (2020). A dynamic model of effective factors on Agile business–IT alignment. Emerald Publishing Limited.

Carayannis, K. (2003). The Story of Managing Projects. Quorum Books.

Chung, R. Jr, Rainer, J., & Lewis, B. R. (2003). The impact of information technology infrastructure flexibility on strategic alignment and application implementations. *Communications of the Association for Information Systems, 11*(1), 11. doi:10.17705/1CAIS.01111

Deeb, A. (2019). *Software development methodologies in industry* [M.S. thesis]. Department Software Engineering, Australian National University.

Girvan, L., & Girvan, S. (2022). *Agile from First Principles*. The Chartered Institute for IT.

Khadem & Khadem. (2017). *Total Alignment. Tools and tactics for streamlining your organization.* Entrepreneur Press (EP).

Madampe, K., & Hoda, R. (2020). Towards Understanding Emotional Response to Requirements Changes in Agile Teams. IEEE/ACM.

Mansoori & Tayab. (2014). Standardized software development model for SME software houses in Pakistan. *Journal of Independent Studies and Research - Computing, 12*(1), 11-17.

Maxwell-Sinclair. (2016). *An Analysis of In-house and Offshore-outsourced Software Development Projects Utilizing Waterfall versus Agile Methodologies: A Simulation Study*. School of Computer Science and Information Systems, Pace University.

Pedersen. (2013). *A Quantitative Examination of Critical Success Factors Comparing Agile and Waterfall Project Management Methodologies*. Capella University.

Pierre, E. L. (2020). From Agile Leader to Agile Leadership: An OD Project in an International Company Operating in the Middle East. Saint Joseph University.

Project Management Professional Body of Knowledge (PMBOK), version 6. (2015). Project Management Institute (PMI).

Rigby, Sutherland, & Takeuchi. (2016). *The Secret History of Agile Innovation*. Academic Press.

Shah, J., Jinwala, D. C., & Patel, S. J. (2016). An excursion to software development life cycle models: An old to ever-growing models. *Software Engineering Notes, 41*(1), 1–6. doi:10.1145/2853073.2853080

Singhto & Phakdee. (2016). *Adopting a Combination of Scrum and Waterfall Methodologies in Developing Tailor-made SaaS Products for Thai Service and Manufacturing SMEs*. IEEE.

Tallon, P. A. (2011). Competing perspectives on the link between strategic information technology alignment and organizational agility: insights from a mediation model. MIS Quarterly, 463-486.

Wirattanapornkul, S. (2012). *Effect of IT capabilities and business–IT strategic alignment on business agility* [Doctoral dissertation]. University of the Thai Chamber of Commerce.

ENDNOTES

1 Agile as a discipline has many methods as well such as Scrum, Kanban, and the Scalable Agile Framework SAFe.

2 As described in the PMBOK that the process is a set of interrelated activities and actions performed to create a predefined product, or service or conclude a result; as per the BABOK, the process is a set of activities designed to accomplish a specific objective by taking one or more defined inputs and turning them into defined outputs.

3 Which is similar to a business analyst but with more product roles and responsibility related.

4 Some environments are called scrum team which is the project members who are going to execute the scope.

5 Requirements specification is divided into business process, business use cases, system use cases, and integration use cases.

6 SMART stand for Specific, Measurable, Achievable, Realistic, and Timely which is limited by time.

7 DevOps stands for Development and Operation is about fast, flexible development and provisioning of business processes. —Christof Ebert.

Chapter 9
Strategic Outlook for Big Data Management

Neeta Baporikar
https://orcid.org/0000-0003-0676-9913
Namibia University of Science and Technology, Namibia & SP Pune University, India

ABSTRACT

In the last two decades, big data has come to prominence in all spheres, from politics to business. Big data is seen as a resource to enhance business operations and also as a tool to help employees work more efficiently and streamline the collection and distribution of information technology (IT). Hence, the prevailing trend is that virtually everyone, ranging from big web companies to traditional enterprisers to physical science researchers to social scientists, is either already experiencing or anticipating unprecedented growth in the amount of data available in their world, as well as new opportunities and great untapped value. The understanding of the role of big data in this interconnected world is still in its nascent stage. What has been studied and highlighted appears massive, but what is yet to be realised is the latent potential of big data from an organisational perspective. Hence, adopting a systematic literature review with content analysis, the core aim of this chapter is to deliberate on the strategic outlook for big data management.

INTRODUCTION

The volume, velocity, variety, veracity, variability, visualisation, and value of data generated and shared by various actors in the (digital) economy has increased immeasurably, paving the way to an era of Big Data (BD) (Sivarajah et al., 2017; Wedel & Kannan, 2016). Raw data as such is futile. Only when purposefully processed, aggregated, and organized into a user-friendly format can they become information that can provide meaning given a specific context (O'Brien & Marakas, 2005). Insights that drive actions (e.g., challenge established norms and push in new directions as would be the case when introducing new touchpoints in the customer journey) are typically more valuable than ones that simply answers questions Against this backdrop, BDM are approaches, methods, and tools (Villarroel Ordenes & Zhang, 2019) that can help organisations develop customer insights from (big) data and information,

DOI: 10.4018/978-1-6684-7416-7.ch009

with the purpose of supporting managerial decision-making. To support managerial decision-making, BDM might encompass four different levels of analysis: descriptive, inquisitive (or diagnostic), predictive, and prescriptive (Sivarajah et al., 2017; Wedel & Kannan, 2016). Academic literature and popular press suggest that considerable value and competitive advantage can be attained by making effective decisions based on BDA (Davenport & Harris, 2017). BDM have the potential to transform business functions like supply chain and operations management, accounting and finance, sales, and marketing and even entire industries like healthcare, finance, and legal services).

Big Data (BD) has come of age and this is an era of it. Computer scientists, physicists, economists, mathematicians, political scientists, sociologists, and many others are clamoring for access to the massive quantities of information produced by and about people, things, and their interactions. Diverse groups argue about the potential benefits and costs of analyzing information from Twitter, Google, Verizon, 23andMe, Facebook, Wikipedia, and every space where large groups of people leave digital traces and deposit data. Especially since 2015, BD has come to prominence within business operations as a tool to help employees work more efficiently and streamline the collection and distribution of information technology (IT). There is a trend that, virtually everyone, ranging from big Web companies to traditional enterprisers to physical science researchers to social scientists, is either already experiencing or anticipating unprecedented growth in the amount of data available in their world, as well as new opportunities and great untapped value (Chen, Chen, Du, Li, Lu, Zhao, & Zhou, 2013). Yet there are many significant questions unanswered: Will Big data Management (BDM) aid in making organizations sustainable or bring in equitable distribution wealth or solve problems of health, reduce diseases or poverty, access to education and digital divide? Will BDM help make people's access to information more efficient and effective? If so then, how will this shape better life for mankind in terms of access, equity and justice? Will it transform how we study human communication and culture? Will organizations do better only in terms of profitability and also ensure sustainability and making the world better place to live?

Further when it comes to utility of big data by organizations there is no doubt it is a resource but will organizations have a strategic outlook and adopt long term approach when using this resource still remains a question. Even if organizations want to use this resource in a more effective and efficient manner, there are challenges (Almeida & Calistru, 2013). But with a strategic oulook and futuristic approach, recognizing that BDM is essential for long term growth and optimal benefits is crticial. Hence adopting a systematic literature review, with content analysis the core aim of this chapter is to deliberate on strategic outlook for BDM. The chapter also proposes a framework for strategic management of BDM.

LITERATURE REVIEW

Top management enthusiasm and compatibility between BDM and the firm's business processes have all been considered important for adoption of big data applications (Esteves and Curto, 2013). There is increasing recognition that the study of BDM and its diffusion has been important for policy makers, academics, businesses and governments (Chen and Zhang, 2014). The adoption of BDM depended upon managerial, organization, environmental and technological factors (Musti & Baporikar, 2023; Esteves and Curtos, 2013; McAfee, Brynjolfsson, Davenport, Patil, & Barton, 2012; Onay & Özturk, 2018).

BD is gradually modifying the way organizations are doing businesses. Previous trends such as BI and business analytics may be considered as the initiation point for BD ideas. Nevertheless, the novelty of BDM is the comprehensive method of providing real-time analytical services using databases to store structured and unstructured data (Chen and Zhang, 2014). While BDM is regarded an important technology that can provide strategic and operational advantages, it has yet to see significant rates of adoption in the firms of emerging economies and for that there is a need to adopt a strategic outlook on BDM.

Data Challenges

- **Access and Information Sharing:** It is common to expect reluctance of private companies and other institutions to share data about their clients and users, as well as about their own operations. Obstacles may include legal or reputational considerations, a need to protect their competitiveness, a culture of secrecy, and more broadly, the absence of the right incentive and information structures. There are also institutional and technical challenges, when data is stored in places and ways that make it difficult to be accessed and transferred.
- **Acquisition Rate:** Typically, given a large data set, it is often necessary to find elements in it that meet a specific criterion, which likely occurs repeatedly. Scanning the entire data set to find suitable elements is obviously impractical and very challenging.
- **Analytical Challenges:** The relevance and harshness of those challenges will vary depending on the type of analysis being conducted, and on the type of decisions that the data might eventually inform.
- **Data Overload:** Analysts and institutions are not used to effectively deal with a large number of variables, which is efficiently done with interactive dashboards. Practitioners still lack a standard workflow that would allow researchers, users and policymakers too efficiently and effectively use and the data which may be lead to issue of data overload..
- **Design of System:** To effectively deal with size is likely also to result in a system that can process a given size of data set faster, but would be costly and not affordable for all size of organizations.
- **Generalizability:** While observational data always represents this source very well, it only represents what it represents, and nothing more. While it is tempting to generalize from specific observations of one platform to broader settings, this is often very deceptive.
- **Harmonization:** Digital trace data still requires international harmonization of indicators. It adds the challenge of so-called "data-fusion", the harmonization of different sources.
- **Privacy:** The privacy is the most sensitive issue, with conceptual, legal, and technological implications. This concern increases its importance in the context of big data. In its narrow sense, privacy is defined by the International Telecommunications Union (Gordon, 2005) as the "right of individuals to control or influence what information related to them may be disclosed". Privacy can also be understood in a broader sense as encompassing that of companies wishing to protect their competitiveness and consumers and stages eager to preserve their sovereignty and citizens. In both these interpretations, privacy is an overarching concern that has a wide range of implications for anyone wishing to explore the use of big data for development in terms of data acquisition, storage, retention, use and presentation.
- **Representativeness:** While traditional development statistics is mainly concerned with the representativeness of random survey samples, digital trace data is never a random sample.
- **Size of Data Structures:** Managing large and rapidly increasing volumes of data has been a challenging issue for many decades. In the past, processors getting faster, which resources had needed to cope with increasing volumes of data, mitigated this challenge. But there is a fundamental shift underway now considering that data volume is scaling faster than computer resources.

Considering the size issue, we also know that the larger the data set to be processed, the longer it will take to analyze.

- **Security in Information Sharing:** Especially in big data use cases many online services today require us to share private information (i.e., facebook, linkedin, etc), but beyond record-level access control we do not understand what it means to share data, how the shared data can be linked, and how to give users fine-grained control over this sharing.
- **Transparency:** To analyze what the data is really telling in a fully transparent manner is difficult and challenging.

Thus, the challenges are intertwined and difficult to consider in isolation, but according to King and Powell (2008), they can be split into three categories: (a) getting the picture right (i.e., summarizing the data), (b) interpreting or making sense of the data through inferences, and (c) defining and detecting anomalies.

Management Challenges

- Management challenges that may prevent companies from succeeding in BDM include leadership and strategy (McAfee, Brynjolfsson, Davenport, Patil, & Barton, (2012).
- Organizational culture is critical to creating the right environment and ensures the effectiveness and drive big data capability with a strategic orientation (Lin, & Kunnathur, 2019). This is vital for BDM as a culture that embraces data and evidence-driven approaches to business decisions, and governance that delineates responsibility and accountability for data, are both catalysts for BDM value creation.
- Companies that have leadership teams with clear BDM strategies with clear goals and can articulate the business case are likely to succeed (Côrte-Real, Oliveira & Ruivo, 2017).
- Data-sharing agreements among multiple parties involved in a BDM need to be reached for data protection and privacy, including anonymization for open data, access control, rights management, and data usage control (George, Haas & Pentland, 2014). Thus, there is an obvious need to address some of the most fundamental concepts of privacy law, including the definition of "personally identifiable information," the role of individual control, and the principles of data minimization and purpose limitation (Tene & Polonetsky, 2012).
- Various surveys and reports indicate that a large proportion of companies are not aware if the ROI on investment in IT enablement and BDM would be positive or negative. This uncertainty highlights the challenge in determining and measuring the business value of BDM. Very few companies have taken steps to quantify rigorously ROI for BDM efforts. They need to get more precise in measuring ROI from BDA and examine the relationship between BDA and business outcomes. Practically, however, this is very difficult because there are so many factors or variables that need to be considered and these transcend dollars represented by revenue or cost savings. It requires mapping data, analytics, and business processes to desired business outcomes, and then measuring the impact or success of the outcomes.
- It is impossible to collect and analyze data across an enterprise and deliver insights to where they are most needed without proper organizational structure and governance mechanisms in place. BDM requires data to be collected and analyzed with centralized governance, which ensures that all big data projects within an organization apply the common standards, protocols, methods, and

tools. Therefore, an organization needs to establish a governance framework that standardizes the operations of BDM across diverse operational areas while also supporting federated project delivery.

DETERMINANTS IN ADOPTING STRATEGIC OUTLOOK ON BDM

- Technological
- Organizational
- Environmental

Inquiring about drivers of organizational success and sustainability, strategy research has pointed to resources (Barney, 1991), knowledge (Grant, 1996), and organizational capabilities (Eisenhardt & Martin, 2000; Helfat & Peteraf, 2009) as being influential. The dynamic capabilities perspective holds that capabilities are developed based on the combined and strategic use of resources, knowledge, and competencies (Teece, 2007). As our early review showed, Big Data is undoubtedly a collection of various resources, from which, analytics, representing competencies, is applied to generate knowledge. However, knowledge generation relies on organizational capabilities (Gold, Malhotra, & Segars, 2001). Further, organizational capabilities assume usage and deployment of resources and knowledge. Thus, organizational capabilities are stronger and sustainable drivers of organizational success than resources and knowledge (Teece, 2007). Thus, the hallmark of the new economy is the ability of organizations to realize economic value from their collection of knowledge assets as well as their assets of information, production distribution, and affiliation (Baporikar, 2020; 2019). Despite the competitive necessity of becoming a knowledge-based organization, senior managers have found it difficult to transform their business processes and firms through programs of knowledge management as there are issues in dealing with big data generated due to the technological waves (Baporikar, 2016; Baporikar 2017).

Data type and amount in human society is growing in amazing speed which is caused by emerging new services such as cloud computing, internet of things and social network, the era of BD has come. Data has been fundamental resource from simple dealing object, and how to manage and utilize big data better has attracted much attention (Xiaofeng, & Xiang, 2013). The term *'big data'* has been in use since the 1990s, with some giving credit to John Mashey, the popular American Computer Scientist for popularizing the term. BD data usually includes data sets with sizes beyond the ability of commonly used software tools to capture, curate, manage, and process data within a tolerable elapsed time. BD philosophy encompasses unstructured, semi-structured and structured data; however the main focus is on unstructured data. BD "size" is a constantly moving target; as the data creation is dynamic and non-stop. It can move fast from few dozen terabytes to many zettabytes of data. BD requires a set of techniques and technologies with new forms of integration to reveal insights from data-sets that are diverse, complex, and of a massive scale. Thus, BD is where parallel computing tools are needed to handle data and this is what represents a distinct and clearly defined change in the computer science used, via parallel programming theories, and losses of some of the guarantees and capabilities made by Codd's relational model. BD uses mathematical analysis, optimization, inductive statistics, and concepts from nonlinear system identification to infer laws (regressions, nonlinear relationships, and causal effects) from large sets of data with low information density to reveal relationships and dependencies, or to perform predictions of outcomes and behaviors.

Features of Big Data

Due to the amount and complexity of these data, it is difficult to process them using traditional tools, so the use of Big Data technology is essential in order to take advantage of this kind of data (Syed, Gillela, & Venugopal, 2013). Big Data technology is able to overcome the difficulties involved in understanding and extracting relevant knowledge from different kinds of data, which include: Diversity in types of fonts, formats and languages; Unstructured information (ideas, emotions, nuances, ambiguities, polysemy, etc.) that is contextual and has complex and fuzzy relations, such as distance, overlap, correlation, similarity, opposition, etc.; Dependence on the context in which it is emitted; Semantic problems due to the fact that language is constantly changing; and Dependence on grammar, language and the medium used. A more subtle aspect of BD which is not frequently mentioned is that the analysis of massive data, which are often incomplete and even slightly inaccurate, seeks to find correlations and detect "things that are happening", largely ignoring the analysis of causality. The emphasis is on the "what", not the "why" (Orenga-Roglá, & Chalmeta, 2016).

BD has certain feature and understanding them are crucial for organizations to develop a better perspective, so as to manage it efficiently. A brief discussion of the characteristics is below:

- **Exhaustive:** Means whether the entire system (i.e. n= all) is captured or recorded or not. BD may or may not include all the available data from sources.
- **Extensional:** Is if new fields in each element of the data collected can be added or changed easily.
- **Fine-Grained and Uniquely Lexical:** Refers respectively, the proportion of specific data of each element per element collected and if the element and its characteristics are properly indexed or identified.
- **Relational:** Means if the data collected contains common fields that would enable a conjoining, or meta-analysis, of different data sets.
- **Scalability:** Is if the size of the BD storage system can expand rapidly.
- **Value:** Is the worth in information that can be achieved by the processing and analysis of large datasets. Value also can be measured by an assessment of the other qualities of BD. Value may also represent the profitability of information that is retrieved from the analysis of BD data.
- **Variability:** Is the characteristic of the changing formats, structure, or sources of big data. Big data can include structured, unstructured, or combinations of structured and unstructured data. Big data analysis may integrate raw data from multiple sources. The processing of raw data may also involve transformations of unstructured data to structured data.
- **Variety:** Means the type and nature of the data. The earlier technologies like RDBMSs were capable to handle structured data efficiently and effectively. However, the change in type and nature from structured to semi-structured or unstructured challenged the existing tools and technologies. The BD technologies evolved with the prime intention to capture, store, and process the semi-structured and unstructured (variety) data generated with high speed (velocity), and huge in size (volume). Later, these tools and technologies were explored and used for handling structured data also but preferable for storage. Eventually, the processing of structured data was still kept as optional, either using big data or traditional RDBMSs. This helps in analyzing data towards effective usage of the hidden insights exposed from the data collected via social media, log files, sensors, etc. Big data draws from text, images, audio, video; plus it completes missing pieces through data fusion.

- **Velocity:** Is the speed at which the data is generated and processed to meet the demands and challenges that lie in the path of growth and development. BD is often available in real-time. Compared to small data, BD is produced more continually. Two kinds of velocity related to BD are the frequency of generation and the frequency of handling, recording, and publishing (Kitchin & McArdle, 2016).
- **Veracity:** Refers to the truthfulness or reliability of the data, which refers to the data quality and the data value (Onay, & Öztürk, 2018). *BD* must not only be large in size, but also must be reliable in order to achieve value in the analysis of it. The data quality of captured data can vary greatly, affecting an accurate analysis.
- **Volume:** Refers to the quantity of generated and stored data. The size of the data determines the value and potential insight and whether it can be considered big data or not. The size of BD is usually larger than terabytes and petabytes (Sagiroglu, 2013).

The Vs of big data represent the qualities of BD in value, variability, variety, velocity, veracity and volume. However the other characteristics also have a significant role when it comes to impact of decisions made based on BD.

Strategic Outlook and Value Proposition

Businesses today are eager to adopt BDM initiatives and strategies because they do not want to face potentially negative consequences of not doing so. However, the long-term strategic implications of BDM implementation are not well understood. Academics have not studied how BDM can lead to a competitive advantage and strategic business value. Success of BDM strategies requires more than just the data asset, the techniques to collect and manage big data, and knowledge and implementation experience of analytics methods and tools. It also requires a strategic perspective of the challenges and opportunities, measures and mechanisms so that BDM can serve as a resource to harness strategic business value and keep firms competitive. But before the chapter discusses the challenges and opportunities BDM, it is critical that organizations apply the strategic tools and do the evaluation of adopting BDM. Significant strategy tools are briefly discussed below.

BDM is one option for organizations to modernize with many benefits including scalability, elasticity, cost savings, and performance gains (Côrte-Real, Oliveira, & Ruivo, 2017). Despite the many benefits, BDM isn't the right fit for every organization or for all businesses. When deciding whether to adopt BDM, there is need to systematically assess your needs in the many areas. Some of the important areas are described below. After that the SWOT analysis must be done so that the decision to adopt BDM or not is rational and well informed decision.

Agility: The "instant infrastructure" characteristics of BDM deployments reduce project delays and enhance agility. Consider this to be a plus when you have or anticipate an ongoing flow of new projects.

Commitment: Politics and people can't be overlooked as real considerations when making the decision to adopt BDM. Are there resources, support, sponsorship, and political will to do it right?

Compliance: Consider carefully the degree to which your data is subject to regulatory compliance. Data privacy, protection of personally identifying information (PII), and data location are primary concerns that sometime lead to hybrid deployments and not holistically.

Disaster Recovery and Business Continuity: When disaster recovery and business resumption are key concerns BDM offers some unique advantages. Give BDM strong consideration when data is business critical or mission critical. Also consider whether data is sufficiently integrated into plan and the time and cost of recovery for a lost or corrupted data can be high.

Governance: BDM adds new dimensions to data governance responsibilities. When adopting BDM it is important that governance practices are recognized and adapt to BDM governance issues.

Networking: Moving data across networks—most commonly the internet—is an inherent part of BDM systems. Limited network bandwidth is only one issue. Concerns about security of data moving over networks may inhibit BDM adoption.

Scalability and Elasticity: Scalability and elasticity are substantial benefits of BDM and are among the top reasons to adopt BDM. Though inviting characteristics they are of little value, however, if you without real business and technical needs for scaling and dynamic resource allocation.

Security: Security is an often-cited concern, a concern that may be more about perception than reality. Evaluate service provider security practices including physical security and hardening of servers. Securing data as it moves across networks is a practical concern.

Technical Debt: Evaluate the amount of technical debt that you have assumed or will assume in the future. When entropy, lack of reliable documentation, and aging technology create future technical issues, BDM offers solutions to reduce or minimize technical debt.

Technology Architecture: Compatibility with technology architecture is an important consideration.

Keeping in mind the above factors, SWOT analysis needs to be done before adopting BDM.

Strengths, Weakens, Opportunities and Threats (SWOT) Analysis: Organizations must first do a SWOT before adopting and initiating the BDM strategy. Figure 1 gives the generic SWOT for BDM below.

Figure 1. Generic SWOT for BDM
Source: Musty and Baporikar (2022)

STRENGTHS	WEAKNESSES
Business impact? Application of technology? Advanced skills? Expertise and specialized knowledge? Most experienced people? Innovative solutions?	Business value? User satisfaction? Resources? Tools and technology? Knowledge and skills? Workload vs. capacity?
OPPORTUNITIES	**THREATS**
Business goals and needs? Advancing BI and analytics? User wants and expectations? Technology utilization? Reach into and across the business? Related projects & initiatives?	Obstacles and barriers? Stakeholder engagement & participation? Technological uncertainties? Data & process uncertainties? Scheduling & critical business events? Competing projects & initiatives?

VRIO Framework: The classic VRIO framework (valuable, rare, costly to imitate, organizationally embedded), based on a resource-based view (RBV) of firms (Baporikar, 2008; Barney & Hesterly, 2010; Knott, 2015), can be adopted to examine and develop BDM as a strategic resource to realize business value and sustain competitive advantage. When a firm considers and initiates a BDM strategy, it can apply the VRIO framework as below to assess whether BDM has potential to generate strategic business value. Table 1 reflects the application of VRIO Framework.

Thus, BDM though a valuable resource may not be sufficient by itself to sustain competitive advantage but without BDM a firm can suffer competitive disadvantage. The combination of BDM with other organizational resources and capabilities provides a new way to sustain competitive advantage. Assessing BDM is challenging, since in many instances of how data come together and how insights are recognized and acted upon are unpredictable. However, firms can get better at this by understanding the challenges and opportunities of BDM from strategic lenses to take advantage of the BDM to yield improved decisions, innovative products, or automated processes.

Advantages BDM

Companies currently have to deal with profound changes in the way they manage their business, their customers and their business models, since they are overrun by a data-driven revolution in management. This revolution is due to the wide availability of big data and the fast evolution of big data technologies. Big data is recognized as one of the most important areas of future technology, and is fast gaining the attention of many industries, since it can provide high value to companies (Raguseo, 2018). Slowly but surely organizations are realizing the value of managing data as it has become a strategic resource. Especially in today's global market the data size is also increasing and this is very adopting BDM will give organizations a strategic advantage and due to the benefits of BDM will help them to achieve competitive advantage too. Some of the major advantages and benefits of BDM due to digital trace of data are providing fine-grained data with many interrelated variables, and new aspects, like network connections. There is enhanced geographical coverage as technology has enabled level playing field for small and big organizations, countires etc. apart from that there is better scientific analysis as data analysis be it time series, trends and graphs can be produced without any errors and efficiency (Baporikar, 2015; 2014). Another advantage is the asepce tof timeliness and more focused thematic coverage as data analysis is fast within hours and days of being collected, it results in timely information for more rational decision-making including areas that were previously difficult or impossible to measure. Further, BD represents not only the factor from environment that confronts the companies with avalanche of data, but also very imporant resource which provide opportunities for companies to make value on the basis of collected data. Characteristics and possibilities which BD technologies offer have positioned them as a valuable factor for gaining and sustaining the competitive advantage in companies (Nikolić, 2017). Hence, it is crucial to recognize that BD technologies impact on competitive advantage of the companies that use them and hence there is need to explore it with a strategic outlook..

Table 1. VRIO framework application

Criteria	Question/s	Confirmation
Valuable	Does the BDM enable your organization to obtain valuable insights to exploit new business opportunities and/or neutralize competition threat?	The key question of data value stems from whether BDM can provide novel and valuable insights to exploit new business opportunities or defend competition threats. If the answer is yes, which is often difficult to determine, then BDM can become a valuable resource for business. The value of BDM exists in: • Insights generated from it can be used to create business value in many areas, such as business process improvement, product and service innovation, customer experience and market enhancement, organization performance improvement, and the creation of symbolic value such as business image and reputation. • Insights about products and services by analyzing both internally generated data and external user-generated content (e.g., online product/service reviews) can be used to increase product/ service differentiation, adjust the price of products/services, and develop innovative products and services. • Insights about customers and markets can be used to improve customer satisfaction and loyalty, lock in customers and suppliers, and create a niche market. • Insights about organization performance can enrich organizational intelligence for decision making and, development of flexible organizational structure to respond to market and environmental changes, make better capacity utilization, and increase return on assets.
Rare	Is your big data content, analytics capability, or the combination of them, rare? Can a few of your competitors acquire or possess them?	BDM can be rare, meaning that few competitors can acquire or possess the same or similar capability. Two key components prevail. • Content of big data itself may be imitable if it is user generated content available on online social media. But it is not so if it is internally generated data obtained from business interactions with employees, customers, suppliers, which are proprietary. But integrated data based on internally generated with externally obtainable data can make it a rare asset. • Analytics capability. Although BDM and analytics tools, such as Hadoop and various data and text mining tools, can be purchased from vendors, analytics knowledge, human talent, expertise, and experience with advanced big data management and analytics tools can be rare, domain-specific, and unique to a business context.
Costly to imitate	Without BDM capability, will your competitors face challenges or obstacles in obtaining or developing it? Is it difficult or almost impossible for your competitors to imitate what you can do with BDM?	Yes as there are many reasons that BDM is difficult and costly to imitate or inimitable. Important reasons include: • The big data asset and analytics capability require a long time to develop and nurture. Firms often engage in "learning by doing" and evolve from exploratory use to a more institutionalized form of use. • A firm may develop its own analytics algorithms and methods, which makes the analytics capability proprietary and inimitable. • The development and implementation of BDM capability are subject to a firm's IT maturity, the decision-making culture, and IT leadership, which makes BDM costly to imitate.
Organizationally embedded	Do your organization's business strategies and culture support the exploitation of valuable, rare, and costly-to-imitate BDM resources?	Yes if viewed from alignment as the implementation of BDM is IT-oriented, but a BDM strategy must be business-oriented. Success of organization depends on the inclusion of BDM in firm's long-term business strategy, and the mechanisms in place to facilitate business alignment with this strategy. This alignment involves processes, policies, procedures, organizational structure/governance, and corporate culture to leverage data for competitiveness.

SOLUTIONS AND RECOMMENDATIONS

Strategies for dealing with big data challenges will differ depending on the data maturity of the organization. How efficiently and effectively can data be collected for analysis, and for that matter, is the organization aware of all of the different types and sources of data that should be included to maximize insight and answers is an important issue. Also how well can the organization reconcile different data formats and what is the cost of collecting and analyzing data, and how is that cost weighed against the anticipated value of the outcome is another important consideration. Hence to ensure that the optimal benefits are reaped by there is need to have a strategic outlook for BDM. Some of the solutions and recommendation to ensure that the organizations do this in a systematic manner include:

- Bring together line of business leaders and IT practitioners to identify which data pools have the greatest value. Additionally, it would be interesting to evaluate the data stores that have been prepared for analysis and consider how they could be expanded or improved, and look at unstructured data sets and prioritize which ones should be converted to more usable formats. Business leaders and IT staff must also work together to highlight use cases for the data based on existing business to determine which approaches will yield the most business value in the shortest window.
- In a perfect world free from budgets, every piece of data that is collectable would be collected, and every byte would be analyzed in as many ways as the mind can consider. But in reality, collecting, storing, and analyzing data comes at a cost. Companies will need to make economic decisions about which data is worth collecting and analyzing. In fact, different parts of the business will have to make compromises. Business leaders are likely to lean towards collecting and analyzing more data, while IT leaders will aware if technology budget limitations and staff restrictions may lean in the other direction. The more data collected, the bigger the economic problem become. It is more expensive to store and manipulate more data, and the more data there is to process the more computational power is required, layering on more cost. Yet more data produces better informed decisions. Approaching big data analytics with finite definitions of what data will be considered sounds counterproductive, is crucial.
- New problems and growing computing power will spur the development of new analytical techniques. There is also a need for ongoing innovation in technologies and techniques that will help individuals and organizations to integrate, analyze, and visualize the growing amount of big data.

FUTURE RESEARCH DIRECTIONS

A rapidly developing and uncertain environment represents a key challenge within which business leaders make decisions. This study can be used by managers and service providers to improve their decision-making process in such an environment. Future research could build on this study by examining BDM adoption in different sectors and industries and in different countries both with quantitative and qualitative methodologies. On a geographical dimension, adoption of tenchnolgy differs therefore, it may not be appropriate to generalize to the whole population of the firms in other developed and developing economies. For this reason, further empirical investigations in different countries are needed. The methodology adopted for this study is content analysis and though this approach is useful in exploring into business-related decision analysis, it limits the ability to generalize. It is difficult to generalize these findings to a larger population of enterprises. Future research could build on this study by examining BDM adoption in different sectors and industries by both qualitative and quantitative methodologies and a careful selection of samples that can help to provide a representative picture of BDM. Similarly, future research on SMEs adoption and strategic value for them of BDM is also suggested. Another interesting thread for future studies is the difficult if not impossibility in collecting and analyzing data across an enterprise without proper organizational structure and governance mechanisms in place. Hence, studies pertaining to relationships between organizational structure, governance and BDM need to be undertaken. Social and economic environment influence on BDM strategies and applications is another interesting and emerging area. Further and because BDM is relatively new, there has been little empirical research on how BDM can harness business value and linkage among BDM assets, impacts, and business performance. There is need to have a better understanding of how, why, and when BDM can be valuable for companies to gain a competitive advantage.

CONCLUSION

Despite the popularity of BDM in industry, many organizations have failed to reach their strategic goals after investing substantial resources. In this chapter, we offer a strategic perspective on challenges and opportunities in BDM and proper a mechanism for effective BDM. Through this mechanism we argue that leveraging big data for insights and actions will successfully help businesses to achieve strategic business value and aid in proper strategic positioning. Businesses need to assess the strategic role of big data analytics and to invest in quality data, state-of-the-art tools, and data-savvy people who understand relevant technologies and data-drive business opportunities. Successful BDM yields value in both functional and symbolic forms as successful initiatives are championed through an integrative BDM strategy and strong leadership. By articulating key challenges and opportunities we offer important research questions that address BDM adoption. Thus, the effective use of big data has the potential to transform economies, delivering a new wave of productivity growth and consumer surplus. Using big data will become a key basis of competition for existing companies, and will create new competitors who are able to attract employees that have the critical skills for a big data world. Leaders of organizations need to recognize the potential opportunity as well as the strategic threats that big data represent and should assess and then close any gap between their current IT capabilities and their data strategy and what is necessary to capture big data opportunities relevant to their enterprise. To conclude, business leaders should start thinking strategically about how to prepare the organizations for big data as data analysis will change, becoming part of a business process instead of a distinct function performed only by trained specialists. Achieving the vast potential of big data demands a thoughtful, holistic approach to data mining, data management, analysis and information intelligence.

REFERENCES

Almeida, F., & Calistru, C. (2013). The main challenges and issues of big data management. *International Journal of Research Studies in Computing*, *2*(1), 11–20. doi:10.5861/ijrsc.2012.209

Baporikar, N. (2008). Global Strategic Management. Himalaya Publishing House.

Baporikar, N. (2014). Information Strategy as Enabler of Competitive Advantage. *International Journal of Strategic Information Technology and Applications, 5*(1), 30–41. doi:10.4018/ijsita.2014010103

Baporikar, N. (2015). Holistic Framework for Evolving Effective Information Systems Strategy. *International Journal of Strategic Information Technology and Applications, 6*(4), 30–43. doi:10.4018/IJSITA.2015100103

Baporikar, N. (2016). Business Process Management. *International Journal of Productivity Management and Assessment Technologies, 4*(2), 49–62. doi:10.4018/IJPMAT.2016070104

Baporikar, N. (Ed.). (2017). *Global practices in knowledge management for Societal and Organizational Development*. IGI Global.

Baporikar, N. (2019). E-Learning Strategies for Emerging Economies in the Knowledge Era. In J. Pelet (Ed.), *Advanced Web Applications and Progressing E-Learning 2.0 Technologies in Higher Education* (pp. 150–171). IGI Global. doi:10.4018/978-1-5225-7435-4.ch008

Baporikar, N. (2020). Learning Link in Organizational Tacit Knowledge Creation and Dissemination. *International Journal of Sociotechnology and Knowledge Development, 12*(4), 70–88. doi:10.4018/IJSKD.2020100105

Barney, J. (1991). Firm resources and sustained competitive advantage. *Journal of Management, 17*(1), 99–120. doi:10.1177/014920639101700108

Barney, J. B., & Hesterly, W. S. (2010). *Strategic management and competitive advantage: Concepts*. Prentice Hall.

Chen, C. P., & Zhang, C. Y. (2014). Data-intensive applications, challenges, techniques and technologies: A survey on Big Data. *Information Sciences, 275*, 314–347. doi:10.1016/j.ins.2014.01.015

Chen, J., Chen, Y., Du, X., Li, C., Lu, J., Zhao, S., & Zhou, X. (2013). Big data challenge: A data management perspective. *Frontiers of Computer Science, 7*(2), 157–164. doi:10.100711704-013-3903-7

Côrte-Real, N., Oliveira, T., & Ruivo, P. (2017). Assessing business value of Big Data Analytics in European firms. *Journal of Business Research, 70*, 379–390. doi:10.1016/j.jbusres.2016.08.011

Davenport, T., & Harris, J. (2017). *Competing on Analytics: Updated, with a New Introduction: The New Science of Winning*. Harvard Business Press.

Eisenhardt, K. M., & Martin, J. A. (2000). Dynamic capabilities: What are they? *Strategic Management Journal, 21*(10-11), 1105–1121. doi:10.1002/1097-0266(200010/11)21:10/11<1105::AID-SMJ133>3.0.CO;2-E

Esteves, J., & Curto, J. (2013, January). A risk and benefits behavioral model to assess intentions to adopt big data. *Proceedings of the 10th International Conference on Intellectual Capital, Knowledge Management and Organisational Learning: ICICKM 2013*. 10.37380/jisib.v3i3.74

George, G., Haas, M. R., & Pentland, A. (2014). Big data and management. *Academy of Management Journal, 57*(2), 321–326. doi:10.5465/amj.2014.4002

Gold, A. H., Malhotra, A., & Segars, A. H. (2001). Knowledge management: An organizational capabilities perspective. *Journal of Management Information Systems, 18*(1), 185–214. doi:10.1080/07421222.2001.11045669

Grant, R. M. (1996). Toward a knowledge-based theory of the firm. *Strategic Management Journal, 17*(S2), 109–122. doi:10.1002mj.4250171110

Helfat, C. E., & Peteraf, M. A. (2009). Understanding dynamic capabilities: Progress along a developmental path. *Strategic Organization, 7*(1), 91–102. doi:10.1177/1476127008100133

King, G., & Powell, E. N. (2008, August). *How not to lie without statistics.* Delivery at the 2008 Annual Meeting of the American Political Science Association.

Kitchin, R., & McArdle, G. (2016). What makes Big Data, Big Data? Exploring the ontological characteristics of 26 datasets. *Big Data & Society, 3*(1). Advance online publication. doi:10.1177/2053951716631130

Knott, P. J. (2015). Does VRIO help managers evaluate a firm's resources? *Management Decision, 53*(8), 1806–1822. doi:10.1108/MD-08-2014-0525

Lin, C., & Kunnathur, A. (2019). Strategic orientations, developmental culture, and big data capability. *Journal of Business Research, 105*, 49–60. doi:10.1016/j.jbusres.2019.07.016

McAfee, A., Brynjolfsson, E., Davenport, T. H., Patil, D. J., & Barton, D. (2012). Big data: The management revolution. *Harvard Business Review, 90*(10), 60–68. PMID:23074865

Musti, K. S., & Baporikar, N. (2023). Industry 4.0-based enterprise information system for P2P lending. *Journal of Science and Technology Policy Management, 14*(1), 6–24. doi:10.1108/JSTPM-06-2020-0093

Nikolić, J. L. (2017). The impact of big data technologies on competitive advantage of companies. *Facta Universitatis-Economics and Organization, 14*(3), 255–264.

O'Brien, J. A., & Marakas, G. M. (2005). *Introduction to information systems.* McGraw-Hill/Irwin.

Onay, C., & Öztürk, E. (2018). A review of credit scoring research in the age of Big Data. *Journal of Financial Regulation and Compliance., 26*(3), 382–405. doi:10.1108/JFRC-06-2017-0054

Orenga-Roglá, S., & Chalmeta, R. (2016). Social customer relationship management: Taking advantage of Web 2.0 and Big Data technologies. *SpringerPlus, 5*(1), 1462. doi:10.118640064-016-3128-y PMID:27652037

Raguseo, E. (2018). Big data technologies: An empirical investigation on their adoption, benefits and risks for companies. *International Journal of Information Management, 38*(1), 187–195. doi:10.1016/j.ijinfomgt.2017.07.008

Sagiroglu, S. (2013). Big data: A review. *2013 International Conference on Collaboration Technologies and Systems (CTS),* 42–47. 10.1109/CTS.2013.6567202

Sivarajah, U., Kamal, M. M., Irani, Z., & Weerakkody, V. (2017). Critical analysis of big data challenges and analytical methods. *Journal of Business Research, 70*(1), 263–286. doi:10.1016/j.jbusres.2016.08.001

Syed, A., Gillela, K., & Venugopal, C. (2013). The future revolution on big data. *Future, 2*(6), 2446–2451.

Teece, D. J. (2007). Explicating dynamic capabilities: The nature and microfoundations of (sustainable) enterprise performance. *Strategic Management Journal, 28*(13), 1319–1350. doi:10.1002mj.640

Tene, O., & Polonetsky, J. (2012). Big data for all: Privacy and user control in the age of analytics. *Northwestern Journal of Technology and Intellectual Property, 11*(5), 239–273.

Villarroel Ordenes, F., & Zhang, S. (2019). From words to pixels: Text and image mining methods for service research. *Journal of Service Management, 30*(5), 593–662. doi:10.1108/JOSM-08-2019-0254

Wedel, M., & Kannan, P. K. (2016). Marketing analytics for data-rich environments. *Journal of Marketing, 80*(6), 97–121. doi:10.1509/jm.15.0413

Xiaofeng, M., & Xiang, C. (2013). Big data management: concepts, techniques and challenges. *Journal of Computer Research and Development, 50*(1), 146.

KEY TERMS AND DEFINITIONS

Barriers: Anything serving to obstruct, or preventing, access, or progress. Anything or something that limits a quality or achievement or the act of limiting or the condition of being limited or cause delay. Barriers come in many forms and from many sources. They can be temporary or permanent. When evaluating a barrier, it is necessary that one looks at all the activities that precede the delay as well as the activities that follow the delay.

Borderless World: A borderless world is a global economy in the age of the internet that is thought to have removed all the previous barriers to international trade.

Challenges: Something that by its nature or character serves as a call to make special effort, a demand to explain, justify, or difficulty in a undertaking that is stimulating to one engaged in it.

Database: A set of data structured to support the storage, retrieval, and analysis of information, often custom-designed for specific business applications. Databases are central to information processing since they allow new and more efficient ways of assembling records and organizing work for better decision-making.

Decision-Making: A rational and logical process of choosing the best alternative or course of action among the available options.

Impact: To have effect on, effect of coming into contact with a thing or person; the force exerted by a new idea, concept, technology, or ideology, the impression made by an idea, cultural movement, social group, it is to drive or press (an object) firmly into (another object, thing, etc.) so as to have an impact or strong effect (on).

Imperative: Absolutely necessary; urgent; compelling; a rule; principle; or instinct that compels a certain behavior.

Information Technology (IT): The umbrella term that encompasses the entire field of computer-based information processing: computer equipment, applications, and services, telecommunication links and networks, digital databases, and the integrated technical specifications that enable these systems to function interactively. IT is study or use of systems (especially computers and telecommunications) for storing, retrieving, and sending information.

Knowledge Development: The development of knowledge includes not only processes of external knowledge procurement (i.e. through cooperative efforts, consultants, new contacts, etc.) or the creation of specific knowledge resources like research and development departments. The formation of personal and technical knowledge networks is also part of the development of knowledge.

Models: An exact representation of something in greatly reduced size for better understanding and adoption if found suitable.

Network: A set of communication paths (or channels) and the points (or nodes) they connect, including switches to determine which channel will be used when more than one is available. Computer networks, like telephone networks, can be thought of as telecommunications highways over which information travels.

Strategies: Method chosen and plans made to bring about a desired future, achievement of a goals or solutions to a problem. Strategies are a result of choices made. It is that set of managerial decisions and actions that determine the long term performance of a business enterprise.

Technology: The branch of knowledge that deals with the creation and use of technical means and their interrelation with life, society, and the environment, drawing upon such subjects as industrial arts, engineering, applied science, and pure science; method for convening resources into goods and services.

Chapter 10
The Role of Social Manufacturing for Entrepreneurship in the Industry 4.0 Transformation

Salih Aka
Erzincan Binali Yıldırım University, Turkey

ABSTRACT

Social manufacturing is an internet- and social network-based platform where different manufacturers' capabilities can be seen and manufacturers with similar skills and hardware levels can come together to form communities. In the horizontal community, manufacturers who have similar socialised manufacturing resources and can perform the same processing activities are brought together. In the vertical community, there are manufacturers who can take part in different production activities of a product, from raw material to final product, and combine their socialised resources in this direction. Social manufacturing allows the bargaining power of the main producer to decrease thanks to the communities it establishes. The social manufacturing platform is a virtual showcase for small-scale entrepreneurs to present their talents, an effective cost management mechanism for customers, and an interaction, coordination, and sharing tool that will maximise production efficiency for countries.

INTRODUCTION

Volatile consumer expectations and dynamic markets are causing manufacturing companies to focus on mass customization. In competitive markets, businesses need to focus on more personalized and innovative product development. However, the current conditions increase the costs and decrease the productivity of the enterprises that perform all the supply, manufacturing, and distribution functions. Many activities that are not the core business of the enterprise make it unwieldy and threaten the economic sustainability. Responding to changing market trends requires being much more agile and flexible. Businesses implement a strategy of focusing on their core ability and obtain professionalized outsourcing support

DOI: 10.4018/978-1-6684-7416-7.ch010

for their inefficient activities. In future, it is expected that outsourcing for machining parts will become a much higher priority for manufacturing enterprises.

Outsourcing has two sides. One of them is the main business that requests various machining services related to the manufacture of the product. The others are the manufacturing enterprises that have the resources to fulfill the requested tasks regarding the product of the parent enterprise. In conventional manufacturing supply chains, the main business meets its outsourcing needs with a limited number of manufacturers. Factors such as mutual distrust, incomplete information about the capabilities of the manufacturer that shares the resource, and miscommunication may require that this cooperation is limited to a small number of stakeholders (Cao et al., 2015). Contemporary production approach adopts new paradigms such as transparency, communication and sharing. Today, while individual and corporate orientation towards service industries and digital content production is observed, new production technologies are increasing, and alternative digital opportunities are being created for the development of physical production (Hamalainen et al. 2018). Social manufacturing is a new resource sharing model shaped around these paradigms. Stakeholders such as small-medium sized businesses, smart factories, workshops, logistics service providers and public warehouse providers who want to share socialized manufacturing resources for outsourced/crowdsourced tasks are united under the social manufacturing platform (Ding et al. 2018).

Social manufacturing is like cloud manufacturing in terms of its working principle. Cloud manufacturing serves to provide integration between resource providers and service requesters. Cloud manufacturing and social manufacturing are seen as cyber-physical and social systems that facilitate the analysis of big data in decision making, thus making business and relationship management efficient, flexible, and easily controllable (Jiang et al., 2016). However, cloud manufacturing has some technological inadequacies in areas such as security, resource management and scheduling, inter-organizational collaboration, logistics, etc. (Cao et al., 2015). Social manufacturing is to bring together the relevant fields of social search, social computing, and social production to connect the next-generation production network of the Internet of Things and 3D printing, and to ensure that manufacturing resources are fully involved in the entire production process (Xiong et al., 2018).

Social manufacturing is a platform that is not centrally managed and powered by social networks. In this platform, individuals can provide services on their own, within a network or within an organization (Hirscher et al., 2018). Zhou et al. (2016) discuss social manufacturing as a kind of service-oriented smart system that uses social networks to outsource production activities tasks in an organized manner between individuals and companies. However, this view emphasizes that manufacturing can also be supported by social networks, as it refers to the need to use social networks (Facebook, Linkedin, etc.) to facilitate interaction and communication with users (Hirscher et al., 2018).

The widespread use of social media and the technology-oriented change in production paradigms have led to the emergence of social manufacturing. Considering that these developments are recent, it is seen that social manufacturing is already a newly developing platform. With the Industry 4.0 era, digitalization is gaining intensity in manufacturing sectors and supply chains. As a matter of fact, digital manufacturing support systems such as cloud manufacturing (Tao et al., 2011; Xu, 2012), networked manufacturing (Xiong et al., 2018) have contributed to the development of social manufacturing. There are also different systems such as artificial neural networks (Cao et al., 2015), natural language processing (Leng and Jiang, 2016), blockchain (Leng et al., 2019), and RFID (Ding et al., 2018), which serve as an auxiliary and support mechanism in the effective use of the social manufacturing. The systems used contribute to the efficient sharing of resources and increase efficiency.

Social manufacturing emerges as a candidate to change today's understanding of manufacturing. Communication and interaction are becoming the most important factor for the globalizing world of production. Social manufacturing has the potential to be at the center of the industry 4.0 revolution, where devices and people can interact with each other. The aging mass production approach is shifting to individual production with industry 4.0 tools. The customer is more part of the product development process than ever before. This situation requires manufacturers to be more agile and flexible. However, companies that play the role of big players trying to do all the manufacturing tasks themselves have difficulty in keeping up with the rapid changes. Social manufacturing can turn small producers that do not have capital power, that are too small to be noticed in the sector and that have limited resources, to become a stakeholder. It also gathers small manufacturers together and increases their bargaining power vis-à-vis large manufacturers. Social manufacturing creates a window of opportunity for small manufacturers who want to expand their business.

Social manufacturing also has the opportunity to create the infrastructure of virtual manufacturing. So much so that startups that set off with just a business idea have the opportunity to produce their products without the need for a production line, thanks to social manufacturing. Social manufacturing can bring manufacturers together according to production tasks and enable the product to emerge. From this point of view, the organization that an entrepreneur needs can be easily established with social manufacturing.

The objective of this study is to describe the paradigm shift towards social manufacturing and to explain how the social manufacturing platform is an entrepreneurial tool. For this purpose, a review on the role of social manufacturing and entrepreneurship has been made by examining a limited number of recent studies. The study makes conceptual suggestions on how social manufacturing functions can be used for entrepreneurship purposes with some other industry 4.0 technologies.

In this section, the components, working principle and usage advantages of the social manufacturing platform, which allows manufacturers who want to share their resources and those who want to receive manufacturing services for their products, to gather in a social network are explained.

PRODUCTION FUNCTIONS LEADING TO SOCIAL MANUFACTURING

The idea of maximizing resource use is the mainstay of many basic paradigms in production issues. The lean production system is one of the approaches that adopts the maximum utilization of resources by reducing waste (Sundar et al., 2014). While lean production directly targets customer satisfaction, it contributes to efficiency with a minimum waste policy against sudden changing demand. However, this approach faces major challenges such as limited resources, unpredictable economic environment and harsh competition conditions with competitors (Palange and Dhatrak, 2021). Innovative approaches such as lean manufacturing are expected to change organizational cultures. This change provides benefits for employees by reducing fatigue and stress, eliminating waste, creating financial benefits, reducing rework, reducing inventory levels and reducing lead times (Gupta and Jain, 2013).

Lean manufacturing has been a pioneer in creating an agile and flexible production environment by activating internal factors. However, the organization of external factors, as well as internal, gains importance for cost advantage. It marks the beginning of a new era for technological and cyber developments. Zeng et al. (2022) express this transformation, which they call digital reform, as creating an integration between the production, management and operational processes of enterprises and controlling all processes through a data chain using digital technology.

In our world where collaborations and networks are digitized, it seems unlikely that the production paradigm will not be affected by digitalization. Alternative digital universes such as social media and the metaverse are key to change. Production systems are in a period where communication opportunities are developing very rapidly, especially under the leadership of industry 4.0. This period has its own parameters. Social media and digital universes enable each individual to do business as an entrepreneur. Each individual can become a stakeholder of the production and value chain. On the other hand, large-scale companies are also individualized thanks to social media and similar platforms. This situation offers a very broad vision to individuals and organizations in terms of production capabilities.

Social manufacturing is emerging as a new platform capable of playing a role in the individualization of mass production. In fact, the innovative potential of some production factors in the industry 4.0 transformation has accelerated new paradigm shifts in production (Alheriani et al., 2021). Internet-based communication between actors and social network-based development of this communication, outsourcing that will increase efficiency and agility in manufacturing and production activities, individualization of mass production, massification of individual production form the basis of this paradigm shift towards social manufacturing.

Manufacturing and Social Networking

Social media and social networks, which emerged with the aim of establishing a digital and virtual relationship network between individuals, have changed many habits of humanity about life over time. Social networks are an effective way of building togetherness. At the same time, social media are easy-to-access and low-cost platforms where talents and experiences can be showcased. After the realization of these features, social media and social networks have turned into convenient tools that allow the development of different business models. It is inevitable that this phenomenon, which changes the lifestyle, consumption and business styles of individuals, will also create a paradigm shift in production. Actually, production and manufacturing systems, which are digitized with decision support systems such as ERP, MRP, and CAD etc. and then supported by IOT and cloud manufacturing, will continue to develop through social networks in the next step. Advances in communication technology, especially 5G, allow production systems to communicate with each other and contribute to the development of autonomous systems. Technological infrastructures that provide efficiency for production systems cause the formation of large manufacturing data and the complexity of decision and control systems. Critical decisions such as evaluation and selection often push the boundaries of the decision maker and increase the possibility of error. Social networking platforms are becoming a convenient tool in the evaluation and selection of alternatives in line with production and manufacturing needs.

Development in Outsourcing Service Concept

In the classical production approach, the manufacturers completed the processing processes of which they were not experts by purchasing parts or semi-finished products from the supplier. With the developments in communication technology, the way of doing business has also begun to change. Communication technology facilitated the establishment of strategic partnerships between the supplier and the manufacturer, contributing to the increase in the total quality and competitiveness of the supply chain. The joint use of product service systems by all stakeholders has successfully served the purpose of maximizing the value provided by the supply chain. However, such cooperation is not enough to overcome the high competition conditions in globalizing economies. The change in customer demands and requests is the fastest of all time. This rate of change has an increasing momentum. In order for manufacturers to continue their existence, they need to keep up with the changes in demand and customer expectations. Businesses whose organizational structure is set up to manage all manufacturing processes remain cumbersome for this change. Strategic cooperation with key supplier can be considered as one of the leading organizational developments changed by communication technology. However, the main change that communication technology has created on large masses through social media is transforming all habits. It is not possible for production to remain indifferent to this innovation.

Manufacturers are becoming much more agile by focusing on their own activities and outsourcing non-specialized activities to third-party service providers. Third party logistics companies carry out activities such as distribution and handling of manufacturing enterprises. However, the main innovation of the third party logistics companies will be to solve some of the processing processes of the main manufacturer with the support of outsourcing. While many small-scale companies specialize only in certain processing services, they can use their limited resources to develop what they do best. Developing the expertise of different companies in different jobs can increase overall productivity. In this way, much faster and higher quality transactions can be performed at less cost. Such an organizational structure may also allow all stakeholders in the system to use their maximum capacities. In order to establish this systemic structure, it is important to establish a strong internet-based communication network and enable stakeholders to interact easily. Social network structure and fast communication infrastructures such as 5G can enable the establishment of this system. Product service systems based on the social network structure are the inspiration for such an application.

Open Design and Innovation Approach

The classical production paradigm has an understanding of innovation from the manufacturer to the end user. Innovation and R&D teams established for product and service development make design and operational decisions in line with the consumer data they obtain from the field. In this case, although the feedback received from the consumers is taken into account, this flow in the value chain is far from directly reflecting all the wishes and expectations of the user.

Digital platforms are useful tools for conveying requests and expectations. Especially open source software platforms offer an unlimited world that will allow users to meet their own needs. These platforms enable users to realize their dreams with their user-friendly interfaces and, software languages that are easy to learn and program.

Social media platforms and various digital channels that use the open design and innovation approach have much more than the limited number of improvement suggestions they can get by employing a certain number of developers. The open system prepares the infrastructure for each individual to contribute as a developer. For companies, this resource is an unlimited offer with zero cost. Global social media and digital platforms already benefit from this resource. Some social media platforms such as YouTube, Wikipedia etc. are some of the digital channels where individuals directly contribute and provide data. Independent of the company, a value chain emerges and grows thanks to the interactions of content providers and users.

The open design and innovation approach also offers development opportunities for manufacturing companies. Since the designs created by the users and the operational innovation suggestions are directly from the consumer, the market research effort of the companies are eliminated. In addition, there will be no need for extra costs such as design and labor. In addition to the opportunities offered by this approach, there are also some drawbacks. The open design option makes it easier for external users to submit their designs directly to the company. The company can use these designs, but in this case, a payment will be made for the service provided by the designer. Currently, some open source applications (e.g., Linux, Android) can solve their legal problems with various prerequisites (Mohajeri, 2015). However, open design and legislative changes supporting innovation and increasing benefit will make this approach preferable for manufacturers.

CONCEPTUAL DIMENSION OF SOCIAL MANUFACTURING

Production has a role similar to the circulatory system in human life for national economies. Over time, technological developments, environmental sensitivity and social awareness have changed the patterns of production and manufacturing function. While manufacturing, which was labor-intensive in the past, first became factory and then automated, we are now witnessing the digitalization of manufacturing (Gebauer et al., 2021).

Digitization has developed with advances in information and communication technology. We are in an age where machines, objects and tools can communicate with each other, make decisions, and implement them. There is a huge data density behind the smart devices and the receiving mechanisms. Artificial intelligence applications, which enable data to be processed, are creating the opportunity for smarter devices to develop themselves day by day. The way that devices communicate and interact with each other is not different from individuals establishing associations with the help of networks. The Internet creates an infrastructure for virtual environments that allow individuals to come together. Individuals can form associations and establish organizations by interacting through social networks. Social networks have begun to be effective on individuals' behavioral patterns and consumption habits. This situation leads to a change in the way of doing business. Xiong et al. (2022) mentions the change in manufacturing paradigms because of industrial revolutions over time and the technological infrastructure behind this change, as seen in Figure 1. In the period until Industry 4.0, mass production is the driving force behind production. However, the rationalization of production and the virtual development of social relations have also changed manufacturing. There is a share of cyber-physical systems (CPS) behind the smartness of manufacturing. Machines that can communicate with each other via the Internet have contributed to the reduction of errors, improvement of efficiency and innovation activities. The effectiveness of communication channels has created an environment where manufacturing is much more personalized and flexible than before, and where resources and production factors can relate to each other (Aheleroff et al., 2021). Along with the development in digital transformation and network applications, the integration of social networking and manufacturing provides further strengthening of manufacturing. This transformation is expressed as cyber–physical–social systems (CPSSs) (Xiong et al., 2022).

Benchmarking can often be used as a tool to inspire new business models. Well, is it possible to use this change created by social media and social networks on consumption and purchasing habits in manufacturing? The concept of social manufacturing can actually be shaped through this question.

Figure 1.

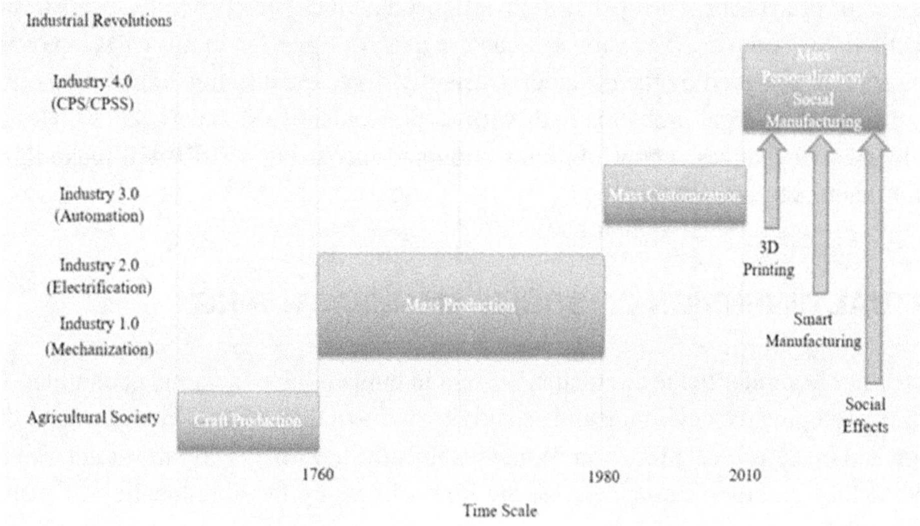

Social manufacturing provides an environment where individual participants can make choices in the process, where individuals can develop cooperation not only with companies but also with other individuals, and where roles can change dynamically (Hamalainen et al. 2018). Social manufacturing is a system based on internet and social network connections and based on outsourcing and crowdsourcing mechanism in business modeling. While this system provides the sharing of socialized resources through a platform with a social media interface, it needs some kind of social networking structure.

The premise of the paradigm is service delivery. Every small-scale manufacturer is actually a service provider. Social manufacturing is a tool that can be used in determining this service need, finding service providers and meeting the service need. This service need of the main manufacturer can be met by outsourcing or crowdsourcing service. In the outsourcing service approach, a large number of service providers are evaluated in terms of the nature of the work, and the most suitable one to do the job is selected. The selected outsourcing service provider is considered a strategic partner for the main manufacturer and the expectations of the main manufacturer are guaranteed with a binding contract between the partners. The main manufacturer can provide feedback on the processes by controlling the service provider. In the crowdsourcing service concept, the main manufacturer calls for service expectations. Service providers who think they can fulfill the call's requirements apply that they want the task. The main manufacturer chooses the enterprise that is the most suitable among the applicant enterprises.

Election processes can be complicated and dependent on subjective decisions for the decision maker. Both types of service requests are time-consuming processes for the main manufacturer. Finding, evaluating and deciding on service providers in oursourcing and crowdsourcing service mechanisms can be costly. In addition, different tools may be needed to reach service providers. Relationships and collaborations can be established by taking into account past work experiences. In other words, references are effective in cooperation. From the point of view of individuals, the structure called social media creates virtual environments in the establishment of relations and cooperation. Social relations are established through the personal characteristics and past experiences of individuals in the virtual environment. If social media and internet-based relationship management can be integrated into the production environment, relationships similar to individual partnerships can be established between businesses. In this way, a digital structure consisting of a network of relations and interaction emerges.

In the social manufacturing platform, such networking is called a community. Communities are vital to the fulfillment of the processing task. Two basic approaches, horizontal and vertical, are taken as basis in the formation of communities. The horizontal approach is based on bringing together manufacturers with the same resources and similar capabilities to perform the same machining tasks. In the vertical approach, it is aimed to create a group of manufacturers with different characteristics, each specialized in different fields, to perform sequential processing tasks in the manufacture of a product. These manufacturers are businesses with a very small structure, with a small number of employees, and with the ability to produce flexible and agile production against demand changes. Social manufacturing provides a new type of entrepreneurial opportunity for such small businesses with its community structure. Horizontal and vertical communities are actually in a structure that can provide the flow of the entire product life cycle at the emergence of a product. Manufacturers in communities are qualified to meet the design, service, software and many other production requirements that may be needed in a product life cycle (Yang and Jiang, 2019).

Contracts are important in eliminating trust problems between the stakeholders who will carry out the production. Contracts include guarantees regarding the execution and timing of the task. Social manufacturing needs to provide similar security guarantees when bringing together the service provider and the main manufacturer requesting the service. Blockchain-style digital assets have recently emerged as a secure payment or exchange tool that has been used frequently. Social manufacturing is one of the internet-based digital platforms. For this reason, the use of digital assets as a means of exchange between stakeholders will also contribute to the vision of establishing innovative relations and cooperation of the social manufacturing paradigm.

SOCIALIZED MANUFACTURING RESOURCES AND SYSTEM STRUCTURE

Main manufacturing companies are established in such a way that they can actually complete a whole product cycle with their large-scale production infrastructure. However, the large-scale manufacturing structure is cumbersome and resists market changes. The concept of social manufacturing leads to the formation of a production infrastructure that can adapt to changes in the market in a much more agile and flexible way. The aim is to increase overall efficiency and capacity utilization within the manufacturing chain by utilizing the resources of small-scale manufacturers rather than large production infrastructures through resource sharing. In other words, it is tried to create a structure focused on obtaining the maximum contribution with a minimalist approach.

Sharing is an approach that underlies the concept of social manufacturing. In an environment where mutual interests are maximized through the sharing of socialized resources, sharing collaborations increases common gains. The communities established by the platform ensure the deepening of cooperation. Socialized resource sharing is carried out within the communities. However, the cooperation of communities is not limited to socialized resource sharing within themselves. Different communities within the platform can also share processing task, service request and capacity.

The vertical manufacturer ecosystem that will enable a product to emerge occurs spontaneously in a network where communities come together. Especially in today's economy where services and goods are globalized, it has become very costly to expect a business to produce all the components of a product itself. Therefore, the need for small and agile manufacturers will require much less effort only with the establishment of this network structure. Social manufacturing can be considered as a system in which many different manufacturers come together in a single product cycle and are actually shaped as if they were a single manufacturer.

The infrastructure includes an internet-based social networking platform. The social manufacturing platform contains the personality traits and past experiences of its users. On the social manufacturing platform, manufacturers provide information about their socialized resources, capacities, skills and experiences to all users. While processing the extremely large data in the system and creating the community, it is quite complex to make matches in line with this data. In addition, with the spread of the social manufacturing platform, it is highly probable that the applications to increase the efficiency of the platform will increase. With the integration of sensors and RFID technology with social manufacturing during machining tasks, there can be instantaneous and very intensive data entry into the platform. Different optimization techniques such as simulation, artificial neural networks and cloud systems can be used in the processing of data, which can also be integrated into the social manufacturing platform. These and similar dynamic structures increase the closeness of decisions such as the formation of communities and the selection of manufacturers to the ideal. Ding et al. (2016) expresses the concept of social manufacturing as a structure consisting of manufacturing service, socialized manufacturing resources, manufacturer communities and social manufacturing platform components.

Service Description

The main manufacturer can request the processing and other manufacturing support services it needs in the product cycle from small businesses specializing in certain subjects. Social manufacturing is shaped by the capabilities of small businesses. Businesses create a kind of curriculum vitae for the main manufacturers for the processing tasks that may come to them by presenting their capabilities within the platform. Social manufacturing helps large-scale enterprises that want to solve their needs for activities include dynamic outsourcing, scheduling, tracking, logistics, etc. with a low level of external manufacturer resources (Jiang et al., 2016). Businesses that want to solve the manufacturing service through outsourcing and crowdsourcing can obtain a much cheaper solution mechanism with the platform.

Socialized Manufacturing Resources

Socialized manufacturing resources are defined as any service capability, machine and device park, or software and programs that small-scale manufacturing companies in the system promise to use within the social manufacturing system (Jiang et al., 2016; Leng et al., 2013). Small-scale manufacturing enterprises display their socialized resources in the interface offered by the social manufacturing platform. Here, the service provider manufacturer provides the capabilities of its machinery, sensors, software or other resources and many more information that the main manufacturer may need in the evaluation. The main producer enterprise can obtain the information about the service it needs in its product cycle through the platform. The social manufacturing platform prepares the environment for the formation of manufacturer communities based on resource notifications. If the main producer carries out all the activities in the product cycle process, it cannot adequately evaluate its own resource capacities and cannot fully benefit from economies of scale. Social manufacturing minimizes the waste of resources throughout the system by pooling the resources of small-scale manufacturers. In the coordination of such a large-scale network in the real life, trust problems, communication infrastructure and motivation of all stakeholders about the benefits of the system are big problems. However, these problems can be eliminated with a strong social network infrastructure such as social manufacturing in the virtual universe.

Horizontal and Vertical Communities

Manufacturer communities are created by the social manufacturing platform, taking into account the similar characteristics of the small business or their ability to do sequential work. Businesses that have previously promised to provide services through the platform are classified according to their manufacturing capabilities or socialized manufacturing resources that can perform some parts of the manufacturing task. Communities can be defined as a formation that supports manufacturers to act collectively and thus to take initiative in the service bargaining process with the main producer (Ding et al., 2016).

Communities have two different clustering structures. Manufacturers take various roles in terms of support they will give to the product cycle. Two different types of clustering offered by the platform are called horizontal and vertical. In communities based on horizontal clustering, manufacturers with similar socialized resources and the ability to perform similar processing tasks are brought together. With horizontal clustering, this community, which consists of businesses doing the same business, gains decision-making power on a sectoral basis. It plays a decisive role in the dynamics of the sector. In the vertical clustering approach, companies with different characteristics and different socialized resources come together. In vertical clustering, many small manufacturers come together to complete all the production processes of a product. Each manufacturer's machining task is different and is responsible for any stage of the product manufacturing process. In this way, it is avoided that only one manufacturer performs each stage of the production of a product. Product-oriented collaborations can be interpreted for vertical communities. In fact, the product emerges because of the coming together of the community, while each small manufacturer is doing their own specialized work.

Vertical communities contribute to the development of the level of expertise in the processing task. While each manufacturer develops their own skills, they indirectly contribute to the improvement of the product. Small manufacturers can move much faster than large manufacturers. This makes it easier to keep up with changes in market conditions.

Platform Operation Logic

The social manufacturing platform is a platform where its members can record their features and collaborate in line with these features. There are two sides to the social manufacturing platform. The first side creates a task offering by presenting its own socialized resources and experiences. The other side is the large-scale manufacturers who demand outsourcing and crowdsourcing services that can fulfill different tasks in the manufacture of their product. The social manufacturing platform creates manufacturer communities by taking into account the manufacturing task demands. These manufacturers' communities may be capable of performing all the manufacturing processes of a product. Xiong et al. (2022) states that the social manufacturing system works as a five-layer structure. Accordingly, while the manufacturers' communities are at the core of social manufacturing, customer and manufacturer matching is ensured at the end-user point of the system after the features specific to the social manufacturing system come into play in the background. Details of the platform are in Figure 2.

- **Layer 1-Resources:** It is the basic building block of social manufacturing as the initial layer. Manufacturers with resources find themselves in the community cluster as a result of similar vertical or horizontal grouping. The community provides an environment for the integration of resource providers and information sharing.
- **Layer 2-Support:** It is the stage where the data of the manufacturers in the source layer are collected and controlled. At this stage, the system analyzes the manufacturing service task to be offered in the light of the data, and the transfer of information about the enterprises is transferred securely. The general framework of the task regarding the service to be provided by the manufacturer is determined by taking into account the user's request.
- **Layer 3-Environment:** Directing the appropriate resources for the task requested by the customer takes place in this layer. A solution mechanism is in operation for filtering the information and taking the most appropriate decision for the correct match.
- **Layer 4-Application:** The model that performs the matching aims to assign the manufacturing resources in the most appropriate way. The coordination mechanism takes action by evaluating the possible outcomes of the match.
- **Layer 5-User:** In the last layer, the match between the manufacturer and the customer requesting the service task takes place. As a result of the feedback received after this stage, it is aimed to continuously improve the service quality related to the task.

The social manufacturing platform offers high entrepreneurial potential for small-scale manufacturers. Small manufacturers and service providers often find it difficult to distinguish themselves in the industry. The acceptance process within the industry can be costly. The social manufacturing platform provides equal opportunity for small enterprises. Demonstrating and discovering features and capabilities within the platform is quite easy. In addition, thanks to communities, there can be enough service providers to perform different tasks in the production of a product. For this reason, everyone actually creates a group of benefit by doing what they are best. The inclusion of small entrepreneurial manufacturers, who have no bargaining power against the main producer alone, helps to strengthen their hands in bargaining. With this feature, the social manufacturing platform is a powerful entrepreneurial support alternative that can prevent small enterprises from disappearing before they even start.

The platform has a three-stage transaction process. First, socialized resource providers create a profile of themselves. In this profile, they indicate their experience, self-abilities, and processing tasks they can perform. The profile also includes the wage expectations for the service they will provide. Similarly, the main producers who request outsourcing and crowdsourcing services also share information about the nature and timing of the service they need on their page. The main producers also indicate the fee scale they are willing to accept for the service request. In the social manufacturing platform, it is not desirable for a service provider small manufacturer to individually respond to a request. Likewise, it is out of the working mentality of the platform for a main producer to contact a service provider individually.

The task of unifying the two parties rests with the social manufacturing platform. The assembly process takes place in line with the processing tasks required in the emergence of the product and the capabilities of the manufacturers who have the resources to fulfill these tasks. Special combination algorithms perform matches in line with the expectations and capabilities defined in the profiles.

Figure 2.

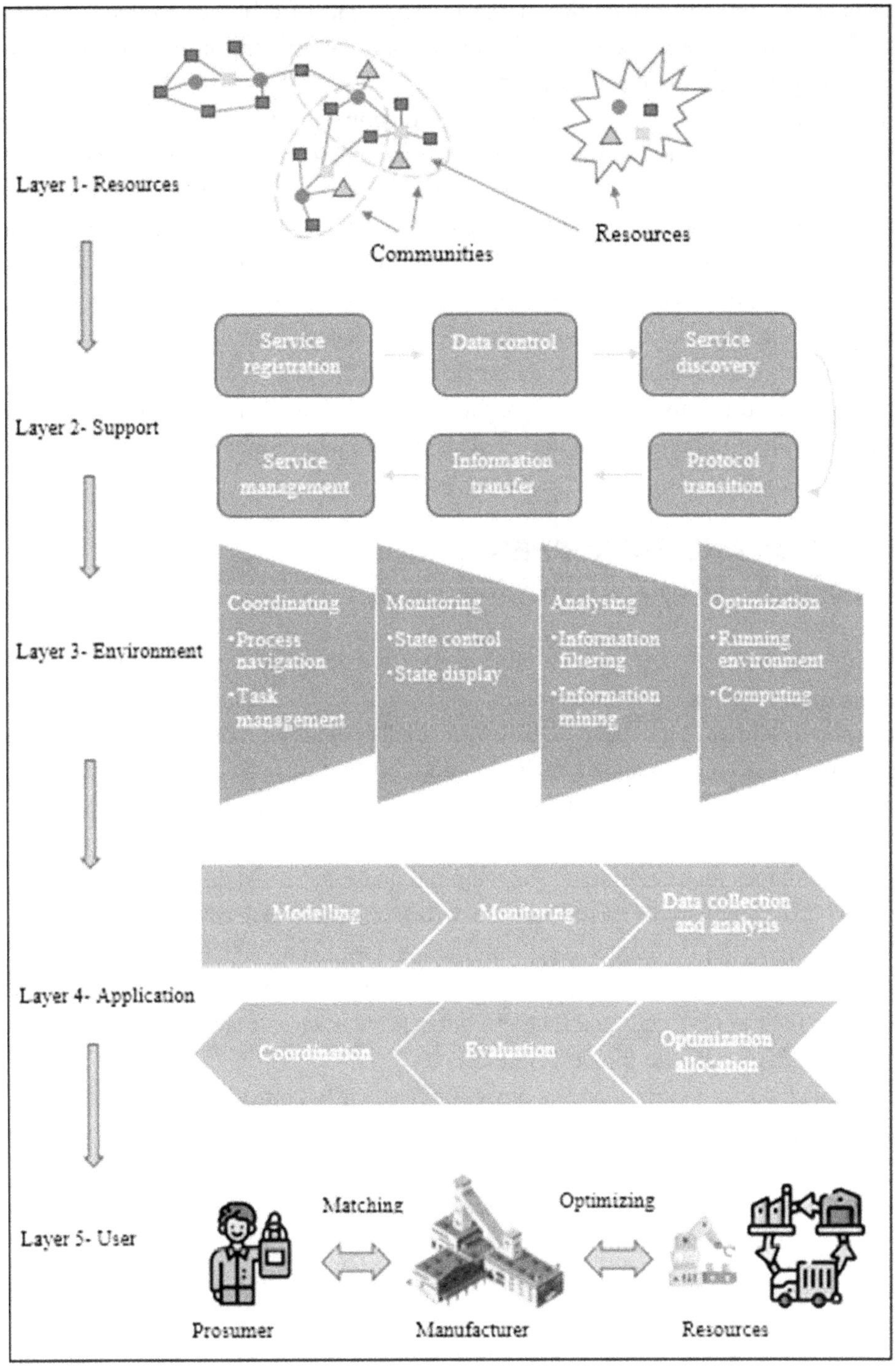

Combination algorithm forms manufacturer communities as horizontally and vertically. Communities are kinds of clusters where many elements come together. Although each cluster has its own boundaries, these boundaries are not isolated from each other. There may be intersections between clusters. This situation can be interpreted as a manufacturer may be in more than one different community. In other words, manufacturers can perform similar manufacturing tasks of different products in line with their capabilities. Communities are a system that protects small entrepreneurial manufacturers in terms of bargaining power against the main producers.

Due to the social network feature of the social manufacturing platform, it is possible to observe the status of the relationship. In other words, the main producer can monitor the efficiency of the service provider during the processing task. This serves the interests of the main producer. The main producer can have information about the efficiency of the manufacturing process through continuous monitoring.

The platform also has a dynamic structure. Service providers and service requesters can update their profiles. The social manufacturing platform can create new communities by considering these updates. This capability helps the main producer with service demand to take a quick position in the face of changes in the market. The main producer can act flexibly in the face of changes and is highly adaptable to market conditions. From this point of view, the social manufacturing platform has a structure that protects both the small entrepreneur and the interests of the main producer.

COLLABORATION AND ENTREPRENEURSHIP BASED ON SOCIAL MANUFACTURING

Digital channels are one of the ways to establish effective economic cooperation. Large-scale main manufacturers attach importance to cooperation with small-scale manufacturers in order to get rid of their cumbersome structures. This makes it easier for small businesses that will not have any say on their own business and wages to be included in the job pool of the big main producers. A large number of businesses that benefit from the power of social media to bring large audiences together are taking part in these collaborations with a new style of entrepreneurship tool called social manufacturing.

The platform provides an environment for scattered and unaware stakeholders to come together to achieve the same goal. Small-scale manufacturers, who share their socialized resources within the platform, are in a network structure thanks to the community. Leng et al. (2019) refers to this structure as a social manufacturing-oriented enterprise relationship network. Stakeholders in the network interact with each other through their experiences and related feedback. Interacting manufacturers may have different tasks. Matches are affected by the job description.

The social manufacturing system allows any enterprise with a product idea to turn into a manufacturer. For example, a company has an innovative product design that will be accepted in the market, but the company does not have a facility infrastructure to produce the product. It is very difficult for such a company to be successful in classical production systems. However, social manufacturing creates an environment for an entrepreneur who does not even have a production line to produce the product, to become an important player in the market. Entrepreneurs may not have a production facility, but they can guarantee the production of the product thanks to the communities.

The system infrastructure allows even small manufacturers to have a large business presence. Thanks to the system, even individuals or small businesses that can perform various manufacturing services as a hobby can become entrepreneurs with access to the platform. The social manufacturing platform can allocate a role and place in the community, regardless of the size of the manufacturer and the complexity of the service. In this way, it becomes possible to evaluate the abilities.

DIGITAL PRODUCT AND SERVICE MANAGEMENT

Digitalization offers manufacturing companies a less costly alternative route to large investments in product design and delivery. Digital product service systems are considered as low investment cost solutions that will ensure high customer satisfaction without the need for any production system (Lerch and Gotsch, 2015). Digital technologies have the effect of revealing new business models that increase service quality (Paschou et al., 2020). The social manufacturing platform is one of the digital products that will truly change the perspective of products and services. Figure 3 presents technologies that are pioneers in the emergence of the reality of social manufacturing (Xiong et al., 2022). The social manufacturing platform is the result of emerging technologies in the Industry 4.0 environment. The social manufacturing platform mediates the emergence of product and service innovations in the field of 3D by utilizing the features of the entire technological infrastructure.

Figure 3.

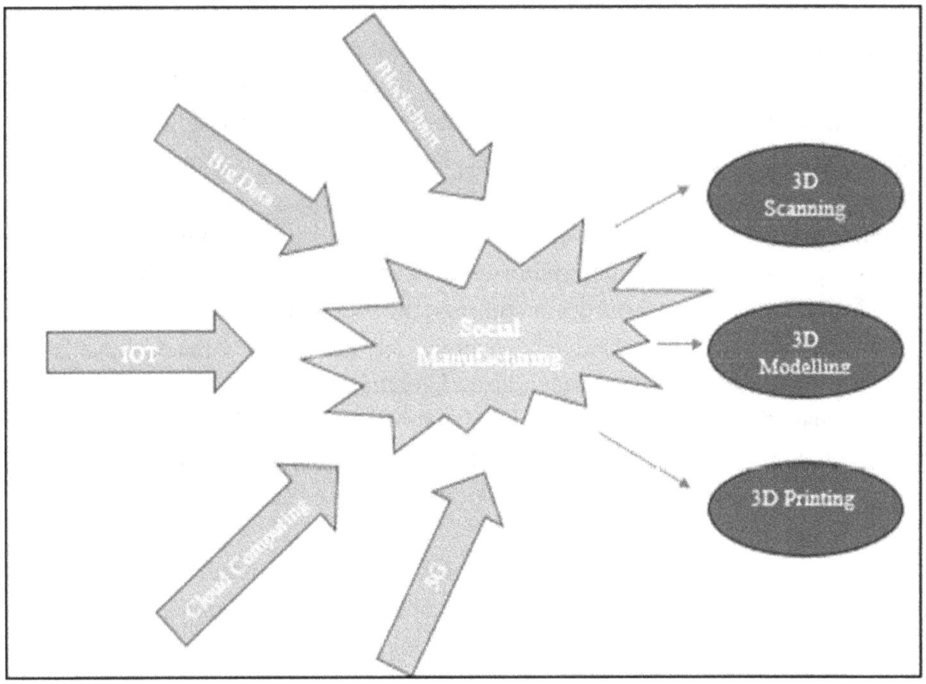

The social manufacturing platform paves the way for product-based innovative work. Open product design practice allows manufacturers within communities to support product development. Since social manufacturing is a social networking platform, it is also possible for stakeholders to comment on product design. With these decentralized interactions, the wishes of consumers and the capabilities of service providers are visible to everyone. In this way, talent information reaches a much wider audience within the network. This situation is called virus-like information spreading mechanism (Yang and Jiang, 2019).

Social media provides users with the opportunity to share their innovative ideas without borders. Thanks to such an environment, both manufacturers have the opportunity to exhibit their talents and products, and customers can get answers to their product and service expectations. An intertwined association between the manufacturer and the customer is not common in conventional production systems. However, with the support of social media, the customer can directly take part in the design of product and service processes. In this context, they can direct their improvement and development suggestions directly to the manufacturer. This situation leads to the development of new business models in production as in social manufacturing.

Technological developments in production infrastructures facilitate the use of social manufacturing by consumers. Actually, 3D printers and digital design applications enable the design and processing service of a manufacturer on a social manufacturing platform with remote access. With the integration of source information systems, different tasks can be combined for the same purpose, such as a single line. This will enrich the number and variety of design alternatives. Digital product and service designs can be shared through social media and the internet. (Yang and Jiang, 2019) defines the version where designs can be shared and developed by everyone as open source design. Open source design, just like open source software, is open to everyone's use, can be changed and improved. Contributors are constantly improving open source designs. In line with the underlying understanding of the social manufacturing paradigm, this creates an opportunity for small entrepreneurs. Individual designers can contribute to the design process without working for any company. On the other hand, small-scale manufacturers can produce solutions by outsourcing without the need for large design teams. The social manufacturing platform creates an environment for small entrepreneurs to realize their design skills.

The social manufacturing platform includes designers within its community structure. After the main manufacturer presents the general framework for the designs, all sub-processes of the design are programmed with the social manufacturing platform. The platform distributes design as well as software and processing tasks within the community. Consumers are also part of the open source design. Consumers can follow every stage of the design through the social manufacturing platform. This ensures that the designs are transparent and traceable. Consumers can contribute to the design at any point. They can share their ideas about design on social media and get the chance to receive feedback from different circles. The social manufacturing platform can involve the consumer in designing products and services like never before. A direct-to-consumer system will enable manufacturers with small-scale production infrastructure to use their resources efficiently. Digital product and service infrastructure helps to adapt quickly to innovations.

The system also includes various risks in return for the high benefit promised in the design processes of products and services. Open source designs will be open to all designers. Optimistic thinking is that all designers will contribute to the process. However, it is unrealistic to think that all designers will provide high quality service in the ideal situation. Gathering of under-talented designers will negatively affect community performance. However, this does not create an obstacle to the social manufacturing platform and open source design approach.

DIGITAL RESOURCE SHARING WITH BLOCKCHAIN

Manufacturers, suppliers and third-party service providers are all components of the value-added chain. The ability of actors to act together results in the emergence of economic benefits. However, multi-actor and globalized production collaborations need much more trust than before. While manufacturers delegate some or all of their production operations to third-party service providers, they entrust both production operations and production targets to external service providers. The fee for this service and the sharing of production secrets depend on the establishment of a mutual trust relationship. In the social manufacturing platform, the employer and the service provider can appear as anonymous characters. The capabilities and features offered by users in their own accounts within the platform are publicly available information on the social networking site. At this stage, it seems unlikely that the employer and the service provider will get to know each other if they have not done business before. Reliable payment systems are needed to guarantee profit sharing in an environment where the parties do not know each other.

The social manufacturing system uses digital possibilities. The concept of resource sharing, which is one of the basic principles of social manufacturing, is united under the concept of Shared Manufacturing thanks to digital concepts such as IOT (Yu et al., 2020). Social manufacturing and Shared Manufacturing principles, which enable vertical and horizontal resource sharing, are often not used effectively due to trust problems. Blockchain applications such as Bitcoin, which are capable of providing secure and efficient solutions in a distributed, decentralized and encrypted manner, are the secure network provider that can solve this problem for platforms like social manufacturing (Nakamoto, 2008).

Cryptology provided by blockchain applications gains importance in terms of security in value sharing and recording job descriptions. Blockchain offers an open manufacturing ecosystem where all stakeholders can monitor production processes, with the promise of a decentralized manufacturing system as opposed to a centralized manufacturing system. In this way, open and reliable sharing of information is guaranteed. Figure 4 shows blockchain-based resource sharing (Yu et al., 2020).

The social manufacturing platform creates a community in line with the qualifications, skills and resource characteristics of resource providers. After customers enter the job description they need into the system, the social manufacturing platform performs the matching process. The blockchain system in Figure 4 ensures transparency for information security and process traceability of consumers and resource providers. Through the encryption mechanism, the data flow cannot be changed and the structure becomes uncontrollable from a single center. Crypto mechanism provide security for the demand data specified by the customer, the job description of the resource provider and the process flow during manufacturing.

Resource sharing system provides resource planning based on demand definition. Afterwards, the blockchain system generates smart contracts that will protect the rights of both parties. Smart contracts provide the tracking of customer requests at the beginning of the job during the transaction execution phase and the job tasks promised by the resource providers throughout the manufacturing process. Transaction execution collects feedback and notifications for the process observed by both parties. This process continues in a closed loop. The resource sharing system responds to new demands according to the availability of resources.

FUTURE RESEARCH

Those encountering the concept of social manufacturing for the first time may have the idea that social manufacturing will only serve manufacturing purposes because of the approach's reference to resource sharing. However, the social manufacturing platform can be a useful tool for many different industries. The rapid communication infrastructure of social manufacturing is conducive to supply chains. Supply chain networks can be built with social manufacturing infrastructure to serve a common purpose, just as in manufacturing communities. The system can contribute to reducing costs by bringing together the most competent stakeholders. Social manufacturing preserves the bargaining power of resource providers. This job guarantee mechanism, established through cooperation, can be easily adapted to different sectors. Social manufacturing promises a sustainable environment and economy through less energy use and less consumption by sharing resources. Just as the platform has a prescriptive effect on bargaining, it can impose rules on more environmentally friendly products and services. Social manufacturing is a new concept that has no boundaries, has been explored by very few people, and offers broad working potential for many more sectors. It is thought that studies on the subject will shape the production and service paradigm of the future.

Figure 4.

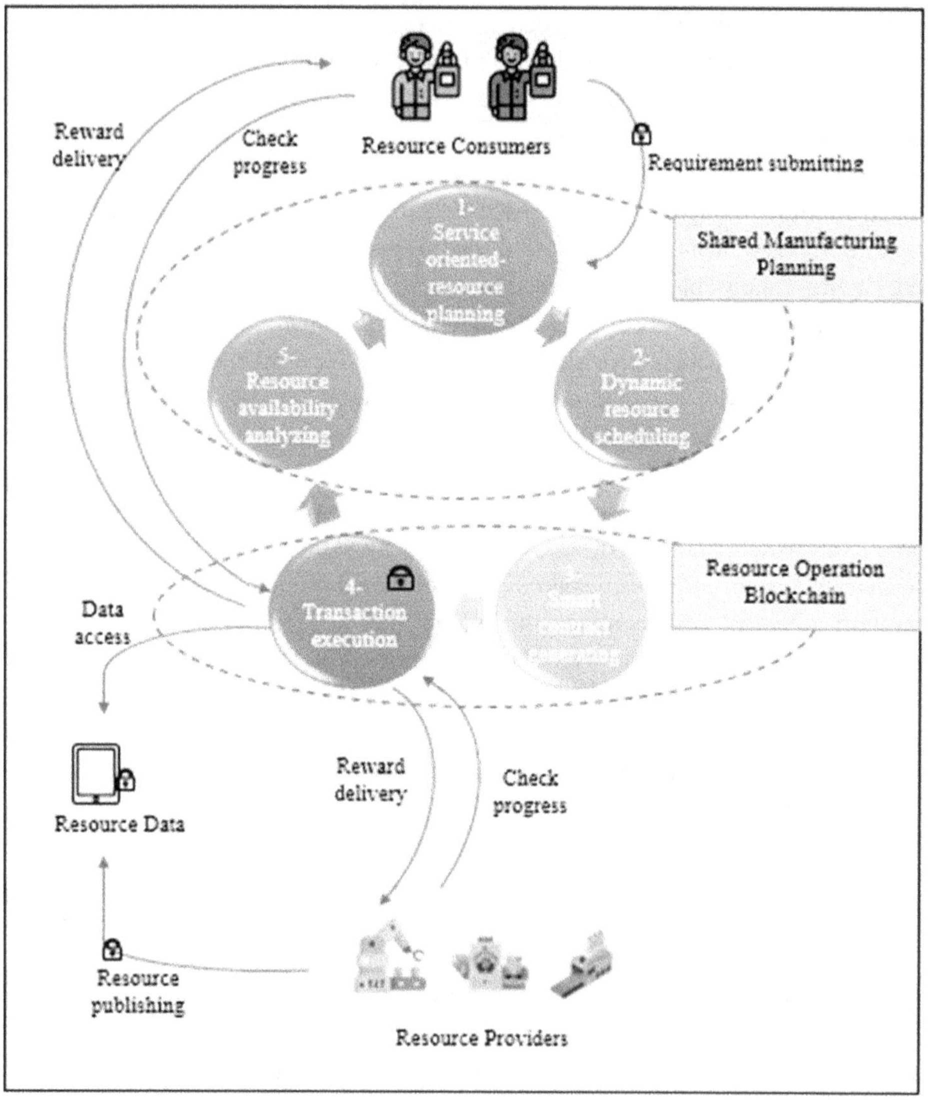

CONCLUSION

This chapter introduces the working mechanism of the social manufacturing platform and the structural layers that make up the social manufacturing system. The social manufacturing platform stands out as an entrepreneurial tool that supports manufacturers, which have limited production resources and specialized in only certain areas. The platform is a low-cost and comprehensive showcase where small entrepreneurs present their individual talents. Community structure brings together small entrepreneurs and increases their bargaining power against big customers. The blockchain-based resource sharing system monitors the business process and ensures mutual payment agreements of the parties. Digitalization, which came with the Industry 4.0 revolution, combined with another technological innovation, social networks, under the concept of social manufacturing. This union opens the door to a new era in production.

REFERENCES

Aheleroff, S., Mostashiri, N., Xu, X., & Zhong, R. Y. (2021). Mass personalisation as a service in industry 4.0: A resilient response case study. *Advanced Engineering Informatics*, *50*, 101438. doi:10.1016/j.aei.2021.101438

Alheriani, N. M. S., Spasojević-Brkić, V. K., & Perišić, M. B. (2021). Novel risk management integrated model implementation: Comparison between manufacturing and service companies. *Journal of Engineering Management and Competitiveness*, *11*(1), 13–19. doi:10.5937/jemc2101013A

Cao, W., Jiang, P., & Jiang, K. (2015). Demand-based manufacturing service capability estimation of a manufacturing system in a social manufacturing environment. *Proceedings of the Institution of Mechanical Engineers. Part B, Journal of Engineering Manufacture*, *231*(7), 1275–1297. doi:10.1177/0954405415585255

Ding, K., Jiang, P., Leng, J., & Cao, W. (2016). Modeling and analyzing of an enterprise relationship network in the context of social manufacturing. *Proceedings of the Institution of Mechanical Engineers. Part B, Journal of Engineering Manufacture*, *230*(4), 752–769. doi:10.1177/0954405414558730

Ding, K., Jiang, P., & Su, S. (2018). RFID-enabled social manufacturing system for inter-enterprise monitoring and dispatching of integrated production and transportation tasks. *Robotics and Computer-integrated Manufacturing*, *49*, 120–133. doi:10.1016/j.rcim.2017.06.009

Gebauer, H., Paiola, M., Saccani, N., & Rapaccini, M. (2021). Digital servitization: Crossing the perspectives of digitization and servitization. *Industrial Marketing Management*, *93*, 382–388. doi:10.1016/j.indmarman.2020.05.011

Gupta, S., & Jain, S. K. (2013). A literature review of lean manufacturing. *International Journal of Management Science and Engineering Management*, *8*(4), 241–249. doi:10.1080/17509653.2013.825074

Hamalainen, M., Mohajeri, B., & Nyberg, T. (2018). Removing barriers to sustainability research on personal fabrication and social manufacturing. *Journal of Cleaner Production*, *180*, 666–681. doi:10.1016/j.jclepro.2018.01.099

Hirscher, A. L., Niinimäki, K., & Armstrong, C. M. J. (2018). Social manufacturing in the fashion sector: New value creation through alternative design strategies? *Journal of Cleaner Production*, *172*, 4544–4554. doi:10.1016/j.jclepro.2017.11.020

Jiang, P., Ding, K., & Leng, J. (2016). Towards a cyber-physical-social-connected and service-oriented manufacturing paradigm: Social Manufacturing. *Manufacturing Letters*, *7*, 15–21. doi:10.1016/j.mfglet.2015.12.002

Leng, J., & Jiang, P. (2016). A deep learning approach for relationship extraction from interaction context in social manufacturing paradigm. *Knowledge-Based Systems*, *100*, 188–199. doi:10.1016/j.knosys.2016.03.008

Leng, J., Jiang, P., Xu, K., Liu, Q., Zhao, J. L., Bian, Y., & Shi, R. (2019). Makerchain: A blockchain with chemical signature for self-organizing process in social manufacturing. *Journal of Cleaner Production*, *234*, 767–778. doi:10.1016/j.jclepro.2019.06.265

Leng, J. W., Jiang, P. Y., Zhang, F. Q., & Cao, W. (2013). Framework and key enabling technologies for social manufacturing. *Applied Mechanics and Materials*, *312*, 498–501. doi:10.4028/www.scientific.net/AMM.312.498

Lerch, C., & Gotsch, M. (2015). Digitalized product-service systems in manufacturing companies: A case study analysis. *Research Technology Management*, *58*(5), 45–52. doi:10.5437/08956308X5805357

Mohajeri, B. (2015). *Paradigm shift from current manufacturing to social manufacturing* [Master's thesis].

Nakamoto, S. (2008). Bitcoin: A peer-to-peer electronic cash system. *Decentralized Business Review*, 21260.

Palange, A., & Dhatrak, P. (2021). Lean manufacturing a vital tool to enhance productivity in manufacturing. *Materials Today: Proceedings*, *46*, 729–736. doi:10.1016/j.matpr.2020.12.193

Paschou, T., Rapaccini, M., Adrodegari, F., & Saccani, N. (2020). Digital servitization in manufacturing: A systematic literature review and research agenda. *Industrial Marketing Management*, *89*, 278–292. doi:10.1016/j.indmarman.2020.02.012

Sundar, R., Balaji, A. N., & Kumar, R. S. (2014). A review on lean manufacturing implementation techniques. *Procedia Engineering*, *97*, 1875–1885. doi:10.1016/j.proeng.2014.12.341

Tao, F., Zhang, L., Venkatesh, V. C., Luo, Y., & Cheng, Y. (2011). Cloud manufacturing: A computing and service-oriented manufacturing model. *Proceedings of the Institution of Mechanical Engineers. Part B, Journal of Engineering Manufacture*, *225*(10), 1969–1976. doi:10.1177/0954405411405575

Xiong, G., Chen, Y., Shang, X., Liu, X., & Nyberg, T. R. (2014, June). AHP fuzzy comprehensive method of supplier evaluation in social manufacturing mode. In *Proceeding of the 11th World Congress on Intelligent Control and Automation* (pp. 3594-3599). IEEE. 10.1109/WCICA.2014.7053314

Xiong, G., Tamir, T. S., Shen, Z., Shang, X., Wu, H., & Wang, F. Y. (2022). A Survey on Social Manufacturing: A Paradigm Shift for Smart Prosumers. *IEEE Transactions on Computational Social Systems*, 1–19. doi:10.1109/TCSS.2022.3180201

Xiong, G., Wang, F. Y., Nyberg, T. R., Shang, X., Zhou, M., Shen, Z., Li, S., & Guo, C. (2018). From mind to products: Towards social manufacturing and service. *IEEE/CAA Journal of Automatica Sinica, 5*(1), 47-57.

Xu, X. (2012). From cloud computing to cloud manufacturing. *Robotics and Computer-integrated Manufacturing*, *28*(1), 75–86. doi:10.1016/j.rcim.2011.07.002

Yang, M., & Jiang, P. (2019). Open product design for social manufacturing. In *Social manufacturing: Fundamentals and applications* (pp. 93–116). Springer. doi:10.1007/978-3-319-72986-2_5

Yu, C., Jiang, X., Yu, S., & Yang, C. (2020). Blockchain-based shared manufacturing in support of cyber physical systems: Concept, framework, and operation. *Robotics and Computer-integrated Manufacturing*, *64*, 101931. doi:10.1016/j.rcim.2019.101931

Zeng, S., Zhou, J., Zhang, C., & Merigó, J. M. (2022). Intuitionistic fuzzy social network hybrid MCDM model for an assessment of digital reforms of manufacturing industry in China. *Technological Forecasting and Social Change*, *176*, 121435. doi:10.1016/j.techfore.2021.121435

Zhou, Y., Xiong, G., Nyberg, T., Mohajeri, B., & Bao, S. (2016). Social manufacturing realizing personalization production: A state-of-the-art review. *IEEE International Conference on Service Operations and Logistics, and Informatics (SOLI)*, 7-11. 10.1109/SOLI.2016.7551653

Chapter 11
How Do Various Social Media Platforms Influence Chinese Tourists' Destination Selections?
From Information Searching and Sharing Perspectives

Khalid Mahmood Abbas
Liverpool John Moores University, UK

Bo Wen
Liverpool John Moores University, UK

ABSTRACT

Underpinned by the rising application of social media to tourism and hospitality, this chapter discussed how various platforms influence tourists' destination selection in China by exploring different types of tourism information and Chinese social media platforms, thus analysing their application and influence on destination selection across the three-stage travel process. This chapter found that tourists' destination selection needs different tourism information produced by individual tourists, destination marketing organisations, and tourism businesses. Thus, Chinese social media platforms have been designed with different functions to apply to tourists' destination choices across three stages of travel. During this process, information characteristics (e.g., positive and negative comments, information variation, richness, and credibility) on these platforms generate positive and negative influences on tourists' destination selection. Based on these, the authors developed a framework for social media for destination selection that suggests several theoretical and managerial implications.

DOI: 10.4018/978-1-6684-7416-7.ch011

INTRODUCTION

Led by the rapid development of the internet and mobile devices, social media remains flourishing (Yoong and Liam, 2019). Notably, live-streaming broadcasts as a new way of sharing information and interacting with people have become increasingly popular (Lin et al., 2021; Xu and Ye, 2020). As such, social media plays an essential role in people's lives, influencing human behaviours (Lyu and Zhang, 2019; Li et al., 2018) and commercial activities organisations in every sector (Li et al., 2021). The tourism and hospitality sector is not exceptional (Valeri and Baggio, 2021; Oliveira et al., 2020). In the marketing dimension, organisations in the public sector, such as destination marketing organisations (DMOs) and tourism businesses uses social media for destination promotion (Tang et al., 2017) because of its low cost and information wide communicability (Lau, 2020). It was confirmed by many practitioners that social media platforms can benefit tourism product and service distribution and promotion (Bowen, 2015). User-generated content (UGC) can facilitate tourism and hospitality organisations to interact with potential customers, increase their online visibility, lift brand recognition and thereby bring about more sales revenues (Asongu and Odhiambo, 2019; Xiang et al., 2017). Hence, DMOs and tourism industries enable to understand their tourism markets and set up business strategies (Noone et al., 2011).

In the tourist dimension, social media platforms have brought about changes in the ways of planning travel and making decisions about destination selection (Gretzel, 2018). On the one side, tourists perceive UGC on social media as a significant and trustful source of information (Li et al., 2021; Lam et al., 2020; Qi and Chen, 2019). On the other side, social media establishes a platform for tourists to enhance their virtual networks and share travel experiences and information (Wang et al., 2021), which sequentially impacts other people to make decisions on destination selection (Yuan et al., 2022, Choe et al., 2017). Social media is widely used by tourists to search, plan and share their travel experiences (Wang et al., 2021). Therefore, for both tourism marketers (DMOs and tourism businesses) and individual tourists, social medial platforms are valuable tools for marketing and social functions (Liu et al., 2022).

China is one of the most essential marketplaces in tourism (China Tourism Academy, 2019) and hospitality (Liu and Hung, 2020). According to the China Statistical Yearbook 2020, there were 6 billion domestic travellers in 2019 (Mo, 2022). In the same year, the number of outbound tourists reached 169 million, which was the highest in the world (World Tourism Organization, 2021). Moreover, China has incredibly advanced information and communication technology and social media within the past decade (Qiu et al., 2019). As of December 2021, the number of social communication Apps reached 211,000, ranking as the No.4 category of mobile Apps (CNNIC, 2021).

Over 90% of Chinese millennials today obtain preliminary information through social media on their smartphones (Wei and Liu, 2019). With the affordance of 4G and 5G technology, China holds a high market share in the live-streaming market worldwide (CNNIC, 2021). Nonetheless, due to unique political and economic systems, China's social media landscape distinctively differs from that of other countries (Luo and Zhai, 2017). For instance, people in many areas of China cannot access western social media platforms such as Instagram, Facebook and Youtube (Hobbs and Roberts, 2018). Thus, numerous domestic social media platforms with parallel functions have been created (Gamage et al., 2022), including WeChat, Weibo, Xiaohongshu, Douyin, Bilibili, etc. In the tourism and hospitality sector, Chinese tourism markets have indigenised travelling (commercial) websites and Apps, such as Ctrip (Liang and Zhang, 2021), Mafengwo (Wu, 2021), Dazhong Dinning (DZDP) (Wang et al. 2021), rather than TripAdvisor, Booking Etc. Therefore, researching social media platforms in the Chinese tourism and hospitality sector has come into being an interesting topic in a wide range of disciplines (Gamage et al., 2022; Yuan et al., 2022).

This chapter will discuss how various information on Chinese social media platforms influence tourists' destination selection. It will start with description of types of tourism information, followed by a discussion of different forms of Chinese social media platforms. The fourth section is to analysis how these Chinese platforms influence tourists' travel-related behaviours for destination choices at 3 stages of travel, and different influences of these platforms on destination during the entire travel process will be explored in the fifth section. Then, combining all above areas, a conceptual framework has been developed and will present in the sixth section. Finally, the key results, implication and future avenue for research out of this chapter will be concluded.

TOURISM INFORMATION

Tourism industry covers a wide range of business activities, such as accommodation, transportation, food, drink, leisure and entertainment, shopping, etc., (Bian and Zhu, 2020). Therefore, tourism-related information mainly generates around these aspects of tourism.

Tourism information usually sources from tourism businesses (DMOs, online agencies, etc.) (e.g. Lei et al., 2022; Zhang et al., 2016) and individual tourists (e.g. Gamage et al., 2022; Xiang and Gretzel, 2010; Daugherty et al., 2008). Regardless of sources of tourism information, studying tourist information is able to help understand the functional positioning of platforms (Li et al., 2021). Hence, the first section draws upon different types of tourism information.

Information From DMOs and Tourism Businesses

Attractions, transportation, services, information and promotion are the key basic infrastructure of destination to sustain (Lei et al., 2022). DMOs and tourism businesses project destination images, videos and introductive messages on the internet through actual or desired perceptions of their offerings (Lei et al., 2022). This information is regarded as a reference to destination selection for potential tourists (Bowen, 2015). For example, Arsal et al., (2010) compared the impacts of different information providers on all aspects of travel experiences and discovered that information provided by experiences local tourism businesses particularly affects tourists' decisions on accommodation and food. But sometimes, the price of travel products provided by DMOs may vary according to hot or cold seasons (Bowen, 2015). As Xu et al., (2021) stated, promotional destination videos produced by DMOs are representations of tourism destinations, which highly rely on the attention of people who are interested in the place, which distinguishes from travel vlogs, a UGC. However, the amount of actual tourism-related information published by DMOs is still low, and these forms of information are basic in destination cities categories (Zhang et al., 2016). Therefore, this field deserves more attention from scholars and practitioners.

User-Generated Content (UGC)

UGC denotes information or content provided and distributed online by the general public rather than paid professionals (Daugherty et al., 2008). Its presence has sparked the tourism and hospitality sector (Xiang and Gretzel, 2010) because it reflects abundant information about tourists' attitudes, opinions and experiences, which is progressively accessible on social media (Gamage et al., 2022). As such, it is widely recognised that UGC is a more credible, authentic, and reliable source of tourism information from prior tourists (Xiang and Gretzel, 2010) than conventional sources, such as travel agents and DMOs (Wang et al., 2021).

Most UGC is textual and image formats on major social media platforms (Xiao et al., 2022; Liang, 2021). Varieties in displayed formats, contents and functions of online platforms may cause considerable differences, such as text length, language styles and use of images, photos and videos (Wang et al., 2022). Differences among various UGC reflecting tourists' needs (Li et al., 2021) affect their decision-making and purchasing behaviours (Liu et al., 2020; Xiang and Gretzel, 2010). Li et al., (2021) investigated the largest Chinese online travel question-and-answer (Q&A) platform, Ctrip (Q&A) and found that information required by tourists can be divided into four types of information, namely, knowledge, efficiency, risk, and hedonic aspects. *Knowledge* is related to certain aspects of destinations and journeys (Dickinson et al., 2014), such as destination climate, accommodation reservations and transportation routes. *Efficiency* refers to travel plans, such as preparation tips on clothing, entertainment, and leisure during the journey etc (Li et al., 2021). *Risk* seeks to avoid various risks during the journey, such as financial risks, security risks, etc (Zou and Yu, 2022). The results of Zhang et al., (2021) exposed that the attention to tourism on Zhihu (a Chinese online community) has grown to risk perceptions and local restriction policies due to the covid-19. Finally, *hedonic information* is entertainment-related, such as destination attractions, shopping, food and other leisure activities (Li et al., 2021). These information needs represent specific aspects of tourism, as shown in Table 1.

Table 1 . Description of the types of tourism elements

Elements of Tourism	Description
Transportation	Traffic-related information during the journey, including flight, ferry, train, coach, bus, underground, car rented, etc.
Attractions	Detailed relevant information about the attraction, such as location, tickets, and open hours
Accommodation	Accommodation-related information, such as accommodation recommendations, types of accommodation, prices, discount and promotion.
Food	Recommendations and introductions to local cuisines and popular restaurant, bars, café, etc.
Climate	Climate-related information and corresponding advice on dressing preparation and protection.
Passing through customs	Including the difficulties and solutions that may happen when passing through customs
Visa	All information related to the visa, such as visa application, validity period, etc.
COVID-19	Information on pandemic situations and corresponding control policies at destinations
Travel guidelines	A series of travel-related suggestions on travel information, such as transportation, accommodation, attractions and food
Time	Time planning issues during the journey and relevant suggestions
Safety	Personal safety issues during the journey and relevant suggestions
Finance	Financial safety issues and preventive measures during the journey
Shopping	Information on speciality items at destinations, famous shopping locations, etc.

Source: Adapted from Li et al. (2021, p. 7)

To summarise, the diverse formats of tourism information available (Li et al., 2021) determine that social media platforms equip different functions to meet different purposes of tourists (Wang et al., 2022). They found that content creators apply photos and headlines for presenting destination or product uniqueness, whereas readers prefer obtaining transportation-related information using detailed texts more than photos (Wang et al., 2022). Especially in the past decade, e-WOM has changed from computer-based to mobile-based formats in the mobile Internet era (Jia and Wu, 2019, Bowen, 2015). It has been discovered that mobile applications (Apps) have gained popularity among millennial tourists to share and receive tourism information (Shi et al, 2020, Wu et al., 2020; Bowen, 2015). Thereafter, multiple functions on those virtual platforms and Apps can facilitate tourists planning and making decisions on their preferred destinations, and meanwhile conveying themselves regarding the journey to potential tourists (Wang et al., 2022).

CHINESE SOCIAL MEDIA PLATFORMS

With the advent of the concepts of Web 2.0 and UGC, Kaplan and Haenlein (2010) defined social media as a cluster of Internet-based Apps to allow people to create and exchange UGC. They have also classified social media into six types: Blogs, collaborative projects, social network sites, content communities, virtual game worlds and virtual social worlds in light of their usage characteristics and functions (Kaplan and Haenlein, 2010). Later on, built on the main marketing application functions, Tuten and Solomon (2013) developed the classification of social media into four zones: social community, social entertainment, social publishing and social commerce, which is demonstrated in Table 2.

Table 2. Classification of social media zones

Social Media Zones	Descriptions
Social Community	Drawing upon relationship building and attracting online users with similar interest to participate in online community activities
Social Entertainment	Mainly for users to play and have fun
Social Publishing	Disseminating information to audiences, including regular updated online content (text, images, and videos). Also viewers can leave comments that cause threaded discussions on certain topics
Social Commerce	Helping online selling and buying of products and services

Source: Adapt from Tuten and Solomon (2013)

Further, Dao (2015) shed light on that this classification has two dimensions. The first is the degree of social presence and the richness of the medium, determining how people communicate and interact with each other on the Internet, whereas the second dimension of social media is a self-presentation and self-disclosure tool (Dao, 2015). Self-presentation and self-disclosure behaviour involves voluntarily and intentionally expressing personal thoughts, feelings and experiences (Krasnova et al., 2010). Yuan et al., (2022) posited that Chinese social media platforms are allocated into the classification with slight modifications based on the degree of social presence or media richness. They added the medium level of self-presentation/self-disclosure to the social media classification of Kaplan and Haenlein (2010) for understanding the media characteristics (Table 3) (Yuan et al., 2022).

Table 3. Classifications of Chinese social media by social presence/media richness and self-presentations/disclosure

Self-Presentation/Self-Disclosure	Social Presence/Media Richness		
	Low	Medium	High
High	-	**Microblogs and blogs** (e.g. Sina Weibo, Tencent Weibo)	**Social networking sites** (e.g. WeChat, Q-zone, LinkedIn)
Medium	**Commercial tourism communities** (e.g., Ctrip, Qunar, DZDP, etc.)	**Third-party tourism communities** (e.g. Qiongyou, Mafentwo, Zhihu, Xiaohongshu)	**Tourism social networking** (e.g. Tuyou)
Low	**Collaborative projects** (e.g. Baidu Baike)	**Content communities** (e.g. Douyin, BliBli, Meipai, Miaopai, etc.)	-

Source: Adapt from Yuan et al. (2022, p. 3)

Regarding self-presentation function, microblogs, blogs and social networking sites are considered higher than commercial tourism communities, third-party tourism communities and tourism social networking (Yuan et al., 2022). The former formats are the welcome sites in which Chinese people are inclined to manage and disclose their personal information publicly (Dao, 2015). In contrast, commercial, third-party tourism communities and tourism social networking are aimed at specific tourism content domains (Kaplan and Haenlein, 2010). Finally, collaborative projects and content communities only allow limited self-disclosure information (Yuan et al., 2022). Collaborative projects spur users to jointly create content (Kaplan and Haenlein, 2010), while content communities allow multiple formats of content sharing, such as videos, pictures and audio clips between users via a user-generated link (Dao, 2015).

People select and use specific types of social media in light of the functions offered (Yuan et al., 2022). Blogs, microblogs and social network sites are designed to deepen socialisation about all aspects of the lives of users (Kaplan and Haenlein, 2010), such as WeChat, Weibo and Xiaohongshu. These platforms gradually combine various functions (e.g. travel vlogs, photo and content sharing) and develop into integrated social Apps for people to share their travel experience (Wang et al., 2022). The strength of integrated social Apps is to attract daily users to interact with friends, online celebrities and various content and allow users to create and share their own experiences (Shi et al., 2020). Commercial and third-party tourism communities aim at more specialised tourism, for example, booking flights and hotels by Ctrip, and travel reviews by Mafengwo and DZDP (Yuan et al., 2022). Some social media platforms introduce a 24-hour Chatbot function to fulfil tourists' needs for instant response (Riley, 2020).

Notably, within recent years, short-video and live-streaming content platforms (e.g. Tiktok, Douyin, Blibli, etc.) (Lin et al., 2021; Qiu et al., 2021; Xu et al., 2021; Lau, 2020; Xu and Ye, 2020) are new and popular means because it creates an immersive climate with real-time and synchronous interactions to obtain viewers' trust (Lin et al., 2022). This novel site exploits a new channel to showcase products, increase sales and clear inventory while spurring authenticity, visualisation and interactivity (Hu and Chaudhry, 2020). Owing to the intangible characteristics of travel products and tourists' needs for travel information, live streaming plarforms have flourished in tourism businesses and individual tourists (Lau, 2020). For example, Ctrip, one of Chinese largest online travel agencies (OTAs), sold $294 million in travel pages and hotel bookings from March to October 2020 (Qiu et al., 2021) and generated transactions of $3.84 million in an hour via a live-streaming sale event (China Travel NEWS, 2020). Accordingingly, based on these classifications, it is necessary to discuss the functions and usage of several most representative Chinese social media platforms.

Social Networking Sites, Microblogs, and Integrated Social Apps

- WeChat was launched by Tencent Holdings in January 2011 in China. It commences as a real-time messaging mobile App, but subsequently, has been equipped with multiple functions in terms of information subscription, socialisation, e-commerce, gaming, shopping, mobile payment services and so forth (Montag et al., 2018). The Moments, the most welcome one in WeChat (Liu et al., 2021), can present users' text, image and video content only with their family, friends or those they know (Zhao et al., 2018). As such, WeChat tends to be a private social media platform. In addition, it is free to download, install and support different mobile operating systems with multiple language choices (e.g. Chinese, English, French, etc.) (Gamage et al., 2022). Compared to major social media sites, WeChat has a widely accessible digital ecosystem, with more than 1308.9 million monthly active members (Statista, 2022).
- Weibo, the Chinese equivalent of Twitter, was launched in 2009. Now, it has become the leading micro-blogging site in China (eMarketer, 2022) and a major integrated social media platform for travel (World Bank Group, 2018). In 2022, it has 584 million monthly active users (Statista, 2022). It enables users to share brief posts including live streams (Qiu et a., 2021). Certain live streaming websites and apps can also be linked via the platform. Chinese people use Weibo more often in daily life (Wang et al., 2022). Unlike WeChat, Weibo aims to post content to the public (Zhao et al., 2018).
- Xiaohongshu, a popular app and fast-emerging social media platform in mainland China, was set up in 2013. The number of monthly active users of Xiaohongshu has achieved 158 million in China in June 2022 (Statista, 2022). Searchable and accessible themes on this platform cover tourism, education and fashion (Xiaohongshu, 2022). In the Xiaohongshu community, people can share their notes and record their positive and fashionable lifestyle through text, images and videos (Mo, 2022).

Xiaohongshu has been successful in combining social media and e-commerce, thus, people often use this site to help them make purchasing decisions (Mo, 2022) via a powerful product review community (Wang et al., 2022). Because it can provide precious corresponding textual and image-related information for users to make decisions (Lei et al., 2022). According to the study by Wang et al., (2022), Chinese people are more likely to use Xiaohongshu to select their destinations via exploring tourism and destination image-related contexts (Lei et al., 2022). In July 2021, there were 3.52 million posts relevant to 'travel' in Xiaohongshu's search engine (Mo, 2022). Intending tourists and millennials particularly welcome this platform in their lives.

Commercial Tourism and Third-Party Communities

- Ctrip is a famous integrated commercial (tourism) website in China. Currently, this platform has nearly 1.5 billion users (Li et al., 2021). It is operated by third parties rather than certain tourism businesses (Yan et al., 2018). Various tourism businesses, including DMOs, OTAs, hotels, etc., are able to set up homepages and promote tourism information (e.g. accommodation, transportation, destination introduction, etc.) on Ctrip. Ctrip combines several websites and is managed to present these forms of information on the site. It offers ticketing services, hotel reservations and delegated tour bookings (Zou and Yu, 2022). Its commercial value in the online travel-booking market constantly ranks first (Chi et al., 2021). Tourists subsequently can use Ctrip to obtain necessary tourism consultation via a 24-hour Q&A chatbox (Riley, 2020) and enjoy network services for planning a trip (Yan et al., 2018; Choi et al., 2007).

- Mafengwo is a major online service through which tourists can share their experiences (Zou and Yu, 2022). This service has set up its official accounts on various social media platforms (WeChat, Weibo, Douyin) and carried out a multi-channel marketing strategy in the tourism sector (Wu, 2021). For instance, according to a Mafengwo market strategy analysis by Wu (2021), Mafengwo commenced its Weibo account "Mafengwo Travel" in May 2010. In December 2022, this account on Weibo posted 46,632 microblogs and has 3.32 million followers. Mafengwo Travel updates 6 posts per day, and these posts and travel tips are from the Mafengwo official App. Mafengwo has an official account on WeChat to publish articles concerning travel destinations with recent news. On the WeChat platform, Mafengwo regularly updates 5 times per week and posts information on Moments to trigger people's continuous focus and discussions on the destinations. Mafengwo has its official mobile app for users to share and seek travel notes and guides. This mobile app has social functions, 'community activities'. Users can meet other tourists in the same place and fulfil their social needs. Mafengwo also released a series of short videos on Douyin in February 2018. Mafengwo mainly uses Douyin to expand the promotion of official materials rather than as a marketing tool (Wu, 2021).

Content Communities and Live-Streaming Broadcasts

- Douyin (Chinese Tiktok) set up in 2016, is a popular short video platform in China. This platform allows people to produce and post 15-second videos concerning various topics. It has gained 100-500 thousand new followers over two-week periods since late January 2020 (Fannin, 2020). Douyin creates two communication functions: audio live streaming and connects that allow followers to initiate a video call (Fitzgerald et al., 2022). It facilitates a real-time messaging function among users in the community (Fitzgerald et al., 2022). Currently, lots of users love to share their travel experience in Douyin (Bian and Zhu, 2020)
- Blibli, a popular Chinese video-sharing website, was launched in 2009 and originally focuses on animation and gaming videos. Similar to YouTube, users are both content viewers and producers (Xu et al., 2021). But now it has widened its video range, including music, beauty makeup, fashion, TV shows, gaming, tourism and celebrities (Wu, 2022; Xu et al., 2022). The average monthly active users on Blibli reached 332.6 million in the third quarter of 2022 (Blibli, 2022). The most distinct function of Blibli is bullet comments available to synchronically interact with video content, providing a sense of sharing and viewing experience virtually for both viewers and video producers (Wu, 2022; Xu et al., 2021).

Comparison Among Chinese Social Media Platforms

As detailed described 4 varieties of social media platforms, people less trust single microblogs and blogs because they have to undertake more information mining before determining (Yuan et al., 2022).

However, the good thing is that WeChat, Weibo and Xiaohongshu have been developed into integrated social media Apps, combining the traditional function of social networking and novel functions, such as media sharing, discussion, content curation, customer review, blogging and shopping (Wang et al., 2022). People present travel blogs in multiple formats, including texts, photos, videos, vlogs, or a mixture of all, which is more vivid and eye-catching than text-based information (Huang, 2012). It is worthwhile that WeChat is for personal networks, whereas Weibo and Xiaohongshu are for the public exchange (Zhao et al., 2018). Weibo and Xiaohongshu have become well-known customer review sites and search engines when tourists need information (Wang et al., 2022).

Compared to microblogs and blogs, Yuan et al., (2022) also pointed out that tourists perceive commercial and third-party tourism communities (e.g. Ctrip, Mafengwo, Xiaohongshu, etc.) more reliable owing to a comprehensive collection of ratings, reviews and comments altogether on one website or application. They also contented that some collaborative projects, like Baidu Baike, is the least trustworthy platform as it is tough to find the accurate and verified tourism information (Yuan et al., 2022).

As for the novel online platforms, even if short videos, travel vlogs and live streaming have a variety of similarities, such as entertainment, social needs, a sense of community, reducing pressure etc. (Qiu et al., 2021), Lin et al (2022) review a wealth of literature and shed light on that these platforms have some fundamental differences (See *Table 4*). Social presence and synchronous interaction between streamers and audiences through live streaming produce a more authentic viewing experience and a stronger purchase impulse than their pre-recorded videos (Ang et al, 2018). Streamers have real-time interactions with viewers through instant text, verbal conversations and body language regardless of the spatial limitation, which creates a strong celebrity-fan tie for any form of business activities (Lin et al., 2022). Additionally, product links, sometimes with special discounts for followers, are placed in the broadcast room to make purchasing process convenient (Zhou et al., 2019). That's why more and more people are fond of buying products and services via live streaming.

Table 4. Differences between pre-recorded video and live streaming

Factors	**Pre-recorded video**	**Live streaming**
Time	Pre-recorded	Simultaneous
Physical Space	Separated	Separated
Psychological Space	Being there	Being together
Social Interaction	Subsequent comments and posts	Instant messages and Synchronous chats
Flow	Scripted	Spontaneous
Production	Embellished (Edited)	Authentic (unedited)
Streamer Identity	Vague (or absent)	Prominent

Source: Adapted from Lin et al. (2022, p. 291)

In summary, social media platforms serve different functions: social networking, entertainment, content publishing and e-commerce (Yan et al., 2018; Tuten and Solomon, 2013). Accordingly, individuals (Yuan et al., 2022) and tourism businesses and DMOs (Zhang et al., 2016; Pike and Page, 2014) select and use specific types of social media in light of the functions offered and preferences (Yuan et al., 2022; Popp and Woratschek, 2016). Nonetheless, few tourists fancy posting their e-WOM on official enterprise websites, probably because official enterprise websites are not very popular or have not opened an online comment function yet (Yan et al., 2018). The results from Yuan et al., (2022) reveal that Chinese tourists prefer applying numerous social media more than picking up one or very few Apps. Therefore, regardless of how functions social media platforms are exerted, it influences tourists' decision-making by forming their destination images, destination choice and expected travel experiences (Liu et al., 2019) at different stages (Wang et al., 2022; Zou and Yu, 2022; Fotis et al., 2011; Cox et al., 2009).

DESTINATION SELECTION PROCESS AND CHINESE SOCIAL MEDIA

Travel behaviours and decision-making for destination selection are complex processes, made up of different stages (e.g., pre-trip, during and post-a trip) and decision types (e.g., destination location, accommodation, dining and leisure activities) (Want et al., 2022; Yuan et al., 2022; Cox et al., 2009). Tourism products are complex, intangible and usually perceived as highly risky without previous experience, thereby visitors need various information to support their decision-making (Fodness and Murray, 1999). Generally, Chinese people often use social media platforms for two purposes: tourism information searching and sociability function (Yuan et al., 2022; Wang et al., 2022).

The role and impact of social media on different stages of making destination choice decisions have been widely investigated by researchers (Want et al., 2022; Yuan et al., 2022; Ge and Gretzel, 2018; Choe et al., 2017; Dwityas and Briandana, 2017; Pabel and Prideaux, 2016). It has been discovered that people usually share travel experiences online during and after the trip and search and receive suggestions from others who visited a destination before (Wang et al., 2017). However, it turns out both similar and contradictory outcomes from previous studies. Wang et al. (2022) highlighted the role of integrated social apps on travel inspiration and destination choice in the pre-trip process. Similar to Cox et al. (2009), social media is mainly adopted to search for information only in the pre-trip stage only, but few are used during and after the trip. That is because tourists need to balance various factors to make a plan and minimise the risk of making unwise decisions (Sirakaya and Woodside, 2005). Conversely, Fotis et al. (2011) believed that social media is a channel to share experiences in the post-trip stage.

At present, with the growing popularisation of 5G and the evolution of social media platforms and new functions, for instance, 3D photos, live streaming and mobile-based Apps, consumer behaviours and preferences have been changing at different stages of travel planning (Wang et al., 2022). Chinese people no longer just use a single or limited number of functions of social media for destination choice in one stage (Yuan et al., 2022), for instance, information searching before the trip, hotel evaluation or experience sharing during and post the journey. Rather, various consumer behaviours and travel activities concur at one stage for tourists to make better destination choices (Yuan et al., 2022; Liu et al., 2020).

Pre-Trip Stage

Before the trip, it is tough for people to judge the landscape and service of the destination in advance. Thus, as proved by numerous studies (Wang et al., 2022; Hu and Yang, 2021; Cox et al., 2009), in this stage, tourists identified their needs for travel and evaluate alternative destinations and risks of potential leisure activities by browsing their preferred information online. For example, Xiao et al., (2022) and Liang (2021) found that tourists are fond of viewing textual and image formats regarding tourism major social media platforms. Before a trip, Chinese people often compare prices of hotels and flights and review the feedback and rate of hotels and destinations provided by tourism businesses and individual tourists (Bowen, 2015). Recently, travel vlogs on Blibli (Xu et al., 2021), short videos on Xiaohongshu (Lei et al., 2022; Mo, 2022), Weibo and tourism live-streaming broadcasts on Douyin (Fung et al., 2022; Lin et al., 2021; Qiu et al., 2021) are growing popular among people. At this moment, the information searched mostly focuses on potential destinations and activities as a whole (Pabel and Prideaux, 2016), which helps tourists modify their choices and finalise their travel plans for destinations (Luo and Zhong, 2015).

Except for information searching, some tourists, especially online celebrities, often post short videos or conduct live-streaming broadcasts concerning what items and how they are preparing for the destination on social media (Fung et al., 2022; Xu et al., 2021). This novel fashion can arouse their followers' and fans' interest in the targeted destinations and give vivid and visualised information to potential tourists.

Amid-Trip

tourists continue searching for information on transportation, dining, accommodation, leisure activities and attractions from different channels (UGC or DMOs and tourism agents) to make specific service-purchasing choices and decisions (Yuan et al., 2022; Liu et al., 2013; DiPietro et al., 2007). In particular, during international trips, people may more rely on social media to look for entertainment information (DiPietro et al., 2007). When having bad experiences at a destination, tourists would rapidly find valuable and real-time information (e.g. location, accommodation, transportation methods, time span, pricing, security, etc.) to make a decision (Bowen, 2015), either changing their destination or withdrawing from the journey in advance. Fotis et al. (2011) revealed that the higher the perceived level of influence from social media on destination choice, the more likely potential travellers would change destination selection. Additionally, the pricing dynamics and promotion information on the social media platforms that are set and changed by DMOs can influence tourists' experience at destinations (Bowen, 2015).

Tourists often disclose their travel stories and post travel photos and videos on various social media platforms simultaneously (Yuan et al., 2022). For example, sharing travel experiences and photos on WeChat, Weibo, and Xiaohongshu (Wang et al., 2022), uploading short video clips on Douyin (Fung et al., 2022; Lin et al., 2021; Qiu et al., 2021 Bian and Zhou, 2020) and even hosting live-streaming broadcasts throughout the entire journey. In doing so, tourists' family members, friends and followers can be attracted by eye-catching travel-related information, thereby increasing their travelling interest in tourism destinations (Yuan et al., 2022). Whilst sharing travel experiences, people also start rating and evaluating the local places they have been to on social media, such as accommodations, restaurants, attractions, and entertainment. Comments and rates from tourists are regarded as important indicators of products, services and infrastructure at destinations for DMOs and tourism businesses to consider improving (Oliveira et al., 2020; Pike and Page, 2014; Sigala et al., 2012).

Post-Trip

the main function of social media is to provide a platform for tourists to recall their trips express their journey experiences and evaluate local products, services and infrastructure at a destination they visited on the various online platforms (Wu, 2021; Dwityas and Briandana, 2017; Cox et al., 2009; Pan et al., 2007). It has been found that sharing travel photos is an autobiographical record and can lead to post-trip behavioural motivations (Zhang et al., 2020). People often provide quantitative rates or textual comments, photos and videos to show how they feel about the destinations. Online celebrities and streamers are willing to tell their fans about their travel experience during live streaming or on exquisite travel vlogs (Xu et al., 2021; Xu et al., 2021; Lau, 2020). It will make those tourists sharing comments consider whether to revisit this destination (Park et al., 2020; Kirilenko et al., 2019) and inspire sequential tourists to decide whether to take trips to this place or not (Yuan et al., 2022; Liu et al., 2019). In the meantime, DMOs and tourism businesses enable to improve their tourism products and services at the destinations (Mo, 2022; Wu, 2021; Zhang e al., 2016).

Therefore, social media platforms play a pivotal role in all stages of travel planning for destination selection. Despite that people usually share travel experiences online during and after the trip and seek suggestions before a trip (Wang et al., 2017), due to the diversity of types and functions of social media platforms, tourists are inclined to take plentiful travel-related actions on different social media simultaneously to make destination selection at a time (Yuan et al., 2022). Specifically, in the pre-trip, other than tourism information exploring for destination selection, information sharing on journey preparation on a variety of social media sites, as a reference to other people's destination choice, has become growing common (Wang et al., 2022; Yuan et al., 2022; Tussyadiah and Fesenmaier, 2009). During the trip, information searching, sharing and destination evaluation co-occur, which simulates tourists to extend, change or end up the trip. Equally, comments shared by tourists help DMOs and tourism businesses to improve products and service management and marketing strategies (Mo, 2022; Wu, 2021; Tussyadiah et al.,2011). By the end, tourists continue engaging in tourism experience sharing and destination evaluation, which keep facilitating DMOs and tourism businesses (Mo, 2022; Wu, 2021). Throughout the entire process of a trip, it can be seen that information from individual tourists and DMOs and tourism businesses mutually interacts with destination selection. Individual tourists obtain the needed tourism information from different online channels (including from DMOs and tourism businesses) to make destination choices. Afterwards, feedback from tourists becomes evidence of destination improvement suggestions for DMOs and tourism businesses, thus, it would help previous tourists' decision on destination revisit and new tourists' destination selection (Tussyadiah et al., 2011).

INFLUENCE OF CHINESE SOCIAL MEDIA PLATFORMS ON DESTINATION SELECTION

Through discussing how social media platforms influence tourists' three main stages of travel process, it can be seen that tourism information and social medial platforms bring both positive and negative influences on tourists' destination selection.

Positive and Negative Comments and Feedback

Experiences during the trip have both positive and negative influences on tourists' emotions to share tourism information and experience on social media (Yan et al., 2018). The results of the research of Yan et al., (2018) uncovered that tourists with positive emotional tendencies may play the role of sharers and share their experiences with others online, while people with negative emotional tendencies prefer to post information on what they witnessed, and they are better at stating their own conditions instead of feelings to remind or warn other tourists. This result was supported by Liu et al. (2019) and Wang et al., (2022). Positive content may heighten higher visiting impulses (Liu et al., 2019). Conversely, the negative comments may reduce their intention to visit (Wang et al., 2022). Thus, positive and negative comments on social media not only influence individuals' travel intention and destination selection (Wang et al., 2022; Liu et al., 2019), but also affect the sales revenue and marketing performance of DMOs, OTAs and tourism businesses (hotels, restaurants etc.) (Bowen, 2015) because they enable to improve their tourism products and services at the destinations based on comments produced by tourists on social media (Mo, 2022; Wu, 2021; Zhang e al., 2016).

Information Variation on Social Media

Due to uneven demand for travel products and their perishability, their price can fluctuate largely. For example, the same hotel room may cost 500 RMB per night in the hot season and 100 RMB per night in the cold season. The pricing dynamics induce people to check and compare prices on expected dates among different platforms to make selections and decisions about destinations before purchasing (Bowen, 2015). They can also attain other indicators of the quality of hotels using UGC on the platforms (Bowen, 2015). In doing so, DMOs and tourism businesses can leverage social media platforms to shift their promotion and pricing strategies to attract more tourists to destinations. However, a danger in this situation is that DMOs and tourism businesses and social media chase advertising dollars at the expense of authenticity (Bowen, 2015). It may not only damage tourists' destination image but cause market shrinkage and profit reduction (Zhao et al., 2018).

Richness and Diversity of Information and Social Media

Travel decisions would depend on more factors. The more active users involved in social media platforms, the more likely they would be affected by the information when making travel decisions (Liu et al., 2013). The narratives and beautiful vlog footage in travel vlogs can tell simulating travel stories to viewers, thereby attracting viewers' continuous attention to the target destinations (Xu et al., 2021). Similarly, Mo (2022) stated that processing photos and modifying text in travel tips in Xiaohongshu can inspire the public's interest and longing for the destination. As a result, richness and diversity of information and social media platforms can help people reach abundant information on various platforms to better make their trip plans.

Different sorts of information on social media platforms not only contribute to individual tourists' destination image (Zhao et al., 2018) and selection (Yuan et al., 2022; Wang et al., 2022) but help DMOs construct and express various themes of destinations (Xiao and Zhao, 2009). Some social media platforms designed with a precious search engine and diverse forms of information (text, images and videos), such as Xiaohongshu, are effective to rescue modern 'choose-disabled' people from overwhelming information (Mo, 2022). However, people may also be overwhelmed by an explosive amount of information, which challenges them to choose destination.

Moreover, unlike UGC from individual tourists, DMOs published a low amount of actual travel-related information on Weibo (microblog platform), and information posted is often irrelevant to tourism (Zhang et al., 2016). However, people need authentic information about local weather, accommodation, food, services, security and transportation at destinations (Zhang et al., 2016). Official information from DMOs can leave good impression on destinations for the public. Hence, DMOS and tourism businesses ought not to ignore the significance of using social media in tourism marketing throughout the course of travel process (Zhang et al., 2016), and active, interesting, humble, informal and honest information posted by DMOs tends to be attractive (Kaplan and Haenlein, 2010).

Information Credibility on Social Media

UGC on various social media platforms is perceived as a more credible and authentic source of tourism information from prior tourists (Xiang and Gretzel, 2010) than conventional sources, such as travel agents and DMOs (Wang et al., 2021), because this type of information comes from authentic travel experiences and stories of those who have already visited the destinations (Gamage et al., 2022). For example, when people make a destination or travel-related decision, they highly depend on the recommendation from their relatives and friends (Berhanu and Raj, 2020). Most of the contacts on WeChat are users' real-life acquaintances (Zhu et al., 2014), and only users' friends and family can see their textual and image contents (Zhao et al., 2018). Due to its high privacy and safety, tourists are inclined to share their tourism photos and thoughts regarding the destination image and meanwhile trust their acquaintances' tourism experience (Zhao et al., 2018; Lien and Cao, 2014).

The aesthetic scenes and first-person narrative of travel vlogs and live-streaming videos and synchronic interplay create vivid and authentic imaginations of destinations in viewers' minds, thereby driving viewers' desire to visit destination (Lin et al., 2022; Xu et al., 2021). People will follow others' videos to a destination and do parallel purchasing behaviour during a trip, like tasting the same food at the same restaurant, or taking photos at the same place (Bian and Zhu, 2020). In particular, this situation has become very common in web celebrities with thousands or even millions of fans (Fung et al., 2022; Xu et al., 2021). Their followers like them and believe their introduction and judgement of the tourism destinations and on-site activities on social media platforms (Reinikainen et al., 2020), thus increasing purchasing tourism products and services (Sandel and Wang, 2022; Xu et al., 2021). In this process, the appreciation of the destination is by-production, because fans are more like to have an attachment to their idols, as known the 'Wanghong economy' (Fitzgerald et al., 2022; Sandel and Wang, 2022) or 'fandomisation' in China (Fung, 2019). Therefore, a number of tourism companies have collaborated with celebrities who act as tour guides to introduce their tourist places (Mo, 2022), hotel offerings (Lau, 2020) and the latest discounts. Online celebrities' real-time responses to viewers' concerns about tourism experiences and products can also save viewers time on destination research and planning (Buhalis and Sinarta, 2019).

Albeit it is widely recognised that social media contributes to Chinese tourism and hospitality, information on social media platforms may raise people's worry regarding its credibility (Sandel and Wang, 2022). This is because web celebrities tend to be capitally oriented (Sandel and Wang, 2022). They may imbue word-of-mouth information and pictures that largely differ from real designations or hotels to their fans because tourism businesses have given them a large number of advertising fees (Fung et al., 2022; Mo, 2022). Currently, some private and public companies manage to take advantage of people's trust to via clickbait strategy (Zhang et al., 2020; Stroud, 2007) to promote their products and services (Zhao et al., 2018). Yet, in fact, information hidden clickbait is not complete and consistent with the content (Zhang et al., 2020; Chen et al., 2015). When people experience their products and services, it turns out that real situations are not what DMOs and tourism businesses introduce in the advertisements (Fung et al., 2022). As a result, tourists are afraid of receiving fake reviews and comments on social media, which online celebrities would lose fans' loyalty and tourists' trust in tourism destinations and hotels (Mo, 2022). In the end, this situation would detrimentally impact tourism and hospitality (Liu et al., 2021).

CONCEPTUAL FRAMEWORK OF SOCIAL MEDIA AND TOURISTS' DESTINATION SELECTION

In this chapter, we discussed the types of tourism information and Chinese social media platforms, the application of social media to the entire travel process and influences of information and social media on tourists' destination selection. Combining all sections together, a conceptual framework (Figure 1) of social media and tourists' destination selection has been developed as below.

Figure 1. Conceptual framework of social media for tourists' destination selection
Source: Authors' self-construct

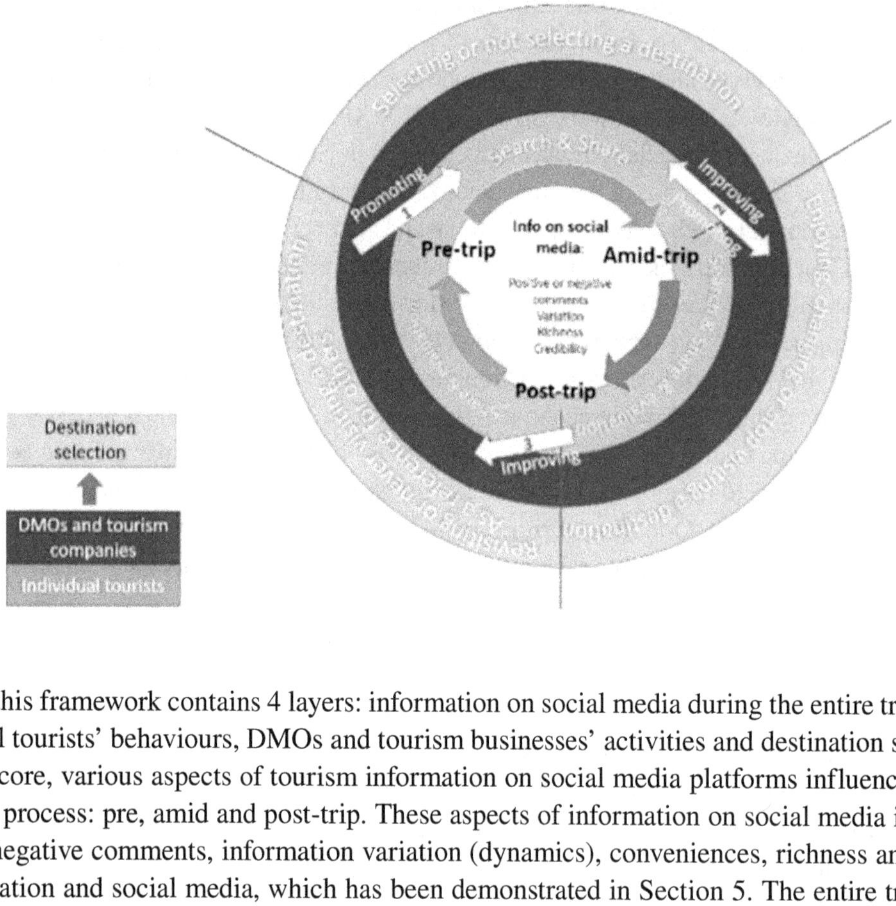

First, this framework contains 4 layers: information on social media during the entire travel process, individual tourists' behaviours, DMOs and tourism businesses' activities and destination selection.

At its core, various aspects of tourism information on social media platforms influence 3 stages of the travel process: pre, amid and post-trip. These aspects of information on social media include positive and negative comments, information variation (dynamics), conveniences, richness and credibility of information and social media, which has been demonstrated in Section 5. The entire travel process with 3 stages is a cycle because tourism experiences from previous tourists can be developed into recommendations and references of destinations for potential tourists.

The second (Green) and third (Purple) layers represent travel-related behaviours/activities of individual tourists and DMOs and tourism businesses across the entire travel process, respectively. However, the behaviours of individual tourists interact with those of DMOs and tourism businesses at 3 stages, as portrayed by 3 white arrows. At its outside layer (Yellow), it describes the destination selection. Both behaviours and activities of tourists and DMOs and tourism companies at every stage of travel can affect the destination selection of previous tourists and future tourists.

To be specific, in the pre-trip stage, DMOs and tourism businesses post various destination information and promotion on social media, which may attract potential consumers' attention to their destinations, as shown in Arrow 1. From the perspective of individual tourists, they mainly search for various tourism information produced by previous tourists and DMOs and tourism businesses on social media to make a travel plan and select a destination. After determining the target destination, people may share what and how they are preparing for this trip on social media. As a result, tourism information posted by previous tourists and DMOs and tourism businesses can affect people whether to select a target destination or not (as presented in the destination choices at the outside layer).

During the trip, individual tourists continue seeking information for enhancing the destination experiences (e.g. food, leisure activities, etc.). Some distinctive local activities and promotion information published by DMOs and tourism businesses may evoke tourists' interest. Meanwhile, they often share their experience at a destination and evaluate local products and services (e.g. hotels, restaurants, attractions, etc.) on multiple social media. The information-sharing and evaluation behaviours can be seen as a reference for DMOs and tourism businesses to improve their information publishing and destination promotion. In this case, the line with two arrows (Arrow 2) depicts the activities between DMOs and tourism businesses and tourists mutually influence. That is, promotion by DMOs and tourism businesses inspires tourists' consumption behaviours at the destination, whereas information sharing and evaluation facilitate DMOs and tourism businesses' strategy improvement. In doing so, current tourists may enjoy visiting destinations. When tourists experience something bad at their current destination, they can make a decision to temporarily change the trip via information searching, or even stop the current trip (as presented in the destination choices at the outside layer).

Finally, when tourists return from the tourist destination, they will share their experiences and evaluate local products and services on social media. Likewise, these comments and feedback enable DMOs and tourism businesses to improve destination management and local infrastructure operations, as portrayed in Arrow 3. Consequently (destination choices at the outside layer in the post-trip stage), the information and experience sharing may trigger previous tourists to recall their fantastic memories and evoke their revisiting intention to the destination. Otherwise, they are disappointed about the destination and decide to not visit it anymore. Also, they would provide warning information about this bad destination to other people, which will affect potential tourists' destination choices.

CONCLUSION AND IMPLICATION

Underpinned by the rising application of social media to tourism and hospitality, this chapter aimed to discuss how various platforms influence tourists' destination selection in China by exploring different types of tourism information and Chinese social media platforms and analysing their application and influence on destination selection across 3-stage travel process. Therefore, this chapter contributes to tourism literature on tourists' destination selection and social media marketing in four ways. Foremost, even though tourism information is explosively growing on social media platforms, it is mostly produced by individual tourists (UGC) but DMOs and tourism businesses (Zhang et al., 2016). Especially, DMOs and tourism businesses often post general information about destination (Zhang et al., 2016) and ignore specific information, such as destination security (Zou and Yu, 2022; Yan et al., 2018), which is not conducive to destination image and local tourism development (Zhao et al., 2018). In reality, tourists have multiple needs of tourism information needs, including accommodation, transportation, food, security, etc. (Lei et al., 2022; Li et al., 2021). Hence, whilst destination marketers absorb and master UGC to improve their strategy and destination management, it is imperative to post more specific and valuable information on local facilities (e.g. restaurants, leisure places, etc).

Second, a large number of Chinese social media platforms with multiple functions are ubiquitous to satisfy people's needs of lives, including travel (Yuan et al., 2022; Wang et al., 2022). In the tourism sector, some microblogs and social network sites are welcomed by individuals and tourism businesses to share and collect information, such as WeChat (Liu et al., 2021), Weibo (Zhao et al., 2018) and Xiaohongshu (Wang et al., 2022; Mo, 2022). Due to continuous combination of functions, these platforms have developed into integrated social apps for a wide usage (Wang et al., 2022). Moreover, the indigenised tourism websites and Apps, such as Ctrip (Liang and Zhang, 2021) and Mafengwo (Wu, 2021), are specifically designed for tourism and hospitality market, to provide travel-related products and services (e.g. ticket booking, hotel reservations, tour guide services, etc.) (Zou and Yu, 2022; Wu, 2021). Recently, short-video and live-streaming content platforms (e.g. Tiktok, Douyin, Blibli, etc.) are new and popular means for people to seek and share travel-related information (Lin et al., 2021; Qiu et al., 2021; Xu et al., 2021; Lau, 2020; Xu and Ye, 2020) because of their immersive climate, synchronous interactions and enjoyment (Lin et al., 2022; Lau, 2020). Accordingly, single social media with simple functions cannot meet tourists' demand for information seeking and self-presentation, entertainment, socialisation and e-commerce (Yan et al., 2018; Tuten and Solomon, 2013). The results from Yuan et al., (2022) revealed that Chinese tourists prefer applying numerous social media more than picking up one or very few Apps. Therefore, DMOs and tourism businesses should consider implementing a multi-channel marketing strategy to expand exposure and promotion (Wu, 2021) for tourists' destination choice and journey experiences throughout the course of their trips (Zhang et al., 2016). Also, Chinese tourism policers may consider widening tourism information flow from foreign countries on the Internet, because it will benefit for Chinese tourists to obtaining more authentic tourism information and understanding international destinations for outbound trip. In the meantime, foreigners can learn and obtain Chinese tourism information on destinations. Thus, it contributes to attract international tourists to visit Chinese destination.

Third, individual tourists, and DMOs and tourism businesses can take advantage of various social media platforms to conduct travel-related behaviours and activities for destination selection at 3 stages of travel: pre-trip, amid-trip and post-trip (Want et al., 2022; Yuan et al., 2022; Cox et al., 2009). In the pre-trip, tourists often seek needed destination information and show journey preparation, which provides valuable suggestions for other people's destination choice and tourism businesses' promotion strategies (Wang et al., 2022; Yuan et al., 2022). During the trip, information searching, sharing and destination evaluation co-occur, simulating individuals to extend, change or end up the trip, simultaneously, inspiring DMOs and tourism businesses to improve destination management and market strategy (Mo, 2022; Wu, 2021). After the trip, people love sharing tourism experience and evaluating destination (Mo, 2022; Wu, 2021). Likewise, it keeps facilitating DMOs and tourism businesses (Mo, 2022; Wu, 2021) and helping previous tourists' decision for next visit and new tourists' destination selection (Tussyadiah et al., 2011). Hence, via a comprehensive understanding of individuals' travel-related behaviours, destination marketers can grasp tourists' preferences and behaviours (Lindsey-Mullikin and Borin, 2017), thereby laying out better destination development programs and marketing promotion for attracting more tourists (Gamage et al., 2022).

Finally, in the process of using social media for destination selection, multiple positive and negative impacts co-generate. Positive and negative feedback (Wang et al., 2022; Yan et al., 2018), information variation (Bowen, 2015) and richness on social media (Yuan et al., 2022; Wang et al., 2022), and information credibility (Lin et al., 2022; Zhao et al., 2018), especially rise of web-celebrities on short-video and live-streaming platforms (Xu et al., 2021), indeed contribute to tourists' destination selection; meanwhile, there are some concomitant issues. For instance, a large amount of tourism information provides an opportunity for people to obtain and compare information to make a better destination choice, however, they may also consume more time in the information waves (Mo, 2022). Also, tourism businesses and online celebrities are capitally oriented (Sandel and Wang, 2022). They collaborate to exaggerate to advertise and promote travel-related products and services at the destination on social media (Fung et al., 2022; Mo, 2022). Even some private and public companies manage to take advantage of people's trust to via clickbait strategy (Zhang et al., 2020; Stroud, 2007). When people see and obtain their products and services, they realised being cheated by the fake promotion (Fung et al., 2022). These situations will detrimentally impact tourists' destination images, destination choice and expected travel experiences (Liu et al., 2019). Hence, destination marketers ought not to ignore the significance of negative feedback and issues of information variation, richness and credibility on social media. They have to set up strict monitoring mechanisms for information and social media to ensure travel-related information stability, specification and authenticity. As Kaplan and Haenlein (2010) proposed, information posted by DMOs need to be active, interesting, humble, informal and honest. In doing so, information and social media platforms can be add-value to tourism and hospitality in China and other countries.

FUTURE AVENUES FOR RESEARCH

Albeit current research highlights the significance of social media to the Chinese tourism and hospitality sector, how different functions on social media affect Chinese tourists' destination selection remains insufficiently understood (Yuan et al., 2022), especially those on short video (Fung et al., 2022; Lin et al., 2022) and living-streaming platforms (Xu et al., 2021). As such, future scholars can conduct more research on different social media platforms at the same time, to compare how similar and different functions influence destination selection.

Furthermore, through reviewing a wide range of literature, WeChat (e.g. Cao et al., 2022; Gamage et al., 2022), Weibo (e.g. Qiu et al., 2021), Xiaohongshu (e.g. Wang et al., 2022; Mo, 2022), Ctrip (e.g. Zou and Yu, 2022; Li et al., 2021) are often investigated by scholars. However, the emerging short video and living-streaming platforms, such as Douyin, Blibli, Kuaishou, need more empirical studies to investigate corresponding advantages and disadvantages for destination selection in Chinese and worldwide context, for instance, information credibility, 'wanghong' economy (Fitzgerald et al., 2022; Sandel and Wang, 2022) or 'fandomisation' (Fung, 2019).

Finally, in combination of types of information and Chinese social media and their application and influence on destination selection across 3-stage travel process, we developed a conceptual framework of social media for tourists' destination selection. It portrays a 3-stage process of tourists' destination selection through the usage of information produced by individuals and DMOs and tourism businesses on social media. This framework may contribute to tourism literature on destination selection. In the future, scholars can adopt different research methods to further test and explore 1) how different information characteristics (positive vs negative, variation, richness, credibility) on social media influence individual tourists' travel-related behaviours at 3 stages; 2) how different information characteristics (positive vs negative, variation, richness, credibility) on social media influence impact DMOs and tourism businesses' marketing activities and strategies at 3 stages; 3) how individual tourists' travel-related behaviours and DMOs and tourism businesses' marketing activities interact with each other throughout the entire process of travel; 4) how social media platforms affect individual tourists to make decision on destinations at each stage (pre-trip, amid-trip and post-trip). Even researchers may develop more interesting research topics based on this framework and apply it to other countries.

REFERENCES

Ang, T., Wei, S., & Anaza, N. A. (2018). Livestreaming vs pre-recorded: How social viewing strategies impact consumers' viewing experiences and behavioural intentions. *European Journal of Marketing*, *52*(9/10), 2075–2104. doi:10.1108/EJM-09-2017-0576

Arsal, I., Woosnam, K. M., Baldwin, E. D., & Backman, S. J. (2010). Residents as travel destination information providers: An online community perspective. *Journal of Travel Research*, *49*(4), 400–413. doi:10.1177/0047287509346856

Asongu, S. A., & Odhiambo, N. M. (2019). Tourism and social media in the world: An empirical investigation. *Journal of Economic Studies (Glasgow, Scotland)*, *46*(7), 1319–1331. doi:10.1108/JES-07-2018-0239

Berhanu, K., & Raj, S. (2020). The trustworthiness of travel and tourism information sources of social media: Perspectives of international tourists visiting Ethiopia. *Heliyon*, *6*(3), e03439. Advance online publication. doi:10.1016/j.heliyon.2020.e03439 PMID:32181382

Bian, R., & Zhu, M. (2020). The Relationship between Ritual, Personal Involvement and Travel Intention: A Study of Check-in-Travel on DouYin. *American Journal of Industrial and Business Management*, *10*(02), 451–467. doi:10.4236/ajibm.2020.102030

blibli.com.cn. (2022). *Bilibili Inc. Announces Third Quarter 2022 Financial Results*. https://ir.bilibili.com/media/vbhaxpxs/q3-2022-bilibili-earnings-release-en.pdf

Buhalis, D., & Sinarta, Y. (2019). Real-time co-creation and nowness service: Lessons from tourism and hospitality. *Journal of Travel & Tourism Marketing*, *36*(5), 563–582. doi:10.1080/10548408.2019.1592059

Cao, X., Luo, Z., Qiu, J., & Liu, Y. (2022). Does ostracism impede Chinese tourist self-disclosure on WeChat? The perspective of social anxiety and self-construal. *Journal of Hospitality and Tourism Management*, *50*, 178–187. doi:10.1016/j.jhtm.2022.02.013

Chen, Y., Conroy, N. J., & Rubin, V. L. (2015). Misleading online content: recognising clickbait as "false news". The 2015 ACM on workshop on multimodal deception detection. doi:10.1145/2823465.2823467

Chi, M., Pan, M., & Wang, W. (2021). A cross-platform comparative study of reviews on sharing accommodation and hotel reservation platform: Combined with LDA-SNA and sentiment analysis. *Library and Information Service*, *65*(2), 107.

China Tourism Academy. (2020). *2019 Annual Report on China's Outbound Tourism Development* http://eng.ctaweb.org.cn/ctaen/c09/202103/9189e906cd044e0ebcd388693e7fb6ff.shtml

China Travel News. (2020). *Trip.com Group Scores Big with Livestreaming Sales Event.* https://www.chinatravelnews.com/article/136944

Choe, Y., Kim, J., & Fesenmaier, D. R. (2017). Use of social media across the trip experience: An application of latent transition analysis. *Journal of Travel & Tourism Marketing*, *34*(4), 431–443. doi:10.1080/10548408.2016.1182459

Chung, M., Ko, E., Joung, H., & Kim, S. J. (2020). Chatbot e-service and customer satisfaction regarding luxury brands. *Journal of Business Research*, *117*, 587–595. doi:10.1016/j.jbusres.2018.10.004

cnnic.com.cn. (2022). *The 49th Statistical Report on China's Internet Development.* https://www.cnnic.com.cn/IDR/ReportDownloads/202204/P020220424336135612575.pdf

Cox, C., Burgess, S., Sellitto, C., & Buultjens, J. (2009). The role of user-generated content in tourists' travel planning behavior. *Journal of Hospitality Marketing & Management*, *18*(8), 743–764. doi:10.1080/19368620903235753

Dao, D. V. (2015). Social media classification scheme in online teaching and learning activities: A consideration for educators. *International Journal of Education and Social Science*, *2*(4), 85–94.

Daugherty, T., Eastin, M. S., & Bright, L. (2008). Exploring consumer motivations for creating user-generated content. *Journal of Interactive Advertising*, *8*(2), 16–25. doi:10.1080/15252019.2008.10722139

Deng, Z., Benckendorff, P., & Wang, J. (2021). Travel live streaming: An affordance perspective. *Information Technology & Tourism*, *23*(2), 189–207. doi:10.100740558-021-00199-1

Dickinson, J. E., Ghali, K., Cherrett, T., Speed, C., Davies, N., & Norgate, S. (2014). Tourism and the smartphone app: Capabilities, emerging practice and scope in the travel domain. *Current Issues in Tourism*, *17*(1), 84–101. doi:10.1080/13683500.2012.718323

DiPietro, R. B., Wang, Y., Rompf, P., & Severt, D. (2007). At-destination visitor information search and venue decision strategies. *International Journal of Tourism Research*, *9*(3), 175–188. doi:10.1002/jtr.600

Dwityas, N. A., & Briandana, R. (2017). Social media in travel decision-making process. *International Journal of Humanities and Social Science*, *7*(7), 193–201.

Fodness, D., & Murray, B. (1999). A model of tourist information search behavior. *Journal of Travel Research*, *37*(3), 220–230. doi:10.1177/004728759903700302

Fotis, J., Buhalis, D., & Rossides, N. (2011). Social media impact on holiday travel planning: The case of the Russian and the FSU markets. *International Journal of Online Marketing*, *1*(4), 1–19. doi:10.4018/ijom.2011100101

Fung, A., He, W., & Cao, S. (2022). Cultural capitals and creative labour of short video platforms: A study of Wanghong on Douyin. *Cultural Trends*, 1–6. doi:10.1080/09548963.2022.2082862

Fung, A. Y. (2019). Fandomization of online video or television in China. *Media Culture & Society, 41*(7), 995–1010. doi:10.1177/0163443719863353

Gamage, T. C., Tajeddini, K., & Tajeddini, O. (2022). Why Chinese travellers use WeChat to make hotel choice decisions: A uses and gratifications theory perspective. *Journal of Global Scholars of Marketing Science, 32*(2), 285–312. doi:10.1080/21639159.2021.1961599

Ge, J., & Gretzel, U. (2017). A new cultural revolution: Chinese consumers' internet and social media use. In Advances in Social Media for Travel, Tourism and Hospitality (pp. 102-118). Routledge.

Gretzel, U. (2018). Tourism and Social Media. The Sage Handbook of Tourism Management, 2, 415-432.

Hobbs, W. R., & Roberts, M. E. (2018). How sudden censorship can increase access to information. *The American Political Science Review, 112*(3), 621–636. doi:10.1017/S0003055418000084

Hu, M., & Chaudhry, S. S. (2020). Enhancing consumer engagement in e-commerce live streaming via relational bonds. *Internet Research, 30*(3), 1019–1041. doi:10.1108/INTR-03-2019-0082

Hu, X., & Yang, Y. (2021). What makes online reviews helpful in tourism and hospitality? a bare-bones meta-analysis. *Journal of Hospitality Marketing & Management, 30*(2), 139–158. doi:10.1080/19368623.2020.1780178

Huang, L. (2012). Social media as a new play in a marketing channel strategy: Evidence from Taiwan travel agencies' blogs. *Asia Pacific Journal of Tourism Research, 17*(6), 615–634. doi:10.1080/10941665.2011.635664

Jia, S. S., & Wu, B. (2019). User-generated information on mobile channels with more concise reviews and more extreme ratings. *IEEE Access : Practical Innovations, Open Solutions, 7*, 83495–83503. doi:10.1109/ACCESS.2019.2924335

Kaplan, A., & Haenlein, M. (2010). Users of the world, unite! The challenges and opportunities of social media. *Business Horizons, 53*(1), 59–68. doi:10.1016/j.bushor.2009.09.003

Kirilenko, A. P., Stepchenkova, S. O., & Hernandez, J. M. (2019). Comparative clustering of destination attractions for different origin markets with network and spatial analyses of online reviews. *Tourism Management, 72*, 400–410. doi:10.1016/j.tourman.2019.01.001

Krasnova, H., Spiekermann, S., Koroleva, K., & Hildebrand, T. (2010). Online social networks: Why we disclose. *Journal of Information Technology, 25*(2), 109–125. doi:10.1057/jit.2010.6

Lam, J. M., Ismail, H., & Lee, S. (2020). From desktop to destination: User-generated content platforms, co-created online experiences, destination image and satisfaction. *Journal of Destination Marketing & Management, 18*, 100490. doi:10.1016/j.jdmm.2020.100490

Lau, A. (2020). New technologies used in COVID-19 for business survival: Insights from the Hotel Sector in China. *Information Technology & Tourism, 22*(4), 497–504. doi:10.100740558-020-00193-z

Lei, W. S., Chen, Z., Zhou, X., & King, B. (2022). Organic destination imagery and social media: Mapping tourism dynamics across China's Greater Bay Area cities. *Journal of China Tourism Research*, 1–24. doi:10.1080/19388160.2022.2047857

Leung, D., Law, R., Van Hoof, H., & Buhalis, D. (2013). Social media in tourism and hospitality: A literature review. *Journal of Travel & Tourism Marketing*, *30*(1-2), 3–22. doi:10.1080/10548408.2013.750919

Li, F., Larimo, J., & Leonidou, L. C. (2021). Social media marketing strategy: Definition, conceptualisation, taxonomy, validation, and future agenda. *Journal of the Academy of Marketing Science*, *49*(1), 51–70. doi:10.100711747-020-00733-3

Li, J. J., Xu, L. Z., Tang, L., Wang, S. Y., & Li, L. (2018). Big data in tourism research: A literature review. *Tourism Management*, *68*, 301–323. doi:10.1016/j.tourman.2018.03.009

Li, L., Song, X., Liu, S., & Huang, K. (2021). Defining High-Quality Answers on a Chinese Tourism Q&A Platform in Terms of Information Needs. *Sustainability (Basel)*, *13*(24), 13884. doi:10.3390u132413884

Liang, B. (2021). Development of rural community-based tourism with local customs from the view of consumer satisfaction. *Annals of Operations Research*, 1–17. doi:10.100710479-021-04302-x

Liang, H., & Zhang, Q. (2021). Do social media data indicate visits to tourist attractions? A case study of Shanghai, China. *Open House International*, *47*(1), 17–35. doi:10.1108/OHI-05-2021-0110

Lien, C. H., & Cao, Y. (2014). Examining WeChat users' motivations, trust, attitudes, and positive word-of-mouth: Evidence from China. *Computers in Human Behavior*, *41*, 104–111. doi:10.1016/j.chb.2014.08.013

Lin, K., Fong, L. H. N., & Law, R. (2022). Live streaming in tourism and hospitality: A literature review. *Asia Pacific Journal of Tourism Research*, *27*(3), 290–304. doi:10.1080/10941665.2022.2061365

Lindsey-Mullikin, J., & Borin, N. (2017). Why strategy is key for successful social media sales. *Business Horizons*, *60*(4), 473–482. doi:10.1016/j.bushor.2017.03.005

Liu, C., & Hung, K. A. (2020). Comparative study of self-service technology with service employees: A qualitative analysis of hotels in China. *Information Technology & Tourism*, *22*(1), 33–52. doi:10.100740558-020-00167-1

Liu, H., Wu, L., & Li, X. (2019). Social media envy: How experience sharing on social networking sites drives millennials' aspirational tourism consumption. *Journal of Travel Research*, *58*(3), 355–369. doi:10.1177/0047287518761615

Liu, I., Norman, W. C., & Pennington-Gray, L. (2013). A flash of culinary tourism: Understanding the influences of online food photography on people's travel planning process on flickr. *Tourism, Culture & Communication*, *13*(1), 5–18. doi:10.3727/109830413X13769180530567

Liu, M. T., Xue, J., & Liu, Y. (2021). The mechanism leads to successful clickbait promotion in WeChat social media platforms. *Asia Pacific Journal of Marketing and Logistics*, *33*(9), 1952–1973. doi:10.1108/APJML-08-2020-0562

Liu, X., Mehraliyev, F., Liu, C., & Schuckert, M. (2020). The roles of social media in tourists' choices of travel components. *Tourist Studies*, *20*(1), 27–48. doi:10.1177/1468797619873107

Liu, X., Zeng, Y., Li, Z., & Huang, D. (2022). Understanding consumers' motivations to view travel live streaming: Scale development and validation. *Tourism Management Perspectives, 44*, 101027. doi:10.1016/j.tmp.2022.101027

Luo, Q., & Zhai, X. (2017). "I will never go to Hong Kong again!" How the secondary crisis communication of 'Occupy Central' on Weibo shifted to a tourism boycott. *Tourism Management, 62*, 159–172. doi:10.1016/j.tourman.2017.04.007 PMID:32287749

Luo, Q., & Zhong, D. (2015). Using social network analysis to explain communication characteristics of travel-related electronic word-of-mouth on social networking sites. *Tourism Management, 46*, 274–282. doi:10.1016/j.tourman.2014.07.007

Lyu, F., & Zhang, L. (2019). Using multi-source big data to understand the factors affecting urban park use in Wuhan. *Urban Forestry & Urban Greening, 43*, 126367. doi:10.1016/j.ufug.2019.126367

Mo, X. (2022). Study on the Content and User Awareness of Travel Promotion in Xiaohongshu APP. *Frontiers in Economics and Management, 3*(1), 352–358.

Montag, C., Becker, B., & Gan, C. (2018). The multipurpose application WeChat: A review on recent research. *Frontiers in Psychology, 9*, 2247. doi:10.3389/fpsyg.2018.02247 PMID:30618894

Noone, B. M., McGuire, K. A., & Rohlfs, K. V. (2011). Social media meets hotel revenue management: Opportunities, issues and unanswered questions. *Journal of Revenue and Pricing Management, 10*(4), 293–305. doi:10.1057/rpm.2011.12

Oliveira, T., Araujo, B., & Tam, C. (2020). Why do people share their travel experiences on social media? *Tourism Management, 78*, 104041. doi:10.1016/j.tourman.2019.104041 PMID:32322615

Pabel, A., & Prideaux, B. (2016). Social media use in pre-trip planning by tourists visiting a small regional leisure destination. *Journal of Vacation Marketing, 22*(4), 335–348. doi:10.1177/1356766715618998

Pan, B., MacLaurin, T., & Crotts, J. C. (2007). Travel blogs and the implications for destination marketing. *Journal of Travel Research, 46*(1), 35–45. doi:10.1177/0047287507302378

Park, E., Kang, J., Choi, D., & Han, J. (2020). Understanding customers' hotel revisiting behaviour: A sentiment analysis of online feedback reviews. *Current Issues in Tourism, 23*(5), 605–611. doi:10.1080/13683500.2018.1549025

Pike, S., & Page, S. J. (2014). Destination Marketing Organizations and destination marketing: A narrative analysis of the literature. *Tourism Management, 41*(2), 202–227. doi:10.1016/j.tourman.2013.09.009

Popp, B., & Woratschek, H. (2016). Introducing branded communities in sport for building strong brand relations in social media. *Sport Management Review, 19*(2), 183–197. doi:10.1016/j.smr.2015.06.001

Porter, C. E. (2004). A typology of virtual communities: A multi-disciplinary foundation for future research. *Journal of Computer-Mediated Communication, 10*(1), 00. Advance online publication. doi:10.1111/j.1083-6101.2004.tb00228.x

Qi, S., & Chen, N. (2019). Understanding Macao's destination image through user-generated content. *Journal of China Tourism Research, 15*(4), 503–519. doi:10.1080/19388160.2019.1577199

Qiu, Q., Zuo, Y., & Zhang, M. (2021). Can live streaming save the tourism industry from a pandemic? A study of social media. *ISPRS International Journal of Geo-Information, 10*(9), 595–610. doi:10.3390/ijgi10090595

Qiu, S., Alizadeh, A., Dooley, L. M., & Zhang, R. (2019). The effects of authentic leadership on trust in leaders, organisational citizenship behavior, and service quality in the Chinese hospitality industry. *Journal of Hospitality and Tourism Management, 40*, 77–87. doi:10.1016/j.jhtm.2019.06.004

Reinikainen, H., Munnukka, J., Maity, D., & Luoma-Aho, V. (2020). 'You really are a great big sister'–parasocial relationships, credibility, and the moderating role of audience comments in influencer marketing. *Journal of Marketing Management, 36*(3-4), 279–298. doi:10.1080/0267257X.2019.1708781

Riley, J. (2020). Sustaining customer engagement through social media brand communities. *Journal of Global Scholars of Marketing Science, 30*(4), 344–357. doi:10.1080/21639159.2020.1766990

Sandel, T. L., & Wang, Y. (2022). Selling intimacy online: The multi-modal discursive techniques of China's Wanghong. *Discourse, Context & Media, 47*, 100606. doi:10.1016/j.dcm.2022.100606

Shi, J., Fan, A., & Cai, L. A. (2020). Leisure mobility of Chinese millennials. *Journal of China Tourism Research, 16*(4), 527–546. doi:10.1080/19388160.2019.1687060

Sigala, M., Christou, E., & Gretzel, U. (2012). *Social media in travel, tourism and hospitality: Theory, practice and cases*. Ashgate Publishing, Ltd.

Sirakaya, E., & Woodside, A. G. (2005). Building and testing theories of decision-making by travellers. *Tourism Management, 26*(6), 815–832. doi:10.1016/j.tourman.2004.05.004

Sobhanifard, Y., & Vaeysi, M. (2020). Mixed modeling of the social network mechanisms for the sustainable development of tourism: The case of Iranian Kurdistan. *Sustainable Development (Bradford), 28*(1), 187–196. doi:10.1002d.1981

Statista. (2022a). *Number of monthly active users of Xiaohongshu app in China from December 2020 to June 2022 (in millions).* https://www.statista.com/statistics/1327421/china-xiaohongshu-monthly-active-users/

Statista. (2022b). *Number of monthly active users of Weibo Corporation from 1st quarter of 2014 to 3rd quarter of 2022 (in million).* https://www.statista.com/statistics/795303/china-mau-of-sina-weibo/

Statista. (2022c). *Number of monthly active WeChat users from the 2nd quarter 2011 to the 3rd quarter 2022 (in millions).* https://www.statista.com/statistics/255778/number-of-active-wechat-messenger-accounts/

Stroud, N. J. (2017). Attention as a valuable resource. *Political Communication, 34*(3), 479–489. doi:10.1080/10584609.2017.1330077

Tang, Y., Zhong, M. L., Qing, F. L., Fang, Y., & He, M. F. (2017). Application of new media in inbound tourism destination marketing – a case study of Sichuan Province. *Skills and Market, 24*(6), 63–67.

Tussyadiah, I. P., & Fesenmaier, D. R. (2009). Mediating tourist experiences: Access to places via shared videos. *Annals of Tourism Research, 36*(1), 24–40. doi:10.1016/j.annals.2008.10.001

Tussyadiah, I. P., Park, S., & Fesenmaier, D. R. (2011). Assessing the effectiveness of consumer narratives for destination marketing. *Journal of Hospitality & Tourism Research (Washington, D.C.), 35*(1), 64–78. doi:10.1177/1096348010384594

Tuten, T. L., & Solomon, M. R. (2013). *Social media marketing*. Pearson Education.

Valeri, M., & Baggio, R. (2021). A critical reflection on the adoption of blockchain in tourism. *Information Technology & Tourism, 23*(2), 121–132. doi:10.100740558-020-00183-1

Wang, G., Qiu, H., & Ren, L. (2022). Determinants of tourists' intention to share travel experience on social media: A fsQCA application. *Current Issues in Tourism*, 1–6. doi:10.1080/13683500.2022.2091428

Wang, J., Li, Y., Wu, B., & Wang, Y. (2021). Tourism destination image based on tourism user-generated content on the Internet. *Tourism Review, 76*(1), 125–137. doi:10.1108/TR-04-2019-0132

Wang, J., Xia, Y., & Wu, Y. (2022). Sensing Tourist Distributions and Their Sentiment Variations Using Social Media: Evidence from 5A Scenic Areas in China. *ISPRS International Journal of Geo-Information, 11*(9), 492. doi:10.3390/ijgi11090492

Wang, X., Huang, Y., & Li, X. (2017). Behavior of Sharing Travel Experiences in Social Media. *Management Review, 29*(2), 97–105.

Wang, Z., Huang, W. J., & Liu-Lastres, B. (2022). Impact of user-generated travel posts on travel decisions: A comparative study on Weibo and Xiaohongshu. *Annals of Tourism Research Empirical Insights, 3*(2), 100064. doi:10.1016/j.annale.2022.100064

Wei, R., & Liu, X. (2019). Insights into the psychology of mobile apps as the new home screen: Evidence from cutting-edge research in Chinese societies. *Chinese Journal of Communication, 12*(1), 1–6. doi:10.1080/17544750.2019.1548662

World Bank Group. (2018, 25 September). *The voice of travelers: Leveraging user-generated content for tourism development 2018*. http://hdl.handle.net/10986/30451

World Tourism Organization. (2021, 16 March). *Yearbook of tourism statistics, data 2015–2019* (2021 ed.). https://www.e-unwto.org/doi/book/10.18111/9789284422487

Wu, J. (2021). Analysis of Mafengwo's Social Media Strategy. *The 2021 4th International Conference on Humanities Education and Social Sciences (ICHESS 2021)*, 2373-2377. https://creativecommons.org/licenses/by-nc/4.0/

Wu, L., Fan, A., & Shen, H. (2020). Embracing the future: New technology and mediated Chinese tourists. *Journal of China Tourism Research, 16*(4), 487–493. doi:10.1080/19388160.2020.1845074

Xiang, Z., Du, Q., Ma, Y., & Fan, W. (2017). A comparative analysis of major online review platforms: Implications for social media analytics in hospitality and tourism. *Tourism Management, 58*, 51–65. doi:10.1016/j.tourman.2016.10.001

Xiang, Z., & Gretzel, U. (2010). Role of social media in online travel information search. *Tourism Management, 31*(2), 179–188. doi:10.1016/j.tourman.2009.02.016

Xiao, L., & Zhao, L. (2009). Tourism destination image spreading on the Internet—Content analysis based on the related websites on Cross-Straint. *Luyou Xuekan, 24*(3), 75–81.

Xiao, X., Fang, C., Lin, H., & Chen, J. (2022). A framework for quantitative analysis and differentiated marketing of tourism destination image based on visual content of photos. *Tourism Management, 93*, 104585. doi:10.1016/j.tourman.2022.104585

xiaohongshu.com.cn. (2022). *About Xiaohongshu.* https://www.xiaohongshu.com/protocols/about

Xu, D., Chen, T., Pearce, J., Mohammadi, Z., & Pearce, P. L. (2021). Reaching audiences through travel vlogs: The perspective of involvement. *Tourism Management, 25*(15), 2518–2533. doi:10.1016/j.tourman.2021.104326

Xu, X., Huang, D., & Shang, X. (2021). Social presence or physical presence? Determinants of purchasing behaviour in tourism live-streamed shopping. *Tourism Management Perspectives, 40*, 100917. doi:10.1016/j.tmp.2021.100917

Xu, Y., & Ye, Y. (2020). Who watches live streaming in China? Examining viewers' behaviors, personality traits, and motivations. *Frontiers in Psychology, 11*, 1607. doi:10.3389/fpsyg.2020.01607 PMID:32848995

Yoong, L. C., & Lian, S. B. (2019). Customer engagement in social media and purchase intentions in the hotel industry. *International Journal of Academic Research in Business & Social Sciences, 9*(1), 54–68. doi:10.6007/IJARBSS/v9-i1/5363

Yuan, Y., Chan, C. S., Eichelberger, S., Ma, H. & Pikkemaat, B. (2022). The effect of social media on travel planning process by Chinese tourists: the way forward to tourism futures. *Journal of Tourism Futures*. doi:10.1108/JTF-04-2021-0094

Zhang, J., Gui, Y., Wu, B., Morrison, A. M., & Li, C. (2016). Is destination marketing organization microblogging in China delivering? An empirical analysis of information supply against consumer information needs. *Journal of Vacation Marketing, 22*(1), 68–85. doi:10.1177/1356766715591869

Zhang, W. (2021). Text Mining Applied in Evolution of Q&A Platforms users' Information Demand on Tourism in COVID-19 Normalization. In *2021 5th Annual International Conference on Data Science and Business Analytics (ICDSBA)* (pp. 29-40). IEEE. 10.1109/ICDSBA53075.2021.00016

Zhang, W., Du, W., Bian, Y., Peng, C. H., & Jiang, Q. (2020). Seeing is not always believing: An exploratory study of clickbait in WeChat. *Internet Research, 30*(3), 1043–1058. doi:10.1108/INTR-09-2019-0373

Zhang, X., Chen, Z., & Jin, H. (2021). The effect of tourists' autobiographical memory on revisit intention: Does nostalgia promote revisiting? *Asia Pacific Journal of Tourism Research, 26*(2), 147–166. doi:10.1080/10941665.2020.1718171

Zhao, Z., Zhu, M., & Hao, X. (2018). Share the Gaze: Representation of destination image on the Chinese social platform WeChat Moments. *Journal of Travel & Tourism Marketing*, *35*(6), 726–739. doi:10.1080/10548408.2018.1432449

Zhou, J., Zhou, J., Ding, Y., & Wang, H. (2019). The magic of danmaku: A social interaction perspective of gift sending on live streaming platforms. *Electronic Commerce Research and Applications*, *34*, 100815. doi:10.1016/j.elerap.2018.11.002

Zhu, W., Zheng, D. Q., Wang, W. C., & Zhou, H. H. (2014). The differences between Weibo and WeChat: The evidence from the social capital theory. *Journal of Intelligence*, *6*, 138–143.

Zou, Y., & Yu, Q. (2022). Sense of safety toward tourism destinations: A social constructivist perspective. *Journal of Destination Marketing & Management*, *24*, 100708. doi:10.1016/j.jdmm.2022.100708

Chapter 12
An Analysis on the Adoption of Chatbots in the Banking Sector of Hong Kong:
A Contemporary System for Improving Customer Experiences in E-Banking

Stuart So
University of Exeter, UK

ABSTRACT

In view of the fierce competition and rapidly changing business environment in the banking and finance industries, many banks have been progressively shifting their retail banking services online. With the aim of streamlining operations and improving customer service, the burgeoning use of artificial intelligence (AI) in the banking industry accelerates the adoption of various AI-based technologies. This chapter conducted a case study on Fubon Bank, researching the adoption of chatbots in the Hong Kong banking industry. A chatbot development framework for e-banking is being developed. Lastly, a comparison of chatbot services among three local banks in Hong Kong is provided.

INTRODUCTION

Adopting artificial intelligence (AI) in a contemporary business system allows organization and analysis of data from all levels of the institution, and it helps increase profitability and productivity and improve decision-making. Furthermore, it also helps the institute to create relevant, well-organized, and reliable information supporting its organizational process.

Chatbot is a combination of the words "chatting" and "robot," as in "chatting with a robot." It's an interactive online conversation tool that allows users to ask inquiries in natural language text and receive automated responses. Both virtual assistants (e.g., Siri or Amazon Alexa) and chatbots are powered by this AI-driven communication technology which is called conversational AI. Client-facing chatbots are

DOI: 10.4018/978-1-6684-7416-7.ch012

commonly employed in sales, marketing, customer service, and technical assistance. Its major purpose is to improve customer experiences, automate processes, and provide quality control. According to the Hong Kong Monetary Authority (HKMA) (2019) survey, chatbot is one of the top three most popular AI applications in Hong Kong's banking sector. 'Customer experience' in the digital era refers to a customer using a digital device (e.g., computer, tablet, or smartphone) and a digital platform (e.g., social media) to look for information about a business or brand (i.e., a business or product inquiry) or to make an online purchase (i.e., a transaction), (Batat, 2022). Batat (2022) further defines digital customer experience that reflects all communications between a brand and its customers via digital channels (e.g., emails, social networks, online advertising).

Aiming at outperforming its competitors, a chatbot can help a bank improve customer experiences in a variety of ways when it comes to customer services. The most prevalent use scenario for chatbots in bank is customer care through the automation of ordinary monotonous duties such as greeting customers, gathering information about their problems, providing clients with requested information, accepting a payment from a receiver, and a range of other basic operations. A Chatbot can also reply more quickly and consistently than a human. Human effort can then be decreased because chatbots answer a lot of repetitive requests. This is especially effective in cities with a high living standard like Hong Kong, where it is difficult to justify investing in property and staff for physical contact centers.

Chatbots use machines learning (ML) to learn and improve over time leading to interact better with the users. Utilizing reviews and ratings in the adoption of Chatbots in e-banking will help better understand user behavior and expectations towards system improvement which helps improve online user experience over time. Hence, the chatbot-based e-banking system should get regular updates to further help personalize user experience. There are various forms of chatbots including Menu/button-based Chatbots, Linguistic Based (Rule-Based) Chatbots, Keyword Recognition-Based Chatbots, and Contextual (Machine Learning/Deep Learning) Chatbots (Engati, 2021; Finwin Technologies, 2020). Shruti (2023) explained the concepts of and relationship between AI, ML and Deep Learning (DL) clearly. AI is the concept of creating smart intelligent machines. ML is a subset of artificial intelligence that helps you build AI-driven applications. Lastly, DL is a subset of machine learning that uses vast volumes of data and complex algorithms to train a model. In this study, we will focus mostly on Contextual Chatbots. In order to avoid misunderstanding, I use AI-driven chatbot or simply chatbot from this point forward.

This study compares chatbots in B2C e-banking of different banks and research how chatbots can help manage global e-banking transactions with the aim to identify benefits to the banking sector. The study adopts a unique four-Step approach on the chatbot development methodology to describe the life of a chatbot from cradle to gate. Through the improved chatbot systems at Fubon Bank (Hong Kong), a case study is used to demonstrate the values of chatbots, and their benefits brought to small-medium sized institutions in the banking sector. Lastly, a comparative testing among three retail banks was performed and suggestions are given for future improvement.

APPLICATIONS OF AI AND CHATBOTS

AI

One of the most enigmatic and intriguing modern technologies is AI. Although many individuals may be familiar with the term "AI," most would not know what it actually means. Copeland (2023) defined AI as 'the ability of a digital computer or computer-controlled robot to perform tasks commonly associated with intelligent beings. Hisrich and Soltanufar (2020) further elaborate on the elements of intelligence, such as learning, reasoning, problem-solving, perception, and language, in order to further develop this idea. Smith (2020) argued that the business world is currently experiencing a supervised-learning revolution where computers are being taught to recognise patterns and learn on their own. Goasduff (2019) revealed the recent developments in AI include chatbots, machine learning, augmented intelligence, and intelligent (business) apps, among others. For the most recent development, generative AI-driven chatbot, or generative AI in short creates unique language combinations rather than choosing from pre-written responses, which can be created using Keras-based seq2seq machine translation models using Python (Codeacademy, 2023).

Codeacademy (2023) also revealed the latest research on generative chatbots involves attempting to determine the most effective way to handle chat context and knowledge from prior turns of discourse. In the banking industry, generative AI will help create marketing images and text, answer customer queries via virtual assistants, and produce data that will make machine learning applications more accurate and efficient (Forbes, 2023). Generative AI could revolutionize various verticals within banking by improving the efficiency of know-your-customer (KYC) processes for retail banking, helping interpret small business loan applications for SMB banking, speeding up back-office tasks in commercial banking, and helping banks stress test balance sheets that contain complex, illiquid financial products for investment banking and capital markets (Brown, 2023).

Forbes (2023) argued that one of the largest challenges in executing Generative AI today is its relative immaturity like other new emerging technology. Though GPT has made considerable strides in natural language processing (NLP), there is a sizable chance that the answers it provides are factually erroneous yet sound correct. In sectors like healthcare or financial services, where precision is crucial, this may not be an option. To reduce this risk, organisations must first carefully select the appropriate application areas, followed by the development of the governance and oversight. Besides, GPT has also opened a Pandora's box of security risks. Schwartz (2023) explained that many think ChatGPT will increase the threat posed by phishing. Phishing is most effective when the emails or social media posts appear convincing, and ChatGPT may easily imitate the voice and demeanor of a famous person, business leader, or company representative through email writing. Even if a valid account is hacked, criminals can send such emails from that account. Counter measurements on this potential threat including multi-factor authentication, user education and corresponding risk management framework can be adopted.

Architecture of Chatbots

Different kinds of chatbots exist, depending on their sophistication and capabilities. Contextual (ML/Deep Learning) chatbots, linguistic-based (rule-based), keyword recognition-based, and menu/button-based chatbots are all options. But in this essay, we'll concentrate mostly on contextual chatbots. Its foundation is three classification techniques. First, it is a pattern matching bot that uses Artificial Intelligence Markup Language (AIML) to identify text and respond to it based on the terms it encounters. The chatbot uses pattern matching to comprehend how to react to questions that have previously been pre-programmed into their models. The second is to employ algorithms, such as Natural Language Processing (NLP), Natural Language Generation (NLG), and Natural Language Understanding (NLU). Chatbots transform the user's speech or text into structured data, which is then used to select an appropriate response. The stages of NLP are as follows: Tokenization, Sentiment Analysis, Normalization, Named Entity Recognition and Dependency Parsing. The third is to use neural networks (NN). NN uses weighted connections and nodes in the data to calculate answers. Every statement a bot receives is split down into a variety of words, and each word serves as an input to an artificial neural network. The neural network gets stronger and better over time, enabling the bot to produce a more accurate set of answers to frequently asked questions. But it is linked to the database for all chatbots. The chatbot uses the database to function and to respond appropriately to every user.

AI-driven Chatbots Applications

Chatbots have gained popularity in recent years with the rise of edge computing and AI as businesses find innovative ways to use them. Today, having a chatbot offers many benefits for organisations because it makes life easier for customers, is available 24/7, saves time, and is easy to use. Below are some typical applications of AI-driver chatbots in various business segments (Maher et al., 2022; Wilson and Daugherty, 2018):

1. Personal Aide

An AI-powered chatbot can operate as a customer's personal aide through speech and text-based conversations. It can automate consumer engagements. According to Maher et al. (2022), 44% of respondents said they would rather interact with a chatbot than a human to get their issues addressed, while two-thirds of those surveyed said AI-powered chatbots would help them give helpful responses to customers' inquiries. Another significant use of AI-enabled personal aides is to conduct dialogue in the banking and finance sector. AI can assist users in acting and handling a lot of information more accurately.

2. Application in Retailing

In the retail sectors, conversational chatbots assist customers with product searches, store locators, package tracking, and recommendation requests. Consumers who are blind or visually impaired would ask questions of the chatbot via speech or text input. These questions will be mapped to the relevant responses, which depending on the circumstance may be trained to discriminate inquiries to look up an answer in a knowledge base, ask for clarification, or refer clients to a human. Voice-enabled chatbots take inquiries from users about the products they are interested in and assist with purchases by guiding users through the checkout and navigation processes. Because there are no cashiers or lines at checkout, the IoT-based self-service supermarkets use AI-driven Chatbot to improve the shopping experience.

3. Application in Legal and Finance

In a legal setting, chatbots could help with document completion, appealing a decision, and other legal issues. They could also provide clarification on legal terms and conditions. The most recent disruptive element that has changed how consumers interact is the rise of chatbots in the financial industry. It is stated that the IT or finance industries employ 76% of respondents who use chatbots. More details on the application of chatbots in banking sector will be discussed in subsequent sections.

4. Application in Entertainment

AI-driven chatbots facilitate the development of emotionally charged and substantive conversational exchanges, hence boosting audience growth and engagement. Chatbots can have an impact on the integration of brand sponsors hips and subscriptions services. With internet chatting, conversational bots can be employed for entertainment. A user can converse with the chatbot whenever they are bored to keep themselves occupied by communicating with conversational AI-driven chatbots. They help us by providing enjoyment, reducing our workload, and finding solutions to challenging problems. Popular entertainment chatbot Cleverbot uses rule-based AI techniques to communicate with people (Wilson and Daugherty, 2018).

5. Application in E-Learning

In order to encourage interaction, assist students in planning their studies and educational activities, and provide real-time information, chatbots are used in e-learning. Chatbots powered by AI and deep learning are able to determine a student's level of competence, alter conversational tones, and gather only the material that is pertinent to that learner. Chatbots in e-learning can help with a range of tasks, such as sharing and submitting application forms, assisting students and teachers by answering frequently asked questions, widely disseminating class and test schedules, making announcements, informing students about extracurricular activities, making sign-ups, registrations, and cancellations easier, and gathering feedback, distributing instructional materials to teachers, and students while building communities.

6. Application in Healthcare

In the healthcare industry, chatbots provide user behaviour, anxiety, dietary information, weight loss tracking, and counselling for delicate and mental health issues. By using symptom analysis and a conversational approach, a spoken language medical chatbot may give an appropriate response and assist in guiding the diagnosis of the patients. Also, the chatbot's comparable performance demonstrates that automated medical devices may develop and assume a larger role in healthcare in the future.

7. Application in E-Commerce

The use of chatbots, particularly on smartphones and the internet, has made it simpler for people to carry out daily tasks like communicating and making purchases through messaging and user interaction with the e-commerce engine. A conversational chatbot for e-commerce, which is gaining popularity in the e-commerce industry, enables customers to make online purchases by communicating with a chatbot through a messaging application. Features include personalisation, branding, human connection, artificial intelligence, real-time dialogue, rich communications, context, and retention, discovery, and installation, engagement and marriage methods, and online payment can help consumers when they shop online.

COMPANY BACKGROUND AND ISSUES

Background

Fubon Bank (Hong Kong) Limited ("Fubon Bank") is a wholly owned subsidiary of Fubon Financial Holding Co., Ltd. ("Fubon Financial Holdings"), one of the largest financial holding companies in Taiwan. Their agenda is to become Asia's top financial organization. So far, they have built a number of good financial services companies. Fubon Bank operates a security company and seventeen branches in Hong Kong. According to Business Source Complete (2022), the bank operated a network 17 branches, one securities service center in Hong Kong. As of December 31, 2020, it reported assets of HKD112.3 billion, customer deposits of HKD76.5 billion, and net loans and advances of HKD54.9 billion. Fubon Bank offers a broad range of financial services surrounding consumer and wholesale banking, investment services, wealth management, securities brokerage, financial markets, which can be classified under three segments: Retail Banking, Institutional Banking, and Financial Markets. He reported that 'Fubon GO' mobile app can offer opening of bank account conveniently and quickly online in 3 simple steps in 5 minutes.

In their 2021 press release, Fubon Bank indicated that they have partnered up with the Hong Kong Telecom (HKT), one of the largest telecom operators in Hong Kong to develop their new mobile app, Fubon GO for all the banking needs of a customer (Fubon Bank, 2021). The press release also mentioned that how they fully invested in the idea of adapting new emerging technologies in order to gain competitive among its competitors and gather more customers. According to Mr. Raymond Lee, the former Chief Executive Officer (CEO) and Managing Director of the bank emphasized that digitalization in the financial sector has accelerated due to the outbreak of COVID-19, and this has changed the ways people manage their financial activities (Business Source Complete, 2022; Fubon Bank, 2021). Mr. Lee also mentioned the trend of the financial sector that, Hong Kong has fully embraced Fintech and the government has also launched multiple initiatives to promote low cost and easy access electronic banking, including the introduction of the Faster Payment System, Open API, and the licensing of virtual banks. Therefore, Fubon Bank has taken note of the Fintech trend over and have developed a strategic plan that will transform the Bank from a traditional physical bank to a dual-platform financial institution that offers a broad range of banking services through both virtual and physical channels.

Existing Systems

Fubon Bank is regarded as one of Taiwan's largest financial holding companies. With the goal of becoming one of Asia's top financial institutions, Fubon Financial Holdings has assembled a sizable lineup of financial service providers. In terms of consumer and wholesale banking, investment services, wealth management, securities brokerage, and financial markets, they provide a wide range of financial services. The high-level systems flow, and operations processes used by banks to support its major online products and services are shown in Figure 1.

Figure 1. Systems flow and operations processes of Fubon Bank services

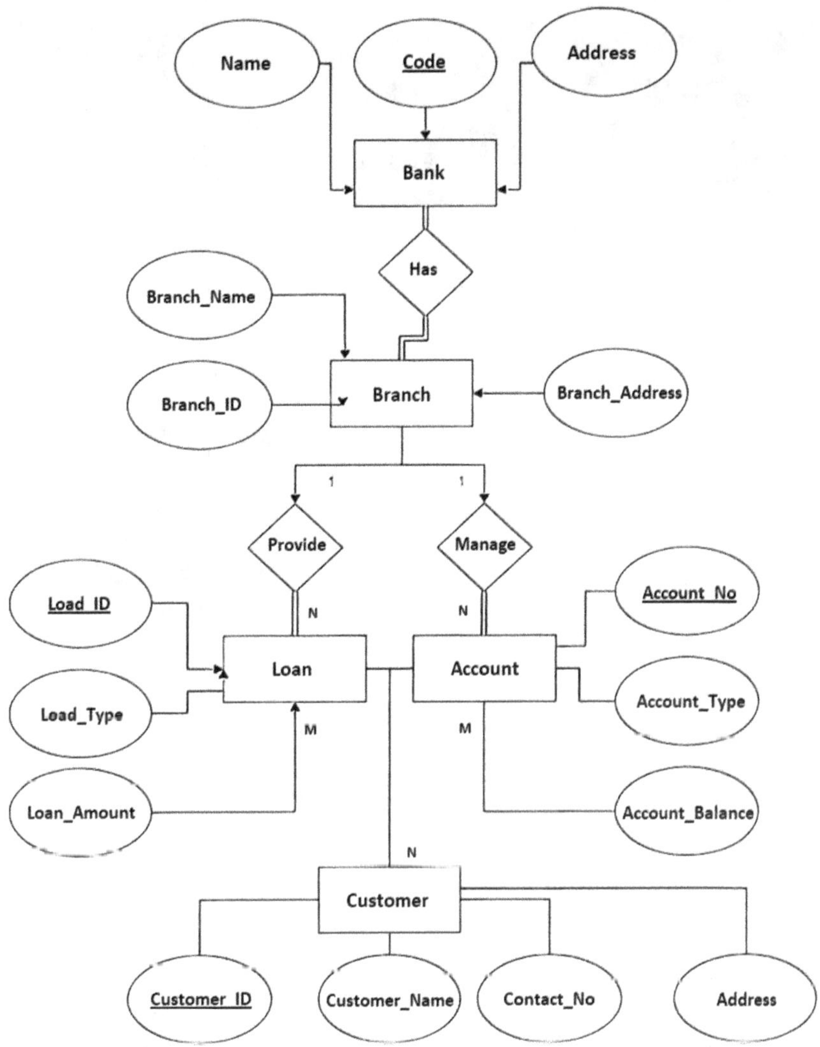

Issues of E-Banking Interface and Comparison With Its Competitor

The e-banking interface that supports Fubon Bank's system flow and operations processes that support its major online products and services of Fubon Bank are explored and analysed through mysteries clients from a multifaceted perspective. The exploration covers all aspects of customer service including marketing, customer service and sales. Clients interact with their e-banking systems through the web-based interface accessing their account and get information from different e-banking services by measuring the response time. Beside expected low turn-around time, a user-friendly interface with features enhancing customer experiences is evaluated as well.

Figure 2. Online loan application menu of e-banking at Fubon Bank

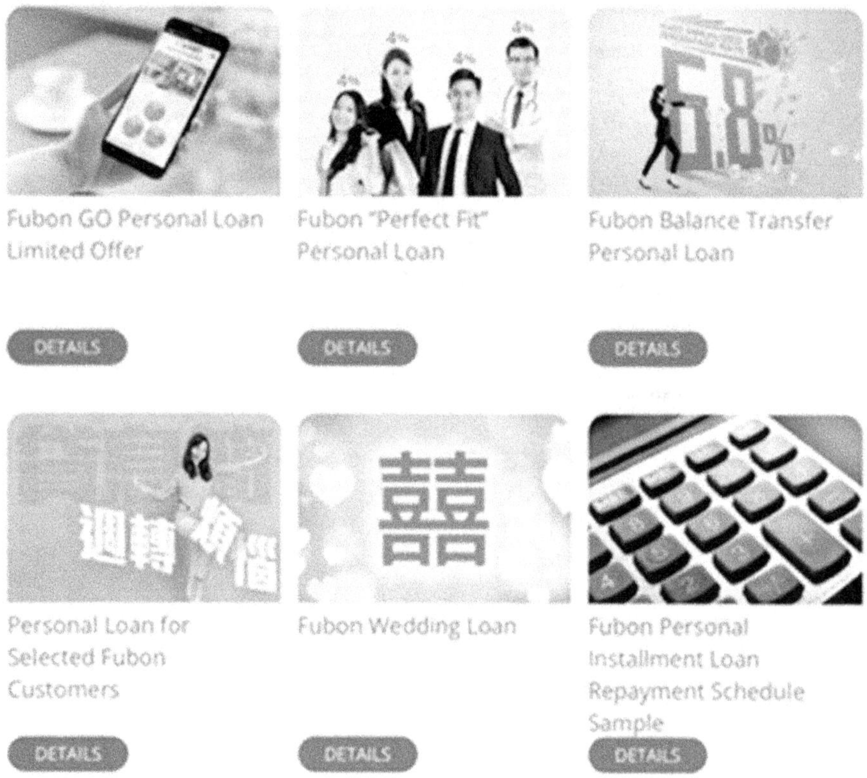

According to Pilarczyk (2016), customer usually switch to different banks if they wait for too long to conduct an online transaction. Keeping this in mind, one of the scenarios is measuring the response time of applying for a loan online from Fubon Bank. The first thing customers would see after clicking on the Loans button on the navigation bar of bank's website is a list of different types of loans a user can borrow (see Figure 2).

For example, if clients want to get a wedding loan and click on the Fubon Wedding Loan tab s/he will be brought to a new tab where the user can get only very basic information about the loan plan. The only way to inquire more about it is the user to call at the personal loan hotline of the bank. The only other online option for the client is to use the chatbot. Since Fubon bank's chatbot is a rule-based chatbot which does not provide interactive queries, the online customer can only have a small number of options chosen from the personal loan section on the rule-based chatbot. This limited service might lead the customer to switch to competitors such as HSBC which provide its client with a ML-based chatbot on their website supported by conversational AI, where an AI-based chatbot can answer virtually whatever questions a client might have about the loan.

Comparatively more flexible and responsive query responses provided by HSBC's AI-based chatbot which could bring a better user experience (see Figure 3). Whereas on Fubon bank's website a client might feel to get some information they have to call the customer service hotline or go to the branch eventually where the number has been largely reduced due to cost saving and the impact of COVID-19 pandemic. Below screenshots provide a view of a quick query from HSBC's live chat about wedding loan questions.

Adding more human responses to the Chatbot such as "Happy Wedding" might increase customer intimacy and improve customer experiences throughout the loan application process. According to Lieberman (2018), CEO of Revenue Scientists, the most preferable way of building better relationship with customers is to provide them with custom and personalized experience. In short, treat customer like people not numbers (Lieberman, 2018). Fubon's e-banking service is not too user-friendly, and its response time is comparatively slow. Implementing an AI-based Chatbot that can improve customer experiences over time through the self-learning/training feature in-built in ML by responding to various user questions in a more human way with a simplified process.

Figure 3. Online loan application process through chatbots at HSBC

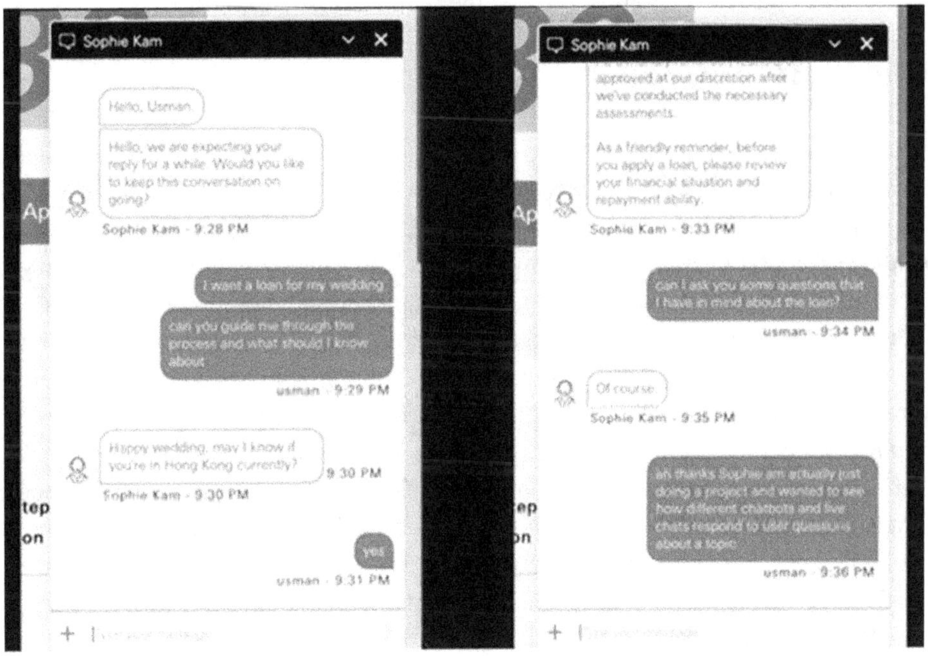

AI AND CHATBOTS IN BANKING SECTOR

Adoption of AI-Based Chatbot

Artificial intelligence (AI) is now widely used and beneficial in both professional and non-professional domains including law and education. Van (2021) asserts that a large number of consumers have shifted from conventional to online shopping, proving the necessity for organisations to utilise IT's benefits. The capability of systems and the customer experiences may both be enhanced by integrating AI.

AI has changed how businesses and customers interact, opening up new business options for the company. A chatbot is an AI-based system that converses with people using natural language via text or speech, (Bernardini et al., 2019). According to Maglogiannis et al. (2020), "Chatbots can be classified using a variety of factors, including the knowledge area, the service provided, the goals, the input processing and answer generation method, the human-aid, and the construction approach". Consequently, it was advised to utilise a chatbot in the e-banking system to help improve customer experiences.

Due to lacking AI an ML, the rule-based chatbot is limited to first-level questions and can only function as intended, which would allow it to learn from its mistakes (So, 2022). This means that simple errors, such misspelt words in customer enquiries, could lead to the chatbot giving false information or misinterpreting what the customer was asking (So, 2022). The company must increase the chatbot's functional capabilities and be prepared for any questions a user may have. The company finds it difficult to compile all user information and respond to every customer issue. In addition, chatbots are less memory-efficient than call centers staffed by real people (So, 2022). Because the chatbot is not designed to recall the entirety of the customer engagement, customers will be frustrated because they have to repeat their questions (So, 2022). In addition, professionals can reply to customer inquiries quickly and provide helpful suggestions or solutions, while chatbots can only respond to pre-defined questions and cannot help customers make decisions or provide the required response.

Chatbots in the Banking Sector

One of the bank's main business purposes is to surpass its rivals in terms of customer service. A chatbot can assist a bank in many ways to enhance the client experience. The most typical use case for chatbots in bank customer care includes welcoming customers, learning about their problems, giving clients the information, they asked, taking payments from recipients, and a number of other elementary duties. Additionally, compared to a person, a chatbot can answer quicker and more reliably. Human work is also decreased because chatbots handle many repetitive queries. This is especially helpful in regions like Hong Kong where it might be challenging to justify investing in real estate and personnel for physical contact centres. According to a report, by 2022, chatbots are predicted to save banks over $8 billion per year. (Juniper Research, 2019).

To further automate account management in core banking and customer care via mobile and online channels, a virtual customer assistant capability can be added to a chatbot. Chatbots have drawn the interest of numerous banking businesses due to all these advantages. In Hong Kong, seventeen banks have already deployed or intend to employ chatbots, and another twenty-five are thinking about doing so (HKMA, 2019). They are able to offer their customers a personal, always open, and effective channel of communication with the bank thanks to the development of Chatbot. Customer services, account enquiry, purchasing help, marketing, investment research, and suggestion are just a few of the marketing applications for the chatbot.

CHATBOTS FOR BANKING IN HONG KONG (HK) CONTEXT

Performance Criteria for Chatbot in HK Banks

Before examining actual chatbot implementation in various Hong Kong banks, we learned that by creating performance criteria on four key perspectives, we can then assess whether a chatbot performed above average or not.

The user-interface (U.I.) of a chatbot is not only the first point of contact for users when they first open the programme, but it is also the first viewpoint from which performance standards may be developed. A chatbot user interface is a collection of linguistic and visual components that allow for human-computer interaction. Users can converse in human languages rather than computer language using chatbots, which are a type of typical language user interface. The ability of a chatbot to converse varies according to the interface used.

Three criteria were developed to assess a chatbot's U.I. performance in light of the aforementioned parameters. We first examine a U.I.'s neatness. In our opinion, a chatbot's U.I. is clean if there are no tightly packed texts on the screen and the entire U.I. is used in a way that is comfortable for the user. Second, we examine if the U.I. enables users to modify the interface directly. For instance, a U.I. provides a clear option (A button in a conspicuous location) for users to customise the application's interface, such as adjusting the font size and background colour. Third, the chatbot would benefit from having sufficient visual accompaniment, such as relevant photos or emoticons.

Next, we look at a chatbot's functionalities. A chatbot can offer customers predefined options, contextual or other rule-based alternatives, and is typically built to comprehend and respond to a wide range of user text and even audio and voice input. A chatbot's functionality performance will be evaluated using four criteria. The initial step is to see if the chatbot can offer simple banking data, like the exchange rate between two different currencies or the time-deposit rate. We would also run user-case testing to see if the chatbot offers basic features like a text box for user input, accurate responses to user input, and distribution of useful suggestion(s) to the user.

Furthermore, we would consider the security precautions. To maintain customers' trust, we think it is crucial for the bank itself to be prepared for unforeseen events like conversation leakage or chatbot system failure. It is preferred to provide a reference code for each conversation record when using chatbot systems. This ensures the veracity of consumer reports on chatbot-related concerns, which also helps the bank officials' investigative process. Additionally, the chatbot is required to clear discussion records in a number of certain circumstances, such as when a user closes or restarts their web browser. This could avoid the user's conversation leaking unexpectedly to others who have the possibility to make use of the same device that the user started the conversation.

Last but not least, we determine whether or not a chatbot has the potential to improve performance. The ideal situation would be for the chatbot to do self-learning from each interaction that was recorded as a sort of machine learning. However, none of the Hong Kong banks we looked into specifically state that their chatbots are capable of self-learning. Instead of the ideal scenario, a chatbot that has a rating system and lets users leave feedback for further enhancement is already a great system, indicating that the application might be expected to continue becoming better over time.

Chatbot Development Methodology: A Four-Step Approach

A chatbot development is proposed for e-banking based on a number of contemporary frameworks and methodologies, including agile software development, design thinking, and AI innovation sprints. the notion that a group should adhere to these guidelines when creating the chatbot.

Figure 4. A chatbot conceptual model for e-banking

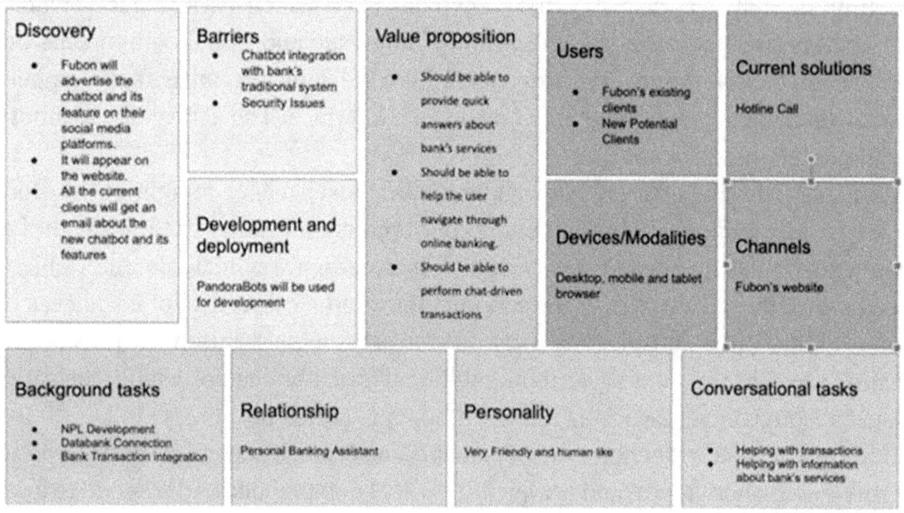

1. Defining Chatbot's Purpose and Expectations: A Conceptual Model for E-Banking

Since the Chabot is essentially an AI software product, the first step is to clearly define its purpose, the problems that it is going to solve, and the value that it is going to bring to the users. This stage is the key to understanding the basic chatbot purpose, scope and value propositions which are important for the rest of chatbot development. Therefore, the expectations and purpose for developing a Fubon bank chatbot is represented by a conceptual model depicted in Figure 4.

2. Chatbot Personality

In step two, chatbot's personality will be determined. This phase is crucial because, according to Chatbots Magazine, one of the top three reasons a chatbot fails is a personality that was badly built (Katz, 2019). The chatbot for Fubon will be programmed to have a very amiable and sympathetic disposition toward the user in order to increase user engagement and produce meaningful experiences.

3. User Journey and Conversation

For step 3, The team needs to analyse the client + chatbot interaction in more depth. They will design the actual content of the conversation between the client and the chatbot. For example, what further questions may a client reply? Any chance that the chatbot doesn't have a clue about an answer? When will the chatbot to divert the question to a help agent? What data does the chatbot need to know to respond to a question?

4. Developing the Chatbot

The last step, the team will actually adapt an appropriate software development cycle methodology and develop the Chabot by coding. After the development is completed, the team will integrate the NLP function to enable the chatbot to understand user queries and instructions in daily language. After both steps are completed, the team will then initiate the testing process.

ADOPTION STRATEGY

The AI-based Chatbot will follow a three-phase adoption strategy as follows:

- **Phase 1:** Quick answers on the public website
- **Phase 2:** Navigating through the bank's website
- **Phase 3:** Chat-drive transactions

Each new phase will begin once the previous one has been implemented and made accessible to users so they may assess the performance of the product. With the above three-phase adoption strategy established, actual U.I. and functional tests will be conducted on the chatbots, and comparison will be made by conducting the same tests on the chatbot of other banks.

TESTING AND COMPARISON

Test Plan

A standardised test plan is formulated as in Table 1.

Table 1. A standardized test plan for chatbots

Identifier	TP-000
Title	Test Plan for all test cases
Description	Present details of test case procedures.
Procedure	1. Observation on user-interface a. Observe tidiness. b. Observe if any visual support. c. Observe if any allowance of interface customization. 2. Test on functionality a. Test if presentation of basic banking information. b. Observe if it allows for text-input. c. Test if English & Chinese as a language is supported. d. Test if text response or button suggestion is accurately referring to user-input. 3. Test on security measurement a. Observe if any reference code. b. Test if any clearance of conversation record automatically. 4. Test on potential to advance a. Test if any customer rating. b. Test if any user comment area for service feedback.

Comparison Test of Chatbots

Table 2. Test results

	Hang Seng Bank	Standard Chartered Bank	Fubon Bank
1. Observation on user-interface			
a. observing tidiness	Pass	Pass	Pass
b. observing if any visual support	Pass	Pass	Pass
c. observing if any allowance of interface customization.	Pass	Fail	Pass
2. Test on functionality			
a. presentation of basic banking information	Pass	Pass	Pass
b. observing if it allows for text-inputs	Pass	Pass	Pass
c. support of both English and Chinese	Pass	Pass	Pass
d. accuracy of response to user inputs	Pass	Pass	Pass
3. Test on security measurement			
a. generation of transaction reference	Pass	Fail	Fail
b. automatic clearance of conversation records	Pass	Pass	Pass
4. Test on potential to advance			
a. customer rating	Fail	Pass	Pass
b. user comment area for service feedback	Fail	Fail	Pass

SUGGESTED FUTURE IMPROVEMENTS

Improvement on Chatbot

The system has to improve on each performance criterion in accordance with the areas for development outlined in the preceding section.

According to the test results, the Fubon Bank is suggested to perform a further refinement of the entire U.I. to address the issue of the lack of visual assistance and text-area for user-input. To begin with, graphics and GIFs should be used for screen decoration rather than the present interface, which is overly text-heavy. This might make the site more appealing to visitors. On the other hand, the latter issue is straightforward to resolve. Implementing a text-box function in the interface is as easy as pie. Additionally, Fubon might offer conversational interaction by combining text-commands with button alternatives.

Improvement on Chatbot Related Operations

When there is a database to support the application, chatbots could play a crucial role in enhancing a company's or organization's customer service. The use-case diagram (Figure 5) that follows demonstrates how the information obtained from the chatbot could be used to enhance customer care is provided.

Figure 5. The unified modeling language (UML) diagram for chatbot improvement

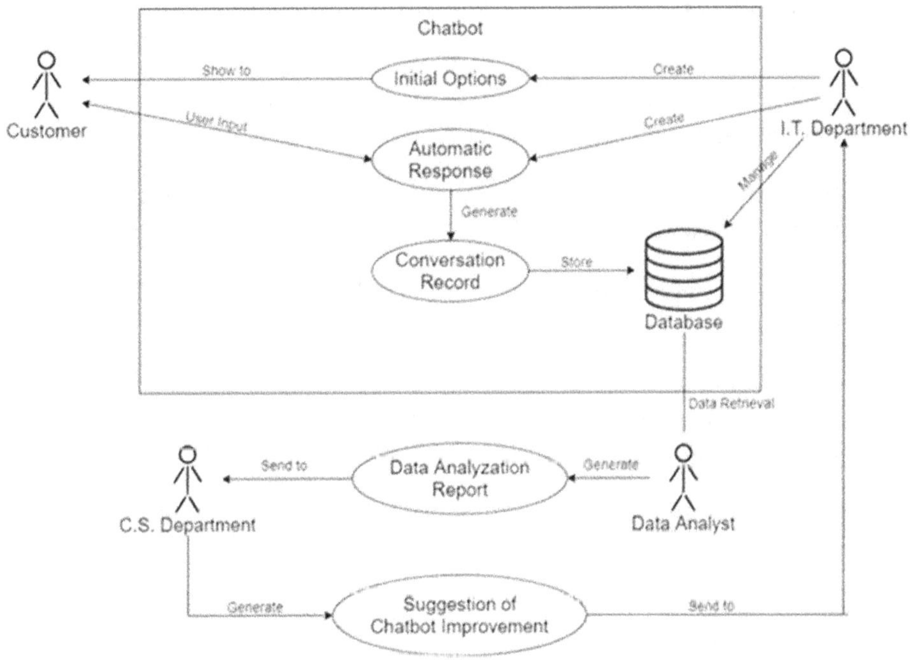

Improvement on Human-Likeness and Perceived Humanness

Chandra et al. (2022) argued that conversational AI's potential economic benefits depend very much on how effectively users interact with these technologies, where this interaction also depends on how closely conversational AI resembles the people it is meant to replace, i.e., "human-likeness".

In a series of experiments conducted by Schuetzler et al. (2020), 450 people conversed with chatbots who varied in their conversational prowess. The results demonstrate that people view a more skilled chatbot as being more anthropomorphic and socially present than a less skilled chatbot, and this improved perceived humanness in turn engages more customers who are delighted to use the chatbot service.

CONCLUSION

Many banks decline to use hybrid chatbot systems because of the complicated configuration needed to give individualised service to each client. This is because doing so exposes them to security risks and introduces them to unfamiliar technology. The effectiveness of a e-banking system with a relatively restricted chatbot is compared and contrasted with other banks' chatbot systems. As soon as all banks begin utilising AI to run their businesses, U.I. design and client feedback are key to the future improvement for Fubon Bank's chatbot in the long term.

REFERENCES

Batat, W. (2022). *Strategies for the digital customer experience: connecting customers with brands in the phygital age*. Edward Elgar Publishing. doi:10.4337/9781800371897

Bernardini, A. A., Sônego, A. A., & Pozzebon, E. (2018). *Chatbots: An Analysis of the State of Art of Literature*. ResearchGate. Available at https://www.researchgate.net/publication/328734789_Chatbots_An_Analysis_of_the_State_of_Art_of_Literature

Brown, T. (2023). *ChatGPT and Generative AI in Banking: Reality, Hype, What's Next, and How to Prepare*. Available at https://www.insiderintelligence.com/content/chatgpt-generative-ai-banking

Business Source Complete. (2022). MarketLine Company Profile: Fubon Bank (Hong Kong) Ltd. Business Source Complete.

Chandra, S., Shirish, A., & Srivastava, S. C. (2022). To Be or Not to Be ...Human? Theorizing the Role of Human-Like Competencies in Conversational Artificial Intelligence Agents. *Journal of Management Information Systems*, *39*(4), 969–1005. doi:10.1080/07421222.2022.2127441

Codeacademy. (2023). *Generative Chatbots*. Available at https://www.codecademy.com/learn/deep-learning-and-generative-chatbots/modules/generative-chatbots/cheatsheet

Copeland, B. J. (2023). *Artificial intelligence*. Available at https://www.britannica.com/technology/artificial-intelligence/Reasoning

Engati. (2021). *The 6 types of chatbots — Which one do you need?* Chatbots Life. Available at https://chatbotslife.com/the-6-types-of-chatbots-which-one-do-you-need-61e3becbdec

Finwin Technologies. (2020). *What are the different types of chatbots?* Medium. Available at https://medium.com/finwintech/what-are-the-different-types-of-chatbots-c99cdd6b3248

Fubon Bank. (2021). *Fubon Bank (Hong Kong) and HKT Form Strategic Partnership to Drive FinTech Innovations*. Available at https://www.fubonbank.com.hk/resources/common/pdf/pr_210121_e.pdf

Goasduff, L. (2019). *Top trends on the Gartner Hype cycle for artificial intelligence*. Available at https://www.gartner.com/smarterwithgartner/top-trends-on-the-gartner-hype-cycle-for-artificial-intelligence-2019/

Hisrich, R. D., & Soltanufar, M. (2020). Unleashing the Creativity of Entrepreneurs with Digital Technologies. In M. Soltanifar, M. Hughes, & L. Göcke (Eds.), *Digital Entrepreneurship: Impact on Business and Society*. Springer.

Hong Kong Monetary Authority (HKMA). (2019). *Report on Artificial Intelligence (AI) Application in Banking*. The Hong Kong Monetary Authority (HKMA). Available at https://www.hkma.gov.hk/eng/news-and-media/press-releases/2019/12/20191223-4/

Juniper Research. (2019). *Chatbot interactions in retail to reach 22 billion by 2023, as AI offers compelling new engagement solutions*. Available at: https://www.juniperresearch.com/press/chatbot-interactions-retail-reach-22-billion-2023

Katz, S. (2019). The ultimate guide to chatbot personality. *Chatbot Magazine*. Retrieved May 23, 2021, from https://chatbotsmagazine.com/the-ultimate-guide-to-chatbot-personality-b9665ab5e99d

Lieberman, M. (2018). *5 Ways to Improve Customer Relationships* [Web log post]. Available at https://www.square2marketing.com/blog/5-ways-to-improve-customer-relationships

Maglogiannis, I., Iliadis, L., & Pimenidis, E. (Eds.). (2020, May 6). An Overview of Chatbot Technology. *Artificial Intelligence Applications and Innovations: 16th IFIP WG 12.5 International Conference, AIAI 2020, Neos Marmaras, Greece, June 5–7, 2020, Proceedings, Part II*. https://www.ncbi.nlm.nih.gov/pmc/articles/PMC7256567/#CR20

Maher, S. K., Bhablc, S. G., Lahase, A. R., & Nimbhore, S. S. (2022). AI and Deep Learning-driven Chatbots: A Comprehensive Analysis and Application Trends. *Proceedings of the Sixth International Conference on Intelligent Computing and Control Systems (ICICCS 2022)*, 994-998. 10.1109/ICICCS53718.2022.9788276

Pilarczyk, K. (2016). Importance of management information system in banking sector. *Annales Universitatis Mariae Curie-Skłodowska, Sectio H. Oeconomia*, *50*(2), 69. doi:10.17951/h.2016.50.2.69

PwC. (2019). *A practical guide to Responsible Artificial Intelligence (AI)*. Available at https://www.pwc.com/gx/en/issues/data-and-analytics/artificial-intelligence/what-is-responsible-ai/responsible-ai-practical-guide.pdf

Schuetzler, R. M., Grimes, G. M., & Scott, G. J. (2020). The impact of chatbot conversational skill on engagement and perceived humanness. *Journal of Management Information Systems*, *37*(2), 875–900. doi:10.1080/07421222.2020.1790204

Schwartz, K. D. (2023). *ChatGPT and Cybersecurity: The Good, the Bad, and the Careful*. ITProToday. Available at https://www.itprotoday.com/vulnerabilities-and-threats/chatgpt-and-cybersecurity-good-bad-and-careful?_mc=NL_DR_EDT__20230318&cid=NL_DR_EDT__20230318&utm_rid=CPNET000013888747&utm_campaign=52417&utm_medium=email&elq2=3b2f518b0ff54d9aa3519366401c1a0e&sp_eh=b1cc10eb664b0f9908d2950be90e1f41ae1dce8fb81536791e5a2df38e9256df

Shruti, M. (2023). *AI vs Machine Learning vs Deep Learning: Know the Differences*. Simplilearn Solutions. Available at https://www.simplilearn.com/tutorials/artificial-intelligence-tutorial/ai-vs-machine-learning-vs-deep-learning

Smith, C. S. (2020). *Computers already learn from us. But can they teach themselves?* Available at https://www.nytimes.com/2020/04/08/technology/ai-computers-learning-supervised-unsupervised.html

So, S. (2022). The Impact of the COVID-19 Pandemic on B2C E-Business and the Challenges to Bonjour Holdings Limited. In H. Taherdoost (Ed.), *Driving Transformative Change in E-Business Through Applied Intelligence and Emerging Technologies*. IGI Global. doi:10.4018/978-1-6684-5235-6.ch003

Srivastava, S. (2023). Generative AI In The Enterprise Produces Early Learnings. *Forbes*. Available at https://www.forbes.com/sites/sanjaysrivastava/2023/03/25/generative-ai-in-the-enterpriseuse-cases--early-learnings/?sh=10cd14973202

Van, L. A. (2021). How the COVID-19 pandemic can stimulate more radical business process improvements: Using the metaphor of a tree. *Knowledge and Process Management*, *28*(2), 107–116. doi:10.1002/kpm.1659

Wilson, H. J., & Daugherty, P. R. (2018). Collaborative Intelligence: Humans and AI are joining forces. *Harvard Business Review*, *96*(4), 114–123.

Compilation of References

Abbas, Gravell, & Wills. (2014). Historical Roots of Agile Methods: Where did "Agile Thinking" Come from? School of Electronics and Computer Science, University of Southampton.

Abbasi, K., Alam, A., Brohi, N. A., Brohi, I. A., & Nasim, S. (2021). P2P lending fintechs and smes' access to finance. *Economics Letters, 204*, 109890. doi:10.1016/j.econlet.2021.109890

Abbate, T., Codini, A. P., & Aquilani, B. (2019). Knowledge co-creation in open innovation digital platforms: Processes, tools and services. *Journal of Business and Industrial Marketing, 34*(7), 1434–1447. doi:10.1108/JBIM-09-2018-0276

Acquier, A., Carbone, V., & Massé, D. (2019). How to create value (s) in the sharing economy: Business models, scalability, and sustainability. *Technology Innovation Management Review, 9*(2), 5–24. doi:10.22215/timreview/1215

Acs, Z. J., Autio, E., & Szerb, L. (2014). National systems of entrepreneurship: Measurement issues and policy implications. *Research Policy, 43*(3), 476–494. doi:10.1016/j.respol.2013.08.016

Adam, S., Ramliy, M. K., Thoo, A. C., Mas'od, A., & Muharam, F. M. (2019). Entrepreneurial orientation and organizational performance of e-business in Malaysia: The moderating role of External Environment. *Advanced International Journal of Business, Entrepreneurship and SMEs, 1*(1), 1–17. doi:10.35631/aijbes.11001

Adidas. (2021). *4DFWD: Data Driven 3d Printed Performance Technology Designed To Move You Forward.* Retrieved 21st April from https://news.adidas.com/running/4dfwd--data-driven-3d-printed-performance-technology-designed-to-move-you-forward/s/514baddb-1029-4686-abd5-5ee3985a304a#:~:text=adidas%204D%20footwear%20is%20amongst,new%20adidas%204DFWD%20lattice%20midsole

Adler, P. S., & Kwon, S. W. (2002). Social capital: Prospects for a new concept. *Academy of Management Review, 27*(1), 17–40. doi:10.2307/4134367

Afele, J. S. C. (2003). Digital Bridges and digital opportunities for developing nations. *Digital Bridges*, 85–159. doi:10.4018/978-1-59140-039-4.ch005

Afonasova, M. A., Panfilova, E. E., Galichkina, M. A., & Ślusarczyk, B. (2019). Digitalization in economy and innovation: The effect on social and economic processes. *Polish Journal of Management Studies, 19.*

Agrawal, M. (2017). *Internet of Things – Business Models.* Retrieved 19th April from https://www.linkedin.com/pulse/internet-things-business-models-mohit-agrawal

Agyei, S. K., Adam, A. M., & Agyemang, O. S. (2019). Financial Literacy, cultural dominance, and financial well-being of SME owners in Ghana. *Poverty & Public Policy, 11*(3), 222–237. doi:10.1002/pop4.254

Aheleroff, S., Mostashiri, N., Xu, X., & Zhong, R. Y. (2021). Mass personalisation as a service in industry 4.0: A resilient response case study. *Advanced Engineering Informatics, 50*, 101438. doi:10.1016/j.aei.2021.101438

Ahmad, I., & Gupta, S. (2021). *Digital transformation: Key technology, cybersecurity and privacy risks*. Retrieved 13th March from https://www.nortonrosefulbright.com/en/knowledge/publications/4318add0/digital-transformation-key-technology-cybersecurity-and-privacy-risks

Ahn, M. J., & Chen, Y.-C. (2022). Digital transformation toward AI-augmented public administration: The perception of government employees and the willingness to use AI in government. *Government Information Quarterly*, *39*(2), 101664. doi:10.1016/j.giq.2021.101664

Aidrous, I. A., Asmyatullin, R. R., & Glavina, S. G. (2021). *The Development of the Digital Economy: GCC Countries Experience. Industry Competitiveness: Digitalization*, Management, and Integration.

Al Naimi, S. M. (2021). Economic Diversification Trends in the Gulf: The Case of Saudi Arabia. *Circular Economy and Sustainability*. PMID:34888575

Albiman, M. M., & Sulong, Z. (2017). The linear and non-linear impacts of ICT on economic growth, of disaggregate income groups within SSA region. *Telecommunications Policy*, *41*(7-8), 555–572. doi:10.1016/j.telpol.2017.07.007

Alexander, M. (2020). *Agile vs. waterfall: Project methodologies compared*. CIO.

Alheriani, N. M. S., Spasojević-Brkić, V. K., & Perišić, M. B. (2021). Novel risk management integrated model implementation: Comparison between manufacturing and service companies. *Journal of Engineering Management and Competitiveness*, *11*(1), 13–19. doi:10.5937/jemc2101013A

Ali, I., Sadiddin, A., & Cattaneo, A. (2022). Risk and resilience in agri-food supply chain smes in the pandemic era: A cross-country study. *International Journal of Logistics Research and Applications*, 1–19. doi:10.1080/13675567.2022.2102159

Ali, M. B. (2021). Internet of Things (IoT) to Foster Communication and Information Sharing: A Case of UK Higher Education. *Fostering Communication & Learning With Underutilized Technologies in Higher Education*, 1-20.

Ali, M. B., Wood-Harper, T., & Ramlogan, R. (2020a). A Framework Strategy to Overcome Trust Issues on Cloud Computing Adoption in Higher Education. In Modern Principles, Practices, and Algorithms for Cloud Security (pp. 162-183). IGI Global. doi:10.4018/978-1-7998-1082-7.ch008

Ali, M., & Abdel-Haq, M. K. (2021). Bibliographical Analysis of Artificial Intelligence Learning in Higher Education: Is the Role of the Human Educator and Educated a Thing of the Past? In Fostering Communication and Learning With Underutilized Technologies in Higher Education (pp. 36-52). IGI Global.

Ali. (2019). Multiple Perspective of Cloud Computing Adoption Determinants in Higher Education a Systematic Review. *International Journal of Cloud Applications and Computing, 9*(3), 89-109.

Ali. (2020). Multi-Perspectives of Cloud Computing Service Adoption Quality and Risks in Higher Education. In D. B. A. Mehdi Khosrow-Pour (Ed.), *Handbook of Research on Modern Educational Technologies, Applications, and Management* (2nd ed.). IGI Global.

Ali, M. (2018). The Barriers and Enablers of the Educational Cloud: A Doctoral Student Perspective. *Open Journal of Business and Management*, *7*(1), 1–24. doi:10.4236/ojbm.2019.71001

Ali, M. (2019). Cloud Computing at a Cross Road: Quality and Risks in Higher Education. *Advances in Internet of Things*, *9*(3), 33–49. doi:10.4236/ait.2019.93003

Ali, M. (2022). *Future Role of Sustainable Innovative Technologies in Crisis Management*. IGI Global. doi:10.4018/978-1-7998-9815-3

Ali, M. (Ed.). (2021). *Remote Work and Sustainable Changes for the Future of Global Business*. IGI Global. doi:10.4018/978-1-7998-7513-0

Ali, M. B., & Wood-Harper, T. (Eds.). (2020). *Fostering communication and learning with underutilized technologies in higher education*. IGI Global.

Ali, M. B., Wood-Harper, T., & Ramlogan, R. (2020b). *The Role of SaaS Applications in Business IT Alignment: A Closer Look at Value Creation in Service Industry*. UKAIS.

Ali, M., & Edghiem, F. (2021). Sustainable Business and Collaboration Driven by Big Data Analytics Amidst the Emergence of the Remote Work Culture. In *Remote Work and Sustainable Changes for the Future of Global Business* (pp. 15–32). IGI Global. doi:10.4018/978-1-7998-7513-0.ch002

Ali, M., Edghiem, F., & Alkhalifah, E. S. (2022). Cultural Challenges of ERP Implementation in Middle-Eastern Oil & Gas Sector: An Action Research Approach. *Systemic Practice and Action Research*. PMID:35668863

Ali, M., Wood-Harper, A., & Ramlogan, R. (2017). Benefits and Challenges of Cloud Computing Adoption in Higher Education: A Systematic Literature Review. *British Academy of Management Conference Proceedings, 14*(4).

Aljarrah, E., Elrehail, H., & Aababneh, B. (2016). E-voting in Jordan: Assessing readiness and developing a system. *Computers in Human Behavior, 63*, 860–867. doi:10.1016/j.chb.2016.05.076

Allen, J. P. (2019). *Digital entrepreneurship*. Routledge. doi:10.4324/9780429506567

Almazaydeh. (2022). Formalization of the prediction and ranking of software development life cycle models. *International Journal of Electrical and Computer Engineering*.

Almeida, F., & Calistru, C. (2013). The main challenges and issues of big data management. *International Journal of Research Studies in Computing, 2*(1), 11–20. doi:10.5861/ijrsc.2012.209

Almeida, F., Santos, J. D., & Monteiro, J. A. (2020). The challenges and opportunities in the digitalization of companies in a post-COVID-19 World. *IEEE Engineering Management Review, 48*(3), 97–103. doi:10.1109/EMR.2020.3013206

Al-Roubaie, A. (2021). *The Digital Economy: Challenges and Opportunities for Economic Conversion in the Gulf Countries*. Academic Press.

Al-Sayed, K. A. (2013). *GCC and Arab Spring*. The Peninsula Publishing.

Amankwah-Amoah, J., Khan, Z., Wood, G., & Knight, G. (2021). COVID-19 and digitalization: The great acceleration. *Journal of Business Research, 136*, 602–611. doi:10.1016/j.jbusres.2021.08.011 PMID:34538980

Amjad, T., Rani, S. H. B. A., & Sa'atar, S. B. (2020). Entrepreneurship development and pedagogical gaps in entrepreneurial marketing education. *International Journal of Management Education, 18*(2), 100379. doi:10.1016/j.ijme.2020.100379

Anderson, G. (2019). Mastering Collaboration. O'Reilly Media, Inc.

Ang, T., Wei, S., & Anaza, N. A. (2018). Livestreaming vs pre-recorded: How social viewing strategies impact consumers' viewing experiences and behavioural intentions. *European Journal of Marketing, 52*(9/10), 2075–2104. doi:10.1108/EJM-09-2017-0576

Appiah-Otoo, I., & Song, N. (2021). The impact of ICT on economic growth-Comparing rich and poor countries. *Telecommunications Policy, 45*(2), 102082. doi:10.1016/j.telpol.2020.102082

Arab News. (2021). *Evaluating Saudi Arabia's Vision 2030 at the five-year mark*. Retrieved 25th Nov from https://www.arabnews.com/node/1850041

Aravindaraj, K., & Rajan Chinna, P. (2022). A systematic literature review of integration of Industry 4.0 and warehouse management to achieve Sustainable Development Goals (sdgs). *Cleaner Logistics and Supply Chain, 5*, 100072. doi:10.1016/j.clscn.2022.100072

Aronowitz, A. A., & Veldhuizen, M. E. (2021). The human trafficking–organized crime nexus. In *The Routledge Handbook of Transnational Organized Crime* (pp. 232–252). Routledge. doi:10.4324/9781003044703-17

Arsal, I., Woosnam, K. M., Baldwin, E. D., & Backman, S. J. (2010). Residents as travel destination information providers: An online community perspective. *Journal of Travel Research, 49*(4), 400–413. doi:10.1177/0047287509346856

Asikhia, O. U. (2016). SMEs, wealth creation and poverty alleviation in Nigeria. *Journal of Economics and Behavioral Studies, 8*(4), 17–31. doi:10.22610/jebs.v8i4(J).1360

Asongu, S. A., & Odhiambo, N. M. (2019). Tourism and social media in the world: An empirical investigation. *Journal of Economic Studies (Glasgow, Scotland), 46*(7), 1319–1331. doi:10.1108/JES-07-2018-0239

Atabekov, A., & Yastrebov, O. (2018). Legal Status of Artificial Intelligence Across Countries: Legislation on the Move. *European Research Studies, 21*(4), 773–782. doi:10.35808/ersj/1245

Atanasova, I. (2019). Copyright infringement in digital environment. *Economics & Law, 1*(1), 13–22.

Ateeq. (2014). Comparison of various SDLC models. *Global Journal of Multidisciplinary Studies, 3*(11), 176-181.

Atkinson, T. C. (2022). *Sex-e-Work: An Exploration on the Rise of OnlyFans as a Space for Sexually Explicit Content* [Doctoral dissertation]. Carleton University.

Autio, E., & Cao, Z. (2019). *Fostering digital start-ups: Structural model of entrepreneurial ecosystems*. Academic Press.

Autio, E., & Levie, J. (2017). Management of entrepreneurial ecosystems. The Wiley handbook of entrepreneurship, 423-449. doi:10.1002/9781118970812.ch19

Autio, E., Kenney, M., Mustar, P., Siegel, D., & Wright, M. (2014). Entrepreneurial innovation: The importance of context. *Research Policy, 43*(7), 1097–1108. doi:10.1016/j.respol.2014.01.015

Avison, D. E., & Wood-Harper, A. T. (1990). *Multiview: An Exploration in Information Systems Development*. Blackwell Scientific Publications.

Avison, D. E., Wood-Harper, A., Vidgen, R. T., & Wood, J. (1998). A further exploration into information systems development: The evolution of Multiview2. *Information Technology & People, 11*(2), 124–139. doi:10.1108/09593849810218319

Avolio, B. J., Sosik, J. J., Kahai, S. S., & Baker, B. (2014). E-leadership: Re-examining transformations in leadership source and transmission. *The Leadership Quarterly, 25*(1), 105–131. doi:10.1016/j.leaqua.2013.11.003

Babajide, A., Lawal, A., Asaleye, A., Okafor, T., & Osuma, G. (2020). Financial Stability and entrepreneurship development in sub-sahara africa: Implications for sustainable development goals. *Cogent Social Sciences, 6*(1), 1798330. Advance online publication. doi:10.1080/23311886.2020.1798330

Babar, M. A., Brown, A. W., & Mistrik, I. (2014). *Agile Software Architecture Aligning Agile Processes and Software Architectures*. Elsevier.

Babcock, H. M. (2018). The Federal Government Has an Implied Moral Constitutional Duty to Protect Individuals from Harm Due to Climate Change: Throwing Spaghetti Against the Wall to See What Sticks. *Ecology Law Quarterly, 45*, 735.

Bahrain EGov Report. (2016). *E-government of Bahrain: Bahrain national eGovernment strategy*. Retrieved from https://www.bahrain.bh/wps/wcm/connect/fc54be3a-a0d6-43ef-9cbe-7ab640c581d3/New+eGovernment+Strategy+2012-2016.pdf?MOD=AJPERES

Bahrain News. (2019). *Bahrain among the first countries to rollout 5G network, says minister*. Retrieved from https://www.bna.bh/en/Bahrainamongthefirstcountriestorollout5Gnetworksaysminister.aspx?cms=q8FmFJgiscL2fwIzON1%2BDv5AaBoS%2Fg96G32BSZLftMo%3D

Bancroft, A. (2020). Crime Is as Smart and as Dumb as the Internet. In *The Darknet and Smarter Crime* (pp. 1–22). Palgrave Macmillan. doi:10.1007/978-3-030-26512-0_1

Baporikar, N. (2008). Global Strategic Management. Himalaya Publishing House.

Baporikar, N. (2014). Information Strategy as Enabler of Competitive Advantage. *International Journal of Strategic Information Technology and Applications*, *5*(1), 30–41. doi:10.4018/ijsita.2014010103

Baporikar, N. (2015). Holistic Framework for Evolving Effective Information Systems Strategy. *International Journal of Strategic Information Technology and Applications*, *6*(4), 30–43. doi:10.4018/IJSITA.2015100103

Baporikar, N. (2016). Business Process Management. *International Journal of Productivity Management and Assessment Technologies*, *4*(2), 49–62. doi:10.4018/IJPMAT.2016070104

Baporikar, N. (2019). E-Learning Strategies for Emerging Economies in the Knowledge Era. In J. Pelet (Ed.), *Advanced Web Applications and Progressing E-Learning 2.0 Technologies in Higher Education* (pp. 150–171). IGI Global. doi:10.4018/978-1-5225-7435-4.ch008

Baporikar, N. (2020). Learning Link in Organizational Tacit Knowledge Creation and Dissemination. *International Journal of Sociotechnology and Knowledge Development*, *12*(4), 70–88. doi:10.4018/IJSKD.2020100105

Baporikar, N. (Ed.). (2017). *Global practices in knowledge management for Societal and Organizational Development*. IGI Global.

Bardhan, I., Krishnan, V., & Lin, S. (2013). Research note—Business value of information technology: testing the interaction effect of IT and R&D on Tobin's Q. *Information Systems Research*, *24*(4), 1147–1161.

Barney, J. (1991). Firm resources and sustained competitive advantage. *Journal of Management*, *17*(1), 99–120. doi:10.1177/014920639101700108

Barney, J. B., & Hesterly, W. S. (2010). *Strategic management and competitive advantage: Concepts*. Prentice Hall.

Barseghian, A. (2019). *How Nike Is Using Analytics To Personalize Their Customer Experience*. Retrieved 21st April from https://www.forbes.com/sites/forbestechcouncil/2019/10/07/how-nike-is-using-analytics-to-personalize-their-customer-experience/?sh=402ac85b1611

Bashir, T., Usman, I., & ur Rehman, J. (2016). Secure digital watermarking using optimized improved spread spectrum and BCH coding for DIBR 3D-TV system. *Multimedia Tools and Applications*, *75*(13), 7697–7713. doi:10.100711042-015-2689-z

Basu, S., & Fernald, J. (2007). Information and communications technology as a general-purpose technology: Evidence from US industry data. *German Economic Review*, *8*(2), 146–173. doi:10.1111/j.1468-0475.2007.00402.x

Batat, W. (2022). *Strategies for the digital customer experience: connecting customers with brands in the phygital age*. Edward Elgar Publishing. doi:10.4337/9781800371897

Bauer, M., & Erixon, F. (2020). *Europe's quest for technology sovereignty: Opportunities and pitfalls* (No. 02/2020). ECIPE Occasional Paper.

Beisheim, M., & Langner, C. (2021). *Lean Startup as a Tool for Digital Business Model Innovation: Enablers and Barriers for Established Companies*. Academic Press.

Belitski, M., & Liversage, B. (2019). E-leadership in small and medium-sized enterprises in the developing world. *Technology Innovation Management Review*, *9*(1), 64–74. doi:10.22215/timreview/1212

Beltrami, M., Orzes, G., Sarkis, J., & Sartor, M. (2021). Industry 4.0 and sustainability: Towards conceptualization and theory. *Journal of Cleaner Production*, *312*, 127733. doi:10.1016/j.jclepro.2021.127733

Ben Hassen, T. (2022). *A Transformative State in the Wake of COVID-19: What Is Needed to Enable Innovation, Entrepreneurship, and Education in Qatar?* Academic Press.

Berger, E. S., Von Briel, F., Davidsson, P., & Kuckertz, A. (2021). Digital or not–The future of entrepreneurship and innovation: Introduction to the special issue. *Journal of Business Research*, *125*, 436–442. doi:10.1016/j.jbusres.2019.12.020

Berhanu, K., & Raj, S. (2020). The trustworthiness of travel and tourism information sources of social media: Perspectives of international tourists visiting Ethiopia. *Heliyon*, *6*(3), e03439. Advance online publication. doi:10.1016/j.heliyon.2020.e03439 PMID:32181382

Bernardini, A. A., Sônego, A. A., & Pozzebon, E. (2018). *Chatbots: An Analysis of the State of Art of Literature*. ResearchGate. Available at https://www.researchgate.net/publication/328734789_Chatbots_An_Analysis_of_the_State_of_Art_of_Literature

Bharadwaj, A., El Sawy, O. A., Pavlou, P. A., & Venkatraman, N. V. (2013). Digital business strategy: Toward a next generation of insights. *Management Information Systems Quarterly*, *37*(2), 471–482. doi:10.25300/MISQ/2013/37:2.3

Bianchini, M., & Michalkova, V. (2019). *Data analytics in SMEs: Trends and policies*. Academic Press.

Bian, R., & Zhu, M. (2020). The Relationship between Ritual, Personal Involvement and Travel Intention: A Study of Check-in-Travel on DouYin. *American Journal of Industrial and Business Management*, *10*(02), 451–467. doi:10.4236/ajibm.2020.102030

Bican, P. M., & Brem, A. (2020). Digital Business Model, Digital Transformation, Digital Entrepreneurship: Is There A Sustainable "Digital"? *Sustainability (Basel)*, *12*(13), 1–15. doi:10.3390u12135239

Bigdeli, E., Motadel, M., Eshlaghy, A. T., & Radfar, R. (2020). A dynamic model of effective factors on Agile business–IT alignment. Emerald Publishing Limited.

Bigliardi, B., & Ivo Dormio, A. (2009). An empirical investigation of innovation determinants in Food Machinery Enterprises. *European Journal of Innovation Management*, *12*(2), 223–242. doi:10.1108/14601060910953988

Bird, L., Hoang, T., Stanyard, J., Walker, S., & Haysom, S. (2020). *Transformative Technologies*. Academic Press.

Bishoge, O. K., & Suntu, S. L. (2018). Opportunies of urban horticulture for poverty alleviation in Dar es Salaam City, Tanzania – A case study of Ubungo Municipality. *Journal of Food. Nutrition and Agriculture*, *12–16*, 12–16. Advance online publication. doi:10.21839/jfna.v1i1.123

blibli.com.cn. (2022). *Bilibili Inc. Announces Third Quarter 2022 Financial Results*. https://ir.bilibili.com/media/vbhaxpxs/q3-2022-bilibili-earnings-release-en.pdf

Bock, A. J., & George, G. (2017). The Business Model Book: Design, build and adapt business ideas that drive business growth. Pearson UK.

Böhm, I., & Lolagar, S. (2021). Open source intelligence. *International Cybersecurity Law Review*, *2*(2), 317–337. doi:10.136543439-021-00042-7

Boh, W. F., Huang, C. J., & Wu, A. (2020). Investor experience and innovation performance: The mediating role of external cooperation. *Strategic Management Journal*, *41*(1), 124–151. doi:10.1002mj.3089

Bollaert, H., Lopez-de-Silanes, F., & Schwienbacher, A. (2021). Fintech and access to finance. *Journal of Corporate Finance*, *68*, 101941. doi:10.1016/j.jcorpfin.2021.101941

Bordeleau, F.-E., Mosconi, E., & de Santa-Eulalia, L. A. (2020). Business intelligence and analytics value creation in Industry 4.0: A multiple case study in manufacturing medium enterprises. *Production Planning and Control*, *31*(2-3), 173–185. doi:10.1080/09537287.2019.1631458

Bosma, N., Hill, S., Ionescu-Somers, A., Donna Kelley, J. L., & Tarnawa, A. (2020). *Global Entrepreneurship Monitor 2019/2020 global report*. Global Entrepreneurship Research Association.

Bourdieu, P. (2011). The forms of capital. *Cultural theory: An anthology, 1*, 81-93.

Bowen, P. (2017). Prosecution of cases of human trafficking in a common law system. In *Routledge Handbook of Human Trafficking* (pp. 213–223). Routledge. doi:10.4324/9781315709352-17

Bradley, S. W., Kim, P. H., Klein, P. G., McMullen, J. S., & Wennberg, K. (2021). Policy for innovative entrepreneurship: Institutions, interventions, and societal challenges. *Strategic Entrepreneurship Journal*, *15*(2), 167–184. doi:10.1002ej.1395

Brassea, M. (2021). *Augmented Reality vs Virtual Reality for Manufacturers*. Retrieved 22nd April from https://www.tacton.com/cpq-blog/augmented-reality-vs-virtual-reality/

Bressan, S. (2012). Criminal Law against Human Trafficking withing the EU: A Comparison of an Approximated Legislation. *European Journal of Crime Criminal Law and Criminal Justice*, *20*(2), 137–163. doi:10.1163/092895612X13333546844554

Brixiová, Z., Kangoye, T., & Yogo, T. U. (2020). Access to finance among small and medium-sized enterprises and job creation in Africa. *Structural Change and Economic Dynamics*, *55*, 177–189. doi:10.1016/j.strueco.2020.08.008

Broad, R., & Muraszkiewicz, J. (2020). The investigation and prosecution of traffickers: Challenges and opportunities. The Palgrave International Handbook of Human Trafficking, 707-723.

Brooks-Gordon, B., & Vickers, E. (2022). Growth and Diversity of the Online Solopreneur and Sexpreneur. *Current Opinion in Psychology*, 101474. PMID:36469962

Brown, T. (2023). *ChatGPT and Generative AI in Banking: Reality, Hype, What's Next, and How to Prepare*. Available at https://www.insiderintelligence.com/content/chatgpt-generative-ai-banking

Brown, I., & Marsden, C. T. (2013). *Regulating code: Good governance and better regulation in the information age*. MIT Press. doi:10.7551/mitpress/8879.001.0001

Brunovskis, A. (2012). *Balancing protection and prosecution in anti-trafficking policies: A comparative analysis of reflection periods and related temporary residence permits for victims of trafficking in the Nordic Countries*. Nordic Council of Ministers. doi:10.6027/TN2012-556

Bryant, K., & Landman, T. (2020). Combatting human trafficking since Palermo: What do we know about what works? *Journal of Human Trafficking*, *6*(2), 119–140. doi:10.1080/23322705.2020.1690097

Bughin, J., & Van Zeebroeck, N. (2017). The best response to digital disruption. *MIT Sloan Management Review*.

Buhalis, D., & Sinarta, Y. (2019). Real-time co-creation and nowness service: Lessons from tourism and hospitality. *Journal of Travel & Tourism Marketing*, *36*(5), 563–582. doi:10.1080/10548408.2019.1592059

Bukht, R., & Heeks, R. (2017). *Defining, conceptualising and measuring the digital economy.* Development Informatics working paper.

Burt, R. S. (2000). The network structure of social capital. *Research in Organizational Behavior*, *22*, 345–423. doi:10.1016/S0191-3085(00)22009-1

Business Source Complete. (2022). MarketLine Company Profile: Fubon Bank (Hong Kong) Ltd. Business Source Complete.

Cainelli, G., De Marchi, V., & Grandinetti, R. (2020). Do knowledge-intensive business services innovate differently? *Economics of Innovation and New Technology*, *29*(1), 48–65. doi:10.1080/10438599.2019.1585639

Caldwell, L. K. (1983). The economy and the environment. *Business Horizons*, *26*(6), 2–5. doi:10.1016/0007-6813(83)90038-1

Campbell, R., Sanders, T., Scoular, J., Pitcher, J., & Cunningham, S. (2019). Risking safety and rights: Online sex work, crimes and 'blended safety repertoires'. *The British Journal of Sociology*, *70*(4), 1539–1560. doi:10.1111/1468-4446.12493 PMID:30318604

Cao, W., Jiang, P., & Jiang, K. (2015). Demand-based manufacturing service capability estimation of a manufacturing system in a social manufacturing environment. *Proceedings of the Institution of Mechanical Engineers. Part B, Journal of Engineering Manufacture*, *231*(7), 1275–1297. doi:10.1177/0954405415585255

Cao, X., Luo, Z., Qiu, J., & Liu, Y. (2022). Does ostracism impede Chinese tourist self-disclosure on WeChat? The perspective of social anxiety and self-construal. *Journal of Hospitality and Tourism Management*, *50*, 178–187. doi:10.1016/j.jhtm.2022.02.013

Carasa, L. L. (2022). *Enhancing international cooperation to fight gender inequality: A comparative analysis of the effectiveness of internet regulations in tackling online violence against women in the EU and the USA.* Academic Press.

Carayannis, K. (2003). The Story of Managing Projects. Quorum Books.

Carlsmith, K. M. (2001). *Why do we punish? Retribution, deterrence, and incapacitation as motives for punishment.* Princeton University.

Carlsmith, K. M. (2006). The roles of retribution and utility in determining punishment. *Journal of Experimental Social Psychology*, *42*(4), 437–451. doi:10.1016/j.jesp.2005.06.007

Carlsson, B. (2004). The Digital Economy: What is new and what is not? *Structural Change and Economic Dynamics*, *15*(3), 245–264. doi:10.1016/j.strueco.2004.02.001

Casino, F., Pina, C., López-Aguilar, P., Batista, E., Solanas, A., & Patsakis, C. (2022). SoK: Cross-border criminal investigations and digital evidence. *Journal of Cybersecurity*, *8*(1), tyac014. doi:10.1093/cybsec/tyac014

Castiglione, D., Charvet, J., Coole, D., & Forsyth, M. (1995). *The social contract from Hobbes to Rawls.* Routledge.

Cenamor, J., & Frishammar, J. (2021). Openness in platform ecosystems: Innovation strategies for complementary products. *Research Policy*, *50*(1), 104148. doi:10.1016/j.respol.2020.104148

Chambers, D., & Munemo, J. (2019). Natural resource dependency and entrepreneurship: Are nations with high resource rents cursed? *Journal of International Development*, *31*(2), 137–164. doi:10.1002/jid.3397

Chandra, S., Shirish, A., & Srivastava, S. C. (2022). To Be or Not to Be ...Human? Theorizing the Role of Human-Like Competencies in Conversational Artificial Intelligence Agents. *Journal of Management Information Systems, 39*(4), 969–1005. doi:10.1080/07421222.2022.2127441

Chauhan, C., Singh, A., & Luthra, S. (2021). Barriers to industry 4.0 adoption and its performance implications: An empirical investigation of emerging economy. *Journal of Cleaner Production, 285*, 124809. doi:10.1016/j.jclepro.2020.124809

Chen, Y., Conroy, N. J., & Rubin, V. L. (2015). Misleading online content: recognising clickbait as "false news". The 2015 ACM on workshop on multimodal deception detection. doi:10.1145/2823465.2823467

Chen, C. P., & Zhang, C. Y. (2014). Data-intensive applications, challenges, techniques and technologies: A survey on Big Data. *Information Sciences, 275*, 314–347. doi:10.1016/j.ins.2014.01.015

Cheng, C.-Y., Chien, M.-S., & Lee, C.-C. (2021). ICT diffusion, financial development, and economic growth: An international cross-country analysis. *Economic Modelling, 94*, 662–671. doi:10.1016/j.econmod.2020.02.008

Chen, J., Chen, Y., Du, X., Li, C., Lu, J., Zhao, S., & Zhou, X. (2013). Big data challenge: A data management perspective. *Frontiers of Computer Science, 7*(2), 157–164. doi:10.100711704-013-3903-7

Chen, Y., & Roldan, M. (2021). Digital innovation during COVID-19: Transforming challenges to opportunities. *Communications of the Association for Information Systems, 48*(1), 3. doi:10.17705/1CAIS.04803

Chesbrough, H. (2007). Business model innovation: It's not just about technology anymore. *Strategy and Leadership, 35*(6), 12–17. doi:10.1108/10878570710833714

Chesbrough, H. W. (2003). *Open Innovation: The New Imperative for Creating and Profiting from Technology*. Harvard Business School Press.

Chesbrough, H., & Bogers, M. (2014). *Explicating open innovation: Clarifying an emerging paradigm for understanding innovation. New Frontiers in Open Innovation*. Oxford University Press. doi:10.1093/acprof:oso/9780199682461.003.0001

Chi, M., Pan, M., & Wang, W. (2021). A cross-platform comparative study of reviews on sharing accommodation and hotel reservation platform: Combined with LDA-SNA and sentiment analysis. *Library and Information Service, 65*(2), 107.

China Tourism Academy. (2020). *2019 Annual Report on China's Outbound Tourism Development* http://eng.ctaweb.org.cn/ctaen/c09/202103/9189e906cd044e0ebcd388693e7fb6ff.shtml

China Travel News. (2020). *Trip.com Group Scores Big with Livestreaming Sales Event*. https://www.chinatravelnews.com/article/136944

Choe, Y., Kim, J., & Fesenmaier, D. R. (2017). Use of social media across the trip experience: An application of latent transition analysis. *Journal of Travel & Tourism Marketing, 34*(4), 431–443. doi:10.1080/10548408.2016.1182459

Choi, B. (2019). The role of firm size and IT capabilities in open and closed innovation. *Asia Pacific Journal of Information Systems, 29*(4), 690–716.

Chuang, J. A. (2009). Rescuing trafficking from ideological capture: Prostitution reform and anti-trafficking law and policy. *U. Pa. L. Rev., 158*, 1655.

Chung, M., Ko, E., Joung, H., & Kim, S. J. (2020). Chatbot e-service and customer satisfaction regarding luxury brands. *Journal of Business Research, 117*, 587–595. doi:10.1016/j.jbusres.2018.10.004

Chung, R. Jr, Rainer, J., & Lewis, B. R. (2003). The impact of information technology infrastructure flexibility on strategic alignment and application implementations. *Communications of the Association for Information Systems, 11*(1), 11. doi:10.17705/1CAIS.01111

Ciborra, C., & Hanseth, O. (2000). Towards a contingency view of infrastructure and knowledge: an exploratory study. Business Information Technology Management Alternative and Adaptive Futures, 178-194.

Cinnioğlu, H. (2020). A Review of Modern Leadership Styles in Perspective of Industry 4.01. *Agile Business Leadership Methods for Industry*, *4*(0), 1–23. doi:10.1108/978-1-80043-380-920201002

Cioboată, M. (2020). The Underground Economy: Determinants and Implications. *Revista tinerilor economişti*, (34), 52-63.

Clough, J. (2014). A world of difference: The Budapest Convention on Cybercrime and the Challenges of Harmonisation. *Monash University Law Review. Monash University. Faculty of Law*, *40*(3), 698–736.

cnnic.com.cn. (2022). *The 49th Statistical Report on China's Internet Development*. https://www.cnnic.com.cn/IDR/ReportDownloads/202204/P020220424336135612575.pdf

Codeacademy. (2023). *Generative Chatbots*. Available at https://www.codecademy.com/learn/deep-learning-and-generative-chatbots/modules/generative-chatbots/cheatsheet

Cohen, J. (2006). Social, emotional, ethical, and academic education: Creating a climate for learning, participation in democracy, and well-being. *Harvard Educational Review*, *76*(2), 201–237. doi:10.17763/haer.76.2.j44854x1524644vn

Colombo, M. G., Foss, N. J., Lyngsie, J., & Lamastra, C. R. (2021). What drives the delegation of innovation decisions? The roles of firm innovation strategy and the nature of external knowledge. *Research Policy*, *50*(1), 104134. doi:10.1016/j.respol.2020.104134

Copeland, B. J. (2023). *Artificial intelligence*. Available at https://www.britannica.com/technology/artificial-intelligence/Reasoning

Côrte-Real, N., Oliveira, T., & Ruivo, P. (2017). Assessing business value of Big Data Analytics in European firms. *Journal of Business Research*, *70*, 379–390. doi:10.1016/j.jbusres.2016.08.011

Cory, N., Atkinson, R. D., & Castro, D. (2019). *Principles and Policies for "Data Free Flow With Trust"*. Information Technology and Innovation Foundation.

Council of Europe. (2001, Nov. 23). *Convention on Cybercrime*. Author.

Covin, J. G., & Slevin, D. (1989). Strategic management of small firms in hostile and benign environments. *Strategic Management Journal*, *10*(1), 75–88. doi:10.1002mj.4250100107

Covin, J. G., & Slevin, D. P. (1991). A conceptual model of entrepreneurship as firm behavior. *Entrepreneurship Theory and Practice*, *16*(1), 7–26. doi:10.1177/104225879101600102

Cox, C., Burgess, S., Sellitto, C., & Buultjens, J. (2009). The role of user-generated content in tourists' travel planning behavior. *Journal of Hospitality Marketing & Management*, *18*(8), 743–764. doi:10.1080/19368620903235753

Cubides Kovacsics, M. I., Santos, W., & Siegmann, K. A. (2022). Sex workers' everyday security in the Netherlands and the impact of COVID-19. *Sexuality Research & Social Policy*, 1–15. doi:10.100713178-022-00729-4 PMID:35637773

Cunningham, S., & Kendall, T. D. (2011). Prostitution 2.0: The changing face of sex work. *Journal of Urban Economics*, *69*(3), 273–287. doi:10.1016/j.jue.2010.12.001

Cutler, S. P. (1999). Building International Cases: Tools for Successful Investigations. *FBI L. Enforcement Bull.*, *68*, 1.

Dacin, M. T., Dacin, P. A., & Tracey, P. (2011). Social entrepreneurship: A critique and future directions. *Organization Science*, *22*(5), 1203–1213. doi:10.1287/orsc.1100.0620

Dahlman, C., Mealy, S., & Wermelinger, M. (2016). *Harnessing the digital economy for developing countries*. Academic Press.

Dalenogare, L. S., Benitez, G. B., Ayala, N. F., & Frank, A. G. (2018). The expected contribution of Industry 4.0 technologies for industrial performance. *International Journal of Production Economics*, *204*, 383–394. doi:10.1016/j.ijpe.2018.08.019

Damiani, L., Demartini, M., Guizzi, G., Revetria, R., & Tonelli, F. (2018). Augmented and virtual reality applications in industrial systems: A qualitative review towards the industry 4.0 era. *IFAC-PapersOnLine*, *51*(11), 624–630. doi:10.1016/j.ifacol.2018.08.388

Danarahmanto, P. A., Primiana, I., Azis, Y., & Kaltum, U. (2020). The sustainable performance of the digital start-up company based on customer participation, innovation, and business model. *Business: Theory and Practice*, *21*(1), 115–124. doi:10.3846/btp.2020.11053

Danielsson, A. (2021). *Economic Activity or Public Order Limitations: The Interplay of the Regulation of Prostitution between National Law, EU Law and Efforts to Combat Human Trafficking* [Thesis].

Danielsson, A. (2017). Legal philosophical considerations of prostitution: A roadmap to understanding diverse legal approaches to prostitution in Europe. *Strathclyde Law Review*, *3*(1), 24–59.

Danielsson, A. (2017a). Competing Ideas of Regulationism-What Can be Learnt from the German Move to a More Comprehensive Regulation of Prostitution. *International Journal of Advanced Research*, *5*(3), 2149–2166. doi:10.21474/IJAR01/3734

Danish, R. Q., Asghar, J., Ahmad, Z., & Ali, H. F. (2019). Factors affecting "Entrepreneurial culture": The mediating role of creativity. *Journal of Innovation and Entrepreneurship*, *8*(1), 14. Advance online publication. doi:10.118613731-019-0108-9

Dank, M. L., Khan, B., Downey, P. M., Kotonias, C., Mayer, D., Owens, C., ... Yu, L. (2014). *Estimating the size and structure of the underground commercial sex economy in eight major US cities*. Academic Press.

Dao, D. V. (2015). Social media classification scheme in online teaching and learning activities: A consideration for educators. *International Journal of Education and Social Science*, *2*(4), 85–94.

Daugherty, T., Eastin, M. S., & Bright, L. (2008). Exploring consumer motivations for creating user-generated content. *Journal of Interactive Advertising*, *8*(2), 16–25. doi:10.1080/15252019.2008.10722139

Davenport, T. H., Barth, P., & Bean, R. (2012). *How 'big data' is different*. Academic Press.

Davenport, T., & Harris, J. (2017). *Competing on Analytics: Updated, with a New Introduction: The New Science of Winning*. Harvard Business Press.

Davila Delgado, J. M., Oyedele, L., Ajayi, A., Akanbi, L., Akinade, O., Bilal, M., & Owolabi, H. (2019). Robotics and automated systems in construction: Understanding industry-specific challenges for adoption. *Journal of Building Engineering*, *26*, 100868. doi:10.1016/j.jobe.2019.100868

de Cock, M., & Woode, M. (2014). *Profits and Poverty: The Economics of Forced Labour*. Academic Press.

De Felice, F., Travaglioni, M., & Petrillo, A. (2021). Innovation Trajectories for a Society 5.0. *Data*, *6*(11), 115. doi:10.3390/data6110115

De Marneffe, P. (2012). *Liberalism and prostitution*. OUP USA.

De Streel, A. (2020). *Online Platforms' Moderation of Illegal Content Online.* Policy Department for Economic, Scientific and Quality of Life Policies, European Parliament.

Dean, J. (2009). Democracy and other neoliberal fantasies. In *Democracy and Other Neoliberal Fantasies.* Duke University Press. doi:10.2307/j.ctv11smj29

Deeb, A. (2019). *Software development methodologies in industry* [M.S. thesis]. Department Software Engineering, Australian National University.

Deeb-Swihart, J., Endert, A., & Bruckman, A. (2022). Ethical Tensions in Applications of AI for Addressing Human Trafficking: A Human Rights Perspective. *Proceedings of the ACM on Human-Computer Interaction, 6*(2), 1-29. 10.1145/3555186

Deng, Z., Benckendorff, P., & Wang, J. (2021). Travel live streaming: An affordance perspective. *Information Technology & Tourism, 23*(2), 189–207. doi:10.100740558-021-00199-1

Denoo, L., & Yli-Renko, H. (2019). Entrepreneurship in a new digital industry: The emergence and growth of mobile health. Digital Entrepreneurship: Interfaces Between Digital Technologies and Entrepreneurship, 79-98.

Devasahayam, T. W. (2019). Sex, Crime and Deceit: Women and Child Trafficking and Sexual Abuse in the Internet Age in Cambodia and Thailand. *Exploring the Nexus Between Technologies and Human Rights,* 1.

Diamond, L., & Plattner, M. F. (Eds.). (2012). *Liberation technology: Social media and the struggle for democracy.* JHU Press. doi:10.1353/book.72079

Díaz-Bonilla, E. (2021). *Food Systems Summit Brief prepared by research partners of the Scientific Group for the Food Systems Summit, May 11th, 2021.* https://sc-fss2021.org/wp-content/uploads/2021/06/FSS_Brief_Science_Policy_Interactions.pdf

Dickinson, J. E., Ghali, K., Cherrett, T., Speed, C., Davies, N., & Norgate, S. (2014). Tourism and the smartphone app: Capabilities, emerging practice and scope in the travel domain. *Current Issues in Tourism, 17*(1), 84–101. doi:10.1080/13683500.2012.718323

Didier, E., Hellweger, A., Powell, R. J., & van Kampen, C. (2022). Exploring Legal Accountability of Global Technology and Social Media Companies for the Cyber Exploitation and Online Human Trafficking of Yezidis and Other Minorities By ISIS. *Journal of Human Trafficking, Enslavement, and Conflict-Related Sexual Violence, 3*(1), 4–44. doi:10.7590/266644722X16563337545111

Digital Oman Strategy. (2018). *Ministry of Technology and Communications: Digital Oman strategy 2018.* Retrieved from https://www.ita.gov.om/ITAPortal/eOman/Main_Strategic_Directions.aspx

Dimitratos, P., Johnson, J. E., Plakoyiannaki, E., & Young, S. (2016). SME internationalization: How does the opportunity-based international entrepreneurial culture matter? *International Business Review, 25*(6), 1211–1222. doi:10.1016/j.ibusrev.2016.03.006

Ding, K., Jiang, P., Leng, J., & Cao, W. (2016). Modeling and analyzing of an enterprise relationship network in the context of social manufacturing. *Proceedings of the Institution of Mechanical Engineers. Part B, Journal of Engineering Manufacture, 230*(4), 752–769. doi:10.1177/0954405414558730

Ding, K., Jiang, P., & Su, S. (2018). RFID-enabled social manufacturing system for inter-enterprise monitoring and dispatching of integrated production and transportation tasks. *Robotics and Computer-integrated Manufacturing, 49,* 120–133. doi:10.1016/j.rcim.2017.06.009

DiPietro, R. B., Wang, Y., Rompf, P., & Severt, D. (2007). At-destination visitor information search and venue decision strategies. *International Journal of Tourism Research*, *9*(3), 175–188. doi:10.1002/jtr.600

Drucker, P. (2014). *Innovation and entrepreneurship*. Routledge. doi:10.4324/9781315747453

Drucker, P. F. (1999). Peter Drucker on the new business realities. *Antitrust Bulletin*, *44*(4), 795–819. doi:10.1177/0003603X9904400403

Duggal, A. S., Malik, P. K., Gehlot, A., Singh, R., Gaba, G. S., Masud, M., & Al-Amri, J. F. (2022). A sequential roadmap to Industry 6.0: Exploring future manufacturing trends. *IET Communications*, *16*(5), 521-531. doi:10.1049/cmu2.12284

Dutta, D., & Sarma, M. K. (2020). Adoption of digital innovation-Formulating adopter categories and levels of adoption in a digital sphere in an emerging economy. *International Journal on Management of Innovation & Technology*, *17*(08), 2050059. https://www.worldscientific.com/doi/epdf/10.1142/S0219877020500595. doi:10.1142/S0219877020500595

Dutta, P., Choi, T. M., Somani, S., & Butala, R. (2020). Blockchain technology in supply chain operations: Applications, challenges and research opportunities. *Transportation Research Part E, Logistics and Transportation Review*, *142*, 102067. doi:10.1016/j.tre.2020.102067 PMID:33013183

Dwityas, N. A., & Briandana, R. (2017). Social media in travel decision-making process. *International Journal of Humanities and Social Science*, *7*(7), 193–201.

Dy, A. M., Marlow, S., & Martin, L. (2017). A Web of opportunity or the same old story? Women digital entrepreneurs and intersectionality theory. *Human Relations*, *70*(3), 286–311. doi:10.1177/0018726716650730

Eaton, D. (2022). *Human Trafficking: Detection and Transaction Monitoring Techniques* [Doctoral dissertation]. Utica University.

EDFI. (2016). *Investing to create jobs, boost growth and fight poverty*. Association of the European Development Finance Institutions.

Egbetokun, A., Siyanbola, W., Olamade, O., Adeniyi, A., & Irefin, I. (2008). Innovation in Nigerian SMEs: types and impact. MPRA Paper 25338, University Library of Munich.

Eisenhardt, K. M., & Martin, J. A. (2000). Dynamic capabilities: What are they? *Strategic Management Journal*, *21*(10-11), 1105–1121. doi:10.1002/1097-0266(200010/11)21:10/11<1105::AID-SMJ133>3.0.CO;2-E

Eisenhardt, K. M., & Schoonhoven, C. B. (1996). Resource-based view of strategic alliance formation: Strategic and social effects in entrepreneurial firms. organization. *Science*, *7*(2), 136–150.

Eisenmann, T.R., Parker, G., & Van Alstyne, M. (2009). Opening platforms: How, when and why. *Platforms, Markets and Innovation*, *6*, 131-162.

Ejsmont, K., Gladysz, B., & Kluczek, A. (2020). Impact of industry 4.0 on sustainability—Bibliometric literature review. *Sustainability (Basel)*, *12*(14), 5650. doi:10.3390u12145650

Elia, G., Margherita, A., & Passiante, G. (2020). Digital entrepreneurship ecosystem: How digital technologies and collective intelligence are reshaping the entrepreneurial process. *Technological Forecasting and Social Change*, *150*, 119791. doi:10.1016/j.techfore.2019.119791

Ellermann, H., Kreutter, P., & Messner, W. (2017). The Palgrave Handbook of Managing Continuous Business Transformation. E-Leadership for SMEs in the Digital Age, 17, 375–416. doi:10.1057/978-1-137-60228-2

Ellison, G. (2017). Who needs evidence? Radical feminism, the Christian Right and sex work research in Northern Ireland. In *Reflexivity and Criminal Justice* (pp. 289–314). Palgrave Macmillan. doi:10.1057/978-1-137-54642-5_13

Engati. (2021). *The 6 types of chatbots — Which one do you need?* Chatbots Life. Available at https://chatbotslife.com/the-6-types-of-chatbots-which-one-do-you-need-61e3becbdec

Essien, E. D. (Ed.). (2022). *Handbook of Research on Present and Future Paradigms in Human Trafficking*. IGI Global. doi:10.4018/978-1-7998-9282-3

Esteves, J., & Curto, J. (2013, January). A risk and benefits behavioral model to assess intentions to adopt big data. *Proceedings of the 10th International Conference on Intellectual Capital, Knowledge Management and Organisational Learning: ICICKM 2013*. 10.37380/jisib.v3i3.74

European Commission. (2013). *Strategic policy forum for digital entrepreneurship: Fuelling digital entrepreneurship in Europe*. Author.

European Commission. (2015). *European Commission (EC), Digital Transformation of European Industry and Enterprises; A report of the Strategic Policy Forum on Digital Entrepreneurship*. http://ec.europa.eu/DocsRoom/documents/9462/attachments/1/translations/en/renditions/native

European Police Office. (2015). *Exploring Tomorrow's Organised Crime*. Author.

Europol, I. O. C. T. A. (2014). https:// www.europol.europa.eu/activities-services/main-reports/internet-organised-crime-threat-assessment-iocta-2014

Europol. (2021). *Internet Organised Crime Threat Assessment (IOCTA) 2021*. Publications Office of the European Union.

Facebook. (2022). *Report something: Facebook help centre*. Facebook Help Centre. Retrieved December 9, 2022, from https://en-gb.facebook.com/help/263149623790594

Fagerberg, J., Fosaas, M., & Sapprasert, K. (2012). Innovation: Exploring the knowledge base. *Research Policy*, *41*(7), 1132–1153. doi:10.1016/j.respol.2012.03.008

Faludi, J., Hoffenson, S., Kwok, S. Y., Saidani, M., Hallstedt, S. I., Telenko, C., & Martinez, V. (2020). A research roadmap for sustainable design methods and tools. *Sustainability (Basel)*, *12*(19), 8174. doi:10.3390u12198174

Farrell, A., DeLateur, M. J., Owens, C., & Fahy, S. (2016). The prosecution of state-level human trafficking cases in the United States. *Anti-Trafficking Review*, (6), 48–70. doi:10.14197/atr.20121664

Federico, G. (2018). *The origin of Big Data*. Retrieved 18th April from https://www.federicomassarottomason.com/2018/01/31/big-data/

Feghali, K., Matta, J., & Moussa, S. (2022). Digital transformation of accounting practices and behavior during COVID-19: MENA evidence. *Accounting and Management Information Systems*, *21*(2), 236–269. doi:10.24818/jamis.2022.02005

Feld, B. (2020). *Startup communities: Building an entrepreneurial ecosystem in your city*. John Wiley & Sons.

Fenwick, T., & Edwards, R. (2016). Exploring the impact of digital technologies on professional responsibilities and education. *European Educational Research Journal*, *15*(1), 117–131. doi:10.1177/1474904115608387

Fernandes, C., Ferreira, J., Veiga, P., Kraus, S., & Dabić, M. (2022). Digital entrepreneurship platforms: Mapping the field and looking towards a holistic approach. *Technology in Society*, *70*, 101979. doi:10.1016/j.techsoc.2022.101979

Finklea, K. M. (2011, July). *The interplay of borders, turf, cyberspace, and jurisdiction: Issues confronting US law enforcement*. Congressional Research Service, Library of Congress.

Finwin Technologies. (2020). *What are the different types of chatbots?* Medium. Available at https://medium.com/finwintech/what-are-the-different-types-of-chatbots-c99cdd6b3248

Flowers, R. B. (2011). *Prostitution in the digital age: Selling sex from the suite to the street.* ABC-CLIO.

Fodness, D., & Murray, B. (1999). A model of tourist information search behavior. *Journal of Travel Research, 37*(3), 220–230. doi:10.1177/004728759903700302

Fotis, J., Buhalis, D., & Rossides, N. (2011). Social media impact on holiday travel planning: The case of the Russian and the FSU markets. *International Journal of Online Marketing, 1*(4), 1–19. doi:10.4018/ijom.2011100101

Freeman, C. (1995). The 'National System of Innovation' in historical perspective. *Cambridge Journal of Economics*, 5–24. doi:10.1093/oxfordjournals.cje.a035309

Frosio, G. F. (2018). Why keep a dog and bark yourself? From intermediary liability to responsibility. *International Journal of Law and Information Technology, 26*(1), 1–33. doi:10.1093/ijlit/eax021

Fubon Bank. (2021). *Fubon Bank (Hong Kong) and HKT Form Strategic Partnership to Drive FinTech Innovations.* Available at https://www.fubonbank.com.hk/resources/common/pdf/pr_210121_e.pdf

Fudge, J. (2018). Modern Slavery, Unfree Labour and the Labour Market: The Social Dynamics of Legal Characterization. *Social & Legal Studies, 27*(414).

Fung, A. Y. (2019). Fandomization of online video or television in China. *Media Culture & Society, 41*(7), 995–1010. doi:10.1177/0163443719863353

Fung, A., He, W., & Cao, S. (2022). Cultural capitals and creative labour of short video platforms: A study of Wanghong on Douyin. *Cultural Trends*, 1–6. doi:10.1080/09548963.2022.2082862

Furfaro, A., Piccolo, A., Parise, A., Argento, L., & Saccà, D. (2018). A Cloud-based platform for the emulation of complex cybersecurity scenarios. *Future Generation Computer Systems, 89*, 791–803. doi:10.1016/j.future.2018.07.025

G20. (2016). *G20 digital economy development and cooperation initiative.* G20 Research Group at the University of Toronto.

Gallagher, A. T. (2010). *The international law of human trafficking.* Cambridge University Press. doi:10.1017/CBO9780511761065

Gamage, T. C., Tajeddini, K., & Tajeddini, O. (2022). Why Chinese travellers use WeChat to make hotel choice decisions: A uses and gratifications theory perspective. *Journal of Global Scholars of Marketing Science, 32*(2), 285–312. doi:10.1080/21639159.2021.1961599

Ganichev, N. A., & Koshovets, O. B. (2021). Forcing the digital economy: How will the structure of digital markets change as a result of the COVID-19 pandemic. *Studies on Russian Economic Development, 32*(1), 11–22. doi:10.1134/S1075700721010056 PMID:33642845

Gans, J. S., & Stern, S. (2003). The product market and the market for "ideas": Commercialization strategies for technology entrepreneurs. *Research Policy, 32*(2), 333–350. doi:10.1016/S0048-7333(02)00103-8

Garcia-Teruel, R. M. (2020). Legal challenges and opportunities of blockchain technology in the real estate sector. *Journal of Property, Planning and Environmental Law.*

Gartner, W. B. (1988). "Who is an entrepreneur?" is the wrong question. *American Journal of Small Business, 12*(4), 11–32. doi:10.1177/104225878801200401

Gawer, A., & Cusumano, M. A. (2002). *Platform leadership: How Intel, Microsoft, and Cisco drive industry innovation* (Vol. 5). Harvard Business School Press.

Ge, J., & Gretzel, U. (2017). A new cultural revolution: Chinese consumers' internet and social media use. In Advances in Social Media for Travel, Tourism and Hospitality (pp. 102-118). Routledge.

Gebauer, H., Paiola, M., Saccani, N., & Rapaccini, M. (2021). Digital servitization: Crossing the perspectives of digitization and servitization. *Industrial Marketing Management*, *93*, 382–388. doi:10.1016/j.indmarman.2020.05.011

Geldenhuys, K. (2019). Bilateral tools for fighting transnational organised crime. *Servamus Community-based Safety and Security Magazine*, *112*(8), 32–37.

George, G., Haas, M. R., & Pentland, A. (2014). Big data and management. *Academy of Management Journal*, *57*(2), 321–326. doi:10.5465/amj.2014.4002

Gerry, F., Muraszkiewicz, J., & Vavoula, N. (2016). The role of technology in the fight against human trafficking: Reflections on privacy and data protection concerns. *Computer Law & Security Report*, *32*(2), 205–217. doi:10.1016/j.clsr.2015.12.015

Ghataka, A., Chatterjee, S., & Bhowmick, B. (2020). Intention Towards Digital Social Entrepreneurship: An Integrated Model. *Journal of Social Entrepreneurship*, 1–22. doi:10.1080/19420676.2020.1826563

Ghezzi, A., & Cavallo, A. (2020). Agile Business Model Innovation in Digital Entrepreneurship: Lean Startup Approaches. *Journal of Business Research*, *110*, 519–537. doi:10.1016/j.jbusres.2018.06.013

Giones, F., & Brem, A. (2017). Digital Technology Entrepreneurship: A Definition and Research Agenda. *Technology Innovation Management Review*, *7*(5), 44–51. doi:10.22215/timreview/1076

Girvan, L., & Girvan, S. (2022). *Agile from First Principles*. The Chartered Institute for IT.

Goasduff, L. (2019). *Top trends on the Gartner Hype cycle for artificial intelligence.* Available at https://www.gartner.com/smarterwithgartner/top-trends-on-the-gartner-hype-cycle-for-artificial-intelligence-2019/

Godec, D., Pilipović, A., Breški, T., Ureña, J., Jordá, O., Martínez, M., Gonzalez-Gutierrez, J., Schuschnigg, S., Blasco, J. R., & Portolés, L. (2022). Introduction to Additive Manufacturing. In D. Godec, J. Gonzalez-Gutierrez, A. Nordin, E. Pei, & J. Ureña Alcázar (Eds.), *A Guide to Additive Manufacturing* (pp. 1–44). Springer International Publishing. doi:10.1007/978-3-031-05863-9_1

Gold, A. H., Malhotra, A., & Segars, A. H. (2001). Knowledge management: An organizational capabilities perspective. *Journal of Management Information Systems*, *18*(1), 185–214. doi:10.1080/07421222.2001.11045669

Goodman, M. (2006). *Mutual Legal Assistance Treaties and Letters Rogatory: A Guide for Judges.* Academic Press.

Goździak, E. M., & Vogel, K. M. (2020). Palermo at 20: A retrospective and prospective. *Journal of Human Trafficking*, *6*(2), 109–118. doi:10.1080/23322705.2020.1690117

Gozgor, G., & Lau, C. K. M. (2021). Editorial: Economic Effects of COVID-19 Related Uncertainty Shocks. *Frontiers in Public Health*, *9*, 760619. doi:10.3389/fpubh.2021.760619 PMID:34650956

Grabowska, S., Saniuk, S., & Gajdzik, B. (2022). Industry 5.0: Improving humanization and sustainability of Industry 4.0. *Scientometrics*, *127*(6), 3117–3144. doi:10.100711192-022-04370-1 PMID:35502439

Grady, N. W., Underwood, M., Roy, A., & Chang, W. L. (2014, October 27-30). Big Data: Challenges, practices and technologies: NIST Big Data Public Working Group workshop at IEEE. *Big Data*.

Grant, M. (2014). *Playing the whore: The work of sex work.* Verso Books.

Grant, R. M. (1996). Toward a knowledge-based theory of the firm. *Strategic Management Journal, 17*(S2), 109–122. doi:10.1002mj.4250171110

Greene, A. S. (2013). What is Constitutional Obligation. *BUL Rev., 93*, 1239.

Gregori, P., & Holzmann, P. (2020). Digital sustainable entrepreneurship: A business model perspective on embedding digital technologies for social and environmental value creation. *Journal of Cleaner Production, 272*, 122817. doi:10.1016/j.jclepro.2020.122817

Gretzel, U. (2018). Tourism and Social Media. The Sage Handbook of Tourism Management, 2, 415-432.

Grossmann, G., Jordan, A., Muruganandha, R., Selway, M., & Stumptner, M. (2013). *Enabling Information Interoperability through Multi-domain Modeling*. Practice-Driven Research on Enterprise Transformation. doi:10.1007/978-3-642-38774-6_2

Gunasilan, U. (2019). Entrepreneurship as a driver of the digital transformation. *International Review of Management and Marketing*, 9(5), 23–29. doi:10.32479/irmm.8264

Gupta, S., & Jain, S. K. (2013). A literature review of lean manufacturing. *International Journal of Management Science and Engineering Management*, 8(4), 241–249. doi:10.1080/17509653.2013.825074

Gurr, D. (2004). ICT, Leadership in Education and E-leadership. *Discourse: Studies in the Cultural Politics of Education, 25*(1), 113–124. . doi:10.1080/0159630042000178518

Gyandoh, M. K. (2001). Foreign Evidence Gathering: What obstacles stand in the way of justice. *Temp. Int'l & Comp. LJ, 15*, 81.

Hamalainen, M., Mohajeri, B., & Nyberg, T. (2018). Removing barriers to sustainability research on personal fabrication and social manufacturing. *Journal of Cleaner Production, 180*, 666–681. doi:10.1016/j.jclepro.2018.01.099

Han, H., Shiwakoti, R. K., Jarvis, R., Mordi, C., & Botchie, D. (2023). Accounting and auditing with blockchain technology and artificial Intelligence: A literature review. *International Journal of Accounting Information Systems, 48*, 100598. doi:10.1016/j.accinf.2022.100598

Hanna, N. (2018). A role for the state in the digital age. *Journal of Innovation and Entrepreneurship*, 7(1), 5. doi:10.118613731-018-0086-3

Hannibal, M., & Rasmussen, E. S. (2014). Digital Entrepreneurship in a traditional production firm. *International Journal of E-Services and Mobile Applications*, 6(3), 48–66. doi:10.4018/ijesma.2014070104

Hansen, S., & Wakonen, J. (1997). *Innovation, a winning solution?* International Journal of Technology. doi:10.1504/IJTM.1997.001668

Harding, R., Hart, M., Jones-Evans, D., & Levie, J. (2002). *Global entrepreneurship monitor*. London Business School.

Harper, J. (2022). *GCC countries must develop 'tech champions' to compete with US and China*. Retrieved from https://www.arabianbusiness.com/industries/technology/gcc-countries-must-develop-tech-champions-to-compete-with-us-and-china

Haugh, H. (2005). A research agenda for social entrepreneurship. *Social Enterprise Journal, 1*(1), 1–12. doi:10.1108/17508610580000703

Hayter, C. S., & Link, A. N. (2018). Why do knowledge-intensive entrepreneurial firms publish their innovative ideas? *The Academy of Management Perspectives, 32*(1), 141–155. doi:10.5465/amp.2016.0128

Helfat, C. E., & Peteraf, M. A. (2009). Understanding dynamic capabilities: Progress along a developmental path. *Strategic Organization*, *7*(1), 91–102. doi:10.1177/1476127008100133

Henderson, E. (1995). Of Signifiers and Sodomy: Privacy, public Morality and Sex in the Decriminalisation Debates. *Melb. UL Rev.*, *20*, 1023.

Henfridsson, O., & Bygstad, B. (2013). The generative mechanisms of digital infrastructure evolution. *Management Information Systems Quarterly*, *37*(3), 907–931. doi:10.25300/MISQ/2013/37.3.11

Hesse, N., & Sternberg, R. (2017). Alternative growth patterns of university spin-offs: Why so many remain small? *The International Entrepreneurship and Management Journal*, *13*(3), 953–984. doi:10.100711365-016-0431-6

Hilbert, M. (2022). Digital technology and social change: The digital transformation of society from a historical perspective. *Dialogues in Clinical Neuroscience*. PMID:32699519

Hinings, B., Gegenhuber, T., & Greenwood, R. (2018). Digital innovation and transformation: An institutional perspective. *Information and Organization*, *28*(1), 52–61. doi:10.1016/j.infoandorg.2018.02.004

Hirscher, A. L., Niinimäki, K., & Armstrong, C. M. J. (2018). Social manufacturing in the fashion sector: New value creation through alternative design strategies? *Journal of Cleaner Production*, *172*, 4544–4554. doi:10.1016/j.jclepro.2017.11.020

Hisrich, R. D., & Soltanifar, M. (2021). Unleashing the creativity of entrepreneurs with digital technologies. Digital Entrepreneurship: Impact on Business and Society, 23-49. doi:10.1007/978-3-030-53914-6_2

Hisrich, R. D. (1990). Entrepreneurship/intrapreneurship. *The American Psychologist*, *45*(2), 209–222. doi:10.1037/0003-066X.45.2.209

Hisrich, R. D., & Soltanufar, M. (2020). Unleashing the Creativity of Entrepreneurs with Digital Technologies. In M. Soltanifar, M. Hughes, & L. Göcke (Eds.), *Digital Entrepreneurship: Impact on Business and Society*. Springer.

Hobbs, W. R., & Roberts, M. E. (2018). How sudden censorship can increase access to information. *The American Political Science Review*, *112*(3), 621–636. doi:10.1017/S0003055418000084

Hodgson, J. S. (2011). Safeguarding Suspects' Rights in Europe: A Comparative Perspective. *New Criminal Law Review*, *14*(4), 611–665. doi:10.1525/nclr.2011.14.4.611

Home Office (HO). (2006). *A Co-ordinated Prostitution Strategy and a Summary of Responses to `Paying the Price'*. Author.

Hong Kong Monetary Authority (HKMA). (2019). *Report on Artificial Intelligence (AI) Application in Banking*. The Hong Kong Monetary Authority (HKMA). Available at https://www.hkma.gov.hk/eng/news-and-media/press-releases/2019/12/20191223-4/

House of Commons Home Affairs Committee, Third Report, Prostitution, HC (2016±17)

Hsiao, R., & Weaver-Lee, Z. (2021). Mutual Legal Assistance in the Digital Age and Taiwan's New Southbound Policy. *Policy*, *21*, 1.

Huang, L. (2012). Social media as a new play in a marketing channel strategy: Evidence from Taiwan travel agencies' blogs. *Asia Pacific Journal of Tourism Research*, *17*(6), 615–634. doi:10.1080/10941665.2011.635664

Hu, C., Yan, X., & Zhou, Z. (2022). The Digital Economy, market-based factor allocation and shared prosperity. *Frontiers in Humanities and Social Sciences*, *2*(8), 119–124. doi:10.54691/fhss.v2i8.1667

Hull, C. E. K., Hung, Y. T. C., Hair, N., Perotti, V., & DeMartino, R. (2007). Taking advantage of digital opportunities: A typology of digital entrepreneurship. *International Journal of Networking and Virtual Organisations*, *4*(3), 290–303. doi:10.1504/IJNVO.2007.015166

Hu, M., & Chaudhry, S. S. (2020). Enhancing consumer engagement in e-commerce live streaming via relational bonds. *Internet Research*, *30*(3), 1019–1041. doi:10.1108/INTR-03-2019-0082

Hüsing, T., Korte, W. B., Fonstad, N., Lanvin, B., Welsum, D., Cattaneo, G., Kolding, M., & Lifonti, R. (2013). *E-Leadership: E-Skills for Competitiveness and Innovation Vision, Roadmap and Foresight Scenarios*. European Commission.

Hu, X., & Yang, Y. (2021). What makes online reviews helpful in tourism and hospitality? a bare-bones meta-analysis. *Journal of Hospitality Marketing & Management*, *30*(2), 139–158. doi:10.1080/19368623.2020.1780178

IFC. (2013). *Assessing private sector contributions to job creation and poverty reduction*. International Finance Corporation.

Ilbiz, E., & Kaunert, C. (2021). Europol and cybercrime: Europol's sharing decryption platform. *Journal of Contemporary European Studies*, 1–14.

ILO. (2019a). *Enabling environment for sustainable enterprises in Sierra Leone*. International Labour Organization.

Ilyas, M., ud din, A., Haleem, M., & Ahmad, I. (2023). Digital Entrepreneurial Acceptance: An Examination of technology acceptance model and do-it-yourself behavior. *Journal of Innovation and Entrepreneurship*, *12*(1), 15. Advance online publication. doi:10.118613731-023-00268-1

InfoSys. (2023). *Industry 4.0 as an evolution, not a revolution*. Retrieved 22nd April from https://www.infosys.com/iki/perspectives/industry-4-0-evolution.html

Instagram. (2022). *Report Violations of our Community Guidelines*. Instagram Help Center. Retrieved December 9, 2022, from https://help.instagram.com/contact/383679321740945

International Labour Organization. (2016). *Occupational Safety and Health Management System: An Applied and Training Guide for Medium and Large Companies*. Available online: https://www.ilo.org/wcmsp5/groups/public/---africa/---ro-abidjan/---sro-cairo/documents/publication/wcms_622420.pdf

Internet World Stats. (2022). *Internet Usage in the Middle East*. Retrieved from https://www.internetworldstats.com/stats5.htm#me

Isenberg, D. (2011). Introducing the entrepreneurship ecosystem: Four defining characteristics. *Forbes*, *14*, 1–8.

ITC. (2018). *Promoting SME competitiveness in Africa: Data for de-risking investment*. International Trade Centre.

ITC. (2019). *SME competitiveness outlook 2019: Big money for small business—Financing the sustainable development goals*. International Trade Centre.

Iyamu, T. (2021). Technology acceptance model. *Applying Theories for Information Systems Research*, 143–154. doi:10.4324/9781003184119-9

Jackson, N. C., & Dunn-Jensen, L. M. (2021). Leadership succession planning for today's digital transformation economy: Key factors to build for competency and innovation. *Business Horizons*, *64*(2), 273–284. doi:10.1016/j.bushor.2020.11.008

Jardine, E. (2021). Policing the cybercrime script of darknet drug markets: Methods of effective law enforcement intervention. *American Journal of Criminal Justice*, *46*(6), 980–1005. doi:10.100712103-021-09656-3

Javaid, M., Haleem, A., Singh, R. P., & Suman, R. (2021). Substantial capabilities of robotics in enhancing industry 4.0 implementation. *Cognitive Robotics*, *1*, 58–75. doi:10.1016/j.cogr.2021.06.001

Jiang, P., Ding, K., & Leng, J. (2016). Towards a cyber-physical-social-connected and service-oriented manufacturing paradigm: Social Manufacturing. *Manufacturing Letters*, *7*, 15–21. doi:10.1016/j.mfglet.2015.12.002

Jiang, X. (2020). Digital economy in the post-pandemic era. *Journal of Chinese Economic and Business Studies*, *18*(4), 333–339. doi:10.1080/14765284.2020.1855066

Jia, S. S., & Wu, B. (2019). User-generated information on mobile channels with more concise reviews and more extreme ratings. *IEEE Access : Practical Innovations, Open Solutions*, *7*, 83495–83503. doi:10.1109/ACCESS.2019.2924335

Johnson, B., & Lundvall, B. Å. (2013). National Innovation Systems (NIS). In E. G. Carayannis (Ed.), *Encyclopedia of Creativity, Invention, Innovation and Entrepreneurship*. Springer. doi:10.1007/978-1-4614-3858-8_458

Jones, A. (2020). *Camming: Money, power, and pleasure in the sex work industry*. NYU Press. doi:10.18574/nyu/9781479842964.001.0001

Jung, T. H., & tom Dieck, M. C. (2017). Augmented reality, virtual reality and 3D printing for the co-creation of value for the visitor experience at cultural heritage places. *Journal of Place Management and Development*.

Jung, T., & tom Dieck, M. C. (2019). *Augmented Reality and Virtual Reality: The Power of AR and VR for Business*. Springer International Publishing.

Jung, T., tom Dieck, M. C., Lee, H., & Chung, N. (2016). Effects of virtual reality and augmented reality on visitor experiences in museum. In *Information and communication technologies in tourism 2016* (pp. 621–635). Springer. doi:10.1007/978-3-319-28231-2_45

Juniper Research. (2019). *Chatbot interactions in retail to reach 22 billion by 2023, as AI offers compelling new engagement solutions*. Available at: https://www.juniperresearch.com/press/chatbot-interactions-retail-reach-22-billion-2023

Kahn, K. B. (2018). Understanding innovation. *Business Horizons*, *61*(3), 453–460. doi:10.1016/j.bushor.2018.01.011

Kallinikos, J., Hasselbladh, H., & Marton, A. (2013). Governing social practice: Technology and institutional change. *Theory and Society*, *42*(4), 395–421. doi:10.100711186-013-9195-y

Kannisto, P., & Hästbacka, D. (2022). Digitalized cross-organizational interoperability in industrial business ecosystems: Implications and models for process industry. *Proceedings of the 3rd International Conference on Innovative Intelligent Industrial Production and Logistics*. 10.5220/0011543900003329

Kaplan, A., & Haenlein, M. (2010). Users of the world, unite! The challenges and opportunities of social media. *Business Horizons*, *53*(1), 59–68. doi:10.1016/j.bushor.2009.09.003

Karlsson, C., Rickardsson, J., & Wincent, J. (2021). Diversity, innovation and entrepreneurship: Where are we and where should we go in future studies? *Small Business Economics*, *56*(2), 759–772. doi:10.100711187-019-00267-1

Katz, S. (2019). The ultimate guide to chatbot personality. *Chatbot Magazine*. Retrieved May 23, 2021, from https://chatbotsmagazine.com/the-ultimate-guide-to-chatbot-personality-b9665ab5e99d

Keating, S. J., Leland, J. C., Cai, L., & Oxman, N. (2017). Toward site-specific and self-sufficient robotic fabrication on architectural scales. *Science Robotics*, *2*(5), eaam8986. doi:10.1126cirobotics.aam8986 PMID:33157892

Kennedy, E. J. (2016). *Digital desire: Commercial, moral, and political economies of sex work and the internet* [Doctoral dissertation]. University of Kansas.

Kenney, M., & Pon, B. (2011). Structuring the smartphone industry: Is the mobile internet OS platform the key? *Journal of Industry, Competition and Trade*, *11*(3), 239–261. doi:10.100710842-011-0105-6

Kesidou, E., Narasimhan, R., Ozusaglam, S., & Wong, C. Y. (2022). Dynamic openness for network-enabled product and process innovation: A panel-data analysis. *International Journal of Operations & Production Management, 42*(3), 257–279. doi:10.1108/IJOPM-06-2021-0380

Kesti, M. (2021). *The digital twin of an organization by utilizing reinforcing Deep Learning*. Deep Learning Applications. doi:10.5772/intechopen.96168

Kethineni, S., & Cao, Y. (2020). The rise in popularity of cryptocurrency and associated criminal activity. *International Criminal Justice Review, 30*(3), 325–344. doi:10.1177/1057567719827051

Keyhani, M., Robinson, M., Lehar, A., & Ashjari, A. (2022). Digital Entrepreneurship and capital acquisition in the global economy. *Digital Entrepreneurship and the Global Economy*, 91-101.

Keyser, M. (2017). The council of Europe convention on cybercrime. In *Computer Crime* (pp. 131–170). Routledge. doi:10.4324/9781315095493-7

Khadem & Khadem. (2017). *Total Alignment. Tools and tactics for streamlining your organization.* Entrepreneur Press (EP).

Khandwalla, P. (1977). *The design of organizations*. Harcourt, Brace.

King, G., & Powell, E. N. (2008, August). *How not to lie without statistics.* Delivery at the 2008 Annual Meeting of the American Political Science Association.

Kirilenko, A. P., Stepchenkova, S. O., & Hernandez, J. M. (2019). Comparative clustering of destination attractions for different origin markets with network and spatial analyses of online reviews. *Tourism Management, 72*, 400–410. doi:10.1016/j.tourman.2019.01.001

Kiron, D., Kane, G. C., Palmer, D., Phillips, A. N., & Buckley, N. (2016). Aligning the organization for its digital future. *MIT Sloan Management Review, 58*(1).

Kitchin, R. (2015). Making sense of smart cities: Addressing present shortcomings. *Cambridge Journal of Regions, Economy and Society, 8*(1), 131–136. doi:10.1093/cjres/rsu027

Kitchin, R., & McArdle, G. (2016). What makes Big Data, Big Data? Exploring the ontological characteristics of 26 datasets. *Big Data & Society, 3*(1). Advance online publication. doi:10.1177/2053951716631130

Kittichaisaree, K. (2017). Regulation of Cyberspace and Human Rights. In *Public International Law of Cyberspace* (pp. 45–152). Springer. doi:10.1007/978-3-319-54657-5_3

Knott, P. J. (2015). Does VRIO help managers evaluate a firm's resources? *Management Decision, 53*(8), 1806–1822. doi:10.1108/MD-08-2014-0525

Konrad, H. (2002). Trafficking in human beings-the ugly face of Europe. *Helsinki Monitor, 13*(3), 260–271. doi:10.1163/157181402401452924

Korte, W. B., Hüsing, T., & Dashja, E. (Eds.). (2015). *E-Leadership: Digital Skills for SMEs*. European Commission.

Koufopoulou, P., Williams, C. C., Vozikis, A., & Souliotis, K. (2019). Shadow Economy: Definitions, terms & theoretical considerations. *Advances in Management and Applied Economics, 9*(5), 35–57.

Kranrattanasuit, N. (2014). ASEAN and human trafficking: Case studies of Cambodia, Thailand, and Vietnam. Martinus Nijhoff Publishers. doi:10.1163/9789004265189

Krasnova, H., Spiekermann, S., Koroleva, K., & Hildebrand, T. (2010). Online social networks: Why we disclose. *Journal of Information Technology, 25*(2), 109–125. doi:10.1057/jit.2010.6

Kraus, S., Palmer, C., Kailer, N., Kallinger, F. L., & Spitzer, J. (2018). Digital Entrepreneurship. *International Journal of Entrepreneurial Behavior & Research*. doi:10.1108/IJEBR-06-2018-0425

Kraus, S., Palmer, C., Kailer, N., Kallinger, F. L., & Spitzer, J. (2019). Digital entrepreneurship: A research agenda on new business models for the twenty-first century. *International Journal of Entrepreneurial Behaviour & Research, 25*(2), 353–375.

Kunze, E. I. (2009). Sex trafficking via the internet: How international agreements address the problem and fail to go far enough. *J. High Tech. L., 10*, 241.

Kuratko, D. F. (2005). The emergence of entrepreneurship education: Development, trends, and challenges. *Entrepreneurship Theory and Practice, 29*(5), 577–597. doi:10.1111/j.1540-6520.2005.00099.x

Kushnir, K., Mirmulstein, M. L., & Ramalho, R. (2010). *Micro, Small, and Medium Enterprises around the World: How Many Are There, and What Affects the Count?* World Bank/IFC.

Kyprianou, C. (2016). Getting to network effects: Social club and open door strategies in two-sided marketplaces. In Academy of management proceedings (Vol. 2016, No. 1, p. 17343). Academy of Management.

Lackéus, M., & Williams Middleton, K. (2015). Venture creation programs: Bridging entrepreneurship education and technology transfer. *Education + Training, 57*(1), 48–73. doi:10.1108/ET-02-2013-0013

Lai, J., & Widmar, N. O. (2021). Revisiting the digital divide in the COVID-19 era. *Applied Economic Perspectives and Policy, 43*(1), 458–464. doi:10.1002/aepp.13104 PMID:33230409

Lamine, W., Anderson, A., Jack, S. L., & Fayolle, A. (2021). Entrepreneurial space and the freedom for entrepreneurship: Institutional settings, policy, and action in the space industry. *Strategic Entrepreneurship Journal, 15*(2), 309–340. doi:10.1002ej.1392

Lam, J. M., Ismail, H., & Lee, S. (2020). From desktop to destination: User-generated content platforms, co-created online experiences, destination image and satisfaction. *Journal of Destination Marketing & Management, 18*, 100490. doi:10.1016/j.jdmm.2020.100490

Lau, A. (2020). New technologies used in COVID-19 for business survival: Insights from the Hotel Sector in China. *Information Technology & Tourism, 22*(4), 497–504. doi:10.100740558-020-00193-z

Lavorgna, A. (2015). Organised crime goes online: realities and challenges. *Journal of Money Laundering Control.*

Layton, R., & Elaluf-Calderwood, S. (2019, November). A social economic analysis of the impact of GDPR on security and privacy practices. In *2019 12th CMI Conference on Cybersecurity and Privacy (CMI)* (pp. 1-6). IEEE. 10.1109/CMI48017.2019.8962288

Le Dinh, T., Vu, M. C., & Ayayi, A. (2018). Towards a living lab for promoting the digital entrepreneurship process. *International Journal of Entrepreneurship, 22*(1), 1–17.

LEAD (2014). E-*Leadership Skills for Small and Medium Sized Enterprises project.* European Commission, Directorate-General for Enterprise and Industry.

Lee, C. (2022). An analysis of global digital knowledge sharing platforms on National Territorial Policy and its implications. *Journal of the Korean Cadastre Information Association, 24*(2), 102–127. doi:10.46416/JKCIA.2022.08.24.2.102

Lee, I. C., & Lewis, M. (2003). Human trafficking from a legal advocate's perspective: History, legal framework and current anti-trafficking efforts. *UC Davis J. Int'l L. & Pol'y, 10*, 169.

Lei, W. S., Chen, Z., Zhou, X., & King, B. (2022). Organic destination imagery and social media: Mapping tourism dynamics across China's Greater Bay Area cities. *Journal of China Tourism Research*, 1–24. doi:10.1080/19388160.2022.2047857

Leng, J. W., Jiang, P. Y., Zhang, F. Q., & Cao, W. (2013). Framework and key enabling technologies for social manufacturing. *Applied Mechanics and Materials*, *312*, 498–501. doi:10.4028/www.scientific.net/AMM.312.498

Leng, J., & Jiang, P. (2016). A deep learning approach for relationship extraction from interaction context in social manufacturing paradigm. *Knowledge-Based Systems*, *100*, 188–199. doi:10.1016/j.knosys.2016.03.008

Leng, J., Jiang, P., Xu, K., Liu, Q., Zhao, J. L., Bian, Y., & Shi, R. (2019). Makerchain: A blockchain with chemical signature for self-organizing process in social manufacturing. *Journal of Cleaner Production*, *234*, 767–778. doi:10.1016/j.jclepro.2019.06.265

Lerch, C., & Gotsch, M. (2015). Digitalized product-service systems in manufacturing companies: A case study analysis. *Research Technology Management*, *58*(5), 45–52. doi:10.5437/08956308X5805357

Leung, D., Law, R., Van Hoof, H., & Buhalis, D. (2013). Social media in tourism and hospitality: A literature review. *Journal of Travel & Tourism Marketing*, *30*(1-2), 3–22. doi:10.1080/10548408.2013.750919

Leuprecht, C., Jenkins, C., & Hamilton, R. (2022). Virtual money laundering: policy implications of the proliferation in the illicit use of cryptocurrency. *Journal of Financial Crime*.

Lewis, J. A. (Ed.). (2003). Cyber security: turning national solutions into international cooperation (No. 25). CSIS.

Li, F. (2020). *Team to market (T2M): Creating high performance teams in the digital age*. Academic Press.

Li, J., Herdem, M. S., Nathwani, J., & Wen, J. Z. (2022). Methods and Applications for Artificial Intelligence, Big Data, Internet-of-Things, and Blockchain in Smart Energy Management. *Energy and AI*, 100208.

Liang, B. (2021). Development of rural community-based tourism with local customs from the view of consumer satisfaction. *Annals of Operations Research*, 1–17. doi:10.100710479-021-04302-x

Liang, H., & Zhang, Q. (2021). Do social media data indicate visits to tourist attractions? A case study of Shanghai, China. *Open House International*, *47*(1), 17–35. doi:10.1108/OHI-05-2021-0110

Li, C., Jiang, Y., & Fang, P. (2019). Innovation in advanced manufacturing driven by supercomputing. *Procedia CIRP*, *83*, 584–589. doi:10.1016/j.procir.2019.04.092

Lieberman, M. (2018). *5 Ways to Improve Customer Relationships* [Web log post]. Available at https://www.square-2marketing.com/blog/5-ways-to-improve-customer-relationships

Lien, C. H., & Cao, Y. (2014). Examining WeChat users' motivations, trust, attitudes, and positive word-of-mouth: Evidence from China. *Computers in Human Behavior*, *41*, 104–111. doi:10.1016/j.chb.2014.08.013

Li, F., Larimo, J., & Leonidou, L. C. (2021). Social media marketing strategy: Definition, conceptualisation, taxonomy, validation, and future agenda. *Journal of the Academy of Marketing Science*, *49*(1), 51–70. doi:10.100711747-020-00733-3

Liggett, R., Lee, J. R., Roddy, A. L., & Wallin, M. A. (2020). The dark web as a platform for crime: An exploration of illicit drug, firearm, CSAM, and cybercrime markets. The Palgrave handbook of international cybercrime and cyberdeviance, 91-116.

Li, J. J., Xu, L. Z., Tang, L., Wang, S. Y., & Li, L. (2018). Big data in tourism research: A literature review. *Tourism Management*, *68*, 301–323. doi:10.1016/j.tourman.2018.03.009

Li, L., Song, X., Liu, S., & Huang, K. (2021). Defining High-Quality Answers on a Chinese Tourism Q&A Platform in Terms of Information Needs. *Sustainability (Basel), 13*(24), 13884. doi:10.3390u132413884

Lima, E., Lopes, R. M., Nassif, V., & Silva, D. (2015). Opportunities to Improve Entrepreneurship Education:Contributions Considering Brazilian Challenges. *Journal of Small Business Management, 53*(4), 1033–1051. doi:10.1111/jsbm.12110

Lin, R.-T., & Koh, D. (2019). Small and medium enterprises: Barriers and drivers of managing environmental and occupational health risks. Encyclopedia of environmental health, 682–692. doi:10.1016/B978-0-12-409548-9.11347-8

Lin, C., & Kunnathur, A. (2019). Strategic orientations, developmental culture, and big data capability. *Journal of Business Research, 105*, 49–60. doi:10.1016/j.jbusres.2019.07.016

Lindsey-Mullikin, J., & Borin, N. (2017). Why strategy is key for successful social media sales. *Business Horizons, 60*(4), 473–482. doi:10.1016/j.bushor.2017.03.005

Lin, K., Fong, L. H. N., & Law, R. (2022). Live streaming in tourism and hospitality: A literature review. *Asia Pacific Journal of Tourism Research, 27*(3), 290–304. doi:10.1080/10941665.2022.2061365

Lin, N. (1999). Social networks and status attainment. *Annual Review of Sociology, 25*(1), 467–487. doi:10.1146/annurev.soc.25.1.467

Lin, N. (2002). *Social capital: A theory of social structure and action* (Vol. 19). Cambridge university press.

Linstone, H. A. (1989). Multiple perspectives: Concept, applications, and user guidelines. *Systems Practice, 2*(3), 307–331. doi:10.1007/BF01059977

Liu, K., Belitski, M., & Li, W. (2014). Leading your company to high performance growth. E-Leadership strategies for SMEs driving innovation and competitive edge in digital integration. *The Henley Accelerator High Growth Accelerator, Executive programme*. https://www.henley.ac.uk/executiveeducation/clopenedp/henley-accelerator/high-growth-accelerator/high_growth_accelerator_2013.pdf

Liu, C., & Hung, K. A. (2020). Comparative study of self-service technology with service employees: A qualitative analysis of hotels in China. *Information Technology & Tourism, 22*(1), 33–52. doi:10.100740558-020-00167-1

Liu, H., Wu, L., & Li, X. (2019). Social media envy: How experience sharing on social networking sites drives millennials' aspirational tourism consumption. *Journal of Travel Research, 58*(3), 355–369. doi:10.1177/0047287518761615

Liu, I., Norman, W. C., & Pennington-Gray, L. (2013). A flash of culinary tourism: Understanding the influences of online food photography on people's travel planning process on flickr. *Tourism, Culture & Communication, 13*(1), 5–18. doi:10.3727/109830413X13769180530567

Liu, M. T., Xue, J., & Liu, Y. (2021). The mechanism leads to successful clickbait promotion in WeChat social media platforms. *Asia Pacific Journal of Marketing and Logistics, 33*(9), 1952–1973. doi:10.1108/APJML-08-2020-0562

Liu, Q., Gu, J., Yang, J., Li, Y., Sha, D., Xu, M., Shams, I., Yu, M., & Yang, C. (2021). Cloud, Edge, and Mobile Computing for Smart Cities. In W. Shi, M. F. Goodchild, M. Batty, M.-P. Kwan, & A. Zhang (Eds.), *Urban Informatics* (pp. 757–795). Springer Singapore. doi:10.1007/978-981-15-8983-6_41

Liu, X. (2022). *Targeted poverty alleviation: China's ingenuity to defeat poverty*. Bangladesh Journal of Public Administration. doi:10.1007/978-981-19-4488-8

Liu, X., Mehraliyev, F., Liu, C., & Schuckert, M. (2020). The roles of social media in tourists' choices of travel components. *Tourist Studies, 20*(1), 27–48. doi:10.1177/1468797619873107

Liu, X., Zeng, Y., Li, Z., & Huang, D. (2022). Understanding consumers' motivations to view travel live streaming: Scale development and validation. *Tourism Management Perspectives*, *44*, 101027. doi:10.1016/j.tmp.2022.101027

Li, W., Liu, K., Belitski, M., Ghobadian, A., & O'Regan, N. (2016). E-Leadership through Strategic Alignment: An Empirical Study of Small- and Medium-sized Enterprises in the Digital Age. *Journal of Information Technology*, *31*(2), 185–206. doi:10.1057/jit.2016.10

Loonam, J., Eaves, S., Kumar, V., & Parry, G. (2018). Towards digital transformation: Lessons learned from traditional organizations. *Strategic Change*, *27*(2), 101–109. doi:10.1002/jsc.2185

Ludbrook, F., Michalikova, K. F., Musova, Z., & Suler, P. (2019). Business models for sustainable innovation in industry 4.0: Smart manufacturing processes, digitalization of production systems, and data-driven decision making. *Journal of Self-Governance and Management Economics*, *7*(3), 21–26.

Lumpkin, G. T., & Dess, G. G. (1996). Clarifying the entrepreneurial orientation construct and linking it to performance. *Academy of Management Review*, *21*(1), 135–172. doi:10.2307/258632

Luo, Y., Liang, P., Wang, C., Shahin, M., & Zhan, J. (2021, October). Characteristics and challenges of low-code development: the practitioners' perspective. In *Proceedings of the 15th ACM/IEEE international symposium on empirical software engineering and measurement (ESEM)* (pp. 1-11). Academic Press.

Luo, Q., & Zhai, X. (2017). "I will never go to Hong Kong again!" How the secondary crisis communication of 'Occupy Central' on Weibo shifted to a tourism boycott. *Tourism Management*, *62*, 159–172. doi:10.1016/j.tourman.2017.04.007 PMID:32287749

Luo, Q., & Zhong, D. (2015). Using social network analysis to explain communication characteristics of travel-related electronic word-of-mouth on social networking sites. *Tourism Management*, *46*, 274–282. doi:10.1016/j.tourman.2014.07.007

Lyman, R. N. (2006). Compulsory process in a globalized era: Defendant access to mutual legal assistance treaties. *Va. J. Int'l L.*, *47*, 261.

Lyu, F., & Zhang, L. (2019). Using multi-source big data to understand the factors affecting urban park use in Wuhan. *Urban Forestry & Urban Greening*, *43*, 126367. doi:10.1016/j.ufug.2019.126367

Mackay, M., Hardesty, B. D., & Wilcox, C. (2020). The intersection between illegal fishing, crimes at sea, and social well-being. *Frontiers in Marine Science*, *7*, 589000. doi:10.3389/fmars.2020.589000

Madampe, K., & Hoda, R. (2020). Towards Understanding Emotional Response to Requirements Changes in Agile Teams. IEEE/ACM.

Maglogiannis, I., Iliadis, L., & Pimenidis, E. (Eds.). (2020, May 6). An Overview of Chatbot Technology. *Artificial Intelligence Applications and Innovations: 16th IFIP WG 12.5 International Conference, AIAI 2020, Neos Marmaras, Greece, June 5–7, 2020, Proceedings, Part II.* https://www.ncbi.nlm.nih.gov/pmc/articles/PMC7256567/#CR20

Maher, S. K., Bhable, S. G., Lahase, A. R., & Nimbhore, S. S. (2022). AI and Deep Learning-driven Chatbots: A Comprehensive Analysis and Application Trends. *Proceedings of the Sixth International Conference on Intelligent Computing and Control Systems (ICICCS 2022)*, 994-998. 10.1109/ICICCS53718.2022.9788276

Maindola, S., & Kumar, S. (2022). Employee perception of the effectiveness of digitalized performance management systems. *Disruptive Innovation and Emerging Technologies for Business Excellence in the Service Sector*,186–195. . doi:10.4018/978-1-7998-9194-9.ch009

Malik, P. (2022). *Improve your customer service with AI-powered chatbots.* Retrieved 20th April from https://www.sprinklr.com/blog/customer-service-chatbots/

Mancarella, F. (2021). *Human rights-based approach to sex-trafficking of women and girls: the analysis of prostitution policies in Italy, Sweden, and the Netherlands* [Doctoral dissertation].

Manickam, V. (2020). *Weak, Strong AI — Do these Terms Matter?* Retrieved 21st April from https://medium.com/@vjmanickam/weak-strong-ai-do-these-terms-matter-4bb57ce3a61f

Manishimwe, T., Raimi, L., & Azubuike, C. J. (2022). Customer-centric influence of entrepreneurial marketing on business performance of hotels in Nigeria during the COVID-19 crisis. *Journal of Revenue and Pricing Management, 21*(6), 668–683. doi:10.105741272-022-00383-w

Mansoori & Tayab. (2014). Standardized software development model for SME software houses in Pakistan. *Journal of Independent Studies and Research - Computing, 12*(1), 11-17.

Marchant, C. A., Briggs, K. A., & Long, A. (2008). In silico tools for sharing data and knowledge on toxicity and metabolism: Derek for windows, meteor, and vitic. *Toxicology Mechanisms and Methods, 18*(2-3), 177–187. doi:10.1080/15376510701857320 PMID:20020913

Marchegiani, L. (2021). Knowledge and (Digital) learning organizations. *Digital Transformation and Knowledge Management*, 105–148. doi:10.4324/9780367628284-4

Marcon, É., Le Dain, M.-A., & Frank, A. G. (2022) Designing business models for Industry 4.0 technologies provision: Changes in business dimensions through digital transformation. Technological Forecasting and Social Change, 185.

Margiono, A. (2021). Digital transformation: Setting the pace. *The Journal of Business Strategy, 42*(5), 315–322. doi:10.1108/JBS-11-2019-0215

Marion, N. E. (2010). The Council of Europe's Cyber Crime Treaty: An exercise in Symbolic Legislation. *International Journal of Cyber Criminology*, 4.

Marr, B. (2020). *Tech Trends in Practice: The 25 Technologies that are Driving the 4th Industrial Revolution.* Wiley.

Marr, B. (2016). *Big Data in Practice: How 45 Successful Companies Used Big Data Analytics to Deliver Extraordinary Results.* Wiley. doi:10.1002/9781119278825

Marr, B. (2017). *Data Strategy: How to Profit from a World of Big Data, Analytics and the Internet of Things.* Kogan Page.

Marston, H. R., & van Hoof, J. (2019). "Who doesn't think about technology when designing urban environments for older people?" A case study approach to a proposed extension of the WHO's age-friendly cities model. *International Journal of Environmental Research and Public Health, 16*(19), 3525. doi:10.3390/ijerph16193525 PMID:31547204

Martin, R.L., & Osberg, S. (2007). *Social entrepreneurship: The case for definition.* Academic Press.

Martin, A., & Grudziecki, J. (2006). DigEuLit: Concepts and Tools for Digital LiteracyDevelopment. ITALICS. *Innovations in Teaching & Learning in Information & Computer Sciences, 5*(4), 246–264.

Mason, C., & Brown, R. (2014). Entrepreneurial ecosystems and growth oriented entrepreneurship. *Final report to OECD, 30*(1), 77-102.

Mathrick, S. (2023). *Understanding The 5 Types Of Cyber Security.* Retrieved 21st April from https://kmtech.com.au/information-centre/understanding-the-5-types-of-cyber-security/

Matlay, H., & Westhead, P. (2007). Competitive advantage in virtual teams of E-entrepreneurs: Evidence from the European Tourism Industry. *Tourism in the New Europe*, 9–27. doi:10.1016/B978-0-08-044706-3.50005-9

Matolcsi, A., Mulvihill, N., Lilley-Walker, S. J., Lanau, A., & Hester, M. (2021). The current landscape of prostitution and sex work in England and Wales. *Sexuality & Culture*, *25*(1), 39–57. doi:10.100712119-020-09756-y

Matt, D. T., Modrák, V., & Zsifkovits, H. (2020). *Industry 4.0 for SMEs: Challenges, Opportunities and Requirements*. Springer International Publishing. doi:10.1007/978-3-030-25425-4

Matthews, R. (1986). Beyond Wolfenden? Prostitution, Politics and the Law. In R. Matthews & J. Young (Eds.), Confronting Crime (p. 188). Academic Press.

Maxwell-Sinclair. (2016). *An Analysis of In-house and Offshore-outsourced Software Development Projects Utilizing Waterfall versus Agile Methodologies: A Simulation Study*. School of Computer Science and Information Systems, Pace University.

McAfee, A., Brynjolfsson, E., Davenport, T. H., Patil, D. J., & Barton, D. (2012). Big data: The management revolution. *Harvard Business Review*, *90*(10), 60–68. PMID:23074865

McKee, K. A. (2010). It's 10: 00 PM Do You Know Where Your Children Are. *Regent UL Rev.*, *23*, 311.

McMenzie, L., Cook, I. R., & Laing, M. (2019). Criminological policy mobilities and sex work: Understanding the movement of the 'Swedish model' to Northern Ireland. *British Journal of Criminology*, *59*(5), 1199–1216. doi:10.1093/bjc/azy058

Mell, P., & Grance, T. (2009). The NIST definition of cloud computing. *National Institute of Standards and Technology*, *53*(6), 50.

Meneses Falcón, M. D. C., Urío Rodríguez, S. J., & Uroz Olivares, J. (2019). *Financing of trafficking in human beings in Spain*. Academic Press.

Michael, K., & Rose, G. L. (2007). *Human tracking technology in mutual legal assistance and police inter-state cooperation in international crimes*. Academic Press.

Miller, D. (1983). The Correlates of Entrepreneurship in Three Types of Firms. *Management Science*, *29*(7), 770–791. doi:10.1287/mnsc.29.7.770

Mingaleva, Z., Deputatova, L., & Starkov, Y. (2020). *Management of organisational knowledge as a basis for the competitiveness of enterprises in the digital economy*. Academic Press.

Mingaleva, Z. A., Deputatova, L. N., Akatov, N. B., Starkov, Y. V., & Mitrofanova, E. (2019). Application of HADI-cycle for providing sustainability of processes of knowledge and innovation. *Entrepreneurship and Sustainability Issues*, *7*(2), 1628–1640. doi:10.9770/jesi.2019.7.2(58)

Mingaleva, Z., & Mirskikh, I. (2015). Psychological aspects of Intellectual property protection. *Procedia: Social and Behavioral Sciences*, *190*, 220–226. doi:10.1016/j.sbspro.2015.04.938

Miniaoui, H., & Schilirò, D. (2016). *Innovation and Entrepreneurship for the growth and diversification of the GCC Economies*. Academic Press.

Mitchelmore, S., & Rowley, J. (2010). Entrepreneurial competencies: A literature review and development agenda. *International Journal of Entrepreneurial Behaviour & Research*, *16*(2), 92–111. doi:10.1108/13552551011026995

Mithas, S., Tafti, A., & Mitchell, W. (2013). How a firm's competitive environment and Digital Strategic Posture Influence Digital Business Strategy. *Management Information Systems Quarterly*, *37*(2), 511–536. doi:10.25300/MISQ/2013/37.2.09

Mkwambisi, D. D., Jew, E. K., & Dougill, A. J. (2021). Farmer Preparedness for Building Resilient Agri-Food Systems: Lessons from the 2015/2016 El Niño drought in Malawi. *Frontiers in Climate*, *2*, 584245. Advance online publication. doi:10.3389/fclim.2020.584245

Mohajeri, B. (2015). *Paradigm shift from current manufacturing to social manufacturing* [Master's thesis].

Montag, C., Becker, B., & Gan, C. (2018). The multipurpose application WeChat: A review on recent research. *Frontiers in Psychology*, *9*, 2247. doi:10.3389/fpsyg.2018.02247 PMID:30618894

Morabito, V. (2021). Digital Entrepreneurship and Digital Business. *Digital Entrepreneurship, Management. Systems Practice*, 5–27. doi:10.1017/9781108979917.002

Morley, L., & Leyton, D. (2022). Queering the Digital Knowledge Economy. *Queering Higher Education*, 71–96. doi:10.4324/9781003257431-4

Morris, M. H., Pryor, C. G., & Schindehutte, M. (2012). *Entrepreneurship as experience: How events create ventures and ventures create entrepreneurs*. Edward Elgar Publishing. doi:10.4337/9781781005187

Morris, M., & Paul, G. (1987). The relationship between entrepreneurship and marketing in established Firms. *Journal of Business Venturing*, *2*(3), 247–259. doi:10.1016/0883-9026(87)90012-7

Motta, V., & Sharma, A. (2020). Lending technologies and access to finance for smes in the hospitality industry. *International Journal of Hospitality Management*, *86*, 102371. doi:10.1016/j.ijhm.2019.102371

Mo, X. (2022). Study on the Content and User Awareness of Travel Promotion in Xiaohongshu APP. *Frontiers in Economics and Management*, *3*(1), 352–358.

Mubarak, M. F., & Petraite, M. (2020). Industry 4.0 technologies, digital trust and technological orientation: What matters in open innovation? *Technological Forecasting and Social Change*, *161*, 120332. doi:10.1016/j.techfore.2020.120332

Mufudza, T. (2019). Dynamic strategy in a turbulent business environment. *Strategic Management - A Dynamic View*. doi:10.5772/intechopen.81250

Mugarura, N., & Ssali, E. (2020). Intricacies of anti-money laundering and cyber-crimes regulation in a fluid global system. *Journal of Money Laundering Control*, *24*(1), 10–28. doi:10.1108/JMLC-11-2019-0092

Muiruri, S. (2017). African small and medium enterprises (SMES) contributions, challenges and solutions. *European Journal of Research and Reflection in Management Sciences*, *5*(1), 36–48.

Mulvihill, N. (2022). Female Independent Sex Workers. In *Experiences of the Sex Industry* (pp. 18–42). Bristol University Press. doi:10.2307/j.ctv2sjj08k.6

Muñoz, P., & Kibler, E. (2016). Institutional complexity and social entrepreneurship: A fuzzy-set approach. *Journal of Business Research*, *69*(4), 1314–1318. doi:10.1016/j.jbusres.2015.10.098

Munro, V. E., & Scoular, J. (2012). Abusing vulnerability? Contemporary law and policy responses to sex work in the UK. *Feminist Legal Studies*, *20*(3), 189–206. doi:10.100710691-012-9213-x

Murphy, A. K., & Venkatesh, S. A. (2006). Vice careers: The changing contours of sex work in New York City. *Qualitative Sociology*, *29*(2), 129–154. doi:10.100711133-006-9012-2

Musti, K. S., & Baporikar, N. (2023). Industry 4.0-based enterprise information system for P2P lending. *Journal of Science and Technology Policy Management*, *14*(1), 6–24. doi:10.1108/JSTPM-06-2020-0093

Nadelmann, E. A. (2010). *Cops across borders: The internationalization of US criminal law enforcement*. Penn State Press.

Nadkarni, S., & Prügl, R. (2021). Digital transformation: A review, synthesis and opportunities for future research. *Management Review Quarterly*, *71*(2), 233–341. doi:10.100711301-020-00185-7

Nakamoto, S. (2008). Bitcoin: A peer-to-peer electronic cash system. *Decentralized Business Review*, 21260.

Nambisan, S. (2017). Digital Entrepreneurship: Toward a digital technology perspective of entrepreneurship. *Entrepreneurship Theory and Practice*, *41*(6), 1029–1055. doi:10.1111/etap.12254

Narver, J., & Slater, S. (1990). The effects of a market orientation on business profitability. *Journal of Marketing*, *5*(4), 20–35. doi:10.1177/002224299005400403

National Rapporteur on Trafficking in Human Beings. (2010). *Trafficking in Human Beings*. Bureau of the Dutch National Rapporteur.

Nchofoung, T. N., & Asongu, S. A. (2022). ICT for sustainable development: Global comparative evidence of globalisation thresholds. *Telecommunications Policy*, *46*(5), 102296. doi:10.1016/j.telpol.2021.102296

New Kuwait Vision. (2019). *Government of Kuwait: New Kuwait Vision 2035*. Retrieved from https://www.newkuwait.gov.kw/home.aspx

Ng, H. S. (2021). Opportunities, challenges, and solutions for industry 4.0. In *Research Anthology on Cross-Industry Challenges of Industry 4.0* (pp. 1–20). IGI Global. doi:10.4018/978-1-7998-8548-1.ch001

Ngoasong, M. Z. (2018). Digital entrepreneurship in a resource-scarce context: A focus on entrepreneurial digital competencies. *Journal of Small Business and Enterprise Development*, *25*(3), 483–500. doi:10.1108/JSBED-01-2017-0014

Ngo, T. D., Kashani, A., Imbalzano, G., Nguyen, K. T. Q., & Hui, D. (2018). Additive manufacturing (3D printing): A review of materials, methods, applications and challenges. *Composites. Part B, Engineering*, *143*, 172–196. doi:10.1016/j.compositesb.2018.02.012

Nguyen, D. H. (2020). International cooperation and mutual legal assistance in criminal matters in handling with transnational wildlife trafficking crimes in Vietnam. In *E3S Web of Conferences* (Vol. 164, p. 11006). EDP Sciences. doi:10.1051/e3sconf/202016411006

Nguyen, T. U. H., Newby, M., & Macaulay, M. J. (2013). Information technology adoption in small business: Confirmation of a proposed framework. *Journal of Small Business Management*, *53*(1), 207–227. doi:10.1111/jsbm.12058

Nikolaev, M. G. (2018). Strategic company management in the Digital Business Environment. *European Journal of Management Issues*, *26*(3-4), 82–91. doi:10.15421/191809

Nikolić, J. L. (2017). The impact of big data technologies on competitive advantage of companies. *Facta Universitatis-Economics and Organization*, *14*(3), 255–264.

Nobanee, H., & Dilshad, N. (2020). Digital Entrepreneurship: Concepts, Applications, and future research agenda. *SSRN* Electronic Journal. https://doi.org/ doi:10.1504/IJBG.2010.035479

Noone, B. M., McGuire, K. A., & Rohlfs, K. V. (2011). Social media meets hotel revenue management: Opportunities, issues and unanswered questions. *Journal of Revenue and Pricing Management*, *10*(4), 293–305. doi:10.1057/rpm.2011.12

Nordina, N., Normanb, H., Zainic, H., Hamdand, F., Md, M., & Yunuse, N.H.A. (n.d.). *Online Innovation of Business Start-up Training for Marginalised Communities via MOOCS*. Academic Press.

O'Brien, J. A., & Marakas, G. M. (2005). *Introduction to information systems*. McGraw-Hill/Irwin.

O'Neill, M. C. (2011). The EU legal framework on trafficking in human beings: Where to from here–the UK perspective. *Journal of Contemporary European Research, 7*(4), 452–467. doi:10.30950/jcer.v7i4.376

OECD. (2014). *Measuring the digital economy: A new perspective.* OECD Publishing.

Oettmeier, K., & Hofmann, E. (2017). Additive manufacturing technology adoption: An empirical analysis of general and supply chain-related determinants. *Journal of Business Economics, 87*(1), 97–124. doi:10.100711573-016-0806-8

Okereafor, K. (2021). *Cybersecurity in the COVID-19 Pandemic.* CRC Press.

Oliveira, T., Araujo, B., & Tam, C. (2020). Why do people share their travel experiences on social media? *Tourism Management, 78*, 104041. doi:10.1016/j.tourman.2019.104041 PMID:32322615

Omand, D., Bartlett, J., & Miller, C. (2012). Introducing social media intelligence (SOCMINT). *Intelligence and National Security, 27*(6), 801–823. doi:10.1080/02684527.2012.716965

Omorede, A. (2014). Exploration of motivational drivers towards social entrepreneurship. *Social Enterprise Journal, 10*(3), 239–267. doi:10.1108/SEJ-03-2013-0014

Onay, C., & Öztürk, E. (2018). A review of credit scoring research in the age of Big Data. *Journal of Financial Regulation and Compliance., 26*(3), 382–405. doi:10.1108/JFRC-06-2017-0054

Onuoha, G. (2007). Entrepreneurship. *AIST International Journal, 10*, 20-32.

Oppong, G. Y. S., Singh, S., & Kujur, F. (2020). Potential of digital technologies in academic entrepreneurship–a study. *International Journal of Entrepreneurial Behaviour & Research, 26*(7), 1449–1476. doi:10.1108/IJEBR-06-2019-0401

Oppong-Tawiah, D., & Bassellier, G. (2017). *Digital innovation, platform orientation and the performance of IT start-ups.* Academic Press.

Orenga-Roglá, S., & Chalmeta, R. (2016). Social customer relationship management: Taking advantage of Web 2.0 and Big Data technologies. *SpringerPlus, 5*(1), 1462. doi:10.118640064-016-3128-y PMID:27652037

Organization for Security and Co-operation in Europe (OSCE), Recommendations on enhancing efforts to identify and mitigate risks of trafficking in human beings online as a result of the humanitarian crisis in Ukraine, Publisher, Organization for Security and Co-operation in Europe, 22 April 2022

Osano & Languitone. (2015). Factors influencing access to finance by SMEs in Mozambique: case of SMEs in Maputo central business district. *Journal of Innovation and Entrepreneurship, 5*(1), 13. . doi:10.1186/s13731-016-0041-0

OSCE Office of the Special Representative and Co-ordinator for Combating Trafficking in Human Beings. (2021). *Discouraging the demand that fosters trafficking for the purpose of sexual exploitation.* OSCE.

Osorno, R., & Medrano, N. (2020). Open innovation platforms: A conceptual design framework. *IEEE Transactions on Engineering Management, 69*(2), 438–450. doi:10.1109/TEM.2020.2973227

Oztemel, E., & Gursev, S. (2020). Literature review of Industry 4.0 and related technologies. *Journal of Intelligent Manufacturing, 31*(1), 127–182. doi:10.100710845-018-1433-8

Pabel, A., & Prideaux, B. (2016). Social media use in pre-trip planning by tourists visiting a small regional leisure destination. *Journal of Vacation Marketing, 22*(4), 335–348. doi:10.1177/1356766715618998

Paché, G. (2022). Prostitution of Underage Girls in France: The Hidden Supply Chain Dimensions. *Journal of Marketing Management, 10*(1), 1–12.

Palange, A., & Dhatrak, P. (2021). Lean manufacturing a vital tool to enhance productivity in manufacturing. *Materials Today: Proceedings, 46*, 729–736. doi:10.1016/j.matpr.2020.12.193

Pan, W., Xie, T., Wang, Z., & Ma, L. (2022). Digital economy: An innovation driver for total factor productivity. *Journal of Business Research, 139*, 303–311.

Pan, B., MacLaurin, T., & Crotts, J. C. (2007). Travel blogs and the implications for destination marketing. *Journal of Travel Research, 46*(1), 35–45. doi:10.1177/0047287507302378

Pan, L. (2022). Maturity assessment for implementing digital technologies in SMEs. *Proceedings of the International Conference on Big Data Economy and Digital Management*. 10.5220/0011157300003440

Park, E., Kang, J., Choi, D., & Han, J. (2020). Understanding customers' hotel revisiting behaviour: A sentiment analysis of online feedback reviews. *Current Issues in Tourism, 23*(5), 605–611. doi:10.1080/13683500.2018.1549025

Paschou, T., Rapaccini, M., Adrodegari, F., & Saccani, N. (2020). Digital servitization in manufacturing: A systematic literature review and research agenda. *Industrial Marketing Management, 89*, 278–292. doi:10.1016/j.indmarman.2020.02.012

Patwary, A. (2020). Private sector SMEs in realizing SDG 1- "no poverty" in the context of Bangladesh. *International Journal of Humanities, Arts, and Social Sciences, 6*(6), 274–288. doi:10.20469/ijhss.6.20005-6

Paul, J. A., & Wang, X. (2019). Socially optimal IT investment for cybersecurity. *Decision Support Systems, 122*, 113069.

Pedersen. (2013). *A Quantitative Examination of Critical Success Factors Comparing Agile and Waterfall Project Management Methodologies*. Capella University.

Peppet, S. R. (2012). Prostitution 3.0. *Iowa Law Review, 98*, 1989.

Pérez-Lara, M., Saucedo-Martínez, J. A., Marmolejo-Saucedo, J. A., Salais-Fierro, T. E., & Vasant, P. (2020). Vertical and horizontal integration systems in Industry 4.0. *Wireless Networks, 26*(7), 4767–4775. doi:10.100711276-018-1873-2

Peukert, C. (2019). The next wave of digital technological change and the cultural industries. *Journal of Cultural Economics, 43*(2), 189–210. doi:10.100710824-018-9336-2

Phuapan, P., Viriyavejakul, C., & Pimdee, P. (2015). Elements of digital literacy skill: A conceptual analysis. *Asian International Journal of Social Sciences, 15*(4), 88–99. doi:10.29139/aijss.20150406

Piccarozzi, M., Silvestri, C., Aquilani, B., & Silvestri, L. (2022). Is this a new story of the 'Two Giants'? A systematic literature review of the relationship between industry 4.0, sustainability and its pillars. *Technological Forecasting and Social Change, 177*, 121511. doi:10.1016/j.techfore.2022.121511

Pierre, E. L. (2020). From Agile Leader to Agile Leadership: An OD Project in an International Company Operating in the Middle East. Saint Joseph University.

Pike, S., & Page, S. J. (2014). Destination Marketing Organizations and destination marketing: A narrative analysis of the literature. *Tourism Management, 41*(2), 202–227. doi:10.1016/j.tourman.2013.09.009

Pilarczyk, K. (2016). Importance of management information system in banking sector. *Annales Universitatis Mariae Curie-Skłodowska, Sectio H. Oeconomia, 50*(2), 69. doi:10.17951/h.2016.50.2.69

Plachkinova, M., & Pittz, T. (2021). Assessing the Awareness of Cybersecurity Within Entrepreneurship Students: The Cyberpreneurship Project. *Entrepreneurship Education and Pedagogy, 4*(3), 564–582. doi:10.1177/2515127420913056

Polyzoidou, V. (2021). Combatting the Cybercrime: Thoughts Based on the Second Additional Protocol (Draft) to the Budapest Convention on Cybercrime. In *EU Internet Law in the Digital Single Market* (pp. 355-375). Springer.

Popp, B., & Woratschek, H. (2016). Introducing branded communities in sport for building strong brand relations in social media. *Sport Management Review, 19*(2), 183–197. doi:10.1016/j.smr.2015.06.001

Porter, C. E. (2004). A typology of virtual communities: A multi-disciplinary foundation for future research. *Journal of Computer-Mediated Communication, 10*(1), 00. Advance online publication. doi:10.1111/j.1083-6101.2004.tb00228.x

Porter, M. E. (1980). Industry structure and competitive strategy: Keys to profitability. *Financial Analysts Journal, 36*(4), 30–41. doi:10.2469/faj.v36.n4.30

Pradhan, R. P., Arvin, M. B., Nair, M., Bennett, S. E., & Bahmani, S. (2019). Short-term and long-term dynamics of venture capital and economic growth in a digital economy: A study of European countries. *Technology in Society, 57*, 125–134. doi:10.1016/j.techsoc.2018.11.002

Prahalad, C. K., Prahalad, C. K., Fruehauf, H. C., & Prahalad, K. (2005). *The Fortune at the Bottom of the Pyramid.* Wharton School Pub.

Preez, N. d., Louw, L., & Essmann, H. (2009). *An Innovation Process Model for Improving Innovation Capability.* Academic Press.

Presutti, M., Boari, C., & Majocchi, A. (2011). The importance of proximity for the start-ups' knowledge acquisition and exploitation. *Journal of Small Business Management, 49*(3), 361–389. doi:10.1111/j.1540-627X.2011.00331.x

Project Management Professional Body of Knowledge (PMBOK), version 6. (2015). Project Management Institute (PMI).

Pronina, E. V. (2022). Increasing the level of digital knowledge as the key to the country's energy security. *Uchenyy Sovet*, (9), 557–564. doi:10.33920/nik-02-2209-01

Proulx, K. (2022). *Anonymity Online and the Perfect Environment for Cybercrime* [Doctoral dissertation]. Utica University.

Prylinski, K. M. (2020). Tech Trafficking: How the internet has transformed sex trafficking. *J. High Tech. L., 20*, 338.

PwC. (2019). *A practical guide to Responsible Artificial Intelligence (AI).* Available at https://www.pwc.com/gx/en/issues/data-and-analytics/artificial-intelligence/what-is-responsible-ai/responsible-ai-practical-guide.pdf

Qatar National Vision. (2018). *Government Communications Office of Qatar: Qatar national vision 2030.* Retrieved from https://www.gco.gov.qa/en/about-qatar/national-vision/

Qermane, K., & Mancha, R. (2021). WHOOP, Inc.: Digital entrepreneurship during the Covid-19 pandemic. *Entrepreneurship Education and Pedagogy, 4*(3), 500–514. doi:10.1177/2515127420975181

Qi, S., & Chen, N. (2019). Understanding Macao's destination image through user-generated content. *Journal of China Tourism Research, 15*(4), 503–519. doi:10.1080/19388160.2019.1577199

Qiu, Q., Zuo, Y., & Zhang, M. (2021). Can live streaming save the tourism industry from a pandemic? A study of social media. *ISPRS International Journal of Geo-Information, 10*(9), 595–610. doi:10.3390/ijgi10090595

Qiu, S., Alizadeh, A., Dooley, L. M., & Zhang, R. (2019). The effects of authentic leadership on trust in leaders, organizational citizenship behavior, and service quality in the Chinese hospitality industry. *Journal of Hospitality and Tourism Management, 40*, 77–87. doi:10.1016/j.jhtm.2019.06.004

Quintel, T. A., & Cole, M. (2018). Transborder Access to e-Evidence by Law Enforcement Agencies: A first comparative view on the Commission's Proposal for a Regulation on a European Preservation/Production Order and accompanying Directive. SSRN *Electronic Journal.*

Rachinger, M., Rauter, R., Müller, C., Vorraber, W., & Schirgi, E. (2019). Digitalization and its influence on Business Model Innovation. *Journal of Manufacturing Technology Management, 30*(8), 1143–1160. doi:10.1108/JMTM-01-2018-0020

Raets, S., & Janssens, J. (2019). The financial approach to tackling trafficking in human beings. In Financing of organised crime: Human trafficking in focus (pp. 97-108). Center for the Study of Democracy (CSD).

Raets, S., & Janssens, J. (2021). Trafficking and technology: Exploring the role of digital communication technologies in the Belgian human trafficking business. *European Journal on Criminal Policy and Research, 27*(2), 215–238. doi:10.100710610-019-09429-z

Raguseo, E. (2018). Big data technologies: An empirical investigation on their adoption, benefits and risks for companies. *International Journal of Information Management, 38*(1), 187–195. doi:10.1016/j.ijinfomgt.2017.07.008

Rahal, R., Ghalamzan-E, A. M., Abi-Farraj, F., Pacchierotti, C., & Robuffo Giordano, P. (2023). Haptic-guided grasping to minimise torque effort during robotic telemanipulation. *Autonomous Robots.* Advance online publication. doi:10.100710514-023-10096-7

Raimi, L., & Manishimwe, T. (2021). *Small Business Survival of Onslaughts of Boko Haram Insurgency, COVID-19 Pandemic, and Economic Crisis in Yola, North-East Nigeria.* Cases on Small Business Economics and Development During Economic Crises. doi:10.4018/978-1-7998-7657-1.ch005

Raj, R. (2023). *How does Blockchain work?* Retrieved 20th April from https://intellipaat.com/blog/tutorial/blockchain-tutorial/how-does-blockchain-work/

Rajan, R., & Aldhaheri, S. K. (2019). *Digital Nation: How the United Arab Emirates is Building a Future Based on Tech Innovation. Motivate Media Group.*

Ramírez-Montoya, M. S., Castillo-Martínez, I. M., Sanabria-Z, J., & Miranda, J. (2022). Complex Thinking in the Framework of Education 4.0 and Open Innovation—A Systematic Literature Review. *Journal of Open Innovation, 8*(1), 4. doi:10.3390/joitmc8010004

Raniya, S. (2019). *Micro-, Small and Medium-sized Enterprises (MSMEs) and their role in achieving the Sustainable Development Goals.* The United Nations Department of Economic and Social Affairs Division for Sustainable Development Goals.

Rathee, R., & Rajain, P. (2017). Entrepreneurship in the digital era. *Asia Pacific Journal of Research in Business Management, 8*(6), 52–63.

Ratten, V. (2018). *Sport entrepreneurship: Developing and sustaining an entrepreneurial sports culture.* Springer. doi:10.1007/978-3-319-73010-3

Rauch, A., & Hulsink, W. (2015). Putting Entrepreneurship Education Where the Intention to Act Lies: An Investigation Into the Impact of Entrepreneurship Education on Entrepreneurial Behavior. *Academy of Management Learning & Education, 14*(2), 187–204. doi:10.5465/amle.2012.0293

Rawat, R., Garg, B., Mahor, V., Telang, S., Pachlasiya, K., & Chouhan, M. (2022). Organ trafficking on the dark web—the data security and privacy concern in healthcare systems. *Internet of Healthcare Things: Machine Learning for Security and Privacy*, 189-216.

Recker, J., & Von Briel, F. (2019, November). *The Future of Digital Entrepreneurship Research.* Existing and Emerging Opportunities. In ICIS.

Reedy, P. (2020). Interpol review of digital evidence 2016-2019. *Forensic Science International. Synergy, 2*, 489–520. doi:10.1016/j.fsisyn.2020.01.015 PMID:33385144

Reinikainen, H., Munnukka, J., Maity, D., & Luoma-Aho, V. (2020). 'You really are a great big sister'–parasocial relationships, credibility, and the moderating role of audience comments in influencer marketing. *Journal of Marketing Management*, *36*(3-4), 279–298. doi:10.1080/0267257X.2019.1708781

Report, D. (2019). *Big Data in the GCC: From strategy to global leadership.* Retrieved from https://www2.deloitte.com/ye/en/pages/about-deloitte/articles/revolution/big-data-gcc.html

Riera, C., & Iijima, J. (2018). Does investment in digital technologies yield Digital Business Value? The Digital Investment Paradox and knowledge creation as enabling capability. *Proceedings of the 10th International Joint Conference on Knowledge Discovery, Knowledge Engineering and Knowledge Management.* 10.5220/0006958202080215

Ries, E. (2011). *The lean startup: How today's entrepreneurs use continuous innovation to create radically successful businesses*. Currency.

Rigby, Sutherland, & Takeuchi. (2016). *The Secret History of Agile Innovation.* Academic Press.

Riley, J. (2020). Sustaining customer engagement through social media brand communities. *Journal of Global Scholars of Marketing Science*, *30*(4), 344–357. doi:10.1080/21639159.2020.1766990

Roe-Sepowitz, D. (2019). A six-year analysis of sex traffickers of minors: Exploring characteristics and sex trafficking patterns. *Journal of Human Behavior in the Social Environment*, *29*(5), 608–629. doi:10.1080/10911359.2019.1575315

Rogers, E. M. (1995). Diffusion of innovations. Academic Press.

Rogers, E. M. (2005). *Diffusion of innovations*. Free Press.

Rosenstand, C. A. F. (2021, June). Governance framework for performance measurement of a regional digital ecosphere. In *Event Proceedings: ISPIM Innovation Conference–Innovating Our Common Future*. LUT Scientific and Expertise Publications.

Ross, E. (2018). Increasing United States-China cooperation on anti-corruption: Reforming mutual legal assitance. *Geo. Wash. L. Rev.*, *86*, 839.

Rubin, S. H., & Dai, W. (2003). An Integrated Knowledge Management Environment: A Study of Counter Terrorism Technologies. *Journal of Information & Knowledge Management*, *02*(03), 203–217. doi:10.1142/S0219649203000401

Ryalat, M., ElMoaqet, H., & AlFaouri, M. (2023). Design of a Smart Factory Based on Cyber-Physical Systems and Internet of Things towards Industry 4.0. *Applied Sciences (Basel, Switzerland)*, *13*(4), 2156. doi:10.3390/app13042156

Saebi, T., & Foss, N. J. (2015). Business models for open innovation: Matching heterogeneous open innovation strategies with business model dimensions. *European Management Journal*, *33*(3), 201–213. doi:10.1016/j.emj.2014.11.002

Sagiroglu, S. (2013). Big data: A review. *2013 International Conference on Collaboration Technologies and Systems (CTS),* 42–47. 10.1109/CTS.2013.6567202

Sakai, T., & Nagai, T. (2022). Explainable autonomous robots: A survey and perspective. *Advanced Robotics*, *36*(5-6), 219–238. doi:10.1080/01691864.2022.2029720

Salerno, M. S., Gomes, L. A., Silva, D. O., Bagno, R. B., & Freitas, S. L. (2015). Innovation processes: Which process for which project? *Technovation*, *35*, 59–70. doi:10.1016/j.technovation.2014.07.012

Samad, W. A., & Azar, E. (2018). Smart Cities in the Gulf: Current State, Opportunities, and Challenges. Springer Singapore.

Samara, G., & Terzian, J. (2021). Challenges and opportunities for digital entrepreneurship in developing countries. *Digital Entrepreneurship, 283.*

Sandel, T. L., & Wang, Y. (2022). Selling intimacy online: The multi-modal discursive techniques of China's Wanghong. *Discourse, Context & Media, 47*, 100606. doi:10.1016/j.dcm.2022.100606

Sanders, T. (2009). UK sex work policy: eyes wide shut to voluntary and indoor sex work. Regulating Sex for Sale: Prostitution Policy Reform in the UK, 67.

Sanders, T., Connelly, L., & King, L. J. (2016). On our own terms: The working conditions of internet-based sex workers in the UK. *Sociological Research Online, 21*(4), 133–146. doi:10.5153ro.4152

Satalkina, L., & Steiner, G. (2020). Digital Entrepreneurship and its role in Innovation Systems: A systematic literature review as a basis for future research avenues for Sustainable Transitions. *Sustainability (Basel), 12*(7), 2764. doi:10.3390u12072764

Saudi Vision 2030. (2020). *Vision 2030.* Retrieved from https://vision2030.gov.sa/en/reports

Schreider, T. (2020). Cybersecurity Law, Standards and Regulations. Rothstein Publishing.

Schrock, W. (2022). Internet-Era Human Trafficking and the Need for a Better International Legal Instrument. *U. Md. LJ Race, Religion, Race, Gender & Class, 22*, 120.

Schroeder, H., Burch, S., & Rayner, S. (2013). Novel multisector networks and entrepreneurship in urban climate governance. *Environment and Planning. C, Government & Policy, 31*(5), 761–768. doi:10.1068/c3105ed

Schuetzler, R. M., Grimes, G. M., & Scott, G. J. (2020). The impact of chatbot conversational skill on engagement and perceived humanness. *Journal of Management Information Systems, 37*(2), 875–900. doi:10.1080/07421222.2020.1790204

Schumpeter, J. A. (1934). The theory of economic development. Harvard University Press.

Schumpeter, J. A. (2017). *Essays: On entrepreneurs, innovations, business cycles and the evolution of capitalism.* Routledge. doi:10.4324/9781351311489

Schumpeter, J., & Backhaus, U. (2003). *The theory of economic development.* Springer.

Schwartz, K. D. (2023). *ChatGPT and Cybersecurity: The Good, the Bad, and the Careful.* ITProToday. Available at https://www.itprotoday.com/vulnerabilities-and-threats/chatgpt-and-cybersecurity-good-bad-and-careful?_mc=NL_DR_EDT__20230318&cid=NL_DR_EDT__20230318&utm_rid=CPNET000013888747&utm_campaign=52417&utm_medium=email&elq2=3b2f518b0ff54d9aa3519366401c1a0e&sp_eh=b1cc10eb664b0f9908d2950be90e1f41ae1dce8fb81536791e5a2df38e9256df

Scoular, J., & Carline, A. (2014). A critical account of a 'creeping neo-abolitionism': Regulating prostitution in England and Wales. *Criminology & Criminal Justice, 14*(5), 608–626. doi:10.1177/1748895814543534

Scoular, J., Pitcher, J., Sanders, T., Campbell, R., & Cunningham, S. (2019). Beyond the gaze and well beyond Wolfenden: The practices and rationalities of regulating and policing sex work in the digital age. *Journal of Law and Society, 46*(2), 211–239. doi:10.1111/jols.12155

Scuotto, V., Nicotra, M., Del Giudice, M., Krueger, N., & Gregori, G. L. (2021). A microfoundational perspective on smes' growth in the Digital Transformation Era. *Journal of Business Research, 129*, 382–392. doi:10.1016/j.jbusres.2021.01.045

Selby, J. (2017). Data localization laws: Trade barriers or legitimate responses to cybersecurity risks, or both? *International Journal of Law and Information Technology, 25*(3), 213–232. doi:10.1093/ijlit/eax010

Seo, H.-J., Lee, Y. S., & Oh, J. H. (2009). Does ICT investment widen the growth gap? *Telecommunications Policy, 33*(8), 422–431. doi:10.1016/j.telpol.2009.04.001

Shah, J., Jinwala, D. C., & Patel, S. J. (2016). An excursion to software development life cycle models: An old to ever-growing models. *Software Engineering Notes, 41*(1), 1–6. doi:10.1145/2853073.2853080

Shaiful Fitri Abdul Rahman, N., Adam Hamid, A., Lirn, T.-C., Al Kalbani, K., & Sahin, B. (2022). The adoption of industry 4.0 practices by the logistics industry: A systematic review of the gulf region. *Cleaner Logistics and Supply Chain, 5*, 100085. doi:10.1016/j.clscn.2022.100085

Shane, S. (2000). Prior knowledge and the discovery of entrepreneurial opportunities. *Organization Science, 11*(4), 448–469. doi:10.1287/orsc.11.4.448.14602

Shane, S., & Venkataraman, S. (2000). The promise of entrepreneurship as a field of research. *Academy of Management Review, 25*(1), 217–226. doi:10.5465/amr.2000.2791611

Sharmeela, C., Sanjeevikumar, P., Joseph, M., & Sivaraman, P. (2023). IoT, Machine Learning and Blockchain Technologies for Renewable Energy and Modern Hybrid Power Systems. River Publishers.

Shekhar, B., & Vincent, V. V. (2022). Technology and human trafficking: Reconstructing the nexus. *Urban Crime. International Journal (Toronto, Ont.), 3*(1), 65–101.

Shelley, L. (2010). *Human trafficking: A global perspective*. Cambridge University Press. doi:10.1017/CBO9780511760433

Shi, J., Fan, A., & Cai, L. A. (2020). Leisure mobility of Chinese millennials. *Journal of China Tourism Research, 16*(4), 527–546. doi:10.1080/19388160.2019.1687060

Shoemaker, D., Sigler, K., & Shoemaker, T. (2023). *Teaching Cybersecurity: A Handbook for Teaching the Cybersecurity Body of Knowledge in a Conventional Classroom*. CRC Press.

Shruti, M. (2023). *AI vs Machine Learning vs Deep Learning: Know the Differences*. Simplilearn Solutions. Available at https://www.simplilearn.com/tutorials/artificial-intelligence-tutorial/ai-vs-machine-learning-vs-deep-learning

Shulzhenko, N., & Romashkin, S. (2020). Internet fraud and transnational organized crime. *Juridical Tribune, 10*(1), 162–172.

Shumpeter, J. A. (1942). *Capitalism. Socialism and Democracy*. Harper and Row.

Sigala, M., Christou, E., & Gretzel, U. (2012). *Social media in travel, tourism and hospitality: Theory, practice and cases*. Ashgate Publishing, Ltd.

Singh, M., Goyat, R., & Panwar, R. (2023). Fundamental pillars for industry 4.0 development: implementation framework and challenges in manufacturing environment. *The TQM Journal*.

Singhto & Phakdee. (2016). *Adopting a Combination of Scrum and Waterfall Methodologies in Developing Tailor-made SaaS Products for Thai Service and Manufacturing SMEs*. IEEE.

Sirakaya, E., & Woodside, A. G. (2005). Building and testing theories of decision-making by travellers. *Tourism Management, 26*(6), 815–832. doi:10.1016/j.tourman.2004.05.004

Siregar, S., & Chang, K. (2022). External Social Capital, Cybersecurity Incident Flexibility, and Cybersecurity Incident Management Effectiveness. *PACIS 2022 Proceedings*.

Sivarajah, U., Kamal, M. M., Irani, Z., & Weerakkody, V. (2017). Critical analysis of big data challenges and analytical methods. *Journal of Business Research, 70*(1), 263–286. doi:10.1016/j.jbusres.2016.08.001

Siyanbola, W., & Olamade, O. (2012). *Innovation Systems and Capabilities in Developing Regions: Concepts, Issues and Cases* (A. Egbetokun, Ed.; 1st ed.). Routledge. doi:10.4324/9781315588674

Skivko, M. (2021). Digital Technologies, Social entrepreneurship and Governance for Sustanable Development. *Research in Social Change, 13*(1), 165–173. doi:10.2478/rsc-2021-0016

Smith, C. S. (2020). *Computers already learn from us. But can they teach themselves?* Available at https://www.nytimes.com/2020/04/08/technology/ai-computers-learning-supervised-unsupervised.html

Sobhanifard, Y., & Vaeysi, M. (2020). Mixed modeling of the social network mechanisms for the sustainable development of tourism: The case of Iranian Kurdistan. *Sustainable Development (Bradford), 28*(1), 187–196. doi:10.1002d.1981

Soliman, M. (2020). *COVID-19 and the digital landscape in the Gulf.* Retrieved 27th Dec from https://www.mei.edu/publications/covid-19-and-digital-landscape-gulf

Soluk, J., Kammerlander, N., & Darwin, S. (2021). Digital entrepreneurship in developing countries: The role of institutional voids. *Technological Forecasting and Social Change, 170*, 1–13. doi:10.1016/j.techfore.2021.120876

Son, N. H., Lam, L. B., Van Duong, H., Bac, H. M., Anh, D. D., Thuy, V. T., Quynh, N. T., Tan, N. D., Giang, L. H., Hai, V. S., Van Khanh, T., van Thi Thanh, T., & Lan, N. T. (2022). VNU-LIC Digital Knowledge Center Model: Transforming Big Data Into Knowledge. *From Born-Physical to Born-Virtual: Augmenting Intelligence in Digital Libraries*, 516–522. doi:10.1007/978-3-031-21756-2_44

Sopjani, X. (2019). *Challenges and opportunities for startup innovation and entrepreneurship as tools towards a knowledge-based economy: The case of Kosovo.* Academic Press.

So, S. (2022). The Impact of the COVID-19 Pandemic on B2C E-Business and the Challenges to Bonjour Holdings Limited. In H. Taherdoost (Ed.), *Driving Transformative Change in E-Business Through Applied Intelligence and Emerging Technologies*. IGI Global. doi:10.4018/978-1-6684-5235-6.ch003

Spiezia, F. (2022, May). International cooperation and protection of victims in cyberspace: welcoming Protocol II to the Budapest Convention on Cybercrime. In *ERA Forum* (Vol. 23, No. 1, pp. 101-108). Springer Berlin Heidelberg. 10.100712027-022-00707-8

Spigel, B. (2017). The relational organization of entrepreneurial ecosystems. *Entrepreneurship Theory and Practice, 41*(1), 49–72. doi:10.1111/etap.12167

Spremic, M. (2017). Governing digital technology–how mature IT governance can help in digital transformation? *International Journal of Economics and Management Systems, 2.*

Srinivasan, M. (2022). *GCC E-Performance Index 2022 reveals strong digital transformation efforts by GCC countries.* Retrieved from https://www.sme10x.com/10x-industry/gcc-e-performance-index-2022-reveals-strong-digital-transformation-efforts-by-gcc-countries

Srinivasan, A., & Venkatraman, N. (2018). Entrepreneurship in digital platforms: A network-centric view. *Strategic Entrepreneurship Journal, 12*(1), 54–71. doi:10.1002ej.1272

Srivastava, S. (2023). Generative AI In The Enterprise Produces Early Learnings. *Forbes*. Available at https://www.forbes.com/sites/sanjaysrivastava/2023/03/25/generative-ai-in-the-enterpriseuse-cases--early-learnings/?sh=10cd14973202

Stahl, B. C. (2021). *Artificial intelligence for a better future: an ecosystem perspective on the ethics of AI and emerging digital technologies*. Springer Nature.

Stam, F. C., & Spigel, B. (2016). *Entrepreneurial ecosystems.* Utrecht School of Economics Working Papers, (16-13).

Stam, E. (2015). Entrepreneurial ecosystems and regional policy: A sympathetic critique. *European Planning Studies*, *23*(9), 1759–1769. doi:10.1080/09654313.2015.1061484

Statista. (2022). *Size of the blockchain technology market worldwide from 2018 to 2025*. Retrieved 10th June from https://www.statista.com/statistics/647231/worldwide-blockchain-technology-market-size/#:~:text=Blockchain%20technology%20market%20size%20worldwide%202018%2D2025&text=Forecasts%20suggest%20that%20global%20blockchain,dollars%20in%20size%20by%202025

Statista. (2022a). *Number of monthly active users of Xiaohongshu app in China from December 2020 to June 2022 (in millions)*. https://www.statista.com/statistics/1327421/china-xiaohongshu-monthly-active-users/

Statista. (2022b). *Number of monthly active users of Weibo Corporation from 1st quarter of 2014 to 3rd quarter of 2022 (in million)*. https://www.statista.com/statistics/795303/china-mau-of-sina-weibo/

Statista. (2022c). *Number of monthly active WeChat users from the 2nd quarter 2011 to the 3rd quarter 2022 (in millions)*. https://www.statista.com/statistics/255778/number-of-active-wechat-messenger-accounts/

Steiber, A., & Alänge, S. (2020). Corporate-startup co-creation for increased innovation and societal change. *Triple Helix (Heidelberg)*, *7*(2-3), 227–249. doi:10.1163/21971927-bja10004

Stockhem, O. (2020). *Improving the international regulation of cybersextrafficking of women and children through the use of data science and artificial intelligence* [Doctoral dissertation].

StoykovaR. (2022). The Right to a Fair Trial as a Conceptual Framework for Digital Evidence Rules in Criminal Investigations. *Available at* SSRN 4232504. doi:10.2139/ssrn.4232504

Strategy. (2020). *Advancing digital maturity a $100+ billion opportunity for GCC*. Retrieved from https://www.consultancy-me.com/news/4488/advancing-digital-maturity-a-100-billion-opportunity-for-gcc

Strohmayer, A., Clamen, J., & Laing, M. (2019, May). Technologies for social justice: Lessons from sex workers on the front lines. In *Proceedings of the 2019 CHI conference on human factors in computing systems* (pp. 1-14). 10.1145/3290605.3300882

Stroud, N. J. (2017). Attention as a valuable resource. *Political Communication*, *34*(3), 479–489. doi:10.1080/10584609.2017.1330077

Sundar, R., Balaji, A. N., & Kumar, R. S. (2014). A review on lean manufacturing implementation techniques. *Procedia Engineering*, *97*, 1875–1885. doi:10.1016/j.proeng.2014.12.341

Sussan, F., & Acs, Z. J. (2017). The digital entrepreneurial ecosystem. *Small Business Economics*, *49*(1), 55–73. doi:10.100711187-017-9867-5

Swierczek, F. W., & Thai, T. (2003). Motivation, entrepreneurship and the performance of smes in Vietnam. *Journal of Enterprising Culture*, *11*(01), 47–68. doi:10.1142/S0218495803000044

Syed, A. S., Sierra-Sosa, D., Kumar, A., & Elmaghraby, A. (2021). IoT in Smart Cities: A Survey of Technologies, Practices and Challenges. *Smart Cities, 4*(2).

Syed, A., Gillela, K., & Venugopal, C. (2013). The future revolution on big data. *Future*, *2*(6), 2446–2451.

Szalavetz, A. (2020). Digital transformation–enabling factory economy actors' entrepreneurial integration in global value chains? *Post-Communist Economies*, *32*(6), 771–792. doi:10.1080/14631377.2020.1722588

Tallon, P. A. (2011). Competing perspectives on the link between strategic information technology alignment and organizational agility: insights from a mediation model. MIS Quarterly, 463-486.

Tamanaha, B. Z. (2004). *On the rule of law: History, politics, theory*. Cambridge University Press. doi:10.1017/CBO9780511812378

Tang, Y., Zhong, M. L., Qing, F. L., Fang, Y., & He, M. F. (2017). Application of new media in inbound tourism destination marketing – a case study of Sichuan Province. *Skills and Market*, *24*(6), 63–67.

Tao, F., Zhang, L., Venkatesh, V. C., Luo, Y., & Cheng, Y. (2011). Cloud manufacturing: A computing and service-oriented manufacturing model. *Proceedings of the Institution of Mechanical Engineers. Part B, Journal of Engineering Manufacture*, *225*(10), 1969–1976. doi:10.1177/0954405411405575

Tapscott, D. (2014). *The Digital Economy Anniversary Edition: Rethinking Promise and Peril in the Age of Networked Intelligence*. McGraw-Hill Education.

Taras, D. (2001). *Power and Betrayal in the Canadian Media: Updated Edition*. University of Toronto Press.

Tarutė, A., Duobienė, J., Klovienė, L., Vitkauskaitė, E., & Varaniūtė, V. (n.d.). *Identifying factors affecting digital transformation of smes*. AIS Electronic Library (AISeL). Retrieved April 4, 2023, from https://aisel.aisnet.org/iceb2018/64

Tashi, U., Ullah, A. M. M., Watanabe, M., & Kubo, A. (2018). Analytical Point-Cloud Based Geometric Modeling for Additive Manufacturing and Its Application to Cultural Heritage Preservation. *Applied Sciences (Basel, Switzerland)*, *8*(5), 656. doi:10.3390/app8050656

Tawalbeh, L. A. A., & Saldamli, G. (2019). Reconsidering big data security and privacy in cloud and mobile cloud systems. *Journal of King Saud University - Computer and Information Sciences*.

Teece, D. J. (2018). Profiting from innovation in the digital economy: Enabling technologies, standards, and licensing models in the wireless world. *Research Policy*, *47*(8), 1367–1387.

Teece, D. J. (1986). Profiting from technological innovation: Implications for integration, collaboration, licensing and public policy. *Research Policy*, *15*(6), 285–305. doi:10.1016/0048-7333(86)90027-2

Teece, D. J. (2007). Explicating dynamic capabilities: The nature and microfoundations of (sustainable) enterprise performance. *Strategic Management Journal*, *28*(13), 1319–1350. doi:10.1002mj.640

Tekic, Z., & Koroteev, D. (2019). From disruptively digital to proudly analog: A holistic typology of digital transformation strategies. *Business Horizons*, *62*(6), 683–693. doi:10.1016/j.bushor.2019.07.002

Tene, O., & Polonetsky, J. (2012). Big data for all: Privacy and user control in the age of analytics. *Northwestern Journal of Technology and Intellectual Property*, *11*(5), 239–273.

The Inter-Agency Coordination Group against Trafficking of Persons (ICAT). (2019). *Human Trafficking and Technology: Trends, Challenges and Opportunities*. The Inter-Agency Coordination Group against Trafficking of Persons (ICAT). Retrieved from https://icat.un.org/sites/g/files/tmzbdl461/files/human_trafficking_and_technology_trends_challenges_and_opportunities_web.pdf

Theoneste, M., & Clinton-Etim, N. (2021). Investigating the level of entrepreneurial orientation and desire for self-employment of students in selected tertiary institutions, north-east nigeria. *The Business and Management Review*, *12*(01). Advance online publication. doi:10.24052/BMR/V12NU01/ART-03

Thukral, E., & Ratten, V. (2021). COVID-19: Entrepreneurial ecosystem approach to bounce back: Implications for the sport industry. In Innovation and entrepreneurship in sport management (pp. 148-158). Edward Elgar Publishing.

Thurnhofer, M. K. (2022). *What we keep in the shadows: Sex work in Germany during the COVID-19 pandemic*. Academic Press.

Tiba, S., van Rijnsoever, F. J., & Hekkert, M. P. (2020). The lighthouse effect: How successful entrepreneurs influence the sustainability-orientation of entrepreneurial ecosystems. *Journal of Cleaner Production, 264*, 121616. doi:10.1016/j.jclepro.2020.121616

Tidd, J., & Bessant, J. (2014). *Managing Innovation: Integrating Technological, Market and Organisational Change*. Wiley.

Tilson, D., Lyytinen, K., & Sørensen, C. (2010). Research commentary—Digital infrastructures: The missing IS research agenda. *Information Systems Research, 21*(4), 748–759. doi:10.1287/isre.1100.0318

Tomy, S., & Pardede, E. (2018). From uncertainties to successful start ups: A data analytic approach to predict success in technological entrepreneurship. *Sustainability (Basel), 10*(3), 602. doi:10.3390u10030602

Tony Yu, F. L. (2012). Turning trash papers into gold: Entrepreneurship and international coordination of China's paper queen, Zhang Yin. *Journal of Chinese Entrepreneurship, 4*(1), 88–96. doi:10.1108/17561391211200957

Torn, A., & Lister, K. (2018, July). Emancipatory sex work research: narratives of a hidden population. *Narrative Matters Annual Conference.*

Tortorella, G. L., Cawley Vergara, A. M., Garza-Reyes, J. A., & Sawhney, R. (2020). Organizational learning paths based upon industry 4.0 adoption: An empirical study with Brazilian manufacturers. *International Journal of Production Economics, 219*, 284–294. doi:10.1016/j.ijpe.2019.06.023

Treloar, C., Cama, E., Stardust, Z., & Kim, J. (2021). 'I wouldn't call the cops if I was being bashed to death': Sex work, whore stigma and the criminal legal system. *International Journal for Crime. Justice and Social Democracy, 10*(3), 142–157.

Trongtorsak, S., Saraubon, K., & Nilsook, P. (2021). Collaborative Experiential Learning Process for Enhancing Digital Entrepreneurship. *Higher Education Studies, 11*(1), 137. doi:10.5539/hes.v11n1p137

Tsiavos, V., & Kitsios, F. (2022). *Technology as Driver, Enabler and Barrier of Digital Transformation: A Review*. Academic Press.

Tussyadiah, I. P., & Fesenmaier, D. R. (2009). Mediating tourist experiences: Access to places via shared videos. *Annals of Tourism Research, 36*(1), 24–40. doi:10.1016/j.annals.2008.10.001

Tussyadiah, I. P., Park, S., & Fesenmaier, D. R. (2011). Assessing the effectiveness of consumer narratives for destination marketing. *Journal of Hospitality & Tourism Research (Washington, D.C.), 35*(1), 64–78. doi:10.1177/1096348010384594

Tuten, T. L., & Solomon, M. R. (2013). *Social media marketing*. Pearson Education.

Tyagi, A. K., Fernandez, T. F., Mishra, S., & Kumari, S. (2021). Intelligent automation systems at the core of industry 4.0. In *International conference on intelligent systems design and applications* (pp. 1-18). Springer. 10.1007/978-3-030-71187-0_1

Ulas, D. (2019). Digital Transformation Process and SMEs. *Procedia Computer Science, 158*, 662–671. doi:10.1016/j.procs.2019.09.101

UN Office on Drugs and Crime (UNODC). (2020). *Global Report on Trafficking in Persons*. UNODC.

UNODC. (2015). *Study on the effects of new information technologies on the abuse and exploitation of children*. https://www.unodc.org/documents/ Cybercrime/Study_on_the_Effects.pdf

Upadhyay, N., Upadhyay, S., & Dwivedi, Y. K. (2021). Theorizing Artificial Intelligence Acceptance and Digital Entrepreneurship Model. *International Journal of Entrepreneurial Behaviour & Research, 28*(5), 1138–1166. doi:10.1108/IJEBR-01-2021-0052

Valeri, M., & Baggio, R. (2021). A critical reflection on the adoption of blockchain in tourism. *Information Technology & Tourism, 23*(2), 121–132. doi:10.100740558-020-00183-1

van der Wilt, H. (2018). Extradition and mutual legal assistance in the draft Convention on Crimes Against Humanity. *Journal of International Criminal Justice, 16*(4), 795–812. doi:10.1093/jicj/mqy037

van Rij, J., & McAlister, R. (2020). Using Criminal Routines and Techniques to Predict and Prevent the Sexual Exploitation of Eastern-European Women in Western Europe. The Palgrave International Handbook of Human Trafficking, 1689-1708.

Van, L. A. (2021). How the COVID-19 pandemic can stimulate more radical business process improvements: Using the metaphor of a tree. *Knowledge and Process Management, 28*(2), 107–116. doi:10.1002/kpm.1659

Verhoef, P. C., Broekhuizen, T., Bart, Y., Bhattacharya, A., Qi Dong, J., Fabian, N., & Haenlein, M. (2021). Digital transformation: A multidisciplinary reflection and research agenda. *Journal of Business Research, 122*, 889–901. doi:10.1016/j.jbusres.2019.09.022

Vervest, P., & Dunn, A. (2000). Digital Business Technologies and Total Action. *How to Win Customers in the Digital World*, 21–79. doi:10.1007/978-3-642-57141-1_2

Villarroel Ordenes, F., & Zhang, S. (2019). From words to pixels: Text and image mining methods for service research. *Journal of Service Management, 30*(5), 593–662. doi:10.1108/JOSM-08-2019-0254

Vision 2030. (2022). Saudi Vision 2030: Financial Development Programme. *Saudi Arabia, 2022*, 39.

Vision, U. A. E. (2010). *The UAE Government Portal: UAE vision 2021.* Retrieved from https://www.government.ae/en/about-the-uae/strategies-initiatives-and-awards/federal-governments-strategies-and-plans/vision-2021

Vivrette, A. T. (2022). *Approach to the Global Human Trafficking Crisis: Analyzing Applications of Social Network Analysis* [Doctoral dissertation].

Vlase, I., & Preoteasa, A. M. (2022). Flexi (nse) curity in adult webcamming: Romanian women's experiences selling digital sex services under platform capitalism. *Gender, Place and Culture, 29*(5), 603–624. doi:10.1080/0966369X.2021.1878114

Volodko, A., Cockbain, E., & Kleinberg, B. (2020). "Spotting the signs" of trafficking recruitment online: Exploring the characteristics of advertisements targeted at migrant job-seekers. *Trends in Organized Crime, 23*(1), 7–35. doi:10.100712117-019-09376-5

Vu, K. M. (2011). ICT as a source of economic growth in the information age: Empirical evidence from the 1996–2005 period. *Telecommunications Policy, 35*(4), 357–372. doi:10.1016/j.telpol.2011.02.008

Waller, L., Johnson, S. C., Satchell, N., Gordon, D., Daley, G. L. K., Reid, H., ... Linton, P. (2022). Woe is the dark Web: the main challenges that governments of the Commonwealth Caribbean will face in combating dark Web-facilitated criminal activities. *Transforming Government: People, Process and Policy.*

Walter, S. G., & Block, J. H. (2016). Outcomes of entrepreneurship education: An institutional perspective. *Journal of Business Venturing, 31*(2), 216–233. doi:10.1016/j.jbusvent.2015.10.003

Wang, B. (2021). *Artificial intelligence technology simulation university three whole education moral education model research.* Academic Press.

Wang, G., Qiu, H., & Ren, L. (2022). Determinants of tourists' intention to share travel experience on social media: A fsQCA application. *Current Issues in Tourism*, 1–6. doi:10.1080/13683500.2022.2091428

Wang, J., Li, Y., Wu, B., & Wang, Y. (2021). Tourism destination image based on tourism user-generated content on the Internet. *Tourism Review*, *76*(1), 125–137. doi:10.1108/TR-04-2019-0132

Wang, J., Xia, Y., & Wu, Y. (2022). Sensing Tourist Distributions and Their Sentiment Variations Using Social Media: Evidence from 5A Scenic Areas in China. *ISPRS International Journal of Geo-Information, 11*(9), 492. doi:10.3390/ijgi11090492

Wang, X., Huang, Y., & Li, X. (2017). Behavior of Sharing Travel Experiences in Social Media. *Management Review*, *29*(2), 97–105.

Wang, Z., Huang, W. J., & Liu-Lastres, B. (2022). Impact of user-generated travel posts on travel decisions: A comparative study on Weibo and Xiaohongshu. *Annals of Tourism Research Empirical Insights*, *3*(2), 100064. doi:10.1016/j.annale.2022.100064

Wasiuzzaman, S., Nurdin, N., Abdullah, A. H., & Vinayan, G. (2020). Creditworthiness and access to finance of smes in Malaysia: Do linkages with large firms matter? *Journal of Small Business and Enterprise Development*, *27*(2), 197–217. doi:10.1108/JSBED-03-2019-0075

Wedel, M., & Kannan, P. K. (2016). Marketing analytics for data-rich environments. *Journal of Marketing*, *80*(6), 97–121. doi:10.1509/jm.15.0413

Wei, R., & Liu, X. (2019). Insights into the psychology of mobile apps as the new home screen: Evidence from cutting-edge research in Chinese societies. *Chinese Journal of Communication*, *12*(1), 1–6. doi:10.1080/17544750.2019.1548662

Wellman, B., Quan-Haase, A., Boase, J., Chen, W., Hampton, K., Díaz, I., & Miyata, K. (2003). The social affordances of the Internet for networked individualism. *Journal of Computer-Mediated Communication*, *8*(3), JCMC834. doi:10.1111/j.1083-6101.2003.tb00216.x

Wellman, B., & Wortley, S. (1990). Different strokes from different folks: Community ties and social support. *American Journal of Sociology*, *96*(3), 558–588. doi:10.1086/229572

West, J., & Bogers, M. (2014). Leveraging external sources of innovation: A review of research on open innovation. *Journal of Product Innovation Management*, *31*(4), 814–831. doi:10.1111/jpim.12125

White, S. (2018). *Creating better business environments for micro and small enterprises', Technical Report*. Donor Committee for Enterprise Development.

Wieltschnig, P., Muraszkiewicz, J., & Fenton, T. (2021). Without data we are fighting blind: the need for human security data in defence sector responses to human trafficking. *Journal of Modern Slavery: A Multidisciplinary Exploration of Human Trafficking Solutions, 6*(3).

Wiliandri, R. (2020). A conceptual approach to identify factors affecting the digital transformation of micro, small and medium-sized enterprises (msmes) during covid-19 pandemic in Indonesia. *Ekonomi Bisnis*, *25*(2), 66. doi:10.17977/um042v25i2p66-85

Willcocks, L. P., Sauer, C., & Lacity, M. C. (2016). *Enacting Research Methods in Information Systems* (Vol. 1). Palgrave Macmillan.

Willcocks, L., Venters, W., & Whitley, E. (2014). *Moving to the Cloud Corporation*. Palgrave Macmillan. doi:10.1057/9781137347473

Williams, L. D. (2021). Concepts of Digital Economy and Industry 4.0 in Intelligent and information systems. *International Journal of Intelligent Networks*, *2*, 122–129. doi:10.1016/j.ijin.2021.09.002

Wilson, H. J., & Daugherty, P. R. (2018). Collaborative Intelligence: Humans and AI are joining forces. *Harvard Business Review, 96*(4), 114–123.

Wirattanapornkul, S. (2012). *Effect of IT capabilities and business–IT strategic alignment on business agility* [Doctoral dissertation]. University of the Thai Chamber of Commerce.

Wolfenden Committee, Report of the Committee on Homosexual Offences and Prostitution (1957; Cmnd. 247) para. 60.

Wood-Harper, A., & Avison, D. (1992). Reflections from the experience of using Multiview: Through the lens of soft systems methodology. *Systemist, 14*(3), 136–145.

Woods, A. K. (2015). *Data beyond borders: Mutual legal assistance in the internet era.* Academic Press.

Woods, A. K. (2016). Against data exceptionalism. *Stanford Law Review, 68*, 729.

World Bank Group. (2018, 25 September). *The voice of travelers: Leveraging user-generated content for tourism development 2018.* http://hdl.handle.net/10986/30451

World Tourism Organization. (2021, 16 March). *Yearbook of tourism statistics, data 2015–2019* (2021 ed.). https://www.e-unwto.org/doi/book/10.18111/9789284422487

Wu, J. (2021). Analysis of Mafengwo's Social Media Strategy. *The 2021 4th International Conference on Humanities Education and Social Sciences (ICHESS 2021),* 2373-2377. https://creativecommons.org/licenses/by-nc/4.0/

Wu, L., Fan, A., & Shen, H. (2020). Embracing the future: New technology and mediated Chinese tourists. *Journal of China Tourism Research, 16*(4), 487–493. doi:10.1080/19388160.2020.1845074

Xiang, Z., Du, Q., Ma, Y., & Fan, W. (2017). A comparative analysis of major online review platforms: Implications for social media analytics in hospitality and tourism. *Tourism Management, 58*, 51–65. doi:10.1016/j.tourman.2016.10.001

Xiang, Z., & Gretzel, U. (2010). Role of social media in online travel information search. *Tourism Management, 31*(2), 179–188. doi:10.1016/j.tourman.2009.02.016

Xiaofeng, M., & Xiang, C. (2013). Big data management: concepts, techniques and challenges. *Journal of Computer Research and Development, 50*(1), 146.

xiaohongshu.com.cn. (2022). *About Xiaohongshu.* https://www.xiaohongshu.com/protocols/about

Xiao, L., & Zhao, L. (2009). Tourism destination image spreading on the Internet—Content analysis based on the related websites on Cross-Straint. *Luyou Xuekan, 24*(3), 75–81.

Xiao, X., Fang, C., Lin, H., & Chen, J. (2022). A framework for quantitative analysis and differentiated marketing of tourism destination image based on visual content of photos. *Tourism Management, 93*, 104585. doi:10.1016/j.tourman.2022.104585

Xiong, G., Wang, F. Y., Nyberg, T. R., Shang, X., Zhou, M., Shen, Z., Li, S., & Guo, C. (2018). From mind to products: Towards social manufacturing and service. *IEEE/CAA Journal of Automatica Sinica, 5*(1), 47-57.

Xiong, G., Chen, Y., Shang, X., Liu, X., & Nyberg, T. R. (2014, June). AHP fuzzy comprehensive method of supplier evaluation in social manufacturing mode. In *Proceeding of the 11th World Congress on Intelligent Control and Automation* (pp. 3594-3599). IEEE. 10.1109/WCICA.2014.7053314

Xiong, G., Tamir, T. S., Shen, Z., Shang, X., Wu, H., & Wang, F. Y. (2022). A Survey on Social Manufacturing: A Paradigm Shift for Smart Prosumers. *IEEE Transactions on Computational Social Systems*, 1–19. doi:10.1109/TCSS.2022.3180201

Xu, D., Chen, T., Pearce, J., Mohammadi, Z., & Pearce, P. L. (2021). Reaching audiences through travel vlogs: The perspective of involvement. *Tourism Management, 25*(15), 2518–2533. doi:10.1016/j.tourman.2021.104326

Xu, X. (2012). From cloud computing to cloud manufacturing. *Robotics and Computer-integrated Manufacturing, 28*(1), 75–86. doi:10.1016/j.rcim.2011.07.002

Xu, X., Huang, D., & Shang, X. (2021). Social presence or physical presence? Determinants of purchasing behaviour in tourism live-streamed shopping. *Tourism Management Perspectives, 40*, 100917. doi:10.1016/j.tmp.2021.100917

Xu, X., Lu, Y., Vogel-Heuser, B., & Wang, L. (2021). Industry 4.0 and Industry 5.0—Inception, conception and perception. *Journal of Manufacturing Systems, 61*, 530–535. doi:10.1016/j.jmsy.2021.10.006

Xu, Y., & Ye, Y. (2020). Who watches live streaming in China? Examining viewers' behaviors, personality traits, and motivations. *Frontiers in Psychology, 11*, 1607. doi:10.3389/fpsyg.2020.01607 PMID:32848995

Yang, G.-Z., Bellingham, J., Dupont, P. E., Fischer, P., Floridi, L., Full, R., Jacobstein, N., Kumar, V., McNutt, M., Merrifield, R., Nelson, B. J., Scassellati, B., Taddeo, M., Taylor, R., Veloso, M., Wang, Z. L., & Wood, R. (2018). The grand challenges of science robotics. *Science Robotics, 3*(14), eaar7650. doi:10.1126cirobotics.aar7650 PMID:33141701

Yang, M., & Jiang, P. (2019). Open product design for social manufacturing. In *Social manufacturing: Fundamentals and applications* (pp. 93–116). Springer. doi:10.1007/978-3-319-72986-2_5

Yar, M. (2012). E-Crime 2.0: The criminological landscape of new social media. *Information & Communications Technology Law, 21*(3), 207–219. doi:10.1080/13600834.2012.744224

Yasmin, T., El Refae, G. A., & Eletter, S. (2022). Digital Healthcare Provision Policies in United Arab Emirates (UAE) Amid COVID-19. In Digital Economy, Business Analytics, and Big Data Analytics Applications (pp. 215-222). Springer.

Yazdinejad, A., Dehghantanha, A., Parizi, R. M., Srivastava, G., & Karimipour, H. (2023). Secure intelligent fuzzy blockchain framework: Effective threat detection in iot networks. *Computers in Industry, 144*, 103801. doi:10.1016/j.compind.2022.103801

Yoong, L. C., & Lian, S. B. (2019). Customer engagement in social media and purchase intentions in the hotel industry. *International Journal of Academic Research in Business & Social Sciences, 9*(1), 54–68. doi:10.6007/IJARBSS/v9-i1/5363

Yoo, Y., Henfridsson, O., & Lyytinen, K. (2010). Research commentary—the new organizing logic of digital innovation: An agenda for information systems research. *Information Systems Research, 21*(4), 724–735. doi:10.1287/isre.1100.0322

Youssef, A. B., Boubaker, S., & Omri, A. (2018). Entrepreneurship and sustainability: The need for innovative and institutional solutions. *Technological Forecasting and Social Change, 129*, 232–241. doi:10.1016/j.techfore.2017.11.003

Yuan, Y., Chan, C. S., Eichelberger, S., Ma, H. & Pikkemaat, B. (2022). The effect of social media on travel planning process by Chinese tourists: the way forward to tourism futures. *Journal of Tourism Futures*. doi:10.1108/JTF-04-2021-0094

Yu, C., Jiang, X., Yu, S., & Yang, C. (2020). Blockchain-based shared manufacturing in support of cyber physical systems: Concept, framework, and operation. *Robotics and Computer-integrated Manufacturing, 64*, 101931. doi:10.1016/j.rcim.2019.101931

Zaheer, H., Breyer, Y., & Dumay, J. (2019). Digital entrepreneurship: An interdisciplinary structured literature review and research agenda. *Technological Forecasting and Social Change, 148*, 119735. doi:10.1016/j.techfore.2019.119735

Zahra, S. A., Liu, W., & Si, S. (2023). How Digital Technology promotes entrepreneurship in ecosystems. *Technovation, 119*, 102457. doi:10.1016/j.technovation.2022.102457

Zeng, S., Zhou, J., Zhang, C., & Merigó, J. M. (2022). Intuitionistic fuzzy social network hybrid MCDM model for an assessment of digital reforms of manufacturing industry in China. *Technological Forecasting and Social Change*, *176*, 121435. doi:10.1016/j.techfore.2021.121435

Zhai, Y., Jiang, D., Gozgor, G., & Cho, E. (2021). The Amplifying Effect of Conflicts on Case Fatality Rate of COVID-19: Evidence From 120 Countries [Brief Research Report]. *Frontiers in Public Health*, *9*, 9. doi:10.3389/fpubh.2021.681604 PMID:34422745

Zhang, W. (2021). Text Mining Applied in Evolution of Q&A Platforms users' Information Demand on Tourism in COVID-19 Normalization. In *2021 5th Annual International Conference on Data Science and Business Analytics (ICDSBA)* (pp. 29-40). IEEE. 10.1109/ICDSBA53075.2021.00016

Zhang, J., Gui, Y., Wu, B., Morrison, A. M., & Li, C. (2016). Is destination marketing organization microblogging in China delivering? An empirical analysis of information supply against consumer information needs. *Journal of Vacation Marketing*, *22*(1), 68–85. doi:10.1177/1356766715591869

Zhang, W., Du, W., Bian, Y., Peng, C. H., & Jiang, Q. (2020). Seeing is not always believing: An exploratory study of clickbait in WeChat. *Internet Research*, *30*(3), 1043–1058. doi:10.1108/INTR-09-2019-0373

Zhang, X., Chen, Z., & Jin, H. (2021). The effect of tourists' autobiographical memory on revisit intention: Does nostalgia promote revisiting? *Asia Pacific Journal of Tourism Research*, *26*(2), 147–166. doi:10.1080/10941665.2020.1718171

Zhao, Z., Zhu, M., & Hao, X. (2018). Share the Gaze: Representation of destination image on the Chinese social platform WeChat Moments. *Journal of Travel & Tourism Marketing*, *35*(6), 726–739. doi:10.1080/10548408.2018.1432449

Zhong, R. Y., Xu, X., Klotz, E., & Newman, S. T. (2017). Intelligent Manufacturing in the Context of Industry 4.0: A Review. *Engineering (Beijing)*, *3*(5), 616–630. doi:10.1016/J.ENG.2017.05.015

Zhou, J., Zhou, J., Ding, Y., & Wang, H. (2019). The magic of danmaku: A social interaction perspective of gift sending on live streaming platforms. *Electronic Commerce Research and Applications*, *34*, 100815. doi:10.1016/j.elerap.2018.11.002

Zhou, Y., Xiong, G., Nyberg, T., Mohajeri, B., & Bao, S. (2016). Social manufacturing realizing personalization production: A state-of-the-art review. *IEEE International Conference on Service Operations and Logistics, and Informatics (SOLI)*, 7-11. 10.1109/SOLI.2016.7551653

Zhu, W., Zheng, D. Q., Wang, W. C., & Zhou, H. H. (2014). The differences between Weibo and WeChat: The evidence from the social capital theory. *Journal of Intelligence*, *6*, 138–143.

Ziemnowicz, C. (2013). Joseph A. Schumpeter and Innovation. Encyclopedia of Creativity, Invention, Innovation and Entrepreneurship, 1171–1176. doi:10.1007/978-1-4614-3858-8_476

Zou, Y., & Yu, Q. (2022). Sense of safety toward tourism destinations: A social constructivist perspective. *Journal of Destination Marketing & Management*, *24*, 100708. doi:10.1016/j.jdmm.2022.100708

Zukin, S. (2020). *The Innovation Complex: Cities, Tech, and the New Economy*. Oxford University Press. doi:10.1093/oso/9780190083830.001.0001

About the Contributors

Farag Edghiem in a Senior Lecturer in Digital Marketing Communications at Manchester Metropolitan University - As an active contributor to numerous academic journals and conferences, the research foci of Dr Edghiem are on the topics of digital service innovation and the critical role of service employees in initiating innovation. Dr Edghiem's research also opts to explore the determinants of automated service encounters, both online and offline, and the digital transformation within the service sector.

Mohammed Ali is a Lecturer in Digital Business and Information Systems and the programme lead for Business Management with Innovation and Technology at the University of Salford Business School, UK. He is a Senior Fellow of Higher Education with extensive teaching experience. His research interests fall under the socio-technical and system complexities of information systems and digital disruption and he has published widely in the area of digital transformation, digital technologies for higher education, and information systems to facilitate remote work and for managing crisis situations. He is currently involved in various academic projects that aim to promote research-informed teaching in areas such as complex issues in information systems development, systemic practice in information systems action research, sociotechnical issues in information systems adoption and digital innovation and sustainability theories.

* * *

Khalid Abbas is a senior lecturer at Liverpool Business School, Liverpool John Moores University, UK where he has been a faculty member since 2018. He is responsible in the learning of global business management and other human resource management modules at Liverpool Business School. He holds an executive MBA and a PhD from Liverpool Business School in the UK. He has a keen interest in employees' intentions and determinants of knowledge sharing behaviours; and the impacts of knowledge sharing on organisational development.

Salih Aka is Assistant Professor in Erzincan Binali Yıldırım University. He is interested in production management, social manufacturing, multicriteria decision-making, artificial neural networks, simulation, and food supply chain.

Neeta Baporikar is currently a Professor/Director (Business Management) at Harold Pupkewitz Graduate School of Business (HP-GSB), Namibia University of Science and Technology, Namibia. Prior to this, she was a Head-Scientific Research, with the Ministry of Higher Education CAS-Salalah, Sultanate of Oman, Professor (Strategic Management and Entrepreneurship) at IIIT Pune and BITS India. With a decade-plus of experience in the industry, consultancy, and training, she made a lateral switch to research and academics in 1995. Prof Baporikar holds D.Sc. (Management Studies) USA, Ph.D. (Management), the University of Pune INDIA with MBA (Distinction) and Law (Hons.) degrees. Apart from this, she is an external reviewer, Oman Academic Accreditation Authority, an Accredited Management Teacher, a Qualified Trainer, an FDP from EDII, a Doctoral Guide, and a Board Member of the Academic and Advisory Committee in accredited B-Schools. With more than 300 scientific publications, and an author of 30 plus books in the area of entrepreneurship, strategy, management, and higher education, she has to her credit many conferred doctorates. She is also an active member of the international and editorial advisory board for international publishers, and a reviewer for Emerald, IGI, Inderscience, Wiley, etc.

Alicia Danielsson is the director of the Centre for Trafficking, Exploitation and Modern Slavery Studies (TEAMS) within the Hume Institute for Postgraduate Studies in Lausanne, Switzerland. She is also an Assistant Professor in Law and Head of the Centre for Contemporary Coronial Law at the University of Bolton. Her particular interests and expertise are in the areas of human rights law, EU law, international business law, jurisprudence, legal research methods, international criminal justice and comparative law. In particular, her subject-specific research interests lie in the fields of comparative and EU law, with a specific focus on the area of freedom, security and justice, as well as EU labour law and human rights protection.

Theoneste Manishimwe is a PhD student at the American University of Nigeria, as well as a research and teaching assistant. He is also the Commonwealth of the Bahamas' International MUN delegate at the UNDP (United Nations Development Programme).

Lukman Raimi is an Assistant Professor at the Universiti Brunei Darussalam in the Department of Business Administration (Entrepreneurship major). Previously, he was the Chair of Entrepreneurship, the Coordinator Graduate Program SBE, and Assistant Director Centre for Entrepreneurship at the American University of Nigeria.

Stuart So teaches and research operations, supply chain, and information management with a special focus on business & supply chain sustainability, corporate social responsibility (CSR), circular economy (CE) and life cycle assessment (LCA). Stuart is a Lecturer in Environmental Analytics and Programme Director for BSc in Business Analytics at the University of Exeter Business School (UEBS). His teaching includes environmental analytics, operations analytics, business statistics & mathematics and capstone project & research methods. Back in Hong Kong, he taught management Information systems (MIS), data curation & information management, and capstone project & research methods at the University of Hong Kong (HKU). Stuart received his doctorate from Macquarie University and completed his fellowship at the City University of Hong Kong. His research focuses on operations sustainability and information management, particularly environmental analytics. Stuart has published more than 50 research articles in major peer-reviewed journals and conferences (Stuart So - Google Scholar) He received two best paper awards and a research acknowledgment prize from the IEEE Conference, ANZAM Conference, and University of Melbourne respectively. Stuart is an editorial board member of the International Journal of Systems and Service-Oriented Engineering (IJSOE) and Library: High-Tech (LHT). He is also a casual reviewer of a number of SCI/SSCI journals. Stuart has been a Guest Editor of the Special Issue "COVID-19 Pandemic and Health Informatics" for Library: High-Tech, a three-part special issue focusing on health information management and analytics in the COVID-19 pandemic. Currently, he is a guest editor of the Special Issue "Circular Economy and Environmental Analytics: Insights for Designing Sustainable Operations and Supply Chains" for Sustainability, a MPDI journal. Stuart is currently working on several research projects. One studies social media users' information-seeking and sharing behaviour under the COVID-19 pandemic from an IS/IM perspective. On the sustainability side, Stuart is researching plastic waste management and recycling in a global context. He is also interested in environmental psychology, Stuart studies the social, cultural, political, and psychological determinants of climate change risk perceptions by exploring the psychological elements, their impact on public individual's pro-environmental attitudes and behaviours. Professionally, Stuart provided consulting on supply chain decarbonization and lean management. He holds a Certified Carbon Auditor (CCA) qualification from Energy Institute (UK), and a Certified Information Systems Auditor (CISA) from ISACA (USA). He is also an IRCA-certified ISO 14001 Environmental Management Systems (EMS) Auditor and ISO22000 Food Safety Management Systems (FSMS) Internal Auditor.

Bo Wen is a member of staff at Liverpool Business School, Liverpool John Moores University, UK. She teaches human resource management and research methods at Liverpool John Moores University. She has been involved in research projects concerning management knowledge transfer partnerships and motivations for international students to do a PhD in the UK. Her overarching interests are knowledge/information sharing and hiding behaviours in the small family business context.

Trevor Wood-Harper holds the Emeritus Chair of Information Systems (IS) and Systemic Change at the Alliance Manchester Business School (AMBS) having been recruited in 2003 to re-vision Information Systems & Management Research and Doctor- al Education on the merger of University of Manchester Institute of Science and Technology (UMIST) with the Victoria University of Manchester (VUM). He has held visiting chairs at the following universities: Oslo; South Australia (A$500K funding); New South Wales, Sydney; Cape Town; Napier, Edinburgh; Georgia State, Atlanta and Copenhagen Business School. Currently AMBS has world ranking 37 and in the UK 6. He has acted as an external examiner for many BSc, MSc and MBA courses including LSE and Warwick. For 10 years he was a member of the British Computer Society (BCS) Validation Panel for undergraduate degrees. Also he has acted, as an advisor on university periodic research review panels with the most recent was Henley Business School, Reading.

Index

G

H

I

K

M

O

P

R

S

T

U

V

W

www.ingramcontent.com/pod-product-compliance
Lightning Source LLC
LaVergne TN
LVHW062143300926
849161LV00010B/2610